AGAPE AND EROS

the text of this book is printed
on 100% recycled paper

AGAPE
AND
EROS

PART I

A Study of the Christian Idea of Love

PART II

The History of the Christian Idea of Love

By
ANDERS NYGREN
Bishop of Lund

Translated by
PHILIP S. WATSON

Harper & Row, Publishers
New York and Evanston

THE LIBRARY

OF RELIGION AND CULTURE

General Editor: Benjamin Nelson

AGAPE AND EROS

Printed in the United States of America.

All rights reserved.

This book was first published in England by the S.P.C.K. House: Part I in 1932; Part II, Vol. I, in 1938; Part II, Vol. II, in 1939; revised, in part retranslated, and published in one volume in 1953. It is here reprinted by arrangement with the Westminster Press, publishers of the United States edition.

First paperback edition: 1969
Harper & Row, Publishers, Incorpated,
10 East 53rd Street, New York, N.Y. 10022

TABLE OF CONTENTS

INTRODUCTION

THE PROBLEM OF AGAPE AND EROS

PART ONE

THE TWO FUNDAMENTAL MOTIFS

CHAPTER ONE

THE AGAPE MOTIF

CHAPTER TWO

THE EROS MOTIF

I. THE PREPARATION OF THE SYNTHESIS

CHAPTER ONE

NOMOS, EROS AND AGAPE

II. THE COMPLETION OF THE SYNTHESIS

CHAPTER TWO

THE CARITAS-SYNTHESIS

III. THE DESTRUCTION OF THE SYNTHESIS

CHAPTER FIVE

THE RENEWAL OF THE EROS MOTIF IN THE RENASCENCE

CHAPTER SIX

THE RENEWAL OF THE AGAPE MOTIF IN THE REFORMATION

AUTHOR'S PREFACE

In the introductory chapter of this work, it is stated that the question there raised for discussion is one of the most central and yet *most neglected* in the theological field. When this statement was originally made, that was in fact the position. But during the last twenty years the situation has entirely changed. The problem of "Agape and Eros" has become a matter of major theological interest, and there has been quite a spate of literature dealing with it. It would take far too long here to name and comment on the relevant books and articles.

Part One of the present work appeared in an English translation—somewhat abridged—by A. G. Hebert in 1932. Part Two was translated by Philip S. Watson and published in two volumes in 1938-39. It has now been thought desirable to make a full version of Part One available to English readers, and I am deeply grateful to Professor Watson for undertaking the task of preparing it. It is a great pleasure to me that this work, which has long been out of print, is now again available, and in an unabridged form.

It is tempting to join issue in this Preface with a number of English authors who have paid more particular attention to my work. I think especially of J. Burnaby's *Amor Dei* (1938) and M. C. D'Arcy's *The Mind and Heart of Love: A Study in Eros and Agape* (1945). But as the reason why these important and interesting works come to different conclusions from my own, is essentially that they start from different premisses, any profitable discussion of them would have to be conducted at considerable length, and for that there is no room in a Preface. I have therefore had to resist the temptation of an otherwise very attractive undertaking. In the discussion of the subject that has so far taken place, I have found no reason to abandon my original position at any point, and my work is therefore being republished without alteration.

ANDERS NYGREN.

TRANSLATOR'S PREFACE

PART I of this work consists of a study of the Christian idea of love as it appears in the New Testament and in contrast to the Hellenistic idea. With this, both the starting-point for the history of the Christian idea of love is given and also the essential distinction between the two " fundamental motifs" (Eros and Agape) which have left their impress upon it. That history is described in Part II up to the point where the problem of " Agape and Eros " finds its natural solution in the Reformation. It is substantially the story of how a synthesis of these two " motifs " was prepared, completed, and destroyed. In his original Preface to Part I the author explained why he had chosen the Reformation as his *terminus ad quem*.[1] It was not that the Christian idea of love had had no history since the Reformation, nor that the problem of " Agape and Eros " had ceased to exist as a result of the solution then found for it. It was rather because the development of Christian thought about love had proceeded along somewhat different lines, and could not very suitably be discussed under the heading of " Agape and Eros ".

Since this work first appeared in English, there have been a number of recurrent misunderstandings of its theme, which may perhaps be obviated if something is said here about the meaning of the major technical terms employed in it.[2] We may begin with the two that are in the title: Agape and Eros.

---

[1] *Den kristna kärlekstanken genom tiderna. Eros och Agape I.* (Svenska Kyrkans Diakonistyrelses Bokförlag. Stockholm, 1930), pp. 3f. (Part II was issued by the same publishers in 1936.)

[2] See also my article on " Some Theological Implications of Agape and Eros " in *The Expository Times*, September 1938.

These are Greek words, both commonly translated as "love". They are used here to represent two quite distinct ideas of love, one of them prevalent in the ancient Hellenistic world, where it was called *eros*, and the other characteristic of primitive Christianity, to which it was known as *agape*. Eros and Agape are thus used in a highly specialised sense. There is no suggestion that, wherever the Greek word *eros* or the Greek word *agape* occurs, it must necessarily have the same meaning as it bears here, or that this meaning cannot be represented on occasion by other words.[1] Nor is there any suggestion that every form of love that existed in the Hellenistic world, or that exists in the non-Christian world generally, must be classified as Eros. That would be as foolish as to claim that pure Agape was the only form of love that ever existed among Christians. The question under discussion is not how the Greeks or the primitive Christians actually loved, but what they thought about love, their ideas or theories of love.

The Eros that is here contrasted with Agape, stands for a quite specific conception of love, of which the classical example is Plato's "heavenly Eros". This is a human love for the Divine, a love of man for God. But it should be observed that not everything which can be called man's love for God is to be identified with Eros. Eros is an appetite, a yearning desire, which is aroused by the attractive qualities of its object; and in Eros-love man seeks God in order to satisfy his spiritual hunger by the possession and enjoyment of the Divine perfections. But the love of man for God of which the New Testament speaks is of a quite different stamp. It means a whole-hearted surrender to God, whereby man becomes God's willing slave, content to be at His disposal, having entire trust and confidence in Him, and desiring only

---

[1] In Gnosticism *agape* came to represent what Plato had called " Vulgar Eros " (*cf. infra* pp. 303 ff.); and elsewhere the idea of Agape was represented by, e.g., *philanthropia* (*infra* p. 374, n. 1).

that His will should be done. This love is not, like Eros, a longing and striving after something man lacks and needs, but a response of gratitude for something freely and bountifully given, namely, God's own Agape; and although it can itself be called Agape, its character as response is more clearly marked when it is described (by St. Paul especially) as "faith". God's love, Agape in the fullest sense of the term, has neither the appetitive nature of Eros nor the responsive character of Faith; it is entirely independent of external stimulus and motivation. God loves because it is His nature to love, and His loving consists, not in getting, but in doing good.

Agape is further distinguished from Eros in that it is "indifferent to value". That is to say, it is neither kindled by the attractiveness nor quenched by the unattractiveness of its object. This is seen most clearly in God's love for sinners, who are loved in spite of their sin. Not that God prefers sinful to righteous men, or that sinners are somehow more worthy of His love. His loving is not determined by the worthiness or unworthiness of those whom He loves, but by His own nature of love. God always retains the initiative in loving. Such a love as this cannot be shown by man towards God, since man's love for God at its best is never more than a response to God's prior love for man. But man can show such a love towards his fellow-men. He can become a child of the heavenly Father and learn to love his enemies as the Father does. Not that he will love his enemies to the exclusion of his friends, any more than the heavenly Father's love for sinful men excludes His love for His sinless Son. But his loving will not be determined by the friendship or enmity shown to him by others. This freedom of Agape-love in relation to its object is the main point when it is said to be "indifferent to value". But indifference to value does not mean indifference to response. Naturally, Agape seeks to be accepted by those to whom it is offered. Why else should it be offered? To Eros, on the other hand, which is far from

" indifferent to value ", the question of a response on the part of the loved object is far less important.[1] For Eros does not seek to be accepted by its object, but to gain possession of it.

Now Eros and Agape are described as two " fundamental motifs "—to which a third, called " Nomos ", is added in Part II—and this whole work is conceived as a " study of motifs " or a piece of " motif-research ". What, then, do these terms mean? Motif-research is the name given to a method of investigation that is directed to discover the fundamental motif of any given outlook or system of thought. And the fundamental motif is that factor in virtue of which a particular outlook or system possesses its own peculiar character as distinct from all others. It is the fundamental meaning behind the outward forms and expressions, which gives them their significance; it is that essential constituent which gives coherence to the whole and makes it what it is. Similar or identical forms and expressions may sometimes conceal totally different motifs, while widely differing forms and expressions may sometimes represent the same motif. Such a motif is discovered as the answer supplied by any given outlook or system to a question of so fundamentally necessary a nature that it can be called a fundamental question; and motif-research sets out to ask and answer such questions.

In the present instance it is solely with religious outlooks or systems we are concerned. With regard to religion, then, what question is of so fundamentally necessary a nature that it can be called a fundamental question? The nature of religion itself supplies the answer. Religion is fellowship with the eternal, with God. The question of questions for any religion, therefore, is: How is fellowship with God conceived; how is it supposed to be realised, in what does it consist? The answer to this question reveals the fundamental

_____

[1] If indeed it is important at all. The loved object may, like Aristotle's God who " moves by being loved ", be itself entirely unmoved.

motif of the religion under discussion. For if the essence of religion is fellowship with God, then the ultimately determinative factor of any actual, historical religion must be the way in which it conceives of fellowship with God. Now the answers given to this question by Hellenism, by Judaism, and by Christianity are conceived respectively in terms of Eros, of Nomos, and of Agape. Man's desire for heavenly things, man's fulfilling of the Law, and God's own love freely bestowed on the sinner—these are three different ways to fellowship with God. Eros, Nomos, and Agape—these are the fundamental motifs of Hellenism, Judaism, and Christianity.

It will be noticed that of these three ways to fellowship with God, the first two are sharply, indeed absolutely, distinguished from the last, inasmuch as the former are centred in man, egocentric,[1] while the latter is centred in God, theocentric.[2] Now it is true that there probably does not exist a religion which entirely lacks all traces of theocentricity.[3] But such traces do not constitute a fundamental motif. They are rather isolated glimpses, and it is first in Christianity that the theocentric way of salvation, of fellowship with God, is fully seen : salvation comes from God and leads to God, and God's will is given unqualified affirmation. This is the way of Agape. In non-Christian sources the theocentric tendency is strongest in the Old Testament; and yet Judaism is an egocentric religion inasmuch as its fundamental motif is Nomos : it regards fellowship with God as something to be achieved in virtue of man's fulfilment of the Law; it is a theology of merit.[4] Hellenistic religion, again, is egocentric inasmuch as

---

[1] "*Egocentric*" because in the matter of *my* fellowship with God the emphasis is all on *my* doing and desiring.

[2] Because the emphasis is on God's action.

[3] *Cf. infra* p. 206.

[4] From the point of view of the New Testament, of course, for which the Old Testament is *Christian* scripture, Judaism with its Nomos motif is a perversion of the religion of the Old Testament, due to a complete failure to understand the true nature and function of the Law.

Eros, the heavenward directed desire, does not seek God for His own sake, but as the *summum bonum* which alone can satisfy man's wants and needs. That is, it seeks God as a means to an end, the satisfaction of itself, so that what it essentially seeks is not God, but its own "highest good", which it happens to identify with God.

Now it is characteristic of a fundamental motif that it sets its mark on every aspect of the outlook or system of thought in which it occurs. We have an example of this in the Christian conception of the creative and the redemptive activity of God. God created us men without our aid, without any doing or deserving or desiring of ours. He created us "out of nothing", and all that we have and are He has given us freely and for nothing. If we ask what moved Him to do this, the answer is that He loved us—with that unmerited and unmeritable love which is Agape. "This" (as St. Augustine somewhere says) "is the grace of creation". But the full depth of divine Agape is not seen until it appears in "the grace of our Lord Jesus Christ". Here God's love is displayed in the redemption of lost, sinful men, who not only could not save themselves from sin and death, but deserved the very opposite of salvation—and can hardly be said to have been looking for the kind of salvation that was actually offered them. Both creation and redemption, therefore, are the work of "grace" or of free, generous Agape. The Divine love that lets the sun shine and the rain fall on the just and the unjust, and the love of God that is in Christ Jesus our Lord, are one and the same. Moreover, every genuinely Christian doctrine gives expression in one way or another to the thought of this love, from which also flows that essential principle of Christian ethical life: "Freely ye received, freely give."

If this point had been duly observed, the mistake would not have been made (as it more than once has) of equating the problem of Eros and Agape with that of "Nature and

Grace ". Grace here represents God's redemptive activity, Nature His creative work, and Eros is regarded as belonging to the sphere of Nature. This may mean that Eros is " natural " to man in the sense that it is an essential characteristic of human nature (or, if we follow Aristotle, of universal nature) as created by God. In that case, God is the author of Eros; and there cannot be any fundamental conflict between Eros and Agape, since both come from the same God. If they seem to conflict, we must seek a reconciliation and a synthesis. But this is an odd argument. We might as well say that God is the author of sin—which in one sense is only too " natural " to man—as that He is the author of Eros; for if God is Agape, Eros is totally contrary to His nature. Agape is a love that loves to give, freely, selflessly; Eros is a love that loves to get, a highly refined form of self-interest and self-seeking. Therefore it must be regarded as sinful by the Agape that " seeketh not its own ". Agape is opposed to all forms of selfishness, however refined they may be—for by no means all forms of human self-interest and egocentricity, even of a refined and spiritual kind, are to be identified with Eros. If the Neoplatonist is egocentric in his Eros, the Pharisee is just as egocentric in his aspiration to a place in the Kingdom of God on the ground of his own righteousness, his observance of the Law. But Hellenistic Eros-religion and the Judaistic religion of Nomos are by no means the same thing, although both are opposed to the religion of Agape.

From the egocentric standpoint of Eros and Nomos, Agape is " irrational ". Eros finds abundant reason for man to love God, in that God possesses what man lacks and seeks; but no reason for God to love man, since man possesses nothing that God could desire. Nomos finds good reason for God to love the righteous, in that they deserve well of Him; but no reason for Him to love sinners—why, the very idea is absurd and blasphemous. For Agape, however, no such eudemonistic and legalistic reasons can be given. The God of Agape loves simply because it is His nature to love—and the children of God love because they take after their Father and delight to do as He does. Agape is by nature so utterly self-forgetful and self-sacrificial that it may well seem (from an egocentric point of view at any rate) to involve the supreme irrationality of the destruction of the self, as some critics have alleged that it does. But in fact, Agape means the death, not of the self, but of selfishness; it is the antithesis, not of selfhood, but of self-centredness, which is the deadliest enemy of true self-hood. Man realises his true self just in so far as he lives by and in Agape. That is what he was created for by God, who is Agape. Man cannot become what he is meant to be, so long as he is self-centred, taken up with himself. He needs to be taken out of himself, out of his cramping preoccupation with himself and his own affairs. And that is precisely what Agape does for him in so far as he accepts it. It delivers him out of the prison of his egocentricity into the glorious liberty of the children of God. From the point of view of Agape, the rationality of Eros and Nomos is that of the "natural man", who can see no sense in doing anything for nothing unless he does it for himself—and who is prepared to "rationalise" even God's Agape by explaining it as an expression of Divine self-love.

Now in the light of what has been said, it is clear that whenever the Nomos or Eros motif encounters the Agape motif there is bound to be conflict, open or concealed. The Agape motif can never enter into a real synthesis with either of the other two, since egocentricity and theocentricity are quite incompatible. But this must not be taken to mean that nothing in Judaism or Hellenism can be regarded as having any value for the Christian. Such a view would be absurd. Christianity is absolutely exclusive in the sense that it admits no religious motif which does not derive by necessity from the idea of Agape, no way of fellowship with God but the way of God's Agape. Yet it is far from the case that every-thing in non-Christian religions, let alone in non-Christian cultures, is false and worthless from the point of view of Christianity. In the Old Testament Judaism has contributed a priceless treasure to the Christian Church; and it is not the cultural values of Hellenism, but Hellenism as religion, that is incompatible with Christianity. To say that Christianity admits only one way of salvation, one way of fellowship with God, which is strictly theocentric, and rejects all other ways, is not to say that it denies the existence of good and valuable things in the non-Christian world. On the contrary, it is quick to perceive them, and to give the glory to God, from whose boundless Agape comes everything that is good.

With such values, however, whether cultural or religious, this work is not concerned. Its aim is not to draw out the wider implications of the Christian idea of love, but simply to understand it; therefore it is not within its province to dis-cuss such questions. It deals strictly with the nature of the idea of Agape and the historical vicissitudes through which it has passed. This or any other fundamental motif is rarely, if ever, found in its quite pure form in practice, but there is a continual interplay in which now one, now another, gains the upper hand and leaves its impress on the whole outlook of the individual or school which it dominates, while the other motifs are subordinated to it, or even transformed by being pressed into its service. This process is illustrated in the following pages by studies of the outstanding representa-tives of the different types in the history of the Church. In a series of conflicts between the rival motifs, the most unex-pected permutations and combinations are revealed, and it is as a story of dramatic struggle, of fierce hostilities and strange alliances, that the history of the Christian idea of love unfolds.

In a work of this kind, two principles must be observed. First, merely to consider formal statements of doctrine is not enough; we must discover the underlying religious motif, the real motive forces behind them. Secondly, while doing this we must take care not to force upon the material a theory alien to it. A study of motifs is only valid in so far as it makes for a better understanding of the material, and its capacity to do justice to this is the test of its tenability. The latter point is no less important than the first. Dr. Nygren has therefore sought to let the authors speak for themselves, avoiding as far as possible traditional labels and accepted characterisations. His aim has been at every point to keep the reader aware in some measure of contact with the sources.

For the sources the chief editions used are indicated in the footnotes, except in the case of the following: For the Apostolic Fathers, *Patrum apostolicorum opera, rec. Gebhardt, Harnack, Zahn, ed. sexta minor,* 1920; for Justin and Tatian, *Die ältesten Apologeten. Texte mit kurzen Einleitungen hrsg. v. Edgar J. Goodspeed,* 1914; for the rest of the Apologists, *Corpus apologetarum, ed. Otto;* for Clement of Alexandria, Origen, Hippolytus, Eusebius, Methodius, Epiphanius, *Die griechischen christlichen Schriftsteller der ersten drei Jahrhunderte, hrsg. von der Kirchenväter-Commission der Königl. Preussischen Akademie der Wissenschaften;* for Irenaeus, *Irenaei Quae supersunt omnia, ed. A. Stieren, Bd. I.,* 1853 (for the " Contra hæreses "), and *Bibliothek der Kirchenväter, Bd. IV.,* 1912 (S. Weber's translation of the " Epideixis "); for Tertullian, the Vienna *Corpus scriptorum ecclesiasticorum latinorum,* and Fr. Oehler's edition of works not yet available in the Vienna Corpus.

In cases of translation from the sources, there has been reference to English versions where these are available, but whenever it has seemed desirable, for the sake of clarity or closer conformity to Dr. Nygren's rendering, to depart from them, this has been done. It has seemed advisable to give an English rendering of the German sources generally and of Luther's German and Latin, while retaining the references to the edition in which the original appears. The original has been given only where a translation or close paraphrase already occurs in the text.

The passage from Luther which stands as a motto for Part II (*infra*, p. 233) comes from the Heidelberg Disputation of 1518, thesis 28—*Weimar Auflage* (*WA*) I, p. 365. This thesis is discussed below (pp. 506 f.).

PHILIP S. WATSON.

Handsworth Methodist College,
    Birmingham.
        August, 1951.

THE PROBLEM OF AGAPE AND EROS

I

THE NATURE OF THE PROBLEM

1. THE TWOFOLD PURPOSE OF THE INQUIRY

THE purpose of the present inquiry is twofold: first, to investigate the meaning of the Christian idea of love; and secondly, to illustrate the main changes it has undergone in the course of history.

It might reasonably have been expected that theologians would have given special attention to these questions, for it is plain that the idea of love occupies a—not to say the—central place in Christianity, both from a religious and an ethical point of view. Yet we have only to glance at the treatment the subject has received from theologians in recent times, to see that it is among the most neglected. In the history of doctrine, comprehensive and painstaking work has been devoted to the elucidation of quite peripheral details, while this central question has been largely left on one side, as though the meaning and structure of the Christian idea of love were self-evident and unambiguous, and were sufficiently defined by the mere mention of the word " love "; and as though the idea of love had had one and the same significance for all Christians in all ages. Nor is the position any different when we turn to the history of Christian ethics. Here, too, the details are often well worked out, and we are given particulars of what were often quite unimportant modifications of current ethical ideas and ideals by individual thinkers; but little is said of the new foundation provided for ethics by Christianity with its new conception of love. The Christian idea of love, which involves a revolution in ethical outlook without parallel in the history of ethics, a revolution rightly described by Nietzsche as a complete " transvaluation of all ancient values "—this idea and the vicissitudes through which it has passed in Christian history are scarcely mentioned in the traditional histories of ethics.

The neglect of these questions on the theological side can be illustrated from the latest edition (1929) of the most modern theological work of reference, *Die Religion in Geschichte und Gegenwart*. The reader who turns to the article "Liebe" for guidance as to the meaning of Christian love finds, in addition to a number of exegetical notes, an attempt at systematic treatment of the subject. But what an attempt! No effort is made to fathom the depths of the Christian idea of love, but it is treated as if it hardly needed explanation; and the writer is chiefly concerned to bolster up Christian love with the aid of a self-respect based on self-love.[1] Nor is anything said of what has happened to Christian love during the long development of Christianity; there is not a hint that it has had an eventful history, full of conflict and dramatic changes. The treatment of the history of ethics in the *Hand-buch der Philosophie* similarly illustrates a widespread failure to see where the great and decisive ethical crises have

---

[1] *R.G.G.*,[2] vol. iii., 1929, cols. 1641-1643. The idea of basing Christian love on self-respect is here worked out in three ways. (1) The question is raised, " Whether love can possibly be commanded and produced at will?" The commandment of love is said to be especially dangerous when it is directed to " children and young people . . . before they have acquired a fund of self-respect and faith in God and men." (2) It is asserted that love " is by no means the root or foundation or source of all Christian morality." The foundation is rather the self-respect that rests on self-love, while Christian love is " the top story of the edifice of Christian character." (3) The importance of Nietzsche's criticism of Christian " slave-morality " is emphasised " as an ally in the struggle for a pure, unvarnished neighbourly love united with a strong self-reliance and a strong sense of honour and justice." That is what we learn from this article about the meaning of the Christian idea of love.

occurred. The Christian idea of love has passed through two such crises—in primitive Christianity and at the Reformation; but in the *Handbuch* the former is treated simply as a background for the ethical theories of the Middle Ages, and Luther is just mentioned in connection with the break-up of Scholasticism.

To describe the changes that the Christian idea of love has undergone through the centuries would be ultimately the same as to write the entire inner history of Christianity. Every generation has had to face the problem of Christian love, and every new period has made a characteristic contribution to its history. These contributions, it is true, have not always been such as to disclose fresh aspects of the Christian idea of love; but then they are all the more revealing in respect of the structure and spiritual temper of their times. It is not the least interesting feature of the history of the Christian idea of love that the characteristics of the several periods are so clearly discernible in it.

It is not, however, our purpose to give a full and comprehensive account of the history of the Christian idea of love and of the way in which the different periods have reacted to it. We are not so much interested in the peculiarities of the different periods as in the distinctive character of the Christian conception of love. There are times, like those of primitive Christianity and the Reformation, when the specifically Christian conception thrusts itself powerfully to the fore; at other times it has to struggle, often against odds, to maintain itself against alien conceptions of love, but just by contrast with these it is compelled to reveal something of its own unique quality. It is on such periods that we shall concentrate our inquiry, and in this way the two tasks we have set ourselves will be interrelated. For although it is only when we understand the inner meaning of the Christian idea of love that we can understand the real significance of the changes it has undergone, yet by noticing these changes we shall be the better able to see what its essential meaning is, and by watching its reactions to other conceptions of love we shall pave the way for an analysis of its content and structure.

2. Two Opposed Fundamental Motifs

Of all the other views that have confronted the Christian idea of love, or *agape*, and have forced it to a decision—whether to the decision of a life-and-death struggle or of a settlement by compromise—by far the most important is that view of love which finds its most complete and classical expression in the Platonic conception of *eros*. When the Christian idea of Agape first enters on the scene it finds a quite different religious and ethical outlook already in possession of the stage, an outlook thoroughly dominated by the idea of Eros in the widest sense of that term. The meeting of Christianity with this basic religious tendency of the ancient world can well be described as its hour of destiny. For although Agape is " the transvaluation of all ancient values ", yet after that meeting it was inevitable that it should in some measure take up those values into itself, or even be itself taken up into the ancient scheme of values; and in either case the idea of Agape was bound to lose something of its original force. Hence arises the problem that has made itself felt in different contexts and in the most varied forms through the whole of Christian history ever since: the problem of Eros and Agape.

No long familiarity with this problem is needed to show that it is of a very peculiar kind. Its peculiarity can be plainly seen from the following facts: first, that in Eros and Agape we have two conceptions which have originally nothing whatsoever to do with one another; and, second, that in the course of history they have none the less become so thoroughly bound up and interwoven with one another that it is hardly possible for us to speak of either without our thoughts being drawn to the other. Any attempt to draw a clear and essential distinction between Eros and Agape, therefore, can easily look like a violent and artificial separation of things that by nature belong together.

At this introductory stage it is most important to insist on the original absence of any relation between Eros and Agape. Wilamowitz-Moellendorff, in his great work on Plato, has rightly expressed sharp condemnation of the common habit of confusing Platonic Eros with New Testament Agape. He says: " A brief but emphatic word of warning must here be given against the old but now no longer always harmless misunderstanding by which Plato's Eros is confused with the Agape to which Paul dedicates his ' Hymn to Love ' in 1 Cor. xiii. . . As the latter knew nothing of Eros, so the former knew nothing of Agape; they could have learnt something from one another here, but being what they were, they would not have done so."[1] There cannot actually be any doubt that Eros and Agape belong originally to two entirely separate spiritual worlds, between which no direct communication is possible. They do not represent the same value in their respective contexts, so that they cannot in any circumstances be rightly substituted for one another.

At first sight this observation seems only to make our inquiry more difficult. Eros and Agape were to be compared and contrasted with one another; but it now looks as if they were essentially incommensurable, since the necessary point of comparison appears to be lacking. It is, however, of the utmost importance that we should accustom ourselves from the beginning to the idea that we cannot count on any *direct* correspondence and commensurability between Eros and Agape. Only as we do so shall we be able to take an unbiased view of the problem and see it as it really is.

There are two influences in particular that tend to distort

---

[1] *Platon*, I., 1919, p. 384. *Cf.* also *op. cit.*, II., 1919, p. 71 : ". . . the kind of nonsense talked by the theologians when they confuse ἀγάπη and ἔρως."

our view of the issue. The first is a more than thousand year old tradition, which tells us that Eros and Agape belong together and must be connected with one another. No great proof is needed to show the binding power of such a tradition. Almost everywhere in the history of the Christian idea of love we find Eros and Agape most intimately connected with one another, and it is therefore difficult to escape the impression that this connection is natural and necessary. The second, and no less powerful, influence is the power of language over thought. Eros and Agape are Greek words, both of which are represented in our language by the one word " love ". What, then, could be more natural than to assume that behind the one word there is one and the same idea, and to conclude that Eros and Agape stand for one and the same reality, or at any rate for closely related realities? Whatever the relation between Eros and Agape may be, at least they appear to have the most essential thing in common, inasmuch as they are both " love ";[1] and from this point of view they are but different versions of the same thing. But the double spell cast upon us by tradition and language is broken as soon as we realise that Eros and Agape have originally nothing whatever to do with one another. Then, however, the connection between them is no longer self-evident, but becomes a problem.

Eros and Agape can be confronted with one another in three different ways. We can take them simply as words, and consider the relation between them mainly from a philological point of view; or we can regard them as two independently developed historical conceptions which call for comparison; or we can conceive of them as two different

[1] The inconvenience of using the word "love" to represent two such different things as Eros and Agape is obvious. In his *Grundlegung der Ethik als Wissenschaft*, 1925, J. Rehmke distinguishes between two meanings of "love", which for lack of suitable terminology he describes as "Liebe¹" and "Liebe² ". The distinction he has in mind does not precisely coincide with that between Eros and Agape, but it illustrates the terminological difficulty we have to face.

general attitudes of mind, two distinct religious and ethical fundamental motifs.

It is an evident fact that when the New Testament speaks of love it makes large use of the word ἀγάπη, but consistently avoids the word ἔρως. This striking linguistic peculiarity can hardly be accidental, and it suggests obvious questions. Why is the one word and not the other an appropriate term for love as Christianity thinks of it? What is the original meaning and derivation of the two words? What is it that gives each of them its peculiar shade of meaning? And so forth. For our present purposes, however, we have no occasion to embark upon this precarious line of inquiry. We are not using the terms Agape and Eros in their general philological sense, but with reference to the special content with which creative minds have filled them. In the case of Eros we may think first and foremost of Plato, and in the case of Agape we may think, say, of Paul. But we obviously can never learn from the simple, common meaning of the words what Plato makes of Eros or what Paul makes of Agape. This we must discover from their writings, where it often assumes a remarkably plastic form.

We pass on, then, to a comparison of Eros and Agape in the second of the senses mentioned above. Two independent historical conceptions, the Eros of Plato and the Agape (say) of Paul, are to be compared with one another. But we are immediately confronted with a difficulty. Will not the original lack of connection between these conceptions, which we noted above, prove an insuperable obstacle to such a comparison? Since Paul knows nothing of Eros, and Plato nothing of Agape, will there be any point in comparing Eros with Agape in this sense? Platonic Eros and Pauline Agape have, so to speak, no common denominator; they are not answers to the same question. Why, then, should we compare them at all? Is it not arbitrary, and therefore meaningless, to compare phenomena that have arisen under such different conditions?

The right answer to the question of the relation between Eros and Agape, when it is stated in this second way, might very well be that there is no relation between them at all.

The position is quite different when we set Eros and Agape over against one another in the third of the ways suggested, as different general attitudes to life. In this sense there is a very real relation between them. There is quite concrete proof of the existence both of an attitude to life of which the hall-mark is Eros, and equally concrete proof of the existence of another attitude to life of which the hall-mark is Agape; and these two general attitudes do not run side by side like parallel lines that never meet, but they constantly run into one another. At every point in the history of the spiritual life there is concrete evidence of a relation between them, inasmuch as each of them strives to put its stamp on the spiritual life as a whole. When we speak of Eros and Agape, therefore, we are thinking of them all the time in this sense—that is, as " fundamental motifs ". Our task is to discover their roots and determine their characteristics. For this purpose, of course, we can draw material from the particular historical forms in which they have appeared; but it is never these forms, as such, that we shall be comparing with one another, but always Eros and Agape as fundamental motifs.

3. Fundamental Motifs and Motif-Research

The term " fundamental motif " requires more precise definition, and two questions in particular call for an answer. First, what do we mean by describing anything as a fundamental motif? And, secondly, what right have we to describe Agape as a fundamental motif of Christianity? The idea of Agape meets us as one among other characteristically Christian ideas. Have we then any grounds for ascribing to the idea of love such a special position and such a fundamental importance as is expressed by the term " fundamental motif "? Before we go on to give a definite answer to these questions, it may be well to prepare the way with some preliminary observations on the meaning of motif-research.

The most important task of those engaged in the modern scientific study of religion and theological research is to reach an inner understanding of the different forms of religion in the light of their different fundamental motifs. For a long time they have been chiefly occupied in collecting a vast mass of material drawn from different religious sources for the purposes of comparison. But when the comparison actually comes to be made, the uncertainty of it immediately becomes apparent; for it is plain that no conclusion can be drawn from the mere fact that one and the same idea or belief occurs in different religious contexts. The idea or belief may have exactly the same form without having at all the same meaning, if in one case it is a basic conception, while in the other it is more loosely attached. Its meaning cannot be the same if —as is naturally most often the case—its setting is different in the different religions. What such an idea, or belief, or sentiment really means, can only be decided in the light of its own natural context. In other words, we must try to see what is the basic idea or the driving power of the religion concerned, or what it is that gives it its character as a whole and communicates to all its parts their special content and colour. It is the attempt to carry out such a structural analysis, whether in the sphere of religion or elsewhere, that we describe as motif-research.

4. MOTIF-RESEARCH AND HISTORICAL-GENETIC RESEARCH

As distinct from historical-genetic research, motif-research is concerned less with the historical connections and origins of motifs than with their characteristic content and typical manifestations. This may suggest that in adopting the method of motif-research we are dangerously departing from the safe and solid ground of empirical fact. Does not the quest for the fundamental motif of a religion introduce an element of valuation, and therefore a subjective element, into the inquiry? When, in dealing with a spiritual phenomenon, we distinguish between "fundamental" and "non-fundamental" conceptions, and regard the latter as at most a development of the former, this distinction seems not to be given in the phenomenon itself, but to be imported into it by our imaginative reconstruction of it. But is not such a procedure more akin to artistic synthesis than to scientific analysis, more a matter of intuition than of investigation? And does not motif-research expose us to the risk of arbitrary subjectivism, from which we are safe so long as we stick to the given facts and refrain from distinguishing between fundamental and more peripheral motifs? In answer to these questions there are two things to be said.

First, it is an illusion to suppose that objectivity and empirical accuracy are guaranteed by sticking to the individual data of the spiritual life. There is nothing to be gained by that except an unrealistic spiritual atomism. A mass of disconnected elements is gathered, which can be arranged in the most diverse patterns, and we can never even be sure that we have rightly understood any single one of them since their meaning depends on the context to which they belong. In order to grasp the meaning of a spiritual phenomenon, it is obviously not enough to know the elements of which it is composed, but we must also know the connection between them; and this connection, it should be noted, is no less empirically given than the elements themselves. When, therefore, motif-research concentrates on this connection—since "fundamental motif" stands for that to which the connection is due—it has in no way departed from empirical ground, but has simply directed our attention from one empirical element to another.

Secondly, the conditions of motif-research are misunderstood if we imagine that it rests on essentially unverifiable intuition and has no use for scientific analysis. It cannot, of course, be denied that the underlying idea or fundamental motif of a religion may be intuitively discerned, or that such an intuition is of inestimable value for motif-research. But intuition alone does not constitute research; and if we are to speak of research in this connection the gains of intuition must be subjected to scientific analysis and verification. The question we have to answer here, therefore, is whether it is at all possible by means of scientific analysis to determine the fundamental motif of any given form of religion. The answer can only be an unqualified affirmative. The purpose of the scientific study of religion is not merely to record the actual conceptions, attitudes, and so forth, that are found in a particular religious *milieu*, but more especially to find out what is characteristic and typical of them all. That is what motif-research deliberately and consistently seeks to do, and is indeed fully capable of doing. What we regard as a fundamental motif need not be a matter of subjective and arbitrary choice, for it is open to objective examination. A religion deprived of its fundamental motif would lose all coherence and meaning; and therefore we cannot rightly regard anything as a fundamental motif unless its removal would have such an effect. This gives us the basic principle on which motif-research must proceed with its analysis. It need only be added, in order to prevent a possible misunderstanding, that the fundamental motif need by no means consist of a clearly formulated idea, but can equally well consist of a general underlying sentiment.

Motif-research, then, is in no more unfavourable a position than any other empirical investigation. Sometimes it can actually produce more fully assured results than historical-genetic research. To discover the origins of a particular motif, the soil from which it has sprung, and how it has found its way into a particular religious outlook, can be extremely difficult. Hypothesis can stand against hypothesis with no possibility of an objective decision between them. But the place and importance of the motif in the outlook in question may nevertheless be unmistakably clear. This indicates a certain difference of approach between the two types of research. Both are concerned with motifs, but historical-genetic research is interested chiefly in their migrations, so to speak, and in the historically demonstrable connections between similar motifs in different places. Motif-research, as we have described it, is primarily interested in the content of the motifs, and it can show us that the same or similar motifs are to be found even in cases where there is no reason to suspect historical dependence.

5. Motif-Research and Value-Judgments

We have distinguished motif-research from historical-genetic research. It is still more important, though it should be unnecessary, to distinguish it clearly from every kind of valuation. We have described motif-research as a type of scientific analysis, and that alone is enough to show that there can be no question of any value-judgment. The task of science is to understand, not to appraise. This elementary fact is still far from generally recognised, however, and therefore it must be explicitly stated.

Unless this point is fully and clearly grasped the whole of the following exposition is likely to be misconstrued. It is as easy as it is wrong, when we set the Christian idea of Agape over against the ancient idea of Eros, to suppose that we are comparing them with reference to their respective values, or even that we are assuming the superior value of the idea of Agape and making it the criterion for an unfavourable judgment on the idea of Eros. Support for such a view is given by the fact that we frequently have occasion to show how an admixture of the Eros motif has weakened the Agape motif and rendered it more or less ineffective. In order to prevent this kind of misunderstanding it may be stated categorically at the outset that our exposition is entirely indifferent to the question of value. Admittedly we are dealing with "values", but our attitude to them is that of an observer who wishes to understand, not of a valuer assessing their worth. Agape and Eros are contrasted with one another here, not as right and wrong, nor as higher and lower, but as Christian and non-Christian fundamental motifs. We are dealing with a difference of type, not of value. It is, of course, true that Eros and Agape are still living forces which can compel us to decide our personal attitude to them; but that is something entirely outside the province of science. Such a decision is a personal affair which is determined by quite other than scientific considerations. If, finally, in our treatment of the idea of Eros we have in view primarily the solvent effects it has had on the Agape motif, that is simply due to the nature of the task we have set ourselves. Our purpose is to give an account of the Christian idea of love and the vicissitudes through which it has passed. If our purpose were to expound the idea of Eros and its vicissitudes, the emphasis of our inquiry would be correspondingly changed, and the idea of Agape would be regarded chiefly from the point of view of its solvent effects on the Eros motif. Hence even at this point there is no question of a value-judgment.

It is not, however, simply in order to prevent possible misunderstanding that the indifference of this exposition to the question of value must be emphasised. The value-judgment has a habit of claiming pride of place even in scientific discussion, greatly to the detriment of theoretical clarity. It is sometimes very plain, for instance, that those who find an indispensable value in the idea of Eros as well as in that of Agape have a certain interest in glossing over and minimising the essential difference between them. Their argument can be put briefly as follows: both are valuable, therefore they cannot be ultimately irreconcilable. Here a third factor, which may be termed the primacy of the practical value-judgment, joins the two already discussed—the power of language and the power of tradition—in encouraging the confusion of Eros and Agape. In opposition to the pressure of all such alien interests it will be our task to delineate as sharply as possible the characteristics of both fundamental motifs and to make clear their relation to one another.

II

THE PLACE OF THE IDEA OF AGAPE IN CHRISTIANITY

1. MORE PRECISE DEFINITION OF THE TERM "FUNDAMENTAL MOTIF"

WE started by saying that the idea of love occupies a central place in Christianity. That is so obvious a fact that it would hardly seem to need any special investigation. But it is also a fact that the idea of Agape in Christianity constitutes the answer to certain quite definite questions; and, obviously, we can only understand the full force of an answer if we are clear about the question that is being answered. The same idea can have very different meanings, according as it represents the answer to one question or another. Hence it is by no means superfluous to inquire more closely into the question or questions to which the idea of Agape is intended as the answer. In this way the idea of Agape will be placed in its proper setting, related to its context.

We have indicated the central importance of love in Christianity by describing it as a Christian "fundamental motif"; but this term can be variously understood and we have still to define it. We raised, but did not answer, the two following questions: (1) What do we mean by describing anything as a fundamental motif? (2) What right have we to ascribe to the idea of Agape, which is after all only one among other characteristically Christian ideas, such fundamental significance as to call it a fundamental motif? These questions must now receive a definite answer.

First, then, what do we mean by calling anything a fundamental motif? The primary associations of the term are perhaps with the realm of art. The fundamental motif is that which makes a work of art into a unified whole, determines its structure, and gives it its specific character. It is the theme that constantly recurs in new variations, imparting its own tone and colour to the whole. But broad and indefinite statements like these are insufficient to show the precise sense in which we are using the term "fundamental motif". For this purpose the following definition may be given: *A fundamental motif is that which forms the answer given by some particular outlook to a question of such a fundamental nature that it can be described in a categorical sense as a fundamental question.* To develop the full meaning of this statement we should have to go into the whole doctrine of the categories, for which this is naturally not the place. All we can do here is to touch on the most necessary points.

If we take the broadest possible survey of human thought, we get a lively impression of the truth of the old saying that there is nothing—or very little—new under the sun. There are a certain few themes which constantly recur in fresh variations and combinations, but in such a way that the old theme can still be recognised in the new forms. Quite early in the history of thought we find the great fundamental questions asked concerning the True, the Beautiful, the Good, and—to crown them all—the Eternal. For our Western civilisation the formal statement of these questions was the work of Plato, though the materials for it were in existence long before his time. And great as the changes may be which these questions have undergone since, we can none the less say that we are still occupied ultimately with these same great questions today when we speak of the problems of Knowledge, of Æsthetics, of Ethics, and of Religion. Indeed, we might very well describe the whole development of civilised thought as a constantly renewed attempt to state these questions and fix their meaning. It happens, however, from time to time in the historical process that the meaning of one or other of these questions is completely altered. This is the way in which new developments take place with respect to the great fundamental questions of humanity. It is not that a traditional question is set aside and a new question substituted for it, but rather that a new meaning is unexpectedly discovered in the old question. The form of the question remains unchanged, but its content is different; it does not *mean* the same; the frame is old but the picture is new.

When we speak of a fundamental motif we are moving in the realm of those comprehensive, ultimate questions which we have just mentioned. The fundamental motif is the answer given by some particular type of outlook to one or more of these questions. This answer need by no means take the form of a theoretical proposition; it can equally well be a general, underlying sentiment which involves a certain attitude towards these questions or—more passively—a certain reaction to them. There is thus a close connection between fundamental motifs and fundamental questions of the "categorical" kind we have described; but it is of the greatest importance to maintain a clear distinction between them. They differ as a question and an answer differ, and this difference cannot safely be ignored.

In all ages it has been the conscious or unconscious endeavour of metaphysics to blur this distinction. Men have believed that by philosophical analysis the answer could be deduced from the question. At this point there is an obvious difference between the metaphysical systems and every religious outlook. Even though the two types may state their answer (often for emotional reasons) in very similar language, yet the difference always remains. The metaphysician always tries in one way or another to deduce his answer as "necessary", while the religious mind firmly refuses to do so, but insists on its answer as axiomatic and thus maintains a synthetic relation between question and answer.

In the case of two of these great fundamental questions, the ethical and the religious, Christianity has brought a revolutionary change not only with regard to the answers but with regard to the questions themselves. It has so altered the way of putting both these questions that they no longer have the same meaning as before, and it has also given them both a new answer. This change, in respect both of questions and answers alike, is essentially bound up with the idea of Agape.

2. The Transformation of the Basic Ethical and Religious Questions by Christianity

It is not difficult to see how the meaning of the *ethical* question has changed in the course of history. Most of the problems treated as ethical by the ancient philosophers fall for us entirely outside the ethical sphere, while what we regard as quite central in ethics is not treated by them at all For this change the ethical contribution of Christianity is chiefly responsible. Yet we can see also how the original form of the question survives even when it has acquired a new content; for ethical discussion is still occupied with the problem of the Good. But this problem clearly has a quite different meaning according as it is looked at from an individualistic point of view or conceived in terms of fellowship or personal relationships. Ancient ethics were individualistic. The problem of the Good was therefore the problem of a "Highest Good"—that is, of something which could in every respect satisfy the individual. The dominant question was that of *eudæmonia*, happiness; and although different answers might be given—the answer of Hedonism, that happiness is the pleasure of the moment; or of Aristotle, that it consists in activity and the attainment of perfection; or of Stoicism, that it is *ataraxia*, independence and indifference towards the external vicissitudes of life—yet the statement of the question remains always the same.

Now it is just in respect of this question that Christianity makes a revolutionary change; for Christianity consistently makes fellowship the starting-point for ethical discussion. The question of the Good is no longer envisaged from the point of view of the isolated individual, but rather from that of man in society, man in his relation to God and to his fellow-men. Here we see the influence of the idea of Agape. Agape, or love, is a social idea which as such has nothing in common with individualistic and eudæmonistic ethics; and when the question of the Good is approached from the point of view of social relationships it takes on an entirely new meaning. It becomes dissociated from eudæmonism and utilitarianism and turns into the entirely independent question of " the Good-in-itself ".[1]

Equally far-reaching is the change that Christianity has brought with regard to the *religious* question, the question of the Eternal or of man's fellowship with God. The meaning of this question must clearly vary according as the centre of gravity in the religious relationship is placed in man's ego or in the Divine : in the former case we get an egocentric, in the latter a theocentric religion. In both cases we speak of " religion ", because both involve a relation between man and God; yet we have really two quite separate questions here, for it makes all the difference whether we are interested in God as the One who can satisfy all the needs and desires of the ego, or as the sovereign Lord who has absolute authority over the ego. In so far as the religious question has now come to be envisaged from a theocentric rather than an egocentric point of view, it is chiefly due to Christianity that the change has come about. Doubtless there is scarcely any religion from which the theocentric tendency is wholly absent; but it has nowhere else been able to overcome those contrary influences

[1] This question is discussed in detail in my *Etiska grundfrågor*, 1926, where the first chapter deals with " The Independence of the Ethical Judgment " and the second with " The Concept of the Good ".

that appeal to man's natural tendency to take everything around him into his own service, and to judge and value everything according as it advances or retards his own interests. The study of the underlying motifs of the different religions shows that there is always a dominant group of motifs of an egocentric character. It is in Christianity that we first find egocentric religion essentially superseded by theocentric religion.[1] We shall see later on that this revolution, too, is intimately connected with the idea of Agape.[2]

It follows that Christianity takes a unique place as a creative force in the history of human thought. It has revolutionised the treatment of the fundamental questions of religion and ethics, and the very way in which it puts these questions reveals a creative power of the highest order. The reason why it has been equally creative in both religion and ethics is that these, from a Christian point of view, are not strictly two separate things, but are so interwoven with one another as to be really only two different aspects of the same thing. Christianity knows nothing either of a non-ethical fellowship with God or of non-religious ethics. The Christian Religion is a thoroughly ethical religion and its ethic is a thoroughly religious ethic.

3. Agape as the Fundamental Motif of Christianity

The fundamental motif of an outlook is its answer to a fundamental question of a "categorical" nature. We have observed that human thought concentrates on a few such questions. There are a certain few great questions, first raised long ago, which recur with extraordinary persistence throughout history demanding an answer. When men grapple with

---

[1] *Cf.* my essay on "Egoism och religion" in *Svensk Teologisk Kvartalskrift*, III., 1927, pp. 129-150, and on "Die kopernikanische Umwälzung Luthers" in *Zeitwende*, VI., 1930, pp. 357 ff. Both essays are reprinted in my *Urkristendom och Reformation*, 1932.

[2] See pp. 200 ff. below.

these questions their concern as a rule is simply to find an answer to them; they rarely think of the questions themselves —that is, the way in which they are stated—as a matter for investigation. The questions are simply taken over from tradition as something given and once for all established. But a question has an extraordinary power of suggestion and constraint. It directs our attention to the different possible answers and so seems to leave all the different possibilities open; yet the number of possible answers may be seriously limited by the very way in which the question is put. To a wrongly stated question there can be no right answer. The question thus indirectly influences the answer. It is in this way, above all, that a fundamental question stated in a certain way can hold the minds of men in bondage for centuries, not to say millennia. What men seek is a better way of answering the question, while the question itself is passed on unaltered. Modifications of the fundamental questions, therefore, generally take place more or less unawares, and it is only rarely that a really radical revolution occurs. When this happens it is the result of a new total attitude to life in general.

Two of these extremely rare revolutions—that which has turned the religious question from an egocentric into a theocentric question, and that which has freed the ethical question from eudæmonism and turned it into the question of " the Good-in-itself "—have resulted, as we have seen, from the contribution made by Christianity. But the creative significance of Christianity is not exhausted in the restatement of questions. It is manifested even more clearly in the answer that Christianity gives to the fundamental religious and ethical questions thus restated. Here we find also that characteristically Christian interpenetration of religion and ethics of which we spoke above, for to both these questions Christianity gives precisely the same answer. To the religious question, now stated in theocentric terms, What is God? Christianity replies with the Johannine formula : God is ἀγάπη.

And to the ethical question, What is the Good, the " Good-in-itself "? the answer is similar : The Good is ἀγάπη, and the ethical demand finds summary expression in the Commandment of Love, the commandment to love God and my neighbour.

We have therefore every right to say that ἀγάπη is the centre of Christianity, the Christian fundamental motif *par excellence*, the answer to both the religious and the ethical question. Agape comes to us as a quite new creation of Christianity. It sets its mark on everything in Christianity. Without it nothing that is Christian would be Christian. Agape is Christianity's own original basic conception.

III

"THE HEAVENLY EROS"

WE have fixed the bearings of the idea of Agape within the context of Christianity and have thus got a preliminary definition of its significance. Our next task should be to give a corresponding definition of that other fundamental idea with which our inquiry is to deal, the idea of Eros. There are, however, several reasons why it is both unnecessary and impracticable to do so. It is unnecessary because the idea of Eros is not the primary object of our inquiry. The Eros motif comes into the picture only in order to shed light on the development of the Christian idea of love, since the changes which this has undergone are unintelligible without reference to it. But even if it were necessary it would be impracticable. We have been able to fix the bearings of the idea of Agape, because it is the fundamental motif of such a concrete new development as Christianity; but with the Eros motif the position is quite different, for it breaks out in the most diverse places. Practically all religious life outside Christianity is characterised by it more or less, and even within Christianity it exerts its influence and shows itself throughout history the real rival of the Christian Agape motif. This widespread occurrence of the Eros motif clearly makes it difficult to fix its precise bearings; for in different contexts it can occupy very different positions. The idea of Agape can be compared to a small stream which, even in the history of Christianity, flows along an extremely narrow channel and sometimes seems to lose itself entirely in its surroundings; but Eros is a broad river that overflows its banks, carrying everything away with it, so that it is not easy even in thought to dam it up and make it flow in an orderly

49

course. When the Eros motif invades Christianity, however, its endeavour is to drive out and supplant the Agape motif; and therefore, since we have shown the place occupied by the latter, we have also shown the place of the former in so far as it is of any importance for our present study.

But even if, for the reasons stated, we have no need to be more specific in our definition of the idea of Eros, we ought at least to indicate the sense in which we are using the term here. Recent writers have used the word " eros " in a great variety of senses, and even if we said that what we are essentially concerned with is " Platonic love "—that is, the traditional and widely influential conception that derives from Plato's doctrine of Eros—we should not thereby avoid ambiguity. For even with regard to the precise meaning of " Platonic love " opinion is very much divided. It used generally to be the purely spiritual, ideal character of Platonic love that was insisted upon, but more recently—as a result, partly, of psychoanalytical considerations—its natural connection with sensual love has been increasingly stressed.[1]

Now undoubtedly there is a connection between sensual and Platonic love, for it can be seen quite clearly in Plato's writings; and it is naturally important that it should be investigated and explained. Yet it is entirely irrelevant for our purposes and we shall do well if we deliberately disregard it; for even apart from it we may very easily be tempted to equate Eros with earthly, sensual love and Agape with heavenly, spiritual love as we seek to compare and contrast them.[2] But if we do that we shall certainly do no justice to Eros. Deep

---

[1] See especially R. Lagerborg, *Die platonische Liebe*, 1926.
[2] Leopold Ziegler appears to be in some measure guilty of this oversimplification when he writes, for example, in his *Gestaltwandel der Götter*, 3rd edn., vol. i., 1922, p. 399: " One would have thought there could be nothing that the developing Christianity of the following period would have found it more desirable and, indeed, necessary to make its own than this distinction, so useful for religious purposes, between sexually and non-sexually rooted impulses, which Plato and the Hellenic and Hellenistic philosophy that followed him had always looked upon as one."

as the sensual roots of Platonic love may be, its whole tendency is to seek deliverance from the merely sensual. Plato does all in his power to prevent the confusion or identification of the Eros which he has in mind, with ordinary sensual love. Whereas the latter merely binds the soul more firmly to things sensible and material, it is the task of the philosophical Eros to set the soul free from the fetters of sense and raise it up to the supersensible, heavenly world. If the word Eros is to be used for the love which stops at the sensible object, allowing itself to be bound by it instead of using it as a stepping-stone in its ascent to the supersensible, then we must distinguish between two different kinds of Eros. That there is such a distinction is an elementary fact, which we must observe if we are to do justice to the Platonic outlook, for it is as fundamental as the distinction between the sense-world and the world of Ideas. It is, indeed, so elementary that in the *Symposium* Plato feels no necessity to make Socrates or Diotima speak about it, but entrusts to Pausanias the task of explaining the difference between what he calls "vulgar (πάνδημος) Eros" and "heavenly (οὐράνιος) Eros".[1]

Between Vulgar Eros and Christian Agape there is no relation at all, and if we had only this form of Eros to consider the problem of Eros and Agape would easily be solved. The heavenly Eros, however, in its most sublimated and spiritualised form, is the born rival of the idea of Agape. Each of them in its own way shines with the light of heaven, and, alien as they are to one another from the beginning, they have nevertheless enough in common to prevent them from entirely passing each other by. Agape displays a heavenly character from the beginning; it needs no spiritualising or sublimating to be recognised as divine and heavenly Agape. With Eros it is otherwise; only the highest form of Eros, Eros in the most sublimated sense, "heavenly Eros", is capable of entering the lists against Agape.

[1] *Symposium* 180 D.

The mistake is commonly made of representing Agape as a higher and more spiritualised form of Eros, and of supposing that the sublimation of Eros is the way to reach Agape. The thought of " the heavenly Eros " reminds us that that is not the case; for heavenly Eros may be a sublimation of sensual love, but it is not itself capable of further sublimation. The heavenly Eros is the highest possible thing of its kind; it has been spiritualised to an extent beyond which it is impossible to go. Agape stands alongside, not above, the heavenly Eros; the difference between them is not one of degree but of kind. There is no way, not even that of sublimation, which leads over from Eros to Agape.[1]

[1] It can therefore be very misleading when R. Saitschick gives his *Schicksal und Erlösung* the sub-title " Der Weg von Eros zu Agape." The fact that he does so, however, is an indication that he uses the two terms in an essentially different sense from that we have given them above.

IV

CONFLICTING FUNDAMENTAL MOTIFS

1. EROS AND AGAPE

THE history of the Christian idea of love begins with an entirely new and peculiarly Christian fundamental motif of religion and ethics—the Agape motif. But the subsequent course of that history is not a smooth and straightforward development; it is a story of struggle and conflict.

The worst thing that can happen to a new conception like the Agape motif, is that it should meet with another conception exhibiting enough similarities and points of contact to be capable of being confused with it. Through such confusion the specific content of the new idea can be drained away from within, so to speak, by the other; and that is exactly what has happened in a very large measure to the Christian Agape motif. Agape entered into a world that had already received the impress of Eros, which therefore had the advantage of being first in the field; and, what is more, Agape had not even the good fortune to encounter it as an open antagonist, since it appeared in the guise of the heavenly Eros. In that form it had gathered up into itself all that there was of idealism in the ancient world; it pointed upward, and all its endeavour was to draw men's minds away from the things of sense up towards the supernatural, heavenly life. It is therefore easily understandable that Eros should appear to be the natural ally of Christianity rather than its principal adversary. Eros and Agape ceased to be recognised as contrary motifs and the tension between them was relaxed. The two streams united, and a considerable part of the force which Agape had gathered came ultimately to benefit the Eros motif. Hence the alliance proved highly disastrous for the Agape motif. The stream of the Christian idea of love flowed partly, at least, into the broad river of Eros, becoming one of the tributaries that fed the idealistic currents of late antiquity; while to the extent that it still flowed along the course of the Agape motif it became itself the recipient of tributaries from alien sources. The Agape motif lost its purity.

There were innumerable channels by which the influx of alien elements into the Agape motif could take place. Christianity has never been hermetically sealed against the outside world, and from the first it was set in the midst of that extensive historical complex of religions which we usually denominate " Hellenism ". It is, moreover, typical of these Oriental-Hellenistic religions, with which Christianity early came into contact and by which it was undoubtedly influenced at many points, that they are shot through and through with the Eros motif in the widest sense of that term. At a later stage Christianity received through Platonism (or Neoplatonism) what we might call an official contribution from the Eros motif. When Platonism found its way into Christianity, or—to put it another way—when Christianity tried to express itself in Platonic terms, the Agape motif inevitably underwent a transformation.

The transformation did not, however, take place entirely without resistance. Even where the Agape motif might seem to have been disposed of by assimilation to the Eros motif, there was always a remnant of it which stubbornly refused to be assimilated. And this remnant has constantly acted as a disturbing factor which has prevented the problem of Agape and Eros from ever being entirely settled. Hence it comes about that throughout the history of Christianity the Agape motif again and again breaks forth afresh. It is therefore impossible to represent the history of the Christian idea of love as a single, continuous line. It is rather the story of how the Agape motif and the Eros motif encounter one another; how they become so intertwined that it is almost impossible to disentangle them; how Agape has always had to be asserting itself afresh lest it should be quite overwhelmed by Eros; and how it sometimes breaks out, if only at isolated points in Christian history, with all its original force. The history of the idea of Agape thus presents itself to us as a tense drama, which forms the inside story, so to speak, of the development of Christianity.

2. EROS AND CARITAS

In a work entitled *Eros und Caritas, Die platonische Liebe und die Liebe im Sinne des Christentums* (1929), Heinrich Scholz treats of a problem that would appear from the sub-title to coincide entirely with our own. But this is not in fact the case, and the main title has already given us a hint of it. When Scholz compares Platonic love with Christian love, he represents them not as Eros and Agape but as Eros and Caritas. This fact in itself, of course, need mean no more than a difference of terminology; but the actual treatment of the subject reveals a far more important difference. Caritas is not simply another name for Agape. By Caritas, Scholz means love as it appears in the Gospels, in Paul, Augustine, Dante and Pascal.[1] Clearly the development of the Christian idea of love is conceived here as an unbroken line which runs from the Gospels and Paul right on through the Middle Ages. Augustine, Dante and Pascal are described as " the three classical interpreters of love in the Christian sense ";[2] Dante is called " the greatest poet of Caritas."[3]

All this may be true enough of Caritas, but it is altogether untrue of Agape. The conception of love in Augustine or Dante is not a simple interpretation of Agape, but a transformation of it. Mediæval Caritas is a complex phenomenon, containing elements both of Agape and of Eros. The problem

[1] *Op. cit.*, p. 44.   [2] *Op. cit.*, p. 2.   [3] *Op. cit.*, p. 95.

of Eros and Caritas is therefore quite different from the problem of Eros and Agape. In the case of the latter, Eros is confronted with the Christian idea of love in its original sense; in the former, with the Christian idea remodelled under the influence, in part, of the Eros motif. Naturally the problem of Eros and Caritas is well worth investigating; but it merely confuses the issue when Caritas, influenced as it is by the Eros motif, is unquestioningly identified with "love in the Christian sense".

This difference between the two problems is connected with yet another. When the problem of Eros and Agape is raised, it cannot be settled simply by a comparison of the two motifs. Eros and Agape are not merely two theoretical ideas that invite comparison, but different attitudes to life, different tendencies, which are in actual conflict with one another. If on the other hand we raise, as Scholz does, the problem of Eros and Caritas, the position is quite different. Of course it can be said that Eros and Caritas, too, are not merely theoretical ideas, but represent definite attitudes to life, definite tendencies. But since Caritas already contains something of Eros, the question of its relation to Eros is not marked by anything like the same tension as the question of the relation between Eros and Agape. In the case of Eros and Caritas there is no such degree of real conflict between opposed fundamental motifs as there is in the case of Eros and Agape. Caritas in the mediæval sense of the term virtually signifies a neutral point in the conflict between Eros and Agape; in Caritas the tension between Eros and Agape has become, at least for the moment, so slight as to be imperceptible.

3. An Outline of the Further Course of the Inquiry

We have now stated and defined our problem, and thereby laid down the main lines on which our subsequent discussion must proceed. Our first task will be to give an account of the original significance of the two fundamental motifs, Eros and Agape, before they lost their purity by association with one another. This will furnish only the starting-point for our discussion, of course; but it will be the most important and, indeed, the all-determining point. In our attempt to understand the continual clash between the two motifs, which we find in the history of the Christian idea of love, everything will depend on our being entirely clear about their primary and essential significance. The extraordinary importance of this question is the reason for our devoting the first main section (Part One) of this work to it.

Naturally we turn first to the Agape motif (Chapter I.) as the motif out of which the Christian idea of love has grown. The Agape motif has its roots in the new and specifically Christian way of fellowship with God, as this is depicted in the Gospels (I.). It finds its highest expression in Paul, in the union of his theology of the Cross with the thought of Divine love and in his preaching of the Agape of the Cross (II.). The supreme formal statement is reached in the Johannine " God is Agape " (III.).

Our next task is to give a corresponding exposition of the Eros motif (Chapter II.). The attempt to trace this motif to its source leads us back to ancient Mystery-piety (I.). It reaches its height in Plato, at whose hands it is also cast into its classical mould (II.). It has, however, a significant history after Plato, quite apart from its meeting with the Agape motif, and this later history is particularly important for an understanding of the Eros motif in the Middle Ages. It is therefore necessary to devote some attention to the remodelling of the Eros motif by Aristotle and Neoplatonism (III.).

After the exposition of the two motifs, the rest of Part One is devoted to a clarification of the fundamental contrast between them (Chapter III.). Nietzsche is right when he describes Christianity—that is to say, Agape—as a " transvaluation of all ancient values ", for those values all centre in

Eros (I.). After a review, in parallel columns, of the points of contrast between the two fundamental motifs (II.), we proceed to show how the opposition between them finds expression in the different " dimensions " of love—that is, in the conception of God's love, of our love for God and for our neighbour, and of self-love (III.). But the opposition between the two motifs extends much further even than this, for each of them has a tendency to associate with itself its own peculiar complex of ideas and feelings (IV.). Hence the question arises how it has ever been possible for these very different motifs to become fused together, as there is abundant evidence in Christian history to show that they have (V.).

The first part of our task being thus completed we turn to the second, where we have to give an account of the conflict between the two motifs in the course of Christian history. For an outline of this, however, the reader may be referred to the Introduction to Part Two of this work, especially the third section of it.

PART ONE

THE TWO FUNDAMENTAL MOTIFS

"Although the poverty of our language is such that in both cases it says 'love', yet the two ideas have nothing to do with one another."

U. v. WILAMOWITZ-MOELLENDORFF.

CHAPTER ONE

THE AGAPE MOTIF

I

AGAPE AND FELLOWSHIP WITH GOD

1. The Starting-Point for the Interpretation of the Idea of Agape

It has long been recognised that the idea of Agape represents a distinctive and original feature of Christianity. But in what precisely does its originality and distinctiveness consist?

This question has often been answered by reference to the *Commandment of Love*. The double commandment, " Thou shalt love the Lord thy God with all thy heart " and " Thou shalt love thy neighbour as thyself ", has been taken as the natural starting-point for the exposition of the meaning of Christian love. Yet the fact is that if we start with the commandment, with Agape as something demanded, we bar our own way to the understanding of the idea of Agape. The error of this procedure should have been evident from the fact that both parts of the Commandment of Love—both the commandment of love for God and that of love for one's neighbour—occur in the Old Testament, and are introduced in the Gospels, not as something new, but as quotations from the Old Testament.

It is equally an error to regard the combination of the two commandments, which in the Old Testament occur separately, as the specific achievement of Christianity. The earliest Christians, at all events, were not conscious of any difference from Judaism on this point. That is clear from the fact that in Luke it is a lawyer, a representative of Old Testament religion, who combines the commandments (Luke x. 25 ff.); and if in Mark it is Jesus Himself who combines them, He does so with a direct reference to the Old Testament, while a scribe is represented as heartily agreeing with Him (Mark xii. 25 ff.).

It can, of course, be pointed out with some justification that in the Old Testament the commandment of love stands as one among many rules and regulations, and that it was Christianity that first gave it its dominant place as a summary of the whole requirement of the Law. Yet, granted that later Judaism bears to a high degree the marks of legalism and externality, there was never lacking in Judaism a tendency to make love central in ethical and religious relationships; and it is not true to say that the commandment of love is merely one among many legalistic regulations. As early as Hosea the principle that love is the central requirement of the Law is clearly recognised; God desires " love and not sacrifice " (Hos. vi. 6).[1] Indeed, love towards God sometimes acquires such importance that it can stand alongside " the fear of the Lord " as an inclusive description of the right attitude of man to God. There are thus to be found in Judaism definite impulses towards making the commandment of love in this sense the " great commandment of the Law ". Not even along this line, therefore, is the qualitatively new and distinctive element in Christianity to be found.

If the Commandment of Love can be said to be specifically Christian, as undoubtedly it can, the reason is to be found, not in the commandment as such, but in the quite new meaning that Christianity has given it. The love it requires does not mean the same in a Christian context as it meant in Judaism. To reach an understanding of the Christian idea of love

---

[1] Where the English R.V. reads " mercy " (mg. " kindness "), the Swedish version has " love ".—*Translator's note.*

simply by reference to the Commandment of Love is therefore impossible; to attempt it is to move in a circle. We could
never discover the nature of Agape, love in the Christian
sense, if we had nothing to guide us but the double command: "Thou shalt love the Lord thy God with all thy
heart" and "Thou shalt love thy neighbour as thyself." It
is not the commandment that explains the idea of Agape,
but insight into the Christian conception of Agape that enables us to grasp the Christian meaning of the commandment.
We must therefore seek another starting-point.

One of the most striking differences between the Commandment of Love as it is interpreted in the Old Testament
and in Christianity, is that in the latter it is universal in its
scope. In Judaism love is exclusive and particularistic: it is
directed to one's " neighbour " in the original and more restricted sense of the word, and it is directed to " neighbours
only ". Otherwise the application of the term " neighbours ",
and therefore the scope of love, can vary a good deal, ranging
from one's immediate kith and kin to any member of the
same nation. When " neighbour " is understood in the latter
sense there comes to be a close correspondence between the
two commandments of love. Love towards God has its
counterpart in love for one's neighbour, which is understood
as love for the Chosen People of God, the " peculiar people ".
The scope of love can also be extended to embrace even aliens
resident among the Chosen People. Yet, even so, love always
preserves its limits. Christian love, on the other hand, over-
leaps all such limits; it is universal and all-embracing. "There
can be neither Jew nor Greek, there can be neither bond nor
free, there can be no male and female " (Gal. iii. 28). For
this reason the attempt has often been made to interpret the
Christian idea of love in the light of the cosmopolitan and
individualistic spirit which was widespread in the ancient
world, especially in circles influenced by Stoicism, and which
transcended national and social barriers with the rational-

istic ethical concept of "man" and "citizen of the world."
For reasons shortly to be given, however, this is quite useless
as a starting-point for the interpretation of the Christian idea
of Agape; it cannot shed light on anything that is essential to
the Christian concept of love. In the first place, the universalism of Christian love is not its most distinctive feature,
and, in the second place, Christian universalism rests on an
entirely different basis from that of Stoicism.

Another, and equally mistaken, interpretation of the ethical
revolution involved in the Christian idea of love represents it
as arising essentially from social considerations. Troeltsch is
right when he says: "In order to understand the foundation
principles of Christianity as a whole, in its relation to social
problems, it is of the utmost importance to recognise that the
preaching of Jesus and the creation of the Christian Church
were not due in any sense to the impulse of a social movement. To put it quite plainly: Christianity was not the product of a class struggle of any kind; it was not shaped, when
it did arise, in order to fit into any such situation; indeed, at
no point was it directly concerned with the social upheavals
of the ancient world."[1] Here we may recall Nietzsche's
attempt to interpret Christian love as a manifestation of "resentment" born of Jewish hatred. He writes: "From the
stem of that tree of revenge and hatred, Jewish hatred—the
deepest and sublimest, ideal-creating, value-transforming
hatred, the like of which has never been seen on earth—
sprang something equally unique, a *new love*, the deepest
and sublimest of all kinds of love. . . . This Jesus of
Nazareth, himself the embodiment of the Gospel of love,
this 'Saviour', bringing to poor and sick and sinners blessedness and victory—was he not Seduction itself in its most
sinister and irresistible form, the seduction by a roundabout

---

[1] E. Troeltsch, *The Social Teaching of the Christian Churches*, E.T.,
1931, vol. i., p. 39. *Cf.* K. Holl, *Urchristentum und Religionsgeschichte,*
1925, p. 27.

way to just those *Jewish* values and innovations in respect of the ideal?"[1] Nietzsche quite rightly saw that Christian love means the transvaluation of those values of antiquity which he himself valued most highly; but he did not see that it means just as complete a transvaluation of all Jewish values. His arbitrary choice of the idea of "resentment" as his starting-point led him to miss the deepest characteristics of Christian love and to treat it as simply synonymous with universal altruism.

Closely related to Nietzsche's view is that which regards Christian love as purely and simply the negation of the Jewish doctrine of retribution. There are several points which might seem to favour this interpretation. One of the most conspicuous facts about the Christian idea of love is that it involves a transvaluation of all previously accepted values. In relation to these values, therefore, it has a negative, critical significance, such as finds typical expression in the sharp antitheses of the Sermon on the Mount. If what chiefly strikes us here is the antithetical style, we may well incline to the view that the Christian Church must quite naturally have felt itself in opposition to the prevailing Judaism, and that this fact would be bound to influence its ethical attitude. What Judaism affirmed, Christianity must deny. If Judaism maintained the principle of exactly equivalent retribution, "An eye for an eye and a tooth for a tooth," then the Christian requirement must naturally be, "Resist not him that is evil" (Matt. v. 38 f.). If Judaism took the commandment of love to mean, "Thou shalt love thy neighbour and hate thine enemy", then Christianity must say, "Love your enemies, and pray for them that persecute you" (Matt. v. 43 f.). But this would mean that the Christian idea of love was determined ultimately by the outlook of its opponents.

---

[1] F. Nietzsche, *Zur Genealogie der Moral*, 1. Abhandlung, 8.—*Cf.* Max Scheler's criticism of Nietzsche in his essay on " Das Ressentiment im Aufbau der Moralen " (*Vom Umsturz der Werte*, 1919, vol. i., pp. 43 ff.).

It might seem as if this view, which clearly recognises that there is an antithesis between Judaism and Christianity, were the direct opposite of that of Nietzsche, who seeks to derive Christian love directly from Judaism. Yet these two views come to much the same thing in the end, for they both deny the independent character of Christian love and treat it as simply the negative reflection of its opponent's position. This, in fact, is the root-fault of all the interpretations we have so far considered; they fail to recognise that Christian love rests on a quite definite, positive basis of its own. What, then, is this basis?

The answer to this question may be found in the text last quoted: "Love your enemies". This text, which at first sight is one of the best arguments for the "negation" theory, actually furnishes a complete refutation of it. It is true that love for one's enemies is at variance with our immediate natural feelings, and may therefore seem to display the negative character suggested above; but if we consider the motive underlying it we shall see that it is entirely positive. The Christian is commanded to love his enemies, not because the other side teach hatred of them, but because there is a basis and motive for such love in the concrete, positive fact of God's own love for evil men. "He maketh His sun to rise on the evil and the good." *That* is why we are told: "Love your enemies . . . that ye may be children of your Father which is in heaven" (Matt. v. 44 f.).

It is no mere accident that we find here so intimate a connection between Christian love and the Christian relationship to God, Agape and fellowship with God. The reason for it is that the Christian ethic is from first to last a religious ethic; and this is not merely in the sense that the ethical demands are attributed to the Divine will, and that Divine omnipotence with its sanctions of reward and punishment is invoked to maintain the ethical order. Such an external and formal connection between ethics and religion can leave them without any real inner relation to one another, for the *content* of the ethical demand need not have anything whatever to do with religion. The Christian ethic is a religious ethic in a far deeper sense, inasmuch as the actual content of the ethical life is wholly determined by the religious relationship, by fellowship with God. There can therefore be no doubt where the starting-point is to be found which we are seeking for our interpretation of the idea of Agape. It is the Christian conception of fellowship with God that gives the idea of Agape its meaning. It will therefore be our next task to consider the nature of Christian fellowship with God.

2. THE DISTINCTIVE CHARACTER OF CHRISTIAN FELLOWSHIP WITH GOD

At the supremely important turning-points in the history of religion, when something really new appears on the scene, it is curious to observe how the consciousness that the new element is emerging is coupled with a conservative retention of the old. Yet it is not as curious as at first sight might appear. It is merely a symptom of the fact that all the really great revolutions begin from within and the new life only gradually bursts asunder the old forms and creates new ones for itself. We have an example of this in the Reformation. Luther does not first appear as the founder of a new Church, but he holds on to the old as long as he possibly can; it is only through force of circumstances that his reforming work leads to the formation of a new, independent Church.

But the supreme instance is furnished by the emergence of Christianity itself. Here is something that is both absolutely new and yet firm in its attachment to the old. Jesus does not come forward as the founder of a new religion; and yet Christianity develops into something altogether new and different in kind from Judaism. Jesus moves within the forms created by Old Testament piety; nothing is further from his mind

than to abolish them, for He has not come to destroy the Law
and the Prophets, but to fulfil them. He has not come to
proclaim a new God; the God of the Old Testament, " the
God of Abraham, Isaac and Jacob ", is His God. His whole
activity is directed to the one end of leading men to fellowship with this God. But it is just at this point that we find
the new and distinctive element. What Jesus seeks to bring
is *not a new conception of God, or new ideas about God, but
a new fellowship with God*; that is to say, the new element is
connected with the very heart of the religious life, for it concerns the very nature of fellowship with God itself. Here we
have the new wine—to use the figure employed by Jesus in
Matt. ix. 17—which in due time was to burst the old wineskins and let Christianity emerge from Judaism as a completely new religion. Christian fellowship with God is different in kind from that of Judaism; and therefore Christianity, in spite of its historical connection with Judaism, and
in spite of any other bonds and affinities between them, is a
fundamentally different thing from Judaism. What, then,
constitutes the uniqueness of Christian fellowship with God?

" I came not to call the righteous, but sinners," says Jesus
(Mark ii. 17); and with these words He turns the entire scale
of Jewish values upside down. He could hardly have expressed in stronger terms what was bound to be felt as an
assault on the traditional outlook. It is only necessary to
remember the associations of the term " the righteous " in the
Jewish mind. There is a universal feeling that the difference
between the righteous and the sinner, the godly and the ungodly, implies a difference of value; and in Judaism this
natural feeling was immensely strengthened by religious considerations. The righteous man loved God's Law, and God's
Law ennobled him. Old Testament piety with its devotion
to the Law was by no means the external legalism it is often
assumed to have been. There was an inward bond that held
the godly man to the Law. The righteous felt no sense of

external compulsion when confronted by the Law, but a sense of inner solidarity with it. He delighted in the Law of the Lord. Its observance gave him value and made him acceptable to God. His prevailing mood was that expressed in Ps. i.:

" Blessed is the man that walketh not in the counsel of the
    ungodly,
Nor standeth in the way of sinners,
Nor sitteth in the seat of the scornful.
But his delight is in the Law of the Lord;
And in His Law doth he meditate day and night.
And he shall be like a tree planted by the streams of water,
That bringeth forth its fruit in its season,
Whose leaf also doth not wither;
And whatsoever he doeth shall prosper.
The wicked are not so;
But are like the chaff which the wind driveth away.
Therefore the wicked shall not stand in the judgment,
Nor sinners in the congregation of the righteous.
For the Lord knoweth the way of the righteous:
But the way of the wicked shall perish."

It is thus between the righteous and the sinners that the decisive distinction is drawn—in the sight both of God and of men.

But now Jesus comes and throws all this to the winds. He eats and drinks with publicans and sinners, and says: " I came not to call the righteous, but sinners." We can see at once that those who had grown up in religious devotion to the Law were bound to see in this a violent assault on the very foundations of their inherited religion and morality. It was not merely an isolated point of doctrine that was attacked, but the very substance of legal piety and the deepest susceptibilities of the traditional religion. And it was the more serious because Jesus did not put forward this revaluation simply as

His private, subjective judgment, but claimed an objective, religious basis for it. Not only He, but God Himself judges thus. When Jesus calls sinners, He is not acting on His own initiative, but in fulfilment of the mission on which He has been sent, the very purpose for which He has " come ". By thus linking the revaluation with His sense of vocation He attributes it to God Himself. It is as commissioned by God that He acts as He does; and His mode of action, as He sees it, is a reproduction of God's own. God seeks the sinner and wills to take him into fellowship with Himself. Fellowship with God is not governed by law but by love. God's attitude to men is not characterised by *justitia distributiva*, but by ἀγάπη, not by retributive righteousness, but by freely giving and forgiving love.

Two different kinds of fellowship with God confronted one another here, and a conflict was inevitable. The more those on either side were in earnest about fellowship with God, the less the clash could be avoided. When, therefore, we find Jesus in the Gospels engaged in ceaseless controversy with the Pharisees, this is not fundamentally, either on His side or on theirs, a commonplace struggle for power. Just because the Pharisees were in earnest about their religion they were bound to resist what seemed to them to be a violation, not merely of the human, but above all of the Divine, order of justice, and therefore of God's majesty. The struggle of the Pharisees against Jesus is the protest of the religion of law against the religion of love.[1]

The contrast between the two kinds of religion must not, of course, be understood to imply that the Old Testament scheme of law had no place at all for the Divine love. On the contrary, Judaism had a good deal to say about God's love. God was the God of love because He was the God of

[1] *Cf.* on this A. Nygren, *Filosofisk och kristen etik*, 1923, pp. 189 and 249 ff. *Cf.* also for a similar point of view K. Holl, *Urchristentum und Religionsgeschichte*, 1925, pp. 16 ff., and G. Aulén, *Den kristna gudsbilden*, 1927, pp. 25 ff.

the Covenant;[1] the very fact that He had established His Covenant and *given His Law*, was the supreme expression of His love. But this meant that His love was bound by the limits of the Law and the Covenant:

" The mercy (love) of the Lord is from everlasting to everlast-
  ing upon them that fear Him,
And His righteousness unto children's children;
To such as keep His covenant,
And to those that remember His precepts to do them."

(Ps. ciii. 17 f.)

God's love is shown, be it noted, to them that fear Him; it is shown to the righteous, not to the sinner. It signifies at most that God is faithful to His Covenant despite man's unfaithfulness, provided that man returns to the Covenant.[2] But it is a far cry from this to that Divine love which comes to call sinners. For such love has no place within a legal scheme, and to those who think of fellowship with God in terms of law and justice it is bound to seem nothing less than blasphemy.

[1] *Cf.* J. Pedersen, *Israel*, 1920, pp. 264 ff.; J. Hempel, *Gott und Mensch im Alten Testament*, 1926, pp. 126 ff., and *Altes Testament und Geschichte*, 1930, pp. 17 ff.

[2] *Cf.* Deut. vii. 6-10: " For thou art an holy people unto the Lord thy God: the Lord thy God hath chosen thee to be a peculiar people unto himself, above all peoples that are upon the face of the earth. The Lord did not set his love upon you, nor choose you, because ye were more in number than any people; for ye were the fewest of all peoples; but because the Lord loveth you, and because he would keep the oath which he sware unto your fathers, hath the Lord brought you out with a mighty hand, and redeemed you out of the house of bondage, from the hand of Pharaoh king of Egypt. Know therefore that the Lord thy God, He is God; the faithful God, which keepeth covenant and mercy with them that love him and keep his commandments to a thousand generations; and repayeth them that hate him to their face, to destroy them; he will not be slack to him that hateth him, he will repay him to his face." This passage is specially interesting as a testimony from the exilic period to God's " unmotivated " love for Israel, a love depending solely on His own will and oath. But at the same time the difference between this love and New Testament Agape is clearly revealed, for the principle of retribution is still maintained.

But in order to understand the meaning of Agape we must look rather more closely at this new kind of fellowship with God; and we may begin by asking what is the cause of this revaluation, this transformation of the religious relationship. Why is it sinners that are called? The old idea that it is in virtue of a righteous life that we gain God's approval and are received into fellowship with Him, is so natural that it seems not to need any explanation. But when Jesus completely reverses this natural order, so that fellowship with God is offered to sinners, while the righteous go empty away, we cannot but ask the reason for such a startling change. Is it merely an inversion of values due to emotional reaction, an unreasoning repudiation of a previously accepted scale of values? Or is there perhaps something in the nature of the sinner that makes him of more value than the righteous in God's sight?

The latter explanation has found many supporters, and it may be of interest to see what one of them has to say for it. Let us take the Roman Catholic author Max Scheler, who in other respects understands as well as any the meaning of the Christian idea of Agape. In his essay on " Das Ressentiment im Aufbau der Moralen " he takes great pains to show how the sinner is in fact better than the righteous man. " The notorious sinner ", he explains,[1] " always makes confession of the evil in his soul. I am not thinking here merely of a confession in words publicly, but also of confession to himself, and of confession through the acts in which his sinful will issues. Granted that what he confesses here is evil and sinful, yet the fact that he confesses it, the fact that he sins, when he already has a sinful heart, is not evil, but good! He thereby cleanses his heart and prevents the infection from spreading—that infection which, in those who inhibit the evil impulses in themselves, takes possession of deeper and deeper levels of the personality. . . . Therefore the sinful

[1] Max Scheler, *Vom Umsturz der Werte*, 1919, vol. i., pp. 133 f.

act and the subsequent repentance (which surely begins in the element of confession contained in the act itself) is in Jesus' eyes better than the suppression of the sinful impulse and the consequent poisoning of a man's inner being, which can very well go together with a serene consciousness of being good and righteous—in the eyes of the Law. That is why there is so much ' more joy in heaven over one sinner that repents than over a thousand righteous ';[1] and that is why ' he that hath little that needs to be forgiven, the same loveth little '."[2]

It is easy to see that Scheler is not particularly happy in his quotations, but what is worse is that his whole argument is false. We look in vain in the Gospels for any evidence that Jesus would have accepted the view that by allowing sin free rein a man "cleanses his heart and prevents the infection from spreading ", and that the sinful act prevents evil from taking " possession of deeper and deeper levels of the personality ". Jesus never regards sin as something that affects only the outer levels of man's nature. For Him sin has its roots in man's inmost being, in his heart: " For from within, out of the heart of men, evil thoughts proceed. . . . All these evil things proceed from within, and defile the man " (Mark vii. 17 ff.). Jesus does not recognise in the sinner any central core which is unaffected by sin, and which a man must keep untainted by sinning—so to speak—outwards from himself. When Scheler sums up Jesus' teaching by saying that " the sinner who sins is better than the sinner who does not sin, and whose sinful impulse strikes inwards and poisons his nature ",[3] this can only be described as a freely constructed theory, which has not the slightest connection with the actual facts, but indeed is plainly refuted by them. At least it is clear that *this* is not the reason why Jesus calls sinners.

[1] Should actually be " ninety and nine righteous "—Luke xv. 7.
[2] Luke vii. 47—but incorrectly quoted, so that its meaning is no longer the same as in its original context.
[3] Scheler, *op. cit.*, I., pp. 134 f.

Where, then, does the error of Scheler's view lie? It lies in the way in which the question is stated. It is taken for granted that if God loves the sinner, He must do so because the sinner is in some way or other better than the righteous; and the question therefore is in what respect he is better. Thus the question itself leads to mistaken arguments like Scheler's, that the sinner has at least this advantage, that by his sinful actions he both confesses his true character and also " sins outwards from himself ". But the prior assumption is one that can by no means be taken for granted. Does it really follow that if God loves the sinner, the sinner is therefore better than the righteous? Must God's love necessarily direct itself to those who are better? Already in the Old Testament there are suggestions that God's love is not bound by the value or importance of its object. " The Lord did not set His love upon you, nor choose you, because ye were more in number than any people; for ye were the fewest of all peoples : but because the Lord loveth you . . . hath the Lord . . . redeemed you " (Deut. vii. 7 f.).

Judaism, it is true, never dared to apply any such principle to God's dealings with the righteous and the sinner; but Jesus goes the whole length. According to Him, God's love is sovereign in this matter also; indeed, it reveals its sovereignty most clearly of all in the fact that it directs itself to sinners. We only obscure the real nature of the fellowship with God, and make the relation between God and man less truly a relation of love, if we seek a basis for it in the idea that the sinner is better than the righteous. To ask in this sense for an explanation of God's love is the same as to deny His love. Such an explanation would imply that the religious relationship was still of the old legal type, and that God loved those whose qualities of character made them more worthy of His love than other men. But then not even the great change made by Jesus would embody any really new principle. He would simply have discovered a hidden value in those who least of all seemed to possess any value, and would have accepted the implications of this discovery in respect of the religious relationship. He would have brought no new fellowship with God, but God's love, still confined within the limits of legality, would simply have been directed to a more worthy object.

There is scarcely a more insidious way of emptying the Christian idea of love and Christian fellowship with God of their vital content than to treat God's love for sinners—that clearest of all expressions of the *new* way of fellowship with God—as merely a special case of the old legalistic religious relationship. *Christian fellowship with God is distinguished from all other kinds by the fact that it depends exclusively on God's Agape.* We have therefore no longer any reason to ask about either the better or worse qualities of those who are the objects of Divine love. To the question, Why does God love? there is only one right answer: Because it is His nature to love.

3. THE CONTENT OF THE IDEA OF AGAPE

Our inquiry has now reached the point where it is possible for us briefly to describe the content of the Christian idea of love in so far as it concerns Divine love. Its main features can be summarised in the following four points:

(1) *Agape is spontaneous and " unmotivated "*. This is the most striking feature of God's love as Jesus represents it. We look in vain for an explanation of God's love in the character of the man who is the object of His love. God's love is " groundless "—though not, of course, in the sense that there is no ground for it at all, or that it is arbitrary and fortuitous. On the contrary, it is just in order to bring out the element of necessity in it that we describe it as " groundless "; our purpose is to emphasise that there are no extrinsic grounds for it. The only ground for it is to be found in God Himself. God's love is altogether *spontaneous*. It does not look for anything

in man that could be adduced as motivation for it. In relation to man, Divine love is " *unmotivated* ". When it is said that God loves man, this is not a judgment on what man is like, but on what God is like.

It is this love, spontaneous and "unmotivated"—having no motive outside itself, in the personal worth of men—which characterises also the action of Jesus in seeking out the lost and consorting with " publicans and sinners ". It was precisely in this action, which from the point of view of legal relationships was inexplicable and indefensible, that He knew Himself carrying out the Father's work and revealing His mind and will. When fellowship with God is conceived of as a legal relationship, Divine love must in the last resort be dependent on the worth of its object. But in Christ there is revealed a Divine love which breaks all bounds, refusing to be controlled by the value of its object, and being determined only by its own intrinsic nature. According to Christianity, " motivated " love is human; spontaneous and "unmotivated " love is Divine.

This being so, we can see why Jesus was bound to attack a religious relationship conceived in legal terms. Had He been concerned only to claim a place for the idea of *love in the most general sense* within the religious relationship, He could have secured it even within the legal scheme. There was no need to smash the legal scheme in order to do that. The love for which there is room in this scheme, however, is the " motivated " love that is directed to the righteous, to those who deserve it. But Jesus is not concerned with love in this ordinary sense, but with the spontaneous, unmotivated love that is Agape; and for this there is fundamentally no place within the framework of legal order. To go back once more to the words of Jesus in Matt. ix. 17, we may say that *Agape is the new wine which inevitably bursts the old wineskins.* Now we see also why there had to be a revolutionary change of attitude towards the righteous and the sinner. If God's love were restricted to the righteous it would be evoked by its object and not spontaneous; but just by the fact that it seeks sinners, who do not deserve it and can lay no claim to it, it manifests most clearly its spontaneous and unmotivated nature.

(2) *Agape is "indifferent to value"*. This does not really add anything new to what has already been said; but in order to prevent a possible misunderstanding, it is necessary to give special emphasis to one aspect of the point we have just made. When Jesus makes the righteous and sinners change places, it might at first sight appear as if this were a matter of simple transvaluation, or inversion of values; but we have already said enough to show that it is a question of something far deeper. It is not that Jesus simply reverses the generally accepted standard of values and holds that the sinner is "better" than the righteous. True as it is to say that He effected a "transvaluation of all values", yet the phrase can easily give rise to a false impression. Actually, something of far deeper import than any "transvaluation" is involved here —namely, the principle that *any thought of valuation whatsoever* is out of place in connection with fellowship with God. When God's love is directed to the sinner, then the position is clear; all thought of valuation is excluded in advance; for if God, the Holy One, loves the sinner, it cannot be because of his sin, but in spite of his sin. But when God's love is shown to the righteous and godly, there is always the risk of our thinking that God loves the man on account of his righteousness and godliness. But this is a denial of Agape—as if God's love for the "righteous" were not just as unmotivated and spontaneous as His love for the sinner! As if there were any other Divine love than spontaneous and unmotivated Agape! It is only when all thought of the worthiness of the object is abandoned that we can understand what Agape is. God's love allows no limits to be set for it by the character or conduct of man. The distinction between the worthy and the

unworthy, the righteous and the sinner, sets no bounds to His love. " He maketh His sun to rise on the evil and the good, and sendeth rain on the just and the unjust " (Matt. v. 45).

(3) *Agape is creative*. When we seek to analyse the structure of the idea of Agape, what first attracts our attention is its spontaneous and unmotivated character. This, as we have described it above, shows that we are dealing with a love of a quite unique kind. The deepest reason for its uniqueness, however, has not yet been stated. What is ultimately decisive for the meaning of Agape can only be seen when we observe that it is *Divine* love and therefore shares in the creativeness that is characteristic of all the life of God. Agape is creative love. God does not love that which is already in itself worthy of love, but on the contrary, that which in itself has no worth acquires worth just by becoming the object of God's love. Agape has nothing to do with the kind of love that depends on the recognition of a valuable quality in its object; Agape does not recognise value, but creates it. Agape loves, and imparts value by loving. The man who is loved by God has no value in himself; what gives him value is precisely the fact that God loves him. *Agape is a value-creating principle.*

We have now reached the deepest and ultimately decisive feature of the idea of Agape—a feature which it must be said has been very much obscured in modern theology. Ever since Ritschl's time it has been common for theologians to speak of " the infinite value of the human soul " as one of the central ideas of Christianity, and to connect it with the idea of "God's fatherly love". Thus A. von Harnack, in *Das Wesen des Christentums*, claims that the teaching of Jesus as a whole can be grouped under three heads, each of such a nature as to contain the whole; and one of these he entitles " God the Father and the infinite value of the human soul."[1] To this, however, we can rightly object that the idea of " the infinite

[1] A. v. Harnack, *Das Wesen des Christentums*, 1913, pp. 33 and 40 ff.; E.T., *What is Christianity?* pp. 51 and 63 ff.

value of the human soul " is by no means a central idea of Christianity. Only a false exegesis has made it possible to find support for this idea in the oft-quoted passage : " What doth it profit a man, to gain the whole world, and forfeit his life (A.V. soul)? For what should a man give in exchange for his life (A.V. soul)?" (Mark viii. 36 f.). Moreover, Harnack's statement that " all who bear a human face are of more value than the whole world "[1] shows very clearly that the thought of an infinite value of this kind as belonging to man by nature has its roots elsewhere than in Christianity.

What chiefly interests us here, however, is the destructive effect that this idea has had on the conception of Divine love. The suggestion that man is by nature possessed of such an inalienable value, easily gives rise to the thought that it is this matchless value on which God's love is set. Even though the Divine spark may seem to have been wholly quenched in a man sunk in sin, it is none the less present in "all who bear a human face ", and its potentialities are capable of being actualised in everyone. Viewed in this light, God's forgiveness of sins means merely that He disregards the manifold faults and failings of the outward life and looks only at the inward, imperishable value which not even sin has been able to destroy. His forgiving love means that He sees and values the pearl of great price, regardless of the defilement that happens at present to cling to it. He overlooks the defects and imperfections and concentrates on the essence of the personality which wins His approbation.[2]

If this interpretation of Divine forgiveness and love were correct, God's love would not in the last resort be spontaneous and unmotivated but would have an adequate motive in the infinite value inherent in human nature. The forgiveness of sins would then imply merely the recognition of an already existing value. But it is evident enough that this is not the

[1] Op cit., p. 43; E.T., p. 67.   [2] Cf. the similar argument in F. C. Krarup, Livsforstaaelse, 1915, pp.97 ff.

forgiveness of sins as Jesus understands it. When He says,
" Thy sins are forgiven thee ", this is no merely formal attesta-
tion of the presence of a value which justifies the overlooking
of faults; it is the bestowal of a gift. Something really new is
introduced, something new is taking place. The forgiveness
of sins is a *creative work of Divine power* (ἐξουσία) which
Jesus knows Himself called to carry out on earth, and which
can be put on a level with other Divine miracles, such as His
healing of the paralytic (Mark ii. 5-12).

(4) *Agape is the initiator of fellowship with God.* Not
only does Agape determine the essential and characteristic
content of Christian fellowship with God, but in virtue of its
creative nature it is also important for the initiation of that
fellowship. In the relations between God and man the
initiative in establishing fellowship lies with Divine Agape.
If we consider the implications of the idea of Agape, it becomes very plain that all the other ways by which man seeks
to enter into fellowship with God are futile. This is above
all true of the righteous man's way of meritorious conduct,
but it is no less true of the sinner's way of repentance and
amendment. Repentance and amendment are no more able
than righteousness to move God to love.

In this connection also the advent of Agape is completely
revolutionary. Hitherto the question of fellowship with God
had always been understood as a question of the way by
which man could come to God. But now, when not only the
way of righteousness but also that of self-abasement and
amendment is rejected as incapable of leading to the goal, it
follows that *there is from man's side no way at all that leads
to God.* If such a thing as fellowship between God and man
nevertheless exists, this can only be due to God's own action;
God must Himself come to meet man and offer him His
fellowship. There is thus no way for man to come to God,
but only a way for God to come to man : the way of Divine
forgiveness, Divine love.

Agape is God's way to man. But here we have reached a point which we shall pursue further when we come to consider the Pauline idea of Agape.

4. THE EVIDENCE OF THE PARABLES

Having outlined the fundamental significance of the Agape motif, we shall now endeavour to give it a more concrete form by illustrating it from the Parables of Jesus. If the idea of Agape really holds the central place we have claimed for it in the life and teaching of Jesus, it can hardly have failed to set its mark on His Parables; indeed, it can be proved to have done so. It can be shown that the Agape motif forms the principal theme of a whole series of Parables—in opposition to the legal motif of traditional religion. But before the Parables can be of service to us here there are two difficulties to be overcome.

The first is a difficulty of long standing. The chief hindrance to a fruitful use of the Parables in the past has been the allegorical method of interpretation, which opened the door wide for all kinds of fanciful expositions. With the aid of this method it has been possible to make the Parables mean almost anything. But as a result the Parables have become practically useless as evidence of what Jesus really intended. No one has done more to overcome this arbitrary method and bring lucidity and logic into the exegesis of the Parables than A. Jülicher in his monumental work, *Die Gleichnisreden Jesu* (2nd edn., 1910), in which he argues very acutely and consistently that the Parables of Jesus are not allegories, but " literal discourse ".

Unfortunately, in getting rid of the old difficulty Jülicher himself has introduced a new one, which makes it that the Parables still seem unpromising as illustrations of the idea of Agape. For, according to Jülicher, a Parable is essentially intended as a form of demonstration, which with inevitable necessity compels the hearer's assent. The purpose of Jesus in His Parables, therefore, is to induce His hearers by means of simple illustrations drawn from ordinary life to acknowledge as " self-evident " a similar situation in the spiritual sphere. If this interpretation were correct we should clearly have no right to expect to find in the Parables any testimony to God's Agape. Agape can never be " self-evident ". Placed in the context of ordinary human life it will always seem more or less of a paradox. Against Jülicher's interpretation, however, we must insist that a number of the Parables, and these the greatest and most central, are completely unintelligible unless they are understood in the light of the idea of Agape. As it would take too long to prove this in detail, we must confine ourselves to giving two examples—the Parables of the Prodigal Son and the Labourers in the Vineyard.[1]

According to Jülicher, the Parable of the Prodigal Son (Luke xv. 11-32) is a particularly good illustration of his thesis that Parables are methods of proof. Every detail of it is " faultlessly established ",[2] so that no room is left for the least doubt in the hearer's mind; he must capitulate, and admit that " that is how it really happens in life ".[3] Then he is forced to go on and draw the conclusion : Therefore, God cannot deal otherwise with the sinner; He must receive him and give him His forgiveness. In this Parable, God's goodness to the sinner, His will to forgive, is " not merely illustrated, but seriously proved ". For just as no one can take exception to a human father's acting in the way here described, so " the application to the Father in heaven is self-evident ".[4]

Now is this really sound? We must remember that for the

[1] *Cf.* on this my article " Till förståelsen av Jesu liknelser " in *Svensk teologisk kvartalskrift*, 1928, pp. 217 ff., and A. Fridrichsen, " Den nyere tids parabelforskning " in the same journal, 1929, pp. 34 ff.

[2] A. Jülicher, *Die Gleichnisreden Jesu*, 1910, I., p. 66.

[3] *Op. cit.*, I., p. 102.   [4] *Op. cit.*, II., p. 361.

traditional Jewish outlook there could not be a more unacceptable and shocking idea than that of God's love for sinners. That Jesus should take lost-sinners to Himself was bound to appear, not only to the Pharisees, but to anyone brought up and rooted in Jewish legal righteousness, as a violation of the order established by God Himself and guaranteed by His justice.

"This man receiveth sinners, and eateth with them"—a more serious accusation could hardly have been made against Jesus; it was as much as to say that He was overturning the very foundations of the entire religion of Israel. The forgiveness of sins which He preached was bound to seem an attack on the Divine righteousness which rendereth to every man according to his works.[1] Yet we are asked to believe that, in face of this compact opposition, this deeply rooted religious conviction, Jesus offered as proof to the contrary the Parable of the Prodigal Son! He is supposed to have told a story from life about a father who receives with open arms his profligate but returning son, thereby compelling His hearers, first, to admit that "that is how it really happens in life", and then, to argue from this to the attitude of God, drawing the "self-evident" conclusion that God acts in the same way towards the sinner. Truly an unconvincing proof! May we not credit Jesus' opponents, the spokesmen for justice in the relation between God and man, with sufficient intelligence to counter the Parable of Jesus immediately with another which would "prove" the precise opposite? What was there to prevent them from telling of a father whose son had wasted his substance with riotous living in a far country and then returned to his father destitute but with good intentions; but the father, who knew from experience what such good intentions are usually worth, met his son's entreaties with the stern reply, "My house is closed to you until by your own honest work you have earned a place for yourself and so

[1] Job xxxiv. 11; Ps. lxii. 13; Prov. xxiv. 12; Jer. xvii. 10; xxxii. 19; etc.

made amends for the wrong you have done "; and the son went out into the world and turned over a new leaf, and when he afterwards returned to his father he thanked him for the unyielding severity that had led to his recovery, unlike the foolish softness and weak indulgence of some other fathers, which would have let him continue in his prodigal ways—why should not such a story have been told, with such " brilliant natural colouring " and so " faultlessly established " that the hearer must at once admit " that is how it really happens in life ", and proceed to find " the application to the Father in heaven self-evident " ?

What is questionable about the treatment of Jesus' Parables as means of proof is the fact that underlying it there is a rationalistic conception of religion. We must distinguish here between two diametrically opposed types of religion : the *demonstrational* and the *revelational*. The former takes its starting-point in ordinary human life and seeks to make its way up from that to the religious life, which it constructs in accordance with the rules it has found applying in human affairs; and its aim in taking this course is to arrive at certain universally valid religious and ethical truths. The revelational type, on the other hand, takes its starting-point in the religious life itself. Only if God Himself comes to meet us and reveals Himself to us can we possibly come to Him. In so far as we can speak of an aim here, it is not certain universal, abstract propositions about God, but fellowship with God. To which of these two types the message of Jesus as a whole belongs there can be no doubt, for it bears throughout the distinctive mark of the revelational type; and this applies also to the Parables. The Parables of Jesus are not essentially means of proof but means of revelation. They do not rest on a rational " It must be so ", but on an authoritative " I say unto you ". It was not without reason that people got the impression from His preaching that He spoke " as one having authority (ἐξουσία), and not as their scribes " (Matt. vii. 29).

Jesus did not regard it as His task to proclaim certain universally valid religious and ethical principles, arguing in their
support that they were most natural and rational. Nothing
could be more alien to His mind than to apply the idea of
nihil rationabilius to God's dealings with men. It is tempting
for the theologically minded to turn Jesus more or less into a
theologian, and ask about His idea or conception of God.
Jesus, however, had not come to propound an idea of God or
to purify men's conceptions of God, but to give them a new
fellowship with God. He was carrying out a mission from
God, and the Parables were a means to that end.

The Parables do not say, " God must, rationally, act thus ",
but, " God does in fact act thus, contrary to all rational calculations ". God is the Holy One . . . what, then, could be
more rational, more " self-evident ", than that He should refuse
to have dealings with sinners? But Jesus proclaims the opposite. God's holiness remains in all its majesty and unyielding
austerity, yet Jesus proclaims that the Holy One seeks sinners;
and He conceives His own mission on the same lines : He
has not come to call the righteous, but sinners. " They that
are whole have no need of a physician, but they that are sick "
(Mark ii. 17). It is vain to seek any motive for this in the
character of the sinners, as if they were in some way better
than the " righteous ". There is no motive for this conduct on
the part of God. The only explanation of it lies in God's
love. But it is characteristic of God's love that it is spontaneous and " unmotivated ".

The Parables of Jesus in general are far from being intended
to deduce from universally accepted premises a certain attitude of God as self-evident and as the only natural thing.
On the contrary, they have as their own background the " unmotivated " Divine love that baffles all rational calculations.
It is this love that seeks expression in the Parable of the
Prodigal Son. The essential thought of the Parable is therefore quite misrepresented if we take it to mean : An earthly

father in real life acts just as the story says; therefore God acts in the same way. In this case God's love is measured by human standards; God is made in the image of man. But the Parable of the Prodigal Son takes the opposite course. God's attitude is the primary thing, and the father in the Parable is made in the image of God. Certainly not every earthly father acts in the way here described; but it is the way God acts. And just as the Parable of the Prodigal Son can only be understood in this light, so also can many other of Jesus' Parables.

A particularly illuminating example of this is found in Jülicher's treatment of the Parable of the Labourers in the Vineyard (Matt. xx. 1-16). In this Parable, as elsewhere, the general background is God's " unmotivated " love, in virtue of which He enters into fellowship with those who are not worthy of it. The point is directed against the thought of worthiness and merit, against every attempt to regulate fellowship with God by the principle of justice. The attitude of the Householder, expressed in the principle of " equal pay for unequal work ", serves as an illustration of that attitude of God which Jesus elsewhere expresses by saying that " He maketh His sun to rise on the evil and the good ". Jülicher takes no account of this background to the Parables; and therefore his treatment of it, and the difficulties in which he becomes involved, furnish the most striking negative proof of the contention that this Parable can rightly be understood only against the background of the idea of Agape.

Jülicher sums up his interpretation of this Parable as follows: " We are bound to agree with the man. If he had ordered more to be paid to the last than to the first, we should have found his action questionable. If he had given the first more than had been agreed upon, since in any case he had started being generous, we should have been delighted. But as we have not to decide how we should act in such a case, nor yet which course of action would be most beneficial from a social-political point of view, our conclusion is : The Householder is within his rights, in spite of the discontent of some of the labourers; he has exercised kindness without infringing justice; he has both strictly fulfilled his duty and made use of his rights to the advantage of men poorer than himself. This judgment on the good and righteous Householder, who is at once just and kind, is demanded of us by Jesus simply in order that honesty may compel us to pass the same judgment in similar cases on a higher level."[1]

Every sentence here calls for criticism. First: regarded as a "proof", this Parable would be as unfortunate as that of the Prodigal Son. Elsewhere Jülicher demands that the story element in a parable shall bear the marks of inescapable necessity. It must compel the hearers' unqualified assent. But where is the unqualified assent here? To his very hesitating assent to the action of the Householder, Jülicher adds the questionable rider that "we" in a similar case might well have acted otherwise, and that if the Householder had acted otherwise "we" should have been delighted. That is not an unqualified assent. Why, then, should we take this Householder's doubtful conduct as a starting-point for our "proof" of God's way of dealing with men? Would it not have been more reasonable to take the course of action with which we should have been delighted? And how in such circumstances could anyone demand or expect of Jesus' opponents an unqualified assent?

Secondly: Jülicher accepts the principle of justice and merit as valid, yet refuses to admit the validity of the complaint of the first-comers among the labourers. But that is unjust! For if it were really a question of merit and worthiness, then the labourers who complained were undoubtedly in the right. It is impossible to make a simple addition of the exercise of kindness and the non-infringement of justice. If the principle of merit and reward is laid down as finally decisive, then there is an "infringement of justice", not only

[1] *Op. cit.*, II., p. 466.

when the good lose their reward and the evil receive it, but also when the more deserving and the less deserving are treated in the same way. The principle of justice requires a due proportion between work and wages. Jülicher has failed to see that the lack of such proportion in this Parable is due to the essential purpose of the Parable, which is to exclude completely the principle of justice from the religious relationship. " Motivated " justice must give place here to " unmotivated " love. That there is something wrong with his way of reckoning, Jülicher himself has evidently felt, as can be seen from his suggestion that " we " in a similar case might perhaps have acted otherwise. And it is only a weak attempt to save the principle of justice in the case of those who received a full day's pay for only an hour's work, when he adds the comment : " What the righteous receive as their due, as the merited reward of their devotion, he bestows on penitent sinners out of free grace . . . and by their coming, by their repentance and amendment, even though at a late hour, these poor wretches show themselves after all worthy of his grace."[1] So, then, God's treatment of them is motivated by their attitude to Him, and they deserve what He gives them ! But then the whole argument immediately threatens to fall to pieces, when Jülicher asserts that it is only " miserable jealousy " that will not thankfully acknowledge the goodness " with which He gives a reward far exceeding merit and worthiness, and pays wages where hour-long, year-long, life-long idleness might have been blamed or punished ".[2] What are we to say from the point of view of justice when a reward is given to those who deserve blame or punishment? In any case, it was not merely " miserable jealousy ", but also purer and loftier motives, that caused the champions of justice in Judaism to react against such teaching.

It is futile to try to eliminate from this Parable that which is offensive in it from a juridical point of view. The offence

[1] *Op. cit.*, II., p. 467.   [2] *Ibid.*

only ceases when the principle of justice itself is eliminated as inapplicable to the religious relationship; and this is precisely what happens in the Parable of the Labourers in the Vineyard. It is equally futile to try to find a motive for God's love for the lost. The offence of this only ceases when we realise that God's love for the righteous is just as " unmotivated ", since it is characteristic of God's love that it is not evoked by its object, it is not " motivated ".

We have lingered over Jülicher's treatment of this Parable because it illustrates so very clearly the impossibility of a sound interpretation, unless we see it against the background of Jesus' new way of fellowship with God, of which the hallmark is the Agape motif. When Jülicher says, " If he had given the first more than had been agreed upon, since in any case he had started being generous, we should have been delighted ", this completely ruins the point of the Parable. It is an attempt to introduce an essentially impossible compromise between unmotivated love and motivated justice. The principle of justice with its demand for due proportion is preserved : everyone has received according to his desert, except that grace has raised the whole transaction to a higher initial standard.

When, however, we notice that the background of the Parable is the Agape motif, its meaning becomes transparently clear. In spontaneous, " unmotivated " love, the Householder gives the late-comers a reward far exceeding what they could claim. Those who have worked longest, bound as they are by the idea of the due proportion that justice demands, now reckon that they ought to receive more than the others. In relation to the Householder, it is true, they cannot demand this; but in relation to their fellows who came later, surely " righteousness " demands that more work should be matched by more pay. When this expectation is disappointed they grumble. Although it is of grace that the others have received more than they have earned, and although the whole idea of merit and reward has thus been completely transcended, yet the grumblers regard themselves as *entitled* to receive more than the others. They use the principle of grace to establish a heightened legal claim. But the Householder replies: If you come with the demands of justice, let us stick to justice. "Friend, I do thee no wrong: didst not thou agree with me for a penny? Take up that which is thine, and go thy way" (Matt. xx. 13 f.). Where spontaneous love and generosity are found, the order of justice is obsolete and invalidated. But to those who still wish to maintain the legal order, goodness itself becomes a cause for offence: "Is thine eye evil, because I am good?" (15). Those who cannot make any claim (the sinners) accept the unmotivated generosity; those who are able to present a claim (the righteous) demand motivated justice and refuse to accept the unmotivated love. "So the last shall be first, and the first last" (16).

Precisely the same testimony to God's spontaneous, unmotivated love is contained in the Parable of the Prodigal Son; and there, lest anyone should still be in doubt about the unmotivated character of the love that is portrayed, the Elder Brother stands in the background representing the legal order. From his point of view, from the point of view of justice, the Elder Brother is entirely right; his younger brother's conduct has furnished no grounds whatever for such a love as his father has shown him. But that makes it so much the more plain that the father's love is an altogether spontaneous love.

The spontaneity of Christian love means that it is directly opposed to all rational computation and calculation. Agape gives and sacrifices even where rational calculation would suggest that any sacrifice was useless. Agape sows its seed in hope, even when there seem to be no grounds at all for hope. When the Sower goes forth to sow (Mark iv. 3 ff.) he knows that by far the greater part of the seed will be lost and yield no fruit; yet he takes no account of that, but sows broadcast in the carefree manner of love. The spirit of Agape breathes through this Parable. And the same is true of the Parable of the Lost Sheep. It is not the cold reflection of reason but unmotivated love that leaves the ninety and nine in the wilderness to go after that which is lost (Luke xv. 4).

Finally, we may notice the Parable of the Unmerciful Steward (Matt. xviii. 23 ff). The feature of the Divine Agape that is most prominent here is its boundlessness and its unconditional character. But if God's love and His will to forgive is boundless and unconditional, it demands of those who receive its forgiveness that their love and forgiveness shall likewise be boundless and unconditional: not " until seven times, but until seventy times seven " (22). " I forgave thee all that debt, because thou besoughtest me: shouldest not thou also have had mercy on thy fellow-servant, even as I had mercy on thee?" (32 f.).

Here it is clearly shown how the Christian ethic is rooted in Christian fellowship with God. *The distinctive character of the Christian ethic, as it arises out of fellowship with God, can be summed up in Jesus' words to His disciples: " Freely ye have received, freely give "* (Matt. x. 8). Those who have freely received God's love are called to pass it on freely to their fellow-men.

5. THE COMMANDMENT OF LOVE IN ITS CHRISTIAN MEANING

Now at last we are in a position to define the Christian meaning of the commandment of love. *The Agape that is required here has its prototype in the Agape manifested by God, and therefore it must be spontaneous and unmotivated, uncalculating, unlimited, and unconditional.*

This is true in the first place of *love towards God.* When a man has experienced God's Agape, when in spite of his unworthiness and absolute nothingness he has been taken into fellowship with God, it follows that he belongs absolutely to God   The unconditional nature of the love he has experienced makes the demand for his surrender to it also unconditional. The attempt sometimes made to interpret man's love for God as meaning that man regards God as his "highest good" is thoroughly misleading. It gives the impression that man has an independent life of his own apart from God. God is measured by human standards, and even though He is judged to be man's "highest good", yet man's attitude to Him is still relative, conditional on His being such a "good". But it is precisely this that the commandment of love seeks to eradicate. Its demand is complete and unconditional. "Thou shalt love the Lord thy God *with all thy heart, and with all thy soul, and with all thy mind, and with all thy strength*" (Mark xii. 30). These words imply absolute devotion and submission. Love towards God is neither *amor concupiscentiæ* nor *amor amicitiæ*, neither "acquisitive love" nor "the love of friendship"—to use the common scholastic distinction; for both of these take their rise and direction from man himself. If love towards God were "acquisitive love", then God, even though He were described as the *highest* good, would in the last resort be the means for the satisfaction of man's desires. Nor is there any room for the "love of friendship" in a theocentric relationship to God, for that love presupposes an equality between Divine and human love which does not exist. It is excluded by the sovereignty of Divine love.

In the conception of "love towards God" there is a difficulty which is not immediately apparent in the Synoptic Gospels, but which becomes a living issue for St. Paul and frequently makes itself felt in the later history of the Christian idea of love. The commandment of love towards God is taken over by Jesus from the Old Testament, but He fills it with new content by setting it in relation to the new fellowship with God which He has brought. God's Agape is the criterion of Christian love. Nothing but that which bears the impress of Agape has a right to be called Christian love. This connection between God's love and the Christian's love is clearest when the latter takes the form of neigh-bourly love.   We may recall here the Parable of the Un-merciful Steward, who ought to have had mercy on his fellow-servant because the king had mercy on him (Matt. xviii. 33); or the commandment that we should love our enemies, which is based on God's attitude to the evil (Matt. v. 44 f.).   But although the connection with God's Agape is plainest in the case of neighbourly love, yet it is no less real whatever the object of the love may be—not excluding even love towards God. Christian love is something other than ordinary human love.   But what gives it its special character is precisely the fact that it is patterned on God's love.   There is therefore no Christian love that does not derive its character from the Agape that is found in fellowship with God.   But it is just this fact that is the source of the above-mentioned difficulty.

God's love is spontaneous and "unmotivated"; consequently man's love for God, if it is really to deserve the name of Agape, must also be spontaneous and "unmotivated".   But what does that imply?   Can our love for God ever be spon-taneous?   And what sense would there be in saying that our love for God was "unmotivated"?   Is not our love for God in fact "motivated" in the very highest degree?   Is it not motiv-ated by the Agape He has shown towards us?   We are here driven into an apparently inescapable dilemma.   The more the spontaneous and unmotivated nature of God's love is em-phasised, the less room there is for a spontaneous and un-motivated love towards God.   On the other hand, if we seek to maintain the demand for spontaneity in Christian love even when it is directed towards God, it seems impossible to do so without reducing the spontaneity of Divine love.

As has already been said, there is little sign of this difficulty in the Synoptic Gospels. Love towards God is there main-tained as the first and greatest commandment, and although the new meaning given to love admittedly strains this old commandment almost to breaking-point, yet the breaking-point is never actually reached. The existence of the difficulty has been pointed out here, however, as it will give rise to a number of complications later on. It is important to observe that the difficulty is present from the beginning, even though it is not yet felt as a difficulty.

What, then, has prevented the difficulty from emerging at this initial stage? The deepest reason is undoubtedly this, that to have love for God means, as Jesus sees it, exactly the same as to be possessed by God, to belong absolutely to Him. This being possessed by God both excludes all thought of absolute spontaneity on man's part, and includes a relative spontaneity, which gives to love for God a quite different character from that of human" motivated " love. It excludes man's spontaneity, inasmuch as it is God's Agape that has "chosen" him and made him a slave of God, so that he cannot be said to have anything he can call his own in relation to God. But this very fact of belonging without reserve to God includes also something that must be described as spontaneity when it is compared with ordinary human love. The latter has an egocentric motive, and the less it is affected by extraneous considerations (and the more it is in that sense " spontaneous "), then the more egocentric it becomes. From such motivation Christian love of God is exempted because it is identical with absolute possession by God. All teleological motivation is excluded here. Love towards God does not seek to gain anything. It most certainly does not seek to gain anything other than God. But neither does it seek to gain even God Himself or His love. The very thought of gaining anything, even of gaining God's love, is fundamentally alien to it. It is the *free*—and in that sense spontaneous—surrender of the heart to God. When God gives His love freely and for nothing, there remains nothing for man to gain by loving God. His love for God loses the character of a deserving achievement and becomes pure and unfeigned. It flows by inescapable necessity from the fact of his belonging unreservedly to God; and being aware of so belonging, it devotes its whole attention to the carrying out of God's will. It is obedience to God, without any thought of reward. "When ye shall have done all the things that are commanded you, say, We are unprofitable servants; we have done that which it was our duty to do" (Luke xvii. 10).

We must now turn to the second part of the commandment of love, which requires *love for one's neighbour*, and seek to make clear its specifically Christian meaning. There are four points in particular that call for our attention.

(1) In order to grasp the Christian meaning of the commandment of neighbourly love, it is above all necessary to bear in mind its religious basis. When we say that the Christian ethic is a religious ethic, this is to be taken without any qualification. It is not the case that while love towards God is of a religious nature, neighbourly love is a more general ethical requirement. Neighbourly love loses its specifically Christian character if it is taken out of context of fellowship with God. This point needs to be the more emphasised because the idea has often been put forward that it is possible to retain Christian ethics even while rejecting the religious content of Christianity. But the "love for one's neighbour", the "general love of humanity", which it is thus intended to retain, turns out in the end to be something quite other than Christian love for one's neighbour. Nothing could be more disastrous for the Christian idea of love than that it should be identified with modern ideas of altruism, fellow-feeling, and so forth. Even though the "humane" ideals of altruism and the ethic of sympathy may present on the surface certain similarities to Christian neighbourly love, they nevertheless have entirely different spiritual roots, and Christian love has really nothing at all to do with such modern ideas.[1]

[1] In this connection reference may be made to Max Scheler's interesting discussion of "the modern love for humanity" (*Vom Umsturz der Werte*,

The second commandment is like the first also in the fact that neighbourly love springs from the same root as love for God—that is, from fellowship with God and experience of God's Agape. It is also from this that the characteristic features of Christian neighbourly love are derived. The love required by the commandment is, like God's Agape, spontaneous and unmotivated. It is not merely a reflection of the attitude of the person who is its object, but has creative power to establish a new fellowship between men. Jesus draws a sharp distinction between human love and Divine, and so also between the love that is a natural growth and that which has its root in God's love. The Divine love is unmotivated, the human motivated. Measured by the standard of Divine love, therefore, human love is not love at all in a deeper sense, but

1919, vol. i., pp. 150 ff.). Scheler attempts to prove that this "modern love for humanity" is based, in contrast to Christian love, on *ressentiment*; and he has undoubtedly put his finger on something that is characteristic of modern altruism and "humanitarianism" with its "love for humanity" But apt as his criticism is in the main, he has nevertheless failed to perceive the ultimately decisive difference between this general love for humanity and Christian love for one's neighbour. He recognises, of course, that what distinguishes modern altruism from Christian love is its separation of love from its religious basis. But on the other hand, he regards Christian love as rooted rather in man's love for God than in God's own love, and consequently fails to recognise its spontaneous and unmotivated character. Christian love, he holds, is not really directed to "the neighbour", but only to the imperishable value, the "divine element" in man. In accordance with this, he says that "love in the Christian sense is always related primarily to the ideal *spiritual self* in man and to his membership of the Kingdom of God" (p. 150); and he speaks of a "Christian unity and harmony of love for God, self and neighbour" (*ibid.*). The most disturbing feature in this context is the introduction of the thought of self-love, which at a later stage leads Scheler to deny that a concern for one's neighbour is either characteristic of, or essential to, Christian love. "For this Christian idea of love is defined as an act of a particular quality towards the *spiritual, ideal person* as such, and it remains a matter of indifference whether this is the person of the lover *or* the person of the 'other'" (p. 165). "He [Comte] fails to observe that 'love' in the Christian sense is understood as a *species of act*, which is of a spiritual nature, and by its very nature is directed primarily to the spiritual person (of God and of men); that consequently the reference to the other is by no means characteristic of its *essence* and that just for this reason Christianity knows, and must know, a 'self-love' that is different in kind from all 'egoism'!" (p. 166).

only a form of natural self-love, which extends its scope to embrace also benefactors of the self. "If ye love them that love you, what thank have ye? for even sinners love those that love them. And if ye do good to them that do good to you, what thank have ye? for even sinners do the same. And if ye lend to them of whom ye hope to receive, what thank have ye? even sinners lend to sinners, to receive again as much" (Luke vi. 32-34). In distinction from this natural love, which is displayed even by sinners, Christian love is spontaneous and unmotivated.

It is true, of course, that even the Christian's love for his neighbour cannot be spontaneous in quite the same sense as God's love is spontaneous; in the last resort it, too, is nothing but a reflection. But the question is of what it is a reflection. Man's *natural* attitude is a reflection of his neighbour's attitude to him : love is met with love, hate with hate. *Christian love*, on the other hand, is a reflection of God's love; this is its prototype and its ultimate ground. To isolate neighbourly love from love towards God, allowing only the latter to have a religious basis, is therefore entirely wrong. The real meaning of Christian neighbourly love can only be understood if we take serious account of the fact that it, no less than love towards God, is dependent on fellowship with God and experience of the Divine love.

(2) The two commandments of love, as we have seen, cannot be isolated from one another without risk of perversion; but the risk is no less great if they are confused with one another. They are for Jesus quite really *two* commandments; and it is the more important to observe this fact inasmuch as the subsequent history of Christianity is full of attempts to make the two commandments into one. In general, the procedure has been to subsume neighbourly love under love for God. Men have started from the conviction that love for God is in the last resort the only legitimate form of Christian love. They have therefore thought it necessary to justify the de-

mand for love to one's neighbour by showing that it is only another way of speaking of love for God. Hence the idea has been put forward—in very diverse forms—that the Christian's love for his neighbour is not strictly directed to the neighbour, but to God. It is love for the neighbour, not as he actually is, but as he can one day become; or it is not love for the neighbour himself, but for " God in my neighbour " —as the common phrase goes.

Such ideas, however, have no connection whatsoever with the Gospel teaching. When Jesus speaks of " the great and first commandment " and " a second like unto it " (Matt. xxii. 38 f.), these are for Him really two quite distinct commandments, each with its own aim and object. Love for one's neighbour is not simply a special case of love for God, nor is the second commandment an unnecessary repetition in other words of the first; but by its addition Christian love is in fact given a new object. The words, " Thou shalt love thy neighbour as thyself ", really do refer to my neighbour and not to God. The one who is to be loved is my neighbour in his concrete situation and his concrete condition, not some imagined ideal of my neighbour and not " God in my neighbour ".

The objection to the common confusion of love for God and love for one's neighbour is not, however, merely that it misses the original meaning of the double commandment of love, but still more that it destroys just what is most characteristic of the Christian idea of love—namely, its spontaneous and unmotivated nature. If my love for my neighbour is not concerned with him himself, but with a supposed Divine kernel or essence within him, then my love is very far from being unmotivated. One of the chief reasons why people are so ready to let neighbourly love be wholly subsumed under love for God is doubtless because this furnishes a satisfactory motivation for something that otherwise seems to elude all rational explanation. It may serve to illustrate the point here if we recall some words of Nietzsche, which are based on the assumption that love for human beings requires justification. "To love man *for God's sake*—this has been until now the most distinguished and exalted emotion that has been attained among men. That a love for man, apart from some ulterior object to hallow it, is a piece of folly and bestiality; that the propensity to this love for man must first receive from a higher propensity its measure, its elegance, its grain of salt and particle of ambergris—whoever the man was who first felt and 'experienced' this, and however much his tongue may have stammered, when it tried to express something so delicate, let him be to us in all ages holy and venerable, as the man who of all men hitherto has flown highest and gone most splendidly wrong!"[1] Nietzsche has quite rightly seen that every attempt to base love for men on the qualities of its objects is bound to fail, and he has also rightly sensed that the ultimate explanation of Christian love is to be found in the relation of the Christian to God. But he has not seen that it is characteristic of Christian love to be unmotivated and uncalculating, and that it is just the Christian's relation to God that makes it so.

God's Agape is a love that makes mockery of all attempts at rational motivation. But if the rationalising tendency will not allow even God's love to retain spontaneity, but insists on finding a motive for it in the value of its object, then it is only to be expected that it should insist even more strongly on treating the Christian's love for his neighbour in a similar way. For Jesus, on the other hand, it is beyond question that God's love is unmotivated and spontaneous; and therefore it is also beyond question for Him that a man's love for his neighbour should be spontaneous and unmotivated. There is no occasion to look behind our neighbour's actual condition for any hidden valuable quality that will explain and justify our love for him. God's love is explanation and sanction

[1] F. Nietzsche, *Jenseits von Gut und Böse*, 60.

enough: " Love . . . that ye may be sons of your Father which is in heaven " (Matt. v. 44 f.).

(3) We have so far reached two conclusions with regard to neighbourly love. First: such love has a Christian content only as it is closely linked with love for God, and rooted along with the latter in fellowship with God, in God's Agape. Second: the two commandments of love nevertheless remain two, and every attempt to make them into one—by merging love for one's neighbour into love for God, for example—inevitably misrepresents the essential character of Christian love by impairing its spontaneity and groundlessness. As it is thus of the greatest importance that the double commandment of love should retain its *duality*, we must now add a third point, which is equally important: *that the two commandments are two only, and no third can be added to them.* Alongside of the attempt to absorb neighbourly love into love for God, there appears throughout Christian history an attempt to find in the commandment of neighbourly love a third commandment—that of *self-love*; for the command is " Thou shalt love thy neighbour *as thyself.*" Must not my love for my neighbour, then, rest on the foundation of self-love? Is not self-love presupposed here as something without which neighbourly love would hang in the air? Thus, while the commandment of love speaks expressly of *two* things, love for God and love for one's neighbour, there has arisen a strong tradition, which has found acceptance both in Catholic and Protestant theology, that *three* things are included in the Christian commandment of love: love for God, for oneself, and for one's neighbour.

It should not need to be said that the commandment of self-love is alien to the New Testament commandment of love, and has grown up out of a wholly different soil from that of the New Testament. If there were not a desire on other grounds to include self-love among the ethical demands of Christianity, no one would be able to find in the commandment of love any reason for doing so. Self-love is man's natural condition, and also the reason for the perversity of his will. Everyone knows how by nature he loves himself. *So,* says the commandment of love, thou shalt love thy neighbour. When love receives this new direction, when it is turned away from one's self and directed to one's neighbour, then the natural perversion of the will is overcome.[1] So far is neighbourly love from including self-love that it actually excludes and overcomes it.

(4) On the other hand, neighbourly love includes *love for one's enemies.* Even here there is no third commandment added to those of love for God and one's neighbour; and if "Love your enemies" is set alongside "Thou shalt love thy neighbour", as if it were something distinct and different, then it has simply not been understood. It is not true even to say that Jesus conceived of the injunction to love one's enemies as an extreme case of the commandment to love one's neighbour. On the contrary, love for one's neighbour is by nature and from its very origin love for enemies. When Jesus says, "Love your enemies, and pray for them that persecute you" (Matt. v. 44), this is neither an exaggerated sharpening of the commandment of love nor yet an arbitrary perversion of natural sentiment. If love for one's neighbour is to be real Agape it must above all be spontaneous and unmotivated. But where does it show itself more spontaneous and unmotivated than when it is directed to enemies, whose behaviour would most reasonably and naturally provoke the precise opposite of love? It is at this point that it first becomes quite clear that neighbourly love is born of God's Agape and is an outflow

---

[1] Compare the apt comment of R. Bultmann on self-love: "It is therefore meaningless to say (what can only be said on the basis of a humanistic ideal of man), that neighbourly love must be preceded by a legitimate self-love, a necessary degree of self-respect, because we are told 'Thou shalt love thy neighbour as thyself.' Self-love is thus presupposed. And it is in fact presupposed, but not as something that man must first learn, something that must be expressly required of him, but as the attitude of the natural man, which has simply to be overcome" (*Jesus,* p. 100).

from its creative life. Just as God's love is a love for sinners, so the Christian's love is a love for enemies. God's love for sinners and Christian love for enemies are correlatives. Therefore Jesus connects them directly together: " Love your enemies . . . that ye may be sons of your Father which is in heaven: for He maketh His sun to rise on the evil and the good, and sendeth rain on the just and the unjust " (Matt. v. 44 f.). When Christian love is directed to enemies, it shows itself to be real Agape, spontaneous and creative. It creates fellowship even where fellowship seemed impossible. Thus it shows that Christian love is action, not merely reaction.

6. LOVE AND JUDGMENT

To conclude our account of the idea of Agape in the Gospels a word may be added on the relation of love to judgment. Does not the love we have described, and all that goes with it, stand in singular contrast to the thought of judgment, to which Jesus undoubtedly gives a central place?

Perhaps the most important contribution of modern exegesis to our understanding of the Gospel has been the clear light it has shed on the eschatological perspective. For quite a long time this aspect of the Gospel had been entirely neglected by theologians; the eschatological outlook of primitive Christianity was set down as a limitation of view typical of its time, which must be discounted in order to penetrate to the real essence of the Gospel. This essence was taken to consist of Jesus' proclamation of the Kingdom of God, which was interpreted as a this-worldly ethical ideal. To use typical phrases from Kant, the Kingdom was " a People of God according to the moral law ", " a Republic under the moral law ",[1] " a Society aiming quite specifically at the prevention of evil and the promotion of good in man, as a permanent

---

[1] Kant, *Die Religion innerhalb der Grenzen der blossen Vernunft* (Reclam), p. 104.

and continually expanding Association founded purely for the upholding of morality ".[1] Kant's conception of the Kingdom of God came to play a great and disastrous part in theology through the work of A. Ritschl.[2]

Now, however, it has been established beyond all possible doubt that this interpretation of the New Testament idea of the Kingdom of God is false. The eschatological aspect is not an accidental encumbrance, but an essential and constitutive element.[3] The Kingdom of God is not an ideal this-worldly state of affairs; it does not come into being through the moral endeavours of men, but by a mighty act of God; it is not built up, it comes. But this fact gives the thought of judgment added weight. God's Kingdom breaks in with salvation and judgment.

What, then, is the relation of the idea of Agape to that of Judgment? Is it not bound to lessen the seriousness of the idea of judgment when love is made absolutely " unmotivated "? Is there not from an ethical point of view a highly questionable blurring of distinctions when the Divine love, and consequently also the Christian's love for his neighbour, are made independent of the difference between evil men and good, righteous men and sinners? That might seem to be so, and if the love in question were merely the same as sentimental love or weak altruism the danger would undoubtedly be real. But it is precisely the absolute character of the Divine love that is the safeguard against this; for a love so conceived is not in any way incompatible with judgment. Agape is not unrelated to the eschatological element; it is itself a bit of eschatology. The revelation of God's Agape means at the same time the coming of God's Kingdom. Thereby human

---

[1] *Ibid.*, p. 97.

[2] For a fuller treatment of this see my *Filosofisk och kristen etik*, 1923, 197-206.

[3] *Cf.* M. Dibelius, *Geschichtliche und übergeschichtliche Religion im Christentum*, 1925, p. 41: "The eschatological faith of Jesus . . . contains the driving motive of the entire Gospel."

life as a whole is set *sub specie æternitatis*—that is to say, under the Judgment of Love. God's Agape faces man with a decision, an inescapable " Either—Or ". Just because Agape means a completely reckless giving, it also demands unlimited devotion. As creative and productive of fellowship, it becomes also an annihilating judgment on the selfish life which will not let itself be re-created into a life of love and refuses the offered fellowship. It is in the presence of the Divine Agape that a man's destiny is ultimately decided. The question is whether he will let himself be won and re-created by God's love, or will resist it, and so encounter it only as a judgment on his life.

There is, consequently, no weakening of the idea of judgment when the spontaneity and groundlessness of Divine love are pressed to the uttermost. Nor does the idea of Agape suffer by being set in the light of judgment. On the contrary, these two ideas belong together, and each gains in depth and significance along with the other. Only that love which pronounces judgment on all that is not love is in the deepest sense a restoring and saving love. At the same time, no judgment pierces so deep as the judgment of love; and whatever refuses to be won by the reckless self-giving of love cannot be won at all.

II

THE AGAPE OF THE CROSS

1. Jesus and Paul

For a long time past New Testament scholars have been inclined to draw a very sharp line between Jesus and Paul. They have held that there is an immense gulf between the teaching of these two, and have therefore regarded it as their chief problem to explain how such a thing as the theology of Paul could take its rise out of the simple teaching of Christ. This idea has found expression in a variety of ways. Paul is said to have been a theologian who dogmatised a previously undogmatic Christianity and replaced the teaching of Jesus with doctrine and Christology. Whereas what chiefly mattered for Jesus was a number of simple ethical imperatives, what we find in Paul is belief in a system of saving facts: belief in Christ as a heavenly being, in His death and resurrection and the Atonement based on them, belief in the regeneration of Christians and their equipment with the Spirit, belief in the mystical union between Christ and His Church, and so forth. Even if Paul was neither the sole author nor the originator of this development, yet—we are told—it was he who contributed most powerfully to the hellenising or orientalising of early Christianity. Hence, however strongly Paul may have felt himself to be nothing but an apostle and servant of Christ, his work must be regarded less as a continuation of that of Jesus than as a completely new beginning; and it has actually been thought legitimate to describe him as the " second founder " of Christianity.[1]   In its earliest period Christianity branched off on a new line and, thanks to the influence of Paul, became something quite different from what its " first Founder " intended. It was essentially the teaching of Paul, not of Jesus, that came to set its mark on later Christianity.

Now it should be observed that the contrast thus drawn between Jesus and Paul has to do not merely with the form of their teaching and their different ways of expressing it, but with the religious essence of it.   Paul's gospel is held to represent, not a peculiar development or re-statement of Jesus' Gospel, but a quite new religion.   In place of Jesus' Gospel about God's fatherly love, Paul is said to have substituted his Gospel about Christ; and whereas in His own Gospel Jesus is quite in the background, His Person forms the very centre of Paul's.   Jesus' message of the Kingdom of God and Paul's theology of the Cross are thus—on this view—contrasted with one another as two different religions.   There is a greater gulf between the Christianity of Paul and the Christianity of Jesus than between the latter and the highest form of Judaism. W. Wrede says of Paul : " He stands much further from Jesus than Jesus Himself stands from the noblest types of Jewish piety."[2]   Ideas like these have been widely prevalent in modern Pauline scholarship.   Whether with an older school of thought chief emphasis has been laid on the theological and dogmatic element in Paul's conception of Christianity, or, in harmony with the more recent " religious-historical " approach, the attempt has been made to link up his outlook with the ancient Mystery religions, in either case what we have in Paul represents an extraordinary transformation as compared with the teaching of Jesus—a transformation which may, of course, have begun in the very earliest days of the primitive Church before Paul's time.

[1] W. Wrede, *Paulus*, 1904, p. 104.   [2] *Op. cit.*, p. 95.

Now it is, of course, undeniable that the Pauline Epistles set before us a world of ideas in many respects very different from that which meets us in the Gospels. But if we wish to form a sound judgment about the relation between Jesus and Paul we must obviously go further than this. We cannot be content merely to compare and contrast their forms of expression and circles of ideas, and to conclude from the differences we find between these that there is a difference in the basic religious outlook. But neither, on the other hand, have we any right to appeal, as is often done, against such differences to Paul's own testimony that he desired to be nothing else but a servant and witness of Jesus Christ. Such a self-judgment is not in itself any sufficient guarantee that a profound change cannot be taking place. The only reliable means of reaching a decision on this question is to go back to the fundamental religious motif and see whether or not at that point the continuity is preserved. If it is, then no matter how different the forms of expression and circles of ideas may be, we have no right to draw any sharp line of distinction or to talk of " different religions ". If, however, the continuity is broken with respect to the fundamental religious motif, then the unity is irrecoverably lost, no matter how many striking formal similarities can be shown to exist, and no matter how strong may be the subjective consciousness of merely drawing out the implications of what was originally given.

We have not referred to the problem of " Jesus and Paul " with any intention of passing judgment on the many complicated questions to which it has given rise in recent times. Modern scholarship has undoubtedly in many respects shed new light on Paul's Christianity, so that we now have a far more living and concrete picture of it; but we have no need here to settle in advance the question of Paul's relation to Jesus in its entirety. That question does not have to be answered before we can go on to the question of Paul's attitude to the idea of Agape. On the contrary, the inquiry we are now to make into the place and importance of the Agape motif in the Pauline writings is itself of such a kind as to make an important contribution towards the solution of the problem of " Jesus and Paul ". It offers us precisely an opportunity of penetrating behind modes of expression, thought-forms, and circles of ideas, to the fundamental religious motif —the point where the final decision on this question must be made. Our preceding discussion has shown the significance and centrality of the idea of Agape in the life and teaching of Jesus. This idea is not one among other equally important ideas; it is the fundamental motif of Christianity, which sets its stamp on everything else. It is the idea of Agape that hall-marks the new way of fellowship with God which Christianity brings, and the idea of Agape that characterises its new ethic and turns the old commandment of love into a " new commandment " with a specifically Christian content.

If there really exists such an immense gulf between Jesus and Paul that at bottom they represent two different religions, this cannot possibly fail to find expression in a difference of attitude to the fundamental religious and ethical motif, the Agape motif. In that case it would be impossible for the Agape motif to play the same central part in Paul's Christianity as it plays in the Gospels. But if we find the idea of Agape in its characteristic sense still living on in Paul, setting its mark on his teaching, his Gospel about Christ and his theology of the Cross, that will be the most signal refutation of those theories that assert an irreconcilable opposition between the Gospel of Jesus and that of Paul. It will also be the most unimpeachable evidence that Paul's judgment was right when he thought of himself, not as the founder of a new religion, but simply as an apostle and servant of Christ. Once this issue has been settled, it is an interesting subject for scholarly inquiry to determine to what extent Paul has derived from his Jewish and Hellenistic environment materials and modes of expression for his evangelical message and its intellectual and theological formulation; but for the decision of the main question and for our total estimate of Pauline Christianity all this is of only secondary importance. If continuity is preserved in the matter of the Agape motif, that is the surest proof that Pauline Christianity is a legitimate sequel to the Gospel of Jesus. Hence, in view of the present position of Pauline scholarship, it is with a certain suspense that we pass from our study of the Agape motif in the Gospels to an investigation of the place and importance it has for Paul.

2. THE IDEA OF AGAPE IN PAUL'S RELIGIOUS DEVELOPMENT

The first point that draws our attention is the place of the idea of Agape in the development of Paul's religious life, the significance it has for him personally.

Students of Pauline Christianity have commonly taken as their starting-point his " experience on the Damascus road ", holding that his religious outlook must be interpreted in the light of it. But this procedure is open to the objection that we know far too little about the psychological significance of the experience and about the process of the conversion to be able to base any sure judgments on it.[1] With this starting-point it is all too easy to be led into doubtful psychological reconstructions; and, speaking generally, it is not too much to say that psychological reconstruction is one of the chief errors of Pauline scholarship. This observation need not prevent us, however, from inquiring into the part played by the idea of Agape in Paul's own life, for it will naturally be of the greatest importance if we can show that it was of personal interest to him. Even if it was not, the idea of Agape might still be present in his thought as part of the tradition he had received; but it is only when the idea awakens sympathy and wins a personal response that it becomes a real power.

[1] Cf. G. P. Wetter, *Die Damaskusvision und das paulinische Evangelium* in *Festgabe für Adolf Jülicher*, 1927 pp. 80 ff.

Now there is fortunately no need to resort to dubious psychological surmising in order to reconstruct the connection between the idea of Agape and Paul's religious life. The connection is perfectly clear; it rests on the most elementary facts, and facts that are quite indisputable on any view of Paul's development. Different views may be taken as to the psychological significance of the "experience on the Damascus road" and as to the process of the conversion; but its essential meaning is quite plain, and that is all that concerns us here.

What it means can be expressed very briefly thus: *the persecutor became a disciple and an apostle*. It was just this that was for Paul himself a source of ceaseless wonder. How was it that he of all men, he who had done all that lay in his power to destroy the Christian Church, should be called to be an apostle? Were it a matter of worthiness, he would least of all have deserved to become an apostle of Christ. "I am not meet to be called an apostle, because I persecuted the church of God" (1 Cor. xv. 9). Yet it had none the less happened. Christ had revealed Himself to him (Gal. i. 12, 16) "as unto one born out of due time" (1 Cor. xv. 8), and had given him "grace and apostleship" (Rom. i. 5). What was this evidence of? It revealed to him the ways of God; it gave him an insight into God's Agape and Christ's Agape; it showed him the absolutely unmotivated character of God's love. For what could show more clearly how unmotivated, how contrary to all human calculations, God's love and calling are, than the calling of a persecutor to be an apostle?

Realising this, Paul realised also the truth about the way to fellowship with God. Previously he had known a way—the way of man—to God through strict observance of the Law and righteousness of life. He was pursuing that way when he set out for Damascus. But whither had that way led him? To the great sin of his life: his persecution of the Church of God. Instead of leading him to God, it had led him as far away from God as possible. Evidently, then, there is no way

—no way of man—to God. The way of the Law leads away from God. This means a complete inversion of values as far as Pharisaic values are concerned; *human righteousness*, the righteousness that is of the Law, *is sin in an enhanced form*. All that the Law can do is to make the trespass abound (Rom. v. 20); what the Law produces is " wrath " (Rom. iv. 15). It causes every mouth to be stopped and makes all the world guilty before God (Rom. iii. 19).

Having himself followed the way of the Law to the end, and having seen that its " righteousness " only leads away from God, Paul could no longer maintain his old system of values. A transvaluation took place that put a different complexion on everything. Of this Paul speaks in his Epistle to the Philippians, where he says: " If any other man thinketh to have confidence in the flesh, I yet more: circumcised the eighth day, of the stock of Israel, of the tribe of Benjamin, a Hebrew of the Hebrews; as touching the Law, a Pharisee; as touching zeal, persecuting the church; as touching the righteousness which is in the Law, found blameless " (Phil. iii. 4 ff.). There are two things that should be particularly noticed here. First, observe how Paul puts together the righteousness of the Law and the persecution of the Church. It was the way of the Law that had landed him in sin; just when he thought he was most of all doing God's will, he had been committing his most grievous sin. His conversion is therefore not a conversion of the usual type, from sin to righteousness. In that sense he was already " converted " when he underwent this other conversion, which was actually a conversion from " righteousness ". Secondly, observe that for this very reason the Law and all that constituted Israel's pride is counted by Paul as belonging to the sphere of σάρξ, or " the flesh ". To all this, the revelation of God and the Agape of Christ at once put an end. A new standard of values was given, which ruled it all out. Therefore Paul continues: " Howbeit what things were gain to me,

these have I counted loss for Christ." Nothing could be more
mistaken than to see in this transvaluation a manifestation of
" ressentiment ". Paul possessed all the advantages of the Jew
and the righteous Pharisee, and he might have made them
his boast; but he has seen that these things lead him away
from God. Furthermore, he gives them up in favour of a
positive value—that is, in order to " gain Christ ".

But there is yet a further point. Just when Paul is utterly
alienated from God, and that not merely in the sense of *feeling*
himself far from God, but in the sense that he actually *is*
as far removed from God as possible—*just in his greatest sin
God's calling and election come to him. That is Agape:
that is God's way to man.*

The revolution that took place for Paul is therefore much
reduced in significance when it is interpreted merely as a conversion from the Pharisaic way of salvation with its self-con-
scious assurance of possessing the righteousness that counts
before God, to the way of salvation of the *anawim*, with its
hunger and thirst after righteousness, its repentance and
humility. The significance of the revolution is diminished
in this way when W. Sattler, for instance, says : " Paul's experience on the road to Damascus consisted in the radical
insight that there are not two ways, but only one way to
righteousness, the way of grace, of repentance, of *anawah*."[1]
It is much rather the case that Paul became aware that there
is from man's side no way whatsoever to righteousness. Man's
repentance, man's humility, can as little as the observance of
the Law be a practicable way to God. Paul takes seriously
the fact that there is no way from man to God, but only a way
from God to man. His religious position is thoroughly theocentric. Nothing proceeds from man : " for there is no distinction; for all have sinned, and fall short of the glory of
God " (Rom. iii. 22 f.). " All things are of God, who recon-

[1] W. Sattler, *Die Anawim im Zeitalter Jesu Christi* in *Festgabe für Adolf
Jülicher*, 1927, p. 14.

ciled us to Himself through Christ . . . God was in Christ reconciling the world to Himself " (2 Cor. v. 18 f.). Paul's story is not that of a proud Pharisee who is transformed by his conversion into a humble penitent. It is rather the story of a sincere and ardent Pharisee who in his very pursuit of righteousness becomes " the chief of sinners ",[1] and in the very midst of his greatest sin hears the call of Him who " came not to call the righteous, but sinners " (Mark ii. 17). And since the way by which God reaches him is directly opposite to the way of merit and the Law, it can also be described as grace. " By the grace of God I am what I am ", Paul says (1 Cor. xv. 10). The grace of God has turned the persecutor into an apostle.

Enough has been said to prove already that the continuity between the Gospels and Paul in the matter of the fundamental motif is not broken. The idea of Agape that is found in the Gospels lives on with its characteristic meaning, and is actually strengthened in Paul's case by its connection with his personal religious development. The question arises, however, has Paul simply taken over the idea of Agape and passed it on just as he found it, or has the idea undergone any development at his hands? The latter being clearly the case, we must proceed to illustrate this development at certain essential points.

3. Agape as a Technical Term for the Christian Love-Motif

The first point to be noticed in considering Paul's contribution to the development of the Christian idea of love concerns rather its form than its content, but it is not the less important for that. We have shown above how the Gospels are, so to speak, saturated with the Agape motif; but the noun ἀγάπη

---

[1] The question whether this is Paul's own description of himself is of no importance here.

is very rarely found in the Synoptists, for it occurs only in **two** isolated passages (Matt. xxiv. 12; Luke xi. 42), and then without any special significance. It seems to have been Paul who introduced it as a technical term for the Christian Agape motif—though not, of course, in the sense that he coined the word. There is very little ground for the old contention that the word ἀγάπη itself is a new creation of Christianity, for even though its occurrence in non-Christian sources is very rare, yet it is not entirely absent from them. But it is not this question that interests us here. What is far more important is that the reality for which Agape stands, and which appears unmistakably in the Synoptic Gospels as the fundamental motif of Christianity, now receives its characteristic name Where the word occurs in non-Christian sources, it does not occur as the name of this reality, does not signify the same thing.[1]

Now if we reflect on the important part played by words and names in enabling us to retain our grasp of the things they signify, we can see how invaluable it was for the preservation and propagation of the Christian love-motif that it thus received its characteristic designation. And it seems to have been Paul who in this sense made ἀγάπη a technical term for Christian love—so far as the sources allow us to trace the matter back; for it is by no means impossible that this designation may have been used in the primitive Church before Paul,

---

[1] *Cf.* R. Reitzenstein, *Die Formel ' Glaube, Liebe Hoffnung,' bei Paulus.* (*Nachrichten von der Königlichen Gesellschaft der Wissenschaften zu Göttingen. Philol. hist. Kl.,* 1916), p. 383: " The history of the word seems to me particularly interesting here, since ἀγάπη is concerned with a fundamental religious idea, and one that peculiarly belongs to Christianity, in whose literature the word quickly attains a dominant place. It is not a Christian invention (*cf.* Passow-Crönert), and hardly one of Hellenistic Judaism, though it occurs in isolated passages of the Septuagint, and (as Deissmann shows, *Neue Bibelstudien,* p. 27) is used in Philo, *Quod Deus immut.,* 69, in the sense of ' love to God,' and in a connection that perfectly corresponds to later Christian usage, as, e.g., 1 John iv. 18. *But here it remains isolated; it is when it has been taken into the Christian vocabulary that the word undergoes its great development.*"

though for lack of information we cannot be certain about it. Perhaps P. Feine's principle is applicable here: "It is only because Paul stands clearly before us in his letters as a theological personality that he has been regarded as the creator of these ideas. But on closer investigation we find that he stands in a line with others, or else has merely given sharper theological definition to what was the common property of primitive Christianity."[1] Yet even if that be so, it is Paul who first develops the use of the term Agape in the Scriptures and thereby establishes it for future generations. There is, moreover, a further consideration. Little is achieved by the mere fixing of a name or term, unless it is accompanied by a clear delineation of the thing it signifies; but Paul gives us both. It may have been chiefly due to his powerful delineation of the Agape motif that the idea of Agape was able to gain any ground at all: think of the importance of the "Hymn to Agape" in 1 Cor. xiii. in this respect. With this, however, we have already left the formal, terminological question behind.

4. AGAPE AND THE THEOLOGY OF THE CROSS

Paul's most important contribution to the development of the Agape motif lies in the inwardness of the relation he establishes between the idea of Agape and his theology of the Cross, as it is called. The Cross of Christ undeniably stands at the centre of his preaching. It is his conscious endeavour "not to know anything among you, save Jesus Christ, and Him crucified" (1 Cor. ii. 2). He knows he is sent to preach the Gospel. But the Gospel is for him nothing else but the word of the Cross of Christ. Anything that might come alongside this and in any way displace it, he carefully avoids, "lest the Cross of Christ should be made void". "For", he continues, "the word of the Cross is to them that are perish-

<hr />

[1] P. Feine, *Der Apostel Paulus*, 1927, p. 6.

ing foolishness; but unto us which are being saved it is the power of God " (1 Cor. i. 17 f.). In this way Paul deliberately goes counter to the demands made on him from different quarters. " Jews ask for signs, and Greeks seek after wisdom : but we preach Christ crucified, unto Jews a stumbling-block, and unto Gentiles foolishness; but unto them that are called . . . the power of God, and the wisdom of God " (1 Cor. i. 22 ff.). The reason why Paul attaches such importance to the Cross is to be found in his conviction that it is the Cross which determines the character of his new, Christian relationship to God, just as the Law had determined the character of his pre-Christian relationship to God. The way of the works of the Law, however, does not lead to any real fellowship with God, as he had previously thought it did; and now a way of fellowship with God has been opened apart from the Law by the action of God Himself in setting forth Christ, the Crucified, as a means of atonement (Rom. iii. 20 f., 25). Paul's Gospel, therefore, necessarily involves a struggle against, and a liberation from, the Law. Fellowship with God is no longer for Paul a legal relationship. The only question is whether it is a relationship of love.

Now if the Cross is thus plainly central for Paul, it is equally plain that the idea of love plays an immensely important part in his thought. Especially when he speaks of God and God's attitude to us, love comes very much into prominence. Even if we do not find in him the formal identification of God with love that we find in John, yet his position is substantially the same. Paul explicitly describes God as " the God of Agape " (ὁ θεὸς τῆς ἀγάπης, 2 Cor. xiii. 11), and Christians, in so far as they exhibit Agape, as " taught of God " (θεοδίδακτοι, 1 Thess. iv. 9).

Now we should have completely misunderstood the position if we concluded from this that Paul's preaching had two focal points : the Cross and Love. These two do not stand side by side, distinct and separate from one another. On the contrary, it is characteristic of Paul's entire thought that the Cross of Christ and the love of God are viewed as one. It is too little to say that he established a connection between the idea of love and the theology of the Cross. Agape and the theology of the Cross are for him quite simply one and the same thing. It is impossible to think of either without the other. Without the Cross of Christ we should never have known God's love and learnt its deepest meaning; and, conversely, without God's Agape Christ's way would not have led to the Cross. Just as Paul made it his rule " not to know anything save Jesus Christ, and Him crucified ", so he knew of no other love than that which is inseparably bound up with the Cross of Christ. If we desire a formal description of the Pauline idea of love, such as will clearly bring out its distinctive character, we can hardly do better than to call it *the Agape of the Cross*.

Of the many passages we might quote from Paul to illustrate this connection between the Cross and Agape, let us look first at the most important, the classical passage for " the Agape of the Cross ", Rom. v. 6-10 : " While we were yet weak, in due season Christ died for the ungodly. For scarcely for a righteous man will one die : for peradventure for the good man some one would even dare to die. But God commendeth His own ἀγάπη toward us, in that, while we were yet sinners, Christ died for us. Much more then, being now justified by His blood, shall we be saved from the wrath of God through Him. For if, while we were enemies, we were reconciled to God through the death of His Son, much more, being reconciled, shall we be saved by his life." Four things should be noticed here.

First : if we ask what Agape is, we are pointed to the Cross of Christ. To all the various ways in which the Synoptic Gospels express the idea of Agape, Paul has added the supreme and final expression, *the Cross*. Nowhere else is there to be found a revelation of Agape comparable to that in the death of Jesus on the Cross.   What Paul says here is exactly the same as we find in other words in the First Epistle of John : " Hereby know we love, because He laid down His life for us " (1 John iii. 16).   If we had not seen the love that is revealed in the Cross of Christ, we should not have known what love, in the Christian sense of the word, is.   We should doubtless have known what love in general is, but not what love in its highest and deepest sense is, not what Divine love, Agape, is.   What, then, has the Cross of Christ to tell us about the nature and content of Agape-love?   It testifies that it is a love that gives itself away, that sacrifices itself, even to the uttermost.

Secondly : the Agape revealed in the death of Christ is in no way independent of God.   Indeed, God Himself is the subject of this Agape.   It is *God*, says Paul, who proves His love in that Christ died for us.   Christ's work is God's own work, Christ's Agape is God's Agape.   After Christ's sacrifice on the Cross we can no longer speak adequately of God's love without referring to the Cross of Christ, any more than we can speak of Christ's love, shown in His death, without seeing in it God's own love.   The two are henceforth one; in Paul's own words, Agape is " the love of God in Christ Jesus " (Rom. viii. 39).   The idea that it is, strictly speaking, God who is the acting subject in the Work of Christ, is found also in other Pauline passages, such as 2 Cor. v. 19 : " God was in Christ reconciling the world to Himself ".   Paul means it quite seriously when he says : " all things are of God " (verse 18).   It is not we who make our way to God, but He who makes His way to us.   The Atonement does not mean that we reconcile ourselves with Him, but that He in Christ reconciles us to Himself; and it is only on this basis that Paul goes on to say : " be ye reconciled to God " (verse 20).   Here, too, Agape is God's way to man.

Thirdly : nowhere is the absolutely spontaneous and un-motivated nature of God's Agape so clearly manifest as in the death of Christ. "Why, scarcely even for a righteous man will anyone die—though perhaps for one who has been good to him someone may have courage to die."[1] To give one's life for the righteous—after all, there would be some accounting for that. But for whom was it that Christ gave His life? Not for the righteous, but for sinners. Paul emphasises this point three times in the passage quoted (verses 6, 8, 10), and with four different expressions: Christ has died for the weak, the ungodly, sinners, and enemies.[2]

Fourthly: the greatest thing ever previously said of God's love and its spontaneous and unmotivated nature, was that it is a love for sinners, for the unworthy and unrighteous. But Paul seeks to outdo even this and say something still greater: Christ has died, not simply for unrighteous and sinful men, but actually for " ungodly " or " godless " men, $\upsilon\pi\grave{\epsilon}\rho$ $\grave{\alpha}\sigma\epsilon\beta\hat{\omega}\nu$ $\grave{\alpha}\pi\acute{\epsilon}\theta\alpha\nu\epsilon\nu$. Even though the actual words must sot be unduly pressed, yet it is significant that this phrase comes in when Paul is seeking to express the unmotivated nature of God's love. When we remember the part played by religious allegiance in those days, we can see how much further Paul goes when he adds: Christ died for the godless, for those who belonged to other religions, those who were devoted to strange gods.

In thus describing " the Agape of the Cross ", Paul has risen to the sublimest conception of God's Agape ever given or capable of being given. No one has ever gone beyond him, and but few have been able to follow him so far. But the characteristic thing is, that Paul has not attained this height

---

[1] Rom. v; 7 according to the Swedish version.—[Tr.]

[2] For Paul, therefore, love is the same as grace. The two words are interchangeable. It is thoroughly misleading to draw a sharp distinction between them, as is done by O. Moe, for instance, in his *Apostelen Paulus' forkyndelse og laere*, 1928. Moe says: " While $\chi\acute{\alpha}\rho\iota\varsigma$ indicates that God's favour to the sinner is unmerited, $\grave{\alpha}\gamma\acute{\alpha}\pi\eta$ signifies that this favour has a deeper reason "; Agape " includes a valuing, a high regard for its object " (pp. 77 f.). Such a distinction robs Agape of its most characteristic feature, its spontaneous and unmotivated nature.

by an act of free creation. He is only seeking to interpret what has happened at the Cross of Christ. God's Agape, as he sees it, is not the creation of his own spirit, but simply the representation of something that has really happened. God has demonstrated His Agape by the giving of His Son. This fact, to which he can turn back himself and to which he can point others, is for Paul the primary thing. Here God's love meets us, not merely as an idea of love, but as the mightiest of realities, as self-sacrificing love, the love that pours itself out even for the most deeply fallen and lost.

When Paul speaks of Christ's death on the Cross he can also represent it as a *sacrifice*: "walk in love, even as Christ also loved you, and gave Himself up for us, an offering and a sacrifice to God " (Eph. v. 2—note how he brings together Christ's love and His offering of Himself as a sacrifice). But the connection Paul sees between God's Agape and the Cross of Christ gives sacrifice a wholly new meaning, which enables it to be included in the new, Christian order of fellowship with God. If we contrast the Pauline theology of the Cross with the old idea of sacrifice, the revolution that has taken place here will be very plainly seen.

It would be possible to distinguish three stages in the development of the idea of sacrifice. The first stage is represented by sacrifice in its ordinary concrete meaning of sacrificial gift, votive offering. Man offers something of his own property as a sacrifice on the altar of his deity. Sometimes men feel themselves constrained to sacrifice the dearest and most precious thing they possess, in order to win God's favour. Then sacrifice no longer means simply the offering of something of one's own to the deity, but the offering at the same time of something of oneself. Gradually, however, it is realised that what God wants from man is not the ordinary sacrifices. "Hath the Lord as great delight in burnt-offerings and sacrifices, as in obeying the voice of the Lord? Behold, to obey is better than sacrifice " (1 Sam. xv. 22). "To do justice and judgment is more acceptable to the Lord than sacrifice " (Prov. xxi. 3).

We now come to the second stage of the idea of sacrifice. The sacrifices man offers here are obedience, justice and righteousness, mercy and love. These are the means by which man seeks to win God's favour. Sacrifice has been spiritualised and become more personal in character. This may be termed the ethical way of sacrifice. But the question still remains, whether man can really stand with this sacrifice in the presence of the holy and righteous God. Are man's obedience, righteousness, and love sufficiently pure to be accounted offerings well-pleasing to God? Is not that idea rather a form of pride, which could never be more out of place than when man is approaching the Holy One, and which is therefore bound to arouse His displeasure? These questions bring us to the third stage of the idea of sacrifice.

The sacrifices now offered no longer consist of man's ethical achievements, but " the sacrifices of God are a broken spirit " (Ps. li. 17). This is the religious way of sacrifice. In the presence of God nothing else is fitting for man but humility, and it is humility alone that gives man worth in the sight of God. Here man has reached, as it seems, the utmost limit of sacrifice. He has offered of his own, his dearest; he has offered his life's work, offered himself in the work of righteousness; he has offered even the claim he might make for himself on that account, offered it in humility. What more can he have to offer? Even so, there remains a hidden something which is not included in the sacrifice, and which at bottom is the very opposite of sacrifice. One who thinks of humility as a way to fellowship with God, and feels that his own humility gives him an imperishable worth in God's sight, is at bottom anything but humble. It has rightly been said: " He who despises himself feels at the same time respect for himself as a despiser."[1]

---

[1] Nietzsche, *Jenseits von Gut und Böse, Viertes Hauptstück*, p. 78.

Sacrifice may be spiritualised and assume an increasingly personal character, yet its different stages turn out in the end to be merely modifications of one and the same thing. Every fresh step in its development is nothing really new, but merely a step further in the same original direction. Sacrifice is still *man's way to God*. Whatever man offers in sacrifice, he offers it in order to open a way for himself to God.

Looking at the matter from Paul's point of view, we might say that the second stage of sacrifice is represented by the Pharisaic way of salvation, the third by that of the Anawim. But for Paul the Cross of Christ is a judgment both on the way of ethical achievement and on that of humility. The Cross has taught him that there is no access to God at all from man's side. Yet at the same time as it has invalidated all man-made sacrifices, the Cross has disclosed to him a sacrifice of a wholly different kind. At the Cross of Christ it is not man who offers sacrifice, nor is it God who receives it. This sacrifice is *God's own sacrifice*. " All things are of God, who reconciled us to Himself through Christ ", for " God was in Christ reconciling the world to Himself " (2 Cor. v. 18 f.). Sacrifice is no longer man's way to God, but *God's way to man*.

It should by now be sufficiently clear how central the Agape motif is in Paul's Christian preaching. At the same time it is plain that he has not simply taken over and passed on unaltered a ready-made idea. The Agape motif has undergone a real and profound development through being connected with the death of Jesus on the Cross. These two, the love of God and the Cross of Christ, are made to interpret and illumine each other. As Paul sees it, the meaning of Jesus' death is only understood if we find God's love in it, and the depth of God's love only begins to be realised when we see it in the Cross of Jesus. Consequently, the Gospel of God is for Paul identical with the Gospel about Christ and Him crucified. This development of the Agape motif is actually a disclosure of its depth, not a distortion of it as has sometimes been asserted.

We can now see how wrong it is to set the Gospel of Jesus about God's fatherly love in opposition to Paul's Gospel about Christ, his theology of the Cross. *When Paul speaks of the Cross of Christ, he is speaking of God's love and nothing else.* But he does not conceive of God's love as something " self-evident ";[1] he knows and expounds it for the paradox that it is, and it is the thought of the Cross that enables him to do so. Properly understood, it is exactly the same conception that finds expression in his doctrine of Justification. When Paul says that God justifies the sinner apart from the works of the Law, he comes very near to the words of Jesus : " I came not to call the righteous, but sinners ".

5. Love towards God

When Paul speaks of Agape in connection with the Cross, or with Justification, he is thinking essentially of God's love, Christ's love, the love God has shown toward us in giving up His Son to die for us. But Paul can also speak of Agape in another connection : " love is the fulfilment of the law " (Rom. xiii. 10). Love is here something to be actualised by the Christian, and by its actualisation the Law is fulfilled. Paul, like Jesus, can sum up the whole meaning of the Law in the commandment of love. But here we meet a surprising, not to say startling, change of emphasis. Whereas for Jesus, according to the Synoptic Gospels, the commandment of love means the *double* commandment of love towards God and one's neighbour, with a decided emphasis on the former as " the great and first commandment ", Paul's position is quite different. With him, the commandment of love for one's neighbour just as decidedly takes first place. All the com-

---

[1] Jülicher's word : *v. supra,* pp. 82 ff.

mandments of the Law are "summed up in this word, namely, Thou shalt love thy neighbour as thyself" (Rom. xiii. 9), and the love that counts as "the fulfilment of the Law" is accordingly love for one's neighbour.

But this peculiar change is not confined to the commandment of love. It has long been observed by commentators how rarely Paul speaks of Agape in the sense of man's love to God or to Christ. Augustine, for instance, for whom the love of God is the sum and substance of Christianity, remarks with some surprise that when Paul uses the word "caritas" he nearly always means love to one's neighbour, and only very seldom love to God. This old observation proves on investigation to be entirely right. Indeed, it may be questioned whether Paul can with certainty be said to use the noun Agape in the sense of love to God at all, since the few cases where it can be taken in this way are also susceptible of other interpretations.[1] But whatever view we take of these exegetical questions, Paul's general tendency is unmistakable. In his work on "The Christian life according to Paul", E. Eidem says: "The fact that Paul so exceedingly rarely uses the word 'love' to express the attitude of man (as subject) towards God (as object) is the more surprising when we remember how in the Old Testament this word is one of the most commonly used to express the attitude of the faithful towards God. We may recall, moreover, that the great commandment to love God with one's whole heart (Deut. vi. 5) had been recited daily by Paul from his childhood. It forms part of the Jewish Creed, the Sh^ema as it is called (which consists of the three passages, Deut. vi. 4-9, xi. 13-21, Num. xv. 37-41). Nor can it well be doubted that the apostle was acquainted with the prominence given by primitive Christianity, and by

[1] Cf. E. Eidem, Det kristna livet enligt Paulus, I., 1927, pp. 182-185; A. Juncker, Die Ethik des Apostel Paulus, II., 1919, pp. 13-19; H. Lietzmann, Handbuch zum Neuen Testament, IX. (2nd edn.), p. 68. (There are a few passages where the verb ἀγαπάω is used in the sense of love towards God: Rom. viii. 28, 1 Cor. ii. 9, viii. 3, Eph. vi. 24.—Translator's note.)

Jesus Himself, to this ' great commandment ' of love towards God (Matt. xxii. 37, Mark xii. 30, 33, Luke x. 27)."[1]

It cannot be a mere accident that Paul thus leaves the term Agape on one side when he is speaking of man's attitude to God. We face here a far-reaching question of principle. Is not the connection which is elsewhere made between love for one's neighbour and love for God the one thing that imparts a religious character to the ethical life? Does not Paul, by his refusal to speak of man's love towards God, fall below the level even of the Old Testament, where the commandment of love to God has already been recognised as " the great and first commandment "? In point of fact, the position is quite the reverse. There cannot be any doubt that the Pauline ethic is religious from start to finish. But it is not the connection between *man's love* for God and his love for his neighbour that guarantees the religious character of the latter. Instead, it is the connection between *God's love* and neighbourly love that Paul emphasises; and the result of this is only to make neighbourly love still more profoundly religious. Hence the virtual exclusion of man's love for God from the Pauline idea of Agape cannot be regarded as a retrograde step. It means rather that Paul has once again risen to a height in the history of the idea of Agape, to which scarcely anyone has since been able to follow him.

In point of fact, Paul was bound to drop the idea of man's Agape towards God: that was simply a necessary consequence of his whole conception of Agape. If Agape is a love as absolutely spontaneous and entirely unmotivated as the love manifested in the Cross of Jesus, then it is plain that the word Agape can no longer fittingly be used to denote man's attitude to God. In relation to God, man is never spontaneous; he is not an independent centre of activity. His giving of himself to God is never more than a response. At its best and highest, it is but a reflex of God's love, by which it is " motivated "

[1] E. Eidem, *op. cit.*, p. 184.

Hence it is the very opposite of spontaneous and creative; it lacks all the essential marks of Agape. Man's devotion to God must therefore be given another name: not ἀγάπη, but πίστις.

If at this point we compare the position in the Synoptic Gospels with that of Paul, we can show that there is a development—and a logical, consistent development—of the Synoptic idea of Agape. There is, as we saw in the last chapter, an element of obscurity in the Synoptic conception of " love towards God ". God's love, which determines the character of fellowship with God, is the archetype of all that can be called Agape. What is ultimately distinctive of God's love, however, is its completely unmotivated and spontaneous nature, so that no love that is not of this character can rightly be called Agape. Now man's giving of himself in love to God can never be in that sense spontaneous; and yet the Gospels speak of man's Agape to God. It is therefore uncertain whether man may not after all possess a certain independence in relation to God, and whether human spontaneity may not clash with the Divine and limit the sovereignty of Divine love. This uncertainty is completely dispelled in Paul. He overcomes it quite simply by giving up speaking of an Agape of man towards God. In view of the enhancement of the idea of Agape brought about by his exposition of it as the love of the Cross, it is quite natural that he should do so. The term Agape is reserved for the Divine love. Everything comes from God. Paul here goes a step further than the teaching of Jesus as we find it in the Synoptic account, and yet he does not thereby part company with Jesus. He simply fixes the interpretation of Agape which Jesus Himself had given, and had given not only with His lips, but in His life, and above all in that act of self-giving whereby He revealed that God's Agape is the Agape of the Cross. It is the Cross of Christ that has taught Paul to be chary of speaking about our Agape towards God.

Naturally, there is no question of Paul's wishing to eliminate the spiritual reality denoted by the phrase " love towards God "; he merely seeks to give it its proper name, which he calls " faith ". Faith includes in itself the whole devotion of love, while emphasising that it has the character of a response, that it is reciprocated love. Faith is love towards God, but a love of which the keynote is receptivity, not spontaneity.

6. NEIGHBOURLY LOVE AND LOVE FOR GOD

Whereas Paul betrays a clear tendency to avoid the term Agape in describing the Christian's attitude to God, he uses it all the more unreservedly to denote the Christian's attitude to his neighbour. Love for one's neighbour is " the fulfilment of the Law ". This thought occurs several times in Paul, and is given particular prominence. We may recall first his " fundamental statement "[1] in Rom. xiii. 8-10 : " He that loveth his neighbour hath fulfilled the Law. For this, Thou shalt not commit adultery, Thou shalt not kill, Thou shalt not steal, Thou shalt not covet, and if there be any other commandment, it is summed up in this word, namely, Thou shalt love thy neighbour as thyself. Love worketh no ill to his neighbour : love therefore is the fulfilment of the Law." And in Gal. v. 14 it is stated explicitly : " The *whole* Law is fulfilled in one word, even in this; Thou shalt love thy neighbour as thyself."

When Paul thus identifies neighbourly love with the whole requirement of the Law, and ignores its traditional connection with love to God, this—as has already been indicated—does not mean that he is divorcing it from its religious basis. On the contrary, Paul constantly shows his concern to refer the Christian's love for his neighbour back to his fellowship with God. The ultimate reason why human relationships are to be governed by Agape is that the religious relationship is

[1] E. Eidem, *op. cit.*, p. 189.

so governed. Thus in Eph. v. 1 f. Paul writes: "Be ye therefore imitators of God, as beloved children; and walk in love, even as Christ also loved you, and gave Himself up for us." The same principle has been applied in the preceding verse to Christian forgiveness: "forgiving each other, even as God also in Christ forgave you" (iv. 32); and it appears also elsewhere, as in: "Receive ye one another, even as Christ also received you, to the glory of God" (Rom. xv. 7).

But the close connection Paul makes between the Christian's love for his neighbour and God's love presents us with a new problem. The love God has shown to us through the death of His Son on the Cross is for Paul so absolute, so utterly spontaneous and unmotivated, that Agape as the name of this Divine love can no longer fittingly be used for human love, which can never be in the same sense spontaneous and creative. We have seen how in consequence Paul hesitates to use the word Agape in connection with man's love to God; and this raises the question whether he ought not in that case to reserve the name Agape exclusively for God's love and Christ's love. How can he use it to denote the Christian's love for his neighbour? Ought he not to have found a new name in that case too? What justification has he for setting man's love on a level with God's creative love?

This takes us back to the question of the religious basis of the Pauline ethic of Agape; and here we find what seems at first a very surprising fact. Those who approach Paul from a more or less Lutheran point of view—and the emphasis Paul lays on faith ($\pi \iota \sigma \tau \iota s$) is an indication that Luther's point of view is very closely related to his—expect to find that in Paul the ethical life of the Christian, or his love for his neighbour, is referred to faith as its religious basis. Nor is this idea entirely lacking in Paul, though its occurrence is remarkably rare. We find it in the familiar formula, "faith working through love" (Gal. v. 6); but this is almost the only passage where it can be shown with certainty. But Paul's ethic does not therefore lack a religious basis; indeed, it is all the more deeply rooted in the religious relationship. For while Paul may be silent about faith as the connecting link, he commonly traces the ethical life directly back to God's or Christ's Agape : " the love of Christ constraineth us " (2 Cor. v. 14).

That is the reason why Paul can use the name Agape for the love the Christian shows to his neighbour; for not even here does he conceive of man as a centre of activity independent of God. In the life that is governed by Agape, the acting subject is not man himself; it is—as Paul expresses it— God, the Spirit of God, the Spirit of Christ, the Agape of Christ. Between Christ and the Christian there is a deep, intimate fellowship,[1] such as Paul describes in Gal. ii. 20 : " I live; and yet no longer I, but Christ liveth in me "; and the basis of this new life is that Christ " loved me and gave Himself up for me ". In virtue of this intimate fellowship, it is Christ who is the real subject of the Christian life. God's Agape can be described by Paul quite realistically as a kind of " pneumatic fluid ", which is " shed abroad in our hearts through the Holy Ghost which was given unto us " (Rom. v. 5). This Divine Agape infused by the Holy Spirit forms the real substance of the Christian life, and in the life that Christians lead among their fellow-men it is meant to be passed on to others. The Christian has nothing of his own to give; the love which he shows to his neighbour is the love which God has infused into him.

Hence the reason why Paul can apply the term Agape to the Christian's love for his neighbour is that here too he is speaking of God's Agape. It is not that he uses Agape as the name of two different things—*God's* love for us and *our* love for our neighbour. When Paul speaks of Agape he always means the Divine love, never a merely human love. The

---

[1] Sometimes referred to as " Paul's Christ-mysticism " or some such phrase, though " mysticism " is an ambiguous and ill-chosen word to use here.

Christian's love for his neighbour is a manifestation of God's Agape, which in this case uses the Christian, the " spiritual " man, as its instrument.   Since πίστις denotes a receptive attitude, it is less suitably taken as a starting-point for the life of Agape, and Paul goes further back to the original source itself, to God's Agape.   It is not the case that I possess in *my* religious life the effective basis of my ethical life; were it so, it might look as if I were resting in myself and simply drawing on my own inner resources.   Paul's entire religion and ethics are theocentric, and he cannot rest until he has referred everything to God.   " All things are of God, who reconciled us to Himself through Christ."   Whoever is " in Christ " is a new creature; he lives no longer for his own ends or by his own resources (2 Cor. v. 15-18).

This brings us to one more feature that is specially characteristic of the Pauline idea of Agape : its *opposition to all that can be called " self-love "*.   It has often been thought necessary to distinguish between a right and a wrong self-love, and the attempt has been made to give a place to the former as a third kind of love alongside of love to God and neighbourly love.   Indeed, it has even been supposed that a commandment of self-love was implicit in the commandment of neighbourly love.   But we have already seen the error of any such attempt to read the idea of self-love into the Gospels, and it is equally wrong to try to find a place for it in Paul's outlook.   Self-love is excluded by Paul's fundamental principle. " The love of God which is in Christ Jesus " (Rom. viii. 39) is for him the archetype of all that can rightly be called Agape, and it is characteristic of this love that it gives itself, sacrifices itself.   It is thus the direct opposite of acquisitive love.   Paul is not, therefore, adding anything new to his conception of Agape when he says in 1 Cor. xiii. 5, " Agape seeketh not its own ", but this is a self-evident consequence of the theocentric nature of his idea of love.   Agape spells judgment on the life that centres round the ego and its interests.   This is most evident in a man's relation to God and Christ. For when God's Agape is shed abroad in a man's heart through the Holy Spirit (Rom. v. 5) his life thereby gains a new centre. The emphasis is transferred from his own ego to Christ—as the words already quoted from Gal. ii. 20 remind us: "no longer I, but Christ liveth in me". When men are brought under the sovereign power of Christ's Agape, they "no longer live unto themselves, but unto Him who for their sakes died and rose again" (2 Cor. v. 14 f.; cf. also Phil. ii. 21). But this means that selfish bondage to the ego is eradicated from a man's relations with his neighbour also. As Christ "pleased not Himself," we also as Christians "ought . . . not to please ourselves," but "let each one of us please his neighbour for that which is good" (Rom. xv. 1-3; cf. Phil. ii. 4).

When in passages like these Paul sets self-love and neighbourly love in opposition to one another, he is not condemning merely a "lower self-love", or the natural propensity to self-assertion, but all self-love whatsoever, even in its most highly spiritual forms. Nothing is more alien to his mind than to base neighbourly love on a "spiritual" self-love, as though the ego must first look after its own spiritual interests and then secondarily show love to its neighbour. No; Christian love must be ready, according to Paul, to sacrifice even its "spiritual" advantages and privileges, if need be, in the service of its neighbour. An example of this is seen in Paul's attitude to the question of marriage (1 Cor. vii.). The ascetic life is in his view the higher and more valuable; celibacy is the ideal.[1] Yet the Christian must give up this higher

---

[1] K. L. Schmidt, *Der Apostel Paulus und die antike Welt* (*Vorträge der Bibliothek Warburg, 1924-1925*), pp. 60 f. "What is Paul's attitude to marriage and asceticism? What he says about marriage in 1 Cor. vii. is typically un-Jewish, in spite of the lax views of many Rabbis on divorce, and it is entirely in harmony with the spirit of contemporary Neopythagoreanism: asceticism is regarded as the more valuable. . . . Paul and the Stoics are agreed that rigorous asceticism is less to the point than calm moderation, and this is applicable to all conditions of life. The Stoic and

spiritual position out of consideration for his partner (1 Cor. vii. 27); that is what Agape-love requires of him. Indeed, as Paul sees it, Agape can go so far in requiring a man to sacrifice his own spiritual advantages for the advantage of his neighbour, that he even declares himself willing to be accursed and cut off from Christ for the sake of his kinsmen according to the flesh, if thereby they might be saved (Rom. ix. 3).[1]

To sum up: the various aspects of Pauline thought about Agape combine to form an impressively consistent and coherent whole of a very markedly theocentric character. "All things are of God"—nothing is of man. God does not wait for man's achievements and sacrifices. In all other religions it is man who offers sacrifice, and God who receives it, but here the sacrifice is made by God Himself; in His incomprehensible Agape He sends His Son, who sacrifices Himself, gives Himself up for weak, ungodly, sinful, hostile men. Here the righteousness of the Law can only do harm, since it binds man to that which is his own, and prevents him from receiving "the righteousness that comes from God" (Rom. x. 3); to seek to be justified by the Law is to fall away from Grace (Gal. v. 4 f.). But when, through faith, a man is laid open to the action of God, God's Agape is shed abroad in his heart through the Holy Spirit (Rom. v. 5), and the founda-

---

the Pauline view very largely agree with one another here." On the other hand, Schmidt emphasises that "Paul and the Stoics differ completely, when we look at the background of their thought." The biggest difference is undoubtedly in the demand of Agape referred to above, that a man should surrender his own spiritual advantage; this would be inconceivable in a Stoic context.

[1] *Cf.* M. Scheler's view, quoted p. 96, note, *supra*, that Christian love is love for the "spiritual, ideal person"; that it is a matter of indifference whether I direct this love to myself or to the "other"; that "a surrender of one's own soul's welfare for the other's sake is for a Christian sinful"; that concern for one's neighbour is in no way characteristic of Christian love; and that Christianity therefore recognises and must recognise a "self-love" that is essentially different from all "egoism". Nothing of this bears any relation to Christianity, at any rate as Paul understood it.

tion is thereby laid for the new, Spirit-given Agape-life, of
which the subject is no longer the man himself, but God,
Christ, God's Agape, God's.Spirit. Constrained by the Agape
of Christ (2 Cor. v. 14), or led by the Spirit (Gal. v. 18), the
Christian now carries out God's work, bears the fruit of the
Spirit. The fruit of the Spirit, however, is first and foremost
love (Gal. v. 22). Thus Agape, the Agape of God and of
Christ, has both the first and the last word in Paul. Divine
love dominates everything from beginning to end, freely
giving and sacrificing itself for man, seeking him out, being
shed abroad in his heart, bearing the fruit of the Spirit in
his life.

7. GNOSIS AND AGAPE

Even if we had none of the other evidence Paul gives in his
epistles of the central importance he attaches to the idea of
Agape, we could infer from the " Hymn to Agape " in 1 Cor.
xiii. what a dominant place it held in his thought. No other
aspect of the Christian life receives comparable treatment
from Paul. It is true that faith and hope are set alongside of
love, but the whole structure of the hymn shows that what
chiefly matters is love, and this is actually stated in its concluding words: " The greatest of these is love." Love is the
" still more excellent way " which Paul proposes to show to
his readers (1 Cor. xii. 31), and after he has sung its praises
his first exhortation is : " Follow after love " (1 Cor. xiv. 1).
We are not now turning our attention to this passage, however, in order to find further proof of the centrality of the idea
of Agape for Paul. Its significance for our present purpose is
rather that it shows us the idea of Agape set in the wider context of contemporary religion. Paul's message of Agape encountered in the Gentile-Christian Churches an atmosphere
that was influenced in very many ways by the prevalent
religious syncretism. This was particularly the case in the

Church at Corinth, with its cultivation of charismatic gifts, speaking with tongues, gnosis, and so forth—all of them things which can only be rightly understood in the light of the general trends of Hellenistic religious thought. Here we can observe, in a sense for the first time in history, the actual meeting of the Agape motif and the Eros motif, or—to put it more guardedly—of Agape and Gnosis.

Different opinions are possible as to the precise nature of the " gnosis " to which Paul refers here,[1] but there is no mistaking his polemical tone. Elsewhere he can claim to possess a certain " gnosis " himself, he can give thanks that the Corinthians are richly endowed with it, and he can reckon it among the " charismata " (2 Cor. xi. 6; 1 Cor. 1. 5, xii. 8). But here, in 1 Cor. xiii., there is a definite opposition, a contrast between two different " ways ", two different kinds of fellowship with God: on the one side, the Gnostic-mystical " vision of God " typical of Hellenism; and, on the other, the primitive-Christian and Pauline way of Agape. Already at the beginning of 1 Cor. viii. Paul has given notice of the opposition between the two ways, characterising them briefly thus: " Gnosis puffs up, Agape builds up." It is this theme that is taken up again in 1 Cor. xiii., where we are told that Gnosis belongs to that which is " in part " and " shall be done away ", while Agape, together with faith and hope, " abideth " eternally (verses 8, 9, 10, 13).

Now, what is the meaning of the Agape that is here opposed to Gnosis? This is a question on which opinions are very much divided.

According to A. von Harnack, Agape here essentially means the Christian's love for his neighbour. He is well aware, of course, that neighbourly love is for Paul inseparable from love to God; but this does not prevent him from identi-

---

[1] *Cf.* A. Fridrichsen, *Gnosis: Et bidrag til belysning av den paulinske terminologi og erkjennelseteori (Religionshistoriska studier, tillägnade E. Lehmann*, 1927), pp. 85 ff.

fying the Agape referred to in 1 Cor. xiii. specifically with the Christian's love for his neighbour. On this basis he sums up his view of the meaning of the "Hymn to Agape", and of its significance in the history of religion, as follows: "In the midst of a civilisation, which in its best tendencies was intellectualistic, but at the same time occupied itself with mysteries and sacraments, Paul has set forth the fundamental ideas of Jesus about neighbourly love in a delightful way and in a language that everyone understands. Love—that is to say, love for one's neighbour—is the best thing in the world, because it is abiding and eternal; it excels all gifts and every kind of knowledge that we are capable of acquiring, and it takes its place by the side of, nay, above the religious virtues of faith and hope. Plain, unvarnished morality is thus revealed as the essence of religion itself. As in the case of Jesus Himself, religion is brought down from heaven into the sphere of the human and necessary, without losing its divine character."[1]

R. Reitzenstein's interpretation is the direct opposite.[2]

[1] A. v. Harnack, *Das Hohe Lied des Apostels Paulus von der Liebe (1 Cor. xiii.) und seine religionsgeschichtliche Bedeutung (Sitzungsberichte der Königl. Preussischen Akademie der Wissenschaften*, 1911, Bd. I., pp. 161 f.). —*Cf.* A. v. Harnack, *Über den Ursprung der Formel 'Glaube, Liebe, Hoffnung' (Aus der Friedens- und Kriegsarbeit*, 1916, p. 3 ff.).

[2] *Cf.* R. Reitzenstein, *Historia Monachorum und Historia Lausiaca: Eine Studie zur Geschichte des Mönchtums und der frühchristlichen Begriffe Gnostiker und Pneumatiker*, 1916, pp. 100 ff., 238 ff., 242 ff.—R. Reitzenstein, *Die Formel 'Glaube, Liebe, Hoffnung'* (*Historische Zeitschrift*, Bd. 116, 1916, pp. 189 ff.).—R. Reitzenstein, *Die Formel 'Glaube, Liebe, Hoffnung' bei Paulus: Ein Nachwort (Nachrichten von der Königl. Gesellschaft der Wissenschaften zu Göttingen, Philol.-hist. Kl.*, 1917, pp. 130 ff.).—R. Reitzenstein, *Die hellenistischen Mysterienreligionen nach ihren Grundgedanken und Wirkungen*, 3. Aufl., 1927, pp. 383 ff.

Cf. also E. Lehmann and A. Fridrichsen, *1 Cor. xiii., Eine christlich-stoische Diatribe (Theol. Studien und Kritiken*, Jahrg. 94, 1922, pp. 55 ff.). —P. Corssen, *Paulus und Porphyrios (Socrates*, Bd. 73, 1919, pp. 18 ff.).— H. Lietzmann, *Handbuch zum Neuen Testament*, IX., 2. Aufl., 1924, pp. 326 ff.—C. Clemen, *Religionsgeschichtliche Erklärung des Neuen Testaments*, 2. Aufl., 1924, pp. 326 ff.—R. Gyllenberg, *Pistis*, 1922, II., pp. 23 f. —G. Rudberg, *Hellas och Nya testamentet*, 1929, pp. 118, 149 ff.—A. Schweitzer, *Die Mystik des Apostels Paulus*, 1930, pp. 295 ff.

According to him, Agape is here essentially love to God. It is true that in the first part of the hymn (verses 4-6) it is used of the Christian's love for his neighbour; but the description of it at the end (verse 13) as the greatest of the things that abide, even in the future life, can only refer to love for God. Only love for God, and not love for one's neighbour, can be grouped with faith and hope to make a unity of the formula with which the hymn ends. The solution of the exegetical difficulties of this chapter is found by Reitzenstein in the hypothesis of a formula current among the Corinthians, consisting of four members, πίστις, ἀλήθεια (γνῶσις), ἔρως, ἐλπίς—faith, truth (gnosis), eros, hope—to which Paul deliberately opposes his triple formula of "faith, hope, and love". These three alone abide. As against the Corinthians, who pride themselves on their gnosis, Paul strikes out the "truth" that rests on "gnosis"; our gnosis is only in part and shall be done away. Thus only three members of the original formula remain. But Paul has yet another change to make in it; he must replace ἔρως by ἀγάπη. This means that "love" is initially re-interpreted in the direction of neighbourly love—an idea which had originally no place in Hellenistic mysticism.[1] At the same time, Paul cannot but agree with the Hellenists "that the love which lives on into the future in God is not the neighbourly love that endureth all things, but can only be love towards God."[2] This explains why the hymn to Agape falls into two parts, beginning with neighbourly love, but ending with love to God.

In the light of what we have previously learnt about the idea of Agape in Paul, it seems clear that neither of these attempted solutions really meets the difficulty. Harnack's interpretation is obviously wrong. Undoubtedly it is true that neighbourly love plays the leading part in Paul when he is speaking of the Agape shown by the Christian; for he

[1] Reitzenstein, *Historia Monachorum und Historia Lausiaca*, 1916, p. 102.
[2] *Historische Zeitschrift*, vol. 116, 1916, p. 206.

clearly has difficulties about speaking of man's Agape towards God. It is also evident that several of the features shown as distinctive of Agape in I Cor. xiii. are drawn from the Christian's love for his neighbour. But the reason why neighbourly love is thus prominent in Paul is quite other than that given by Harnack. Paul assuredly is not a theologian of the Enlightenment, for whom the essense of religion " is revealed as plain, unvarnished morality ". Agape is not for him an elementary " moral " virtue, which " takes its place alongside, nay, above the religious virtues." And as for the judgment that " religion is brought down from heaven into the sphere of the human and necessary, without losing its divine character ", it is as little true of Paul as of Jesus. The precise opposite would be nearer the mark; with both of them the theocentric tendency is dominant throughout.

Reitzenstein's interpretation seems by comparison to come much nearer to Paul's view. By his intensive researches Reitzenstein has shed more light than any other interpreter on Paul's Agape-hymn. In particular, he has made it impossible for us any longer to miss the polemical note that sounds through it. Agape takes the field against Gnosis; Gnosis is excluded from the formula that speaks of what is essential and abiding. " This is unhellenistic, but authentically Christian and authentically Pauline. Nowhere does the Apostle come so near to us as in this *struggle against Hellenism.*"[1] We must not, of course, overlook the fact that even on his own admission Reitzenstein's interpretation represents only a possibility;[2] yet whatever may be the truth about his hypothetical four-fold formula,[3] it would seem that the essential

---

[1] Reitzenstein, *Die hellenistischen Mysterienreligionen*, 1927, p. 391.

[2] ". . . a question which I am bound to put forward, but cannot answer definitely " (*Hist. Monachorum*, p. 100). " The possibility of such an assumption having been proved, it has the value of a scientific working hypothesis at least until such time as a true interpretation provides another solution for the difficulties that are on all sides acknowledged " (*Nachrichten v. d. Königl. Ges. der Wissenschaften zu Göttingen*, 1916, pp. 413 f.).

[3] *Cf.* J. Moffatt, *Love in the New Testament*, 1929, p. 185: " It is futile

purport of Paul's opposition to Hellenism has been rightly grasped. A few sentences from his concluding summary, which are specially illuminating for the actual position, may therefore well be quoted here. "The significance of this hypothesis as regards Paul may be briefly indicated. First, naturally, each of the terms ἀγάπη, πίστις, and even ἐλπίς, had for him a meaning and importance that was already fixed. If in this Hellenistic formula that he was attacking he found the term ἔρως θεοῦ or ἔρως θεῖος (an idea which prevails in all Hellenistic mysticism and need not at all be derived from Plato) it would not only be clear to him that he could not render this term otherwise than by the word ἀγάπη, but he is so strongly conscious of the dual significance of this word for Christians that he drags in the whole exhortation about loving one's neighbour, which to him is a matter of immense importance. What ' faith ' means to him everyone knows, and it was certainly not from the formula that he learnt the value of hope. What is important is not that he adopts some of its terms, but that he uses them to combat the over-estimation of the Hellenistic Gnosis."[1]

Admirably as Reitzenstein has expounded the Hellenistic background and polemical character of Paul's Agape-hymn, we cannot accept his interpretation of Agape as equivalent to love for God, even though he himself regards this as part and parcel of his whole hypothesis. ' The consequence ", he says, " for me and for all who insist on the interpretation that love *lives on* beyond death is certainly this: it is in that case no longer the all-forbearing, long-suffering and peaceable love for one's neighbour, but love for God, which there attains its

---

to seek the origin of such a phrase in Hermetism or elsewhere ", and p. 186 f. : " There is therefore no need to imagine any source for ' faith, hope and love ' other than the original spontaneous mind of the apostle himself." —Cf. also C. Clemen, *Religionsgesch. Erklärung des N.T.*, pp. 329 f., and A. Schweitzer, *Die Mystik des Apostels Paulus*, p. 297.

[1] *Nachrichten v. d. Kgl. Ges. der Wissenschaften zu Göttingen*, 1916, pp. 415 f.

perfection."[1] But Reitzenstein has obviously been misled here by the thought of a connection between the Pauline formula, " faith, hope, love ", and the Hellenistic formula he postulates. His argument is more or less as follows: the conflict is between Gnosis and Agape; the latter makes it necessary to take the Christian's love for his neighbour into account; but indifference to neighbourly love is one of the plain characteristics of Hellenistic Gnosis. Now Paul " as a Jew, and still more as a follower of Jesus, cannot possibly separate neighbourly love from love to God, of which it is for him the necessary complement. He therefore broadens out the concept of ἔρως θεοῦ into a new, indeterminate concept, ἀγάπη, and no longer distinguishes the objects of this love; but even for him this ἀγάπη can only be reckoned among the things that abide, the μένοντα, the στοιχεῖα, inasmuch as it is *love to God*."[2]

What is wrong with this argument is that Reitzenstein makes Paul arrive at the concept of Agape by *extending* that of Eros, so as to include neighbourly love in his concept of love, yet insists with regard to the love that *lasts on* into the future life, that this newly added, complementary, idea of love must be dropped, so that there remains for Paul only love in pretty much the Hellenistic sense of desire or longing for God. Reitzenstein has here forgotten his own insight, noted above, that the meaning and importance of the term ἀγάπη were fixed for Paul before ever he met the alleged Hellenistic formula, so that he did *not* arrive at the idea of Agape by " broadening out " the concept of Eros, or by adding to the Hellenistic idea of love something that in certain circumstances might be taken away again. Even granted that the Pauline formula was produced in opposition to a Hellenistic formula, what happened was not that Paul produced a revised version of Eros and called it Agape, but that he did

---

[1] *Historische Zeitschrift*, vol. 116, 1916, p. 193.
[2] *Historia Monachorum*, p. 255.

away with Eros altogether and replaced it by the Agape of which the meaning was already fixed for him. In other words, the idea of Agape which Paul uses in 1 Cor. xiii for his attack on Hellenistic Gnosis and Eros, is precisely the same as that which we have already analysed in our earlier discussion.

Neither Harnack's attempt to interpret the idea of Agape morally, as synonymous with neighbourly love, nor Reitzenstein's attempt to interpret it in Hellenistic fashion as exclusively love to God, can be regarded as satisfactory. Here, as so often happens, both answers are misleading, because both rest on a false assumption—the assumption contained in the question to which they are answers—namely, whether Agape means love for God *or* love for one's neighbour. This is a false alternative—at least as far as Paul's idea of Agape is concerned. In Hellenistic Eros-theory, of course, love can only be one of these two—namely, love for God, a yearning for the Divine life; for there is no place for neighbourly love in the context of Eros. But in the case of Pauline Agape it is false to assume that we are faced with an " either—or " of this kind. *Agape has for Paul a value and significance of its own, entirely independent of its object;* it is not necessary to ask every time the word occurs, to whom the love is directed. Agape is primarily God's own love, which is by nature self-giving, overflowing. This love of God is now " shed abroad in our hearts through the Holy Spirit which was given unto us " (Rom. v. 5), and the life of God has thereby taken possession of man's innermost being. The Christian henceforth lives " in Christ ", and Christ lives and works in him; he is "constrained by the Agape of Christ", or "led by the Spirit", and the stream of love that has been poured out in his heart flows forth to his neighbour. This love " beareth all things, believeth all things, hopeth all things, endureth all things " (1 Cor. xiii. 7); its nature is such that it cannot be dammed up, but makes its way out to its neighbour; for " love seeketh not its own " (verse 5). In all its various manifestations it is one and the same Agape, no merely human love, but an outflow from God's own life. This Divine Agape is the love that is the theme of Paul's Agape-hymn; this is the Agape that " never faileth ", and the Agape that " abideth " when Gnosis, like everything else that is " in part ", shall be done away (verses 8-13).

Here the question no longer arises whether Agape is love to God or love to one's neighbour. It is just simply Agape, the life of Agape shining its own light, regardless of any significance it might acquire from its object.

Hence it is least of all possible to say with Reitzenstein that the Agape which " abides " even in the future life must be love to God, longing for the life of God, and that it cannot be " the all-enduring, long-suffering, and peaceable love for one's neighbour."[1] Neighbourly love of this kind is, after all, an outflow of *God's* Agape, and as such it is something that eternally abides, whereas that " love of God " which means yearning desire for God, *Gottessehnsucht*, is essentially an expression of *man's* longing and pining which is destined, in common with Gnosis and all else that is " in part ", to be done away " when that which is perfect is come " (verse 10). Whether human love is one of the things that pass away, or one of those that abide, depends not on whether it is love for one's neighbour or love for God, but on whether it is a merely human love or a love born of God's own and in its image. If it is the latter, then it belongs to the things that abide, no matter what its object may be. It is not of this kind or that kind of Agape, but of Agape as such, of all Agape whatsoever as proceeding from God, that Paul says, " Agape never faileth " (verse 8).

The correctness of this interpretation is confirmed by the

---

[1] *Cf.* also *Nachrichten v. d. Kgl. Ges. der W. zu Göttingen*, 1916, p. 407: " The all-enduring and long-suffering neighbourly love here described has really no place in the next world."

fact that it alone secures unity of meaning for Paul's Agape-hymn. As Reitzenstein interprets it, the hymn shows only a haphazard and confusing oscillation between love to God, which alone fulfils the conditions for abiding in the future life, and neighbourly love, which Paul has also very much at heart as necessary and important for the present life. Paul cannot possibly deny—according to Reitzenstein's theory of the " connection of thought " in the hymn—" that the love which lives on into the future in God is not the neighbourly love that endureth all things, but can only be love to God. But from Judaism, or, rather, from the most authentic Christianity, he has learnt the imperative demand for neighbourly love, and wishes to impress this on the Corinthians as something new, as a necessary expression of love for God in this life. Hence it is this alone that he portrays as love in the inspired words of the main part of the hymn, and yet he says in the conclusion that it ' abideth '. This is certainly unclear."[1] Indeed it is unclear—so unclear that it is impossible to believe Paul capable of anything like it. We are asked to believe that while he is compelled to admit that only love to God abides, he has such a deep concern for neighbourly love that he depicts it alone as love, and then finally says that it, despite its transient nature, abides. An exegesis that results in such " unclarity " assuredly rests on false assumptions, and the error lies in the alternative: *either* love to God *or* love to one's neighbour. For Paul it is not a question of the object of the love, but of its nature and ground. Where love is truly Agape it is grounded in God, and for that reason belongs to the things that " abide ".

But whatever else may be said of Paul's Agape-hymn, it is certain that we have in it a first encounter between the Christian Agape motif and the Hellenistic spirit, which here appears in the form of Gnosis. *Gnosis*, however, *is only another name for the Eros motif*. It is this fact above all that

[1] *Historische Zeitschrift*, vol. 116, p. 206 f.

makes 1 Cor. xiii. of such extraordinary interest in the history of the Christian idea of Agape. Paul has felt and expressed very acutely the opposition that exists between this idea and the Hellenistic idea of love, whether it be called Eros or Gnosis—for these two come to the same thing in the end. Eros is the soul's longing and yearning to attain to the blessed vision of the supersensible world and its beauty, while Gnosis is nothing other than this " vision of God " itself. In 1 Cor. xiii. Paul decisively repudiates this love and this vision of God. With a quite astonishing sensitiveness and sureness of touch he has exposed the fundamental difference of structure between Gnosis-eros and Agape, two things which superficially are so very much alike. *Gnosis is egocentric, Agape theocentric.* This contrast is for Paul absolute : whatever applies to the one does not apply to the other. Whereas he says of Gnosis that it " puffs up ", of Agape he says it " is not puffed up"; ἡ γνῶσις φυσιοῖ, ἡ ἀγάπη οὐ φυσιοῦται (1 Cor. viii. 1; xiii. 4). Agape seeketh not its own, but considers what " edifies ", builds up. In this Paul finds the criterion for judging the value of the different spiritual gifts. The reason why the gift of prophecy ranks higher with him than speaking with tongues he explains thus : " He that speaketh in a tongue edifieth himself; but he that prophesieth edifieth the church " (1 Cor. xiv. 4).

By representing it as the Agape of the Cross, Paul has given the Christian idea of Agape its highest and, in a sense, final expression, and he has also clearly marked it off both from the legal piety of Judaism and from the Eros-piety of Hellenism. The Agape of the Cross is opposed to both of these, for the Cross is to Jews a stumbling-block and to Greeks foolishness (1 Cor. i. 22 ff.); hence, in preaching Agape, Paul has to fight a battle on two fronts. Of these the struggle against " the Law " takes up most space in the Epistles; but documentary evidence is not lacking, especially in the Corinthian Epistles, concerning the second front and the conflict with Hellenistic Eros-religion. It is not, of course, impossible that certain aspects of Pauline thought may be traceable to current Hellenistic ideas; but if we go back, as we ought, to the fundamental motif, the distinguishing feature of his whole view of Christianity, there cannot be the least doubt that his attitude to Hellenistic religion is essentially negative. When he is fighting to maintain the Agape motif he is absolutely uncompromising—as is admitted even by scholars who are otherwise inclined to find a great deal of Hellenistic influence in Paul's religious outlook.[1] The climax of this conflict between the Agape motif and Hellenistic Eros-religion is reached when Paul in 1 Cor. xiii. extols Agape in inspired words as the " still more excellent way " and as that which " abideth " when Gnosis and all other imperfect human attainments shall pass away.

If we could assume with Reitzenstein that " Faith, Hope, Love " was a formula produced by Paul to displace a Hellenistic formula, "Faith, Gnosis, Eros, Hope ", which was current in the Corinthian Church, and from which he eliminated Gnosis and replaced Eros by Agape, then this would mean that Paul actually knew and dealt with the problem we are studying, precisely in the form in which we have stated it— namely, as the problem of " Agape and Eros ". But be that as it may, there can be no doubt that he was alive to the reality of the problem in one form or another, for he sets out in the clearest light the Christian meaning of the idea of Agape

[1] *Cf.* Reitzenstein, *Historische Zeitschrift*, vol. 116, 1916, p. 207: " Since I gained a deeper understanding of the polemical character of the hymn, I have become more firmly convinced that the originality of a religion and a religious personality is not to be found in the language or the imagery, nor even altogether in the conceptions, which they happen to use, but in the emotional quality, that is, in what they make of the material they necessarily take over." Notice also the passage from *Die hellenistischen Mysterienreligionen*, p. 391, quoted above, p. 137, where Reitzenstein speaks of the " authentically Pauline " character of the polemic against Hellenism in 1 Cor. xiii. Here, in the conflict of Agape with Gnosis-eros, we see something of Paul's originality.

and its contrast with Hellenistic Eros-religion. In the subsequent history, however, it was not Agape as preached by Paul that came to set its mark on the conception of the meaning of Christian love. The religion of Gnosis-eros which Paul rejected was far too deeply rooted in the consciousness of late antiquity to be easily supplanted. But even though Paul's conception of Agape did not immediately win general acceptance, yet it formed a mighty bulwark against all attempts to interpret the Christian love-motif in terms of the Eros motif. Whenever in later history we come across a strong Pauline influence, whether in Marcion, Augustine, Luther, or elsewhere, we find that it is always associated with a renewal of the Agape motif.

GOD IS AGAPE

1. THE FINAL FORMULATION OF THE AGAPE MOTIF

WE have followed the Agape motif from its earliest beginnings in the Synoptic Gospels to its supreme expression in Paul. One of the most striking things we have noticed in doing so is the intimate connection that exists from the very beginning between the thought of Agape and the thought of God. In the Gospels, Agape and fellowship with God belong inseparably together, so that each implies the other. We cannot speak of love without speaking of fellowship with God, nor of fellowship with God without speaking of love. It is Agape that distinguishes the new fellowship with God which Christianity brings, a fellowship not governed by law but by love. And, conversely, when we wish to say what love is, in the Christian sense of the word, we cannot avoid referring to Christian fellowship with God. This is so even in the case of love for one's neighbour and love for enemies, for the meaning of that also is determined by its connection with God. God's love for sinners is the basis of the Christian's love for his enemies.

In Paul the connection between God and Agape is even more firmly established. What Agape is we come to know only through God's way of dealing with us; and the supreme manifestation of God's Agape is the Cross of Christ. " God commendeth His own ἀγάπη toward us, in that, while we were yet sinners, Christ died for us " (Rom. v. 8). Paul is convinced that it is God who acts in Christ. When Christ dies for us who are weak, ungodly, sinful, and enemies, this is the supreme revelation of Agape; but it can just as truly be said to be the supreme revelation of God. In the Cross of Christ, God and Agape are seen to be one; Paul has learnt from the Cross that God's mind and will towards us men is mere love, and that Agape and God are quite simply inseparable. Now it is this intimate connection between God and Agape that makes Paul speak at once so sparingly of our love for God and so profusely of love for our neighbour. If God and Agape are ultimately one and the same, there would seem to be no longer any room for the thought of Agape towards God. On the other hand, the Christian's love for his neighbour is no longer merely something of his own, but an outflow of God's Agape. That is why Paul can speak of it in the most exalted terms and describe it as eternally abiding.

Broadly speaking, then, it can be said that already in the Snyoptic Gospels, and still more in Paul, the thought of God and the thought of Agape are so closely associated as to be virtually identified. Paul often suggests their identity, and at times comes very near to putting it into words. God is for him " the God of Agape ". The identification is simply waiting to be expressed, for in all essentials it is already complete. One step more and we should have had the formal statement of it. But that step is nowhere taken by Paul; the phrase that was to make explicit the already existing unity was never uttered by him.

This final step is taken in the First Epistle of John, where the *identity of God and Agape* is asserted in the twice repeated formula : " God is Agape " (1 John iv. 8, 16). Whereas the Pauline " Agape of the Cross " gives the supreme description of the content of the primitive Christian Agape motif, the Johannine " God is Agape " gives the supreme formal statement of it. Nothing greater can be said than this : *God is love, and love, Agape, is God.*

It has long been customary to speak of John as "the Apostle

of love ". The title is justified inasmuch as the Johannine identification of God and Agape places the coping-stone, so to speak, on the edifice of the primitive Christian conception of Agape. To this, however, it may be added that very nearly all the characteristic features of the Agape motif, which we find elsewhere in the New Testament, are also to be found in the Gospel and First Epistle of John. Here, as elsewhere, the starting-point is God's own Agape: " Herein is love, not that we loved God, but that He loved us " (1 John iv. 10). But this Divine Agape of necessity calls forth love in man: " *We* love, because *He* first loved us " (*ibid.*, 19). The love shown by Jesus is the pattern for His disciples' love towards one another, and their love to one another is the token that they are His disciples (John xiii. 13 ff., 34 f.; xv. 12). Furthermore, the Johannine agrees with the Synoptic idea of Agape in that it represents Christian love as manifested in two directions: towards God and towards men. There is no trace here of the Pauline reserve in speaking of love for God. Love for God and love for the brethren belong so inseparably together that the one can be inferred from the other (1 John iv. 20 f.), though brotherly love can be connected either with love for God or, as in Paul, directly with God's love and Christ's love (1 John v. 1; iii. 16; iv. 11).

Johannine love for God is sometimes spoken of as " mystical "—with very doubtful justification. For even in John, to have love towards God is essentially the same as to be absolutely possessed by Him, under His absolute lordship, and it finds expression primarily in obedience to His will, in the keeping of His word and commandments (1 John ii. 5; John xiv. 15, 23 f.). The double commandment of love accordingly occupies a central place. It is an " old commandment " given " from the beginning "; but through Christ and the love He has revealed both in word and deed, it has received a quite new meaning, so that it can be called a " new commandment " (1 John ii. 7 f.; iii. 11; John xiii. 34). What unites the

Johannine with the Synoptic idea of Agape and produces this wide range of agreement is chiefly the fact that they are both based on the new conception of fellowship with God. In this respect, indeed, the Johannine outlook can very well be said to mark an advance on the Synoptic, inasmuch as the thought of fellowship with God forms the foundation on which the entire First Epistle is based (1 John i. 3, 6 f.).

There is likewise a wide range of agreement between the Johannine and the Pauline idea of love. Just as love is for Paul essentially " the Agape of the Cross ", so for John it is the Cross that reveals the deepest mysteries of Divine love. Only at the Cross of Christ, according to John, do we learn what true Agape is. " Hereby know we love, because He laid down His life for us " (1 John iii. 16). The revelation of Divine love consists precisely in the fact that God sent His only-begotten Son into the world and gave Him " to be the propitiation for our sins " (1 John iv. 10), and that the Son " having loved His own . . . loved them unto the end " (John xiii. 1). In John, as in Paul—though perhaps not with the same clarity—it is God who is the acting subject in Christ's sacrificial work of love. Moreover, when we are considering the points of connection between the Johannine and the Pauline idea of Agape, we ought not to forget that the problem of " Gnosis and Agape ", which we have met in Paul, appears also in John—especially in the First Epistle— and that here, too, it is decided in favour of Agape. " He that loveth not knoweth not God " (1 John iv. 8).

A brief survey of the material thus shows that all the essential points of the New Testament doctrine of Agape are reproduced in the Johannine writings, though John takes us a stage further by his identification of God and Agape, which gives to the primitive Christian idea of Agape its final form. Yet it would not be entirely true to the facts to say without qualification that the Johannine idea of love marks the culminating point of the New Testament Agape motif; for while

John says the last word as to its form, Paul has a deeper insight into its essential meaning and content. Nor does the Johannine view of love display the strict unity and consistency that we found in Paul, for at many points there is a certain doubleness to be observed in what John says about Agape. Just when the Agape motif is brought to its highest expression it is also in a peculiar way weakened down.

This raises the very difficult question of the general spiritual environment in which the Johannine writings and their conception of Agape arose. It has been commonly held that the environment might be described as Hellenistic-Oriental; and in recent times the matter has been complicated by a widespread tendency to associate the Johannine literature with the much-discussed Mandæan religion.[1] If such a Hellenistic environment could be historically proved we should once more have an example of an encounter between Agape and Eros. In the Johannine idea of Agape we should see the Agape of primitive Christianity set in an environment of Hellenistic Eros, and this environment might in some measure explain the modifications that can be observed in the Johannine conception. As the Hellenistic, or, alternatively, the Mandæan, theory is historically very dubious, however, we must let this mention of it suffice, and in the account we shall give of the doubleness that is characteristic of the Johannine idea of Agape we must rely solely on the evidence furnished by this idea itself. We can do so the more readily since our present study is principally concerned with the question of its typical structure and this can be satisfactorily

[1] On the Mandæan question, which has been raised chiefly by the investigations of M. Lidzbarski, R. Reitzenstein and H. H. Schraeder, see J. Behm: *Die mandäische Religion und das Christentum*, 1927. Its influence on New Testament exegesis is illustrated by W. Bauer's commentary on the Gospel according to John in the *Handbuch zum Neuen Testament*, 2nd edn., 1925, and by a series of discussions in the *Zeitschrift für die neutestamentliche Wissenschaft*, where the weighty objections brought by E. Peterson should be noted. A summary in W. F. Howard, *The Fourth Gospel in Recent Criticism and Interpretation*, 1931 (3rd edn., 1945), pp. 91 ff.

answered without waiting for the question of its environment and origin to be settled.

2. The Duality of the Johannine Idea of Agape

There are three points in particular at which the above-mentioned duality of the Johannine idea of Agape is evident: (1) in the Johannine " metaphysic of Agape " and its relation to spontaneous, unmotivated love; (2) in Christian love for " the brethren " and the particularism that is closely connected with it; (3) in the question of love for God and love for the world.

(1) *The " metaphysic of Agape " and unmotivated love.* In the Synoptic Gospels and Paul we found that Agape had a threefold meaning. Its connection with the old commandment of love gave it the double sense of love to God and love to one's neighbour, and these two forms of love derived their Christian content from their connection with a third form: God's love revealed in Christ, which is the basic form of all that can be called Agape. The tendency to trace love back to God's love, and to place the main emphasis there, is shared by John; but he does not stop at this, he seeks to go even further back and penetrate to a still greater depth. Love is one with the substance of God; God *is* love, and He is love not only in relation to fallen humanity, but eternally in Himself. In this way the Johannine idea of love acquires a peculiar cosmic-metaphysical aspect, so that we can justly speak of a " metaphysic of Agape " in John, which forms the background of his view of love as a whole. God's Agape is in the first instance the Father's eternal love for the Son: " Thou lovedst me ", He says, " before the foundation of the world " (John xvii. 24; *cf.* iii. 35; v. 20; xv. 9). Love means here the self-communication of God to the Son,[1] and it furnishes the starting-point of a series of self-communications—from God to

---

[1] M. Dibelius, *Joh. 15, 13. Eine Studie zum Traditionsproblem des Johannes-Evangeliums: Festgabe für Adolf Deissmann*, 1927, pp. 168 ff.

Christ, from Christ to the disciple, from the disciple to the
brethren. Just as God has loved Christ and imparted Himself to Him (John iii. 35; v. 20), so Christ has loved His disciples and imparted Himself to them (John xv. 9); and so
they also are called to love one another and impart themselves
to one another (John xiii. 34; xv. 12).

The dual character of this metaphysic of Agape is quite
plain. On the one hand, we find the thought of God's spontaneous, unmotivated love carried to its utmost limit; God's
love is in no sense whatsoever based on anything outside itself;
it has its ground in God Himself, for it is His very essence.
It is not even so far dependent on anything extraneous as to
need an external object to which to direct itself. Love expresses something eternal and transcendent, something that
was "before the foundation of the world"; for even then
God was love—in relation to the Son. On the other hand,
this metaphysic of Agape, like all genuine metaphysics, has
something rationalising and "motivated" about it. If the
eternal love of the Father for the Son is the prototype of all
that can be called Agape the question inevitably arises: Does
Agape here retain its original character? Is it still absolutely
unmotivated? Is it not rather the case that the inherent
worth of the Son is what makes Him the object of the
Father's love? If so, will not this have its effect, at least in
some measure, on God's love towards men, so that not even
it is conceived as altogether spontaneous and unmotivated?
That this is no imaginary difficulty is shown by the fact,
among others, that in John we sometimes find—especially
where God's love for the disciples is concerned—a clause explanatory of the love, introduced by "because", as in xvi. 27:
"The Father Himself loveth you, *because* ye have loved Me."
The Johannine idea of Agape thus actually occupies a somewhat uncertain position between unmotivated and motivated
love.

The curious thing is that both of these find expression in

the Agape-metaphysic; for this both represents the tendency to lay the utmost stress on the spontaneity and eternity of Divine love, and yet at the same time constitutes an incipient weakening of that very spontaneity. Its positive significance lies in its attempt to do full justice to the fact that God is in His very " essence " Agape. When we speak of God's love we are not speaking of something contingently displayed by God, but of that which in every respect and all circumstances characterises His mind and will towards us. God is not only love in relation to sinners, but His love is eternal; before the foundation of the world the Father loved the Son. Yet even though God and Agape are in this way so closely united as to be quite really identified with one another, the Johannine metaphysic of Agape none the less has its perils, and perils precisely for the nature and content of the Christian Agape motif. When the Father's love for the Son is made the prototype of the life of Agape in general, there is always a danger that the unmotivated nature of Divine love may be insufficiently recognised. This is specially evident in the particularistic conception of neighbourly love that is characteristic of John.

(2) *Brotherly love and particularism.* One of the most characteristic features of the Johannine conception of Agape is the substantial equation of neighbourly love with love for the brethren. This modification has already been hinted at in the general movement of Agape which we noted above : God —Christ—the disciple—the brethren. Just as the Father loves the Son, and the Son loves His own, so " the brethren " are the natural object, so to speak, of the Christian's love. It is only this fellowship of love—the love of the brethren for one another—that can in the deepest sense conform to the pattern of the mutual love of the Father and the Son. Only the brethren can become one as the Father and the Son are one (John xvii. 11).

But now at this point also there appears a certain duality

in the Johannine idea of love. On the one side it acquires as brotherly love a depth, warmth, and intimacy that are without parallel elsewhere. Here something essential to Christian love is clearly brought to light: Agape is the *fellowship* of love. But there are limits, and limits that are very soon reached, to what can be achieved in the way of fellowship by neighbourly love or love for one's neighbours in general. Unlimited spiritual fellowship and unity are possible only between " the brethren " who are united in God. That, however, is only one side of the picture. On the other side, neighbourly love becomes *particularistic*. It loses something of its original, all-embracing scope; it becomes love for those who bear the Christian name. When love is said to be the evidence that will convince the world that the disciples of Jesus really are His, it is the love they show to each other as Christians that is meant (John xiii. 35), not the love that directs itself to those who are outside. Of love to enemies there is no longer anything said at all. This clearly means that neighbourly love has lost something of the meaning it had in the Synoptic Gospels, where love to enemies is neither an arbitrary addition to the demand for neighbourly love nor an incidental sharpening of it, but an essential and inseparable feature of Christian love.

Here, then, we have a repetition of the peculiar duality of the Johannine idea of love. That which from one point of view represents an enhancement of the idea of Agape appears from another point of view to constitute a danger to it. Just because love in John is limited to the narrower circle of " the brethren ", it is able to develop a far greater warmth and intimacy than it otherwise could; but this limitation involves for Christian love the risk of losing its original unmotivated character, and of being restricted to the brethren to the exclusion of outsiders and enemies.

It is interesting to compare the Johannine with the Pauline view at this point, for the difference in general attitude between them is very marked. Paul is the persecutor who by a miraculous intervention of God becomes a disciple and apostle. This fundamental fact sets its mark on his view of Agape. God's Agape is for him the supreme paradox. No words are too strong for him to use in order to press home its spontaneous and unmotivated character. He knows, moreover, that he is called to carry the message of the Gospel to those who are most completely lost and estranged from God. After all, he had himself come into the Church of God by a side door, so to speak, thanks to God's Agape. He, too, was lost and estranged from God when God's call came to him. In the Johannine writings the basic mood is altogether different. The author's interest centres primarily in the little circle of believers whom Christ has taken out of the world, that circle which is the object of Christ's special love and care and of which the chief distinguishing mark is the members' brotherly love for each other. To this circle Jesus will manifest Himself, and for it He prays, not for the world (John xiv. 21 ff.; xvii. 9). To this circle the Johannine author belongs as it were by nature. No miracle, no conversion such as Paul's has brought him into it. Nor, therefore, is the idea of Agape presented in such a sharply paradoxical light by him as by Paul. That the Father should love those whom He has taken out of the world and given to the Son, and who have kept His word (John xvii. 6), is not indubitably "unmotivated", or rationally inexplicable; it is in one way very much what we should expect. In a word, we have in Paul the former persecutor of God's Church who now by God's grace and Agape alone is what he is; in John we have "the disciple whom Jesus loved" (John xxi. 7), for whom it is self-evident that Christ's love is bound up with membership of the circle of his disciples.

(3) *Love for God and love of the world.* One more modification remains to be noticed in the Johannine idea of Agape. In the Synoptic Gospels, and still more in Paul, "love" has a

definite religious and ethical quality of its own, in itself and quite independently of its object. Hence Paul can say without further qualification: "Follow after Agape" (1 Cor. xiv. 1). He has no need to specify the object to which this love is to be directed. He knows nothing of any distinction between a true and a false Agape. The moment that love shows itself to be Agape-love its ethical and religious legitimacy is for him beyond doubt. Such love is an outflow of the Divine love whatever its object may be. In John the position is substantially similar. Here also Agape possesses its own definite quality, and we have no need to ask what its object is in order to be able to determine its quality. Hence it can be said of Agape without further qualification: "Agape is of God; and everyone that loveth is begotten of God, and knoweth God. He that loveth not knoweth not God; for God is Agape" (1 John iv. 7 f.). Here we have the high-water mark of the Johannine conception of Agape. God and Agape are one. Agape as such, regardless of the object to which it is directed, is participation in the life of God: Agape is born of God.

Yet it is just at this point that we can observe the modification and weakening already spoken of. It is principally evident in the fact that John does not, after all, find it entirely meaningless to let the object of Agape determine its significance. He knows of a form of Agape which must be repudiated, a kind of love against which he must warn us: *love of the world*. "Love not the world, neither the things that are in the world. If any man love the world, the love of the Father is not in him" (1 John ii. 15). The change of view noticeable in this passage has often been interpreted as having to do solely with the conception of "the world". "The world", it has been said, no longer means here "the world which is in need of salvation, and which, according to John iii. 16, God Himself loves, but the world which is eternally given over to sin and corruption, eternally separated from

God ".[1] That is undoubtedly true; but it is by no means adequate as an account of the change involved. It is not only the meaning of " world ", but also that of " love ", which has been modified. When we are warned against love of the world, it obviously cannot be the generous, self-giving Agape-love that is meant, but only " the love of desire", or *acquisitive love*. Only in the latter sense can " love of the world " be set in opposition to love for God; though when it is, there is always the risk that even love for God will be understood as acquisitive love.

When this happens the difference between the two kinds of love is determined simply by reference to their objects, in the one case to the world, in the other to God. Then Agape, which otherwise is a love that gives and sacrifices, and the very opposite of acquisitive love, becomes itself a species of acquisitive love—namely, the desire that is directed to God and heavenly things.

It is now clear why the quality of the love must in this case be defined in terms of its object, although to define Agape-love in that way is, as we have seen, meaningless. God shows His Agape both to the evil and the good, but can we therefore say that Agape is in the latter instance good, in the former evil and condemnable? As freely giving and self-giving love, Agape is entirely independent of the value of its object. But the position is different with regard to acquisitive love; its quality is determined by the value of its object. The love is of a higher or lower order according as it is set upon higher or lower objects of desire. Here there is real point in opposing to one another love for God and love for the world—love for God as the Highest Good, and love for the world as a lower, temporal, sensible good, or even as evil and sinful. But—be it noted—in both cases the love in question is not Agape, but acquisitive love.

[1] H. Windisch, *Handbuch zum Neuen Testament*, vol. iv., Part Two, 1st edn., 1911, p. 112.

Now it can, of course, rightly be said that there need not be anything more in the Johannine passage quoted above than a certain vagueness of expression and terminology, so that we should not be justified in drawing any conclusions from it with regard to the meaning of Agape in John. Yet even with this qualification there is still a certain difference between the Johannine and the Pauline idea of Agape. Agape is a less sharply defined term in John than in Paul and the purity of the Agape motif is not so consciously guarded as to exclude the possibility of such a modification as that suggested above.

The significance of Johannine thought for the Christian Agape motif can be summed up in two points.

First, John produced for future generations the formulæ that have carried the Agape motif forward through history. We think here primarily of the great text, " God is Agape " (1 John iv. 8, 16), but also of the no less important " God so loved the world, that He gave His only begotten Son, that whosoever believeth in Him should not perish, but have eternal life " (John iii. 16). These two texts, along with Paul's Agape-hymn in 1 Cor. xiii., have played an effective part in preserving for Agape its central position in Christianity. If the primitive Christian Agape motif reaches unsurpassable heights as to its content in Paul's preaching of the Agape of the Cross, it receives supreme expression as to its form in the Johannine identification of God and Agape.

Secondly, as a result of the weakening of the idea of Agape, which we have noticed above, the Johannine conception of love represents in a measure the transition to a stage where the Christian idea of love is no longer determined solely by the Agape motif, but by " Eros and Agape ". The Agape-metaphysic, the particularism, the uncertain position between unmotivated and motivated love, the modification in the direction of acquisitive love—all these contribute in their various ways to that development. Furthermore, even if the attempts to interpret Johannine Christianity in essentially Oriental-Hellenistic terms should prove unsuccessful, it still remains that John's use of such terms as " light ", " life ", " know ", " spirit ", " glory ", which can easily strike a Hellenistic-Gnostic note, creates a spiritual environment in which there would be at least some points of contact for the otherwise alien Eros motif.

CHAPTER TWO

THE EROS MOTIF

I

THE DOCTRINE OF EROS AS A DOCTRINE OF SALVATION

1. Eros-Piety, Christianity's Forerunner or Rival?

WHEN we turn to the Eros motif after studying the primitive Christian Agape motif, we find ourselves in a quite different spiritual world. But it is the world into which Christianity with its Agape motif had to make its entry. It was not virgin soil of which Christianity took possession, but soil that had been intensively cultivated by Eros-piety. In the Eros motif Christianity encountered far and away the most powerful fundamental religious motif of declining antiquity. An important question therefore confronts us. What did it mean for Christianity that it had to enter an environment dominated by the Eros motif, and occupy ground that had therefore already been worked over? Two different answers are possible here. (1) We might argue that Eros-piety had already done a preparatory work that Christianity itself would otherwise have had to do; in which case Eros-piety could be regarded as a forerunner of Christianity. (2) We might take the opposite course and regard the relation between ancient Eros-piety and Christianity as primarily a matter of rivalry; in which case we should chiefly emphasise the peril and menace of Eros for Christianity. Weighty arguments can in fact be advanced for both these views.

We sometimes find the phrase " the fulness of the time "

used to express the thought that when Christianity first appeared the world was in many respects prepared for its reception. One of the most important factors commonly mentioned in this connection is the religious longing and yearning which had taken a wide hold on the decaying world of antiquity, and which found expression in the doctrines of salvation and Mystery-rites in which the age abounded. It should, however, be observed that, although these doctrines and rites were very widespread and in outward appearance exceedingly diverse, yet in their inner structure they were pretty nearly uniform, and the fundamental motif of them all was none other than the Eros motif. The implication, therefore, is that ancient Eros-piety played into the hands of Christianity; and it cannot be denied that there are elements of truth in this view of the matter. In Eros the religious longings and the idealistic trends of late antiquity met and united with one another. The result was the creation of a spiritual atmosphere which at least superficially favoured Christianity, an atmosphere in which the religious question became life's greatest and most serious concern. Here was a point of contact for Christianity when it came with its message of salvation; for it could count on finding everywhere a sense of need for salvation, which had chiefly been awakened through the influence of Eros-piety. Had it not found this religiously fertile soil Christianity could never have achieved the success it did.

Nevertheless, it must be questioned whether this view does not rather obscure than clarify the situation in which Christianity found itself when it entered the ancient world. Eros-piety was far from being—as the above account might suggest—merely an indefinite and vague longing. It was not simply a question, so to speak, which remained unanswered until Christianity brought the answer. The Mysteries and the doctrines of salvation certainly regarded it as one of their main tasks to foster and develop the sense of need for salvation;

but they were able to do so just because they were confident that they possessed the means of satisfying that need. Each of them had its own definite answer to give, its instructions which man must follow in order to secure salvation. It is therefore a very questionable procedure to envisage the relation between Eros-piety and Christianity in terms of question and answer, preparation and fulfilment. If a piety of which the hall-mark is the Eros motif is to be thought of as a preparation for Christianity, it is above all necessary that we should be clear about the risks to which Christianity was exposed through having to make contact with it. Instead of being described as the forerunner of Christianity, Eros-piety could far rather be described as its most dangerous rival. It was the Eros motif which, once accepted into Christianity, threatened more than anything else in its subsequent history to empty the Christian Agape motif of its specific content.

From a purely historical point of view, therefore, it is scarcely possible to reach a definite decision as to whether Eros-piety should be regarded primarily as a forerunner or a rival of Christianity. In our present discussion, where we are concerned to show the essential difference between the Agape motif and the Eros motif, the main emphasis will naturally have to be placed on the rivalry between them. Even where the Eros motif prepared the way for Christianity, it prepared at the same time for a confusion of the two motifs.

2. Mystery-Religion as the Source of the Eros Motif

If we proceed to base our account of the Eros motif on Plato's theory of Eros, we do not mean to suggest by this that Plato was the creator of this motif, for he found it ready to hand and took over essential features of it from Mystery-religion. But there are two reasons why we should base our account on Plato: first, because it was he who gave the Eros motif a characteristic form, in which its meaning and structure are revealed with special clarity; and, secondly, because it was from this source that the Eros motif found its way, through Neoplatonism, into the later development of Christianity.

If it were our purpose to expound the philosophical implications of the Platonic doctrine of Eros and its place in the doctrine of Ideas as a whole, we should find ourselves faced with very considerable difficulties. It is always extremely hard in a case like this, where Plato presents what he has to say in the form of a myth, to be quite sure how much of it he is putting forward as his own serious view, intending it to be taken as genuine theory. Moreover, it is significant that in the *Symposium* he does not put the doctrine of Eros directly in the mouth of Socrates, but simply makes him recount what he has heard from Diotima, the prophetess of Mantinea. But what would otherwise be a difficulty is for our purposes a help, since it reminds us that *the doctrine of Eros is fundamentally a doctrine of salvation.* The spirit that lives in the Platonic doctrine of Eros has previously existed independently in the context of Mystery-piety; and it is with the religious significance of the doctrine, not with its possible philosophical implications, that we are here concerned.

In attempting to trace the Eros motif back to its source in ancient Mystery-piety, our attention is drawn first to the intimate connection between Plato's view and Orphism. Orphism in fact contains all the presuppositions of the doctrine of Eros, as can be clearly seen from its central myth, the myth of Zagreus. This tells how Zeus had resolved to give his son Zagreus (Dionysus) dominion over the world; but while Zagreus was still a child the Titans succeeded in getting him into their power, and killed and devoured him. But Zeus smote the Titans with his thunderbolt and destroyed them; and out of the Titans' ashes he then formed the race of men.[1] "The story of the Titans' treatment of Zagreus may be re-

---

[1] *Cf.* E. Rohde, *Psyche*, II., 3rd edn., 1903, pp. 116 ff.; M. P. Nilsson, *Den grekiska religionens historia*, 1921, pp. 242 ff.; R. Eisler, *Orphisch-dionysische Mysteriengedanken in der christlichen Antike*, 1925, pp. 290 ff.

garded as an ætiological myth designed to explain the central rite in the Dionysiac orgies, the dismemberment and devouring of the deity incarnated in an animal; but in Orphism this is inseparably connected with the myth of the creation of mankind out of the Titans' ashes."[1]

It is this latter part of the myth that is of particular interest for our purposes. It contains the explanation of man's double nature, as being at once akin to the Divine and at enmity with it. This double relation is explained by man's double origin. As created out of the Titans' ashes, he is evil and hostile to God; but since in the Titans' ashes there was also something of the god they had consumed, there is also something Divine in the composition of man. Man thus belongs by origin to two worlds; he is an earthly being with a " titanic " nature, but he also has in him a " divine spark ". It is this Divine element in man that must be liberated from its unwarrantable bondage to the earthly and sensual element; the Divine reason or Divine soul needs above all things to break its bonds, to purify itself from the defilement of the senses, and to pass out from this unnatural environment into the Divine life to which it is by nature akin. The way of salvation for the Divine soul is therefore in Orphism the way of purification and ecstasy, and the goal is the final reunion of the soul with the Divine and its absorption into it.

This conception of the double nature of man, of the Divine origin and quality of the soul, its liberation from the things of sense, and its ascent to its original Divine home, is the common basis on which every theory of Eros rests. Around this basic idea, however, a whole series of characteristic ideas group themselves, all intimately connected with the Eros motif, such as belief in a pre-existent Fall, the conception of the body as the prison-house of the soul, the idea of the transmigration of souls, belief in the soul's natural immortality; and hand in hand with these go the basic mood of asceticism and the mystical-ecstatic way of salvation.

[1] M. P. Nilsson, *op. cit.*, p. 246.

The circle of ideas in which we now find ourselves is by no means confined to Orphism, but reappears with insignificant variations wherever we turn in the world of the ancient Mystery-religions. There is in man a Divine essence which is held captive contrary to its nature in the fetters of sense. The soul is a pearl which has sunk into the darkness at the bottom of the sea.[1] It is this immortal, divine, essential being of man that the Mysteries seek to redeem. These scattered Divine sparks are to be led back and absorbed into the primal Divine fire. Man is the offspring of God; the rational part of his nature is a fragment of the Divine cosmic reason. What he needs, therefore, is to be made aware of the degradation of his present state, put off the earthly trappings that prevent his true nature from coming to light, and being thus purified ascend to his heavenly home. What he needs is to enter into himself, learn to know himself (that is, to know his transcendent worth), and then go out from himself (that is, from his subjection to the conditions of time and sense) and enter into the Deity. Only so does man truly become himself. Even though ancient Mystery-piety is vividly conscious of the human soul's helplessness and need of help, its cardinal assumption is none the less always the original Divine dignity of the soul. This is the presupposition which alone makes possible man's ascent to the Divine sphere; there is no insuperable barrier between the human and the Divine, because the human soul is fundamentally a Divine being.

As time goes on, this complex of motifs becomes more and more the common property of ancient religion. The religion of the Mysteries becomes the truly living religion, and the Eros motif becomes the dominant motif of the religious syncretism which Christianity encounters as soon as ever it comes into contact with the spirit of antiquity.

[1] R. Eisler, *op. cit.*, p. 272. *Cf.* Lehmann-Haas, *Textbuch zur Religionsgeschichte*, 2nd edn., 1922, pp. 218 ff.: " Remember that thou art the son of a King; see whom thou hast served in bondage. Think on the pearl for the sake of which thou hast betaken thyself to Egypt " (p. 219).

II

THE PLATONIC IDEA OF EROS

1. Eros and Dialectic

It was an event of immense importance in human history when Plato in his doctrine of Ideas effected a synthesis of Greek rationalism and Oriental mysticism. Unless account is taken of both these sources of the Platonic outlook its deepest significance cannot really be understood. Its dual aspect is apparent even to superficial observation from the fact that the dialectical argument of the Dialogues is here and there interrupted by a piece of myth, the material for which is mainly drawn from current religious conceptions.

This alternation between *logos* and *mythos* has long been regarded as a difficulty. Among philosophers the chief stress has very naturally been laid on *logos*, so that Plato has been interpreted primarily from the dialectical-methodological side,[1] while the mythical element has been kept in the background as inadmissible evidence for Plato's thought. It ought not to be forgotten, however, that in Plato we do not find philosophy in the modern sense of a critical, scientific discipline, but rather in the sense of a philosophy of life built up partly on a religious basis. It might, indeed, be described as a philosophy that is at the same time a doctrine of salvation; for in it " the exhortation is heard again and again to

---

[1] Among modern interpreters special reference may be made to the Marburg school, which starts from *logos* and interprets Plato in close harmony with its own transcendental-critical outlook. *Cf.* H. Cohen, *Platons Ideenlehre und die Mathematik*, 1878; P. Natorp, *Platos Ideenlehre*, 2nd edn., 1921; N. Hartmann, *Platos Logik des Seins*, 1909. Essentially the same line is taken by O. Wichmann, *Platon und Kant*, 1920.

take thought for our own soul's welfare."[1] Ancient thought was unaware of any sharp distinction between religion and philosophy. Both sought to give directions as to the way of salvation; both sought to help men to attain the true and blessed life. Furthermore, even with regard to the more precise definition of this goal there is far-reaching agreement between Plato and the ancient Mysteries. For both of them salvation means the deliverance of the soul from the prison-house of the body and the senses, and its restoration to its original heavenly home. It is only in respect of the means to this end that they differ, and the difference is only partial. In the Mysteries, the soul's salvation is attained through initiations, purifications, and ritual observance, while in Plato it is through philosophy. But even for the philosopher it involves a " conversion " and a " purification "; and not even the philosopher can get all the way to the goal by means of dialectic, but he reaches it only in a state of " divine madness " ($\mu\alpha\nu\iota\alpha$). The myths yield valuable information about these cosmological, psychological, and religious aspects of Platonism.[2]

Whereas the traditional tendency with regard to the question of *logos* and *mythos* in Plato has been to lay all stress on *logos*, a very evident change of view can be observed in more recent interpreters. The general awakening in modern times of interest in *mythos*[3] has been accompanied by a growing tendency to make the mythical element of decisive importance for the interpretation of Plato.[4] We are now told that it is

[1] U. von Wilamowitz-Moellendorff, *Platon*, I., 1919, p. 325.

[2] There is, however, no justification for regarding the Platonic Academy as simply an " *Erlösungssekt*," as P. L. Landsberg does in his *Wesen und Bedeutung der platonischen Akademie*, 1923, p. 62.

[3] Evidenced, e.g., by the republication of selected works of J. J. Bachofen in *Der Mythos von Orient und Occident: Eine Metaphysik der alten Welt*, ed. M. Schroeter, 1926.

[4] Cf., e.g., K. Reinhardt, *Platons Mythen*, 1927; K. Singer, *Platon der Gründer*, 1927. Even Natorp has·recognised this change, for in the 2nd edn. of his *Platons Ideenlehre* (1921) he says: " When this book was first written it seemed, and perhaps actually was, necessary to keep Plato the

in the myths, and not in the intellectual exercises of dialectic, that Plato says his last word and reveals what he really has at heart. This is obviously a favourable development for us, when our purpose is to investigate the problem of Eros; for Eros lies more on the line of *mythos* than of *logos*. The myth of Eros can in fact be described as the central Platonic myth, the one which gives us the best insight into the deepest motifs of the Platonic outlook.

But the fact that in dealing with Plato's idea of Eros we are likely to find ourselves chiefly in the realm of *mythos*, by no means makes it necessary for us to thrust *logos* into the background. Plato's dialectic and his doctrine of salvation are not unconnected with one another, but there is an inner relationship between them. The doctrine of Ideas and the doctrine of Eros are not two separate things which he merely adds together, but he has succeeded in making a real synthesis of them. The Eros motif, which is the fundamental motif of the doctrine of salvation, is not excluded from the doctrine

---

mystic quite separate from the author of the doctrine of Ideas. It looks today as though we must agree with those critics who hold that this distinction can no longer be maintained" (p. 467). The change in question was to be found, incidentally, as long ago as 1905 in Leop. Ziegler's *Der abendländische Rationalismus und der Eros*, where it is stated that "alongside the scientific element, or we might say *above* it, there is another. The intellectual intuition, or Eros, makes the abstract tale of abstract categories into the wonderful confession of a deep and humanly beautiful instinct" (Preface, p. vii.); and that "here Plato's science transcends itself" (p. 27). Eros thus means a break with science and dialectic; it bases itself on intuition, and therefore takes us into the realm of myth and symbol.— According to U. v. Wilamowitz-Moellendorff, too, " Plato is conscious that the Ultimate and Highest is never scientifically demonstrable" (*Platon*, p. 1); " We apprehend the Highest only in the divine madness, not with the understanding but through inward experience, intuitively. In truth he gives here the supreme height of his philosophy, when he confesses its insufficiency" (p. 418). This view is attacked by O. Wichmann, *Platon und Kant*, 1920, pp. 43 f. : " No mystery, no poetry, no divinity can give that which is the inescapable requirement in this sphere, namely, certainty." *Cf.* further the full discussions of Plato's doctrine of Eros in J. Stenzel, *Platon der Erzieher*, 1938 (vol. 12 of *Die grossen Erzieher, ihre Persönlichkeit und ihre Systeme*, ed. by Rudolf Lehmann), pp. 191-248, and R. Lagerborg, *Die platonische Liebe*, 1929.

of Ideas, for the whole structure of this doctrine is such that it leads up to the thought of Eros as its natural conclusion. W. Windelband is right when he says of Plato: " The world-view which he reached by means of scientific inquiry as the gathered result of all previously propounded theories, was of such a nature that the dogmas of the Dionysiac doctrine of the soul found a place within it, and might appear to be the necessary consequence of it."[1]   Our first task, therefore, will be to illustrate briefly the connection of the Eros motif with the Platonic doctrine of Ideas as a whole.

The most characteristic feature of Plato's outlook is its sharp dualism between the two worlds, the world of sense and the world of Ideas.   Yet it would be an undue simplification to represent this dualism as a mere reproduction of the cosmological dualism of Oriental religion, between the heavenly world of light and the world of darkness.   However close the relation between the two forms of dualism may be, the Platonic dualism preserves its own distinct character by the fact that Plato's doctrine of the two worlds rests ultimately on reasoned grounds.   " It is not simply the old distinction between the light-world of heaven and the darkness of earth, which already dominated *mythos*, nor yet a religious and ethical postulate of two opposing forces, good and evil, that Plato has taken over and transferred from the realm of *mythos* to that of *logos*.   Instead, what is characteristic of genuine Socratism, and what also distinguishes the new and creative element in Plato's teaching from everything pre-Platonic, is the fact that the dualism which dominates Plato's system is deduced by him from a purely logical dis-

[1] W. Windelband, *Platon*, 6th edn., 1920, p. 123.   *Cf.* also: " His method is to assimilate the intellectual content of that doctrine of the soul to his dialectic, and to interpret it in terms of the conception of the Two Worlds that goes with his doctrine of Ideas.   When in this way the essential elements of his religious view appear to have been scientifically established, Plato is at liberty to add to them, in his Myths, the graphically living form which the thoughts had assumed either in the religious society and its cultus or in the free play of his own imagination with this material."

tinction between that which is a concept and that which lies below the level of a concept."[1]

But no matter how much we concentrate on the logical aspect and treat it as the sole determinant of the Platonic outlook, we arrive of necessity, even from this starting-point, at the idea of Eros. The two worlds, the world of Ideas and the world of the senses, the world of necessary rational knowledge and the world of contingent sense-perception, stand admittedly side by side unrelated to one another, but not—be it noted—on a par with one another. To man, who is placed between them and has connections with both of them, it falls as his lot to effect the transition from the one to the other. Not that his intermediate position means that he should unite the two worlds in his own person; but, on the contrary, it is his business to cut himself loose from the lower world and ascend to the higher; and when he does so, when he turns away from the things of sense to the world of Ideas, then the latter achieves a conquest, as it were, over the former. This, however, is possible only in virtue of the Eros that indwells the human soul. The Ideas as such are quite incapable of making any conquests; they are not forces, they exercise no influence in the sense-world. The relation between the two worlds is entirely one-sided; the movement is all in one direction, from below upwards. No helping action proceeds from the world of Ideas, reaching out towards the lower world. The Ideas do not participate in things, but things participate in the Ideas. When man glimpses the Idea in the things, he is seized by Eros, the longing for the pure world of Ideas. *Eros is man's conversion from the sensible to the supersensible; it is the upward tendency of the human soul; it is a real force, which drives the soul in the direction of the Ideal world.* If there were no such thing as Eros, intercourse between the two worlds would be at a standstill, and they

[1] E. Hoffman, *Platonismus und Mittelalter*, p. 23 (*Vorträge der Bibliothek Warburg, Vorträge 1923-1924*, Leipzig und Berlin, 1926, pp. 17-82).

would lie unmoved side by side. It is Eros that sets in motion the ascending process; Eros is the big opportunity of the Ideal world over against the sense-world. For while the Idea cannot reach out to give active assistance in human life, man with his equipment of Eros is called to enable the Idea to assert its authority.

We have now reached the point where the Platonic dialectic culminates in the idea of Eros, and Plato's philosophy is seen to be at the same time a doctrine of salvation.[1] The door now stands wide open for Orphic and Dionysiac notions, and the ideology of the Mysteries is freely drawn upon. It is no longer possible to decide whether what we have here is primarily a philosophical theory or a religious doctrine of salvation, for these two are so interwoven as to form an inseparable unity. This is plainly shown, for example, by the famous allegory of the Cave in the seventh book of the *Republic*.[2] Our position in the sense-world is there compared to that of men sitting chained in an underground cave, able only to see the shadows on the cave wall. Those who have never seen anything else but these shadows believe them to be the true reality. But the philosopher, who has got rid of his chains, climbed up out of the dark cave, and ascended from the gloom of the sense-world to the brightness of the Ideas, knows that true reality is only to be found in this upper world, and that the sense-world shows us only the shadow of real being. But in order to make this discovery a complete conversion is necessary; man must turn—and the turning may be painful—away from lower things, the things of sense, to the super-sensible and that which truly *is*.

The substance of this allegory is that of the doctrine of Ideas, but its colouring is that of the doctrine of salvation.

---

[1] To that extent there is sound observation behind Vilh. Andersen's statement that " Plato's *theory of knowledge*, his doctrine of Ideas, is thus not merely the work of speculation but the fruit of a primitive religious experience, the Dionysiac vision " (*Bacchustoget i Norden*, 1904, p; 75).

[2] *Rep.* 514 ff.

Here an appeal is made to man to turn from the transitory and seek the eternal; here we are told of the soul's imprisonment in the lower world, of the shadows and illusions of the sense-world, and of the pains of conversion when the soul begins to turn towards the heavenly world; we are told of Divine contemplation and human misery, and are given a hint that " those who have come thus far are unwilling to trouble themselves with mortal affairs, and their souls are ever eager to dwell in that upper region ".[1]   Here, as in the *Phædo*, philosophy and soteriology are one and the same.

2. The Myth of Eros

In his magnificent myth of Eros in the *Phædrus*, Plato starts from the assumption common to the Oriental doctrines of salvation, that the human soul has a supernatural, divine origin and worth.   In a pre-existent state the soul has had a vision of the Ideas, or of that which is in itself true, beautiful and good;[2] and this has made so deep an impression on it that even after it has fallen and become bound and fettered in the body " like an oyster in its shell ",[3] it still retains a memory (ἀνάμνησις) of the glory of the world above, and feels an upward attraction which it often cannot itself understand.   Just as the stone in virtue of its nature is attracted downwards, so the soul in virtue of its divine nature is attracted upwards; for everything in existence strives to find its own natural place. *This upward attraction of the soul is Eros.* It is something in the world of souls analogous to the law of

---

[1] *Rep.* 517; *cf.* 519: " But what if from earliest childhood such a nature had been clipped and pruned, and if it had been freed from those sensual enjoyments, such as food and drink, which hang like leaden weights upon the soul from birth and drag its gaze downwards?   If it were thus free from all these, and were turned towards the truth, then this same man would look away to the true with the same keen eyes with which he now looks upon the false." *Cf. Phædo* 65 ff.

[2] *Phædrus* 249. *Phædo* 75.

[3] *Phædrus* 250. Was it perhaps the thought of the soul as a pearl that suggested the choice of this image? *Cf.* p. 165 above.

gravitation in the material world. It prevents the soul from settling down in things temporal, and reminds it that here it is but a stranger and sojourner. The love that Plato teaches is the "heavenly Eros",[1] a love for the bright world of Ideas, a longing to participate in the Divine life.

Eros is very closely associated with the Platonic doctrine of *anamnesis*; it is nourished by the recollection of what the soul in its pre-temporal existence has beheld in the world of Ideas. The strength of this recollection varies in different souls; in most it is only latent, like hot embers under ashes; but in all it must be brought to actuality. This comes to pass through the sight of beautiful things. When the soul perceives the radiance of the beautiful, it gains wings and is able to ascend to the super-sensible.[2] The reason why it is the beautiful that has this effect, is that the Idea of beauty is the brightest and most radiant of all the Ideas. "Beauty once shone for us in brightness, when in the train of Zeus or of some other god we saw the glorious sight and were initiated into that which is rightly called the most blessed of mysteries."[3] Therefore the Idea of beauty is the last to be forgotten and the first to be recollected when we come across its image in the things of sense.

The sight of the beautiful, which comes to man in the sense-world, has for its function to awaken Eros in his soul; not, however, in order that his love may be fixed on the beautiful object, but rather that it may pass beyond it in the continual ascent which is of the very essence of Eros. The beautiful thing is to be a reminder of the soul's true fatherland; it is to point away from itself to the Absolute Beauty, in which it participates and from which it derives its own beauty. Thus, even where Eros is kindled by the sight of the sensuously beautiful, it proves itself to be the " heavenly

---

[1] The distinction between "heavenly Eros" and "vulgar Eros", discussed above, pp. 50 ff., should perhaps be emphasised here.—*Translator's note.*
[2] *Phædrus* 251.   [3] *Phædrus* 250.

Eros " by the fact that it seeks to rise above this to the super-sensible, heavenly beauty. Sensuous beauty is merely the starting-point of the ascending movement, which reaches its goal only in the world of Ideas.

The manner and stages of this ascent of the soul are sketched by Plato in the *Symposium*, and his description might well be called the *ordo salutis* of Eros. He employs here an image which was later to become a favourite with the mystics, and which is typical of every kind of Eros-piety : the image of the " Heavenly ladder " on which the soul has to climb to the world above. Starting from the beauty of sense, the soul ascends as it were on a ladder to ever higher forms of beauty, till at last it comes to the Idea of beauty itself. " When anyone ", Plato says, " under the influence of the right kind of Eros mounts up from these earthly things and begins to see this beauty, he is not far from the final goal. For the right way to the things of Eros, whether one goes alone or is led by another, is to begin with the beautiful things that are here, and mount ever upwards in order to reach the beauty that is above, as if one were ascending a ladder from one beautiful body to two, and from two to all the others, and from beautiful bodies to beautiful actions, and from beautiful actions to beautiful forms of knowledge, till at length one reaches that knowledge which is the knowledge of nothing other than Absolute Beauty, and so knows at last what Beauty really is. It is then, if ever, that life is worth living for man, when he beholds Beauty itself."[1] He who has reached this stage has attained to the highest thing of all, the contemplation of the Idea of beauty, the Beauty which is " eternal, which has had no beginning and does not pass away, which undergoes neither growth nor decay."[2] He has attained to the vision of Absolute Beauty, which is at the same time Absolute Being.

Eros, according to Plato, has by nature a certain duality

[1] *Symposium* 211; *cf. Republic* 514 ff.   [2] *Symposium* 211.

about it. It is neither purely Divine nor purely human, but something in between ($\mu\epsilon\tau\alpha\xi\acute{u}$) the two, "a great dæmon". It is intermediate between the mortal and the immortal, between having and not having, between wisdom and unreason. This duality is explained mythically in the *Symposium* by the story of Eros' parentage. Eros is the son of Penia and Poros; that is, of poverty and need on the one side, and of resourceful initiative and energy on the other. As his mother's son, Eros is poor, coarse, and squalid, a vagabond, who "takes after his mother in always keeping company with want." But he is like his father in always having designs on the beautiful and good, and in being bold and enterprising.[1] Eros himself is neither beautiful nor ugly, neither good nor evil,[2] but occupies a position intermediate between the two; not, however, a neutral position, for he always has a definite tendency in one direction: *Eros is love for the beautiful and the good.*[3]

3. The Content of the Idea of Eros

The account we have so far given of Plato's conception of Eros, drawn mainly from the *Phædrus* and the *Symposium*, has been largely of a mythological character; but it is not difficult to discern the underlying rational idea. It now remains for us to fix more precisely the content of the idea of Eros, or to show the distinctive features of the Platonic conception of love. The chief points to be noticed here can be summed up under three heads: (1) Eros is the "love of desire", or acquisitive love; (2) Eros is man's way to the Divine; (3) Eros is egocentric love.

(1) *Eros as acquisitive love.* When giving a closer definition of Eros, Plato says it is intermediate between having and not having. The most obvious thing about Eros is that it is a desire, a longing, a striving. But man only desires and

---

[1] *Symposium* 203.   [2] *Symposium* 201 f.   [3] *Symposium* 204.

longs for that which he has not got, and of which he feels a need; and he can only strive for that which he feels to be valuable. Hence love, as Plato sees it, has two main characteristics: the consciousness of a present need and the effort to find satisfaction for it in a higher and happier state. The sense of need is an essential constituent of Eros; for without a sense of need acquisitive love would never be aroused. An Eros that was rich, and had everything it wanted, would be a contradiction in terms; and the same is true, fundamentally, of any thought of Eros as freely giving anything away. G. Simmel is right when he says: "The Greek Eros is a Will-to-possess, even when it carries the nobler sense of possessing the beloved object as a recipient of ideal instruction and morally improving attention. That is why love can be for him [Plato] the middle state between having and not having; and the logical consequence is that love must inevitably die away when the possession of its object is secured."[1] It should be specially noted that even where Eros seems to be a desire to give it is still in the last resort a "Will-to-possess"; for Plato is fundamentally unaware of any other form of love than acquisitive love.

By classifying Eros as a type of acquisitive love, Plato has fixed the limits within which we must look for Eros-love. Like all acquisitive love, Eros necessarily directs itself to an object which is regarded as valuable. Love and value belong together here; each suggests the other. Only that which is regarded as valuable can become an object of desire and love. From this it is plain that there can be no room in Plato for any spontaneous and unmotivated love: for acquisitive love is motivated by the value of its object. Eros, however, is not adequately defined by being simply described as acquisitive love. For there is a kind of acquisitive love that drags the soul downwards and only binds it the more firmly to things temporal; and that is sensual love. In contradistinction from

[1] G. Simmel, "Fragment über die Liebe," in *Logos*, vol. x., 1921-22, p. 27.

this, Eros is a love that is *directed upwards*; it is the soul's upward longing and striving towards the heavenly world, the world of Ideas.

It would, of course, be an undue simplification to assert that this difference in the direction of the love was entirely without influence on the structure of the love itself. The plain fact is rather that the character of the desire varies with the quality of the desired object. "Desire for something different is a different desire" (Simmel).[1] It is not the same desire that is directed in the one case downwards and in the other case upwards. Yet however great the difference, it cannot alter the fact that even upward-directed Eros-love has an acquisitive aim.

(2) *Eros as man's way to the Divine.* Plato's description of Eros as an intermediate thing has also a religious significance. Eros is the mediator between Divine and human life. It is Eros that raises the imperfect to perfection, the mortal to immortality. In this connection Plato can speak of love as something Divine, though only in the sense that it unites man with the gods, *not in the sense that the gods feel love.* The gods live their blessed life wanting for nothing. They do not need to love. "Man loves and desires only that which he wants and has not got", Plato says;[2] for "who in the world would desire what he already has?"[3] Since the gods have everything and need nothing, there can be no question of their feeling love. The only relation they can have to love is to be the objects of love. In virtue of its beauty the Divine sets all things in movement towards itself; but the Divine itself is unmoved; it is absolute rest. "A god holds no intercourse with a man," Plato says, "but by means of this intermediary [Eros] all intercourse and discourse between gods and men is carried on."[4] Love, as activity and movement, belongs exclusively to man's side. For love is always the desire of the lower for the higher, the imperfect for the per-

[1] *Op. cit.*, p. 53. [2] *Symposium* 201; *cf.* 200. [3] *Ibid.*, 200. [4] *Ibid.*, 203.

fect. *Eros is the way by which man mounts up to the Divine, not the way by which the Divine stoops down to man.* This is the simple consequence of the twofold presupposition of Eros-love—namely, the recognition of a value in the loved object and the consciousness of needing this value.

The direction of love towards the super-sensible is constitutive of the Platonic idea of Eros. It has often been stated that there is a sharp contrast between the pessimistic outlook on the world which we find in the *Phædo* and the optimistic view which prevails in the *Symposium* and the *Phædrus*. The ethical programme of the *Phædo* is one of sheer flight from the world. The right attitude to the sense-world is to turn one's back upon it. The things of sense merely drag the soul downwards. In this world we have only dim shadow-images of true being. The soul is held in the body as in a prison-house, and waits for the hour of its deliverance. But in the *Phædrus* and the *Symposium* we find a quite different æsthetic-ethical programme. The sense-world is given a positive value. Sensible beauty is a reminder of the Absolute Beauty, and the thought of the beautiful provides a connecting link between the Ideal world and the sense-world. The sharp dualism is overcome and a more harmonious world-view is attained.[1]

Now the difference of tone between these Dialogues is certainly not to be denied; but to conclude from this that the fundamental dualism of Plato's world-view is overcome by the Eros-doctrine of the *Symposium* and the *Phædrus* is completely to misapprehend the facts of the case.[2] The sharp dualism between the two worlds is not done away by the

---

[1] *Cf.* R. Eucken, *Die Lebensanschauungen der grossen Denker*, 13th and 14th edns., 1919, 29 ff. : " Weltflucht und Weltverklärung."

[2] Even in the *Phædrus* the body is described as the prison-house of the soul (250). *Cf. Theætetus* 176 f. : "Evil cannot exist among the gods, but must of necessity dwell in our mortal nature and in our lower world. *Therefore we must seek as quickly as possible to fly from it and escape thither.* But to fly thither is the same thing as to become as much as possible like God."—" World-flight " and the doctrine of Ideas are simply inseparable from one another.

doctrine of Eros, for this doctrine only shows man how he is to be saved out of the one world into the other. That there was a practicable way of escape from the sense-world to the super-sensible Plato never doubted; but this does not imply any weakening of the dualistic opposition between the two worlds. Furthermore, Eros is in no sense an affirmation or acceptance of the sense-world; on the contrary, it is the turning of the soul away from it. *Eros is itself a form of flight from the world.* It is not beautiful things as such that are the object of love and desire. It is only because of the memory they awaken of the higher world that they have any place in the scheme of Eros. Plato's interest in them attaches, not to their singularity and individuality, but to their being " paradigms ", particular instances, which " participate in " the universal beauty. They exist for him only as stepping-stones to this universal. " Beauty in one body ", he says, " is sister to the beauty in any other body; and therefore, as our purpose is to seek after the Idea of the beautiful, it would be very unreasonable not to regard beauty as always one and the same."[1] Hence the *ordo salutis* of Eros, as Plato teaches it, is as follows : from one beautiful body to all beautiful bodies, from these to the beauty of the soul, from this to the beauty in human laws and institutions, then to the beauty of the sciences, and finally to that which is absolutely beautiful, the Idea of beauty itself. Not even in the doctrine of Eros do we find any other way of salvation than this : escape from the sense-world.

(3) *Eros as egocentric love.* The entire structure of Platonic Eros is egocentric. Everything centres on the individual self and its destiny. All that matters from first to last is the soul that is aflame with Eros—its Divine nature, its present straits while it is in bondage to the body, its gradual ascent to the world above, its blessed vision of the Ideas in their unveiled

[1] *Symposium* 210. For the religious significance of the æsthetic in Plato, see H. Ording, *Estetikk og kristendom*, 1929, pp. 14-25.

glory. The very fact that Eros is acquisitive love is sufficient to show its egocentric character: for all desire, or appetite, and longing is more or less egocentric. But the clearest proof of the egocentric nature of Eros is its intimate connection with *eudæmonia*.[1] The aim of love is to gain possession of an object which is regarded as valuable and which man feels he needs. Plato is specially concerned to emphasise this point. "It is by the acquisition of good things [*i.e.*, advantageous, satisfying things]", he says, "that the happy are made happy."[2] And since all men wish to be happy, the same point can be made by saying that all men love the good. Who would not strive to obtain that which was advantageous to himself? To love the good, therefore, is the same as to desire to possess the good and to possess it *permanently*. Love is therefore always a desire for immortality. But in this desire, too, the egocentric will is in evidence.

If we still had any doubt about the egocentric character of the love in question here, it certainly would be removed by such passages of Plato as the following: "Do you think that Alcestis would have died for Admetus, or Achilles have followed Patroclus to death, or that your own Codrus would have sacrificed himself to preserve the kingdom for his sons, if they had not believed that they would win thereby an immortal renown—as in fact they have? Nay, most certainly not. On the contrary, I believe that all men will do anything

---

[1] Socrates' conversation with Diotima in the *Symposium* (204 f.) is instructive on the point: "Tell me, Socrates, what does he desire who loves the good?—He desires to possess it, said I.—And what does he gain who possesses the good?—That is easier to answer, I replied, he gains happiness. —Yes, she said, it is by the acquisition of good things that the happy are made happy. And now there is no need to go on and ask what a man desires who is happy; for we have already reached finality.—You are right, I replied.—Do you now think that this desire and this love is common to all men, and that all wish to have the good always in their possession, or what do you think?—Indeed, said I, I think the desire is common to all."
"Finality" is thus reached only when love is referred back to the egocentric quest for happiness that is common to all men.

[2] *Symposium* 205.

to win immortal fame and such glorious renown, and the better they are, the more eager they are about it: for they love the immortal."[1] Of such a love it could scarcely be said that it "seeketh not its own". Wilamowitz-Moellendorff comments on the passage thus: "But the motive alleged for the self-sacrifice of Alcestis, Achilles and Codrus is not, we hope, to be taken as Plato's real meaning."[2] It may be readily admitted that the egocentric interest appears here in a particularly startling form, which brings it into immediate proximity with the lower egoism. But there is no fundamental reason for dismissing this passage on account of its egocentric colouring; for never in any circumstances, not even in its highest form as yearning for the Divine, does Eros shed its egocentric habit of mind.[3] In order to prevent any misunderstanding, however, let it be clearly stated that the word "egocentric" is not used here in any derogatory sense. It expresses neither approval nor disapproval, but is simply descriptive of the type of love to which Eros belongs.

[1] *Symposium* 208.   [2] *Platon*, vol. ii., 1919, p. 173.
[3] Further evidence of the egocentric nature of Eros is found in Plato's description of the endeavour of souls to rise to the higher world as a chariot-race, in which each "strives to get in front" of the rest (*Phædrus* 248). *Cf.* what is said of friendship in the *Lysis*. There cannot be friendship without desire. The good cannot be the friend of the good, since the good man, "in so far as he is good, is self-sufficient" (214). The object of friendship is to gain some good for oneself. The sick man is a friend to the physician in order that by his aid he may gain health (218 f.). Thus egocentric desire is the basis of friendship (220 f.). "*The ground of friendship*, then, *is purely and simply desire*. A man desires that which is lacking to him, yet is necessary to him (for his existence or the fulfilment of his appropriate tasks); in other words, that which is peculiarly his own." —F. Überweg, *Grundriss der Geschichte der Philosophie*, vol. i., *Die Philosophie des Altertums*, 12th edn., ed. K. Praechter, 1926, p. 238.

III

THE ARISTOTELIAN AND NEOPLATONIC
DEVELOPMENTS OF EROS

1. The Importance of the Later Developments

IF we take a broad survey of the various forms and phases of the Eros motif in antiquity, we shall hardly avoid the impression that it reaches its zenith in Plato. He portrays it with such classical simplicity and purity of line, and in such fascinating colours, as none of its subsequent representations can show. Neither the dry theorising of Aristotle's treatment of the subject, nor the abstruse mythological notions of Plotinus and still more his successors, whereby the universe is populated with a multitude of Erotes which furnish a link between earth and heaven, can successfully compete with Plato. Plato is both the creator and the perfecter of the classical idea of Eros—though he did not create it out of nothing; for the Eros motif, as we have sees, existed independently of him and before his time.

A similar conclusion will be reached if we ignore the treatment of the subject and consider simply the subject itself. All the essential features of the Eros motif—everything necessary for determining its structure—can be found in Plato. For our immediate purpose, therefore, of comparing and contrasting the Eros motif and the Agape motif in respect of their constitutive principles, it might suffice simply to take the idea of Eros in its original Platonic form.

But we must not therefore overlook the extraordinary importance of Aristotle and Neoplatonism in the history of the Eros motif. It was only as a result of their contribution that this motif came to play the significant part it did in human history.   When the Eros motif found its way into Christianity it was not exclusively, nor even primarily, in the form given to it by Plato; it was primarily in the form, on the one hand, of Mystery-piety (as can be seen above all in Gnosticism), and, on the other hand, of Aristotelian and Neoplatonic Eros-theory.   In the early Church and well on into the Middle Ages, it was Neoplatonism that took the lead; and through Augustine and Dionysius the Areopagite the Neoplatonic idea of Eros secured a central and permanent place in Catholicism.   When Aristotelianism afterwards triumphed through Thomas Aquinas, this in no way meant a weakening of the influence of Eros in Scholasticism.   The quarrel between Platonism and Aristotelianism is a quarrel on common ground; and chief among the things they have in common is the idea of Eros.

2. THE EROS MOTIF IN ARISTOTLE

The relation between the Aristotelian and the Platonic theory of Eros might be formulated briefly as follows: Aristotle presents us with an expansion of the Platonic theory, in which the idea of Eros acquires cosmic significance.   In Plato, Eros is the soul's striving after the object of its desire, its urge towards the ultimately beautiful and desirable, the expression of a deep home-sickness for its heavenly fatherland. In Aristotle this conception is given a wider reference and applied, in so far as it can be applied, even to the physical world. " Platonic love as modified by Aristotle ", says Scholz, " is thus a striving after that which is worth striving after, and is so conceived that the existence of this love is claimed, not only for individuals with souls in our sense of the term, but for all the elements of the cosmos."[1]   Accordingly, in order to see the significance of the idea of Eros in Aristotle,

[1] H. Scholz, *Eros und Caritas*, 1929, p. 16.

we must turn not so much to his ethics as to his metaphysics, and especially to his doctrine of motion.

The whole process of nature is seen by Aristotle as a move ment, a successive ascent from matter to form, from imper fection to perfection of being, from potentiality to actuality.[1] The cause of this movement is to be found in the influence of form on matter, an influence which shows itself in two ways: partly as an inherent bias, so to speak, of matter towards form,[2] partly as an active influence of form on matter. This latter, however, is attributable to form only in so far as it is itself matter for a higher form; for as far as Pure Form is con cerned, it is absolutely transcendent over all movement what soever. It is the Pure Form that in the last resort sets the whole process in motion, but it does so without being itself involved in any motion or change; itself unmoved, it is the principle of all movement. But how is it possible for that which itself is completely unmoved to set anything else in motion? Aristotle's answer is the famous κινεῖ ὡς ἐρώμενον " it moves by being loved."[3] That is to say, it sets things in motion in the same way as the beloved object moves the lover, by the desire it awakens. The influence of Pure Form on matter is not exerted through any activity of its own, but solely through the Eros which it kindles, the desire to receive form which it awakens in matter by reason of its perfection. *We thus find in Aristotle the Eros of Plato raised to the level of a cosmic force.* However different Aristotle may other

[1] *Cf.* H. Siebeck, *Aristoteles*, 3rd edn., 1910, p. 37: "This distinction between the ideas of potentiality and actuality (δύναμις and ἐνέργεια) is fundamental both to Aristotle's conception of nature and to his philosophy. The philosopher needs it in order to render fluid the contrast between matter and form, and to represent the whole of nature as a graded series of lower and higher forms of existence in the sense of a total structure arranged in steady gradations from bottom to top." On Aristotle's doctrine of motion, see also H. Scholz, *op. cit.*, pp. 20 ff., and W. Jaeger, *Aristoteles*, 1923, pp. 366 ff.

[2] H. Siebeck, *op. cit.*, p. 35: "There is thus in the very nature of matter the urge and drive towards form and shape; it is the nature of matter to be accessible to (*i.e.*, capable of being moulded by) the influence of form."

[3] *Metaphysics*, 1072 b 3.

wise be from Plato, with regard to the idea of Eros he is Plato's faithful disciple.[1]

The development of Plato's doctrine of Eros on cosmic lines shows itself also at other points in Aristotle's metaphysics. Specially interesting here is the *Stufenleiter der Dinge*, the " Scale of Existence ", which forms the substance of his natural philosophy.[2] Since Eros represents an upward tendency it is not unnatural that he should employ the ladder-symbolism in describing it. In Plato this occurs in what we described above as his *ordo salutis*,[3] where the soul, fired with Eros by the sight of the sensuously beautiful, has to mount up as it were on a ladder to the absolute beauty. For Plato, however, this is no more than a psychologically helpful suggestion as to the way of ascent from the lower world to the higher. It does not in the slightest degree diminish the opposition between the two worlds. The stages through which the soul has to pass, the ladder up which it climbs, do not represent objective realities which connect the sense-world with the Ideal world and make of the two one continuous universe. There is no such connection between the two worlds; Plato is thoroughgoing in his dualism. In Aristotle, however, the cosmic development can be observed again here. The ladder-symbolism, which is used in Plato to illustrate the ascent of the individual soul, appears in Aristotle as a real *Stufenleiter der Dinge*. The whole of existence becomes a continuous *Stufenkosmos*, in which the lower everywhere strives upwards towards the higher and the whole process of movement converges towards the Divine, which exercises its attraction on the lower while remaining itself unmoved. Everything in existence displays this upward tendency; there is in everything an ineradicable longing for likeness to God. The whole universe bears the marks of Eros, the lower reach-

---

[1] *Cf.* Wilamowitz-Moellendorff, *Platon*, vol. i., 1919, p. 420, n. 1.
[2] W. Windelband, *Lehrbuch der Geschichte der Philosophie*, 9th and 10th edns., ed. E. Rothacker, 1921, p. 122.   [3] pp. 174, 179.

ing out after the higher and striving to become like it. This striving manifests itself from sphere to sphere, " in the stars as a striving after likeness to God; in the sun as a striving after likeness to the stars; in nature, with its everlasting growth and decay, as a striving to become like the sun ".[1]

Aristotle's doctrine of motion and his metaphysics are thus based on the idea of God; but—be it noted—a characteristically Greek idea of God. The Deity is the absolutely Unmoved, which exercises its influence on the world " not through any movement or activity of its own, but through the world's longing for the Divine: the world and all that happens in it arises from the longing of matter for God ".[2]

Finally, we may refer to Aristotle's famous doctrine of friendship in the eighth and ninth books of the *Nicomachean Ethics*. The importance of this doctrine in the history of the Christian idea of love is chiefly that it provides the basis of the scholastic distinction between *amor concupiscentiæ* and *amor amicitiæ*, the love of desire and the love of friendship.[3] But it must be observed that even the latter, the nobler form of love, is built in the last resort, according to Aristotle, on self-love.[4]

3. THE EROS MOTIF IN NEOPLATONISM

1. *Plato and Plotinus. " The Alexandrian world-scheme"*. Between Plato and Plotinus there is an interval of more than

---

[1] H. Scholz, *op. cit.*, pp. 42 f. Hence Scholz can sum up by speaking of " the grand threefold pull, exerted upon ever-growing, ever-decaying nature by the gravitational field of the sun, upon the sun by the gravitational field of the starry heavens, and finally upon the starry heavens by the gravitational field of the Deity " (*op. cit.*, p. 40).

[2] W. Windelband, *op. cit.*, p. 122. *Cf.* E. Rolfes, *Die Philosophie des Aristoteles als Naturerklärung und Weltanschauung*, 1923, pp. 368 ff.—though Aristotle is here, as generally in Rolfes, interpreted in the light of Thomistic philosophy.

[3] M. Wittmann, *Die Ethik des Aristoteles*, 1920, p. 233, treats Plato and Aristotle as representing two different conceptions of love: " Whereas Plato has in view a love of *longing* or *desire*, Aristotle thinks of a love of *benevolence.*"

[4] M. Makarewicz, *Die Grundprobleme der Ethik bei Aristoteles*, 1914, pp. 189-206.

five hundred years. During this time the spiritual climate underwent a complete transformation, of which the outstanding feature is a powerful movement of interest towards religion. In late antiquity, philosophy was not thought of as primarily a scientific discipline but as a practical religious affair. What men asked of it was less a theoretical discussion of the problems of objective existence than a basis and support for the inner life, and finally a way to the Divine and blessed life. The importance of this development for the Eros motif is obvious. It means that this motif, which originated in Mystery-piety with its longing for salvation, but which in course of time had been partially secularised, now returned to its source. That the doctrine of Eros is a doctrine of salvation and intimately connected with Mystery-piety is still pretty evident in Plato, but in Aristotle its religious associations are much less apparent; in Plotinus, on the other hand, the religious interest is uppermost and dominates his entire thought.

In all his thinking Plotinus moves within the sphere of that religious and cultural syncretism which is typical of the centuries around the beginning of our era. Perhaps the best description we could give of Neoplatonism would be to call it a *synthesis of Platonism and the Mystery-piety of late antiquity*. This, however, means that the Eros motif takes an even more central place than before. In Plato and Aristotle, it is true, we can trace back a great variety of trains of thought to the Eros motif as their foundation; but in Plotinus there is no need for any tracing back, since the Eros motif is in fact the whole content of his thinking. From the manifoldness of things Plotinus withdraws to the one thing needful, the return of the soul to God. In comparison with this major theme all else is for him of but secondary importance.

The centuries that lie between Plato and Plotinus are also in another respect important for the development of the idea of Eros, for during this period the conception of the universe underwent a far-reaching structural alteration. F. Heinemann, in his work on Plotinus, strongly urges the importance of this new cosmology, which he names " the Alexandrian world-scheme ".[1] Its main features are a sharp dualism between God and matter, and an attempt to establish communication between them by the introduction of a sufficient number of intermediate beings. This communication is conceived as proceeding in both directions: as a *descent* from God to matter, which accounts for the creation of the world, and as an *ascent* of man back to God, which is equivalent to man's salvation.

Certainly the " Alexandrian world-scheme " does not lack points of contact with Plato. Its background is the Platonic doctrine of the Two Worlds; and the more sharply the dualism of this doctrine is conceived the more the need for mediation between the Two Worlds is felt. The more the transcendence of the Ideal world (or the world of the Divine) over the sense-world (or matter) is emphasised, the more necessary it becomes to introduce intermediaries unless all possibility of ascending from the lower world to the higher is to disappear. In Plato himself Eros is just such an intermediary (μεταξύ). In Aristotle also there are significant developments in the direction of the Alexandrian world-scheme, notably in his *Stufenleiter der Dinge*.[2] Yet this " world-scheme " contains one element that is quite foreign to genuine Platonism

---

[1] F. Heinemann, *Plotin, Forschungen über die plotinische Frage, Plotins Entwicklung und sein System*, 1921, pp. 6 ff., 243 ff. For other expositions of Plotinus and Neoplatonism see M. Wundt, *Plotin,* 1919; G. Mehlis, *Plotin,* 1924; A. Drews, *Plotin und der Untergang der antiken Weltanschauung,* 1907; W. R. Inge, *The Philosophy of Plotinus,* 1918. On Plotinus' attitude to the Mystery-religions and Christianity, see Picavet, *Plotin et les mystères d'Eleusis,* 1903; Cocez, *Plotin et les mystères d'Isis,* 1903; C. Schmidt, *Plotins Stellung zum Gnostizismus und kirchlichen Christentum,* 1901 (*Texte und Untersuchungen zur Geschichte der altchristlichen Literatur,* ed. O. v. Gebhardt and A. v. Harnack); H. Leisegang, *Der Heilige Geist,* 1919.

[2] E. Hoffman, *op. cit.,* p. 70: " It [the motif of the Scale] can be traced

and Aristotelianism—namely, the descending movement in the cosmos, or the idea of emanation. Plato's emphasis lies on the ascent of the soul to the world of Ideas; how it happened that a Divine soul ever came down to earth and became imprisoned in a body is a question of merely secondary interest for him, and at most it receives only mythological treatment. But for Plotinus, as for the Alexandrians generally, this is a question of primary importance. In their view, the ascent presupposes the descent and is conditioned by it; for the stages exhibited by the cosmological process (the Descent) must be reproduced, though in the reverse order, by the human soul on its return to God (the Ascent). For Plotinus, therefore, the whole world-process is summed up in the double conception of the out-going of all things from the One, the Divine, and the return of all things to the One.[1]

2. *The Descent and the Ascent.* In Plotinus, the idea of Eros is set within the cosmological framework we have just described, with interesting results. When Plotinus treats of the Ascent of the soul to the Divine he can in large measure follow Plato; but the Descent is his own special problem. How is it that the soul, whose nature is heavenly and Divine, has ever come to find itself down in the alien and unnatural environment of the world of sense? "Often", he writes, "when I awake to myself from the sleep of bodily life, and pass out from the external world and come home to myself,

---

back from Plotinus, through the Jewish-Alexandrian doctrine of emanations and the Stoic *syndesmos*, directly to Aristotle and his mounting climax of spheres and elements, forms and ends, up to the Prime Mover of the heaven of fixed stars. Just here is the great difference between the Stagirite and Plato. It is Aristotle who first makes the μέσα into the rungs of a ladder; in Plato they are never more than symbols of the one and only *metaxy*."

[1] This is also the scheme of thought that dominates all attempts to give a systematic account of the Christian Faith well on into the Middle Ages. The persistence of the "Alexandrian world-scheme", and the strength of its hold on Christian thought, are sufficiently indicated by the fact that the entire *Summa Theologica* of Thomas Aquinas is constructed with its aid.

I behold a wondrous beauty, and believe fully and firmly that I belong indeed to a higher world. Then I feel in myself a most glorious life, and I become one with the Divine. . . . And when after this repose in the Divine I descend from reason's contemplation to discursive thought, then I ask myself how it comes to pass that I am now descending, and how it was that my soul ever entered into this body, the soul which, even though it is in the body, is nevertheless the exalted being which it has shown itself essentially to be."[1] Plotinus finds the answer to this question in the thought of the emanation of all things from the Divine " One ". Just as light, without ceasing to be light, sends out its beams till they lose themselves in the darkness, so the whole of existence streams out from the One in a continually descending scale, without the One ever " passing out from itself ".[2] Every new stage in the series illuminates the stage below with the light it has received from the stage next above. "The more the soul becomes absorbed in contemplation, the more beautiful and the stronger it becomes, and what it draws from its vision, it communicates to the beings next below; thus, as it is constantly illuminated, so it constantly illuminates."[3] This is especially true of the world-soul and its creative activity. That which the world-soul has beheld of the things above, in the intelligible world, it seeks to reproduce in the empirical world. But in this process of receiving from the higher and caring for the lower, there is so far nothing degrading or defiling; it is the soul's normal condition, so to speak, and the soul is quite at liberty to mount up again from what it has created to the archetype after which it has created it.[4]

---

[1] *Enneads*, IV., 8, 1.   [2] V., 3, 12; VI., 5, 3.   *Cf.* also the whole of VI., 4 and 5.   [3] II., 9, 2; II., 3, 17.

[4] II., 9, 4: " The creative cause we take to be not a descending but rather a not-descending." *Cf.* III., 2, 7; IV., 8, 7: " Since there now exists a double nature, the intelligible and the sensible, it is assuredly better for the soul to remain in the intelligible; but it is compelled to have part also in the sensible, since it now has such a nature; and it must not be dissatisfied that it is not in every respect the most perfect being, but occupies

Abnormality occurs only when the individual soul severs
its connection with the world-soul, forgets its Divine origin,
and seeks satisfaction in the world of sense.[1]

When the descending movement has reached its extreme
limit in the world of matter, it turns round into the ascending
movement. Matter is like a mirror, in that it shows us not
reality, but empty and deceptive shadow-images; but it is also
like a mirror in that it reflects the rays from the One that fall
upon it.[2] That is what makes it the turning-point in the
world-process. When the soul allows itself to be caught in
the toils of sense, this is due partly to an over-valuing of
sensible things, as though these had a real existence of their

---

an intermediate station. It is certainly of divine character, yet it is last
among the intelligibles, so that it borders on the sensible nature; and while
it imparts to this realm something of its own nature, it also receives
something from it whenever it fails to hold fast to its unity with the world-
soul and plunges down into the midst of the subordinate object. It has,
however, the capacity for rising up again. . . . But just as in the sphere
of reason the outgoing is a descent to that which is as far below reason
as reason can go (for it belongs not to its nature to ascend to that which
stands above it, but when it acts out from itself and cannot remain in
itself, it must according to a compelling law of nature go to the soul,
which is its end and its limit, and hand over the following stage to the
soul, in order that it may itself ascend again), so it is likewise with the
activity of the soul : here below its activity is directed to that which comes
after it, but the beholding of true being is directed towards that which
lies in front of the soul." Only individual souls can sink down into
matter, not the world-soul. For the world-soul " both things are possible,
to receive from the other world and to give to this world, since as a soul
it must, of course, concern itself with this world " (*ibid.*).

When we are comparing the Eros motif and the Agape motif, it should
be borne in mind that the idea of " receiving from the other world and
giving to this world " can occur also in the context of the Eros motif.

[1] V., I, I : " What can it be that has brought the souls to forget God,
their Father, and though parts of the Divine and wholly belonging to It,
to lose their knowledge both of themselves and of Him ? The source of
this evil in them was their reckless temerity, their birth into the world of
sense, the first difference and the desire to belong to themselves. Since
they manifestly delighted in their self-glory, in that they often indulged
their own motion, they set off on the wrong path, and went very far
astray, and lost the knowledge of their divine origin, like children who
have been early separated from their father and nurtured for a long time
in a far country, so that they know neither themselves nor their father."

[2] III., 6, 7; *cf.* also III., 8.

own, and partly to an under-valuing of the soul's own worth. Therefore, if the sense-bound soul is to participate in the cosmic turning-process by which the Descent turns into an Ascent, it must learn two things: it must come to see the worthlessness of the things which it now values so highly, and it must recall to mind its own high, Divine origin and value.[1]   Here Plotinus reaches the point where he can take up the Platonic Eros-tradition with its teaching about the soul's ascent from the beauty of sense to Absolute Beauty.[2] Certainly the sense-world is beautiful—Plotinus never tires of insisting on this against the Gnostics and the world-despisers[3]—but its beauty is only that of a copy, an image, and he who pursues it pursues a phantom.   The real object of his pursuit is, of course, beauty; but beauty is found in this world only in so far as this world participates in and reflects something of the higher world.   Hence the beauty of the sense-world is a challenge to pursue the Primal Beauty; for it is this that the soul, consciously or unconsciously, most deeply desires.[4]

When the soul has been set in motion by Eros towards the beautiful, it has turned in the direction of the Ascent, and its task is now to mount up to ever higher forms of beauty.   It must now pass in reverse order through the stages which were passed in the Descent.   Bodily things derive their beauty from the soul, the soul from reason, and reason from the One, the Divine; these four, therefore, mark the stages of the up-

[1] V., 1, 1; cf. V., 1, 3.

[2] The chief passage for this is *Ennead* I., 6, which is entitled " Concerning the Beautiful."

[3] Especially in the voluminous 9th book of the 2nd *Ennead*, " Against the Gnostics and those who say that the Demiurge is evil and the world is bad."

[4] VI., 7, 31 : " The soul that has Eros living and present in it needs not the reminder that is given by beautiful things here below; possessing Eros, even if it knows not that it possesses Eros, it is ever in quest; in its longing to attain to the heavenly, it despises the earthly, and when it perceives earthly beauty it is suspicious because it sees a thing clad in flesh and matter . . . not the real Beauty itself."

ward way. " We must ascend again ", says Plotinus, " to the
Good, for which every soul longs. . . . We reach it when
we climb up to the higher world, turn altogether to it, and
divest ourselves of all that we have put on in our descent;
just as they who go to celebrate the holy initiation of the
Mysteries must put off the clothes they were wearing and
go forward naked. We must proceed by this way, till in the
ascent we have left behind us all that is other than God, and
each with himself alone beholds Him alone, the Divine, un-
defiled, simple, pure, that on which all things depend, towards which all things look, in which all have their being,
life and thought, the Ground of all life and reason and existence. What a glow of love shall he not feel who beholds
this! What a burning desire for most intimate union with
it! With what awe and gladness shall he not be thrilled!
For even those who have not yet seen it long for the Divine
as their true Good " (I., 6, 7).

But to the highest height, to perfect union with God, we
cannot attain by dialectic or any discursive thinking, but only
by ecstasy, in which the beholder becomes one with that
which he beholds. " Then shall we see Him and see ourselves: ourselves wrought to splendour, brimmed with Intellectual light . . . *having become, or rather being, God* "
(VI., 9, 9). Only then shall we have reached the goal, when
the copy has returned and been taken up into the Original.
Then the soul has found rest, for it has found the ultimate
object of its longing and desire. For it was this that it really
desired, even when, driven by an earthly and mortal
Eros, it was pursuing transient, temporal advantages (VI., 9,
10).

The possibility of the soul's ascent to the Deity, however,
rests ultimately on the assumption familiar from Orphism
centuries before: that the soul is a Divine being which, contrary to its nature, has been dragged down and imprisoned
in matter. Plotinus is much concerned to maintain that the

soul is by nature essentially good; evil becomes attached to it from outside, through its entanglement with matter.[1] It is the essential kinship of the soul with God that makes its salvation possible. "For the eye could never have seen the sun, if it were not like to the sun in nature; and the soul could never behold the beautiful, if it were not beautiful itself. Let everyone, therefore, first become beautiful and god-like, if he would behold the beautiful and good."[2]

3. *The idea of Eros in Plotinus compared with Plato's Eros and Christian Agape.* The main theme of Plotinus' thought could hardly be better summarised than in the brief formula which he himself borrows from Heracleitus: ὁδός τε κάτω καὶ ἄνω, the downward and the upward way (IV., 8, 1). The doctrine of Eros stands in the centre, dominating both those ways. But it is the upward way in which Plotinus is chiefly interested, for he has ultimately only one thing at heart—namely, the return of the fallen souls to their Divine origin. The story related by Porphyry about his last words on his death-bed is illuminating; to his friend Eustochius, who did not arrive till just before the end, Plotinus said, " I was waiting for you, that you might help to bring the Divine in me to the Divine in the All."[3]   In the account he gives of the

---

[1] On the nobility, divine nature, and pre-existence of the soul, see *Ennead* I., 6, 5 f.; IV., 2, 1; V., 1, 1 ff.; VI., 4, 14; *et al.* For its entanglement with matter as the cause of evil, see I., 8, 4; and *cf.* F. Heinemann, *op. cit.*, pp. 83 ff.

[2] I., 6, 9. On the " eye like to the sun in nature ", *cf.* J. Lindblom, *Det solliknande ögat. En religionshistorisk skiss till ett litterärt motiv. (Svensk teologisk kvartalskrift*, 1927, pp. 230-247.)

The widespread notion of a " beautiful soul ", and the idea that it is our business to cultivate our own soul and fashion it into a work of art, finds one of its earliest expressions in Plotinus: "How canst thou see what beauty a soul has? Enter into thyself and look. And if thou findest thyself not beautiful yet, then do as a sculptor does with a statue which is to be made beautiful : he cuts away here, he smooths there, here he polishes, there he cleans, until he has caused a lovely face to appear upon his statue. So do thou also : cut away all that is excessive, straighten all that is crooked, purge away all that is dark and make it bright, and cease not to work on thine own image until the divine splendour of virtue shines forth in thee "
(I., 6, 9).   [3] Porphyry, *De vita Plotini, 2.*

upward way, Plotinus is in the main dependent on Plato;[1] but in working out his theory of the downward way he had to depend chiefly on himself.

The question now arises, What is the importance of this added feature for the Platonic Eros motif? Is it a logical development of that motif, or does it involve a radical alteration of its structure? We are not here concerned with minor modifications of the Platonic *ordo salutis* resulting simply from the fact that the Ascent has to pass (in reverse order) through the same stages as the Descent. The question is far wider than that. It is a question as to whether any thought whatsoever of a " downward way " can be associated with the Eros motif without a risk of destroying that motif. Eros is, after all, the way of ascent, the longing of man for the Divine life; how, then, can it be combined with something directly contrary to it? We might even be tempted to go a step further and say: it is Agape that is the way of descent, for Agape means that God comes down to lost and sinful men. And if we ignore the difference it makes that the downward way of Christian Agape leads from God to sinful man, while the Plotinian way of descent leads from the Divine to matter, is there not, after all, a definite similarity of structure between them? Plotinus, too, can say that " the higher cares for the lower and adorns it " (IV., 8, 8). Have we not here, then, something like a compromise between the Eros motif and the Agape motif, when the upward tendency

---

[1] Plotinus' treatment of the Eros motif consists largely of paraphrases of Plato, as in I., 6; IV., 7, 10; V., 8, 10; V., 9, 1 f.; VI., 7, 31. We have no occasion to linger over this point, any more than over Plotinus' attempt to allegorise the Myth of Eros, into which he introduces a multitude of good and evil " Erotes ", and so forth (see esp. III., 5). On this, Zeller rightly says: "However great the affection with which our philosopher develops these expositions, and however much his successors may have admired and imitated him in them, the philosophical value of this fanciful interpretation of myths is, even from the point of view of Plotinus' own system, very small " (*Die Philosophie der Griechen*, 5th edn., 1862, vol. iii., p. 601).

of Eros is adapted to the Alexandrian world-scheme and combined with the idea of a Descent of the Divine?

There can be no doubt that by adopting the Alexandrian world-scheme Plotinus departs from Plato. In genuinely Platonic theory there can in principle be only one direction of movement: that from below upwards. The Ideas of Plato are not real forces, and they cannot either directly or indirectly intervene in the lower world. The sharp cleft between the two worlds is a matter of major importance for Plato.[1] The concern for continuity that underlies Plotinus' interest in the " downward way " is more akin to Aristotle's *Stufenkosmos* than to Plato's sharp dualism; and when Plotinus speaks of an eternal union between the world of reason and the world of sense (IV., 8, 6) he is without question un-Platonic. Nevertheless, it would be completely wrong to suppose that the " downward way " of Plotinus bears any real resemblance to the condescending Agape of Christianity; the two have nothing to do with each other. For, in the first place, Plotinus is here thinking of a cosmological process, explaining how the lower world has come into being out of the One; he is not thinking of salvation. Where salvation is concerned, he speaks exclusively of the upward way. Fellowship with God is not brought about by God's coming down in His love to man, but by man's climbing up in Eros to God. Furthermore, in spite of all he says of the downward way, there is in Plotinus no real descent of the Divine. The Divine One remains ever in its transcendence; and the same is true of reason and the world-soul and those individual souls that maintain their connection with the world-soul, for " they do not descend from their royal throne " (IV., 8, 4). When the higher cares for the lower and " sets it in order and adorns it ", it does so from its heavenly height ($\mu\epsilon\tau\epsilon\omega\rho\sigma\pi\sigma\rho\epsilon\hat{\iota}\nu$), without becoming in any way subject to the conditions under which the lower exists; it remains completely inert, exercising

[1] *Cf.* pp. 169 f. above.

its influence only by " passive rule " (ἀπράγμονι ἐπιστασίᾳ, IV., 8, 2). It is fundamental to Plotinus' thought of God that the Divine is self-sufficient and never issues forth from its sublime repose (VI., 7, 41; V., 1, 6). Any suggestion of a spontaneous coming down is out of the question here. In harmony with this—lastly—there is the fact that the Descent, in so far as it is a reality, means *not an act of Divine condescension, but the Fall of the soul into sin and guilt.* Anyone who descends to a lower level always does so involuntarily, according to Plotinus; and that is a proof of weakness and of an inability to maintain the higher position. It is consequently unthinkable that the Divine Being should ever really descend (IV., 8, 5).

Clearly, then, the " downward way " of Plotinus and the condescending Agape of Christianity have nothing whatsoever in common. Zeller aptly expresses the contrast between Christianity and Plotinus thus : " The former tells of a descent of the Godhead into the lowest depths of human weakness; the latter calls for an elevation of man to superhuman Divinity."[1] Here we have the unmistakable contrast between Agape and Eros.

4. *God is Eros.* The same conclusion will be reached if we consider finally the remarkable passage in which it is said of the Divine One : " He is worthy to be loved, and is Himself love, namely, love of Himself, as He is beautiful only from Himself and in Himself."[2] Here God is explicitly described as Eros, and a comparison at once suggests itself with the Johannine " God is Agape ". Plotinus can say " God is Eros " (ἔρως ὁ αὐτός). Yet whereas the Johannine formula can truly be said to be the final consequence and the highest expression of the New Testament Agape motif, it can certainly not be said of the Plotinian " God is Eros " that it is the consequence

---

[1] E. Zeller, *op. cit.*, p. 444.
[2] VI., 8, 15; καὶ ἐράσμιον καὶ ἔρως ὁ αὐτὸς καὶ αὐτοῦ ἔρως, ἅτε οὐκ ἄλλως καλὸς ἢ παρ᾽ αὐτοῦ καὶ ἐν αὐτῷ.

and the highest expression of the Platonic Eros motif. The idea that the Divine is ἐράσμιον, that it is above all else "*worthy* to be loved", is undoubtedly in harmony with the Platonic view. As the Highest Good and the sum of all that can be desired and longed for, the Divine draws to itself all longing and love; for it, and it alone, in the last resort, can claim to be the ultimate object of all Eros whatsoever. But just for this reason there can be no question in Plato of an identification of Eros with the Divine. God is not Eros and Eros is not God. The Divine life is the blessed life, in which is complete satisfaction because there is no want or need; hence no thought of longing and desire, no thought of Eros, can be associated with it. Eros is a demigod (a " dæmon "), which conducts us on our ascent to the Divine. It presupposes the wants and needs of human existence. Where these are not to be found, as in the fully satisfied and self-sufficient Divine life, it is meaningless to speak of Eros.

On the face of it, Plotinus' statement that God is Eros seems to mean a complete abandonment of the Platonic idea of Eros.[1] Yet it only seems to be so. Plotinus gets out of the difficulty by means of a metaphysical construction of the kind employed when God is spoken of as His own Cause. As standing at the head of the causal series, God does not stand within it; the scheme of causality is not applicable to God. But the fact that we cannot look for a cause of God's existence outside Himself is expressed by saying that He is His own Cause. The category of cause is thus at once maintained and set aside; and by means of this metaphysical finesse it is made to appear that God can be fitted into the scheme of causality without infringement of His position as First Cause.

[1] In view of the difficulties involved in the idea, it is tempting to see in Plotinus' statement an attempt to counter the Christian formula, " God is Agape "—the more so, since his contemporary, Origen, who like Plotinus reckoned himself a disciple of Ammonius Saccas, in his Preface to his *Commentary on the Song of Songs*, actually puts Agape and Eros side by side, and maintains that we can say with equal right : " God is Eros " and " God is Agape ".

It is in this kind of way that Plotinus deals with the question of Eros. God, as the Highest Good, is the ultimate goal of all longing and striving; but He Himself cannot strive or long for anything, since He has in Himself everything that can possibly be desired. Beyond God there is no further end that could be sought; hence the Eros-scheme is not applicable to God. As the ultimate goal of all Eros, He cannot be Himself caught up in the movement of Eros. This fact, that there is nothing outside God which could be the aim of His striving and Eros, Plotinus expresses by saying that God is certainly Eros, but *Eros to Himself*. In this way he succeeds in applying the Eros-scheme to God, without infringement either of His position as ultimate end, or of His absolute *eudæmonia*, self-sufficiency and autarchy. God is at once the ultimate source and the ultimate goal of all things. He is *causa sui* and αὐτοῦ ἔρως.

Here we have the clearest demonstration of the difference between Eros and Agape. Eros is not really applicable to God, yet it is applied to Him; and when it is so applied, its acquisitive and egocentric character so far asserts itself that it can only mean a love which is entirely taken up with itself and the enjoyment of its own perfection. The contrast between this and the idea of Agape can be expressed most simply as follows: the assertion that " God is Eros " has no meaning unless Eros is understood as αὐτοῦ ἔρως, self-love; but to speak of God's Agape as self-love, as an ἀγάπη directed to itself, would be sheer nonsense.[1]

[1] It is true that, as we have seen, the Fourth Gospel represents the love of the Father as directed to the Son, and since the Son is true God, this Agape is a love of God directed to God. But since the Son is distinct from the Father, Agape is here, as always, self-giving love.—*Hebert's note.*

CHAPTER THREE

THE FUNDAMENTAL CONTRAST BETWEEN AGAPE AND EROS

I

THE TRANSVALUATION OF ALL ANCIENT VALUES

1. THE GENERAL SIGNIFICANCE OF THE TRANSVALUATION

IN seeking to express the relation between Christianity and the ancient world, Nietzsche coined the well-known formula that Christianity meant a "transvaluation of all ancient values". This formula contains a great deal more truth than is generally recognised. It is also capable of a far wider application than its author had in mind. It holds good, not only with respect to Classical antiquity, but also with respect to Judaism and, indeed, the entire pre-Christian and non-Christian world. The "transvaluation" is seen, above all, in the central Christian motif, the Agape motif. Agape is like a blow in the face to both Jewish legal piety and Hellenistic Eros-piety.

From the point of view of Jewish legal piety, it is self-evident that God loves the righteous and the godly, and that He does not love the unrighteous and the sinner. That is a simple corollary of the conception of fellowship with God as governed by the Law. But Jesus declares: "I came not to call the righteous, but sinners" (Mark ii. 17); and the reason for this lies in God's Agape, for by its very nature Agape means the forgiveness of sins. Agape shatters completely the legal conception of the relationship between God and man. That is the reason for the conflict of Jesus with the Pharisees and Paul's campaign against "the Law". Agape is the opposite of "Nomos", and therefore a denial of the foundation on which the entire Jewish scale of values rested.

But the idea of Agape is no less opposed to the ancient Græco-Hellenistic scale of values, of which the hall-mark is Eros. For the Greeks it is self-evident that the gods do *not love*. Why should they, when they possess all that they can wish? Having no lack of anything, no unsatisfied desire, they have no need to love; that is, they have no need to desire anything, to seek longingly to acquire anything. Against this, Christianity confesses its fundamental faith that "God is love". This love, however, has nothing to do with acquisitive desire, but is characterised by sacrifice and self-giving; for it is Agape. The question, "Why should God love?" has no meaning in a Christian context. God does not love in order to obtain any advantage thereby, but quite simply because it is His nature to love—with a love that seeks, not to get, but to give. This means, in other words, that no teleological explanation or motivation of His love can be entertained.

It is plain that Greek thought has no place for fellowship with God in the strict sense of that term. The gods live their blessed, immortal life high above the transience and change of human existence. "A god holds no intercourse with a man", says Plato (*Symposium* 203). But in Christianity, Agape means precisely fellowship between God and man instituted by God. No doubt the Greek philosophers can speak at times, in harmony with popular religious ideas, of the love of the gods for men; yet even then the contrast between ancient thought and Christianity is not lessened. We have only to ask *who* it is that is loved by the deity, and the difference at once becomes clear. Aristotle's answer to this question is as follows: "He who lives according to reason will be the special object of the deity's love. For if the gods have any care for human affairs, as men think they have, we must surely assume that they take delight in the best and that which is most akin to them—which is our reason—and that they reward those who most love and honour this. ... But it is plain that these things are to be found supremely in the wise man. Hence he is most loved by the deity."[1] Obviously the love in question here is diametrically opposed to Christian Agape. According to Aristotle, it is only reasonable to assume that God most loves the wise man; but according to Paul, the love and election of God are the direct opposite of what we might reasonably assume. " God ", he says, " chose the foolish things of the world, that He might put to shame them that are wise; and God chose the weak things of the world, that He might put to shame the things that are strong; and the base things of the world, and the things that are despised, did God choose, yea and the things that are not, that He might bring to nought the things that are " (1 Cor. i. 27 f.).

Nietzsche is therefore undoubtedly right in speaking of Christianity as a transvaluation of all ancient values; and not only so, but also as regards the meaning and content of this transvaluation he puts his finger on the decisive point. His words are important enough to be quoted as they stand. " Modern men," he says, " hardened as they are to all Christian terminology, no longer appreciate the horrible extravagance which, for ancient taste, lay in the paradox of the formula, ' God on the Cross '. Never before had there been anywhere such an audacious inversion, never anything so terrifying, so challenging and challengeable, as this formula; it promised a transvaluation of all ancient values."[2]

[1] *Eth. Nic.*, X., viii., 9. *Cf.* H. Meyer, *Platon und die aristotelische Ethik*, 1919, pp. 187 f.

[2] *Jenseits von Gut und Böse*, Drittes Hauptstück, 46. Nietzsche can well be described as the modern exponent of Paul's statement in 1 Cor. i. 23. His worship of antiquity opened his eyes to the immense and fundamental difference between antiquity and Christianity, a difference which in the interests of apologetics there has all too often been a readiness to obscure.

Nietzsche was not the first to discover that Christianity with its "God on the Cross" means the transvaluation of all ancient values. That was realised in the earliest days of Christianity, among both its friends and its foes. "God on the Cross"—it was in this that Paul, too, saw the great transvaluation introduced by Christianity. "We preach Christ crucified," he says, "unto Jews a stumbling-block, and unto Gentiles foolishness" (1 Cor. i. 23). But "God on the Cross" is only another name for the Agape of the Cross. To the Jews it was bound to be a *skandalon*, not merely because of the difficulty they had in conceiving a crucified Messiah, but also, and above all, because the Agape of the Cross rules out the entire scheme of values on which their conception of the religious relationship was based. And to the Græco-Hellenistic mind no less, the preaching of Christ crucified and the Agape of the Cross was bound to seem foolishness. Both ethically and religiously Agape is hopelessly in conflict with the mental outlook of antiquity. From an ethical point of view, it cannot but appear as sheer unrighteousness. It conflicts with the ideal of the wise man and the notion of upward endeavour. It runs directly counter to the idea of Eros and man's ascent to the sphere of the Divine. It seems to put a premium on sin; it looks very like ethical laxity, and lenience towards those to whom no lenience should be shown. Hence, as the ancients see it, it is defective also from a religious point of view. It is, indeed, a blasphemy against God; for it represents Him as worse than human judges, who do after all take pains to secure objectivity and truth. Agape cannot but seem sheer godlessness, for it contradicts everything that is characteristic of the ancient conception of God. It conflicts with the Divine immutability, incorruptibility and eternality; for how can the Immutable descend and subject Himself to the changes and chances of human life? And it conflicts with God's *eudæmonia*, His beauty, happiness and blessedness; for what could induce Him who knows no unsatisfied desire, to leave His blessedness and self-sufficiency and go to such a length of self-emptying as to endure the death of the Cross? Such in brief is the kind of criticism which in the second century was directed against the Christian idea of Agape by a Platonist like Celsus.[1]

Putting it in terms that are often used—and misused—we might say that Agape gives expression to the paradoxical and irrational nature of Christianity. In saying this, however, it is important that we should make it clear that the idea of Agape is *not* paradoxical or irrational in the sense in which those terms are commonly used. There is in many quarters today an unhealthy cult of the paradoxical and irrational, almost as if the lack of clarity and consistency were sufficient evidence of religious or Christian truth. When we describe the idea of Agape as paradoxical and irrational, we do not for a moment suggest that it contains any logical contradiction or implies a *credo quia absurdum*. The idea of Agape is by no means self-contradictory. On the contrary, it is a quite simple and clear and easily comprehensible idea. It is

[1] For an impression of the way in which an ancient mind, in no way " hardened to all Christian terminology ", reacted to the idea of Agape, we cannot do better than turn to Celsus. " What great deeds ", he asks, " did Jesus perform as being a God? Did he put his enemies to shame, or bring to a ridiculous conclusion what was designed against him? . . : If not before, yet why not now, at least, does he not give some manifestation of his divinity, and free himself from this reproach, and take vengeance upon those who insult both him and his Father?" (Origen, *Contra Celsum*, II., 33 ff.). We have only to listen to questions like these to realise in a flash how completely contrary the ancient sense of values is to the Agape of Christianity. *Cf.* K. Holl, *Urchristentum und Religionsgeschichte*, 1925, pp. 19 f. : " Celsus with his characteristic acuteness of vision has seen this point too in Christianity, and he never tires of pointing out to Christians the absurdity, the contemptibleness, the revoltingness of their conception of God. Every other religion has some regard for itself, and admits only respectable, cultivated, irreproachable people into its fellowship; but Christianity runs after the riffraff of the streets. As if it were positively a bad thing to have committed no sin, or as if God were a robber chief who gathered criminals around him! In this, Celsus was only expressing the objection that every Greek or Roman must have felt against Christianity. That ' the Deity has dealings only with the pure ', was for them a sacred, inviolable axiom."

paradoxical and irrational only inasmuch as it means a trans-valuation of all previously accepted values.

2. THE RELIGIOUS-HISTORICAL BACKGROUND OF THE TRANSVALUATION

In order to bring out the deepest meaning of the contrast between Agape and Eros, however, we must do more than simply show them to be two opposed ideas of love. Otherwise we may easily give the impression that nothing is involved but an opposition at one particular point, whereas in fact it is a universal, all-embracing opposition, touching every point. Here, therefore, we must take, if only very briefly, a wider survey.

Eros and Agape are the characteristic expressions of two different attitudes to life, two fundamentally opposed types of religion and ethics. They represent two streams that run through the whole history of religion, alternately clashing against one another and mingling with one another. They stand for what may be described as the egocentric and the theocentric attitude in religion.

In the egocentric type, the religious relationship is dominated essentially by man. The distance between man and the Divine is not insuperable. Man is akin to the Deity, or is maybe himself a Divine being, though at the moment he is confused and distracted by the things of sense that surround him. To come to himself, therefore, is to come to the Divine; and therein lies man's true end, his satisfaction and blessedness. Between the Divine and the human there is thus presupposed an unbroken continuity, and no matter how great the difference between them may be, it is but relative. Hence it is possible for man to mount up successively towards an ever-increasing likeness to God, and to draw step by step nearer the Divine.

In the theocentric type, on the other hand, everything

centres in God. Between God and man there is an absolute
distinction, a border-line that can never be crossed from man's
side. Any thought of man's raising himself up to the Divine
life is felt to be sheer titanic pride, which, so far from bringing man into a right relation to God, represents the highest
degree of godlessness. The gulf that is fixed between God
and man is absolute, so that man has no possibility of working his way up to the Divine level. Only God Himself can
bridge the gulf. Man cannot by means of Eros attain to God.
Real fellowship with God is possible only if God in his
Agape condescends to man.

It is the egocentric type that has generally predominated in
the history of religion. From primitive beginnings it rises to
the spiritual heights of Mysticism. It makes it its aim to
awaken in man a longing and questing for the eternal; it
seeks to induce him to turn from this transitory and corruptible life and mount up on the wings of the soul to the higher
world from which the soul originates. A high-water mark
of this development is reached in Platonism, which has not
only a philosophical but also a thoroughly religious aspect.
Religiously, the great gift of Platonism to the world is its
passionate love and longing for the super-sensible, the self-
subsistent, the Divine.

The opposite, theocentric, tendency has never been wholly
lacking, though it has remained more in the background.[1]
Not until Christianity appears does it break decisively through
and claim complete supremacy. It is in its theocentric character that we see the deepest reason why Christianity necessarily involves a transvaluation of all ancient values.

Religion is fellowship with God. But two different conceptions are possible of the way in which this fellowship is
brought about. It can either be thought of as achieved by the

---

[1] It appears in the Old Testament, of course, but it is present in other
religions as well. *Cf.* A. Nygren, *Det bestående i kristendomen*, 1922, pp.
38 f., and *Försoningen, en Guds gärning*, 1932, p. 19.—*Translator's note.*

raising up of the human to the Divine—and that is the contention of egocentric religion, of Eros; or else it is held to be established by the gracious condescension of the Divine to man—and that is the contention of theocentric religion, of Agape.

II

TABULATION OF THE ESSENTIAL POINTS OF CONTRAST

WE have seen the contrast between Eros and Agape widen out into a fundamental opposition between two whole attitudes to life. With this we have reached the point which has all along been the main purpose of our study. We stated already in the Introduction that we were not, strictly speaking, concerned with a comparison of two isolated historical phenomena.[1] Such a comparison would easily lead to all kinds of arbitrariness. Indeed, it is questionable whether there would be any possibility of comparison; for Eros and Agape grew up in such different circumstances that they are bound to appear incommensurable when set over against one another in their simple historical form. In this connection we may recall the saying of Wilamowitz-Moellendorff about Plato and Paul, that " they could have learnt something from one another here, but, being what they were, they would not have done so."[2] What reason is there, then, for taking Plato as the starting-point for a discussion of Paul's outlook, or Paul for a discussion of Plato's? In the present instance, however, as has been said, we are not concerned simply with two such historical individuals and their views, but with two fundamentally different attitudes which set their mark on the whole of life. We are concerned with two competing fundamental motifs, two contrary ideals, or conceptions of what life means. This entirely alters the situation, and pro-

[1] See above, pp. 34 ff.   [2] *Platon, I.*, 1919, p. 384.

vides much more favourable conditions for the purposes of comparison and contrast.

For a comparison to be possible, the objects to be compared must, of course, have something in common as well as their points of difference; and this appears to revive our difficulty. For what could Eros and Agape have in common? There seems in fact to be no possibility of discovering any idea common to them both which might serve as a starting-point for the comparison; for at every point the opposition between them makes itself felt. It is, however, unnecessary to look for anything common to them in that sense. What is common in a case like this, where we are dealing with fundamental motifs, is the question to which they are answers. The common question furnishes a common denominator, so to speak, for the answers, despite all differences between them. Both Eros and Agape claim to give expression to man's relation to the Divine, and both exercise a formative influence on his ethical life. It is these ultimate, universal questions that concern us here. We can speak of Eros-religion and Agape-religion, of Eros-ethics and Agape-ethics; and it is the content of these general concepts that we have to try to determine.

One further observation must be made. When we are comparing and contrasting two general attitudes to life, it is easy to slip over from the consideration of facts to an appraisal of values. The terms that are used to describe the different attitudes to life are then taken as indicative of the value attached to them. For example, when we describe the contrast between Eros and Agape by saying that Eros is egocentric love, Agape unselfish love, or that Eros means self-assertion, Agape self-sacrifice, we readily associate the idea of unselfishness and self-sacrifice with that of something estimable, and the idea of self-assertion and egocentric conduct with that of something unestimable. It is owing to the transvaluation wrought by Christianity that this has come to seem natural and inevitable to us. To the men of antiquity, how-

ever, self-assertion and egocentric conduct were not less obviously estimable. We have thus two ultimate standards of
value confronting one another here, and it is our purpose
simply to describe them, not to act as judge between them.
In setting Agape and Eros side by side, *our aim is to bring
out a difference in type, not a difference in value.*

Bearing this in mind, we may now go on to ask what are
the characteristic features of the Eros-attitude and the Agape-
attitude respectively. The principal and ultimately decisive
contrast between them has already been clearly brought out
in the preceding pages. In order to sum up and conclude our
account of the two fundamental motifs and their contrary
tendencies, we append here a tabular survey. The various
particulars it contains have, of course, emerged here and there
in the course of our investigation, but now we are less concerned with these details as such, than with the antithetical
arrangement of them, which will enable us to see how the
difference in type is manifested throughout.

Eros is acquisitive desire and long-ing.	Agape is sacrificial giving.
Eros is an upward movement.	Agape comes down.
Eros is man's way to God.	Agape is God's way to man.
Eros is man's effort: it assumes that man's salvation is his own work.	Agape is God's grace: salvation is the work of Divine love.
Eros is egocentric love, a form of self-assertion of the highest, noblest, sublimest kind.	Agape is unselfish love, it " seeketh not its own ", it gives itself away.
Eros seeks to gain its life, a life divine, immortalised.	Agape lives the life of God, there-fore dares to "lose it."
Eros is the will to get and possess which depends on want and need.	Agape is freedom in giving, which depends on wealth and plenty.
Eros is primarily *man's* love; God is the *object* of Eros. Even when it is attributed to God, Eros is patterned on human love.	Agape is primarily *God's* love; God *is* Agape." Even when it is attri-buted to man, Agape is patterned on Divine love.
Eros is determined by the quality, the beauty and worth, of its object; it is not spontaneous, but " evoked ", " motivated ".	Agape is sovereign in relation to its object, and is directed to both " the evil and the good "; it is spontaneous, "overflowing", "un-motivated ".
Eros *recognises value* in its object—and loves it.	Agape loves—and *creates value in its* object.

III

THE CONTRAST AS IT APPEARS IN THE
DIFFERENT DIMENSIONS OF LOVE

LOVE expresses a relation between a subject who loves and an object that is loved. If we turn our attention to the object, and confine ourselves to personal objects, love will be seen to take four different forms, which we shall here describe as the " dimensions " of love. These are (1) God's love for man, (2) man's love for God, (3) man's love for his fellow-men, and (4) man's self-love. With regard to the last-named, we might well have doubts about describing it as a relation, since the loving subject and the loved object coincide. But as the thought of man's self-love has played a very prominent part in the history of the Christian idea of love, it is necessary to take account of it here.

In the earlier part of this chapter we have had opportunity to assure ourselves of the contrast in essential principle between the Eros motif and the Agape motif. We shall now have an excellent illustration of this contrast if we notice what a difference it makes to the meaning and content of these four forms of love when they are interpreted in terms of Eros and of Agape respectively. It is especially interesting to observe how the emphasis falls with a certain inevitability on directly opposite points in the two cases.

1. We will begin with the question of *God's love* and see how different it looks in the light of Eros and the light of Agape.

In the context of the Eros motif there is not much sense in speaking of God's love. It is, indeed, impossible to speak of it if we seriously bear in mind what " love " means in this context. Eros is the upward tendency; but there is no way upwards for God. Eros is yearning desire; but with God there is no want or need, and therefore no desire nor striving. God cannot ascend higher. Least of all is it possible that He should have any love for man, for that would imply a descent from His Divine perfection and blessedness to something inferior.

Where the religious relationship is marked by Agape, on the other hand, the tendency is all the other way. Here the thought of God's love is central. All love that has any right to be called Agape is nothing else but an outflow from the Divine love. It has its source in God. " God is Agape." This, too, is a simple consequence of the meaning of Agape. Since Agape is a love that descends, freely and generously giving of its superabundance, the main emphasis falls with inescapable necessity on the side of God.

2. When we turn to the question of *love towards God* the contrast again manifests itself in characteristic fashion.

Whereas the thought of God's love is quite out of place in the sphere of the Eros motif, there is no difficulty in finding a place for love towards God. In love man reaches up towards God and seeks to secure participation in His riches and blessedness. Here the upward-striving tendency of Eros comes into its own : human want and need seeks for satisfaction in the Divine fullness. Eros-love is acquisitive desire, appetite, which as such strives to obtain advantages. Since God is the Highest Good, the sum of all conceivable good or desirable objects, it is natural that He should attract to Himself all desire and love. It is of course possible for man to love other things than the Divine, but anyone who does this, and no more, has no real understanding of his desire, no perception of its true nature and its insatiability. In his blindness he chooses the lower instead of the higher and cheats himself of the highest satisfaction.

In the context of the Agape motif, too, love for God has a central place. " Thou shalt love the Lord thy God with all thy heart, and with all thy soul, and with all thy mind. This is the great and first commandment " (Matt. xxii. 37 f.). There are, however, two comments to be made on this. First, we must recall how love for God begins in Paul to occupy a somewhat uncertain position. Agape is spontaneous, unmotivated love. But in relation to God, man's love can never be spontaneous and unmotivated. God's love always comes first and awakens man's love in response. This explains the remarkable reticence we notice in Paul with regard to man's love for God. Man's loving surrender of himself without reserve to God is still, of course, the central thing in the Christian life, but Paul shrinks from applying the term Agape to it. To do so would suggest that man possessed an independence and spontaneity over against God, which in reality he does not. It would obscure the fact that man's love for God is only his response to God's love for him, and that only God is in His essence love.

The second thing to be said is that love has here acquired a quite new meaning. Just as God's love is not an appetitive longing, but signifies that God graciously wills to take man, despite his unworthiness, into fellowship with Himself, so man's love for God signifies that man, moved by this Divine love, gratefully wills to belong wholly to God. The idea of appetitive desire can only be applied in a metaphorical sense to man's attitude to God. God transcends everything that can be made an object of human desire and longing. He is not the " Highest Good ", in the sense that He is more desirable than all other objects of desire, but He is simply not to be classed with any objects of desire whatsoever. What we have here is a purely theocentric love, in which all choice on man's part is excluded. Man loves God, not because on comparing Him with other things he finds Him more satisfying than anything else, but because God's unmotivated love has overwhelmed him and taken control of him, so that he cannot do other than love God. Therein lies the profound significance of the idea of predestination; man has not selected God, but God has elected man.

3. This sets its mark also on *love for one's neighbour*. Here the contrast between Eros-love and Agape-love becomes if possible even more striking. Admittedly we have in both cases an ethic based on religion, and to that extent neighbourly love can in both cases be said to be practised " for God's sake ". But this phrase has a quite different meaning in the two cases.

Eros does not seek the neighbour for himself; it seeks him in so far as it can utilise him as a means for its own ascent. In Plato, we may recall, Eros is strictly speaking not concerned with its immediate object, but it is its nature to be always detaching itself from its object and using it as a stepping-stone to higher things. The object *must* be left behind. Love is directed only to that in the object which participates in the Idea of the Beautiful; and in the last analysis it is only this Idea that is the object of Eros. Love may begin with sensible objects, but it is its business to mount up to increasingly abstract objects. It takes the same upward way as we follow in rising from particulars to universals and the world of Ideas. It is not only in Plato, however, that Eros is thus committed to detachment from its immediate object, for throughout its subsequent history the idea of Eros retains this characteristic feature. It displays it above all in the case of neighbourly love, which is never love pure and simple, but has always an ulterior motive in the thought that it is " for God's sake ". The neighbour is merely an intermediate object of love, while its ultimate object is God. It is not man as such, but " God in man ", that is loved. It is typical of the Eros-outlook that a place can only with difficulty be found in it for neighbourly love. Where the only proper object of man's love and longing is God, a serious problem is posed by the question: Have I any right to love my neighbour? For will not the love that I devote to my neighbour be diverted from God? A place is found, however, for neighbourly love in the thought of man as fundamentally a Divine being. To the extent that man participates in the Divine, and only to that extent, is it right for me to love him. But this means that it is no longer the concrete human being, but the Divine Idea of him, " God in him ", that I really love. Moreover, from " God in my neighbour " my love must seek to pass on to God Himself. For a love that actually seeks no other object beyond its neighbour there is no room whatsoever. The showing of love towards one's neighbour is regarded as a meritorious act, a step up on the way to God, and therein lies its justification.

The neighbourly love that bears the stamp of Agape is quite different in character. Agape-love is directed to the neighbour himself, with no further thought in mind and no sidelong glances at anything else. Hence the question arises what grounds there are for this love. What can induce a man to love just simply his neighbour, with no further object in view? What, above all, can induce him to love an enemy? The fact that neighbourly love includes love for one's enemies reveals most clearly the acute difficulty of the problem. When my neighbour happens to be also my enemy, obviously no reason for my loving him can be found in his own character or conduct. So long as my love for my neighbour and my enemy is regarded as a meritorious achievement, whereby I make myself worthy of God's love, solid grounds can be given for loving my neighbour. But when this ulterior motive disappears—as it does when God's love for us is completely unmotivated, so that our love for our neighbour and our enemy cannot in any way help us to win God's love— does it not look as if neighbourly love were bereft of any actuating principle, and therefore itself reduced to unreality? Love, after all, implies motion, a movement towards an object; and if it is real we ought to be able to show what sets it in motion. But that is just what seems to be impossible here; there seems to be no demonstrable motive. There is no motive for the love in the loved object itself, and no motive must be found outside the object, in some ulterior purpose, or else the love will not be true and unfeigned, will not be Agape. For unless love for one's neighbour is directed to the neighbour alone, unless it is concerned exclusively with him and has literally no other end in view—not even that of gaining God's love—then it has no right to the name of neighbourly love. If it is asked what motive there is for Christian love towards one's neighbour, what inspires it and sets it in motion, there can only be one answer: God Himself. Christian neighbourly love is a love " for God's sake "—though this phrase, we must hasten to add, has now a quite different meaning from what it had before. God is not the end, the ultimate object, but the starting-point and permanent basis of neighbourly love. He is not its *causa finalis*, but its *causa efficiens*. It is not as the " Prime, Unmoved Mover " that God sets love in motion, but He is Himself involved in its motion. Being Himself Agape, He brings forth Agape. It is not as being loved, but as loving, that God sets love in motion. Here, therefore, the phrase " for God's sake " has no teleological but only a causal significance. Since God is Agape, everyone who is loved by Him and has been gripped and mastered by His love cannot but pass on this love to his neighbour. In this way God's love passes over directly into the Christian's love for his neighbour.

4. Finally, the contrast between Eros and Agape finds expression also in their different attitudes to *self-love*.

Eros is essentially and in principle self-love. In confirmation of this it is sufficient to recall what has already been said of the egocentric character of Eros-love. It is not too much to say that self-love is the basic form of all love that bears the stamp of Eros. Love for God and love for one's neighbour (or for any other object than God) can alike be reduced to self-love. Neighbourly love, for which there would seem to be no room in the realm of Eros, is none the less provided with a satisfactory motive in the thought that it represents a stage in one's own ascent to higher things. And love for God is firmly founded on the conviction that He is the satisfaction of all man's needs and desires.

Agape, on the other hand, excludes all self-love. Christianity does not recognise self-love as a legitimate form of love. Christian love moves in two directions, towards God and towards its neighbour; and in self-love it finds its chief adversary, which must be fought and conquered. It is self-love that alienates man from God, preventing him from sincerely giving himself up to God, and it is self-love that shuts up a man's heart against his neighbour. When, quite early in the history of Christianity, self-love began to be spoken of as a third form of Christian love, and as the true basis of love for God and one's neighbour, this meant nothing else but a compromise between Eros-love and Agape-love. Agape was being accommodated to the essential principles of Eros, and was assuming its characteristic traits. The result of this compromise could only be that Agape succumbed to Eros; for a love towards God and one's neighbour that is based on self-love cannot be anything else but Eros-love. We must not, of course, overlook the fact that when a place is sought for self-love within the context of Agape, it is always a higher, refined and spiritualised self-love, a love for one's "ideal self" that is intended, and that a distinction is therefore drawn between a legitimate and a sinful self-love. But not even this distinction can prevent the love from losing its Agape-character. Agape recognises no kind of self-love as legitimate.

In conclusion, a summary review of the different " dimensions " of love as seen from the point of view of Eros and

Agape respectively will enable us to verify that there is a clear tendency for the emphasis to fall on directly opposite points in the two cases. For Eros, chief weight is undoubtedly given to self-love. Eros demands satisfaction for its own desire and longing. Hence it can find ample room also for love towards God, since God as the Highest Good is the satisfaction of every desire. It has less room, however, for neighbourly love. Indeed, it would be truer to say that the thought of neighbourly love is alien to the Eros-outlook, into which it was first introduced through a compromise with the Agape-outlook. When Eros-love is directed to a fellow-man, it is because he is regarded, not as a " neighbour ", but as an object which participates in the Idea of the Beautiful, or in the higher world generally, and which can therefore be used as a means of ascent to that world. One form of love has absolutely no place at all in the scheme of Eros, and that is God's love.

Agape runs directly counter to all this. For Agape it is precisely God's love, God's Agape, that is both the criterion and the source of all that can be called Christian love. This Divine love, of which the distinctive feature is freedom in giving, has its direct continuation in Christian neighbourly love, which having received everything freely from God is prepared also to give freely. Here, therefore, we have no need to try to make room for neighbourly love, nor to find any external motivation for it. It is God's own Agape which seeks to make its way out into the world through the Christian as its channel. As regards love towards God, on the other hand, we can certainly not say that it has no place within the scheme of Agape, but we must say that its meaning is quite other than in the context of Eros. It has got rid of the egocentric, acquisitive character that is irreconcilable with the unreserved devotion of a man to God and his complete possession by God. We therefore notice a certain reserve in speaking about love towards God. The self-surrender of love is expressed for preference by other words than Agape, words such as unequivocally reveal its character as a response to the Divine love. But one form of love has absolutely no place in the context of Agape motif, and that is self-love.

Hence, if we arrange the various forms of love in the order of their importance for Eros and Agape respectively, giving three marks to the form which in each case dominates the conception of love as a whole, and no marks to any form which is completely absent from it, we get the following result:

Agape			*Eros*	
3	(Downward Movement)	God's love	(Upward Movement)	0
2		Neighbourly love		1
1		Love for God		2
0		Self-love		3

IV

THE AGAPE-SYSTEM AND THE EROS-SYSTEM

THE distinction between the two great conceptions of love, Agape and Eros, should by now be sufficiently clear for us to proceed further and point out how each of these two motifs tends to carry with it a whole complex system of associated ideas, images and sentiments in such a way that we can distinguish between an "Agape-system" and an "Eros-system". It would take too long here to outline the entire system of ideas in which the Christian Agape motif finds expression, and to show how it differs from that dominated by the Eros motif, but before we go on to study the later history and the conflation of the two motifs, it will be in place to give at least a few examples of the kind of ideas which belong to each system, so that we may have a readier eye for the occurrence of either motif. The ideas in question are primarily forms in which the different fundamental attitudes of mind represented by Agape and Eros find expression, and they are therefore of particular importance for our purpose as *symptoms*, enabling us to detect which of the two is the underlying motif. They can, however, also be of more practical importance. For just as words both give expression to thought and can also give rise to it, so certain ideas or conceptions are not only expressive of a fundamental attitude of mind, but they are also vehicles of it, and actually capable of inducing it even where there was originally no trace of it.

1. A question which has often been discussed is that of the contrast between *Mysticism* and "*Revealed religion*". For this contrast, too, our preceding discussion is illuminating. All true Mysticism belongs decidedly to the Eros-tradition.

Its main preoccupation is with man's way to God. It is essentially self-salvation by means of an ascent to the Divine. There is a continuous line of Eros-tradition running from Neoplatonism and Alexandrian theology through Dionysius the Areopagite (and, in part, also through Augustine) to Scotus Erigena and the Mediæval mystics, and thence to German Idealism and the post-Kantian speculative systems. Although we have to reckon here with an important degree of influence from the Agape motif, the fact nevertheless remains that both religious Mysticism and philosophical Idealism have their deepest roots in the Eros motif. The religion of Revelation, on the other hand, belongs to the Agape-tradition. Here nothing but a Divine revelation can establish communication between God and man. It is not a question of man's way to God, but of God's way to man.

2. The contrast between Eros and Agape has a habit of appearing as the contrast between " *works* ", or human achievement, and *faith*. We have seen how Plato describes the return of the soul to its original abode under the figure of a successive ascent—an idea which afterwards constantly recurs, especially in the Mystics. When we come across the notion of the soul's ascent of the heavenly ladder, we can generally take it as a sign that we are within the sphere of the Eros motif. Ladder-symbolism is one of the favourite forms of expression of the Eros motif.[1] It gives very apt expression to the thought that the goal of man's striving is an other-worldly ideal, and that its attainment is dependent on man's own effort and achievement. In contrast to this, the presence of Agape is marked by a receptive attitude. It is no accident that Agape is constantly found in the most intimate connection with faith; for it is not here a question of something to

[1] *Cf.* R. Reitzenstein, *Die hellenistischen Mysterienreligionen,* 3rd edn., 1927, p. 183. E. Briem, *Zur Frage nach dem Ursprung der hellenistischen Mysterien,* 1928, p. 53. W. Bousset, *Die Himmelsreise der Seele. Archiv für Religionswissenschaft,* IV., pp. 136 ff., 229 ff. *Cf.* also Reitzenstein, *op. cit.,* p. 21.

which man works his way up, but of something offered to man by the Divine Agape which comes down. The humble receptivity of faith is therefore the proper attitude of mind and heart in Agape-religion. It is true that mystical Eros-religiosity, too, can lead to humility as its crowning virtue; but then humility is in that case a " work ", a result of human endeavour, something achieved by self-emptying.

3. The contrast between Eros and Agape is characteristically revealed in the disparity of the estimates they involve as to the value of one's own person. *Eros starts with the assumption of the Divine origin and worth of the soul.* The soul is a pearl, which has become lost and defiled, but which retains none the less its imperishable value. Neoplatonism can speak of the soul as a part of the World-soul, and Mysticism speaks of the "Divine spark", the *Fünklein*, as the inmost essence of the soul. What makes possible the union of the soul with God is its natural kinship with Him, and the fact that there is in the depths of the soul a Divine element which forms a point of contact for God, something for Him to work on. Our task in this life therefore is—as Plotinus puts it—to bring the Divine in ourselves back to the Divine in the all. *Agape, on the other hand, starts with the conviction of one's own lack of worth.* When man has fallen away from God, he is wholly lost and has no value at all. But just in this is the " point of contact " for God's Agape, since God seeks that which is lost. All thought of " merit " is here excluded. The idea of merit has an intimate connection with the Eros-tradition, even though it can exist independently of it.

4. We are carried a stage further by observing the contrast between Eros and Agape in respect of their *ethical outlook*. From the point of view of Eros, there lies behind the ethical dualism of Good and Evil a metaphysical dualism of Spirit and Matter, and the thought of the spiritual as good and the material as evil is expressed in a variety of ways. The soul is in itself and by nature good, but it is held in the body as in

a prison, and this enforced association with the corporeal is the root of all evil. Man's ethical task, therefore, is to liberate himself from the bondage of sense. Consequently, the ethics of Eros tend to be of an ascetic character. Evil lies in the downward direction, looking towards the things of sense, while good lies in the upward direction, towards things spiritual; and man's conversion, which the Eros-ethic preaches, means a change in the direction of his desire. The desire which was previously directed downwards to the sense-world is now directed upwards to the spiritual, transcendent, heavenly world.

The ethics of Agape are of a quite different stamp. Here, the opposition between good and evil is conceived exclusively in terms of the will. Sin has nothing essentially to do with the bodily or sensual nature. Sin is the perversion of the will, ungodliness, disobedience to God; it is man's self-centred rebellion against God. Hence " conversion " also has a quite different meaning. It no longer signifies simply the transference of desire from one object to another, from a lower to a higher, but it signifies a complete change of heart, whereby the selfish will is transformed into a theocentric will, a will determined by God.

5. If we ask *what it is that awakens love in man* we get completely different answers from Eros and from Agape. Eros is of a markedly æsthetic character. It is the beauty of the Divine that attracts the eye of the soul and sets its love in motion. Hence " beholding ", " contemplation ", " vision ", are important words in the sphere of Eros. True, the thought of " seeing God " is also found in the sphere of Agape,[1] but there its meaning is quite different; for the awareness is never absent that " no man can see God and live ", and that God dwells in a light that renders Him unapproachable under the conditions of earthly life—though we can behold something of God's glory in Christ (John i. 14; 2 Pet. i. 16). To speak

[1] Matt. v. 8; 1 Cor. xiii. 12; 2 Cor. v. 7; 1 John iii. 2; Rev. xxii. 4.

of the "beauty" of God in the context of Agape, however, sounds very like blasphemy. Although the thought of "the glory of the Lord" is of frequent occurrence, it is not this that draws out man's love: the glory of the Lord has generally more of the *tremendum* than of the *fascinosum* about it. What awakens love in man is nothing else but the Agape shown to him by God.

6. Lastly, we must allude to two sets of ideas which are intimately connected with the Eros motif and the Agape motif respectively, and which bring out with special clarity the contrast between them. When Plato speaks of the soul, the thought of the *immortality of the soul* is always present.[1] Immortality is a natural endowment of the soul, which bespeaks its Divine origin. All that is required is that the soul should purify itself and set itself free from its bondage to sense in order to return to its Divine origin. The Divine life of immortality is its normal condition. This idea of the natural immortality of the soul is completely foreign to the Agape motif. Instead, we find a belief in the *resurrection of the dead*. In the course of history these two—belief in the immortality of the soul and belief in the resurrection of the dead—have constantly been blended together; yet in fact they belong to two opposite religious and ethical worlds. Wherever the natural immortality of the soul becomes the fundamental religious dogma, we can be fairly certain that we are within the sphere of Eros. But where the Agape motif is dominant, it regularly expresses itself in belief in the resurrection of the dead. If participation in the eternal life of God is possible for man, the possibility is not based on any natural quality or endowment of man, but simply and solely on a mighty act of God. Just as it is God who makes the sinner righteous, so it is God who makes the dead to live. Resurrection is the sign-manual of the Divine Agape. It has nothing to do with the contrast between soul and body, as if one part of man's being

[1] H. Barth, *Die Seele in der Philosophie Platons*, 1921, pp. 49 ff.

were by nature divine and immortal while the other was impure and perishable. Death is the judgment of God upon human life in its entirety, and resurrection is the renewal of human life, likewise in its entirety, by God's love. It was a true sense of the issues involved in the contrast in question that led early Christian writers to insist on the belief in the " resurrection of the flesh " in opposition to the " spiritualising " tendencies of Græco-Hellenistic thought. It is therefore highly misleading when modern scholars treat this belief as evidence of a " naturalistic " outlook. So far from its being a piece of naturalism, it shows a determination to resist the naturalism of Eros-religion, which treats eternal life as a natural product dependent on the inborn quality of the soul, instead of seeing in it the personal operation of God's omnipotence and love.[1]

We have been able to give only a few examples here of the ideas and conceptions belonging respectively to the Eros-system and the Agape-system. The picture will be filled out further when we come to discuss the historical development of the idea of love. All that matters for the present is that we should have a general appreciation of what is involved. It should, however, be emphasised once more that what we are dealing with here are only " symptoms "; otherwise we may be in danger of drawing far too rigid and mechanical a distinction between the two systems of Eros and Agape. For, of course, it is not the case that certain conceptions belong of necessity to one motif, while certain others of necessity go with the other. Real life is so full of inconsistencies that we can never be quite sure that a certain motif is present, even when the conceptions usually associated with it are clearly observable. It can happen that a group of conceptions becomes detached from its usual motif and united with its

---

[1] On the subject of the immortality of the soul and the resurrection of the dead, cf. especially C. Stange, *Die Unsterblichkeit der Seele*, 1925, and the interesting discussion that followed between Stange and P. Althaus.

opposite, so that it acquires a quite new meaning. Our historical study will furnish a number of examples of such interchanges between the two motifs. Hence it is important that rigidly preconceived notions should not lead us astray. Yet the natural connection of each of the different groups of ideas and conceptions with its own particular motif at least justifies our taking steps to discover how far the motif in question is really present. The outward symptom may prove deceptive, but it will at least have served a useful purpose by leading us to make a closer investigation, even if this produces a negative result. It is only by letting the motif and the symptoms shed light on each other that we can achieve our purpose. We can arrive at the motif only by paying attention to the symptoms that are characteristic of it. On the other hand, we do not truly understand the significance of the particular ideas until they no longer stand in isolation, but have been successfuly referred back to their central motif.

V

POSSIBILITIES OF CONFUSION BETWEEN THE
TWO MOTIFS

IF Eros and Agape are not only two entirely opposite motifs, but have also each developed their own characteristic group of representations, we cannot but ask how it has ever been possible for them to be confused and conflated with one another, as the history of Christianity shows that they have. The answer is very simple. The illustrations we have given of the two groups have been presented in an isolation and artificial purity such as does not occur in actual history. There are within each of the two groups plenty of ideas and imagery capable of furnishing a point of contact for the contrary motif. In order to see quite clearly how it has been possible for the two motifs to be blended together, we need only pay attention to the following three points.

1. We must on no account allow ourselves to imagine that the Eros motif and the Agape motif ever encountered one another as total strangers. Certainly they belong to two fundamentally different worlds, but this fundamental difference is not the same as actual isolation from one another. It is impossible to name any occasion as that on which they first met, and before which they had been entirely unaffected by one another. Already before Christianity appeared on the scene, Judaism had gone through a process of Hellenisation on a large scale, as the Jewish Wisdom Literature testifies. We must therefore reckon with a mixture of motifs from the very beginning. For a concrete illustration of the way in which this Hellenisation of Judaism assisted the entry of the Eros motif into Christianity we may turn to Wisdom ix. 15: " For a corruptible body weigheth down the soul, and the earthly

frame lieth heavy on a mind that museth on many things "
(R.V. mg.). Again and again during the early centuries of
Christianity this text came to serve as a bridge over which
Eros-theory was able to pass into Christianity.[1] The idea of
the rational soul, which in virtue of its Divine nature seeks to
mount up to the super-sensible world, but is hampered and
dragged down by the weight of the corruptible body, seems
in the light of this text to be no longer an alien idea, but to
find support in Holy Scripture.

2. If on the one hand the civilisation in the midst of which
Christians lived during the early centuries was thoroughly
permeated with the Eros motif, and if on the other hand
support for this motif seemed not to be entirely lacking in
their own Holy Scriptures, then the way lay open for an increasingly far-reaching confusion of motifs. Although for
a time the Agape motif was in the ascendant in that primitive Christianity which was " foolishness " in the eyes of the
world, yet the Eros motif was the mainstay of contemporary
" educated religion ". It therefore seemed to be a matter of
first importance for apologetic purposes to show that the
deepest intentions of Christianity were quite in harmony with
the universally accepted Eros motif. Particularly important
in this connection was the allegorical method of interpreting
Scripture, for it greatly eased the passage of the Eros motif
into Christianity. Thanks to this method, it was possible to
read into many a Biblical text which only superficially suggested it, a deeper, hidden meaning dictated by the Eros
motif. The thought of the mystical vision of God, for instance, which is one of the most prominent features of Eros
religion, has always been able to attach itself to the text,
" Blessed are the pure in heart, for they shall see God "
(Matt. v. 8), without any notice being taken of the deep
cleavage between the mystical and the eschatological vision

[1] So particularly in Augustine; see below, pp. 466, 483, 485.—*Translator's
note.*

of God, of which alone the text speaks, and which is only another way of speaking about perfected fellowship with God.[1] Paul, too, of course, speaks of seeing face to face (1 Cor. xiii. 12), and here also it was overlooked that the thought is entirely eschatological and that the " seeing " belongs only to the coming Æon, the " Age to come " (2 Cor. v. 7). The conception of a mystical vision of God was securely established, and it was enough that Paul spoke of " seeing " and thereby apparently gave support to this basic conception of Eros-piety.[2]

In a similar way, the Græco-Hellenistic dualism of spirit and matter, soul and body, together with the idea of the Divine nature of the soul and its imprisonment in the corporeal world, found points of contact in the Mosaic account of Creation. It was not difficult to read into the text which tells how God formed man out of the dust of the ground and breathed into his nostrils the breath of life (Gen. ii. 7), the

---

[1] On this see esp. W. W. Baudissin, ' Gott schauen ' in der alttestamentlichen Religion. Archiv für Religionswissenschaft, 1915, pp. 173-239. Baudissin tries to show here how the New Testament idea of " seeing God " is derived from, and satisfactorily explained by, Old Testament precedents, so that there is no need to suppose any influence from the language of the Hellenistic mystery-religions (p. 175). " Quite generally, for the religious experience of the New Testament, ' sight ' is reserved for the Coming Æon, in contrast to the ' faith ' which belongs to the present Age " (p. 173).

[2] Cf. K. Deissner, Paulus und die Mystik seiner Zeit, 1918, esp. ch. iii., ' Glauben und Schauen,' pp. 93-106. " Paul knows this mystical ideal, but for himself he rejects it, when he plainly declares: ' We walk by faith and not by sight.' This is not a phrase thrown out as it were accidentally by the Apostle; it occurs in a passage in which he carefully and deliberately weighs up against one another his present religious possession and that which awaits him in eternity " (p. 97).

E. Lohemeyer, on the other hand, in Σὺν Χριστῷ, Festgabe für Adolf Deissmann, pp. 237 ff., points out various passages in which Paul seems to show the influence of Platonic and Hellenistic philosophy and religion —as, for instance, when he speaks of his desire to depart and be with Christ. Cf. also G. Rudberg, Hellas och Nya Testamentet, 1929, 151 ff. But A. Schweitzer, in Die Mystik des Apostels Paulus, takes just these and similar passages to support his thesis that Paul's mysticism is essentially eschatological in character and entirely different in kind from Hellenistic mysticism.

idea that man is possessed of a double nature, of which the corruptible part is to return to the earth, while the incorruptible soul returns to its Divine source (Eccles. xii. 7). Moreover, in the passage that speaks of man as created in the image of God (Gen. i. 26 f.), additional support was found for the idea that man is by nature akin to the Divine.[1] Again, the story of Jacob's dream about the ladder set up to heaven (Gen. xxviii. 12) or the words of Jesus in John i. 51, " Ye shall see the heaven opened, and the angels of God ascending and descending upon the Son of Man ", have been used times without number as a text for the exposition of the soul's successive ascent to the heavenly sphere. And we need hardly mention the disastrous part played by the mystical interpretation of the Song of Songs in assisting the identification of the Eros motif with the Christian idea of Agape.

3. While points of contact (real or apparent) for the Eros-motif were thus by no means lacking on the Christian side, the process of conflation was also materially aided by the approach which the Eros motif itself, at least in certain of its forms, appears to make towards the idea of Agape. We have in mind particularly the " Alexandrian world-scheme ", as we have called it, and the " downward way " or " Descent ".[2]

---

[1] E. Lehmann, in his *Skabt i Guds billede* (*Lunds universitets årsskrift*), 1918, writes: " The strongest argument against ' creation in God's image ' is the complete silence of the rest of the Old Testament on this subject, which, if it had been a prevalent idea, might have been expected to be very frequently used, and used to the full, in the constantly recurring treatment of the relation between God and men. But no Prophet, no Psalm, not Job, not even the humane Deuteronomy, has any suggestion of such a likeness of nature between God and man " (pp. 11 f.). " It is no accident that this doctrine of the image of God was first developed at a time when the Greek language was making its way into the religious literature of the Jews " (p. 17).

[2] See above, pp. 186 ff., 194 ff. In illustration of the way in which even modern scholars find it natural to treat Eros and Agape as parallel to one another, we may quote from O. Thune Jacobsen, *Antikken og Kristendommen*, 1922, pp. 30 ff.: " Not only the form, but also the content of John xiii.-xvii. invites comparison with Plato's *Symposium*. In the *Symposium* we see Socrates rise, and carry the others with him, above the contemplation of the beauty in a particular thing or a particular human

This both preserves the Eros motif and at the same time appears to do justice to the Agape motif. It contains both a Divine descent and a human ascent, and so furnishes us with the compromise formula which at least seems to reconcile Eros and Agape: the cosmological Descent of the deity and the soteriological Ascent of man. That such a compromise means the victory of Eros need hardly be said, for the cosmological version of Agape is not Agape at all.

In ways such as we have described the two opposed motifs have again and again been joined together. From the point of view of essential principle, their union cannot be described as anything but a self-contradictory compromise, which contains the seeds of its own dissolution from the beginning. But from a historical point of view this compromise is seen to have been inevitable. If Christianity had not sought contact with the most powerful religious motif of the time, it could only have continued to exist as an obscure

---

form, to delight in Beauty itself in its ideal perfection. . . . In a similar way, Jesus in the Christian *Symposium* of the Fourth Gospel opens His disciples' eyes to the *good* in its divine perfection, when He answers Philip's request, ' Show us the Father!' with the words: ' He that hath seen me hath seen the Father.' Both in Plato and in John the point is the opening of the eye to the Idea—in Plato the Idea of perfect beauty, in John of perfect goodness. But whereas the Ideal perfection, according to Plato, is not revealed through any particular thing or human form, it has been revealed, according to John, through the conduct of a particular person, namely Jesus, who has expressed it in His dealings with His disciples in their daily life together and—in a specially pregnant way—at their solemn farewell meeting. Here, according to John xiii., Jesus carries to the uttermost [*cf.* R.V. mg.—TR.] the love wherewith He has loved His own. . . . Since John sees in this perfect love of Jesus a revelation of the nature of God Himself, a revelation of ' the Father,' he sees perfect goodness as something that not merely exists in men's thoughts as an Idea, but as having the support of reality, just as surely as for John ' God' is the *Almighty*. For Plato, love for the pure Idea of Beauty becomes a virtue, which makes its possessor beloved of the gods and—possibly—immortal. Similarly, recognition of the love of Jesus as a revelation of the nature of God becomes for John an expression of the fact that the person concerned has made God's loving point of view his own and therefore is already here in time living his life in the depths of eternal life."

sect. The Agape motif might have been longer preserved in its purity, but only at the price of becoming ineffective. What seems as a matter of principle to be an impossible compromise was the form in which the Agape motif could gain access to the mind of the contemporary world. If Agape was to be of any importance at all, a *modus vivendi* between it and Eros had to be found. There cannot be any real synthesis between two forces so completely contrary to one another as Eros and Agape—the Eros which, beginning with a sense of poverty and emptiness, seeks God in order to find in Him satisfaction for its own wants, and the Agape which, being rich through God's grace, pours itself out in love. The measure in which such a synthesis appears to have been successful is from the point of view of the Agape motif the measure of its failure, for it has meant the betrayal of Agape. Whenever a synthesis seems to have been reached and the two motifs are united, it becomes the task of a succeeding generation to untie the knot and thereby bring about a deeper understanding of the true nature of the Christian love-motif.

SECOND PART

FUNDAMENTAL MOTIFS IN CONFLICT

Amor Dei non invenit sed creat suum diligibile, Amor hominis fit a suo diligibili. Et iste est amor crucis ex cruce natus, qui illuc sese transfert, non ubi invenit bonum quo fruatur, sed ubi bonum conferat malo et egeno.—LUTHER.

INTRODUCTION

I. The Confusion of Motifs in the Christian Idea of Love

THE history of the Christian idea of love is understood only as we keep in mind the fact that two separate spiritual worlds contribute to its making. It starts from the New Testament message of Agape, but its development is not simple and straightforward from this point, since important elements of the Hellenistic idea of Eros have been mingled with it. In the later history of Christianity it may often be doubted whether what is there called Christian love really has anything in common with the Agape of primitive Christianity, or whether it does not rather represent the Eros motif.

The first part of this work has contrasted the two worlds and shown that the word 'love' bears entirely different meanings in the New Testament and in Hellenism.

Eros, the central motif of the Hellenistic theory of salvation, is desire, egocentric love, for which man occupies the dominant position as both starting-point and goal. The starting-point is human need, the goal is the satisfaction of this need. It is characteristic of this Way of salvation that the human is to be raised to the Divine. The human soul is regarded as in essence divine, requiring only to reflect upon its high estate and cease to seek satisfaction in changing and transient things. True wisdom is to turn from things temporal and rise on the wings of the soul to that higher world which was the soul's home before it became confined in the prison-house of the body. Eros is the soul's homesickness, its longing for what can give it true satisfaction, at once the mark of its nobility and a symptom of its present humiliation, a testimony both that it belongs to a higher existence and that in its present situation it painfully lacks that which by nature it needs. In Eros the soul undertakes its heavenly journey, whether this takes the form of spasmodic aspiration or of ecstatic vision and rapturous enjoyment; and it manifests thereby a spirit akin to that of the heaven-storming Titans. Even in its loftiest form Eros retains the egocentric trait.

Agape, Christian love, is of a wholly different nature. It has nothing to do with desire and longing. It " seeketh not its own," does not ascend, like Eros, to secure advantages for itself, but consists in sacrifice and self-giving. And it bears this character ultimately because its prototype is God's own love. The human is not here raised to the Divine, but the Divine, in compassionate love, descends to the human. Agape is primarily God's love, unveiled at its deepest in the Cross of Christ, in His offering of Himself for sinners.

From these two sources is derived that view of love which, with all kinds of modifications, is found in the history of Christianity as " the Christian idea of love." Strictly, it is improper to speak of the Christian idea of love as a single idea, for in fact it includes a series of different conceptions, which arose out of the encounters of primitive Christian Agape and Hellenistic Eros with one another. Now one, now the other predominates, but in general there is a mixture of the two.

Thus far we have been able to examine the two conceptions of love in relative independence, for reasons both of principle and of history. As regards principle, it was necessary first clearly to distinguish the two fundamental motifs, with a view to a profitable appreciation of the different outlooks and understanding of the forces at work. But, furthermore, the two motifs are at the beginning historically quite distinct. There was, it is true, continual communication between the two worlds from the moment Christianity appeared, and their relationship does not first begin when Christianity leaves a Palestinian for a Hellenistic environment. It is vain to seek an 'earliest form of Christianity' absolutely free from Hellenistic influence, since Judaism—despite its exclusiveness—had already undergone a not insignificant process of Hellenisation before Christianity arose. Even so the two views of love can be treated in relative independence at the outset, especially with reference to their fundamental motif. For difficult as it may be, in matters of detail, to draw a definite line between Hellenistic and Christian, the distinction of fundamental motif is clear and certain. One who knows Hellenistic piety cannot doubt that it is dominated by the Eros motif and has, in principle, no room for the Agape motif. No less clearly, primitive Christianity is dominated by the Agape motif, and Eros is alien to it.

It is not surprising that the two fundamental motifs at the outset so clearly exclude one another. There is something so compelling about them both that it is difficult to understand how anyone who had come under the influence of either could have any use for the other. How can one borne irresistibly in the upward movement of Eros, one who sees in the Divine simply a self-sufficient, blessed life whose fascinating loveliness awakes in all lower beings a yearning desire to participate in it, one who regards the Divine as the Absolutely Unmoved which, by the Eros it awakens, sets all things in motion towards itself—how can such an one find anything at all divine in a love which, like Agape, empties itself and descends to the weak and the lost? Must it not seem sheer folly to him? On the other hand, how can one who has been conquered and compelled by the Cross of Christ and has learnt from His self-offering what Divine love is, connect with it an ascending, egocentric love? So long as the two love motifs live with their original force, they simply must exclude one another. That is why it has been possible to deal with them independently and show their fundamental contradiction. For even though quite early we can detect some contact between them—for instance, Paul's polemic against Gnosis, the incipient modification of Agape in John, the "Alexandrian world-scheme" and the "Descent," or Plotinus' formula "God is Eros"—yet there is no question of their coming to terms.

The situation is entirely different when we come to the continuation of the story. The dams are soon broken down and the streams can contend or mingle unimpeded; and the result is a conflict waged throughout the history of Christianity, in which each of the two motifs strives to determine the meaning of Christian love and the interpretation of Christianity in general.

2. The Hellenisation of the Christian Idea of Love

In so far as the Eros motif forces its way into Christianity, we may speak of the Hellenisation of Christianity. This apparently introduces an idea which has long dominated the history of dogma, and recalls Harnack's well-known judgment: "Dogma in its conception and development is a work of the Greek spirit on the soil of the Gospel."[1] Reasons in favour of this view are not far to seek. In attempting to express the content of Christianity, dogma borrows concepts and formulæ from Greek thought; and it is easy to suspect that the specifically Christian meaning may have been lost in the process of translation, while the Hellenistic spirit has gained an entry into Christianity along with Hellenistic forms of thought.

Nevertheless a thoroughgoing revision of the common view is probably necessary on this point.[2] It was natural and inevitable that the Early Church should speak the language of its time, but it is in no way a foregone conclusion that

[1] Harnack: *History of Dogma*, vol. i., p. 17.
[2] *Cf.* G. Aulén: "Innebär den gammalkyrkliga kristologien en 'hellenisering' av kristendomen?" Art. in *Svensk teologisk kvartalskrift*, v., 1929, pp. 3 ff.

this means a perversion of Christianity. The decisive question is, what motif these terms were meant to express and how they succeeded. The answer can only be supplied by motif-research, that is, by an enquiry which detects the motif behind the formal expression. Such an enquiry into the development of dogma in the Early Church largely shows that, far from this being a Hellenisation of Christianity, it actually stands guard against a Hellenising tendency and seeks to preserve the peculiar character of Christian fellowship with God. The motif behind early Christological dogma is not Eros, as the idea of *homousios* demonstrates. Ultimately, the affirmation of the Son's *homousia* with the Father means nothing but a confession of God's Agape and the rejection of the Eros theory. Christ is not, in Hellenistic fashion, a man or demi-god who has ascended to the Divine sphere; He is by nature one with the Father, and in Him nothing less than God Himself meets us. The self-offering of Christ is God's own Agape.

This does not mean that no Hellenisation took place; but it did not occur at the points usually indicated. It went on not so much *in* the construction of dogma as *alongside* of it. Christology and the question of the Trinity, where the first direct construction was done, are perhaps the points at which the Early Church had most success in maintaining the idea of Agape. As a matter of fact, the doctrinal disputes of the Early Church were not so fruitless as is usually supposed. A later age, which has difficulty with the old formulations, readily regards the whole development of dogma as simply an unfortunate side-track, where the practical, religious content of Christianity is lost in theoretical speculations. But this is a superficial and unhistorical attitude. The dogmas of the Early Church have played a part extraordinarily important for the preservation of Christianity, by effectively preventing its dissolution in the religious syncretism which surrounded it. The doctrinal disputes are important because at certain essential points they sharpen the consciousness of the peculiar character of Christianity, and are a reminder that there was in these questions something specifically Christian which had to be fought for.

One who has seen the syncretistic confusion in which the Christian idea of love soon became involved can scarcely be contemptuous of the service rendered by early dogmatic construction in guarding the specifically Christian conception. *Christian love, Agape, has never, strictly speaking, been the subject of dogmatic treatment.* Although, or perhaps we should say, because Agape is the centre of Christian faith and life, the fundamental Christian motif, it has not been made the subject of conscious reflection in the manner of controversial dogmatic issues, and what is characteristic of it has not been fixed in a binding creed. This fact has had dire results, for it has consequently been possible for ideas and motifs entirely alien to Christianity, especially the Hellenistic Eros motif, to invade Christian thought and exert their influence in the name of Christian love. Here is a real Hellenisation of Christianity, and that in the deepest sense of the word. It is not simply that certain formulæ and ideas, produced on Hellenistic soil, have been taken over by Christianity, but the fundamental Hellenistic motif itself has victoriously invaded Christian territory and transformed it from within. The Hellenistic Eros motif has achieved a hegemony, which has been won, however, not in open conflict, but in such a way that the tension between it and the Christian Agape motif has often not even been suspected.

3. SYNTHESIS AND REFORMATION

The history of Christian ideas proceeds in a definite rhythm, alternating between two tendencies, which we may call synthesis and reformation.[1] By synthesis is meant the

[1] See my *Urkristendom och reformation*, 1932, pp. 147-175.

tendency to adapt Christianity to its environment by combining material drawn from both Christianity and elsewhere,
so as to fuse into one, as far as possible, Christianity and the
world of spiritual culture which it enters.   By reformation
is meant the tendency to present Christianity in a pure form,
by distinguishing it as sharply as possible from everything
else, so that its own peculiar character is made clear.

There are two possible kinds of synthesis, cultural and
religious.   In the case of the former, Christianity is exposed
to less risk, since it can enter into relations with this or that
culture, indifferent in itself, without necessarily endangering
its own special character.   But with a religious synthesis,
in which Christianity is joined to an alien religious outlook,
the case is different.   Christianity is plainly made easier of
acceptance for those who previously held that alien outlook,
but no less plainly it runs the risk of losing what is peculiarly
characteristic of it.   Christianity is easier to accept, but can
what is so accepted really be Christianity in the strictest sense
of the word?   Is it not so impaired as to merit the description of salt which has lost its savour?

By a natural reaction of Christianity itself, a period of
synthesis is commonly followed by a period more on the
lines of reformation, in which the chief interest is to consider the uniqueness of Christianity.   But the need for
assimilation soon reappears and leads to a new synthesis,
which in turn proceeds to its dissolution in a new reformation, and so on.   Successive stages in the evolution of Christianity are thus marked by the construction and destruction
of syntheses.   Now this might suggest that the task of reformation is essentially negative and destructive; but that is
only so from the point of view of the synthesis.   The work
of reformation in itself is entirely positive; for even when it
attacks an existing synthesis, it does so merely in order to
remove an obstacle to the apprehension of the proper nature
of Christianity which it is the great positive concern of

reformation to set forth clear and complete. *Synthesis and reformation—that is the rhythm of the history of Christian ideas.* The movement is often repeated at short intervals, but—and this is of chief importance—the great epochs of Christian history themselves take the same course. There are comprehensive periods which bear essentially the stamp of synthesis.

This general observation has special significance in relation to the history of the Christian idea of love. Christianity introduced a new love motif into the world in Agape; but the world it entered was mainly Hellenistic, and possessed already its own love motif, Eros, and from the beginning the synthetic tendency is seen at work to blend the two. This process is often described as merely the meeting of Christianity and ancient culture, and nothing more than a cultural synthesis is supposed to be in question. But this is an undue simplification, since in fact the issue is nothing less than a religious synthesis, in which two separate religious phenomena are fused into one. What really happens is that the Christian motif is remodelled until it readily unites with a similarly modified Hellenistic motif to form, apparently at least, a single idea of love. Even though the contrary tendency to assert the uniqueness of Christianity never quite died out, and reasserted itself time after time, yet as regards the Christian idea of love, the period from primitive Christianity to the Reformation bears, on the whole, the marks of Hellenistic synthesis. For half a millennium it was in preparation, and when completed it persisted for a thousand years, until the tendency to reformation fully asserted itself in Luther.

With this, the task and scheme of the following study are given. It will be clear from what has been said above that our purpose is not to survey the history of Christianity, testing the various views we find by the standards of Eros and Agape and assigning them to one or the other category.

Such a procedure would deny all real significance to the historical development, which could then at most supply interesting examples of the two motifs. But our interest in the Christian idea of love is directed positively to its historical growth. We have distinguished the two motifs, not so as to possess a convenient standard by which to judge what is valuable and what is of less worth in the history of Christian ideas, but because the conflict between these two motifs provides the key to an understanding of what has actually happened in the history of Christian thought. We are not to single out what bears the stamp of Eros or of Agape in the various ideas of love, but we are to see how these ideas have been built up in the meeting of the two motifs. The analysis of the motifs is a *means*, not the *end* of the enquiry. The end is to understand the historically given views, to understand how they were synthetically formed out of the tension between Eros and Agape. The Christian idea of love is like a tree nourished by different soils, and to understand why it grows as it does, it is necessary to investigate the different strata; but this is not the same thing as to split up the tree. The aim is to understand the tree as it grows.

To write the history of the Christian idea of love is a two-fold task.

First of all we must show how the primitive Christian and the Hellenistic ideas of love are fused into one: this is the stage of synthesis.

Secondly we must show how the specifically Christian idea of love breaks through again and shatters the artfully contrived synthesis; this is the stage of reformation.

Our presentation is grouped round these two main points. Chapter I. deals with the preparation of the synthesis in the Early Church, when the different motifs existed side by side with, as yet, no real connection between them. Chapter II. shows how the synthesis comes to a head in Augustine's doctrine of Caritas, the classic union of the Christian Agape motif and the Neoplatonic Eros motif, which was decisive for posterity; though Pseudo-Dionysius also introduced, more directly, the Eros motif into Christianity. Chapter III. shows how the Eros motif thus reached the Middle Ages. Chapter IV. describes the Mediæval view of love. This is mainly a reproduction of Augustine and Dionysius, although there are original contributions at certain points (*Minnefröm-migkeit*, Passion-mysticism). The Middle Ages, however, experienced supremely the inner difficulties of the old synthesis and indirectly prepared for its dissolution. This came through the Reformation, and, in a measure, through the Renascence as well. The Renascence brings a renewal of the old Eros motif (Chapter V.), in the Reformation the Agape motif breaks powerfully through (Chapter VI.), and the two motifs fall apart. But in spite of the fact that the problem of " Eros and Agape " was solved in principle by the breakdown of the *caritas*-synthesis, this latter continued after the Reformation to be, practically speaking, the dominant idea of love.

1
THE PREPARATION OF THE SYNTHESIS

CHAPTER ONE

NOMOS, EROS AND AGAPE
ACCENTS IN THE EARLY CHURCH

I

THE THREE MAIN TYPES

WITHIN a few decades, the specific and original fundamental motif of primitive Christianity, the idea of Agape, begins to grow dim and blurred. As usually happens when the second generation takes over the inheritance from the first, its full depth and comprehensiveness is not preserved. Primitive clarity and originality are lost, the contours begin to fade in a process of levelling and assimilation which goes on in two directions, partly in relation to the world of the past, partly in relation to the contemporary world.

This is the position of the Christian idea of love in post-apostolic times. Love is clearly an inalienable possession of Christianity, and it can be highly praised; but at times the treatment it is accorded suggests rather an old and venerable tradition than an actually living reality. What it does and does not mean can be plainly inferred from the great hymn to Agape in the First Epistle of Clement, which reads, in obvious imitation of I Cor. xiii.:

"Let him who has Agape in Christ perform the commandments of Christ. Who is able to explain the bond of the Divine Agape? Who is sufficient to tell the greatness of its beauty? The height to which Agape lifts us is not to be expressed. Agape unites us to God. 'Agape covereth a multitude of sins.' Agape beareth all things, is long-suffering in all things. There is nothing base, nothing haughty in

Agape; Agape admits no schism, Agape makes no sedition, Agape does all things in concord. In Agape were all the elect of God made perfect. Without Agape is nothing well-pleasing to God. In Agape did the Master receive us; for the sake of the Agape which He had towards us did Jesus Christ our Lord give His blood by the will of God for us, and His flesh for our flesh, and His soul for our souls."[1]

This passage is especially interesting as illustrating the rise of the various tendencies. First of all, it shows that the primitive Christian idea of Agape was still alive; but it also shows the double tendency to assimilation mentioned above. The idea of Agape is slipping back to the Old Testament level, while at the same time the primitive Christian and the Hellenistic conceptions of love are beginning to merge.

The centrality of the Cross of Christ proves that some-thing of the primitive Christian idea of love remains. It is the " Agape of the Cross " that is praised, God's own love, by which He chose and received us, supremely manifested in that Christ " gave His blood for us." Apart from its context, this seems to be in essential agreement with the Pauline view of love, but an analysis of the passage as a whole reveals the presence and predominance of other ideas, alien to the primitive Christian Agape motif.

As a whole, this hymn to Agape exalts love as incom-parably the greatest human *achievement*. The Old Testa-ment attitude is unmistakable, especially in respect of love to neighbour, which is regarded as a meritorious work. The idea is widespread in the post-apostolic period, that love to neighbour has the effect of atoning for sin. Displayed especially in almsgiving, it is a means of winning forgiveness for sins committed. The saying, " Agape covereth a multi-tude of sins,"[2] is quoted to mean, not the readiness of Agape to forgive and cover its neighbour's sin, but the ability of Agape to win forgiveness from God. This is a love which

[1] 1 Clem. xlix.   [2] *Cf.* 1 Pet. iv. 8; Jas. v. 20.

covers, not another's sin, but one's own, by making restitution for previous offences and winning the favour of God. "Blessed are we, beloved, if we perform the commandments of God in the concord of Agape, that our sins may be forgiven for Agape's sake."[1]

This is mainly in the spirit of the Old Testament, but there is also a *Hellenistic* element present. Love in primitive Christianity is a love which descends; here we find a *love which ascends*. If the thought that God chose us and condescended to us in Christ is not absent, yet the emphasis is not upon it, but upon the fact that man can, by the exercise of his love, ascend to God. "The height to which Agape lifts (ἀνάγει) us is not to be expressed." And the words "Agape unites us to God," are no different from the old idea of Eros as mediator between the human and the Divine. In the New Testament, Agape is God's Way to man; here it is man's Way to God, a means to his ἀναγωγή. Undoubtedly the Eros motif is invading Christian territory —a fact to which confirmation is lent if we recall the part played by the concept of beauty in the doctrine of Eros, for this, too, is represented in Clement's hymn to Agape.[2]

The foregoing illustrates the difficulty of depicting the Christian idea of love in post-apostolic times. Everything is vague and indefinite owing to the interplay of the separate motifs, and it would clearly be valueless to attempt an account of all the different statements made with reference to Christian love. We must, if the material permits of such a procedure, present it under a number of main types. The justification of this method can only appear from the dis-

---

[1] 1 Clem. l. 5.

[2] So also R. Knopf in *Handbuch zum Neuen Testament*, hrsg. von H. Lietzmann, *Ergänzungsband : Die apostolischen Väter*, 1923, pp. 125 f.: " Iη καλλονή a Greek note seems to be struck." On the conclusion of 1 Clem. xlix., A. v. Harnack remarks: " Again the author feels it necessary to mention the Blood of Christ. If he is thinking of the Lord's Supper, then the addition of ' soul ' is proof that the writer is a Greek " (*Einführung in die alte Kirchengeschichte*, 1929, pp. 117 f.).

cussion itself, but for the sake of clarity we may anticipate the result.

Broadly speaking, there are *three main types* of view with regard to the Christian idea of love in the post-apostolic period, according as (1) the *Old Testament Nomos motif*, (2) the *Hellenistic Eros motif*, or (3) the *New Testament Agape motif* predominates.

It is important to note that it is only a question of the dominant motif. There can, in view of the character of the period, be no pure types, but one motif can be dominant in the mixture of motifs, and can set its mark upon any particular conception. Of this Clement's hymn to Agape is a concrete example. In it motifs are plainly mixed, for all three fundamental motifs are represented; but the Old Testament Nomos motif is ultimately predominant.

We may now pass to a brief general consideration of the three main types.

1. The Christian idea of love points both positively and negatively back to Judaism. Love is of central importance in the Old Testament, and the Commandment of Love, requiring love both to God and to neighbour, is an Old Testament commandment. For Judaism especially, the command to love God was the " first commandment in the Law." Love to God is the deepest and most inward expression of man's relation to God which the Old Testament knows. Even so, fellowship between God and man is based on justice and regulated by the Law. Nomos is the controlling idea, and love has its place within the legal framework.

Christianity, however, effects a complete revolution. Jesus accepts, widens and deepens the Old Testament Commandment of Love—this is true, but not the decisive factor. Central for Him is not our love, the love required of and exercised by us, but God's love, whose work He knew Himself called to fulfil. But *God's* love cannot be contained within the framework of the Law, and the legalistic scheme falls to pieces: " I came not to call the righteous, but sinners " (Mk. ii. 17). Paul proceeds further on the same road. The term " justification," it is true, recalls the old Jewish legalism, but Paul's doctrine of justification shatters the legalistic conception of fellowship with God, and makes God's Agape the supreme, controlling idea. God justifies not on the ground of merit and the works of the Law, but of free Grace, groundless, spontaneous and unmotivated. His Agape is love for sinners, and it is characteristic of justification that the sinner is made the object of God's Agape. Pauline Christianity bears therefore an anti-legalist stamp; the Law no longer expresses God's relation to man or man's to God, and in this respect it is made obsolete and abolished by God's Agape.

The difference between the Jewish and the primitive Christian view of love can be formulated thus: *love set within the scheme of law—love breaking down the scheme of law.* Only this latter is Agape in the deepest sense of the word. But the post-apostolic period shrank from accepting its consequences; and although Paul's message of the Agape of the Cross might have shown the way, there is hardly a trace of Paulinism in this early period—much to the detriment of the idea of Agape. The *Commandment* of Love was easier to grasp, and it led back to the Old Testament level, so that Agape was again brought under the scheme of Nomos. This is the type mainly found in the Apostolic Fathers and Apologists.

2. Alongside this tendency to slip back to the Old Testament level, a second type shows the influence of the encounter of Agape with Eros in the contemporary world with its religious syncretism. As converts from Judaism brought their legalistic scheme with them and tried to fit Christian Agape into it, so converts from Hellenism brought the Eros

scheme and tried to introduce something of the idea of Agape into it. The combination was at first quite superficial, and Eros naturally retained its predominance, in a type of thought of which Gnosticism is the chief representative. Gnosticism is a species of religious syncretism which really appears Christian only because the name of Agape is sometimes given to what is in reality Eros. From the point of view of the Agape motif this process is one of complete distortion.

3. The reaction of the Agape motif against both Eros and Nomos came through Marcion. He is above all opposed to legalism and Judaism, which is probably why he has usually been regarded as a Gnostic. He could on the whole make common cause with Gnosticism in his attack on Judaism and the Old Testament, and there are other points of contact; but the motif fundamental to his thought proves that he is anything but a Gnostic. In Gnosticism Eros is fundamental; Marcion's foundation, beyond all doubt, is Agape. To describe his attempt at reformation simply as the reaction of the Agape motif against rival theories is possibly to go too far. But no one in this period asserted the Christian idea of love with such force as he, and we may therefore speak of the reaction of the Agape motif, while reserving its limitations for later consideration.

At the beginning of the post-apostolic period the three main types already confront each other; and the conflict that rages round Gnosticism and Marcion in the second century results in the rise of a *churchly theology*. Certain factors gradually emerge which characterise all interpretation of Christianity in the following period; earlier indefiniteness disappears as the Church begins to form a common theological basis. This also has its influence upon the Christian idea of love. If Gnostic extravagances were branded heretical, so was Marcion's idea of love. Extreme views were excluded, and the Christian idea of love had to move within narrower limits than before. But the three main types persisted, and of the three most influential representatives of ante-Nicene theology, Irenæus, Tertullian and Origen, each represents one of these. Tertullian is decidedly dominated by the Old Testament Nomos motif; Alexandrian theology (Origen) shows how, in spite of the rejection of Gnosticism, the Eros motif persists in seeking entry into Christianity; whilst Irenæus' outlook is evidence that, in spite of the rejection of Marcion's interpretation, the primitive Christian Agape motif remains a powerful factor in Greek theology.

This sketch of the history of the Christian idea of love in the early centuries now remains to be filled out in greater detail. There were, so to speak, two rounds in the contest between the three main types. We must therefore see how the different motifs fare at each stage, and our account will have seven subdivisions. The first three will show the three main types in the *first stage*: the Nomos type in the Apostolic Fathers and the Apologists, the Eros type in Gnosticism, the Agape type in Marcion. The next three sections deal with the *second stage*: the Nomos type in Tertullian, the Eros type in Alexandrian theology, the Agape type in Irenæus. These conflicts, however, issue in victory for none of the three main types, but rather in a *compromise*, such as we find in Methodius, Athanasius and the Cappadocian Fathers, and this will occupy the seventh section.

II

THE NOMOS TYPE IN THE APOSTOLIC FATHERS AND THE APOLOGISTS

1. THE INFLUENCE OF THE OLD TESTAMENT

THE Nomos motif stands in the most intimate relation to the Old Testament, and the use made of the Old Testament is the main reason why this motif largely dominates the understanding of Christianity in the early centuries. The problem of Jewish Christianity, so pressing for Paul, loses its actuality with the passage of Christianity from Palestinian territory, but the Old Testament retains its authority. And with it remains the tension between Agape and Nomos, which was the ultimate ground of Paul's attack on " the Law " and " the works of the Law." The Old Testament was the sacred document of Christianity before the New existed, and the first contributions to Christian theological thought are based on it, through the attempt to find evidence in it that Jesus was the Messiah promised of God.

What significance has it for the Agape motif that Christianity was tied to the sacred writings of Judaism?

Undoubtedly it involved a risk. The idea of Agape first appeared in *opposition* to the Jewish system of values and the consequent conception of fellowship with God; but now the sacred documents of Judaism are accepted without qualification and given canonical authority for Christianity. From this source the second century largely draws its Christianity, and it is not surprising that, for the Apostolic Fathers and the Apologists, the Old Testament Nomos motif becomes the framework into which they try, as far as possible, to fit fragments of the Agape idea, often in the form of individual " words of the Lord " which still further sharpen or deepen the Old Testament commandment. But such sayings, transferred from the context of Agape to that of Nomos, inevitably lose their original meaning. There is therefore some justification for regarding the dependence of Christianity on the Old Testament as a disaster; for it was a superhuman task to assert the idea of Agape in circles which so essentially derived their spiritual nourishment from the Old Testament, and what was specifically Christian was almost bound to be obscured.

Yet it would be most biassed and misleading to suppose that the Old Testament had only this negative significance for the idea of Agape. It had a *positive* value, not easily overestimated, that transcends those general grounds which are usually adduced for the primitive Christian use of the Old Testament. It is said, for example, that the Old Testament was " the Bible of Jesus and the Apostles "; that Jesus proclaimed no other God than the God of the Old Testament, of Abraham, Isaac and Jacob, and that this continuity had to be preserved; that the Old Testament rendered incalculable service in the first Christian missionary activity, since on the basis of it Christianity could claim to represent the most ancient revelation and commend itself to an age which regarded antiquity as an indispensable mark of true religion; and so forth. Now all this is of minor importance compared with the attendant risk of losing what was specifically Christian; but, as a matter of fact, the Old Testament was, in two respects, of the very greatest importance *for the preservation of the idea of Agape.*

First, it is no exaggeration to say that primitive Christianity succeeded only with the help of the Old Testament in making any sense of Agape at its profoundest—the Agape of the Cross. This Agape reverses natural human valuation, and the message of a Crucified Christ was not only for Jews and Greeks a stumbling-block and foolishness, but a hard paradox for Christians themselves. It was only tolerable if they could see in it the "foolishness of God" (1 Cor. i. 21, 25). Here the Old Testament came to their aid. The Cross of Christ was simply the fulfilment of what God had already proclaimed and promised there. Primitive Christianity reads the Old Testament in the light of Christ; it is full of prophecies of Him, and He is the key to its understanding. But it is perhaps even more true to say: *the Old Testament provides the key to the understanding of Christ.* The offence of the Cross was insuperable until they could point to "Moses and all the prophets" and say: "Behoved it not the Christ to suffer these things, and to enter into His glory?" (Lk. xxiv. 26). God has said it Himself in the Holy Scriptures: this raises the apparently absurd to the level of absolute truth. The offence is gone, for "the foolishness of God is wiser than men." The importance of the Old Testament in this respect is illustrated by the remarkable part played by Psalm xxii. and Isaiah liii., first in the New Testament and then in the Apostolic Fathers and the Apologists.[1] Searching the Old Testament Scriptures for passages applicable to the Passion of Christ was not an unnecessary theological luxury, but a necessity for the apprehension of the Divine Agape revealed in Christ, for only so could the full force of the paradox be retained. It is not by accident that the oldest form of Christian theology is the *proof from Scripture,* the attempt to show from the Old Testament that the Crucified is Messiah.[2] This is not, as has often been asserted, a sign of superficiality, but an attempt at that early stage to grasp the new fundamental motif of Christianity.

Secondly, to eliminate the Old Testament, even in the interests of the Agape motif, can easily mean weakening the Christian idea of love. Agape must, it appears, be seen

---

[1] 1 Clem. xvi.; Barn. v.; Justin, Dial. 97-106.

[2] Acts ii. 23; iii. 18; iv. 28; viii. 32-35; xvii. 2 f.; xvii. 11; xviii. 28; 1 Cor. xv. 3. *Cf.* also Matt. xxvi. 56; Mark ix. 12; Luke xxii. 37; xxiv. 46; John xix. 24; xix. 28; xix. 36 f.

against its original background, the Old Testament Nomos motif, if it is to retain its seriousness and depth. It is essentially a transvaluation; it is the conquest of Nomos, and exists only in this tension. Agape is destroyed if, by the removal of the tension, it ceases to be an actual transvaluation and becomes a new, permanent scale of values. Against such a removal of necessary tension the Old Testament stands on guard, as the controversy with Marcion made abundantly clear.

This, then, is the situation in the early centuries. On the one hand the Old Testament must be retained for the sake of the Agape motif; on the other, its retention involves the constant risk of legalistic interpretation, a risk to which post-apostolic Christianity succumbed. Instead of Nomos being the background and being at the same time superseded by Agape, it becomes the leading motif and Agape is subordinated to it.

2. THE "TWO WAYS"

A good illustration of the interweaving of Jewish and Christian, of Nomos and Agape, is provided by that concentrated edition of the Christian ethos known as the "Two Ways." Here we have direct evidence of how fragments taken from the context of the Christian idea of Agape were fitted into the Jewish framework of Nomos. We may confine ourselves to the version found in the Didache.[1] Jewish propaganda literature had been accustomed to present its ethical teaching under the heading of the "Two Ways," the Way to Life and the Way to Death, the Way of Light and the Way of Darkness, and the Didache takes over this tradi-

---

[1] Didache, chaps. i.-vi.; the version in the Epistle of Barnabas, chaps. xviii.-xxi., contains hardly any specifically Christian trait, and so is less suitable for illustration. On "The Two Ways," cf. A. Harnack: *Apostellehre*, PRE³, vol. i., pp. 711-730. A. Seeberg: *Der Katechismus der Urchristenheit*, 1903; *Die beiden Wege und das Aposteldekret*, 1906; *Die Didache des Judentums und der Urchristenheit*, 1908. G. Klein: *Den första kristna katekesen*, 1908.

tion. It adopts, however, not only the formal scheme, but also a number of special ethical requirements and precepts, to which it adds " words of the Lord " from the Christian tradition, calculated to intensify and surpass the Jewish demands. It uses, naturally, the catalogue of virtues and vices inseparable from the doctrine of the " Ways," but more important is the fact that it had already found in its Jewish source the Commandment of Love to God and neighbour as the primary and fundamental mark of the Way to Life.

" There are two ways, one to life and one to death; and there is a great difference between the two ways. The way to life is this : first, thou shalt love the God who made thee; secondly, thy neighbour as thyself; and whatsoever thou wouldst not have done to thyself, do not thou to another "— so the Didache opens, following closely its Jewish model. But there is a Christian note in its comment and exposition— " Now the teaching of these words is this : Bless those that curse you, and pray for your enemies, and fast for those that persecute you. For what credit is it to you if you love those that love you? Do not even the heathen do the same? But, for your part, love those that hate you, and you will have no enemy. Abstain from carnal and bodily lusts. If any man smite thee on the right cheek, turn to him the other cheek also, and thou wilt be perfect. If any man impress thee to go with him one mile, go with him two. If any man take thy coat, give him thy shirt also. If any man will take from thee what is thine, refuse it not—not even if thou canst. Give to everyone that asks thee, and do not refuse; for the Father's will is that we give to all from the gifts we have received. Blessed is he that gives according to the mandate, for he is innocent. . . ." After this digression the Didache returns to its Jewish model, which it then follows closely throughout.

How does the love spoken of here compare with the New Testament idea of Agape?

At first sight it seems to be the same. Its connection with the Old Testament Commandment of Love does not necessarily imply a legalistic conception, for the same connection appears in the Synoptic Gospels, and in any case the Old Testament commandment is given a Christian explanation. Even the most characteristic trait of Agape is not lacking, the " unmotivated " love, love to enemies, love which gives freely and for nothing and " fasts for persecutors." Should we not say at once, then, that instead of Agape being degraded to the level of Nomos, Nomos has been raised to the level of Agape?

Nevertheless, an examination of the view of Christianity underlying the theology of the " Two Ways " shows that, in spite of all, Nomos has the ascendency. The expressions used may be partly the same as in the New Testament, but the motive is different. It is no longer the overmastering, paradoxical love from God which calls forth in the Christian an entirely new kind of love, by which all ordinary human limitations are broken down; but instead, love meets us here as the *loftiest human achievement.* But love regarded as achievement is no longer Agape. The Didache, as 1 Clement, is concerned with the height to which Agape raises one who exercises it. " If any man smite thee on the right cheek, turn to him the other cheek also, *and thou wilt be perfect.*" Love has thus become literally " the Way to Life "; it has become the Way of salvation. It is not, however, the Way of Agape, whereby the Divine love in its groundless compassion finds a way to the sinner and freely gives him salvation, but the directly opposite way, by which man, through exercising so sublime a love, finally reaches perfection. The centre of gravity has changed; love is no longer God's Way to man, but man's Way to God.

This has serious consequences for *love to neighbour* as well. When love means God's love revealed in Christ, given to us without reference to our merits, then love to neighbour is inevitable, almost self-evident; it is the outflow of the Divine love man has received, seeking its way through him to others. We need not, indeed cannot, point to anything else but God's love as the reason for our love to our neighbour. It is "unmotivated" like God's love with which it is given, of which it is an extension. If a motivation can be found, it is purely causal, inasmuch as love to one's neighbour springs by inner necessity out of the experience of Divine love. Otherwise it is not true love to neighbour, since any other motivation introduces an ulterior purpose, and distracts attention from the neighbour.

But love in the Didache is not such an "unmotivated" love, free from all ulterior motives. *The Didache has replaced the causal motivation, which is legitimate from the point of view of Agape, by a teleological motivation.* In the post-apostolic period it becomes increasingly common to regard love (almsgiving) as compensation for sin committed.[1] He who shows love to his neighbour gains deliverance from death.[2] And the Didache urges: "Of whatsoever thou hast gained by thy hands, thou shalt give a ransom for thy sins."[3] The love I show, as a Christian, to my neighbour, not only helps him, but is to my own advantage. This is the first step towards that *combination of love to neighbour and "self-love,"* which was to play so large and, for the idea of Agape, so disastrous a part in the future.

3. THE NOMISTIC MODIFICATION OF THE AGAPE MOTIF

What has been said of the theology of the "Two Ways" may be regarded as representative of the Apostolic Fathers. Their idea of love is to a large extent qualified by nomism.

---

[1] On this idea in 1 Clem. xlix. and l., *cf. supra* pp. 248f.

[2] "Cum possitis benefacere, nolite differre, *quia eleemosyna de morte liberat.*" Polyc. ad Phil. x. 2. *Cf.* also 2 Clem. xvi. 4 and Barn. xix. 10.

[3] Didache iv. 6. For Jewish parallels to this idea, *cf.* G. Klein, *op. cit.*, pp. 253 f. ("Come and wonder at God's mercy towards man; for he can with money redeem himself out of God's hands." *Ibid.*).

This is not to deny that there are individual passages where the full message of Agape appears. *Ignatius* is the chief example, since he, in his dependence on Paul and John, comes nearer the primitive Christian Agape motif than any other of the Apostolic Fathers. In Faith and Love he finds the whole content of Christianity; Faith is the beginning of the Christian life, Love its end.[1] But whether he speaks of Faith or Love he has always one and the same thing in view, the Cross of Christ. Thus he can call Faith Christ's flesh, and Love Christ's blood.[2] The Pauline thought of the *Agape of the Cross* has become for Ignatius a living reality; and he has also the *Johannine identification of God and Agape.* God is the unity of Faith and Love, of Pistis and Agape.[3]

Another witness that the paradox of God's Agape was not forgotten is the beginning of the *Second Epistle of Clement,* the oldest extant Christian homily, which is usually quoted with the *Shepherd of Hermas* as an example of legalistic tendencies. It speaks in the highest terms of all that Christ suffered for our sake, and regards the love He thereby showed as in no way motivated by anything in ourselves. In us He found nothing but blindness and sin; no undamaged kernel in human nature occasioned His saving work, but this was grounded solely in His spontaneous love. "For He had pity on us, and saved us in His mercy, and regarded the great error and destruction which was in us,

---

[1] Ign. ad Eph. xiv. 1: ἀρχὴ μὲν πίστις, τέλος δὲ ἀγάπη.—Ign. ad Smyrn. vi. 2: τὸ γὰρ ὅλον ἐστὶν πίστις καὶ ἀγάπη.

[2] Ign. ad Trall. viii. 1: ἐν πίστει, ὅ ἐστιν σάρξ τοῦ κυρίου, καὶ ἐν ἀγάπῃ, ὅ ἐστιν αἷμα Ἰησοῦ Χριστοῦ.

[3] Ign. ad Eph. xiv. 1: τὰ δὲ δύο, ἐν ἑνότητι γενόμενα, θεός ἐστιν.—On Ignatius and the 'theology of Asia Minor,' cf. F. Loofs: *Leitfaden zum Studium der Dogmengeschichte,* 4 Aufl., 1906, pp. 98 ff.

Ignatius has suffered the peculiar fate, though he most clearly of the Apostolic Fathers represents the Agape motif, of becoming chief authority and patron saint of the invasion of Eros piety. It is, of course, not his fault, but due to a misinterpretation by Origen of one of his sayings, which, apart from this, has no importance in the history of the Christian idea of love. We shall therefore leave consideration of it till we come to Origen; cf. pp. 390 f.

and our hopelessness of salvation save from Him."[1]   It is significant that the words of Jesus are quoted in this context: "I came not to call the righteous, but sinners" (Mk. ii. 17). And equally significant is the comment: "He means that those who are perishing must be saved, for it is great and wonderful to give strength, not to the things which are standing, but to those which are falling. So Christ willed also to save the perishing, and He saved many, coming and calling us who are already perishing."[2]   Such expressions make the conclusion inevitable that 2 Clement clearly perceives the paradox of the Divine love.

Nevertheless, such observations in no way alter the general impression of legalistic modification in the Apostolic Fathers. If 2 Clement so emphasises the spontaneous and unmotivated nature of the Divine love, the author never tires, on the other hand, of talking about the holy and righteous works by which we can become partakers of Christ's mercy, and win blessedness as our merited reward.[3] Love occupies the highest place in the Christian life, yet it is so superficially conceived as to be almost a synonym for almsgiving. 2 Clement has an ascending scale of meritorious works— prayer, fasting and almsgiving: "Fasting is better than prayer, but the giving of alms is better than both; and Agape covers a multitude of sins."[4] Hermas goes even further in this direction; and the same trend is also observable elsewhere.[5] It would be wrong to suppose that the writers of this period are unaware that Christianity has brought something new as compared with Judaism and the Old Testa-

[1] 2 Clem. i. 7.   [2] 2 Clem. ii. 5 ff. *Cf.* also Barn. v. 8-12.
[3] 2 Clem. vi. 9; xvi. 2; xi. 6 f. *Cf.* also viii. 4.
[4] 2 Clem. xvi. 4; *cf. supra*, pp. 248, 260.
[5] Hermas, Sim. v. 3, 3: "If you do anything good beyond the commandment of God, you will gain for yourself greater glory, and shall be more honourable with God than you were destined to be. If, then, you keep the commandments of God, and add these services also, you shall rejoice if you keep them according to my commandment." *Cf.* Sim. viii. 3, 5 ff.; Mand. iv. 3, 7; viii. 9; viii. 12; xii. 6, 5; Vis. iii. 1, 8 f.; iii. 2, 1 f.

ment. They are very conscious of it, but they lack a sense of the difference between Law and Gospel. Christianity is *law*, "*the New Law of our Lord Jesus Christ*," as the Epistle of Barnabas characteristically puts it.[1] Much in the Old Law is made obsolete through Christ, but is replaced by a New Law, which is, it is true, no longer the law of external sanctions, but "the perfect law, the law of liberty,"[2] though its demands, by reason of their very inwardness, are more exacting than those of the Old Law. Christianity and even Christ Himself are understood, in this period, mainly in the light of the New Law. To it Christ has a threefold relation, as (1) Lawgiver, (2) Example of its fulfilment, (3) Judge, who is to judge the world in accordance with it.[3] The all-embracing requirement is Agape, and the demand for love of enemies, in particular, shows how far it transcends the Old Law, in requiring an "extraordinary goodness," which leaves ordinary humanity far behind, and arouses the astonishment and admiration of all.[4]

Interestingly enough, occasional passages in the Apostolic Fathers show a tendency to try to outdo even the New Testament Commandment of Love. This is in itself quite logical, once Agape comes to be regarded as the requirement of a new and more exacting law, for there is no reason why it should not be made still more exacting. The New Testament stops at the simple command: "Thou shalt love thy neighbour as thyself," but the version of the "Two Ways" in the Epistle of Barnabas says: "Thou shalt love thy neighbour *more than* thy own life" ($\dot{\upsilon}\pi\grave{\epsilon}\rho$ $\tau\grave{\eta}\nu$ $\psi\upsilon\chi\acute{\eta}\nu$ $\sigma\upsilon$).[5] Such an intensification of the commandment has sometimes been taken as proof that the Christian idea of love persists

---

[1] Barn. ii. 6: ὁ καινὸς νόμος τοῦ κυρίου ἡμῶν ᾽Ιησοῦ Χριστοῦ.

[2] Jas. i. 25; 1 Clem. ii. 8.

[3] On Christ as Lawgiver and World-judge, *cf.* W. Bousset: *Kyrios Christos*, 2 Aufl., 1921, pp. 299 ff.

[4] 2 Clem. xiii. 4.

[5] Barn. xix. 5.

with its original force;[1] but there are two objections to this view. First, even from the point of view of law and commandment, a formal does not necessarily mean an actual intensification. In fact, if we compare the commandment of love to neighbour as given in the New Testament and in Barnabas, we can hardly fail to see that the latter form is weaker. *The commandment has been re-thought in quantitative categories, and is intensified on this lower level.*[2] But, secondly, even if the commandment were really intensified, this does not mean that the Agape motif is deepened. There is such an antithesis between Agape and Nomos that to sharpen the commandment means weakening the idea of Agape. If the thought of *God's love* recedes into the background, and *the Commandment of Love* comes to the fore, then Agape's fate is sealed. Love to neighbour is no longer a love born of God, which, being of the same nature as the Divine love which is its source, overflows its channel, but it is the highest possible human achievement. We have here not the indicative of Agape, but the imperative of Nomos.

What has been said of the Apostolic Fathers is, in the main, applicable to the Apologists. Both take, in essence, the same view of Christianity, and when they are definitely distinguished it is only because insufficient attention has been paid to the fundamental motif. We may mention, however, a specially characteristic trait.

W. Bauer has pointed out that *love to enemies* is more central in the Apologists than in the Apostolic Fathers,[3] and

---

[1] *Cf. e.g.* H. Preisker: *Die Liebe im Urchristentum und in der alten Kirche*, Theologische Studien und Kritiken, 95 Jahrg., 1923-24, p. 283, where, with reference to Barn. xix. 5, he says: " This love reveals once again something of the first glow." He is not, however, considering the point of view mentioned above, but has in view the universal range of love.

[2] This transformation in a quantitative direction is even clearer in Didache ii. 7, where, however, the text is uncertain.

[3] W. Bauer: *Das Gebot der Feindesliebe und die alten Christen* (in *Zeitschrift für Theologie und Kirche*, 27 Jahrg., 1917), pp. 43 ff.

that not so much as a commandment as an existing fact. But this is due less to a deepened understanding of Agape and a movement away from Nomos than, as Bauer suggests, to the apologetic value of the idea of love to enemies. Christians were accused of "hatred of the human race"; and what better answer could be found than to point to the centrality of love in Christianity, a love shown to enemies, which love was not a dead letter, but a living reality among Christians? The Apologists assert that Christians do not hate, but love all; they persecute none, yet themselves are persecuted—and pray for their persecutors. As the Epistle to Diognetus puts it: "They love all men, and are persecuted by all men."[1] This was a powerful argument against the persecutor. But whatever the motive, the fact remains that the Apologists helped to increase the consciousness that love is a constitutive element in Christianity, and that Christian love is "unmotivated." Nevertheless their general view is that of the Apostolic Fathers. In both cases the point of departure is *not the love God gives, so much as the love He requires of man.*

This, however, is not all that is to be said. If the idea of Agape fares badly in the doctrine of love itself, yet at other points of Christian teaching it has free scope. But before turning to this problem, we must look at the prevalent conception of Christianity in this period from a somewhat unusual angle. For this purpose we may concentrate on a single figure, the chief of the period, Justin Martyr.

4. CHRISTIANITY AS "THE TRUE PHILOSOPHY" AND "THE NEW LAW"

Historians of dogma commonly quote *rationalism and moralism* as distinctive of the theology of the Apologists. Harnack holds that they transformed Christianity into a rational philo-

[1] Epist. ad Diognetum, cap. v., 11: ἀγαπῶσι πάντας, καὶ ὑπὸ πάντων διώκονται.

sophy. " They made Christianity a deistical religion for the whole world without abandoning in word at least the old ' teachings and knowledge' of the Christians."[1] *In content* their theology hardly differs from contemporary idealistic philosophy,[2] and many a pagan philosopher expresses more strongly the need of revelation and salvation than they.[3] Their religion contains little more than the three rational ideas of the Enlightenment, God, virtue and immortality; and it is Christian in so far as this " rational theology " is guaranteed by Christ as divine revelation and therefore absolute truth. " The philosophical doctrines of God, virtue, and immortality became through the Apologists the certain content of a world-wide religion, which is Christian because Christ guarantees its certainty."[4] This view distinguishes two completely disparate elements in the " Christianity " of the Apologists, a *content* lacking anything specifically Christian, and a *form*, that of revelation, which represents Christian influence, but whose sole importance is to guarantee the truth of the content.[5] Harnack says forcefully that " the Church appears as the great insurance society for the ideas of Plato and Zeno."[6]   And alongside this rationalism we are supposed to find a moralism which betrays both Stoic and Jewish influence.

But this is pure construction, and construction which seriously misrepresents the real situation. At least it does not apply to Justin, who, far from turning Christianity into Hellenistic philosophy, is remarkably alive to their funda-

---

[1] Harnack: *History of Dogma*, vol. ii., p. 224.   [2] *Op. cit.*, p. 228.

[3] *Op. cit.*, p. 225.   [4] *Op. cit.*, p. 224.

[5] *Op. cit.*, p. 201, this distinction between form and content is sharply drawn: " If, however, strictly speaking, it is *only the form and not the content of revelation that is supernatural* in so far as this content coincides with that of reason, it is evident that the Apologists simply took the content of the latter for granted and stated it dogmatically." (Italics mine.)

[6] *Op. cit.*, p. 228.   F. Wiegand goes even further: *Dogmengeschichte der alten Kirche*, 1912, p. 24: " The question could be raised whether the Apologist Justin was a Christian at all."

mental incompatibility. We must not be misled by the picture of " the Christian in the philosopher's mantle," and assume that he has rationalised and intellectualised Christianity, missing its deeper religious significance, when he calls it " the only safe and profitable philosophy,"[1] or that the reproach of moralism is just because he describes it as " the New Law."[2] Justin has not, as a rule, been given his proper place in the history of Christianity. He is, in fact, one of the great figures, with whom few can compare. Especially is this true in relation to our present question, for it would be difficult to find anyone who so clearly recognises and expresses the fundamental opposition between Platonism and Christianity.

What, then, does Justin mean when he speaks of Christianity as " the True Philosophy " or " the New Law "? The answer to the first question will show us his attitude to the Eros motif, the answer to the second, his attitude to the Nomos motif.

(i) CHRISTIANITY AS THE TRUE PHILOSOPHY

If we are not to be misled by the associations which the word " philosophy " has for ourselves, we must ask what it means for Justin. In late antiquity, philosophy undergoes an important change. Its emphasis falls more and more on the religious and ethical problems; its great questions become those concerning God and salvation. Philosophy is occupied not with pondering theoretical, rational problems, but with the cure of souls, to bring help to a troubled and suffering generation. The philosopher is often a wandering preacher, seeking to proclaim the Way of salvation, and no clear line can be drawn between philosophy and other doctrines of salvation, Mysteries, Gnostic sects, Mantic arts, and the like. The philosophical schools become increasingly like rival

---

[1] Justin, Dial. viii. 1.   [2] Dial. xi.

sects, each recommending its own special Way to the Vision
of God.   Accordingly it is not a theoretical, but a practical,
religious interest which drives Justin to philosophy, and for
him its task is to give instruction about God and set man
in relationship with Him.   He does not recognise as true
philosophers those who are not interested in this supreme
question, but busy themselves with all kinds of other
problems.   True to the manner of late antiquity, he starts
from the problem of eudæmonism, which he wants philosophy to answer, and which is therefore the standard by
which he tests the different philosophies.   In this Justin
may be compared with Augustine.   Both are in search of
eudæmonia; both are sure that it can only be found by
finding God and entering into relationship with Him; both
test and reject the various philosophies by this standard,
until Christianity remains the only one able to lead to a real
relationship with God and so to true blessedness.[1]   On the
ways pointed out by the Greek philosophers one does not
find God, but travels farther from Him: Christianity alone
can show the right way; it alone is " the safe and profitable
philosophy."

There can be no doubt about what Justin sought in
philosophy.   " Philosophy " means for him virtually the
same as " religion," the Way to fellowship with God.   That
is why he did not seem to find what he sought either in the
Stoics or in the Peripatetics; they had nothing essential to
tell him about God.[2]   And his disappointment is understandable, when a Pythagorean teacher, instead of answering
his burning question, advised him to study music, astronomy
and geometry, as a necessary condition for attaining the
Vision of the Beautiful and Good in itself.   He was not
interested in these sciences; he wanted the Vision of God,

---

[1] Cf. the conclusion of the Dialogue, where he says of Christianity: . . . διὰ
ταύτης τῆς ὁδοῦ δίδοσθαι παντὶ ἀνθρώπῳ εὐδαιμονεῖν (142, 3).
[2] Dial. ii.

fellowship with God. For a time he thought he could find it in Platonism, and he describes his eager study of this, with his special interest in the doctrine of pure spirituality free from all corporeal taint. " The contemplation of ideas furnished my mind with wings, so that in a little while I supposed that I had become wise; and such was my stupidity, I expected forthwith to look upon God, for this is the end of Plato's philosophy."[1]   What Justin was after is clear. Platonism interests him, not as a more or less " scientific " philosophy, not even as a world-view, but as a Way of salvation, as religion. Now he had seriously tried this way, the Way of Eros, and risen on the wings of the soul; what, then, does his change of front mean, when he calls Christianity the True Philosophy instead? It certainly does not mean that he turns Christianity into rational philosophy. It simply means that Christianity is *the true religion, the right Way of salvation, the only one that can lead to real fellowship with God*. But it also implies that *Eros is rejected as a Way of salvation*.

Justin is specially interesting as the first example of a Christian to take up a *direct* attitude to the Hellenistic Eros theory. The fusion of Platonism and Christianity did not take place so easily and unnoticed as is often believed. Both sides marked the contrast between the two quite early, not only in externals, but in fundamental motif. The objections of Platonism to Christianity are best seen in Celsus, whose main line of attack is to show the absurdity of the Christian Agape motif.[2] But Christianity was equally aware of the contrast, and its objections to the Platonic Way of salvation are best seen in Justin. His polemic is doubly important as coming from a man who had himself been a wholehearted Platonist. It might be supposed that he would have retained Platonic elements which would prevent a clear insight into what is central for Christianity, but his attack on the Platonic

---

[1] Dial. ii. 6.   [2] *Cf. supra*, p. 204, n. 1.

Way of salvation is the most indisputable evidence to the contrary. His criticism of Platonism at the beginning of the Dialogue with Trypho is one of the most significant documents of the conflict between Eros and Agape in postapostolic times.

With extraordinary accuracy he touches the crux of the matter. The fundamental error of Platonism is that it presupposes a natural ability in man to make a Way to God and to attain the immediate Vision of God. Justin will not have it that man is, in his essential nature, akin to God, as Plato held, so that he needs only to consider his own Divine nature to find the Way to God; and he is a determined opponent of the fundamental Platonic doctrine of the immortality of the soul. Fellowship with God is unattainable by the method of Eros, whereby human reason makes a Way for man to God, but is possible solely as God in Agape comes down to man and meets him *through revelation*. The resources of rational nature are insufficient to gain fellowship with God; this is possible only through God's gift of His Holy Spirit. Eternal life is not won as a natural right, in virtue of the quality of the soul or spirit, but is a gift of God.[1]

Justin's description of Christianity as the True Philosophy, far from implying a tendency to Hellenisation, means rather that he rejects the Hellenistic Way of salvation and proclaims the Christian.

(ii) CHRISTIANITY AS THE NEW LAW

Justin is not the first to use the term "New Law" of Christianity.[2] It seems to have been common in very early times, and to have contributed in a measure to a nomistic conception of Christianity. What, then, does Justin mean by it?

---

[1] Dial. iv.-v.   [2] *Cf. supra*, p. 263.

Normally it is taken to imply that his Christianity was of the legalistic type. But what we have seen above with regard to his use of the term "True Philosophy" must make us hesitate here. There is much to suggest that the common view is wrong in this case as in that.

First of all, we should observe that Justin's accent is not so much upon the New *Law* as upon the *New* Law, which has made the Old obsolete and invalid.[1] To regard the term "New Law" as a sign of Old Testament or Stoic legalism means a failure to take account of the polemical point of the formula. As Justin's description of Christianity as the "True Philosophy" was not accidental in his polemic against Hellenistic philosophical opinions, neither is it an accident that he describes Christianity as the "New Law" for the precise purpose of his polemic against Jewish legal piety. The Old Testament Law was never intended as the final expression of the relation between God and man, but was to be superseded by something new. In support of this idea Justin can invoke the Old Testament itself, for it speaks of a New Covenant by which God will one day replace the Old. "Behold, the days come, saith the Lord, that I will make a new covenant with the house of Israel and with the house of Judah : not according to the covenant that I made with their fathers in the day that I took them by the hand to bring them out of the land of Egypt; which my covenant they brake, although I was an husband unto them, saith the Lord. But this is the covenant that I will make with the house of Israel after those days, saith the Lord; I will put my law in their inward parts, and in their heart will I write it; and I will be their God, and they shall be my people."[2] This and similar passages enable Justin to retain continuity with the Old Testament at the same time as he insists that Christianity is something absolutely new. Christianity knows no other God than the God of the Old

[1] Dial. xi.   [2] Jer. xxxi. 31 ff. *Cf.* Justin, Dial. xi. 3.

Testament, the God of Abraham, Isaac and Jacob; and the same God who made His Law-covenant with Israel has now made a New Covenant through Christ, which is for all peoples and therefore no longer bound either to the Law or to Israel. Christianity has not revealed a new God, but a *new Way to God*.

The expression "New Law" thus connects Christianity with certain Old Testament passages which Justin regards as prophecies, and is in line with earlier Christian usage; but it by no means implies that the New Covenant is, like the Old, of a legal nature, and that old commandments and precepts have been replaced by new. If the Law had been adequate as a Way of salvation, "what need is there of a New Covenant?" Justin asks.[1] No covenant based simply on Law can lead to salvation—and that is finally decisive for Justin. Christianity is the "New Law" and Christ the "New Lawgiver,"[2] yet the meaning is not legal. It is true that he says Christ enjoined upon us the Law of Love, but he does not on this ground regard Jesus as "Lawgiver" in the ordinary sense of the word, for he expressly says that Jesus by His Commandment of Love to God and neighbour simply summed up that Law which God had proclaimed from the beginning for every generation of the human race.[3] But if all possess the Law, all are under the curse of the Law, for none fulfils all it requires.[4] The New Covenant consists, therefore, not in the giving of a new law, but in the fact that God Himself through the Crucified, who is " God's Christ," saves " all that have committed things worthy of a curse."[5] The New Covenant is not commandments and ordinances, but Christ Himself. " What is the Covenant of God? Is it not Christ?"[6] And it is Christ, not as one who has given new laws, but just as the Crucified. " If, therefore, God pro-

---

[1] Dial. cxxii. 5.   [2] Dial. xviii. 3: ὁ καινὸς νομοθέτης.
[3] Dial. xciii. 1, 2.   [4] Dial. xcv. 1.
[5] Dial. xciv. 5.   [6] Dial. cxxii. 6.

claimed a New Covenant which was to be instituted, and this for a light of the nations, we see and are persuaded that men approach God, leaving their idols and other unrighteousness, through the name of Him who was crucified, Jesus Christ, and abide by their confession even unto death, and maintain piety. Moreover, by the works and by the attendant miracles it is possible for all to understand that *He is the New Law, and the New Covenant, and the expectation of those who out of every people wait for salvation from God.*"[1]

Clearly, for Justin the " New Law " means simply the " New Covenant." God made His Covenant with Israel and gave it His promises; promises which, however, do not belong to Israel after the flesh, but to the spiritual Israel; so that Christianity is now ready to enter into the inheritance from the fathers : " For the true spiritual Israel . . . are we who have been led to God through this crucified Christ."[2] Justin never tires of emphasising the contrast between the Law and the Cross of Christ, and insisting that it is only through the Crucified we are led to God. Not by way of the Law, but only by way of the forgiveness of sins do we come to Him.[3] " Through His stripes those who approach the Father by Him are healed."[4]

A second point which tells against the view that Justin's Christianity is nomistic, is the extraordinary significance he attaches to *the Cross of Christ*. The great theme of the Dialogue is that the Crucified is Christ; and Justin's theology might well be called theology of the Cross, for his entire thought centres solely upon it. Hence his great interest in the Old Testament, for it furnishes proof that the Crucified and no other is the Saviour promised by God. Probably no one has used more than he the two classical Old Testament

---

[1] Dial. xi. 4.   *Cf.* Dial. xliii. 1, where Christ is " the Eternal Law " and " the New Covenant."

[2] Dial. xi. 5.   [3] Dial. xliv. 4.   [4] Dial. xvii. 1.

texts in which the young Church found the chief prophetic utterances concerning the Passion of Christ and His death on the Cross, Isaiah liii. and Psalm xxii. Large parts of the Dialogue are nothing but a paraphrase of these and similar passages and their application to Christ.[1] But he does not merely use passages which can be taken as direct prophecies. The Old Testament is from beginning to end a system of symbols which point forward to the Crucified. The commandments were given because of the hardness of men's hearts, but also to point, in a mysterious manner, to Christ.[2] Justin finds the Cross indicated in the most unlikely places. The uplifted hands of Moses while Israel fought with Amalek are a type of the Cross; and when Moses remained "until evening" (Ex. xvii. 12), this was not for nothing, but a prophecy that Christ should remain on the Cross until evening.[3] The tree of life in Paradise, Moses' rod, with which he redeemed Israel, divided the Red Sea, and smote the rock so that it gave water, Aaron's rod that blossomed, the scion of the root of Jesse, the righteous man of the Psalm, who "shall be like a tree planted by the rivers of water," or the saying from another Psalm, "Thy rod and thy staff, they comfort me"—in all these Justin finds allusion to the wood of the Cross.[4]

There is a serious motive behind these apparently childish interpretations so common in the Early Church. As we said above, the word of the Cross was such a paradox that it could not be accepted without the aid of the Old Testament.[5] So it is with Justin, for whom Christ's death on the Cross is the great mystery[6] which is confirmed because already prophesied—if only darkly—in the Old Testament.[7] Yet not only the Old Testament, but the whole universe bears

---

[1] *Cf.* Dial. xcvii.-cvi., the whole of which is an allegorical treatment of Ps. xxii. On Isa. liii., *cf. e.g.* Dial. xiii. and Apol. i. 50 f.

[2] Dial. xliv. 2.   [3] Dial. xcvii. 1. *Cf.* xc. 4 f. and xci. 4.

[4] Dial. lxxxvi. For other O.T. types of the Cross, *cf.* Dial. xl. 3; xci. 1-4.

[5] *Supra,* pp. 255ff.   [6] Dial. xcvii. 4.   [7] Dial. xcvii. 3. *Cf.* c. 1.

the sign of the Cross. "For consider all things in the world, whether they could be administered or have any community without this σχῆμα·'" The sails of a ship, the plough and other implements, these too remind us by their form, of the Cross. The human form differs from irrational animals only in that it is upright; and if man stretches out his arms, he makes the sign of the Cross, while the very fashion of his face shows the σχῆμα of the Cross. Military symbols, standards and trophies are emblems of the power of the Cross.[1]

All this is abundant proof of the centrality of the Cross in Justin's Christianity and in his thought in general. The Cross is the greatest symbol of Christ's power and rule.[2] Christians have been called by God "through the despised and shameful mystery of the Cross."[3] To be a Christian is the same as "admitting the Crucified Jesus to be both Lord and Christ."[4]

We conclude, then, that when Justin speaks of Christianity as the "True Philosophy" and the "New Law," so far is he from surrendering it to Hellenistic rationalism and Jewish moralism, that he actually intends by these very descriptions to affirm its peculiar character against both of these.[5]

---

[1] Apol. i. 55.

[2] Apol. i. 55, 2: τὸ μέγιστον σύμβολον τῆς ἰσχύος καὶ ἀρχῆς αὐτοῦ.

[3] Dial. cxxxi. 2: διὰ τοῦ ἐξουθενημένου καὶ ὀνείδους μεστοῦ μυστηρίου τοῦ σταυροῦ κληθέντες ὑπὸ τοῦ θεοῦ.

[4] Dial. xxxv. 2.

[5] This is, at any rate, the tendency, too little observed by historians of dogma. They (cf. e.g. Harnack's treatment) are too much guided, partly by A. Ritschl's Die Entstehung der altkatholischen Kirche, partly by M. v. Engelhardt's Das Christenthum Justins des Märtyrers, 1878. The question of motif never occurs to Engelhardt, so that he deals merely with external traits and judges Justin by completed dogma instead of by ruling motif. But a revision of the commonly accepted view as indicated above does not mean to deny that there is a strong Stoic element in the Apologists (including Justin). We must observe (1) that Justin is decidedly outstanding, and what is true of him is not necessarily true of all the Apologists, and (2) that Justin himself is not always on the Christian level we have described. His trend, however, is clear, and must be emphasised as it has not been hitherto.

Christianity is the " True Philosophy," that is, the " True Way of salvation," the Way which really leads to fellowship with God : it is *the Way of the Christian Agape motif*, which is asserted against that of the Hellenistic Eros motif.

Christianity is the " *New Law*," that is, the " New Covenant," that Covenant which is nothing other than the Crucified Himself : it is *the Agape of the Cross*, which is asserted against every form of Jewish nomism.

5. THE THREE FUNDAMENTAL DOGMAS OF THE EARLY CHURCH

The Agape motif, as we have seen, influenced the doctrine of love very little in post-apostolic times;[1] but it was not lost, for it was able to assert itself at other points of Christian teaching.

Three fundamental dogmas give chief expression to the Christian thought of the time : (1) Belief in God as *Creator of heaven and earth*; (2) Belief in the *Incarnation*, which is intimately linked to the Cross of Christ; (3) Belief in the *Resurrection of the flesh*.

Historians of dogma have often judged post-apostolic Christianity by Reformation standards, and have not unnaturally been impressed by its comparative poverty. The ideas of justification and the forgiveness of sins are very much in the background, and Pauline influence in the period is very limited. This applies even to Justin, who stands otherwise nearest to Paul. But a judgment of this kind is entirely arbitrary. It submits an historical study to a subjective valuation for which there is no ground in the situation actually given. To do justice to this period we must observe the general rule that every age must be considered in the light of the special problems which confront it. What, then, is the special problem of post-apostolic times? It is, in

---

[1] *Cf. supra*, p. 265.

brief, to assert Christianity in a Hellenistic environment. And this is done with remarkable consciousness of purpose and power just in the three fundamental dogmas. Or perhaps we should say that the problem was twofold, to assert the peculiar character of Christianity on the one hand against Jewish nomism, on the other against Hellenistic Eros religion. If the Apostolic Fathers and Apologists had but little success in dealing with the former, and often were not even conscious that it presented a problem, they came to grips far more effectively with the latter. *In the confession of God as "Creator of heaven and earth," of the Incarnation and of the "Resurrection of the flesh," the primitive Church raised three mighty bulwarks against the Hellenistic theory of salvation.*

1. The confession of God as "Creator of heaven and earth" is a clear and conscious rejection of the Hellenistic view of salvation. It is not from the material world we need to be saved, for that is a creation of God Himself, and like all that God has made, it is in itself good. God is as much Creator and Lord of the earth as of heaven. "The earth is the Lord's and the fulness thereof; the world, and they that dwell therein. For He hath founded it upon the seas and established it upon the floods" (Ps. xxiv. 1 f.). Special emphasis is laid upon the fact that matter is also God's work.[1] Originally it has no more to do with evil than spirit has. Evil (sin) is not due to the fact that the soul, contrary to its nature, is bound up in corporeality—that is according to God's ordinance at Creation—but it consists in our disobedience and rebellion against His will. The denial that God is Creator of the temporal world is therefore often regarded as the arch-heresy in the ancient Church.[2] Another thought which occasionally occurs is Theophilus' objection to the Platonists, that God's sovereignty ($\mu o\nu a\rho\chi i a$ $\Theta\epsilon o\hat{v}$) is im-

---

[1] Tatian, Oratio ad Græcos v. 7 and xii. 2 ff.
[2] *Cf.* Justin, Dial. xxxv. 4 ff.

pugned if anything is assumed to exist that is not absolutely dependent upon Him for its existence. God's omnipotence is shown precisely in the fact that He created everything *out of nothing*.[1]

2. The confession of the Incarnation still more clearly distinguishes Christianity from Hellenism. Here, as elsewhere, Justin is in the foreground. When with the Fourth Gospel he speaks of Christ as the Logos, the Hellenist could understand him; but when with the Fourth Gospel he goes on to say that this " Logos became flesh,"[2] the Hellenist could only find it absurd. The Logos might be the Saviour, for Hellenism too can speak of a σωτήρ, a saviour, but not one who could conceivably have " become flesh." It is just from the flesh we need to be saved. Justin has no doubt about the difference. Christian salvation is not a sort of spiritualisation by which we put off the corporeal and become pure spirit, but consists in the fact that God Himself (God's Logos) becomes flesh, really comes to us, and accepts our conditions without reserve. Christian salvation does not mean that we mount up to God and meet Him on His spiritual level, but that God Himself comes down to meet us on our human, fleshly level. This mark of Agape is consummately expressed in the idea of Incarnation : " The Word became flesh and dwelt among us." Christ is God among men, " God in the form of man."[3] He is the Incarnate, the Word become flesh. In Christ, says Justin, God Himself has come and taken upon Himself suffering.[4] For Justin the Incarnation

---

[1] Theophilus, Ad Autolycum, lib. ii. 4. *Cf.* Hermas, Mand. i. 1.

[2] John i. 14: ὁ λόγος σὰρξ ἐγένετο.. *Cf.* Dial. lxxxiv. 1 f.

[3] Θεὸς ἐν ἀνθρώπου μορφῇ (Tatian, Oratio ad Græcos xxi. 1). The centrality of the idea of Incarnation is best seen in early Christian art. H. W. Beyer remarks: " The specific quality of Christian art lies primarily in the fact that it possesses a quite definite content, in that it proclaims in sensibly perceptible corporeality the Incarnate Word of the holy Love of God " (H. W. Beyer: *Die Eigenart der christlichen Kunst im Rahmen der Spätantike*, in " Von der Antike zum Christentum," Festgabe für Victor Schulze, 1931, p. 76).

[4] Dial. lxviii. 9. Tatian (Oratio ad Græcos xiii. 6) speaks of Christ as " the suffering God " (ὁ πεπονθὼς Θεός).

is always closely connected with the *Cross*, and all that has been said above about his theology of the Cross gives content to his thought of the Incarnation. For the ancient Church as a whole, both in creed and Christian consciousness, Incarnation and Cross form an indissoluble unity, and the two phrases "born of the Virgin Mary" and "suffered under Pontius Pilate" stand always together. "Born and crucified"—the phrase well describes Justin's outlook.[1] The Agape of the Cross is the background of the idea of Incarnation; not for His own sake, but for the sake of the human race, Christ became man and suffered the death of the Cross.[2]

Justin is fully aware of the *paradox* in the idea of the Incarnation. God's coming to us in Christ cannot be rationally comprehended and proved, but is an expression of the will of God which far transcends all human thoughts, and which therefore can only be stated as a fact and thankfully accepted. To the objection: "You endeavour to prove an incredible and well-nigh impossible thing; that God endured to be born and become man," he retorts that it would never occur to him to try to establish this by any human considerations, but we must seek to learn God's mind and will as He Himself has revealed it in the Holy Scriptures.[3] The paradox of the Incarnation thus becomes a necessary prelude to the Agape of the Cross.

But an important qualification must be added to the above. That is only one side of Justin's position; on the other side, he sharply distinguishes between God and Christ, and frequently expresses himself in ways which contradict what we have so far seen. He can say: "He who has but the smallest intelligence will not venture to assert that the Maker and Father of all things, having left all supercelestial matters,

---

[1] Dial lxxxviii. 4. For close connection of Incarnation and Passion, *cf*. also Barn. v.; Ign. ad Smyrn. i.
[2] *Ibid*.   [3] Dial. lxviii. 1.

was visible on a little portion of the earth."[1]   The Logos is in a way divine, but not in the strictest sense of the word. In the absolute sense He alone is God " whom we believe to be Maker and Father of all things."[2]   He alone is " unbegotten and incorruptible, and therefore God."[3]   He did not come to us; He remains always above the heavens and never reveals Himself to anyone, and has dealings with no one.[4] In relation to Him, Christ is of lower rank, a δεύτερος Θεός, " another God than He who created all things."[5]   This subordinationist trait in the Christology of the Apologists is undoubtedly to be attributed to the Greek idea of God.   It is a compromise due to the attempt to retain the abstract idea of an immovable God along with the Christian idea of Incarnation.   Consequently the genuine Christian paradox has been replaced by another: it is both God and yet not God who meets us in Christ.   Loofs' judgment of the Christology of the Apologists is right, when he says: " Their Logos doctrine is not a ' higher ' Christology than usual, but is rather on a lower level than the genuinely Christian estimate of Christ.   It is not God who reveals Himself in Christ, but the Logos, the reduced (*depotenzierte*) God, a God who *as God* is subordinate to the highest God."[6]

3. The ancient Church differs most of all from Hellenism in its belief in Resurrection.   Christian tradition affirmed the " Resurrection of the flesh," which the Apologists opposed to the Hellenistic doctrine of the " Immortality of the soul." The antithesis was conscious and intentional, for at no point so much as this was their opposition to the Hellenistic spirit

---

[1] Dial. lx. 2.   [2] Dial. lvi. 1.   [3] Dial. v. 4.

[4] Dial. lvi. 1.   *Cf.* Dial. cxxvii. 1-3: "You must not imagine that the unbegotten God Himself came down. . . .   He remains in His own place, wherever that is. . . .   He is not moved or confined to a spot in the whole world, for He existed before the world was made.   How, then, could He talk with anyone, or be seen by anyone, or appear on the smallest portion of the earth ?"

[5] Dial. lvi. 11: Θεὸς ἕτερός ἐστι τοῦ τὰ πάντα ποιήσαντος Θεοῦ, though he goes on to add: ἀριθμῷ λέγω ἀλλὰ οὐ γνώμη.

[6] Fr. Loofs: *Leitfaden zum Studium der Dogmengeschichte*, 4 Aufl., 1906, p. 129.

felt by the early Christians. The Platonic, Hellenistic doctrine of the Immortality of the soul seemed to the Apologists a godless and blasphemous doctrine, which above all they must attack and destroy.[1] Their motto in this regard might well be Tatian's word: "*Not immortal, O Greeks, is the soul in itself, but mortal. Yet it is possible for it not to die.*"[2] The difference between Christian and non-Christian in this matter was so great that belief in the "Resurrection of the flesh" could become a shibboleth. One who believes in the "Immortality of the soul" shows thereby that he is not a Christian. As Justin says: "If you have fallen in with some who are called Christians . . . and who say that there is no resurrection of the dead, but that their souls, when they die, are taken to heaven; do not imagine that they are Christians."[3]

The idea of the Immortality of the soul causes offence primarily because it is an expression of man's hybris (insolence) towards God. For Christian faith, salvation from death is a mighty act of God; in the Platonic, Hellenistic view, immortality is a native possession of the human soul. But such a doctrine, from the Christian point of view, is in line with the Fall; it is man's attempt to make himself like God, to make himself God; it is an assault on God's divinity. Instead of taking eternal life from God's hand as a gift of his unmerited Agape, man insists that he possesses it in his own right in virtue of the divine nature of the soul. That is why the idea is godless and blasphemous; it implies the claim that the soul is akin to God, and itself a divine being.[4] Justin's polemic from this point of view against the Platonic position is especially interesting (Dial. iv. ff.). He first attacks the view that the soul can attain the Vision of God on the ground of its *kinship* to Him and of the *Eros* that therefore

---

[1] Justin, Dial. lxxx. 3-4.

[2] Tatian, Oratio ad Græcos xiii. 1: οὐκ ἔστιν ἀθάνατος, ἄνδρες Ἕλληνες, ἡ ψυχὴ καθ' ἑαυτήν, θνητὴ δέ.

[3] Dial. lxxx. 4.   [4] Dial. iv 2.

dwells in it.[1] No natural endowment and no Eros can deliver the soul from corruption. If we consider merely its natural endowment, " it ought not to be called immortal."[2] But Justin does not mean that the soul must necessarily perish; he is simply attacking the doctrine of its natural immortality, the idea that its nature is such that it cannot perish. This would mean the soul's emancipation from God, so that it would not be in every respect dependent upon Him; and against this Justin's theocentric conviction rebels. God alone is eternal and incorruptible.[3] The human soul lives, not because it *is* life, as God, but because it *has* life,[4] because God imparts life to it. Life does not belong to the soul as it belongs to God.[5] If man that dies does not remain in death, that can only be due to an act of the Divine will. Here, in characteristic fashion, Justin combines the ideas of Creation and Resurrection; both bear witness to God's sovereign power. As the soul did not exist from eternity, but was called into existence by the will of God, so its future destiny depends wholly on God's will: so long as God wills that it shall live, it lives, and when God wills that its existence shall cease, then " the soul is no more, but it returns to the place from whence it was taken."[6] To this sovereignty

---

[1] Dial. iv. 1: διὰ τὸ συγγενὲς καὶ ἔρωτα.

[2] Dial. v. 1: οὐδὲ μὴν ἀθάνατον χρὴ λέγειν αὐτήν. *Cf.* Dial. v. 2: οὐκ ἄρα ἀθάνατοι.

[3] Dial. v. 4.

[4] Dial. vi. 1: ἡ ψυχὴ ἤτοι ζωή ἐστιν ἢ ζωὴν ἔχει . . . ὅτι δὲ ζῇ ψυχή, οὐδεὶς ἀντεῖποι. εἰ δὲ ζῇ, οὐ ζωὴ οὖσα ζῇ, ἀλλὰ μεταλαμβάνουσα τῆς ζωῆς.

[5] Dial. vi. 2.

[6] Dial. vi. 1: ζωῆς δὲ ψυχὴ μετέχει, ἐπεὶ ζῆν αὐτὴν ὁ θεὸς βούλεται. Dial. vi. 2: οὕτως ἄρα καὶ οὐ μεθέξει ποτέ, ὅταν αὐτὴν μὴ θέλοι ζῆν . . . καὶ οὐκ ἔστιν ἡ ψυχὴ ἔτι, ἀλλὰ καὶ αὐτὴ ὅθεν ἐλήφθη ἐκεῖσε χωρεῖ πάλιν.

Theophilus represents a somewhat similar view. He, too, links the ideas of Creation and Resurrection (*cf.* Ad Autolycum i. 7). The main passage for his doctrine of Resurrection is Ad Autol. ii. 27: Man is by nature neither mortal nor immortal, but is created with possibilities in both directions. If God had created him immortal from the beginning, He would have made him God. If He had made him mortal, He would have seemed responsible for his death. This thought is worked out with a moralistic trend, so that the emphasis is less theocentric than in Justin. Since God gave him both possibilities, man could

of God the Resurrection faith bears witness. When God through Christ awakens the dead to life on the Last Day, there can no longer be any doubt that eternal life is His gift. By setting the Resurrection faith over against the Hellenistic doctrine of the Immortality of the soul, the Apologists maintained a position of the utmost importance for Christianity.

Now it must be further noticed that the Apologists were not interested in a merely general belief in Resurrection. It is not only the soul that is to be recalled to life by the will and mighty act of God; but they show a special concern that the bodily side of man's nature, too, shall have a share in the Resurrection. That is why they speak not simply of "the Resurrection" or "the Resurrection of the dead," but precisely of "the Resurrection of the *flesh*" ($\sigma\alpha\rho\kappa\grave{o}\varsigma\ \grave{\alpha}\nu\acute{\alpha}\sigma\tau\alpha\sigma\iota\varsigma$). Here is evidence that the primitive eschatological tradition still survives in the Church; but it is with more than a tradition the Apologists are concerned. Belief in "the Resurrection of the flesh" is not simply an idea that survived; it actually plays a far greater part in the Apologists than in primitive Christianity, and the reason is undoubtedly their reaction against the Hellenistic doctrine of salvation. If the Resurrection faith in itself is already a powerful weapon in their hands, it is a far more powerful weapon when it appears as the "Resurrection of the flesh." The "flesh," corporeal

---

turn to immortality by observing God's commandments, and so receive immortality as a reward from God, and himself become God. But if, in disobedience to God, he turned to the works of death, he would himself be responsible for his death. At Creation, God endowed man with freedom and the possibility of self-determination. What man lost through disobedience God now gives on the ground of His love to man ($\varphi\iota\lambda\alpha\nu\theta\rho\omega\pi\acute{\iota}\alpha$). For as man brought death upon himself through disobedience, so now anyone who will can obtain eternal life by obedience to God's will. For God gave us His Law and His holy commandments that everyone who fulfils them may be saved, attain the Resurrection, and inherit incorruptibility.

On the connection between the ideas of Creation and Resurrection *Athenagoras* bases his "proof of the Resurrection" (*cf.* De resurrectione cadaverum 2 ff., 12 f., 18). Here, too, the moralistic, rationalising element puts his view on a much lower level than Justin's more definitely theocentric doctrine of Resurrection.

nature, is just that from which, in the Hellenistic view, man longs above all to be delivered. The body is the prison and tomb of the immortal, divine spirit. Yet, according to the Apologists, the body is to have a part in the Resurrection life, the source of this world's tragedy is to be immortalised; a thing which must have seemed the height of folly to the Platonist and Hellenist. The Apologists, however, see it in a different light. The tragedy of existence is not due to matter, to the corporeal, for this, as much as spirit, is the good creation of God. To them the Hellenistic tendency to spiritualisation and to contempt for the material and corporeal was an attack on God Himself as Creator of the material world.

If the Resurrection faith in general is determined by the conception of God, and in contrast to the doctrine of the " natural " Immortality of the soul asserts God's sovereignty, the idea of the " Resurrection of the flesh " in particular attacks the Hellenistic conception of sin. According to this last, man's innermost, spiritual self is good and perfect; evil lies in its connection with the corporeal world of sense, which degrades and sullies it. The genuinely Christian idea of sin is the absolute opposite; sin is connected with the innermost being, the will, the spiritual self of man. The corporeal, sensible world is God's good creation, which is, however, corrupted when used as an instrument for the will at variance with God, the spirit hostile to Him. God has made man with body and soul, and their union is in accord with His will. Through death and resurrection He wills to bring to completion the work He began in Creation, but which sin has spoiled; and there is no reason to suppose that this completion refers merely to one side of His creation, the spiritual, while the bodily is left out of account. Such a one-sided view, the Apologists plainly see, implies both an unjustifiable criticism of God's original plan and an unchristian conception of the nature of evil. Hence their extraordinary interest in the "Resurrection of the *flesh*," which receives all the more emphasis in face of strong Hellenistic opposition. In these circumstances, the Apologists' enthusiasm for the participation of the " flesh " in the Resurrection life is understandable;[1] the central things of Christianity are at stake: God's sovereignty, the significance of His creation, the meaning of sin and salvation. We can understand why Justin has to reckon the " Resurrection of the flesh " as an integral part of true Christian doctrine.[2]

Yet despite the Apologists' clear grasp of this issue in the main, there are serious weaknesses to be found, of which Tatian provides the outstanding example. It was he who raised the challenge quoted above: " Not immortal, O Greeks, is the soul in itself, but mortal. Yet it is possible for it not to die." Yet the same man, in developing this thesis, shows himself to be in the highest degree dependent on Gnostic—that is, Hellenistic—views. What determines whether the soul shall be saved from death, is whether or not it has participated in the divine Gnosis.[3] " If the soul continues solitary, it tends downward towards matter, and dies with the flesh; but, if it has 'communion with the divine Pneuma,'[4] it is no longer helpless, but ascends to the regions whither the Pneuma guides it: for the dwelling-place of the Pneuma is above, but the origin of the soul is from beneath. Now, in the beginning the Pneuma was a constant companion of the soul, but the Pneuma forsook it because it was not willing to follow."[5] Yet even after this separation, the soul has retained a spark of the power of the Pneuma, which is the only reason why it can form any con-

---

[1] *Cf. e.g.* Athenagoras' work " De resurrectione cadaverum."
[2] Dial. lxxx. 5: ἐγὼ δέ, καὶ εἴ τινές εἰσιν ὀρθογνώμονες κατὰ πάντα Χριστιανοί, καὶ σαρκὸς ἀνάστασιν γενήσεσθαι ἐπιστάμεθα.
[3] Oratio ad Græcos xiii. 1: ἡ ἐπίγνωσις τοῦ Θεοῦ.
[4] Here is used the typically Gnostic expression συζυγία τοῦ θείου πνεύματος.
[5] Oratio ad Græcos xiii. 4: τοῦ μὲν γάρ ἐστιν ἄνω τὸ οἰκητήριον, τῆς δὲ κάτωθέν ἐστιν ἡ γένεσις.

ception of the Divine at all, though its conception can of course be nothing but a caricature, since the soul separated from Pneuma cannot attain the perfect Vision.[1] A glance at this passage is sufficient to show the large Gnostic influence on Tatian's conception of the soul and consequently on his idea of the Resurrection. Little is gained, from a Christian point of view, by rejecting the natural immortality of the soul, if at the same time it is allowed to possess a 'pneumatic' divine spark, in virtue of which it can win immortality. Tatian has travelled far from the clear and simple theocentric basis for Resurrection given by his teacher, Justin, who says that the soul partakes of life because God wills that it shall live. These views of Tatian cannot, however, be taken as representative, if for no other reason than that the ancient Church generally—on different, but kindred grounds —regarded him as a heretic.[2]

Historians of dogma have as a rule simply noted as a fact, without further consideration, the attitude of the Apologists to the Hellenistic doctrine of Immortality.[3] How little that which lies behind their polemic has been understood, the example of Harnack shows. He quotes from the "De resurrectione" (by an unknown author): "If the Redeemer had only brought the message of the (eternal) life of the *soul,* what new thing would he have proclaimed in addition to what had been made known by Pythagoras, Plato, and the band of their adherents?" and comments: "This remark is very instructive, for it shows what considerations led the Apologists to adhere to the belief in the resurrection of the body (Sw. flesh)."[4] This seems to mean that the Apologists

---

[1] *Ibid.* xiii. 5. The divine "spark" is referred to here as ἔναυσμα τῆς δυνάμεως αὐτοῦ [τοῦ θείου πνεύματος].

[2] Irenæus, Contra hær. i. 28, 1; *cf.* A. Hilgenfeld: *Die Ketzergeschichte des Urchristentums,* 1884, pp. 384 ff.

[3] Harnack mentions it (*History of Dogma,* vol. ii., p. 213, n. 1): "Most of the Apologists argue against the conception of the natural immortality of the human soul."

[4] Harnack, *op. cit.,* p. 195, n. 1.

held the " Resurrection of the flesh " in order to outdo the Greek philosophers, who only taught the Immortality of the soul. But even if there are passages which suggest this thought, that is not the Apologists' real concern. Belief in the " Resurrection of the flesh " is not the complement of the Immortality of the soul, but the contradiction of it. We are faced here with an " Either—Or " : either immortal life as something which belongs to the natural constitution of man, or eternal life as a gift of God, founded upon His work of grace and power, which calls into existence that which does not yet exist and summons the dead to life.

*　　*　　*　　*　　*

If we now finally survey the Apologists' interpretation of Christianity as seen in the three fundamental dogmas of God as Creator of heaven and earth, of Incarnation, and of the Resurrection of the flesh, we shall see that they all have a common reference. An obvious interest in the material, sensible side of existence is an element, at first sight striking, common to them all. The dogma of Creation is presented with great stress on the fact that God is Creator, not only of heaven, but also of earth; the sensible as well as the spiritual world is His work, and it is most strongly asserted that matter ($\mathring{v}\lambda\eta$) is God's creation. As for the Incarnation, the world itself (caro) shows where the accent falls. God's entry into human life in Christ, it is insisted, is not a matter of mere " spiritual " presence, but of nothing less than that God's Logos became " flesh " ($\sigma\acute{a}\rho\xi$). And the doctrine of Resurrection, in the form of " Resurrection of the flesh " ($\sigma\alpha\rho\kappa\grave{o}s$ $\mathring{a}\nu\acute{a}\sigma\tau\alpha\sigma\iota s$) manifests the same trend. In view of this, it is easy to understand the judgment of traditional history of dogma, that the conception of salvation in the early Church is " naturalistic," that salvation is thought of in " physical-hyperphysical " and not in personal or ethical terms. Such naturalistic ideas may have crept in here and there, but it should be clear from what we have seen above that the traditional view is quite mistaken. The chief interest which the three fundamental dogmas are meant to preserve is not naturalistic. Yet it would be no less a mistake to conclude that the chief interest is "personal" and "ethical." The alternatives, "physical-ethical," "naturalistic-personal," are quite inapplicable here. These categories do not touch the issues with which the earliest Christian theology was concerned. When historians of dogma insist upon the crudity of the ideas employed, they have considered only the external garb in which the ideas are presented—and on this superficial level they are undoubtedly right. Their mistake is simply not to have looked behind the outward forms for the motif to which they give expression. And here there is no room for doubt. The three fundamental dogmas of the Early Church exist to give expression to the theocentric Agape motif. They are, as stated above, three bulwarks raised by the ancient Church in defence of the Christian Agape motif against the assaults of Hellenistic Eros piety. The latter, with its spiritualising tendency, with its disposition to find evil in the connection with matter and to conceive salvation as an ascent and spiritualisation, of necessity forces the attention of its opponent towards matter and the "flesh." These "crude" conceptions are thus legitimate expressions of the Agape motif in its conflict with Eros piety.

The Agape motif had to prosecute its campaign on two fronts in post-apostolic times: against the Nomos motif inherited from Judaism, and against the Eros motif that threatened it from the surrounding world. On the latter, the anti-Hellenistic front, the Apostolic Fathers and the Apologists were in many points victorious. On the former, however, they did not succeed in rescuing the Agape motif from the clutches of Nomos.

III

THE EROS TYPE IN GNOSTICISM

1. Gnosis and the Eros Motif

WE have seen the effect of the Nomos motif on the Christian idea of love in post-apostolic times, and we are now to turn to the second type, in which Eros is the central and ultimately determinative motif.

Dependence on the Old Testament offered protection to the Apostolic Fathers and the Apologists against the Eros motif. The great Old Testament tradition, with its faith in the Living God at work in history, has naturally little room for such a motif. Yet the protection it afforded was far from effective. Already in pre-Christian times Judaism had been considerably Hellenised, which means that vital elements of Eros theory had been adopted by late Judaism; and therefore similar elements are, quite naturally, found in the Apostolic Fathers and the Apologists. Apart from direct contact with its Hellenistic environment, the connection of early Christianity with late Judaism lays it open, in a measure, to influences from the Eros motif as well as to the dangers of Nomos. These are, however, never more than influences; in the nature of the case the Eros motif could not be dominant. The strength of a position like Justin's lies in the fact that in the midst of a Hellenistic environment —and he himself had previously tried the Way of Eros—he is so clearly conscious of the contradiction between the Hellenistic and Christian fundamental motifs, and is relatively untouched by the outlook of Eros.

Quite different is the picture presented by Gnosticism. Here the Eros motif overwhelms Christianity as a flood. Gnosticism is a disastrous attempt to involve Christianity in the religious syncretism of late antiquity, and to transform it into a Hellenistic-Oriental Mystery religion of the usual type.

Gnosticism, in spite of the energetic study devoted to it,[1] is still one of the more obscure points in the history of Christianity. This is partly due to the nature of the sources, which are mainly the polemical and therefore biassed accounts of the Fathers. But there are also very diverse opinions about the origins of Gnosticism; some think it is Babylonian, others suggest Iranian models, or influences from Orphism, and so on. There is, however, the less reason to accept any one of these theories, since the Gnostic sects, in accordance with their generally syncretistic character, derive their material from widely different sources. A glance at the extraordinarily variegated mythology of Gnosticism will show at once that this must be the case.

We need not, however, stay to discuss these still disputed points, as our interest is in the general structure of Gnosticism as a whole, upon which more definite agreement is being reached. Chiefly important is the realisation that, although extant sources almost without exception show us only "Christian Gnosticism," yet Gnosticism is not really a native Christian phenomenon at all. It is not merely a sect within Christianity, but a sample of the widespread general syncretism in which virtually the whole of the religious world of antiquity was involved before Christianity arose. But—and this is what is important in our context—what

---

[1] Of the extensive literature on the subject may be mentioned—A. Hilgenfeld: *Die Ketzergeschichte des Urchristenthums, urkundlich dargestellt*, 1884; W. Bousset: *Hauptprobleme der Gnosis*, 1907; E. de Faye: *Gnostiques et gnosticisme. Étude critique des documents du gnosticisme chrétien aux IIe et IIIe siècles* (1913), 1925; R. Reitzenstein: *Die hellenistischen Mysterienreligionen* (1910), 3 Aufl., 1927, pp. 66 ff., 284 ff., 393 ff.; H. Leisegang: *Die Gnosis*, 1924; W. Bauer: *Rechtgläubigkeit und Ketzerei im ältesten Christentum*, 1934; H. Jonas: *Gnosis und spätantiker Geist. I. : Die mythologische Gnosis*, 1934. On source-critical questions—E. de Faye: *Introduction à l'étude du gnosticisme aux IIe et IIIe siècles*. Revue de l'histoire des religions, tome 45-46, 1902.

supremely sets its mark upon this syncretism is precisely *the Eros motif*. The syncretistic religions of late antiquity, including the Gnostic sects, are all essentially doctrines of salvation founded on the idea of Eros. The main question for them all is that of the *destiny of the soul*, which originally belonged to a higher world; its fall and present misery; its desire and longing for something higher and better; its return to its heavenly origin; the way and the stages it must traverse for this purpose; the discipline and the purifications which are conditions of this return—that is, purely things which belong to a pronounced Eros outlook.

A very different view of the Gnostics, frequently held, represents them as the first Christian *theologians*, who were primarily attempting to work out a consistent Christian theology or philosophy of religion. Their concern was thus not syncretism, but unambiguous definition of the specific nature of Christianity. This is Harnack's view in his " History of Dogma " and, still more pronounced, in his latest work on Marcion. He holds it to be " characteristic " of the Gnostic heretics, " that *they refused to admit the syncretism of religious motifs*, and opposed to it a more or less unambiguous religiosity and doctrine. They rightly perceived that the source of this impure syncretism lay chiefly in the Old Testament," which they therefore entirely or in part rejected.[1] Now Harnack can neither deny nor ignore the fact that Gnosticism distinguishes itself by a far-reaching syncretism, but he finds this to be a " paradoxical fact." " In the Gnostics," he says, " we have the remarkable phenomenon, that they . . . by segregating numerous religious and ethical *leitmotifs*, gave Christianity an unambiguous structure, but at the same time to a large extent lived by borrowing from alien Mystery speculations."[2]   Harnack

---

[1] A. v. Harnack: *Marcion : Das Evangelium vom fremden Gott.* 2 Aufl., 1924, p. 13.
[2] *Op. cit.*, pp. 13 ff.

tries to escape the difficulty by saying that these Mystery and myth speculations were used by Gnosticism as the means to carry through that consistent interpretation of Christianity which he supposes to have been the main task of the Gnostics. "We forget," he says, "that Gnosticism means, negatively, the rejection of late Jewish syncretism with its disparate religious motifs, and positively, the attempt to carry through an *unambiguous* religious motif on the basis of the Christian message, because we allow ourselves to be confused by the motley mass of myth speculations which the Gnostics employ. But these are only intended to serve as support for a fundamentally simple religious faith, since they were thought to provide the philosophical and historical expression of the chief theological idea which was to be pursued."[1]

This view does no justice to the real situation. The double sense, above all, in which the word "syncretism" is used is most misleading. It is not the case that the primary interest of the Gnostics was to give an unambiguous account of the unique nature of Christianity, that they were thus obliged to surrender the Old Testament, and that, as a secondary consequence, certain mythological, syncretistic elements entered in. Gnosticism is primarily syncretistic, and that in the strictest sense of the word. The Gnostics approach Christianity with a ready-made, alien motif, by which they put it to rights; and the syncretism in question consists not merely in the combination of certain external ideas and conceptions, but in the *confusion of motifs*. We may admit Harnack's claim that it is a "simple religious faith" that is concealed behind the medley of fantastic speculations, but we may not stop there; we must ask what motif it is which finds expression in this "simple religious faith." Harnack thinks it obvious that this simple faith can mean nothing but "an unambiguous religious motif on the

[1] *Op. cit.*, p. 14, n. 1.

basis of the Christian message "; but here the apparently obvious is in the highest degree problematical. Harnack's chief mistake is in using the formal idea of "an unambiguous religious motif" as if it must necessarily mean a Christian motif; but this is just what needs investigation. To the question, what motif dominates the Gnostic type of piety, there can only be one answer: *the Eros motif.* Plainer proof of this could not be wished than is furnished by a closer examination of the Gnostic Way of salvation.

2. THE GNOSTIC WAY OF SALVATION

What first attracts attention in Gnosticism is its cosmology. This mainly occupies the foreground in the Fathers' attack on the Gnostic heretics. It is easy to regard Gnosticism as primarily a world-view, an explanation of the world, and indeed, Gnosis means the unveiling of a mystery, the imparting of a knowledge not previously possessed. But it is not knowledge in the ordinary sense, not any knowledge whatsoever, that interests the Gnostic; his motto is not knowledge for its own sake. He desires a quite definite knowledge only: knowledge of the Way of salvation, of the mysterious formulæ and passwords which give the soul access to the higher world and bring about its perfect union with the Divine.[1] Hence comes the intimate connection between Gnosis and the Vision of God. Gnosis is knowledge of " who we are and what we have become; whence we are and whither we come; whither we hasten, whence we are redeemed; what our birth is and what our rebirth."[2] Gnosticism can very easily lose itself in cosmological speculations, speculations about æons, and so on, but it is always

[1] " The aim of Gnosis is not to give an answer to the questions posed by a thirst for knowledge that boldly presses forward over the bounds of intellectual cognition, but its aim is to show the way and the means for the salvation of the soul." W. Anz: *Zur Frage nach dem Ursprung des Gnostizismus,* 1897, p. 24.

[2] Clem. Alex., Excerpta ex Theodoto lxxviii. 2.

speculation on a practical religious basis and with a practical religious aim. Its interest, for example, in the planetary spheres and their rulers arises primarily because it sees in them stages which the soul has to pass through, and obstacles which it must overcome, in its ascent to the heavenly fatherland. *The centre of the Gnostic outlook is thus undoubtedly the problem of salvation.*

The root idea is simple enough. This world in which we live is an unnatural mixture of spiritual and material, of elements from the higher light-world and the world of darkness. Salvation consists in the dissolution of this misalliance, and the return of the pneumatic, divine element in man to its natural home in the world of pure spirit.

In structure and general content this idea is closely akin to the Platonic doctrine of salvation, the doctrine of Eros. Yet the differences are not slight. With the Platonic dualism of spirit and matter, the intelligible and sensible worlds, is linked here that of Oriental religious cosmology, the dualism of the heavenly light-world and the world of darkness.[1] Thus there arises real opposition, actual conflict, between the two worlds, as there does not in Plato. Further, what in Plato concerns the individual soul becomes, in Gnosticism, a comprehensive world-drama. But there is also a marked difference in very atmosphere, inasmuch as the distance between the Divine world and the world of matter is infinitely greater in Gnosticism; the Divine has been removed to a far greater height, the world of sense to a far greater depth. God is no longer the Idea of the Ideas, but is unapproachably enthroned high above the Ideal world. This extreme transcendence corresponds closely to the spirit of the age; more peculiarly Gnostic is the degradation of the material world. Granted that appeal could be made to Plato, for he is sharply critical of the sensible world, yet he

[1] On the difference between the two sorts of dualism, *cf.* *supra,* p. 169.

never degrades it as the Gnostics do. It participates in the Ideas, and, despite all, the Cosmos is beautiful; and all that is beautiful, even sensible beauty, points upward to what is Beautiful in itself. Gnosticism, on the other hand, cannot find words strong enough to express its abhorrence of the world we live in. It is not beautiful, but full of misery, filth and uncleanness. The difference between Platonism and Gnosticism on this point can best be seen in Plotinus' polemic " against the Gnostics, or those who say that the Demiurge is evil and the world is bad " (Enn. II., 9). Admitted that this world's beauty is only that of a copy, and it is dangerous for man to surrender himself to anything that cannot give him genuine satisfaction, nevertheless it reminds us of, and points us to, the higher world.

This Gnostic exaggeration of transcendence and degradation of the sensible world makes the problem of the relation between God and the world much more acute. A double question arises: first, how can God, the absolutely Transcendent and Good, have created so evil and impure a world? and secondly, how can we deliver ourselves from this world and attain the Divine life? The former question is cosmological, the latter soteriological.

Gnosticism finds the answer to both questions in the " Alexandrian world-scheme," with its double perspective, the Descent of the Divine and the Ascent of the human spirit, the issue from God and the return to Him, emanation and 'remanation.' As regards the cosmological question, the Descent of the Divine, there is introduced, in accord with the general practice of the time, a large number of intermediaries, æons, which emanate in descending scale from God. The farther such an intermediate being is removed from God, the less of His substance it includes. It was one of these lower beings, the Demiurge, that produced the material world, and hence comes its impurity and corruption. Therefore the Highest God is not responsible for it; the lower, Creator god, the Demiurge, is god of this world.

Just as in the "Alexandrian world-scheme," the cosmological Descent now turns into the soteriological Ascent, though it should be observed that there is, in the Gnostic view, no ground in the descending movement itself for this return. This impure, material world cannot be saved and raised to the Divine world; everything in existence must obviously occupy the place for which it is by nature designed; the spiritual takes the highest, the material the lowest place. This is as it should be, and this is as it is in reality. Existence is an ordered whole, in the sense that everything occupies the place which natural necessity assigns. Yet at one point—that is, in man—this order is broken. By his bodily nature, he belongs to the material world, and therefore is rightly in the low position he actually holds. But the human being includes elements of the higher, pneumatic world; man's spirit is a divine being imprisoned contrary to its nature in the body, a divine seed sown in hostile matter, a spark from the primal divine fire, that has fallen into the world of darkness; it is the pearl that has sunk down into the dim depths of the sea. By reason of its true nature, the human spirit ought to occupy the highest place in existence, but, fettered as it is by the material and corporeal, it occupies the lowest. It lives as a stranger in a most unhappy land; it longs to escape, but is held back by matter and its Ruler, the Demiurge, who will not let the noble prisoner go. As regards his spirit, man is thus infinitely higher than all that belongs to this world. He is higher than the Demiurge, who holds him prisoner in his world,[1] higher than the "Archons" that bar his way as he seeks to return to his heavenly fatherland. "I am of those above,"[2] is the Gnostic's proud boast in the face both of this

---

[1] Hippolytus, Elenchus vii. 23.

[2] ἐγὼ γάρ, φησί, τῶν ἄνωθέν εἰμι.   Epiphanius, Panarion hær. xxvi. 13, 2.

world's God and of the Rulers of the various planetary spheres.

Gnosticism is thus, in the strictest sense, a *Way of salvation*; Gnosis is salvation technique. There is a definite way the human spirit must traverse, certain stages it must pass step by step, in order to return to God. The symbol of the ladder, which we found in Plato and, with certain modifications, in Aristotle,[1] is also found, though in a markedly mythological form, in Gnosticism. On its heavenly journey, the human spirit must ascend through the various spheres which separate it from the Highest God, and in each must put off something of its bodily covering—not only the crude, material body, but also the finer and lighter ethereal or astral body—until finally, freed from all contamination of sense, it becomes altogether spiritual. Obscure and complicated as the Gnostic system is in detail, the scheme employed here is simple, clear and suggestive : salvation consists in this, that the human spirit breaks away from the sensible and material, and returns to the higher world, passing in its Ascent through the same stages as the Divine traversed in its Descent.

This might suggest that Gnosticism was only a simple application of the " Alexandrian world-scheme " with its cosmological Descent and soteriological Ascent; but that is by no means the case. *Gnosticism goes further than this scheme at a decisive point, inasmuch as it speaks of a Divine Descent not only in a cosmological, but also in a soteriological connection.* The Gnostic development of the " Alexandrian world-scheme " is specially interesting as a symptom of a movement—faint and groping, it is true—towards the Christian Agape motif. A comparison of Gnosticism with Plato and Neoplatonism on this point is illuminating. In Plato we find the simple, unambiguous doctrine of Eros; there is only one movement between the two worlds, the

[1] *Cf. supra*, pp. 174, 179, 185.

upward Way of Eros. Salvation is the soul's Ascent, and nothing else. Plotinus is more complicated in that he fits the doctrine of Eros into the " Alexandrian world-scheme." He speaks not only of the " Way up " but also of the " Way down," not only of the Ascent of the human soul, but also of the Descent of the Divine. This might be thought to indicate a development towards Agape, for Agape means primarily the Descent of the Divine; but it is not so, because the Divine Descent is here purely cosmological and has nothing to do with salvation.[1] Salvation is still nothing but the Ascent of the soul. In Gnosticism, however, the situation is quite different. There is a Divine Descent, whose aim is precisely the salvation of man. Salvation is no longer simply the Ascent of the soul to the Divine life, but it also includes *a Divine action, an intrusion into human life from above.*

This is very closely connected with the difference in the view taken by Gnosticism and by Platonic-Neoplatonic teaching of the position of the human soul here in the world. There is on the whole, it is true, considerable agreement between them. Both agree that the human spirit sojourns by accident and under compulsion as guest and stranger here below, for it belongs by its whole constitution to the higher world. The idea of its divine origin and nature is for both the necessary metaphysical condition of the possibility of salvation at all. Further, both are conscious that the divine possibility dwelling in man cannot become actuality except by awakening and prompting from without. The divine spark in man is hidden under the ashes, on the point of extinction; if it is to burst into full flame, oxygen must, so to speak, be brought to it from outside. Thus far, Platonic and Gnostic theory is in complete agreement, but when they come to define this external, awakening influence, they part company.

[1] On this *cf. supra*, pp. 196 f.

For Platonism, with its sharp separation (χωρισμός) of the two worlds, all thought of help from above is excluded. The higher world has no connection with the lower, and cannot intervene. But intervention is unnecessary, since the soul, in the midst of this lower, sensible, material world, is surrounded on all sides with things which can awaken the memory of the higher. The beauty of sensible things points beyond itself to that which is in itself Beautiful, and so gives the soul occasion to reflect that it belongs to the supersensible world. Thus the soul finds the external aid it needs in the very world where it is held prisoner. It is characteristic of the Platonic theory of salvation to operate with this dual significance of the world of sense: on the one hand, the world of sense is opposed to that of the Ideas, it is the prison-house of the soul, that from which the soul is to be saved; on the other hand, it participates in the Ideas, and so can supply the motives required to awaken the soul from its lethargy. And what has been said of Platonism applies equally to Neoplatonism.

For Gnosticism, however, this solution is out of the question, for it finds no such dual significance in this world. From the point of view of salvation, this world has only negative value; it is simply the prison-house of the soul; in it there is nothing, with the exception of the human spirit itself, which can bear witness to a higher world. The spirit, sunk in matter, lacks anything to make it conscious of the high origin it has forgotten. If it is to be awakened from its slumber at all, it must be reached by a message from above, from the higher world.

At this point the figure of the saviour (σωτήρ) becomes important, and contact with Christian tradition is closest. Alien as Gnosticism is to Christianity, stamped as it is by the Eros motif, yet the Gnostics claimed to be Christian, and claimed it with apparent justification inasmuch as they consciously connected salvation with the Person of Jesus

Christ. He is the Messenger from the higher world, the Ambassador of the Highest God to us. Through all the spheres which separate this God from our world, He came down to bring salvation to the spirit imprisoned in matter. The Platonic χωρισμός between the two worlds has disappeared; and though Plotinus' dictum, that He " does not descend from the kingly throne,"[1] might well apply to the Highest God of Gnosticism, yet its meaning would then be essentially different. Plotinus means that the frontier of the different worlds is respected, and although intermediate stages have been introduced into the Platonic scheme, these are kept sharply distinct. There is therefore no immediate relation between the Divine and our world. Quite otherwise is it in Gnosticism. Even if the Highest God does not Himself leave His throne in order to descend, yet the advent of the Divine saviour makes a direct connection with the Divine world.[2] His Descent means precisely that the frontiers of the different spheres are crossed, and—a thing which must be strongly emphasised—*crossed from above*. This is something new in Eros piety.

What is the relation of this new element to the opposition between the Eros and the Agape motifs? Has Gnosticism seriously broken through the Eros scheme and reached a really Christian view of the content of salvation?

In answering this question we must guard equally against overestimating as underestimating the Christian contribution to the Gnostic doctrine of salvation. It is an underestimation to represent Gnosticism as a wholly pagan religion that has nothing whatever to do with Christianity, or has at most received a very thin Christian veneer.[3] For Gnosticism took not only the *name* of its saviour from Christianity; it was con-

---

[1] Enn. iv. 8, 4.

[2] On the other hand, we are told, *e.g.* : " And [the Gospel] came in reality, *although nothing descended from above ; nor did the blessed Sonship . . . leave its place*." Hippolytus, Elenchus vii. 25, 6.

[3] *Cf. e.g.* W. Bousset: *Hauptprobleme der Gnosis*, 1907, pp. 323 ff.

vinced—in varying degrees in different Gnostic sects[1]—that it represented genuine Christianity. Jesus Christ is the great turning-point of world history. He succeeded where all His predecessors failed, in leading the souls imprisoned in matter up to their Divine origin. For the Gnostics He is therefore *Saviour* in an exclusive sense, and so they can lay claim to be reckoned as Christians. On the other hand, the Christian element would be overestimated, if the part here played by Christ the Saviour were supposed to indicate a Christian conception of salvation. The whole Gnostic doctrine is built up on the Eros scheme, and the thought of Christ is introduced without destroying this scheme. Salvation means nothing but the deliverance of the spirit from the toils of matter. Furthermore, Christ is not, in Gnosticism, Saviour in the full Christian sense. He is rather Teacher and Revealer of the Gnostic secrets and Forerunner on the Gnostic Way of salvation. His task is to awaken rather than, strictly speaking, to save. Power to ascend to the Divine life exists already in the imprisoned human spirit; it only needs to be awakened and made effective. Not that the Gnostic preaches mere self-salvation; he is too well aware of man's helplessness for that, and without the Saviour and the message from above no salvation would be possible. On the other hand, the Saviour fulfils much the same function as the beauty of the sensible world in Platonism. In both cases it is a question of setting in motion the possibilities already present in the human spirit, but unable to function without such external stimulus. We might most accurately say that *the task of the Gnostic Saviour is that of Forerunner and Example for the self-salvation of the human spirit*. Gnosticism compromises between self-salvation and salvation

---

[1] E. de Faye is right in saying that we should speak of a series of " Gnosticisms " rather than of " Gnosticism." But here, as throughout this study, we are dealing with the general distinguishing features of the Gnostic structure, and can therefore neglect individual differences.

through Divine intervention, with a leaning to the former. "*Through its own instrumentality*"[1] the soul ascends to the heavenly world. Anything that does not possess this power, that does not belong to the higher world by nature from the beginning, even the heavenly Saviour cannot save.

If corruption, in the Gnostic view, consists in the improper union of spirit and matter, then salvation consists in the separation of the disparate elements so that each comes again to its rightful, natural place. The saving significance of Jesus is due to the fact that in Him the first beginning is made of this separation and return home. It is this that gives the death of Jesus special significance for the Gnostics; its purpose is to bring about the final separation. His suffering does not touch His spiritual nature, but only the lower, bodily and psychical side, which through death returns to its material or psychical origin, whereas the spirit is set free and soars aloft through all the severing spheres to the Highest God.[2] Awakened by the Saviour, the pneumatic part of every man must now arise and undertake the same heavenly journey as He, in accord with the principle that "What has come down from above shall through Him ascend."[3]

To sum up, we may say that the Gnostic Way of salvation manifests a uniform tendency, that of Eros. It is the way upwards from below, κάτωθεν ἄνω.[4] "All things hasten upwards from below, from things inferior to those that are superior. For not one of those things that are among things superior is so silly as to descend beneath."[5] This is the unmistakably Hellenistic basis of Gnosticism.

---

[1] . . . ὡς δύνασθαι δι' αὐτῆς ἀναδραμεῖν, Hippolytus, Elenchus vii. 26, 10; cf. vii. 22, 9.

[2] Elench. vii. 27, 8 ff.

[3] Elench. v. 12, 6: τὰ μὲν γάρ, φησίν, ἄνωθεν κατενηνεγμένα κάτω ἀνελεύσεται δι' αὐτοῦ.

[4] Elench. vii. 22, 8.   [5] Elench. vii. 22, 16.

3. THE TRANSFORMATION OF AGAPE INTO VULGAR EROS

The above account of Gnosticism might seem to suggest that, dominated as it is by the Eros motif, it has nothing to say of Agape at all. But the contrary is in fact the case; for Agape receives frequent and prominent mention. Yet we may not conclude from this that the Agape motif played any real part in Gnostic theory. Merely the name is used, and the Eros motif really holds complete sway. Agape loses its original meaning and is transformed into Eros; not, however, be it observed, into the sublimated " heavenly Eros " of which Plato and his followers speak, but into that despised variety, "vulgar Eros." And it is not difficult to see how this happened. It was bound to be the result of the Gnostic confusion between Eros and Agape, since Gnosticism in principle knows no other love than Eros, yet seeks to force Agape into its scheme. What, then, does ' God's love ' mean in this context? Two ideas are combined: first, since Eros theory dominates the whole, love can only mean longing, appetite, desire; secondly, as it is God's love, it cannot ascend, for there is nothing above God on which He could set His love, and consequently it must be directed downwards to the world beneath Him. These two ideas in combination result in downward-directed desire—that is, vulgar Eros.

The process by which Agape was transformed into vulgar Eros can be studied in the *Diagram of the Ophites*,[1] or in the Justinian *Book of Baruch*.[2]

The *Diagram of the Ophites* is an attempt to portray Gnostic cosmology, which Origen preserves in his work against Celsus. The latter, in his attack on Christianity, had described and ridiculed the Diagram of the Ophites; and Origen replies by saying that Christianity cannot be held responsible for the inventions of heretics. He also gives a

---

[1] Origen, Contra Celsum vi. 24-38.   [2] Hippolytus, Elenchus v. 23-28.

more exact description of the Diagram than Celsus, "to show," as he says, "that we know those things better than he, even although we also disapprove of them." In this way, the points of chief interest to us have been preserved.

According to the Diagram of the Ophites, existence is divided into three realms, which are represented by three circles: uppermost is the Kingdom of God or the realm of pure spirit, Pneuma, which can also be called the pure light-realm; beneath this is the middle realm or realm of the soul, since soul is a mixture of light and darkness; and lowest is the realm of Cosmos. Our interest here is in the uppermost realm, God's realm in the strict sense. It is represented by two concentric circles, the larger described as that of the Father, the smaller as that of the Son. But like a leaden weight, there hangs at the bottom of these two circles yet a third, with the inscription "*Agape*": it is the love-longing that draws the Divine down towards the lower world.[1] 'Αγάπη thus becomes the same as ἐπιθυμία; the Divine love becomes the same as desire, or downright sensual passion.

[1] *Cf.* Origen, Contra Celsum vi. 38. During the last century the descriptions of the Diagram of the Ophites by Celsus and Origen have been the subject of several attempts at interpretation. *Cf.* J. Matter: *Histoire critique du gnosticisme,* 1828, vol. ii., pp. 222 ff.; R. A. Lipsius: *Über die ophitischen Systeme, II.: Celsus und Origines* (Zeitschrift für wissenschaftliche Theologie, 1864, pp. 37-57); A. Hilgenfeld: *Die Ketzergeschichte des Urchristenthums,* 1884, pp. 277-283; H. Leisegang: *Die Gnosis,* 1924, pp. 168-174.

The accompanying figure illustrates the Diagram, in so far as it is of importance for our purposes.

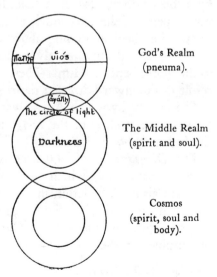

God's Realm (pneuma).

The Middle Realm (spirit and soul).

Cosmos (spirit, soul and body).

Justin's *Book of Baruch* offers a good commentary on this Diagram, the order of events being described as follows. When Elohim looked down, he was inflamed with desire for the lower world, which is pictured as a fabulous being, half maiden, half snake, and named Eden or Israel. The union (γάμος) of Elohim and Eden produced men, who received the soul from below, from Eden, and Pneuma from Elohim. Thus the double nature of man is a constant reminder of his double origin, from God and from the lower world.[1] But as there dwelt in Elohim's nature an upward impulse, he could not for ever remain in the lower world. He deserted Eden and ascended again to the higher regions, accompanied by his angels. But men, who were the result of his union with the lower world and had in themselves something of Elohim's Pneuma, were left here below.[2] This is the source of the world's suffering and distress,[3] since that which belongs by nature to the upper world has been imprisoned in the lower, but has an unquenchable longing to ascend. The cause of the whole tragedy of the world is God's love-longing downwards, God's Agape or God's ἐπιθυμία.[4] *Agape is Elohim's Fall;* his descent to which it led is the origin of all evil, just as his return on high shows man by what way he, too, must ascend to gain the redemption of Pneuma.[5] As leader on this heavenly way, Elohim has again and again sent out his angel Baruch—hence the title, *Book of Baruch.* He was sent to Moses, then to the Old Testament prophets and, on Hellenistic ground, to Herakles. But all these succumbed,

---

[1] Elench. v. 26, 25: ἡ μὲν γὰρ ψυχή ἐστιν 'Εδέμ, τὸ δὲ πνεῦμα 'Ελωείμ, ἑκάτερα ὄντα ἐν πᾶσιν ἀνθρώποις.

[2] Elench. v. 26, 21: . . . τὸ πνεῦμα τοῦ 'Ελωείμ τὸ ὂν ἐν τοῖς ἀνθρώποις.

[3] Elench. v. 26, 14: γέγονε δὲ ἡ τῆς κακίας ἀνάγκη ἐκ τοιαύτης τινὸς αἰτίας.

[4] Elench. v. 26, 19: . . . εἴ πως εἰς ἐπιθυμίαν ἐλθὼν ὁ 'Ελωείμ κατέλθη πρὸς αὐτήν. *Cf.* v. 26, 2: ἦλθεν εἰς ἐπιθυμίαν αὐτῆς.

[5] Elench. v. 26, 24: ἀναβὰς γὰρ πρὸς τὸν ἀγαθὸν ὁ πατὴρ ὁδὸν ἔδειξε τοῖς ἀναβαίνειν θέλουσιν, ἀποστὰς δὲ τῆς 'Εδὲμ ἀρχὴν κακῶν ἐποίησε τῷ πνεύματι τοῦ πατρὸς τῷ ἐν τοῖς ἀνθρώποις.

more or less, to the temptations of the lower world, until finally, in the days of King Herod, Baruch was sent to Jesus of Nazareth, who withstood all temptations and so became the Saviour who could go before men on the heavenly way. In His death, above all, He demonstrates how Pneuma is to be separated from the soul, which belongs to earth. For when on the Cross the bond was broken between His earthly soul and heavenly Pneuma, He gave back His earthly, psychic man to its lower source, to Eden, with the words: " Woman, thou retainest thy son "; but His spirit (Pneuma) He commended into His Father's hands and ascended to the Good One.[1]

Against this background it is easy to understand why Agape, when it occurs in Gnosticism, is readily made the *principle of Creation.* Hippolytus describes the view of the Valentinians thus : In the beginning the Father existed alone, " but since He had power to generate, it seemed good to Him to generate and bring forth the most beautiful and perfect which He had within Himself, for *the Father was not fond of solitariness. For,* says he, *He was all Agape, but Agape is not Agape except there may be some object of affection.*"[2] So the Father brought forth Nous and Aletheia, these brought forth Logos and Zoe, and these in turn brought forth man.[3] Now Christianity can say, rightly, that God created the world by reason of His love; but in a Gnostic context, Agape as the ground of Creation has nothing whatever to do with the Christian idea of love, but is developing towards Eros. In the oldest Greek poetry Eros appears as

---

[1] Elench. v. 26, 31 f.: ἐποίησεν αὐτὸν σταυρωθῆναι· ὁ δὲ καταλιπὼν τὸ σῶμα τῆς Ἐδὲμ πρὸς τὸ ξύλον, ἀνέβη πρὸς τὸν ἀγαθόν. εἰπὼν δὲ τῇ Ἐδέμ· γύναι, ἀπέχεις σου τὸν υἱόν, τουτέστι τὸν ψυχικὸν ἄνθρωπον καὶ τὸν χοϊκόν, αὐτὸς δὲ εἰς χεῖρας παραθέμενος τὸ πνεῦμα τοῦ πατρός, ἀνῆλθε πρὸς τὸν ἀγαθόν.

[2] Elench. vi. 29, 5: φιλέρημος γὰρ οὐκ ἦν. ἀγάπη γάρ, φησίν, ἦν ὅλος, ἡ δὲ ἀγάπη οὐκ ἔστιν ἀγάπη, ἐὰν μὴ ᾖ τὸ ἀγαπώμενον.

[3] Elench. vi. 29, 6 ff.

the driving force in the Cosmic process;[1] and *it is just this original function of Eros that Agape assumes in Gnosticism.*

From these fundamental principles ethical consequences can be drawn in two opposite directions, *ascetic* and *antinomian,* and examples of both are found in Gnosticism.

Asceticism is the more obvious. Since things bodily derive from an evil, or at least a weak and worthless Creator, naturally they must as much as possible be suppressed and mortified. It is man's misfortune that, in him, something of the divine Pneuma is in bondage to the low, vile world of the Demiurge. His struggle for freedom is therefore a struggle against the material, sensible world and its Creator. Everything that weakens and destroys the bodily side of existence is a link in the process of salvation. The place and importance of asceticism are thus given; it is a way of undermining the tyranny of the Demiurge.

The tendency to asceticism, however, readily turns into its opposite, the tendency to *antinomianism.* If the divine Pneuma is our innermost being, our true self, then the main thing is to save this, whatever happens to our lower, inferior part, our outward man. It is of sole importance to free Pneuma from the chains of sense. But this is done less by ascesis than by Gnosis, not by a moral life, but by the rebirth which takes place in the Gnostic Mystery-cults. Hence arises great indifference to ethical life in general. A pure ethical life is for the lower, merely psychical man, who is preserved by ascesis and good works from total corruption,[2] but it is not for the pneumatic man, who is *by nature* above the risk of corruption and can live in the world as he pleases. As things material are by nature incapable of salvation, so pneumatic

---

[1] Hesiod, Theog. v. 116-133. *Cf.* Pauli-Wissowa, RE vi., 1909, col. 489: " In this sense Eros played an important part also in cosmogonies, as in Hesiod's Theogony; but especially in the doctrines of the Orphics, probably before Hesiod, in the poem about the world's egg from which Eros springs and which the Orphics called Phanes."

[2] Irenæus, Contra hær. i. 6, 4.

things by reason of their nature simply *cannot* be overtaken by corruption—quite independently of how the pneumatic man conducts his life. " For even as gold, when submersed in filth, loses not on that account its beauty, but retains its own native qualities, the filth having no power to injure the gold, so they affirm that they cannot in any measure suffer hurt, or lose their pneumatic substance, whatever the material actions in which they may be involved. Wherefore it also comes to pass, that the ' most perfect ' among them addict themselves without fear to all those kinds of forbidden deeds of which the Scriptures assure us that ' they who do such things shall not inherit the kingdom of God.' "[1]   It could indeed be a definite duty of the pneumatic man to yield to all kinds of vices. The Law is given by the god of this world; by transgression of it we oppose him with that part of our being which is rightly under his sway, and so help to break his power. Vice spoils his creation, while Pneuma, being superior to the world, takes no harm from it.[2]

This is the darkest point in the whole history of the Christian idea of love. In Gnosticism, Christian Agape is drawn into the syncretistic whirlpool of late antiquity, is dragged down and associated with the lowest and most repulsive cult forms in the history of religion. It is not merely transformed into Eros, not merely into vulgar Eros, but into the very lowest forms of this. Epiphanius, who himself had been present at the rites of a Gnostic sect which he calls Phibion-

---

[1] Irenæus, Contra hær. i. 6, 2 f.

[2] Eusebius, Eccles. hist. iv. 7, 9: " In accordance with these things they [the followers of Carpocrates] taught that it was necessary for those who wished to enter fully into their mysteries, or rather into their abominations, to *practise all the worst kinds of wickedness, on the ground that they could escape the cosmic powers* [archons], *as they called them, in no other way* than by discharging their obligations to them all by infamous conduct." From this point of view, anything like ascesis is naturally rejected. Far from being of value, it still further confirms the power of the Demiurge and the Archons; *cf.* Epiphanius, Panarion hær. xxvi. 5, 8: " They condemn those who fast, and say that it is not lawful to fast. For *fasting is a work of the archon that created this æon.*"

ites, describes them as follows. They begin with a sumptuous meal, at which even the poor eat flesh and drink wine to excess. After they have inflamed themselves in this way " the husband leaves his place at his wife's side, and says to his own wife : ' *Get up and perform Agape with the brother.*' And the wretches unite themselves with one another."[1] Then follows the sperma-communion : " They communicate their own shame and say : ' This is the Body of Christ.' "[2] What Epiphanius relates of this Gnostic sect is, moreover, not an isolated case. There are often indications of similar things at different times and with reference to different sorts of Gnosticism. Hippolytus writes, about a century earlier, of the Simonists : " They say : ' All earth is earth, and there is no difference where anyone sows, provided he does sow.' And they congratulate themselves on their intercourse with strange women, asserting that this is perfect Agape."[3]

" Asserting that this is Agape "—with this, judgment is pronounced on the Gnostic interpretation of Christianity.

---

[1] Epiphanius, Panarion hær. xxvi. 4, 4: ἀνάστα, ποίησον τὴν ἀγάπην μετὰ τοῦ ἀδελφοῦ. The charges of immorality levelled by the heathen against the Christians were evidently not wholly fictitious, though they applied not to the Christian churches, but to the Gnostic sects. But the heathen could not be expected to make this distinction, since the Gnostics, too, claimed to be Christian. Just as the Gnostics compromised Christianity in the eyes of the heathen, so it was probably partly due to them that the " love feasts " (agapai) fell into disrepute within the Christian Church.

[2] Panarion hær. xxvi. 4, 7.

[3] Hippolytus, Elench. vi. 19, 5: πᾶσα γῆ γῆ, καὶ οὐ διαφέρει ποῦ τις σπείρει, πλὴν ἵνα σπείρῃ, ἀλλὰ καὶ μακαρίζουσιν ἑαυτοὺς ἐπὶ τῇ ξένῃ μίξει, ταύτην εἶναι λέγοντες τὴν τελείαν ἀγάπην. The following from Clem. Alex., after the Gnostic Basilides, shows the same trend: " As a part of what is called God's will we have received that we are to have loved all things in order to rescue the Logos entire for the All " (Stromata IV., cap. xii. 86, 1). The underlying idea is this: Just as the Divine seed, by reason of God's Agape or ἐπιθυμία, was joined to the lower existence and thereby produced the human race, so human seed is the bearer of Divine creative power and can give rise to new human beings, in whom the Divine Spirit (Pneuma) is joined to matter. The more of this creative power that is lost without resulting in new human lives, the better, for it is thus delivered from the dominion of the Demiurge, and the imprisoned spirit is set free to return to its Divine source. *Cf.* also Jude 12-14, and Justin, Apol. i. 26, 6 ff. and 27. For the idea of " perfect Agape," *cf.* Clem. Alex., Strom. VII., cap. xvi. 102, 1.

Nothing could betray more clearly than this grotesque perversion of the fundamental Christian motif, that the Gnostics
in fact had nothing in common with Christianity, although
they claimed the Christian name. And it is no unjustifiable
application of modern standards to a primitive phenomenon
to say that Gnosticism transformed Christian Agape into the
lowest form of " vulgar Eros," for this was also the verdict
of its contemporaries. Clement of Alexandria is particularly
interesting in this connection. He is clearly aware of the distinction between two sorts of Eros underlying Plato's Eros
doctrine. The Eros Plato praises is the noble, sublimated
Eros, born of the heavenly Aphrodite and therefore called
the " heavenly Eros."[1] From this Plato sharply distinguishes
the " vulgar Eros," which is the son of the " vulgar Aphrodite," πάνδημος Ἀφροδίτη, of which he says in the Symposium : " Now the Eros that is the son of the vulgar Aphrodite is really vulgar and lends himself to anything. This
is the Eros we see in the meaner sort of men."[2] It is the
" vulgar Eros " and his mother, πάνδημος Ἀφροδίτη, that
seduce men to levity and dissipation.[3] Clement employs this
distinction for his protest against the Gnostic travesty of
Agape. How dare these impudent heretics seize upon the
name of Agape and use it for a description of their shameful
deeds, their πάνδημος Ἀφροδίτη?[4]

4. Gnosticism and the Three Fundamental Dogmas of Early Christianity

In the Apologists we saw that although the Agape motif
was eclipsed in their doctrine of love, it was represented elsewhere, especially in the three fundamental dogmas of Creation, Incarnation, and the Resurrection of the flesh. We

---

[1] Cf. supra, pp. 49 ff., 172 f.   [2] Symposium 181.   [3] Ibid.
[4] Clem. Alex., Strom. III., cap. ii. 10, 1 : . . . μελετήσαντας δὲ ἐν τοιαύτῃ
ἀγάπῃ τὴν κοινωνίαν. Cf. cap. iv. 27, 1 : εἰσὶν δ᾿ οἱ τὴν πάνδημον Ἀφρο-
δίτην κοινωνίαν μυστικὴν ἀναγορεύουσιν ἐνυβρίζοντες καὶ τῷ ὀνόματι.

cannot say anything similar of Gnosticism.   It has as little
room for the idea of Agape at other points in its system as
in its doctrine of love.   Its Way of salvation, as we saw above
(par. 2), is governed by the Eros motif; even when it speaks
of Agape, it means nothing but the most vulgar Eros (par. 3);
and its attitude to the fundamental dogmas confirms its
absolute opposition to the Christian Agape motif.   It is no
accident that the Gnostics reject these three ideas; indeed,
they regard it as one of their chief duties to attack them.

1. God is not the Creator of heaven and earth.   The
Highest God has nothing to do with the world of sense.
This is produced by a lower being, the Demiurge, and the
best proof of his imperfection is the fact that the creation is
such as it is: material, uncouth, impure.   It is this Creator
the Jews worship as their God, and the Law is the expression
of his will.   He threatens with a curse all who transgress
his will, but is instead himself " the accursed God."   This
title is applied by the Ophites, mentioned above, to the
Creator of the world, the God of the Jews.[1]   The Serpent
which seduced men to fall from the Creator, did them, in
fact, a kindness; he taught them to know the distinction
between good and evil and unmasked for them the real character of the Creator-God.   Therefore the Ophites named their
sect after the Serpent (ὄφις).

2. The idea of Incarnation is equally rejected.   Although
Gnosticism has something corresponding to or reminiscent
of this in its doctrine of the Saviour who comes down to the
lost world with a message from the Highest God,[2] yet it has
no place at all for " the Word became flesh," it knows no
real σὰρξ ἐγένετο.   It has a sort of Christology, but it is,
characteristically, docetic.   The Gnostics never tire of insist-

---

[1] Origen, Contra Celsum VI., cap. xxvii.: . . . λέγοντες θεὸν κατηραμένον
τὸν Ἰουδαίων, τὸν ὄντα καὶ βροντῶντα καὶ τοῦδε τοῦ κόσμου δημιουργὸν
καὶ Μωϋσέως καὶ τῆς κατ᾽ αὐτὸν κοσμοποιίας θεόν.   On " the accursed
God " see Contra Celsum VI., cap. xxvii.-xxix.

[2] Hippolytus, Elench. vii. 25-26.

ing that Christ did not really become man. If, like other men, He had had anything to do with the sensible, material world, He could not be a Saviour and Guide to the higher world. Despite all they say of the necessity of the Saviour's advent in the world, it is one of their chief concerns to deny the "foul mysteries" of His Birth.[1] They can assert that something real happened when the Gospel came into the world, yet they still more emphatically affirm that this cannot mean that the Divine Son really left His place at the Father's side and actually came down to us: "The Gospel came in reality, though nothing descended from above; nor did the Son ('the blessed Sonship') retire from that Inconceivable, and Blessed, and Non-Existent God."[2]

This docetism reacts upon the view taken of the Cross. The suffering of Jesus is not real, but apparent. Basilides says it was not Jesus who suffered; He had no real body and so could not be held by His enemies, but was able, whenever He wished, to ascend to God. At the Crucifixion He stood by, invisible, and watched Simon of Cyrene crucified in His stead, and He laughed His cheated adversaries to scorn.[3] It is therefore wrong to confess Christ as "the Crucified"; we should rather confess Him who was believed to be crucified. "If anyone confesses the Crucified, that man is still a slave and under the power of those who formed our bodies."[4] Nothing could show more clearly how far Gnosticism is from the Christian idea of Agape. Christ proves His heavenly mission not so much in that He gives Himself in love and endures suffering, as by deceiving and laughing to scorn His adversaries—a truly Hellenistic thought. We are reminded of Celsus' query: "What great deeds did Jesus perform as being a god? Did he put his enemies to shame, or bring to

---

[1] Hippolytus, Elench. v. 19, 21: τὰ ἐν μήτρᾳ μυστήρια μυσερά.

[2] Elench. vii: 24, 6: ἦλθε δὲ [τὸ εὐαγγέλιον] ὄντως, καί <τοι>, οὐδὲν κατῆλθεν ἄνωθεν οὐδὲ ἐξέστη ἡ μακαρία υἱότης ἐκείνου τοῦ ἀπερινοήτου καὶ μακαρίου οὐκ ὄντος Θεοῦ.

[3] Irenæus, Contra hær. i. 24, 4.　　　[4] Ibid.

a ridiculous conclusion what was designed against him? If not before, yet why now, at least, does he not give some manifestation of his divinity, and free himself from this reproach?"[1]

3. Finally, Gnosticism rejects absolutely belief in the Resurrection of the flesh. Salvation refers exclusively to the spirit and means its deliverance from corporeality. To refer it to the body as well would be meaningless, for as the spirit is divine and immortal by nature, so the body is by nature perishable;[2] it must suffer disintegration and be annihilated, and no power can save it from this fate. And it is good that this is so, for if things bodily were also to participate in eternal life, that would mean the perpetuation of the ground of this world's misery.

5. GNOSTICS AND APOLOGISTS

We must notice finally the completely altered aspect which post-apostolic Christianity presents on an examination of the fundamental motif.

Recent historians of dogma have been in the habit of exalting the Gnostics at the expense of the Apologists. The former are described as the first Christian theologians, whose work was an attempt to maintain the uniqueness of Christianity; and it has even been said, they had a far clearer sense of this than the Apostolic Fathers and the Apologists.[3] The chief representative of this view is Harnack, who finds " the deepest distinction between Christian philosophers like Justin and those of the type of Valentinus " in the fact that the latter sought for a *religion*, the former for *assurance* as to a theistic

---

[1] Origen, Contra Celsum ii. 33 and 35. *Cf.* on this, *supra*, p. 204, n. 1.

[2] Irenæus, Contra hær. i. 24, 5: " Animæ autem solam esse salutem: corpus enim natura corruptibile exsistit."

[3] E. de Faye: *Gnostiques et gnosticisme*, 1913, p. 442: " Strictly speaking, these Gnostics have a finer sense of what is properly Christian than the Apostolic Fathers, and *a fortiori*, than the mass of Christians of their time."

and moral conception of the world which they already possessed. At first the complexus of Christian tradition was foreign to them both. The Gnostics sought to make it intelligible; the Apologists were content to accept a revelation, which witnessed to the one, spiritual God, to virtue and to immortality. Superficially, says Harnack, the Apologists were the conservatives, but that was because they did not meddle with the contents of tradition. " The Gnostics, on the contrary, sought to understand what they read and to investigate the truth of the message of which they heard." He sums up his view as follows: " The Gnostics sought to determine what Christianity is as a religion, and, as they were convinced of the absoluteness of Christianity, this process led them to incorporate with it all that they looked on as sublime and holy, and to remove everything they recognised to be inferior. The Apologists, again, strove to discover an authority for religious enlightenment and morality and to find the confirmation of a theory of the universe, which, if true, contained for them the certainty of eternal life; and this they found in the Christian tradition."[1]

There is a sound observation behind Harnack's statement. The Apostolic Fathers and Apologists did, in fact, take over the Christian tradition without the thorough revision to which the Gnostics subjected it. But Harnack's explanation of this is entirely misleading, especially when he sees in the opposition between Apologists and Gnostics a conflict between morality and religion. *The conflict is between two separate religious-ethical principles, two religious and ethical outlooks, each with its central motif.* The Apologists are in the tradition that goes back through primitive Christianity to the Old Testament, and granted that they are to a large extent influenced by Old Testament nomism, yet they have far more right than the Gnostics to be considered guardians of the Christian tradition. The Gnostics are on the line of

[1] Harnack: *History of Dogma*, vol. ii., pp. 172 f.

Hellenistic tradition, and their outlook is completely dominated by the Eros motif. Naturally they could not accept. Christianity in the form in which they found it. If it was to be of any use to them at all, it had to be revised and adapted to the fundamental religious motif they already possessed. It is this process of religious transformation, this syncretism of opposed religious motifs, that we have witnessed above. There is no need of such far-fetched explanations as Harnack's for the fact that Gnosticism in general rejects the Old Testament. That is the natural reaction of the Hellenistic spirit to an incompatible tradition. Yet not only the Old Testament, but the fundamental Christian motif equally, suffers the reprobation of Gnosticism. With their Hellenistic idea of fellowship with God, the Gnostics were bound to assail not only the Old Testament, but also the specifically Christian faith in God. When they waged war on the God of Creation and the Law, proclaimed by the Old Testament, and the Early Church replied by throwing all its weight on the side of the Old Testament, this did not mean that it simply fell back to the Old Testament level. *Ultimately the conflict is between a theocentric and an egocentric religion.* Gnosticism is an *egocentric religion of salvation.* Believing in the divine nature of his own self, and with a sense of superiority to the world, the Gnostic launches an assault on the Cosmic world and its Creator. Aided by illumination from above, he ascends to his natural home and, become divine, triumphs over the lower powers. All this is thoroughly Hellenistic, and at the same time completely egocentric. And it is absolutely different in kind from the Christian faith. Christianity is a *theocentric religion of salvation.* Creation as well as Redemption is God's own work, and salvation is not a stage in the spiritual self-assertion of man, but a work of God's compassionate, loving will to fellowship. That modern history of dogma has not sufficiently observed this obvious difference in fundamental motif is probably due largely to the fact that the historians themselves have been unconsciously working with Hellenistic presuppositions. The acceptance of certain of the premises of Hellenistic religion was involved when Ritschlian theologians saw the significance of religion in the fact that it helped man to assert himself in his spiritual superiority to nature, and tried to interpret salvation on the basis of the conflict between spirit and nature, reason and sense.[1]   It was thought self-evident that every religion of salvation must be egocentric; and there was therefore no occasion to subject the content of the idea of salvation to closer analysis.   Wherever the need of salvation was to the fore—as it undoubtedly is in Gnosticism—it was taken for granted that here was something akin to Christianity.[2]   But, in fact, the need and longing for salvation are by no means proper only to the sphere of the Agape motif, but are at least equally strong in Hellenistic Eros piety.   The Early Church understood the difference better than traditional history of dogma has done.   Justin saw what was the root of all Gnostic heresies: it was Hellenistic *self-deification*.[3]

---

[1] *Cf.* my *Urkristendom och reformation*, 1932, pp. 88 ff.

[2] *Op. cit.*, pp. 11 f.: "One of the gravest weaknesses of the traditional history of dogma lies in the fact that it works with the concept of 'salvation' as though it were capable of only one meaning.   Even in scholars of the standing of Harnack and de Faye one can observe how the simple statement that a particular view is marked by a strong 'interest in salvation' is allowed to serve as proof that this view bears a specifically Christian stamp or at least is closely related to Christianity.   They are satisfied so long as they find 'salvation' spoken of, and do not trouble to analyse more closely the content of that 'salvation,' to discover whether it means a Hellenistic or a Christian conception of salvation, Eros' or Agape's way of salvation.   But in this way they also lose the possibility of a real understanding of the development of Christian dogma, which was actually impelled by the conflict between these two opposed views of salvation."

[3] Justin, Apol. i. 26, 1: . . . ἀνθρώπους τινὰς λέγοντας ἑαυτοὺς εἶναι θεούς.   A. Hilgenfeld, *Die Ketzergeschichte des Urchristenthums*, 1884, p. 23, remarks on this passage: "Heresy as it opens with the two Samaritan Magi, Simon and Menander, is still *self-deification*.   Heresy as it finally appears in Marcion of Pontus is the degradation of the Creator into an imperfect being far below the Highest God.   But the former kind of blasphemy remains the basis, in which the latter is forthwith included."

IV

THE AGAPE TYPE IN MARCION

1. THE REDISCOVERY OF THE IDEA OF AGAPE

THUS far we have seen how the Agape motif was thrust into the background in post-apostolic times. In the Gnostics it was wholly supplanted by Eros; in the Apologists it survived, but was adapted to a nomistic scheme, which prevented it having serious effect. Yet there was in this age one instance where the Agape motif powerfully asserted itself and became central for the interpretation of Christianity. And this occurred, peculiarly enough, in Marcion, the man whom the Early Church regarded as the arch-heretic of all.

Harnack's monograph on Marcion describes him as incomparably the most significant religious personality between Paul and Augustine.[1] Without further qualification this judgment perhaps contains a measure of exaggeration; but with specific reference to the history of the Christian idea of love, there is probably no other between Paul and Augustine who could rival Marcion in importance.

The first impression on turning to Marcion from the Apologists and Gnostics is that here at last someone has understood how absolutely new the Christian message is, someone who has also perceived what its newness ultimately is. In sublime language Marcion can describe the miracle of the Divine love. Absolutely new and undreamed, it enters the world through Christ; without warning it comes as an astounding revelation from above. " O miracle above all miracles, rapture, might, and wonder, so that we can say

---

[1] Harnack: *Marcion*, 2 Aufl., 1924, p. 20.

nothing at all about the Gospel, nor think anything about it, nor compare it with anything!"—so runs what was probably the opening sentence of Marcion's "Antitheses."[1] The thought of the absolute newness of Christianity is intimately connected with Marcion's basic idea of the contrast between the God who created us, and the God who in Christ effected our salvation. The world we live in bears clear testimony to the weakness and imperfection of its Maker; it is crude and impure, and Marcion, like the Gnostics, has nothing but contempt for it. But what is true of the world in general—here Marcion parts company with Gnosticism—applies equally to man; he too, body and soul, is a work of the Creator-God, and his weakness and infirmity are convincing evidence of his Maker's inferiority. Further, the Creator is also the God of the Law, who holds men prisoner under his commandments and ordinances. In this situation, against this background, the great and amazing miracle takes place. The Highest God is seized with sympathy for the misery of men, and descends Himself in Christ to bring them deliverance. In compassionate love He wills to save what not He but another created. In abounding mercy He adopts the children of another. Being the Stronger, He vanquishes the Creator-God, despoils him, and leads his oppressed children to a new and better home.

It is easy to see why Marcion so stresses the idea that the Highest God, the Father of Jesus Christ, has nothing to do with the creation, but is an entire stranger to us. He is plainly concerned for Agape. The more he emphasises that God is the Stranger, the greater is the miracle of the Divine love, the greater the paradox of God's Agape. The denial of all connection between Creation and Redemption is meant to assert the absolutely "unmotivated" nature of the Divine love. Nothing was farther from Marcion than the idea that God's love is something self-evident; on the contrary, it is

---

[1] Harnack, *op. cit.*, pp. 74 f., 87, 94, 256.*

the greatest conceivable paradox. What could there be in humanity, the wretched work of the Creator-God, to motivate the saving intervention of the Highest God? What joy or gain could He have of taking for His own these neglected and mis-shapen children of another? Try as we will, we can find nothing in men themselves, nor in their condition, to explain the Highest God's dealings with them. The explanation lies solely in Himself, in His goodness and mercy; this is the only reason for His interest in them. " The Good One had sympathy with those strange to Him as sinners. Neither as good nor as evil did He love them (desire them), but being moved with compassion He pitied them."[1] Here is revived Paul's thought in Rom. v. 8, that God proved His love to us " while we were yet sinners." Marcion sees clearly the difference between the two sorts of love, Eros and Agape, the love that desires to possess and the love that freely bestows. He knows that Agape has nothing at all to do with ἐπιθυμία, but derives its character from God's mercy and His will to give. The chief characteristic of the Highest God for Marcion is His unmotivated goodness; He is " ultro bonus ";[2] and the Divine salvation is unmotivated goodness just because it comes to those who are originally strangers to Him. Tertullian puts into the mouth of Marcion, or a disciple of his, the plea " that that is rather a primary and perfect goodness which is shed voluntarily and freely upon strangers without any obligation of friendship, on the principle that we are bidden to love even our enemies, such as are also on that very account strangers to us."[3] Elsewhere he writes: " If Christ was the Creator's

---

[1] Adamantius, Dialogue i. 3: Συνεπάθησεν ὁ ἀγαθὸς ἀλλοτρίοις ὡς ἁμαρτωλοῖς· οὔτε ὡς ἀγαθῶν οὔτε ὡς κακῶν ἐπεθύμησεν αὐτῶν, ἀλλὰ σπλαγχνισθεὶς ἠλέησεν. Quoted from Harnack, op. cit., Beilage V. (8), p. 264.

[2] Tertullian, Adv. Marcionem iv. 36.

[3] Tert., op. cit., i. 23: " Scio dicturos atquin hanc esse principalem et perfectam bonitatem, cum sine ullo debito familiaritatis in extraneos voluntaria et libera effundatur, secundum quam inimicos quoque nostros et hoc nomine iam extraneos diligere iubeamur."

Son, it was with justice that He loved His own creature; if He comes from another God, His love was excessive, since He redeemed a being who belonged to another."[1]

In the nature of the case, such a living and clear idea of Agape as we find in Marcion was bound to attack both the Nomos and the Eros motif. We must therefore proceed to examine this double reaction somewhat more closely.

2. The Reaction against the Nomos Motif

The most prominent feature of Marcion's thought is his violent opposition to the Old Testament, and this is very closely connected with his interest in Agape. Marcion has a lively conviction that what is given through Christ is absolutely new, and so he will not permit it to have any connection with what went before. To take the view common in the Church, that the Gospel of Christ was simply a continuation and a new phase of the Old Testament revelation, would be to undervalue and endanger its newness. It would be to put a new patch on an old garment or new wine into old bottles—a procedure condemned by Jesus Himself in Luke v. 36 ff. Marcion emphatically rejects all attempts to fit Christian love into the framework of Nomos. He wants the idea of Agape alone.

What made possible the confusion of Agape with both Nomos and Eros was the *allegorical interpretation of Scripture*. In general, it may be observed that allegorism and syncretism readily go hand in hand—for obvious reasons. Allegorism is arbitrary, and can make anything mean anything; contours are obliterated and different motifs run easily into one another. This method had been developed especially in Hellenistic Judaism (Philo) and was carried further by Gnosticism; but even the Apologists welcomed it,

---

[1] Tert., De carne Christi iv.: " Si Christus creatoris est, suum merito amavit; si ab alio deo est, magis adamavit, quando alienum redemit."

and thanks to it elements from totally different spiritual spheres could be inoffensively united. Against this, Marcion demands a *literal interpretation of the Holy Scriptures*.[1] Conscious that Christianity had brought something absolutely new, he had to try to determine in what this consisted and how it differed from all else. But for this purpose a method of interpretation which could make words mean what it pleased and obliterate distinctions was of no value. It was of the greatest importance to let everything be just what it is.

In view of this, Marcion finds in the Old Testament a totally different spirit from that of Christianity: the spirit not of Agape, but of Nomos. The message of Christ is marked by the spontaneous love and mercy of the Highest God, shown to ' strangers,' unmotivated and uncalculated. In the Old Testament, on the other hand, man's relation to God is dominated by the idea of retribution, of reward and punishment. It is to be noted that Marcion does not so much object to the Old Testament in itself, as to its invasion of Christian territory. Before the revelation through Christ, it was all man had; the Highest God was still unknown, and he could only know of the Creator, the God of this world. But since the message from the Highest God has now come, all the old is passed away, and we must no longer cling to it in any form. Our relation to the old is not to be one of co-ordination but one of conflict. It is not a question of two different stages of which the earlier is included in the later and lives on in it, but their relationship is purely *antithetical*. Significantly enough, Marcion's chief work was entitled " Antitheses," and there is reason to suppose that it was mainly constructed so that Old and New Testament sayings were set antithetically side by side.[2] But Marcion carried his distinctions into the New Testament as

[1] Evidence in Harnack, *op. cit.*, p. 260.*
[2] Harnack, *op. cit.*, p. 256* ff. (Beilage V.: Die Antithesen Marcions).

well. As genuine Christian writings he recognised only ten
Pauline epistles and the Gospel according to St. Luke, after
duly purging these of supposed Judaising additions. Only
in these writings, and above all in Paul's attack on "the
Law" did he find that contrast of Gospel and Law which
was the basis of his whole interpretation of Christianity.[1]
So they confront each other, the God of the Old and the
God of the New Testament, the merely "righteous God"
(ὁ δίκαιος Θεός) and the "good God" (ὁ ἀγαθὸς Θεός),[2]
the God of Law and the God of Love; and "no man can
serve two masters."[3] We must refuse faith and obedience
to the Creator, the God of the Law, and give ourselves
wholly to the "good God." The age of the Law is irrevocably past, and the age of the Gospel has entered with
the rule of love. Away, then, with the Old Testament!
And away with its inferior ethical principle: "An eye for
an eye, and a tooth for a tooth!" Only the principle of love
is valid for Christianity.

3. THE REACTION AGAINST THE EROS MOTIF

In opposition to the Old Testament, Marcion could make
common cause with the Gnostics, and his arguments against
the Creator and the God of the Jews are largely those with
which Gnosticism has made us familiar. It is not surprising,
therefore, that the Fathers regarded him as a Gnostic pure
and simple. More recent study, however, especially that of
Harnack, has plainly proved that such a view is unjust to
Marcion. And this is further confirmed by his attitude to
the fundamental religious motif of Gnosticism, the Eros
motif, for he is strongly opposed to this, too.

For Marcion, as for Gnosticism, everything ultimately

---

[1] Tert., Adv. Marcionem i. 19: "Separatio legis et euangelii proprium et
principale opus est Marcionis."
[2] Harnack, *op. cit.*, pp. 262* f.
[3] Luke xvi. 13; *cf.* Harnack, *op. cit.*, p. 260.*

turns on the question of salvation; but, unlike the Gnostics, he has nothing that can strictly be called a Way of salvation; which at once gives an indication of his complete divergence from them. The Gnostic doctrine of salvation includes two ideas: (1) God is *the Unknown*; He is enthroned in remote transcendence and has no direct connection with our world, in which there is nothing that bears witness to Him. (2) Yet He is *not a Stranger*[1] to us, nor we to Him; we are His off-spring, a divine essence dwells within us, and the Gnostic doctrine of salvation is meant to describe that Way of salvation by which the Divine within us can return to its source above. The Gnostic outlook depends upon and derives its peculiar character from the combination of these two ideas: God is the Unknown, yet not a Stranger to us. But this connection is broken by Marcion, for according to him, God is the Unknown and the *absolute Stranger* to us. " For centuries, so long as the Marcionite Church survived, and in every language which Marcionites spoke, ' the Stranger ' remained the proper name for their God. On the other hand, from God's point of view, men were also ' the strangers.' That they had none the less come together and that the strangers had become God's children, was acknowledged the great mystery of this religion."[2]

On this basis, Marcion criticised most sharply a number of the basic tenets of Gnosticism. It is false, he holds, to say that our innermost being derives from another world. We are the work, not of the Highest God, but of the Creator alone; there is no divine spark in us; even the highest we possess comes from the Demiurge. We cannot, therefore, with the Gnostics, speak of man as a stranger and sojourner

---

[1] It should be noted, however, that the distinction between " the Unknown " and " the Stranger " is not everywhere rigidly observed. So, *e.g.*, the word *strange*, " the strange life," is used in Mandæan literature *in the same sense* in which Gnosticism employs the expression " the *Unknown* God." *Cf.* H. Jonas: *Gnosis und spätantiker Geist*, i., 1934, p. 96.

[2] Harnack, *op. cit.*, pp. 118 f.

here in the world, and of the body as the prison of the spirit. Man is at home in the world and belongs by nature entirely to it. Likewise, it is improper to say that Christ "came to His own": He did not come to His own, but to those who were strangers to Him. Only by His revelation did they obtain any knowledge of the higher world and of their new home. Now the Gnostics, it is true, can speak of a revelation, and say that it is only through a message from above that we know anything of the higher world; yet the difference between them and Marcion on this point is obvious. As regards the Gnostics, we may compare the external revelation with oxygen, which must be applied so that the divine spark hidden under the ashes may burst into full flame. The revelation really brings nothing new, but helps to make actual what already exists potentially in us; by its means, the Divine within us is awakened to life. Quite different is the situation in Marcion. The function of revelation is not simply to awaken slumbering powers and possibilities, but it brings something really new. If the Gnostic doctrine of salvation combines self-salvation and the salvation that comes from God, Marcion wants to make salvation exclusively a Divine work. And this he thinks he secures by rejecting all thought of a point of contact in man for this Divine salvation.

4. THE LIMITATION OF THE IDEA OF AGAPE

The above account might suggest that Marcion preached a full Gospel of Agape permitting of no limitations. His teaching about the "Stranger God" was opposed at once to the Old Testament and to Hellenism, both to Eros and to Nomos. Neither of them has any room for an unmotivated Divine love, and in both cases salvation loses, in Marcion's view, its paradox. The impression is given that it is just as it should be. If, as Hellenism teaches, man is akin to God, perhaps actually a bit of the Deity Himself, then salvation is the most natural thing of all. In the end, it is simply God saving Himself. And there is little difference if, as the Old Testament teaches, man, though not indeed akin to God, is God's creature; for then He is obliged to care for the work of His hands. Against both these views, Marcion preaches his " Stranger God." God is bound by no tie at all, whether of kinship and natural likeness or of creation and father-hood. When He descends in Christ to save mankind, He does so out of pure mercy alone, out of sympathy with the misery of man, out of spontaneous and unmotivated love. He takes to Himself those who are not His children, but are wholly strangers to Him; He cares for those who are not His creatures, but creatures of the lower Creator-God. He is "ultro bonus"—to revert to Marcion's own words. He bestows freely and for nothing, as His nature moves Him. His loving will finds expression in the Gospel, but nowhere else. What more can be required of the preacher of Agape?

Yet this is only one side of the matter. Marcion's message of Agape suffers from very definite limitations, which are so important and far-reaching that we must ask whether he really preaches Agape at all.

First, we may look at his attitude to the three fundamental dogmas of the Early Church: Creation, Incarnation, and the " Resurrection of the flesh." In each case he decidedly takes the Hellenistic point of view.

1. This is quite obvious in respect of Creation. One of Marcion's basic tenets is that the Highest God, the Father of Jesus Christ, is not the Creator of our heaven and earth, and has originally nothing to do with them. Here Marcion disagrees with primitive Christian tradition, but is in com-plete agreement with Gnosticism; and at the root of his idea is the Hellenistic dualism of spirit and matter, with its corre-sponding conception of sin. He was able, as we have seen, to apply this dualism in such a way as apparently to produce

a deeper conception of Agape. God's love is all the greater and purer when shown to those who are not His own, but *strangers*. Yet it is not difficult to see that, in denying Creation to be the work of God Himself, Marcion, in the end, goes beyond the idea of Agape and robs it of its real point. Marcion says " the stranger," where the New Testament says " the sinner." He means to assert that God has no obligation whatever towards man; but in that case, man has no obligation towards God. Man is a stranger to God, but this does not imply that he has cut himself adrift from the One who gave him life and all that he has, and towards whom he has unlimited obligation. The whole point of the primitive Christian idea of Agape is that it is sinners God loves—that is, those who in disobedience and rebellion have turned away from Him. With his Hellenistic idea of Creation, Marcion could not go so far as this. On the whole, his last word is that the objects of God's love are " strangers." For him, therefore, the chief obstacle the Divine love has to surmount in its object is absence of worth, absence of kinship with God; whereas the Divine Agape, in its primitive Christian sense, has to overcome the positive unworth of sin and rebellion against God. In the nature of the case, one who is a stranger to God from the first cannot become so much a stranger to Him as one who by disobedience has broken the tie that bound him to God. Only the latter stands under a Divine " ought," and only he, by disobeying this imperative, this obligatory Divine will, can become in the deepest sense a stranger to God. For primitive Christianity, it is his *guilt* that separates man from God, for Marcion it is primarily his *misery*. Hence Marcion never realises the ultimate implications of primitive Christian teaching, for which the Divine love is not merely sympathy with human misery, but also, and primarily, a will to fellowship that overcomes all sin and wrong. His failure to see this gives his view of love a certain sentimental tinge.

The ideas of love and judgment are isolated from one another, and judgment is relegated to the sphere of the lower God, so that the idea of Agape is reduced to a general altruism. Marcion's system is sure proof that if the ideas of Creation and Judgment are set aside, although at first sight this might seem the way to assert the idea of Agape in its purest form, actually the result is prejudicial to Agape.[1]

2. If Marcion's rejection of the primitive Christian belief in Creation reveals a Hellenistic tendency, the same is no less true of his rejection of the idea of Incarnation. In this idea, primitive Christianity had concentrated, perhaps more than anywhere else, its concern for the Agape motif. Christianity has always regarded it as the greatest deed of Divine love, that in Christ God Himself came to us, and dwelt among us, and gave Himself for us to death on the Cross. For primitive Christianity, all else depended upon the infallible reality of this, that the Son of God *really* "became flesh" and *really* suffered death on the Cross.[2] And this intimately affects the question of God's love; for only if it is true, is a *real* Divine love revealed in the life and death of Christ. By this test the spirits are tried. Hellenistic-Gnostic thought finds it unworthy of God to descend in this way, and really "empty" and give Himself. The Incarnation and Death on the Cross can only be thought of as apparent, the Divine nature being in reality untouched. For primitive Christianity, again, it is just this apparency that is most unworthy of God. When God has proved His love to us

---

[1] On "Love and Judgment" *cf. supra*, pp. 102 ff. The greatest weakness in Harnack's interpretation of Marcion is his failure to perceive this limitation in Marcion's understanding of Christianity, so that he accepts Marcion's idea of love as adequately expressing the Christian conception. This is plainly due to Harnack's own interpretation of Christian love, in which he is dependent on Ritschl. The result has been to set Marcion in a false perspective.

[2] *Cf.* Ign. ad Trall. ix., with its repetition of "really" (ἀληθῶς): "Be deaf therefore when anyone speaks to you apart from Jesus Christ . . . who was really born, both ate and drank, was really persecuted under Pontius Pilate, was really crucified and died . . ., who also was really raised from the dead . . . without whom we have no real life."

through the Incarnation and Sacrifice of His Son, we im-
pugn the Divine nature itself, which is love, if we refuse to
see anything but apparent events in the Incarnation and
Death on the Cross. They are realities, as surely as God's
love is not appearance but reality. From the first, Christianity had to be on its guard against docetic views influenced
by Hellenism. " Beloved, believe not every spirit, but prove
the spirits, whether they are of God: because many false
prophets are gone out into the world. Hereby know ye the
Spirit of God: every spirit which confesseth that Jesus Christ
is *come in the flesh* is of God: and every spirit which confesseth not Jesus is not of God."[1] On this issue, Marcion

---

[1] 1 John iv. 1 ff. The ideas of Agape and Incarnation are strikingly interwoven in 1 John. The whole epistle is dominated by the dual thought:
(1) " Everyone that loveth is begotten of God . . . for God is love " (iv. 7 f.).
(2) " Every spirit which confesseth that Jesus Christ is come in the flesh is of
God " (iv. 2). These two ideas are not, however, treated separately and in isolation, but are woven together, which is easily done, since both represent one and
the same interest, and express at bottom the same thing. The following will
give an idea of their interdependence:

  1 John i. 1 (Incarnation): " That which was from the beginning, that which
we have heard, that which we have seen with our eyes, that which
we beheld, and our hands handled, concerning the Word of
life."

      ii. 5 (Agape): " Whoso keepeth His word, in him verily hath the love
of God been perfected. Hereby know we that we are in
Him."

      ii. 22 (Incarnation): " Who is the liar but he that denieth that Jesus
is the Christ ?"

      iii. 10 ff. (Agape): " In this the children of God are manifest, and the
children of the devil: whosoever doeth not righteousness is not
of God, neither he that loveth not his brother. . . . We know
that we have passed out of death into life, because we love the
brethren."

      iii. 16 (Incarnation-Cross-Agape): " Hereby know we love, because He
laid down His life for us: and we ought to lay down our lives for
the brethren."

      iii. 23 (Incarnation-Agape): " And this is His commandment, that we
should believe in the name of His Son Jesus Christ, and love one
another."

      iv. 2 f. (Incarnation): " Every spirit which confesseth that Jesus Christ
is come in the flesh is of God: and every spirit which confesseth
not Jesus is not of God."

characteristically takes sides with the Hellenistic-Gnostic viewpoint. His Christology is markedly *docetic*, with no room for any real idea of Incarnation. At first sight this seems illogical: he wants to show how the Good God, in His compassionate love, came down to us and espoused our cause; and one would think that nothing could serve his purpose better than Incarnation—a real Incarnation, that is. But as a matter of fact, his docetism and denial of the Incarnation are an inevitable consequence of his outlook as a whole; and this in turn illuminates his conception of Agape and its limitations. If the Highest God has nothing to do with the material world, and if salvation consists in our deliverance from it, then naturally the Saviour of men must not be joined by any real bond to this world. How could the Son of the Highest God besmirch Himself with the conditions of human life? If He had, He would Himself have fallen under the dominion of the Creator, from which He was to save us. For this reason Marcion feels it a prime duty to contest the Johannine σὰρξ ἐγένετο. The Son of the Highest God did not become flesh. Nothing material attached to Him when He " was found in fashion as a man " (Phil. ii. 7). In outward appearance He was like any other

---

iv. 7 f. (Agape): "Everyone that loveth is begotten of God, and knoweth God. He that loveth not knoweth not God; for God is love."

iv. 10 (Agape-Incarnation): "Herein is love, not that we loved God, but that He loved us, and sent His Son to be the propitiation for our sins."

iv. 14 ff. (Incarnation-Agape): "And we have beheld and bear witness that the Father hath sent the Son to be the Saviour of the world. Whosoever shall confess that Jesus is the Son of God, God abideth in him, and he in God. And we know and have believed the love which God hath in us. God is love."

v. 1 (Incarnation-Agape): "Whosoever believeth that Jesus is the Christ is begotten of God: and whosoever loveth Him that begat loveth also him that is begotten of Him."

On the Incarnation and the rejection of Gnostic views, *cf*. also Barn. v.; Ign. ad Trall. vi.-x.; Ign. ad Eph. vii. 2; Ign. ad Smyrn. ii.-v.; Tert., Adv. Marcionem iii. 8 ff.

man, but in appearance only. His outward form was nothing but a φάντασμα. How far Marcion, as his churchly critics affirm, drew from this the same conclusion as certain Gnostic schools,[1] that the suffering of Jesus, too, was merely apparent, cannot be determined with certainty. That he could not appreciate the Agape of the Cross as Paul saw it, is none the less evident.

3. As with Creation and Incarnation, so with the "Resurrection of the flesh"; Marcion, as might be expected, again taking the prevalent Hellenistic-Gnostic point of view, wholly rejects any such idea. His Hellenism is more patent at this point than at any other, since he could, one would think, have taken a different attitude in view of his special premises. The Gnostics had to reject belief in the Resurrection of the flesh, in simple consequence of their idea that salvation meant the return of the divine kernel in man to its heavenly origin. For them, it is in the nature of the body to perish and of the spirit to be saved.[2] With Marcion it is different: salvation is the natural destiny of no part of man's being; it is a paradox, the deed of a love from an external source, from the Highest God; the soul has no advantage over the body, for they are both works of the Demiurge, both alike worthless and wretched. Thus Marcion invites the very question his critics put to him: When God has mercy on man, why does He only let it affect the soul? "Now whence comes this halving of salvation, if not from a failure of goodness? What could have been a better proof of a perfect goodness, than the recovery of the whole man to salvation? Totally damned by the Creator, he should have been totally restored by the most merciful God."[3] Even so,

---

[1] Cf. supra, pp. 311 f.

[2] According to the Gnostics (Basilides, Valentinus) the "pneumatic" person is, in virtue of his nature, saved (φύσει σωζόμενος). Clem. Alex., Strom. IV., cap. xiii. 89, 4. Cf. also supra, pp. 307 f., 313.

[3] Tert., Adv. Marcionem i. 24: "Sufficit ipsos, quos saluos facit, imperfectæ salutis inuentos imperfectam bonitatem eius ostendere, scilicet anima tenus

Marcion will not hear of the "Resurrection of the flesh," but limits salvation to the soul alone; which only shows how firmly rooted he is, after all, in Hellenistic soil. Bodily existence is too much bound up with matter, and matter with evil, for him even to consider the idea of the Resurrection of the flesh. And his strongly ascetic ethic points in just the same direction.[1]

5. MARCION'S SIGNIFICANCE FOR THE CHRISTIAN IDEA OF LOVE

If we ask, finally, what is the importance of Marcion in the history of the Christian idea of love, the answer, in accordance with the dual trend we have seen in his thought, must be twofold. More than any other second-century theologian, Marcion made love the centre of Christianity. More than any other, he proclaimed that God is love and nothing but love. That is where Christianity is absolutely new; and that he seeks to assert in a conflict on two fronts, against both Old Testament nomism and Hellenistic Eros piety. If he was less consistent on the latter front, as we see from his dependence on Hellenistic ideas as regards Creation, Incarnation, and the Resurrection of the flesh, yet he conducts his campaign against Nomos in such a way as to leave

---

saluos, carne deperditos, quæ apud illum non resurgit. unde hæc dimidiatio salutis nisi ex defectione bonitatis? quid erat perfectæ bonitatis quam totum hominem redigere in salutem, totum damnatum a creatore, totum a deo optimo adlectum?"

[1] *Cf.* Harnack, *op. cit.*, pp. 148 f.: " Marcion's ethic, also, makes a protest here; for no Christian community has prescribed a more world-renouncing and difficult rule and practice of life than the Marcionite. Marcion forbade his followers marriage and all sexual relations completely. . . . Marriage is not only a filthy abomination (πορνεία), but also brings forth death (φθορά). The motive for this prohibition was primarily the common one, deliverance from the sinful flesh. Not only, however, was this demand presented with an unprecedented force of aversion, but there was a second motive as well: we must not help to enlarge the realm of the Creator, but we must limit it as far as is humanly possible; we must annoy, irritate, and defy this evil god and thus show him that we are no longer in his service but belong to another."

Agape itself behind. His main object is to separate Law from Gospel—"separatio legis et euangelii proprium et principale opus est Marcionis"—and this is the important thing in his interpretation of Christianity. In this respect he displays far keener insight than any of his contemporaries. Christian fellowship with God is essentially, he sees, not regulated by law but by love. Like Paul, he knows that the Way of the Law is no Way of salvation; as such it is obsolete, abolished through Christ. But he then concludes that there must be no further talk of law at all. In other words, he has attempted to transform Agape from a transvaluation of existing values into a new and permanent system of values—an attempt which, as we saw above (pp. 40 f.), can only end by destroying Agape. "Through the law cometh the knowledge of sin" (Rom. iii. 20), and only against the background of sin is the depth of Divine love revealed as the paradox of real Agape. When this side of the matter is missed, then the idea of Agape is inevitably weakened; the Gospel of the forgiveness of sins is lost, and there remains only "the Gospel of the poor soul," "das Evangelium der armen Seele."[1]

The churchly theologians of the second century thus had reason, even from the point of view of the Agape motif, to refuse Marcion's interpretation of Christianity. They rightly felt that it was an abridged and weakened version. Something essential was omitted.[2] And they had the support of the churchly tradition, which had already begun to take shape. When Marcion denied Creation, Incarnation, and the Resurrection of the flesh, it was easy to see that he was proclaiming a strange Christianity. He was attacking a point on which the Early Church was sensitive, and so he established a reputation as the most dangerous of all heretics, the arch-heretic, the "mouthpiece of the devil," "the first-

---

[1] Harnack, *op. cit.*, p. 233.
[2] Irênæus, Contra hær. i. 27, 2.

born of Satan."[1] Outwardly, too, Marcionism was for long a serious menace to the Church. After separating from the Great Church in A.D. 144, not satisfied to form a mere sect, Marcion founded a church of his own, which in a short time grew so large that Justin Martyr could write, about 150, that it extended " over the whole human race."[2] The gravity of the situation is best reflected in the zeal with which the Church attacked the heresy. Scarcely any pre-Arian heretic was the object of such comprehensive refutation as Marcion.[3]

It was disastrous for the later history of the Christian idea of love that Marcion thus became the great arch-heretic. The dangers of his teaching were seen, but the deepest reason for them was not. Consequently the polemic of the Church came to be partly directed against the idea of Agape itself. Any view which sought to give unqualified affirmation to the Agape motif was suspect; and it was felt necessary to temper the Divine love by the addition of elements from the Nomos motif. Marcion had put the alternative: either the righteous God or the good God, and had identified it with the alternative: either Nomos or Agape. Without questioning his statement of the problem, the Church advances to the attack and declares: Here is no " Either-Or," but a " Both-And." God is both the Righteous and the Good. It is wrong to say that God is only love; while describing Him as love we must add the saving clause that He is *also* righteous. Fellowship with God is not determined solely by Agape, but *also* by Nomos. To put it somewhat strongly, the history of the conflict that was waged round Marcion is, in a measure, the story of how the fundamental Christian motif itself, the Agape motif, became a heresy. When the idea of Agape attempted subsequently to assert itself, it could

---

[1] Contra hær. i. 27, 3; iii. 3, 4.
[2] κατὰ πᾶν γένος ἀνθρώπων. Justin, Apol. i. 26, 5.
[3] Thus, *e.g.*, Tertullian's " Adv. Marcionem " occupies more than 350 pages in the Vienna edition (CSEL).

in general not do so at the centre of Christianity, but had to take refuge in the realm of the three dogmas of Creation, Incarnation, and the Resurrection of the flesh. The immediate result of the controversy was undoubtedly to strengthen the position of the Nomos motif. The attack on the Old Testament gave it a further chance in the Church.

V

THE NOMOS TYPE IN TERTULLIAN

1. THE RESULT OF THE FOREGOING CONTESTS

THE Christian idea of love in post-apostolic times is formed under stress of the conflicts between Nomos, Eros and Agape, which issued, in the latter part of the second century, in the development of a churchly theology. This does not mean, however, that any one of the three types succeeded in entirely displacing the others. In fact, they all survive within the Church itself; so much so, indeed, that of the three outstanding ante-Nicene theologians, Irenæus, Tertullian and Origen, each represents one main type.

But even though the second century did not finally settle the issue between the three rivals, yet its verdict is unmistakable. The three main types still appear side by side and to some extent in conflict, but under conditions essentially different from their first encounter. Thanks to Gnosticism, Eros had been unmasked as heretical, and from this it never quite recovered. But even Agape had been compromised by Marcion. Any unqualified proclamation of the Divine love, irrational, paradoxical, spontaneous, was suspect. Agape found itself bordering on heresy. It is no longer proclaimed with the same enthusiasm as it once was by Marcion. On the whole, the Agape motif had to take refuge in the three fundamental dogmas of the Early Church. The Nomos type alone had had no doubt cast upon it. The theology of the Apostolic Fathers and Apologists won the day; and with its aid the Early Church succeeded in warding off the dangers of Gnosticism and Marcionism. Whereas both the Eros and the Agape motif had to be put forward with the greatest caution, the Nomos motif could assert itself unhindered, indeed it could come forward with heightened claims. The chief representative of such a nomistic position is Tertullian.

2. TERTULLIAN's DEFENCE OF THE THREE FUNDAMENTAL DOGMAS

The titles of Tertullian's works indicate at a glance how much of them he devoted to an affirmation of the three fundamental dogmas of the Early Church and to their defence against heretical attacks. Undoubtedly he regarded this as his chief task. His most comprehensive work, *Adversus Marcionem*, centres round the question of *Creation*; against Marcion's blasphemous talk of two Gods, the Creator and the Highest God, the Good God who brought us salvation through Christ, Tertullian insists that the God of Creation is the same as the God of Redemption. But he also devotes a special treatise to the *Incarnation*, with the significant title *De carne Christi*, while an independent work treats " *Of the Resurrection of the Flesh* " (*De carnis resurrectione*). His interest in these subjects is not accidental, but pursues a quite definite plan. He introduces his work " On the Resurrection of the Flesh" with an explanation of the connection between his anti-heretical writings, and states his program thus : Since the heretics have been convinced by his earlier writings that God is the Creator of the flesh, and Christ the Saviour of the flesh, they are now to be convinced of the Resurrection of the flesh. Tertullian attaches great importance to the observance of this logical order in dealing with heretics.[1]

---

[1] " *Obducti dehinc ‹et› de deo carnis auctore et de Christo carnis redemptore, iam et de resurrectione carnis reuincentur.* Congruenter scilicet hoc ferme modo dicimus ineundam cum hæreticis disceptationem,—nam et ordo semper a principalibus deduci exposcit—ut de ipso prius constet, a quo dicatur dispositum esse quod quæritur, atque adeo et hæretici ex conscientia infirmitatis numquam ordinarie tractant." De carnis resurrectione 2.

The three fundamental dogmas have, however, according to Tertullian, an importance going far beyond the more incidental refutation of heresies. They represent for him the Catholic Faith in the most literal sense of the word. Among heretics every little group has its own private opinions, but in the Church one and the same teaching prevails everywhere. In Achæa, Macedonia, Asia, Italy, or Africa—everywhere one and the same message is heard. The Church acknowledges " One Lord God . . ., the Creator of the universe, and Christ Jesus born of the Virgin Mary, the Son of God the Creator, and the Resurrection of the flesh."[1] Nor did the Church first reach this unanimity in opposition to heresy; she has had it from the very beginning, according to the principle that true doctrine is always older than false.[2]

His emphatic reiteration of " the flesh "—God is Creator of the *flesh*, Christ is Saviour of the *flesh*, Resurrection is Resurrection of the *flesh*—reveals a strong anti-Hellenistic bias. He is well aware that the Hellenistic spirit is the source of Gnostic heresies.[3] He laments that Plato, though not through his own fault ("bona fide "), has become caterer to all the heretics.[4] Here Tertullian has in mind primarily the idea of the divine nature of the soul. A right instinct has told him that the fundamental difference between Hellenism and Christianity is to be found at this point. It is characteristic of the Hellenistic outlook, whether represented by

---

[1] " Unum deum dominum novit, creatorem universitatis, et Christum Jesum ex virgine Maria filium dei creatoris, et carnis resurrectionem." De præscriptione hæreticorum 36.

[2] " Quo peræque aduersus uniuersas hæreses iam hinc præiudicatum sit id esse uerum, quodcumque primum, id esse adulterum, quodcumque posterius." Adv. Praxean 2. *Cf.* De præsc. hær. 29.

[3] " Ipsæ denique hæreses a philosophia subornantur. . . . Eadem materia apud hæreticos et philosophos volutatur, idem retractantur implicantur. . . . Hinc illæ fabulæ et genealogiæ interminabiles, et quæstiones infructuosæ, et sermones serpentes velut cancer, a quibus nos apostolus refrenans nominatim philosophiam contestatur caveri oportere." [Col. ii. 8.] De præsc. hær. 7.

[4] " Doleo bona fide Platonem omnium hæreticorum condimentarium factum." De anima 23.

Hellenic philosophers or Christian heretics, to regard man as in essence a Divine being who is in bondage to matter. Salvation then means spiritualisation, the deliverance of the divine part from its captivity in matter and sense. Against this idea of salvation and this whole conception of God, man and the world, Tertullian, in the name of Christianity, protests. To make man a part of the Divine substance, or an appendage to it, is godless presumption. "We, however, who allow no appendage to God, by this very fact reckon the soul as far below God."[1] From this point of view Tertullian's position is one of conscious antithesis to the spiritualising doctrine of Hellenism; and part of his protest is his " materialistic doctrine of the soul." The heretics have taken upon themselves to smuggle a Divine seed into the human soul,[2] and Tertullian objects that not only is the soul not divine, but it is actually of a corporeal nature,[3] and he speaks of the " body of the soul " or " the corporeality of the soul."[4] He rejects the Hellenistic idea of the pre-existence of the soul, in favour of the view that the soul is conceived and born together with the body.[5] The soul has therefore no occasion whatever to look down on the body; the body is the neighbour and brother of the soul. "Why, then, O soul, should you be averse to the flesh? There is none, after the Lord, whom you should love so dearly; none more like a brother to

[1] ". . . quia tantam illi [animæ] concessit diuinitatem, ut deo adæquetur. Innatam eam facit, quod et solum armare potuissem ad testimonium plenæ diuinitatis. . . . Quid amplius proscriberet animam, si eam deum nuncuparet ? Nos autem, qui nihil deo adpendimus, hoc ipso animam longe infra deum expendimus." De anima 24.

[2] " Nec diutius de isto, nisi propter hæreticos, qui nescio quod spiritale semen infulciunt animæ de Sophiæ matris occulta liberalitate conlatum ignorante factore." De anima 11.

[3] De anima 6-11.

[4] "Animæ corpus." De anima 9. "Corporalitas animæ." De anima 7. The soul has its special corporeality (habet corpulentiam propriam). De carnis resurrectione 17.

[5] " Simulne conflata utriusque substantia corporis animæque an altera earum præcedente ? Immo simul ambas et concipi et confici et perfici dicimus, sicut et promi." De anima 27.

you."[1]   Things bodily are thus in every respect worthy of
honour; and because the heretics speak of them with contempt, Tertullian feels it his special duty to praise and glorify
them.[2]   In spite of his asceticism he can praise the material,
sensible world, for, as he points out, it has its ground in the
will of God.[3]

As against the Hellenistic division of human nature, Tertullian firmly holds a *totus-homo* view based on the Old
Testament and primitive Christian tradition.   God has
created *the whole man*, body and soul; owing to the Fall,
the whole man is lost; Christ is come to save not merely a part
of man, but *the whole man*; and in the Resurrection *the
whole man*, body and soul, is to appear before God.[4]   Soul
and body are so intimately united that it is impossible to
speak of any activity of the soul without the body.   What
the soul does, it does in the flesh, and with the flesh, and
through the flesh.[5]   Indeed, the body and the soul are so far
grown together, that it can actually be doubted which should

---

[1] De carn. res. 63.

[2] " Hucusque de præconio carnis aduersus inimicos."   De carn. res. 11.
" Persequar itaque propositum, si tamen tantum possim carni uindicare, quantum
contulit illi qui eam fecit."   De carn. res. 6.   " Exorsi enim sumus ab auctoritate
carnis."   De carn. res. 14.

[3] " . . . necessario et a nobis carnis primum condicio munietur, uituperatione
laudatione depulsa."   De carn. res. 5.   " Caro autem et sermone dei constitit
propter formam."   *Ibid.*   " Age iam, perora in illa sanctissima et reuerenda opera
naturæ."   Adv. Marcionem iii. 11; *cf.* Adv. Marcionem i. 13, ii. 4.   " Hanc
venerationem naturæ, Marcion, despuis ?"   De carne Christi 4.   " Natura
ueneranda est, non erubescenda."   De anima 27.   " Non tamen suo nomine
caro infamis."   De anima 40.

[4] " . . . *totum hominem* elogio transgressionis inscripsit atque exinde merito
perditionis impleuit.   *Totus itaque saluus fiet qui perit totus delinquendo.*"   De
carn. res. 34.   " In primis cum ad hoc uenisse se dicit, uti quod periit saluum
faciat, quid dicis perisse ?   Hominem sine dubio.   Totumne an ex parte ?
Utique *totum.*"   *Ibid.*   *Cf.* also Tertullian's objection to Marcion, who wanted
to limit salvation to the soul alone: " quid erat perfectæ bonitatis quam *totum
hominem* redigere in salutem, *totum* damnatum a creatore, *totum* a deo optimo
adlectum ?"   Adv. Marcionem i. 24.

[5] " . . . in carne et cum carne et per carnem agitur ab anima quod
agitur in corde. . . .   Nihil non cum illa agit, sine qua non est."   De carn.
res. 15.

be regarded as the bearer of the other.[1] In all their temporal
activity they are *one*; why should they not also be one in
eternity?[2]

The fundamental error of the heretics, according to Tertullian, is that they mix up Christian and Hellenistic opinion.
"What has Athens to do with Jerusalem, the Academy with
the Church, the heretics with the Christians?"[3] Tertullian
will hear of no Stoic, Platonic or "dialectic" Christianity.
For one who has found faith in Christ, such a thing can be
nothing but a hindrance.[4] In opposing Greek philosophy
Tertullian is not, however, as is often supposed, moved by
a general hostility to culture, but by the sound observation
that Greek philosophy is largely based on a fundamental
motif incompatible with Christianity. At times when this
point does not arise, Tertullian can go far in recognition of
the philosophers. He frankly admits that they sometimes
reached conclusions approximating to Christianity,[5] and in
such case he gladly agrees with them.[6] What he really fears
is not a cultural synthesis, but a religious synthesis, such as
he found in the heretics. When God has revealed Himself
to us in Christ, why will these heretics insist on learning
their Christianity from the Greeks? Scornfully he cries:
"The fault, I suppose, of the Divine doctrine lies in its
springing from Judæa rather than from Greece. Christ made
a mistake, too, in sending forth fishermen to preach rather

---

[1] "Tanta quidem concretione, ut incertum haberi possit, utrumne caro animam an carnem anima circumferat, utrumne animæ caro an anima pareat carni."
De carn. res. 7.

[2] "Si temporalium, cur non et æternorum?" *Ibid.*

[3] De præsc. hær. 7.

[4] "Viderint qui Stoicum et Platonicum et dialecticum Christianismum protulerunt. Nobis curiositate opus non est post Christum Jesum, nec inquisitione
post evangelium. Cum credimus, nihil desideramus ultra credere." *Ibid.*

[5] "Plane non negabimus aliquando philosophos iuxta nostra sentisse." De
anima 2. *Cf.* De carn. res. 1.

[6] "Utar ergo et sententia Platonis alicuius pronuntiantis: omnis anima
immortalis; utar et conscientia populi contestantis deum deorum; utar et reliquis
communibus sensibus, qui deum iudicem prædicant." De carn. res. 3.

than sophists."[1]   The interweaving of two traditions so different in kind as Hellenism and Christianity can only result in casting doubt on the Christian message. If the heretics were right, Christ would have to recant part of His teaching. With biting irony Tertullian concludes the *De præscriptione hæreticorum* by making Jesus say: " I once gave a Gospel and a doctrine to my apostles; but afterwards it was my pleasure to make considerable changes in it ! I had promised a resurrection, even of the flesh; but, on second thoughts, it struck me that I might not be able to keep my promise ! I had shown myself to have been born of a virgin; but this seemed to me afterwards to be a discreditable thing ! I had said that He was my Father, who is the maker of the sun and the showers; but another and better father has adopted me ! I had forbidden you to lend an ear to heretics; but in this I erred !—Such blasphemies, it is possible, do enter the minds of those who go out of the right path, and who do not defend the true faith from the danger which besets it."[2]   The Christian message is such a unity that it stands or falls as a whole. It is not surprising, then, that the heretic in one point is a heretic in all. If we embrace the spiritualising piety of Hellenism, we must, logically, reject not only Creation, but also Incarnation and the Resurrection of the flesh. If we are enemies of the Creator, then we shall hate the flesh He made and not wish it to be raised; nor shall we have any use for the Word that became flesh.[3]

To sum up: in Tertullian, the anti-Hellenistic front is

---

[1] " Deliquit, opinor, diuina doctrina ex Iudæa potius quam ex Græcia oriens. Errauit et Christus piscatores citius quam sophistam [sophistas conj. Fulvius Ursinus] ad præconium emittens." De anima 3.

[2] De præsc. hær. 44.—Note here, too, the recurrence of the usual theme, the fundamental dogmas of the Resurrection of the flesh, the Incarnation, and God as Creator.

[3] " Tu potius illi exorare debueras *resurrectionem*; . . . Sed nihil mirum, si odisti, cuius *auctorem* quoque respuisti, quam et in Christo aut negare aut mutare consuesti, proinde et ipsum sermonem dei, qui *caro* factus est, uel stilo uel interpretatione corrumpens. . . ." De carn. res. 63.

remarkably clear. If the heretics have confused Hellenism and Christianity, Tertullian will sharply distinguish between them. He urges: Give back to the Greeks what belongs to them! Why use the shield of another, when the Apostle gives you armour of your own?[1] But now we must ask whether Tertullian's attack on Hellenistic Eros is also a defence of Christian Agape. We have more than once observed that in this period the Agape motif took refuge in the three dogmas of Creation, Incarnation, and the Resurrection of the flesh. And who preached these more fervently than Tertullian? Nor were they merely a matter of venerable tradition for him. There were vital Christian interests he wished to preserve by their means. That is quite clear from his treatment of the Incarnation. What makes the Incarnation so important? Plainly, its connection with *the Cross*. "Forma moriendi causa nascendi est."[2] On the Incarnation depends the reality of salvation. If Christ did not really become flesh, but assumed the form of a man only in appearance, what guarantee have we that His suffering and death, too, were not merely apparent, and our salvation an illusion?[3] Tertullian's campaign against Hellenism would seem, then, unquestionably to be the campaign of Agape against Eros. Closer examination, however, shows that this is by no means the case. His starting-point is certainly not the Agape motif, but the Nomos motif. And this becomes still clearer when he is seen, in the interests of the Nomos motif, actually attacking the Agape motif itself.

---

[1] "Redde illi suos sensus. . . . Quid alieno uteris clipeo, si ab apostolo armatus es?" De carn. res. 3.

[2] De carne Christi 6.

[3] "Iam nunc, cum mendacium deprehenditur Christi caro, sequitur, ut et omnia, quæ per carnem Christi gesta sunt, mendacio gesta sint. . . . *Sic nec passiones Christi eius fidem merebuntur.* Nihil enim passus est qui non uere est passus; uere autem pati phantasma non potuit. *Euersum est igitur totum dei opus. Totum Christiani nominis et pondus et fructus, mors Christi, negatur.* . . . Porro, si caro eius negatur, quomodo mors eius adseueratur." Adv. Marcionem iii. 8.

3. TERTULLIAN'S CAMPAIGN AGAINST THE IDEA OF AGAPE

Tertullian is as unsuccessful in making his own position a specifically Christian expression of Agape as he is right, from a Christian point of view, in confuting both the Gnostics and Marcion on the subject of Creation, Incarnation, and the Resurrection of the flesh. He chiefly objected to the heretics that they " mixed " Christianity and Hellenism; but he himself " mixes," without hesitation, Christianity and Judaism, Agape and Nomos. The Gnostics and Marcion had attacked the Old Testament. The double attitude of primitive Christianity and, in particular, of Paul, to " the Law," an attitude at once of recognition and rejection, was followed, in Marcion, by unequivocal rejection. The Old Testament belongs to the Jewish God, and Christians have now no use for it; the " Legal " relation to God is finally antiquated through Christ. No wonder Tertullian, in opposing Marcion, goes to the other extreme in complete recognition of " the Law." Both Testaments stand for him on the same level, from both he draws his faith in exactly the same way, unaware that the New Testament has something essentially new, over and above the Old, to say about the Way of salvation. The Church " mixes the Law and the Prophets with the writings of the Evangelists and Apostles; from thence she drinks her faith."[1] The result in Tertullian is a confusion of motifs. He " mixes " Old Testament Nomos with New Testament Agape, and from the mixture " drinks " his own faith. His defence of the Old Testament is equally a defence of the " Legal " relation to God and the " Legal " Way of salvation. Marcion has asserted that the Highest God acts solely by the principle of goodness and love, the Creator-God solely by that of retributive justice. Tertullian replies that there is

---

[1] " Legem et prophetas cum evangelicis et apostolicis litteris miscet; inde potat fidem." De præsc. hær. 36.

no God but the Creator, and that He is at once both good and righteous.[1]   But when the tension between the God of love and the God of rewards and punishments is inevitable, he decidedly takes the part of the latter. " Eye for eye does our God require; but your God does an even greater injury, when he prevents an act of retaliation. For what man would not repeat a blow, if he were not struck in return?"[2]   Tertullian seems oblivious that this is an argument against the Christian idea of Agape itself, and a criticism not only of Marcion, but of Jesus, who says: " An eye for an eye, and a tooth for a tooth: but I say unto you, Resist not him that is evil " (Matt. v. 38 f.).

It is the *irrational* element in God's Agape that offends Tertullian. For him, the supreme court in which even Divine things must be judged, is reason, *ratio*. Nothing can be upheld that cannot justify itself there.[3]   And he applies this principle to God's goodness and love. " I require reason in His goodness, because nothing else can properly be accounted good than that which is rationally good; much less can goodness itself be detected in any irrationality. More easily will an evil thing which has something rational belonging to it be accounted good, than that a good thing bereft of all reasonable quality should escape being regarded as evil."[4]   When Marcion makes the Highest God in pure mercy espouse the cause of wretched man, that, according to Tertullian, is an " irrational " goodness. Why? Because it was shown to " strangers."[5]   Now Tertullian is aware that Marcion's intention was to exalt God's Agape; its nature is

---

[1] Adv. Marcionem ii. 29.   [2] Adv. Marcionem ii. 28.

[3] " Aliam illi regulam prætendo: sicut naturalia, ita rationalia esse debere in deo omnia." Adv. Marcionem i. 23.

[4] " Exigo rationem bonitatis, quia nec aliud quid bonum haberi liceat, quod non rationaliter bonum sit, nedum ut ipsa bonitas inrationalis deprehendatur. Facilius malum, cui rationis aliquid adfuerit, pro bono habebitur quam ut bonum ratione desertum non pro malo iudicetur." *Ibid.*

[5] " Nego rationalem bonitatem dei Marcionis iam hoc primo, quod in salutem processerit hominis alieni." *Ibid.*

such that it is shown without any obligation, spontaneously, voluntarily, in accord with the commandment that we are to love our enemies.[1] Tertullian's reply to this shows how little he understands the idea of Agape.

His answer is, briefly, as follows. The commandment to love our enemies is, so to speak, a secondary commandment. In the first place comes the commandment to love our neighbour as ourselves. The secondary commandment is intended to inculcate still more forcibly the duty of loving our neighbour. Strictly speaking, we are obliged only to love our neighbour; not, however, an enemy or a stranger. The imposition of the latter is equivalent to an enhancement of the love required of us. "But the due precedes the undue, as the principal quality and of higher worth."[2] Towards my own people I owe the debt of love; it has a rational motivation, is a love demanded by justice, a love "ex iustitia." That love, on the other hand, which goes beyond these natural ties, and embraces the stranger as well, is a superabundant love, a love "ex redundantia."[3] To find, as Marcion does, the essence of Christian love in this latter would be to set unreason and injustice on the throne. The most we could admit is that a love at variance with justice would be rational if it were exercised to the advantage of a relative; but shown to a stranger, towards whom we are under no obligation, it has no rational justification for its existence.[4] The result of Tertullian's exposition is this: *If we really needed to ascribe to God a goodness so at variance with reason, it would be better that there should be no God at all.*[5] And Marcion's declaration that the Highest God

---

[1] *Cf. supra*, pp. 318 f.

[2] "Antecedit autem debita indebitam, ut principalis, ut dignior." *Ibid.*

[3] *Ibid.*

[4] "Fortasse enim pro domestico aliquatenus rationalis habeatur bonitas iniuriosa. Pro extraneo uero, cui nec proba legitime deberetur, qua ratione tam iniusta rationalis defendetur?" *Ibid.*

[5] ". . . quod scilicet in quantum deo congruat, in tantum deum non esse conueniat. . . ." Adv. Marcionem i. 25.

revealed Himself in Christ as pure love evokes the outburst:
"Listen, ye sinners; and ye who have not yet come to this,
hear, that you may attain to such a pass! A better God has
been discovered, who never takes offence, is never angry,
never inflicts punishment, who has prepared no fire in hell,
no gnashing of teeth in the outer darkness! He is purely
and simply good."[1]

Granted that the ambiguity of Marcion's view provoked
such passages as this, yet Tertullian's reaction is plainly due
not to Agape, but to Nomos. He protests not only against
that in Marcion which is untenable or doubtful from a
Christian point of view, but against Agape itself. The
paradox of unmotivated Agape is too great; it has not
sufficient legal sanction. Tertullian is quite unable to conceive of fellowship with God except as based on justice. The
only motive, in his opinion, that can securely bind man to
God is fear of punishment and hope of reward. But this
motive is endangered by the idea of Agape. If God is pure
love and shows His goodness even to the undeserving, then
there is no incentive to goodness. The righteous has no
advantage over the sinner. "Come, then, if you do not fear
God since He is good, why do you not boil over into every
kind of lust, and so realise that which is, I believe, the main
enjoyment of life to all who fear not God?"[2] Now Tertullian knows Marcion's answer quite well: "God forbid,
you say, God forbid!"[3] It is Paul's answer to the critics
who thought his preaching of grace to imply that we should
"continue in sin." Paul answers: "God forbid!"[4] It is
indicative of Tertullian's blindness to the Agape motif that
he can attach no meaning to this *immediate* rejection of sin,
which needs no mediate, egocentric motivation,[5] but arises
directly out of the experience of God's grace. That he cites

---

[1] Adv. Marcionem i. 27.   [2] *Ibid.*   [3] "Absit, inquis, absit!" *Ibid.*
[4] Rom. vi. 1 f.: "Quid ergo dicemus? permanebimus in peccato, ut gratia
abundet? Absit."
[5] Such as fear and hope.

without understanding his opponent's "God forbid!" is surest proof that not Tertullian, but his opponent, at least on the point at issue here, represents the deeper Christian view.

We might be tempted to conclude from this that Tertullian has no place at all for love; but such a conclusion would be too hasty. Even for Tertullian, love and goodness are the primary attributes of God.[1] Out of love God created the world;[2] and love must always be our first word in speaking of God as He is in Himself. Owing to the Fall, however, He has been forced to bring another side of His nature to the fore—namely, His judging and retributive righteousness. But His goodness never ceases, for He defers the restoration of man and the annihilation of the devil. Originally man succumbed to the devil because the devil managed to get man's free will on his side; but now God in His goodness leaves time and space for a continued struggle, to give man opportunity in a fresh contest to defeat the enemy by the use of that same freedom of will, which was the means of his undoing before. Thus God shows His love in giving man an opportunity, through a victory of his own, "worthily to recover his salvation."[3] Even God's retaliatory justice is an expression of His love. Punishment serves the ends of goodness, for it deters man from evil; and that is best for him. "Who would otherwise desire that good which he could despise with impunity?"[4] Would not all take the evil way if they had nothing to fear? But however much Tertullian may talk in this vein of the goodness of God, it all finds a place within the scheme of Nomos. Of Agape, which destroys this scheme, there is not a trace.

Tertullian's outlook unites Old Testament nomism and Roman moralism and jurisprudence. The result is a *theology*

---

[1] "Ita prior bonitas dei secundum naturam, seueritas posterior secundum causam. Illa ingenita; hæc accidens; illa propria, hæc accommodata." **Adv. Marcionem** ii. 11.

[2] Adv. Marcionem ii. 12.   [3] Adv. Marcionem ii. 10.

[4] Adv. Marcionem ii. 13.

of merit whose influence on the later history of Christianity was calamitous. The idea of retribution is central to his interpretation of Christianity. Nothing, he says, can more become God, as the good and righteous Judge, than to elect and reprobate men according to their deserts.[1] God simply cannot disregard man's merit; He cannot condemn those who have not deserved it, nor refrain from reprobating those who have sinned.[2] The Law is thus the proper Way of salvation. As a condition of salvation, God requires man to have fulfilled His will as revealed in the Law; He requires man to give Him complete " satisfaction " (satisfacere deo).[3] By doing what is well pleasing to God, man has in the strictest sense of the word to merit his salvation; and the best means to this is an ascetic life. By good works man can make God His debtor.[4] The highest degree of merit attaches to the highest conceivable achievement, *martyrdom.* To the martyr who following His Lord takes up his cross, the words apply : " The whole key to Paradise is thine own blood."[5]

In Tertullian *Nomos* has taken concrete form as nowhere else in the history of Christianity. Those remnants of the Agape motif which can be found have been fitted into the nomistic scheme and rendered ineffective. Christianity has been thoroughly transformed into a religion of law. Yet even though Tertullian's outlook has affected the Western interpretation of Christianity to a high degree, the circumstance of his own exclusion from the Church, owing to his attachment to Montanism, has in a measure contributed to the limitation of its influence and to the prevention of the complete submergence of the Agape motif in the Nomos motif.

---

[1] " Nihil tam et bono et iudici conuenit quam pro præsentibus meritis et reicere et adlegere." Adv. Marcionem ii. 23.

[2] *Ibid.*

[3] De pænitentia 7; De ieiunio adv. psychicos 3.

[4] " *Bonum factum deum habet debitorem,* sicuti et malum, quia iudex omnis remunerator est causæ." De pænitentia 2.

[5] " . . . in martyriis, si crucem tuam tollas et sequaris dominum, ut ipse præcepit. *Tota paradisi clauis tuus sanguis est.*" De anima 55.

VI

THE EROS TYPE IN ALEXANDRIAN THEOLOGY

1. THE GENERAL CHARACTER OF ALEXANDRIAN THEOLOGY

THUS far in the history of the Christian idea of love, the Eros motif has appeared either sporadically and at isolated points—as in the Apostolic Fathers and Apologists—or else outside the precise sphere of the Christian Church—as in Gnosticism. With Alexandrian theology, the problem of "Agape and Eros" enters on a new phase. Here the influence of Eros is displayed not merely in solitary instances, but dominates the whole structure. At the same time, the Alexandrians, warned by the example of Gnosticism and consciously opposed to it, seek to avoid heresy and produce churchly theology. In short, the Eros motif obtains official admission to the Church.

If we would picture the spiritual milieu in which Clement and Origen lived and worked, and which also, naturally, set its stamp upon their thought, the name "Alexandrian" is instructive. Alexandria was not merely the great junction of contemporary world communications; it was also the spiritual metropolis of late antiquity, where all the separate streams of culture met and mingled. Above all, it was the home of *religious syncretism*. Here Philo had combined the Jewish and the Hellenistic spirit; here Christianity, too, had been drawn into the religious medley, and Gnostic syncretism had flourished under leaders like Basilides and Valentinus. Alexandria was also to a large extent the home of *philosophical syncretism*. Distinctions between the different schools had grown less and less clear; Plato, Aristotle, the Stoa, Neopythagoreanism, and others, had been laid under contribution for the eclectic philosophy of the day. At the same time, the distinction between philosophy and religion had become more and more vague. Philosophical thinking had moved far towards the moral and religious. Though much time and energy were devoted to cosmological speculations, these were not the object of primary interest. " Know thyself "— this became the sole task of philosophy. But "Know thyself" now meant: Know thy Divine nature, and provide for its return to the Divine world! At no time so much as this has philosophy borne the character of a doctrine of salvation. The chief questions of the idealistic philosophy of late antiquity are those of the Way of salvation and the Blessed life. Philosophy is required, in fact, simply to supply a satisfactory normative ethic and a reliable indication of the Way of salvation. It was no mere accident that Neo-platonism, the most syncretistic philosophy late antiquity produced, arose in Alexandria. But no more was it accidental that views like those of Clement and Origen developed here; it was the most natural environment for them.

But the name of Alexandria further recalls *the Alexandrian world-scheme*.[1] Centuries before, this scheme had developed and become the unquestioned assumption from which everybody started. According to it, the cosmic process moves in two contrary directions: the " Downward Way " and the "Upward Way," cosmological Descent and soteriological Ascent. We have met this view already, in Gnosticism and Neoplatonism, for example, and its reappearance in Alexandrian theology simply proves that the latter moves in the same spiritual sphere as they, and that its general theory is determined by its unquestioning assumption of the Alexandrian world-scheme. And it need not be said how nearly this theory agrees with Hellenistic Eros piety.

Such is the milieu out of which the thought of Clement and Origen grew, such the air it breathed. Their interpretation of Christianity is only to be understood against this

[1] On the Alexandrian world-scheme, *cf. supra*, pp. 186 ff.

background. But this means the abandonment of the traditional approach to Alexandrian theology. It has sometimes been assumed that second-century Christianity, as found in the Apostolic Fathers and the Apologists, is the natural background of Alexandrian theology. This was the Christianity, it has been supposed, that Clement and Origen inherited; and the question is, what they did with it, how it was transformed in their hands. Such a statement of the question, however, inevitably leads to over-emphasis of their purely personal contribution. Clement and Origen did not start with the average type of Christianity characteristic of the second century and remodel it to suit the requirements of the Greek spirit. They never regarded it as their task to transform Christianity. The transformation and adaptation had occurred already before their time, and even then not of conscious intent; it was an obvious and inevitable thing in a world permeated by Hellenism. Behind the theology of Clement and Origen is that Hellenised Christianity which had long had its centre in syncretistic Alexandria. If we take note of this and of the particular presuppositions given in Alexandrian culture and the Alexandrian world-scheme, then much that otherwise might appear to be the purely personal ideas of Clement and Origen is seen to be nothing but just such assumptions as they and their environment alike took for granted and lived upon.

It has often been pointed out that the conflict in the Early Church was largely due to the question how far Christianity ought to take ancient culture and thought into its service, and that Alexandrian theology represented the point of view more friendly to culture. And there is an element of sound observation behind this. No one can deny that the positive attitude of Alexandrian theology to Hellenistic philosophy and culture is entirely different from that, for example, of Tertullian. Yet to regard the question as one merely of cultural synthesis is to miss its main point. The sharpness and religious gravity of the conflict are due rather to the fact that ultimately the question at issue is not cultural, but religious synthesis. The Alexandrian theologians lived, in matters religious, on a double tradition. Two separate spiritual streams flowed together in them. Eros and Agape both actively contributed to their Christianity, and they felt no tension between them. Clement and Origin readily took up Greek philosophy, not merely in order to make contact with contemporary "worldly" culture, but above all because they felt themselves allied with the fundamental *religious* view which found expression in the philosophical doctrines. Hellenistic Eros piety represented for them an indisputable value, for which a place must obviously be found in Christianity, inasmuch as the latter united all truth and all value in itself. But there were other circles in the Church, which did not share these Hellenistic presuppositions, circles whose tradition pointed in another direction. Perhaps a synthesis was involved there, too, but of a different kind. Tertullian, for example, has little affinity with the spiritualising outlook of Platonism, but this does not mean that his Christianity shows no signs of synthesis; only it is another synthesis—namely, with the Jewish Nomos motif. These circles, to which in one way or another the religious tradition of Hellenism was foreign, could not but regard the introduction of Greek philosophy into Christianity as a corruption.

It is undeniable that the religion of Clement and Origen rests upon two distinct fundamental motifs. The question is, how was this possible? How could they fail to perceive the dualism? How did they, purely psychologically, manage to combine the two motifs? The answer is in *the allegorical interpretation* of Scripture, which they themselves had no need to invent, for it lay ready to hand in Hellenistic Judaism and Gnosticism, as well as in the more churchly theology of the Apologists. Allegorism was an instrument which enjoyed general recognition, even within the Church; it also well agreed with their syncretistic trend, for it offered them a freedom in relation to the individual texts of Holy Scripture, which at the same time meant that they were unfettered by the fundamental Christian motif. For a right understanding of the Scriptures, on this view, the literal interpretation, which holds to the simple wording of the text, is not enough. Behind every word of Scripture lies a deeper, spiritual, pneumatic meaning, to which allegorical interpretation holds the key. Thus the conflict between Hellenistic piety and Christianity is settled for the Alexandrian theologians; Eros and Agape have come to terms. *But the Eros motif retains the ascendancy, for it is allowed to represent the deeper, spiritual meaning of Christianity.* If the simple Christian clings to the outward wording of Scripture, it is given to the Christian " Gnostic " to penetrate its deeper, spiritual meaning; and what he finds there is in closest accord with Hellenistic Eros piety.

2. FAITH AND GNOSIS IN CLEMENT OF ALEXANDRIA

The syncretistic trend of Alexandrian theology is clearly apparent in Clement of Alexandria.[1] His interpretation of Christianity is founded on the idea of God's Pedagogy, the idea that God, through the Logos, guides and disciplines the human race towards perfection. From this point of view, Hellenistic piety (or philosophy) and Christianity are not rivals, but are related as " preparation and fulfilment." By various ways, God has led humanity forward to Christ. What the Law was for the Jews, philosophy was for the Greeks. Both, in the last resort, come from God, and both have the same purpose—namely, to be pedagogues and

[1] Of literature on Clement we may mention—E. de Faye: *Clément d'Alexandrie*, 1898 (2nd edn. 1906); and J. Meifort: *Der Platonismus bei Clemens Alexandrinus* (Heidelberger Abhandlungen zur Philosophie und ihrer Geschichte, hrsg. von E. Hoffmann und H. Rickert, nr. 17), 1928.

"schoolmasters to bring us to Christ," who is their goal and fulfilment.[1] In Old Testament Law and in Greek philosophy, the Divine Logos has revealed Himself, but in a preparatory manner only; so that, in this respect, they stand more or less on the same level. Clement, it is true, following Jewish and Early Christian tradition, claims that the Greek philosophers "stole" their wisdom from the Old Testament revelation, as Prometheus stole the Divine fire; and he applies to them the words of Jesus in Jn. x. 8: "All that came before me are thieves and robbers." Nevertheless, he uses this idea in such a way—even stolen gold is still gold —that it provides evidence, not against, but for the truth of Greek philosophy, and a proof that it, too, comes ultimately from God.[2] It is the same Logos that is found among Jews and Greeks. The goal, therefore, is the unity of these two in Christ, who is the perfect and final revelation of the Logos here in the world. In Christianity the two converge and find fulfilment; there the separate streams are meant to join.[3]

What, then, is the content of Clement's synthesis? And how are the two motifs related to each other? As has been said, the Old Testament and Greek philosophy are regarded as preparations for Christianity. Does this perhaps mean that the Old Testament Nomos motif and the Hellenistic Eros motif are regarded by Clement as stages preparatory to the Christian Agape motif? And are we therefore justified

---

[1] ἐπαιδαγώγει γὰρ καὶ αὕτη [ἡ φιλοσοφία] τὸ Ἑλληνικὸν ὡς ὁ νόμος τοὺς Ἑβραίους εἰς Χριστόν. προπαρασκευάζει τοίνυν ἡ φιλοσοφία προοδοποιοῦσα τὸν ὑπὸ Χριστοῦ τελειούμενον. Stromata I., cap. v. 28, 3; cf. Strom. VI., cap. v. 41-42.

[2] Strom. I., cap. xvii. 81, 1-87, 7. Cf. esp. 81, 4 and 87, 1.

[3] μία μὲν οὖν ἡ τῆς ἀληθείας ὁδός, ἀλλ' εἰς αὐτὴν καθάπερ εἰς ἀέναον ποταμὸν ἐκρέουσι τὰ ῥεῖθρα ἄλλα ἄλλοθεν. Strom. I., cap. v. 29, 1. μία μὲν γὰρ τῷ ὄντι διαθήκη ἡ σωτήριος ἀπὸ καταβολῆς κόσμου εἰς ἡμᾶς διήκουσα, κατὰ διαφόρους γενεάς τε καὶ χρόνους διάφορος εἶναι τὴν δόσιν ὑποληφθεῖσα. ἀκόλουθον γὰρ εἶναι μίαν ἀμετάθετον σωτηρίας δόσιν παρ' ἑνὸς θεοῦ δι' ἑνὸς κυρίου " πολυτρόπως " ὠφελοῦσαν, δι' ἣν αἰτίαν τὸ " μεσότοιχον " αἴρεται τὸ διορίζον τοῦ Ἰουδαίου τὸν Ἕλληνα εἰς περιούσιον λαόν. Strom. VI., cap. xiiii. 106, 3 f.

in supposing his view, in essence, to be formed by the Agape motif, so that the other two motifs, though they do occur, are merely obsolete survivals?

The possibility of such an interpretation is excluded by Clement's view of the relation between *Faith and Gnosis*. Faith, of course, represents a higher stage, in so far as the Christian faith is the goal to which God willed to lead Jews by means of the Law and Greeks by means of philosophy. But, arrived at the goal, we discover that there are different stages in the Christian life, too. And here the scene changes completely. Within the Christian life, Faith represents the lowest stage. High above " mere Faith " ($\psi\iota\lambda\grave{\eta}$ $\pi\acute{\iota}\sigma\tau\iota\varsigma$) towers Christian " Gnosis."

The mere believer has, it is true, what is essential. The first and decisive step is taken; he has been brought by God from paganism to the saving Christian faith. Yet he is still far from perfection. Faith is a gift, placed in man's heart by God, which makes him able to confess and praise God without even needing to seek Him.[1] That is at once the significance and the limitation of Faith: its significance, because it really brings man into relationship with the true God; its limitation, because it is content with a more superficial acceptance of the content of Faith and does not go on to a deeper, personal appropriation. A Christian at the stage of Faith cleaves to the letter of Scripture, while its spiritual meaning is hidden from him. What keeps him in Faith is neither insight into its necessity nor love to the God who reveals Himself in it, but simply fear and hope.[2] Therefore Faith, too, points beyond itself to a higher and more perfect stage, to Gnosis.[3]

[1] πίστις μὲν οὖν ἐνδιάθετόν τί ἐστιν ἀγαθόν, καὶ ἄνευ τοῦ ζητεῖν τὸν θεὸν ὁμολογοῦσα εἶναι τοῦτον καὶ δοξάζουσα ὡς ὄντα.   Strom. VII., cap. x. 55, 2.

[2] Strom. II., cap. xii. 53.

[3] ὅθεν χρή, ἀπὸ ταύτης ἀναγόμενον τῆς πίστεως καὶ αὐξηθέντα ἐν αὐτῇ χάριτι τοῦ θεοῦ, τὴν περὶ αὐτοῦ κομίσασθαι ὡς οἷόν τέ ἐστιν γνῶσιν. Strom. VII., cap. x. 55, 3.

The true Gnostic (ὁ ὄντως γνωστικός) is, so to say, a
Christian of higher rank. He does not stop at the husk of
Faith, but finds the kernel; he is no longer bound by the letter
of Scripture, but cleaves to its deeper, pneumatic meaning.
Faith, it is true, remains the foundation on which he builds,[1]
not, however, because of any external authority, but because
of his own personal insight into its nature and value. His
motive is not fear and hope, but love to God, and he does
the good for its own sake, not in order to win outward
advantage.[2] Only on this higher level does Faith, or the
believing man, come to perfection.[3] But Clement goes still
further and says that Gnosis is the perfecting of man as man.[4]
This implies, moreover, that through Gnosis man transcends
the human sphere and becomes divine. The true Gnostic is
himself a God.[5]

Clement's distinction between "mere believers" and
"true Gnostics" recalls a distinction we found earlier, in the
heretical Gnostics. But the analogy must not be exaggerated,
for Clement differs radically from Gnosticism at a particularly important point. Faith and Gnosis are, for him,
primarily two different stages of development, not the marks
of two fundamentally distinct classes of people. Indeed, he
protests most strongly against the Gnostic idea of different
sorts of people, predestined, as it were, by their original endowments, to different lots; and he expressly rejects the

---

[1] Strom. II., cap. xi. 48, 1.—To this extent the formula "credo ut intelligam" applies to Clement's view of the relation between Faith and Gnosis.

[2] Strom. IV., cap. xviii. 112, 1.

[3] διὰ ταύτης γὰρ τελειοῦται ἡ πίστις, ὡς τελείου τοῦ πιστοῦ ταύτῃ μόνως
γιγνομένου. Strom. VII., cap. x. 55, 2.

[4] ἔστιν γάρ, ὡς ἔπος εἰπεῖν, ἡ γνῶσις τελείωσίς τις ἀνθρώπου ὡς ἀνθρώπου.
Strom. VII., cap. x. 55, 1.

[5] τούτῳ δυνατὸν τῷ τρόπῳ τὸν γνωστικὸν ἤδη γενέσθαι θεόν· "ἐγὼ
εἶπα· θεοί ἐστε καὶ υἱοὶ ὑψίστου." Strom. IV., cap. xxiii. 149, 8. καὶ
θεοὶ τὴν προσηγορίαν κέκληνται, [οἱ] σύνθρονοι τῶν ἄλλων θεῶν, τῶν ὑπὸ
τῷ σωτῆρι πρώτων τεταγμένων, γενησόμενοι. Strom. VII., cap. x.
56, 6. . . . πῇ ποτε ἄρα ἄνθρωπος γένηται θεός. Protrepticus, cap. i.
8, 4. *Cf.* also Strom. IV., cap. xxiii. 152, 2 f.; VII., cap. iii. 13, 2.

view prevalent in Gnosticism that the Gnostic possesses, in the 'pneumatic' disposition given him by nature, a guarantee of his salvation.[1]

How, then, is Clement's idea of the relation between Faith and Gnosis to be interpreted from the point of view of motif?

R. Seeberg interprets it as follows: "The two stages which Clement assumes in Christianity give expression to his strong sense of the specific character of Christianity as a religion of redemption. The mere believers are those Christians who have remained on the level of a religion of law, the Gnostics with their inner experience of effective, vital fellowship with God rise to the sphere of the religion of redemption. But owing to the fact that Clement himself has only been able to describe this in Hellenic forms, he has himself obscured the greatness of his thought."[2] Against such an interpretation it must, however, be remarked that to talk of Clement's strong sense of the specific character of Christianity hardly seems compatible with the material cited above. We may give all possible weight to his polemical attitude to heretical Gnosticism, we may add that he emphatically asserts the Christian belief in Creation against Hellenistic denials; nevertheless his whole outlook so clearly betrays the Eros motif that we cannot say it gives any considerable expression to what is peculiarly Christian. Seeberg has rightly seen that Clement's two stages represent two forms of religion different in kind, so that the religion of the " mere believer " is essentially a religion of law, whereas the " Gnostic's " is the religion of redemption. Seeberg, however, regards this in the light of a modern, evolutionistic

---

[1] οἱ δὲ ἀπὸ Οὐαλεντίνου τὴν μὲν πίστιν τοῖς ἁπλοῖς ἀπονείμαντες ἡμῖν, αὐτοῖς δὲ τὴν γνῶσιν, τοῖς φύσει σωζομένοις κατὰ τὴν τοῦ διαφέροντος πλεονεξίαν σπέρματος ἐνυπάρχειν βούλονται, μακρῷ δὴ κεχωρισμένην πίστεως, ᾗ τὸ πνευματικὸν τοῦ ψυχικοῦ, λέγοντες. Strom. II., cap. iii. 10, 2. Cf. Pædagogus I., cap. vi. 31, 2.

[2] R. Seeberg: Lehrbuch der Dogmengeschichte, Bd. i., 2 Aufl., 1908, p. 397.

theory, which considers the religion of law to be the lower, the religion of redemption the higher stage in the evolution of religions, Christianity being placed in the latter class. Hence his impression that Gnosis represents what is peculiarly Christian. But Seeberg naturally could not fail to notice that Clement's Gnosis bears, in the highest degree, the stamp of Hellenistic piety. So he cannot but conclude that while Clement's strong sense of the specific character of Christianity drove him to set up the ideal of the "true Gnostic" who refuses to remain at the stage of the religion of law and raises himself to the level of the religion of redemption, yet in his more detailed exposition of this he made far too much use of Hellenic thought-forms inadequate to his Christian outlook.

Without Seeberg's evolutionistic theory, however, the situation in Clement is considerably simpler. Behind the two stages of Christianity lies not the anxiety to present Christianity in its uniqueness, but on the contrary, the syncretistic tendency to find room in Christianity for fundamentally different religious positions. Clement has met post-apostolic Christianity as modified by Nomos. It is in the main foreign to him, yet he will not wholly reject it, but grants it relative authority. It is Christianity, but of a lower order; it is *merely* Faith. But he has also met Hellenistic piety and the Alexandrian Christianity moulded by it, and found them of indisputable value. Within this framework his own religious life at its deepest is lived and hence derives its structure. Thus, in Faith we recognise the *Nomos motif*; but it is not faith in the primitive Christian sense, it is faith to a large extent modified by Nomos. In Gnosis, again, we meet the *Eros motif*; without doubt it is a religion of redemption, but its essential mark is not Agape but Eros. By comparison the Agape motif falls into the background; yet that must not be taken to mean that Clement would feel strange to Christianity and ought really to be classed as a Hellenistic thinker.

The very common question, whether Clement should rather be regarded as a Christian or a Hellenic thinker, ought never to be asked. That alternative does not exist for him. Personally he is a Christian, and wants to be nothing else but a Christian. So that matter is not under debate here; it is a self-evident postulate. Our interest is rather in the structure of his Christianity, with reference to its motif. And if from this point of view we analyse his Christian outlook as we find it in his writings and especially in his conception of the relation between Faith and Gnosis, it is revealed as a synthesis founded principally on the Nomos and Eros motifs, of which the latter, as dominating the highest stage of Christianity, decidedly has the ascendancy.

3. Gnosis and Agape in Clement of Alexandria

The above analysis has shown that Clement's interpretation of Christianity is, in the main, characterised by the Eros motif. Gnosis is the highest, the ideal form of Christianity, and here as always Gnosis proves to be inseparable from Eros and, at bottom, merely another name for it. Clement may most vigorously attack "heretical" Gnosis, but the very "Christian" Gnosis he would put in its place bears substantially the mark of Eros piety. The situation is complicated, however, because in giving the characteristics of "the true Gnostic" Clement has a predilecton for the word ἀγάπη. Does not this suggest that the Agape motif occupies, after all, a more central place than is apparent from what has been said above?

The Clementine scholar, E. de Faye, asserts that this really is so. The true Gnostic, he argues, unites two characteristic traits, ἀπάθεια and ἀγάπη. If the former is Stoic and indicates Clement's debt to antiquity, especially to Plato and Stoicism, the latter is specifically Christian and bears witness to the importance of the Christian contribution to his thought.[1] It is Agape that makes Clement's "true Gnostic" into a real Christian, makes him, indeed, a living figure at all.[2] Love occupies, says de Faye, the same place in Clement's morality as the Christ-Logos in his theology; it is the centre and the Christian inspiration of his ethics.[3] Agape shares with Gnosis the place of honour in Clement's thought. He can express his ideal with now one, now the other of these terms, and often it is impossible to decide whether Gnosis or Agape is the Gnostic's ultimate goal. This oscillation, de Faye holds, is extremely characteristic of Clement; it illustrates how Christianity and philosophy strive for mastery in his thinking.[4] Agape, however, is plainly the soul and vital force in the Gnostic, since in all his classifications of the virtues Clement places Agape supreme. It is the virtue which includes and fructifies all the rest.[5] But de Faye's entire argument presupposes that the word Agape is used by Clement in its specifically Christian sense. Even if he has not failed to notice that certain features of Clement's idea of Agape strongly suggest Platonic influence,[6] yet that does not prevent him from declaring categorically that Clement's idea of Agape is the authentically Christian idea of love.[7]

Attractive as de Faye's theory may be at first sight, yet on closer examination it proves untenable. It illustrates strikingly how easily we can be misled by accepting words and expressions at their face value without submitting them to a motif-analysis. De Faye is fully aware that Clement's Gnosis is "a conception entirely alien to Christianity."[8]

---

[1] E. de Faye: *Clément d'Alexandrie*, 1898, p. 274.

[2] *Op. cit.*, p. 285.   [3] *Op. cit.*, p. 282.

[4] *Ibid.*   [5] *Op. cit.*, p. 283.

[6] "Ἀγάπη, which is the Gnostic virtue *par excellence*, is Christian love. A few isolated traits reminiscent of Plato must not make us lose sight of this essential fact." *Op. cit.*, p. 283.

[7] *Op. cit.*, p. 285.

[8] *Op. cit.*, p. 273: "It must be admitted that Clement's Gnosis is a conception completely foreign to Christianity."

But it is, further, a plain fact that the principle of Clement's Gnostic morality is love.[1] Surely that is enough to arouse the suspicion that the love here spoken of is not exactly identical with love in the specifically Christian sense? And there would have been the more reason for a closer investigation of this point, inasmuch as love in the form of Eros is the fundamental motif itself of Hellenistic piety and of the philosophy influenced by it. De Faye, however, stops short of this question. Clement speaks of $\dot{\alpha}\gamma\dot{\alpha}\pi\eta$, and that is proof positive for de Faye that the specifically Christian idea of love is meant. Altogether, de Faye is singularly obscure and uncertain when he is supposed to be stating what exactly is the difference between Christianity and Greek philosophy. In philosophy, according to him, the rational element preponderates, in Christianity the mystical[2]—as if mysticism were not just as characteristic of Hellenism as ever rationalism was! But since de Faye works with such vague standards of reference, it is not surprising that his conclusions are misleading. There is therefore every reason to view with reserve the result of his enquiry—namely, that to erect his Christian edifice Clement had to borrow sundry material from Greek philosophy, yet it is not this but Christianity which, in the last resort, gives the building its necessary form and determines its type.[3] One cannot help asking : What does de Faye mean here by " Christianity "? His statements

[1] *Op. cit.*, p. 257: " The principle . . . of Gnostic morality is exclusively love."

[2] *Op. cit.*, p. 296: " Greek philosophy and apostolic Christianity are not things of the same kind. The character of the one is predominantly *rational*, and of the other, *mystical*."

[3] " At the basis of Clement's Gnostic Christianity is the Christianity of his time. That is the foundation. The architect who builds upon this foundation the edifice of higher Christianity is Philosophy. To carry out his work the architect borrows from Plato, Zeno, or some such person, a great deal of the materials he requires. But, in the last analysis, what gives the edifice its necessary form, the general lines of the building, and to some extent the type and character which distinguish it, is the foundation, Christianity. Thus you have an edifice which at first sight seems to be entirely the work of Philosophy, but which in reality owes its peculiar features and its plan to Christianity." *Op. cit.*, pp. 297 f.

would be better reversed, to read: In constructing his thought, Clement has used sundry material taken from Christianity; but in the last resort the necessary form and definite type of the edifice is due not to Christianity, but to Hellenism, not to the Agape, but to the Eros motif. This clearly proves to be the case, when the function and nature of Clement's idea of love (Agape) is more closely examined.

Even if Clement's speech falters somewhat when it comes to defining the relation of Agape to Gnosis, so that now Gnosis, now Agape appears to be the ultimate goal of the Christian life,[1] yet in the main he has a consistent conception of the Christian Way of salvation and its various stages. The first step on the Way of salvation is the transition from unbelief (paganism) to Faith, the second, the transition from Faith to Gnosis. But Gnosis leads on to Love, Agape, which is characterised as that inner bond of friendship which binds the Gnostic to God as the object of his Gnosis, and causes him more and more to be transformed into likeness to God. In and through Agape the Gnostic has, so to speak, anticipated the "angelic" life, and that is as near perfection as a man can possibly come under the conditions of earthly life. This explains what Clement understands by the saying he adopts from Ignatius, that Faith is the beginning and Love the end.[2] Faith is the substructure on which the higher Christian life characteristic of the true Gnostic is erected, but this Gnostic life reaches its completion in Agape. Beyond Agape, beyond the desire that continually reaches out towards God, it is impossible to go in this present life. That is the limit of human perfection. But Agape does not stop at any temporal limit; it is a dynamic principle which refuses

---

[1] De Faye rightly says, *op. cit.*, p. 282: "It is sometimes uncertain whether it is γνῶσις or ἀγάπη that is the final end which the Gnostic is to pursue. Clement seems to hesitate, and in different passages it is now Gnosis, now Love which inspires him."

[2] *Cf. supra*, p. 261. Strom. VII., cap. x. 55, 6; . . . ἥ τε ἀρχὴ καὶ τὸ τέλος, πίστις λέγω καὶ ἡ ἀγάπη.

to be circumscribed. Agape is the force that drives the true Gnostic ceaselessly upward and comes to rest only in the future life, when he has urged his way through the seven holy spheres of heaven to the abode (μονή) of the Lord, where the perfected spirit becomes a light, steady, and continuing eternally, entirely and in every part immutable.[1]

Obviously, the Hellenistic ' ordo salutis ' lies at the basis of Clement's conception of the Christian Way of salvation. He differs from the Hellenistic view in maintaining ' mere faith,' but he has raised an edifice upon it whose whole design is dominated by the Eros motif. As God is the eternally immutable and immovable, Himself eternal rest and peace, so the aim of man is to find rest in Him.[2] Man's destiny is ultimately to stand before God as a light " continuing eternally, entirely and in every part immutable." The Way to this goal is marked by the stages of (1) *believing*, (2) *knowing*, (3) *loving* (desiring), (4) *possessing* God. " For it is said : ' To him that hath shall be given,' to faith, knowledge; and to knowledge, love; and to love the possession."[3] Only the first three stages belong to this life; the fourth, possession, is reserved for the life to come, but it is to that we reach out. Agape, with its desire and longing for God, is thus the highest to which a man here in time can attain. We have spoken of " stages " in this connection; yet it should be noted that there is no sharp line of demarcation

---

[1] Strom. VII., cap. x. 57, 4 f. In view of its fundamental importance, this passage may be quoted *in extenso*: καί μοι δοκεῖ πρώτη τις εἶναι μεταβολὴ σωτήριος ἡ ἐξ ἐθνῶν εἰς πίστιν, ὡς προεῖπον, δευτέρα δὲ ἡ ἐκ πίστεως εἰς γνῶσιν. ἡ δέ, εἰς ἀγάπην περαιουμένη, ἐνθένδε ἤδη φίλον φίλῳ τὸ γιγνώσκον τῷ γιγνωσκομένῳ παρίστησιν. καὶ τάχα ὁ τοιοῦτος ἐνθένδε ἤδη προλαβὼν ἔχει τὸ " ἰσάγγελος " εἶναι. μετὰ γοῦν τὴν ἐν σαρκὶ τελευταίαν ὑπεροχὴν ἀεὶ κατὰ τὸ προσῆκον ἐπὶ τὸ κρεῖττον μεταβάλλων, εἰς τὴν πατρῴαν αὐλὴν ἐπὶ τὴν κυριακὴν ὄντως διὰ τῆς ἁγίας ἑβδομάδος ἐπείγεται μονήν, ἐσόμενος, ὡς εἰπεῖν, φῶς ἑστὸς καὶ μένον ἀιδίως, πάντῃ πάντως ἄτρεπτον.

[2] Strom. VII., cap. x. 57, 1 f.

[3] Strom. VII., cap. x. 55, 7: . . . . τῇ μὲν πίστει ἡ γνῶσις, τῇ δὲ γνώσει ἡ ἀγάπη, τῇ ἀγάπῃ δὲ ἡ κληρονομία.

between them.   Although Agape denotes the highest point of the higher Christian life, yet according to Clement it is present as the motive force even in the lower stages.   Not even faith, the lowest stage of the Christian life, can exist apart from Agape.[1]

Now that we have thus seen Clement's idea of love in its concrete form and in its context, we can no longer be in doubt as to its content.   Clement uses the New Testament term Agape, but the reality he intends to convey corresponds most closely to what Plato calls " the heavenly Eros."   Furthermore, his description of how this love is attained is reminiscent of Platonic, Hellenistic ideas.   Man must break the bonds that bind him to the material world, must purify himself from the taint of things sensible.   Of the man thus practised in the art of apathy, and thereby made " angellike," Clement says that by means of love to God he hastens to his holy abode (μονή).[2]   Clement calls this love Agape; he could have called it Eros—the name makes little difference. When he characterises it as apathy towards the lower world and as desire and longing to find one's μονή in the higher, then its connection with the Eros motif is in any case evident. In such circumstances, to find two opposed tendencies in Clement and to make his talk of ἀπάθεια represent the Greek philosophical, whilst ἀγάπη represents the Christian contribution to his thought, is simply playing with words. Both belong to a consistent line of thought and express one and the same tendency.

This conclusion is further confirmed by the way in which Clement defines both God's love and love to neighbour— that is, those two forms of love to which Agape most owes its special stamp and which distinguish it from Eros love.

What, then, is the meaning and content of the idea of

---

[1] Strom. II., cap. vi. 30, 3: ἡ μὲν γὰρ ἀγάπη τῇ πρὸς τὴν πίστιν φιλίᾳ τοὺς πιστοὺς ποιεῖ.

[2] Strom. VI., cap. xiii. 105, 1.

God's love in Clement? First, we may state that this idea falls much into the background in comparison with that of man's love to God. It is this latter that decidedly stands at the centre of Clement's interest. But even when he does speak of God's love, this has not its primitive Christian significance. Altogether, Clement shows little sense of anything unexpected, any paradox, in the message of God's love. On the contrary, it is quite proper, in his opinion, that God should love man. How could He not? Man is His creature, and that in a special sense. All else He has created simply by means of His omnipotent word, but man He has created and fashioned by His own hand and has breathed into him part of His own substance.[1] God's substance is good, and so when He loves man it is something good that He loves. The depths of man's being contain a good and valuable quality, in which God can take delight. There is a something within man (τὸ φίλτρον), which awakens and wins God's love.[2] Being by nature akin to God, man is pleasing to Him and worthy of His love. The sequence Clement observes here is typical. First he proves that man is worthy to be loved, then asks: "But what is lovable for anyone and is not also loved by Him?"[3] So far from conceiving God's love as paradoxical and unmotivated, Clement actually starts by postulating that man as such is worthy of God's love, and then goes on to prove that God loves him. No clearer evidence could be desired to show that his view—in spite of the term "Agape"—essentially bears the stamp of Eros.

Similarly as regards love to neighbour. This is a theme by no means rare in Clement, and he often describes the true

---

[1] Pædagogus I., cap. iii. 7, 1: εἰκότως ἄρα φίλος ὁ ἄνθρωπος τῷ θεῷ.

[2] Pædagogus I., cap. iii. 7, 3: εἰ μὲν οὖν δι' αὐτὸ αἱρετὸν ὁ ἄνθρωπος, ἀγαθὸς ὢν ἀγαθὸν ἠγάπησεν, καὶ τὸ φίλτρον ἔνδον ἐστὶν ἐν τῷ ἀνθρώπῳ, τοῦθ' ὅπερ ἐμφύσημα εἴρηται θεοῦ.

[3] Pædagogus I., cap. iii. 8, 1: ἀλλὰ καὶ φιλητὸν μέν τί ἐστί τινι, οὐχὶ δὲ καὶ φιλεῖται ὑπ' αὐτοῦ; φιλητὸς δὲ ὁ ἄνθρωπος ἀποδέδεικται, φιλεῖται ἄρα πρὸς τοῦ θεοῦ ὁ ἄνθρωπος.

Gnostic's relation to his neighbour in such a way that we seem to recognise the Christian idea of Agape. De Faye writes: "When we read such passages, where Clement shows us the Gnostic full of indulgence towards his brother, helping him in his need, ministering to his wants, well-doing with discrimination and justice, good even to his persecutors, etc., we have no hesitation in recognising their Christian inspiration."[1] Undoubtedly the influence of the Christian love motif is at its strongest here. Yet we must beware of exaggerating its significance. In the first place, even the passages mentioned far too clearly display at once Stoic apathy and a spirit of general philanthropy, to be readily acceptable as legitimate expressions of Christian love to neighbour. Further, the commandment of love to neighbour itself proves to have caused Clement such difficulties as he has only managed to overcome by reinterpreting the command. Just as God's love loses its Agape character, as we saw above, because he furnishes it with a motive, so now love to neighbour also loses its Agape character—because he spiritualises it. Love to God finds a place without difficulty in his outlook, coloured as this is by Hellenism; and in so far as love to neighbour is referred back to this love to God, interpreted on the lines of Eros, he gets rid of what the Hellenistic mind finds offensive in the idea of love to neighbour. An argument he works out in the $\tau \acute{\iota} s$ $\acute{o}$ $\sigma \omega \zeta \acute{o} \mu \epsilon \nu o s$ $\pi \lambda o \acute{\upsilon} \sigma \iota o s$[2] is specially interesting. Greatest among the commandments, according to Christ's own word, is the commandment of love to God. But side by side with it He sets the second: "Thou shalt love thy neighbour as thyself." Who can be meant by this commandment? Who is our "neighbour" whom we are obliged to love? Christ Himself has given the answer in the parable of the Good Samaritan. For who was the neighbour of the man who had fallen into the hands of robbers? Answer: the one

[1] E. de Faye, *op. cit.*, p. 285.   [2] Quis dives salvetur xxvii. 3 ff.

who showed mercy to him. Who, then, is our neighbour?
Who else but the Saviour, for who has shown us such mercy
as He? " Him then we must love equally with God."[1] In
this way Clement makes the commandment of love to neighbour virtually equivalent to that of love to God. In both
parts of the Commandment of Love there is required essentially one and the same thing: love to God and love to
Christ. But if we love Christ, it follows that we keep His
commandments and so care for those who believe in Him.[2]
In this roundabout way love to neighbour in the Christian
sense is finally introduced, yet even so it is bereft of its point
in the traditional fashion: " Agape covereth a multitude of
sins."[3] For Clement, as for post-apostolic Christianity in
general, Agape is the chief means of cancelling sin. Love to
neighbour is the work that most surely leads to salvation.
If a man has Agape dwelling in his soul, he can, though he
has sunk never so deep in sin and transgression, cancel his
guilt, if only he continues and grows in Agape.[4]

Clement's Gnostic, pneumatic mind, trained in the atmosphere of Eros piety, was bound to find love to neighbour,
in its simple, concrete sense, far too earthbound. So he must
spiritualise it. This may also explain his strong disapproval
of the love-feasts customary at the time, which went by the
name of " agapæ."[5] We have already mentioned his attack
upon certain Gnostic sects for their desecration of the holy·
name of Agape, with which they signified their vulgar Eros,
their πάνδημος Ἀφροδίτη.[6] But it was not only against
Gnostic abuses he reacted; he also turned against the custom

---

[1] *Ibid.* xxix. 2: τίς δ' ἂν ἄλλος οὗτος εἴη πλὴν αὐτὸς ὁ σωτήρ; ἢ τίς μᾶλλον
ἡμᾶς ἐλεήσας ἐκείνου. . . . *Ibid.* xxix. 5: τοῦτον οὖν ἀγαπᾶν ἴσα χρὴ
τῷ θεῷ.

[2] *Ibid.* xxx. 1.

[3] Quis dives salvetur xxxviii. 2. *Cf.* 1 Pet. iv. 8. On the traditional post-
apostolic interpretation of this saying, *cf. supra*, p. 248 f.

[4] Quis dives salvetur xxxviii. 4.

[5] *Cf.* K. Völker: *Mysterium und Agape*, 1927, pp. 153 ff.

[6] *Cf. supra*, p. 310.

of holding love-feasts in the Church. " But such entertainments the Lord has not called agapæ."[1] We need not enquire whether these agape-feasts in general gave occasion for justifiable criticism. Clement's point is that the holy name of Agape is degraded when used in connection with things so low and earthly as a meal.[2] For him, Agape is that heavenward longing whose place is above. It is a " celestial food " and " the banquet of the Logos."[3] Of it the Apostle Paul has said that it never falls.[4] But what fall can be more dreadful than that Agape should be cast down from heaven to earth and land right in the sauce-boat?

Clement's Agape has its closest parallel in the " heavenly Eros " of Plato. From this starting-point he attacks the " vulgar Eros " which masquerades in Gnosticism under the holy name of Agape. But from the same starting-point he also attacks Christian Agape, when, in the form of love to neighbour, it appears to him to be all too earthbound.

4. Origen's Religious Synthesis

The fusion of the Eros and Agape motifs, which had occurred personally in Clement of Alexandria, is *systematically* worked out by Origen.[5] Origen's historical importance

---

[1] Pædagogus II., cap. i. 4, 4: τὰς τοιαύτας δὲ ἑστιάσεις ὁ κύριος ἀγάπας οὐ κέκληκεν.

[2] *Op. cit.*, i. 7, 1: ἀγάπη μὲν οὖν δεῖπνον οὐκ ἔστιν. *Op. cit.*, i. 4, 3: " Whence some, speaking with unbridled tongue, dare to apply the name agape to pitiful suppers, redolent of savour and sauces. Dishonouring the good and saving work of the Logos, the consecrated agape . . . and desecrating that name."

[3] *Op. cit.*, i. 5, 3: ἀγάπη δὲ τῷ ὄντι ἐπουράνιός ἐστι τροφή, ἑστίασις λογική.

[4] Here Clement plays on Paul's word in 1 Cor. xiii. 8: " Love never faileth," ἡ ἀγάπη οὐδέποτε πίπτει. Note the pun on the word πίπτει. " χαλεπώτατον δὲ πάντων πτωμάτων τὴν ἄπτωτον ἀγάπην ἄνωθεν ἐξ οὐρανῶν ἐπὶ τοὺς ζωμοὺς ῥίπτεσθαι χαμαί." Pæd. II., cap. i. 5, 4.

[5] Of the abundant recent literature about Origen the following chief works may be mentioned—E. de Faye: *Origène, sa vie, son œuvre, sa pensée*, i.-iii., 1923-1928; Anna Miura-Stange: *Celsus und Origenes*, 1926; Walther Völker: *Das Vollkommenheitsideal des Origenes. Eine Untersuchung zur Geschichte der Frömmigkeit und zu den Anfängen christlicher Mystik*, 1931; Hal Koch: *Pronoia und Paideusis. Studien über Origenes und sein Verhältnis zum Platonismus*, 1932.

is due supremely to the fact that the two great religious streams of late antiquity, the Christian and the Hellenistic, mingle in his thought. Already before him, as we have seen, Christianity had been drawn into the religious confusion of late antiquity, above all in Gnosticism. With this, however, in spite of his syncretistic inclinations, Origen would not make common cause. He rather regards the Gnostics as his chief opponents, whom he must resist at all costs. He is far more clearly aware than Clement that Christianity risks disintegration and the loss of its individuality, when it enters into relations with the surrounding world. Origen will surrender nothing of Christianity, and in a far higher degree than Clement he can be described as a churchly and a biblical theologian. At the same time, he is a Platonic philosopher. This dual strain, however, means that he not only, as often supposed, pours the content of the Christian faith into Greek moulds, but he produces a real religious synthesis. Origen, in fact, lives his religious life in both of the two rival spiritual worlds. He is by fullest conviction a Christian, but an equally convinced Platonist. Beside Augustine, he ranks as the most interesting example of such a blend of religious motifs. The possibility of a reconciliation of the conflicting motifs he finds in the allegorical method of interpretation. By its aid he could reinterpret the Platonic arguments and myths in a biblical direction.[1] But, still more important, thanks to the allegorical interpretation of Scripture, he could also regard Platonism as the hidden,

---

[1] An interesting example is his interpretation of Plato's myth of the Birth of Eros (Symposium 23) to agree with the biblical story of the Fall: "Now I have brought forward this myth occurring in the writings of Plato, because of the mention in it of the garden of Zeus, which appears to bear some resemblance to the paradise of God, and of the comparison between Penia and the serpent, and the plot against Porus by Penia, which may be compared with the plot of the serpent against the man. It is not very clear, indeed, whether Plato fell in with these stories by chance, or whether, as some think, meeting during his visit to Egypt with certain individuals who philosophised on the Jewish mysteries, he learnt of them." Contra Celsum iv. 39.

spiritual meaning of Christianity. For in the last resort it is the Eros motif, the Hellenistic outlook, that is dominant with him. His younger contemporary, the Neoplatonic philosopher Porphyry, aptly writes of him : " His outward life was that of a Christian and opposed to the law, but in regard to his views of things and of the Deity, he thought like the Greeks, inasmuch as he introduced their ideas into the myths of other peoples."[1]

According to circumstances, now one, now the other side of this synthesis comes to the fore. Usually, indeed, Origen displays no very great understanding of the Christian Agape motif, but when it is threatened by direct attacks from its pagan environment he can awake to its significance. In his defence of Christianity, therefore, essential traits of the Christian idea of love sometimes find unexpected expression. When not on the defensive, however, he merely states his own point of view, with no interest but to expound it systematically, and then it is soon enough evident that he is dominated by Eros theory. We may therefore concentrate upon these two points: *Origen's defence of Christianity,* with its relative appreciation of the Agape motif, and *Origen's system,* in which the Eros motif is patently the determinative factor. After making clear the elements of which it is composed, we shall return to the synthesis itself, sealed as it is by Origen's twofold affirmation : *God is Eros,* and *God is Agape.*

5. ORIGEN'S DEFENCE OF CHRISTIANITY

For an understanding of Origen's religious synthesis, his work *Contra Celsum* offers splendid material. It is particularly valuable for our purpose, since here Origen

---

[1] Eusebius, Hist. Eccl. vi. 19, 7 (tr. in Harnack, H.D. ii., p. 341). Eusebius quotes from Porphyry's work, now lost, κατὰ χριστιανῶν. *Cf.* A. Harnack, *Porphyrios, ' Gegen die Christen,'* 15 *Bücher* (in Abhandlungen der Königl. preussischen Akademie der Wissenschaften, Jahrg. 1916, Philos.-hist. Kl.).

comes to the defence of Christianity against an attack directed precisely from the side of Hellenistic piety. Whatever else may be said about Celsus the Platonist's polemical work, the ἀληθὴς λόγος, it can at all events not be denied that in its criticism of Christianity its aim is both central and, in its way, sure. Unlike the usual cheap criticism, it has taken account of what is essential for Christianity, the fundamental motif itself, the Agape motif; but that is to say, it attacks just that in Christianity which was bound to give most offence to antique sensibility. In brief, Celsus' attack on Christianity can be described as the attack of the Eros motif on the Agape motif. Now it is extremely interesting to see how Origen handles this situation. Here is concrete confirmation of the thesis set up above, that he lives on a double spiritual tradition and is moulded by two opposed religious motifs. When Celsus impugns the Agape motif, Origen feels that an irreplaceable value is at stake, and hastens to its relief. When Celsus, again, gives a positive exposition of his own Eros theory and quotes Plato in its support, Origen will be in at this, too; he exerts himself to make it fit in with Christianity. A few examples may make the situation clear.

Celsus has woven together a whole network of ideas to demonstrate the absurdity of the Christian Agape outlook. In the first place, he attacks the conception of God which lies at its root. What sense is there in talking, as the Christians do, of a Divine Descent? " I make no new statement, but say what has long been settled. God is good, and beautiful, and blessed, and that in the best and most beautiful degree. But if He come down among men, He must undergo a change, and a change from good to evil, from beauty to ugliness, from happiness to misery, and from best to worst. Who, then, would make choice of such a change?"[1] This argument of Celsus plainly rests upon the typically Greek conception of God. From this point of view, to talk of a

[1] Contra Celsum iv. 14.

Divine *Descent*[1] is utterly absurd. It contradicts everything
the Hellenistic mind regards as self-evident with respect to
the Divine: it contradicts God's immutability and incorruptibility, but also His *eudæmonia*, His self-sufficiency and
blessedness. The very idea of a god or son of god descending
to earth is senseless and blasphemous to such a degree that it
really does not need any refutation, says Celsus.[2] But even
assuming God had descended to the earth, why should He
reveal Himself in Jesus in particular? If we are to believe
there was something divine in Him, then this must somehow
appear and attest itself. "For as the sun, which enlightens
all other objects, first makes himself visible, so ought the
Son of God to have done."[3] And even if, during His lifetime, He had taken great care to conceal this divinity, at
least it should have burst forth in might and beaten down all
opposition when His enemies led Him to the cross. But
what sign of this is there in Jesus? "What great deeds did
Jesus perform as being a God? Did He put His enemies to
shame, or bring to a ridiculous conclusion what was designed
against Him?"[4] "If not before, yet why now, at least, does
He not give some manifestation of His divinity, and free
Himself from this reproach, and take vengeance upon those
who insult both Him and His Father?"[5]

It is the Agape trait in the person of Jesus, His humiliation,
self-offering and death on the Cross, that repels Celsus; and
the same trait arouses his hostility to the message and activity
of Jesus in general. For who is it that Jesus, and Christianity
after Him, calls to Himself? Not, as in all other religions,
the righteous, but just sinners. "Is it, then, an evil thing
not to have sinned?"[6] asks Celsus. And, alluding to the

---

[1] Contra Celsum iv. 5: . . . ὅτι αὐτὸς κάτεισι πρὸς ἀνθρώπους ὁ Θεός.

[2] *Op. cit.*, iv. 2: . . . τοῦτ' αἴσχιστον, καὶ οὐδὲ δεῖται μακροῦ λόγου ὁ
ἔλεγχος.

[3] *Op. cit.*, ii. 30.   [4] *Op. cit.*, ii. 33.   [5] *Op. cit.*, ii. 35.

[6] *Op. cit.*, iii. 59: " Those who invite to participation in other mysteries make
proclamation as follows: ' Everyone who has clean hands, and a prudent tongue;'

parable of the Pharisee and Publican, he adds: "God will receive the unrighteous man if he humble himself on account of his wickedness, but He will not receive the righteous man, although he look up to Him, adorned with virtue from the beginning."[1]

Celsus must be given his due; his attack did not simply touch externals, but went to the heart of the matter. And, we may add, his objections could not but seem justified on his premises. They would have to be accepted by anyone who accepted the scale of values of antiquity.

What has Origen to say in reply? In one respect, he has a considerable advantage over Celsus; he is serious, and willing to understand and do his opponent justice. If, even so, he is not always as happy in defence as Celsus in attack, that is because of the uncertainty in his own views. For Celsus, the situation was simple. He stood securely on the ground of Eros theory and from this position could forcefully combat his opponent. Origen's position is more precarious. He will surrender nothing of the Christian belief that God has really come to us in Christ, and that Christ, in sacrificial love, has given Himself for us. On the other hand, that Eros piety which Celsus affirms is such a living reality in Origen's own soul that he cannot but be impressed by the criticism.[2]

At one point, however, Celsus' criticism did force Origen

---

others again thus: ' He who is pure from all pollution, and whose soul is conscious of no evil, and who has lived well and justly.' Such is the proclamation made by those who promise purification from sins. But let us hear what kind of persons these Christians invite. Everyone, they say, who is a sinner, who is devoid of understanding, who is a child, and, to speak generally, whoever is unfortunate, him will the kingdom of God receive. Do you not call him a sinner, then, who is unjust, and a thief, and a housebreaker, and a poisoner, and a committer of sacrilege, and a robber of the dead ? What others would a man invite if he were issuing a proclamation for an assembly of robbers ?"

[1] Contra Celsum iii. 62.

[2] For the relation between Origen and Celsus, cf. Anna Miura-Stange: *Celsus und Origenes*, 1926 (Beihefte zur Zeitschrift für neutestamentliche Wissenschaft, Heft 4), where what is common to the views of both is clearly set out.

to take a firm stand, and that was on the question of the *Descent of the Divine Love.* Celsus is offended by the humiliation of Christ, but this, Origen says, is because the only love he knows is one that seeks its own " eudæmonia "; he has no understanding of that love whose nature is to help and to give. Celsus has stared himself blind at the outward lowliness, and therefore cannot discover the Divine glory that reveals itself in the very humiliation. He has not understood that it was for love that Christ emptied Himself, since only so could He be received by men.[1] Here Origen, as a Christian, feels himself infinitely superior to his Platonic opponent. " Celsus, then," he says in one place, " is altogether ignorant of the purpose of our writings, and it is therefore upon his own acceptation of them that he casts discredit, and not upon their real meaning; whereas, if he had reflected on what is appropriate to a soul which is to enjoy an everlasting life, and on the opinion which we are to form of its essence and principles, he would not so have ridiculed the entrance of the immortal into a mortal body, which took place not according to the metempsychosis of Plato, but agreeably to another and higher view of things. And he would have observed one ' descent,' distinguished by its great benevolence ($\phi\iota\lambda\alpha\nu\theta\rho\omega\pi\iota\alpha$), undertaken to convert (as the Scripture mystically terms them) the 'lost sheep of the house of Israel.' "[2]

This emphatic rejection of Hellenistic objections to the Divine Love which descends and gives itself, is evidence that Origen was not a stranger to the Agape motif. Granted it was perhaps Celsus' attack that first opened his eyes to the

---

[1] Contra Celsum iv. 15: διὰ φιλανθρωπίαν " ἑαυτὸν ἐκένωσεν " ἵνα χωρηθῆναι ὑπ' ἀνθρώπων δυνηθῇ. Although the Agape motif plays a much larger part in Origen than in Clement, the actual word ἀγάπη is more seldom used. For God's love Origen likes to use the word φιλανθρωπία. *Cf.* also vi. 15.

[2] Contra Celsum iv. 17: οὐ κατὰ τὴν Πλάτωνος μετενσωμάτωσιν ἀλλὰ κατ' ἄλλην τινὰ ὑψηλοτέραν θεωρίαν. εἶδε δ' ἂν καὶ μίαν ἐξαίρετον ἀπὸ πολλῆς φιλανθρωπίας κατάβασιν. . . .

real essence of Christianity; yet the fact that he reacts as he does on so central an issue, and is not satisfied, as he usually is, with a modification, surely merits attention when the structure of his interpretation of Christianity is in question.

But although Origen had some understanding of the central Christian motif, it was not this, but Eros that formed the centre of his religious outlook. Proof of this is his treatment of the two questions, decisive for religion, concerning (1) Fellowship with God, its nature and content, and (2) The Way to this, the Way to salvation.

First, as regards *fellowship with God*, Origen has derived his definitive ideas directly from Eros piety. To an astonishingly high degree, he has assimilated Platonic or Neoplatonic ways of thinking. The goal of the Christian life is the blessed contemplation of the Deity, as Plato has described it in the dialogue *Phædrus*.[1] The Eros myth of the Phædrus contributes, significantly enough, both modes of expression and general atmosphere to Origen's interpretation of the Christian hope.[2]

As plainly dependent on Eros theory is his view of the *Way of salvation*. It is entirely dominated by the upward movement, the idea of *ascent*. Celsus, following Plato, says there is for the soul a way up from the earth, and that the soul ascends through the planets; and to this Origen has no material objection to make. He merely rejoins that a similar conception had already, earlier, been asserted by Moses, " our most ancient prophet," who, in Gen. xxviii. 12, tells how the Patriarch Jacob saw in a dream a ladder reaching right up to heaven, on which the angels of God ascended and descended.[3] Here, as so often elsewhere in the history of Christianity, the story of Jacob's Ladder is used as biblical legitimation for

---

[1] Contra Celsum vi. 17.

[2] Contra Celsum vi. 20: ἐλπίζομεν πρὸς ἄκροις γενέσθαι τοῖς οὐρανοῖς. Cf. Phædrus, cap. 26, 247 B. Contra Celsum vi. 19: τὸν ὑπερουράνιον τόπον. Cf. Phædrus, cap. 27, 247 C.

[3] Contra Celsum vi. 21

the introduction of the Eros motif into the Christian doctrine of love.

In accordance with Platonic tradition, Origen's Way of salvation starts in the things of sense. The disciples of Jesus, he says, use the sense-world "like a ladder," upon which they mount to knowledge of the spiritual or intelligible world (τὰ νοητά). This is not, however, their final goal. They proceed still higher. When the soul has made itself at home in the heavenly world and has been sufficiently trained by eager communion with spiritual things, it becomes able to ascend even to the Divine Being itself (ἐπὶ τὴν Θεότητα).[1] For he who has thus done all that is required of him is even here counted worthy to see God, in so far as that is possible for a soul still in the body.[2] What Plato says in the Phædrus about the ascent of the soul is thus realised in the Christian. "He rises above the whole universe, 'shutting the eyes of sense, and raising upwards the eyes of the soul.' And he stops not at the vault of heaven; but passes in thought to the place beyond the heavens under the guidance of the Spirit of God."[3]

But how, we cannot help asking, was Origen able to achieve this union of such opposites? How could he at once so completely adopt the scheme of the Eros motif, and yet retain the basic Christian conception of the Descent and self-offering of God's love in Christ?

This difficulty he solved, like Clement, by distinguishing between two levels of Christianity—a lower, marked by "mere

---

[1] Contra Celsum vii. 46. This typically "Platonic" view Origen thinks he can get directly from Rom. i. 20. Cf. also In Cant. Canticorum, liber iii. (on Cant. Cantic. ii. 9): " . . . ab his quæ deorsum sunt, ad ea, quæ sursum sunt, possimus adscendere atque ex his, quæ videmus in terris, sentire et intelligere ea, quæ habentur in cælis." Ibid. " . . . quo per hæc adscenderet mens humana ad spiritalem intelligentiam et rerum causas in cælestibus quæreret."

[2] Contra Celsum vii. 42.

[3] Contra Celsum vii. 44. Cf. Plato's description in the Phædrus (cap. 26-30) of the ascent of the souls to " the place beyond the heavens " under the guidance of the gods.

faith," and a higher, characterised by Gnosis and the Vision of God. That Platonism as expounded by Celsus ideally represents the high-water mark of religion, Origen is more or less willing to admit. He repeatedly assures us that his intention is not to attack what Plato and his followers have said as well as it can be said.[1] Not that Platonism is in any respect superior to Christianity, for Christ and the apostles cherished fundamentally the same doctrine; only their opportunities to expound it were rare, since their environment was not ripe for so deep a view. For Origen, Platonism and Christianity differ not so much in religious theory (still less in fundamental religious attitude), but rather in manner of exposition, which is dependent upon their respective audiences. Platonism speaks to a little, select company, Christianity to all men. Plato and his followers, says Origen, are like people who prepare a meal—sound food in itself, of course—thinking only of some few epicures, and unconcerned that it will be uneatable for the great majority of men with their simpler tastes.[2] The great advantage of Christianity is that it really can be all things to all men. It deals with everyone according to his special capabilities; for every individual a Way of salvation is opened such as he in particular needs and can take. The educated are taught to mount "as on a ladder" from the visible world to the invisible, to God's world.[3] To the uneducated, who could not take that path, Christ has, instead, come down.[4] Thus, the Ways both of Eros and of Agape perform their function in Origen; but there is no doubt as to which of them is the higher. For Origen, as for Clement, Gnosis is far superior to "mere faith."[5] Origen's position might be summarised

---

[1] Cf. e.g. Contra Celsum vii. 42, 46, 49, 51.
[2] Contra Celsum vii. 59 f.   [3] Contra Celsum vii. 46.
[4] Contra Celsum vii. 60: οὕτως ἡ προνοουμένη θεία φύσις οὐ τῶν πεπαιδεῦσθαι νομιζομένων μόνον τὰ Ἑλλήνων ἀλλὰ καὶ τῶν λοιπῶν (Ἑλλήνων) συγκατέβη τῇ ἰδιωτείᾳ τοῦ πλήθους τῶν ἀκροωμένων.
[5] Contra Celsum i. 13.

to the effect that *in principle the Eros Way of salvation is the right one, but subsidiary to it and in order that men in their weakness should not be left without help and support, the Agape Way of salvation has been provided in addition.*[1]

Still, this must not be taken to mean that Origen felt himself really a Hellenic philosopher and a stranger to Christianity, for which he found a place merely on practical, pedagogical grounds. For him, it is all Christianity from beginning to end. Christianity, as he sees it, includes both the above-mentioned Ways of salvation. Not only Hellenistic piety, but Christianity too, is for him, in the last resort, "Eros religion." But the Way of Eros is not easy for an ordinary person to take; and here Christianity shows its superiority. If the great mass of mankind is lost so far as the "philosophers" and Hellenistic piety are concerned, Christianity can reach even those and, at least preparatorily, lead them into the right way. When, therefore, Celsus attacks Christianity because its appeal is to *sinners*, and contrasts it with all other Mystery religions, which first demand of their adherents complete purification before they are allowed to proceed to communion with the Deity, Origen rejects this as a highly unwarrantable objection, for it turns the very strength of Christianity into an accusation against it. Christianity appeals to sinners, it is true; but not in order immediately to surrender the Divine mysteries to them. Sinners must first receive in faith instruction which deters them from sin. Then, when the more advanced have been purified and have improved their life as much as possible—"then and not before do we invite them to participation in our mysteries."[2] We Christians, Origen will say, certainly have our Gnosis and our mysteries, and to them we admit no sinners; there, for us also, the customary condition of

---

[1] *Ibid.*
[2] Contra Celsum iii. 59.

entry obtains: ' Let him who is pure come hither.'[1] To call sinners that they may be healed, and to invite those who have already been purified to the mysteries, these are two very different things.[2] And to attack Christianity because it reckons with the lower stage as well as the higher, is the more unwarranted as the former points away from itself to the latter, and is simply a preliminary to it.[3]

Thus, according to Origen, Christianity and Platonism both represent ideally the same lofty standpoint; but Christianity, to its great advantage, is able to express this in such a way as immediately to capture even the masses. A lawgiver, says Origen, was once asked whether he had given his countrymen the best laws. He replied: "that he had not given them absolutely the best, but the best which they were capable of receiving." So also Christ can say. He has given the best laws that could be of any use to the great majority for improving their lives. He has given them a doctrine which, by threats of punishment, compels the recalcitrant to repent.[4] Christianity simply says what is both true and seems to be clear for the many, though naturally it is not so clear for them as for the few who devote themselves to a philosophical study of these things.[5]

Origen's conception of the relation between Platonism and Christianity is attractively illustrated by the opening of the seventh book against Celsus. Citing both Plato and the

[1] Contra Celsum iii. 60: ἐπεὶ δὲ καὶ " ἡ χάρις " τοῦ θεοῦ ἐστι " μετὰ πάντων τῶν ἐν ἀφθαρσίᾳ ἀγαπώντων " τὸν διδάσκαλον τῶν τῆς ἀθανασίας μαθημάτων, ὅστις ἁγνὸς οὐ μόνον ἀπὸ παντὸς μύσους ἀλλὰ καὶ τῶν ἐλαττόνων εἶναι νομιζομένων ἁμαρτημάτων, θαρρῶν μυείσθω τὰ μόνοις ἁγίοις καὶ καθαροῖς εὐλόγως παραδιδόμενα μυστήρια τῆς κατὰ Ἰησοῦν θεοσεβείας.

[2] Contra Celsum iii. 60: . . . διαφορὰν καλουμένων ἐπὶ μὲν θεραπείαν φαύλων ἐπὶ δὲ τὰ μυστικώτερα τῶν ἤδη καθαρωτάτων.

[3] Contra Celsum iii. 59: εἰς τὸ ἀναβαίνειν φρονήματι ἐπὶ τὸν ἄνδρα.

[4] Contra Celsum iii. 79: οὐ τοὺς καθάπαξ καλλίστους ἀλλ᾽ ὧν ἐδύναντο τοὺς καλλίστους.

[5] Contra Celsum iii. 79: λέγομεν γὰρ περὶ αὐτοῦ καὶ ἀληθῆ καὶ τοῖς πολλοῖς σαφῆ μὲν εἶναι δοκοῦντα οὐ σαφῆ δ᾽ ὄντα ἐκείνοις ὡς τοῖς ὀλίγοις, φιλοσοφεῖν ἀσκοῦσι τὰ κατὰ τὸν λόγον.

Christian sources, Celsus had declared that Plato expressed these things much better than Christianity, and that with no pretence of having received his wisdom by divine revelation. Origen will not directly contradict this, but refers, as usual, to the fact that Christianity addresses itself to the masses, and consequently must use language which they can appreciate. "For our prophets, and Jesus Himself, and His Apostles, were careful to adopt a style of address which should not merely convey the truth, but which should be fitted to gain over the multitude, until each one, attracted and led onwards, should ascend as far as he could towards the comprehension of those mysteries which are contained in these apparently simple words."[1] To this Origen characteristically adds, that even if we can agree that the Hellenes have certain theoretical doctrines in common with the Christians, yet they have not the same ability to win souls.[2]

It remains, then, that the way of philosophy and of Gnosis is, in principle, alone fully satisfying. Faith is an expedient of necessity, since most men are incapable of travelling by any other road. If all men could leave their concern with the affairs of life and devote themselves exclusively to philosophy, no other course should be taken than this. But since neither the cares of life nor the spiritual equipment of men permit of this, there is for the masses no way better than that indicated by Jesus.[3] By this way, all without exception can now reach the goal. Since the Logos Himself has come to us, He has brought it about—to use a phrase of Clement, which Origen might equally well have coined—that "the whole world has already become Athens and Hellas."[4]

---

[1] Contra Celsum vi. 2.   [2] Ibid.

[3] Contra Celsum i. 9: λεκτέον δὲ πρὸς τοῦτο ὅτι εἰ μὲν οἷόν τε πάντας καταλιπόντας τὰ τοῦ βίου πράγματα σχολάζειν τῷ φιλοσοφεῖν, ἄλλην ὁδὸν οὐ μεταδιωκτέον οὐδενὶ ἢ ταύτην μόνην . . . εἰ δὲ τοῦτ' ἀμήχανον πῇ μὲν διὰ τὰς τοῦ βίου ἀνάγκας πῇ δὲ καὶ διὰ τὴν τῶν ἀνθρώπων ἀσθένειαν, σφόδρα ὀλίγων ἐπὶ τὸν λόγον ἀττόντων, ποία ἂν ἄλλη βελτίων μέθοδος πρὸς τὸ τοῖς πολλοῖς βοηθῆσαι εὑρεθείη τῆς ἀπὸ τοῦ Ἰησοῦ τοῖς ἔθνεσι παραδοθείσης.

[4] Clem. Alex., Protrepticus, cap. xi. 112, 1.

6. Origen's System

In Origen's defence of Christianity, Eros and Agape encounter one another. That they are not however equally matched is evident, since his system, as set forth in the " De principiis " (Περὶ ἀρχῶν), is built up almost exclusively on the Eros motif.

In the foreword to this work, Origen starts with the Christian position as generally received in the Church. That is (1) that God is One, that He has created and brought forth everything from nothing, and that in the last days He has sent the Lord Jesus Christ; (2) that this Jesus Christ was begotten of the Father before every creature, that the creation came into being through Him, that He humbled Himself and became man, and that while retaining His Divine nature He became flesh, that He really, and not merely in appearance, was born and suffered, that He really died and really rose from the dead; (3) that the Holy Spirit, who is equal with the Father and the Son in honour and dignity, has inspired the prophets and the apostles; (4) that the soul, when it leaves this world, is to receive recompense according to merit, either eternal life and blessedness or eternal fire and punishment, that there will be a resurrection of the body, and that all souls have free will and are engaged in strife with the devil; (5) that this world is created and transient; (6) that the Holy Scriptures are written by the Spirit of God, and that they have not merely their literal meaning which is obvious to all, but also a hidden meaning to which but few can find their way.[1]

Everything thus established by Christian tradition from the days of the apostles Origen accepts without question.[2]

[1] De principiis I., Præf. 4-8.

[2] " . . . servetur vero ecclesiastica prædicatio per successionis ordinem ab apostolis tradita et usque ad præsens in ecclesiis permanens, illa sola credenda est veritas, quæ in nullo ab ecclesiastica et apostolica traditione discordat." I., Præf. 2.

There is, he holds, no alternative but simple acceptance.[1] But there exist, besides, many as yet undetermined points still capable of different interpretations; and it is these that hold his real interest, upon these he bestows all his pains.   The simple Christian may find the above-named articles of faith sufficient, but to gain real insight into its meaning the Christian Faith must be reconstructed systematically, so that every affirmation of faith is illumined by its relation to all the rest and to the whole.[2]   True, Origen emphasises time on time[3] that much of what he says is merely his own personal opinion, his private interpretation of Christianity, and must not be given out as the generally received Christian Faith: but this makes it the better evidence of what Origen himself thought about Christianity.   We may now observe that at all these still unsettled points his interpretation is consistently in the direction of Hellenistic piety, from which—what is more— he also borrows the general scheme for his interpretation of Christianity as a whole.

Origen rejects the Hellenistic idea of emanation, and speaks, instead, of a Divine act of creation; yet none the less, his theory bears essentially the stamp of emanation. Its whole structure is determined by the *Alexandrian world-scheme* with its double movement: the outgoing of everything from God and the return of everything to Him, the degeneration of the pure spirit, so that it becomes a soul bound to the sense-world, and its regeneration, by which it is restored to the state of pure spirit.

God is conceived in the Greek manner as Absolute Being,

---

[1] " Est et illud definitum in ecclesiastica prædicatione. . . ."   I., Præf. 5.

[2] " Oportet igitur velut elementis ac fundamentis huiusmodi uti secundum mandatum, quod dicit: ' inluminate vobis lumen scientiæ,' omnem qui cupit seriem quandam et corpus ex horum omnium ratione perficere, ut manifestis et necessariis assertionibus de singulis quibusque quid sit in vero rimetur, et unum, ut diximus, corpus efficiat exemplis et affirmationibus, vel his, quas in sanctis scripturis invenerit, vel quas ex consequentiæ ipsius indagine ac recti tenore reppererit."   I., Præf. 10.

[3] Or is it, perhaps, Rufinus who inserts this reservation at doubtful points ?

pure, undifferentiated Unity (μονάς, ἑνάς).[1] As God has begotten the Logos from eternity, so from eternity He has created a spirit-world. So Origen teaches an eternal creation. It would, he thinks, be both absurd and godless to suppose that God ever allowed the creative power which is His, to be inactive.[2] Since, however, God has equipped with free will the rational beings He created, it was possible for them to fall away from Him. This possibility became actuality when they misused their freedom and in disobedience and inertia sank down from their' original estate. Whilst Origen stresses the element of free will in the Fall, nevertheless he looks upon it very nearly as a natural process. Owing to the cooling of the Divine Agape, the pure, rational beings are, so to speak, condensed into souls;[3] and as at once a penal and an educative institution for the fallen and now psychic spirits, God created the sense-world.[4] According to

---

[1] De principiis I., cap. i. 6.

[2] De principiis I., cap. iv. 3.

[3] " Si ergo ea quidem, quæ sancta sunt, ignis et lumen et ferventia nominantur, quæ autem contraria sunt, frigida, et ' caritas ' [=ἀγάπη] peccatorum dicitur ' refrigescere,' requirendum est ne forte et nomen animæ, quod græce dicitur ψυχή, a refrigescendo de statu diviniore ac meliore dictum sit et translatum inde, quod ex calore illo naturali et divino refrixisse videatur, et ideo in hoc quo nunc est et statu et vocabulo sita sit." De princ. II., cap. viii. 3. Cf. the parallel quoted by Koetschau from Epiphanius, Panarion hær. lxiv. 4, 6: ψυχὴν γάρ φησι διὰ τοῦτο καλοῦμεν, διὰ τὸ ἄνωθεν ἐψύχθαι. In general, as regards the origin of the soul, on which Origen's views would be particularly objectionable, Rufinus has endeavoured to tone them down. In this chapter, therefore, there are many gaps in his translation; cf. Koetschau's introduction to the " De principiis," pp. cxviii ff. The "anathemas," however, pronounced by the Synod of Constantinople, 553, against Origen's teaching, supply information about the passages Rufinus has suppressed. In the fourth anathema, which deals with the " Sturz und Einkörperung der λογικά," it is expressly stated: τὰ λογικὰ τὰ τῆς θείας ἀγάπης ἀποψυγέντα καὶ ἐντεῦθεν ψυχὰς ὀνομασθέντα τιμωρίας χάριν σώμασι παχυτέροις τοῖς καθ' ἡμᾶς ἐνδυθῆναι καὶ ἀνθρώπους ὀνομασθῆναι. The parallel to this in the Emperor Justinian's rescript reads: καὶ διὰ τοῦτο τῆς θεοῦ ἀγάπης ἀποψυγείσας καὶ ἐντεῦθεν ψυχὰς ὀνομασθείσας καὶ τιμωρίας χάριν τοῖς σώμασιν ἐμβληθείσας. De princ. II., cap. viii. 3. Cf. also Koetschau's introduction, p. cxxii.

[4] De princ. II., cap. i. This world can therefore be described as τόπος κακώσεως τῆς ψυχῆς. Exhort. 20. In accord with this, Origen interprets the story of the Fall in Genesis as referring to the pre-existent Fall. That God

the depth of their fall, they have been bound to finer or grosser bodies, angels having the finest, demons the grossest, and man being in between. As he appears concretely in the sense-world, man has thus a dual nature: on the one hand, the fallen spirit, on the other, the body which is the spirit's prison-house.

If the first act in cosmic evolution explains how all things, through creation and a pre-existent Fall, have gone out from God and away from Him, the second act shows how everything returns again to Him, and how the soul, dragged down in sense, is restored to its original pure spirituality.[1] To this end the Logos has been throughout the ages immanently active in men, to this end He has come to us in the fulness of time and become flesh. He teaches us to raise ourselves by the right use of free will, step by step, to ever-increasing likeness to God. The way we are thus led is the Way of salvation described above. The lowest step is faith, but this is equally the foundation on which all else rests. Above it rises the Hellenistic Eros ladder, of which the principal stages are: (1) sensible things, (2) $\tau\grave{\alpha}$ $\nu o\eta\tau\acute{\alpha}$, (3) contemplation of God in His creation, (4) contemplation of the Divine Being itself.[2] In virtue of its free will, the immortal soul has the possibility of withdrawing during immeasurable spaces of time from God, who is the soul's highest good, and of descending to the very lowest evil. But in virtue of the same free will, it has also the possibility, with God's help and guided by the Logos, of ascending again from the lowest evil to the

---

made " coats of skins " for the fallen Adam and Eve (Gen. iii. 21) means that He created the sense-world, and clothed the fallen spirits with corporeality. *Cf.* Methodius, De resurrectione i. 4, 2 ff.; Epiphanius, Panarion hær. lxiv. 4, 9.

[1] " Ex quibus omnibus illud videtur ostendi, quod mens de statu ac dignitate sua declinans, effecta vel nuncupata est anima; quæ si reparata fuerit et correcta, redit in hoc, ut sit mens." De principiis II., cap. viii. 3. As the Fall means that mens or $\pi\nu\varepsilon\tilde{\upsilon}\mu\alpha$ sank down and became anima or $\psi\upsilon\chi\acute{\eta}$, so salvation means the restoration of anima to its original character of mens, so that $\psi\upsilon\chi\acute{\eta}$ becomes $\pi\nu\varepsilon\tilde{\upsilon}\mu\alpha$.

[2] Contra Celsum vii. 46.

highest good.[1] So through a series of epochs the cosmic process moves towards the restoration of all things, ἀποκατάστασις πάντων, when the circle is completed, when the end coincides with the beginning, and God, as at the first, is all in all.[2]

When the Christian position, " as generally received in the Church," is to be fitted into this scheme, the natural result is that at every point it is pressed in the direction of the Eros motif. This compromise is apparent in Origen's attitude to the three fundamental dogmas of Creation, Incarnation, and the Resurrection of the flesh. As regards *Creation*, Origen, it is true, maintains that God is Creator not merely of heaven but also of earth. Against Gnosticism and Marcion he asserts that not only the spirit-world but also the corporeal, material world is God's work. And yet the eternal creation of the spirit-world is of a totally different kind from the creation of the temporal world. Only the former is God's own work in the strictest sense, sprung from Himself, from His eternal, creative will. The creation of the material world, on the other hand, is dictated and motivated by sin, by the need of a penal and remedial institution for the fallen spirits. Then, as regards *Redemption*, Origen of course rejects the docetism characteristic of Hellenistic theories. Christ has really become man, really suffered the death of the Cross. And yet, according to Origen, neither the Incarnation nor the death of the Cross has any real meaning for the perfect Christian, the Christian Gnostic. Finally, the same doubleness is also found with regard to the *Resurrection of the flesh*. It is indisputable that Origen holds the Hellenistic belief in the " Immortality of the soul." Yet the constant affirmation, in the Christian tradition, of faith in the " Resur-

---

[1] " Ex quo opinamur, quoniam quidem, sicut frequentius diximus, immortalis est anima et æterna, quod in multis et sine fine spatiis per inmensa et diversa sæcula possibile est, ut vel a summo bono ad infima mala descendat, vel ab ultimis malis ad summa bona reparetur." De principiis III., cap. i. 23.

[2] De principiis I., cap. vi. 2. " Semper enim similis est finis initiis." *Ibid.*

rection of the flesh " has not left him unmoved. He only ventures with the greatest caution to admit his attachment to the philosophical doctrine of the " Immortality of the soul,"[1] and is unable to stop at a purely spiritualising theory, which would otherwise best have answered to his general position. But being thus compelled, half against his will, to accept the belief in the " Resurrection of the flesh," he seeks as far as he possibly can to neutralise it by his interpretation of Paul's words, in 1 Cor. xv., about the " pneumatic body."[2] Further, the final stage is reached only when all corporeality is entirely done away. Thus, in Origen, primitive Christian eschatology is replaced by a spiritualising, evolutionary process, working almost by natural necessity and having *apokatastasis* as its goal. For it belongs to the being and nature of the rational soul to ascend, even if by long detours, to the Divine, and to unite itself with it. Thus the idea of *apokatastasis* in Origen is a spiritualising expression of a tendency which is ultimately naturalistic.[3]

---

[1] *Cf.* Contra Celsum iii. 81. After having referred to the ideas of certain philosophers on the immortality of the soul, including what Plato says of the soul in the Phædrus (cap. 26 and 30), as by nature able to ascend to the height of heaven and to the place beyond the heavens (*cf. supra*, p. 376), Origen adds: " And do not suppose that it is not in keeping with the Christian religion for me to have accepted, against Celsus, the opinions of those philosophers who have treated of the immortality or after-duration of the soul; for, holding certain views in common with them, we shall more conveniently establish our position, that the future life of blessedness shall be for those only who . . ."

[2] *Cf. e.g.* De principiis II., cap. x. 3; III., cap. vi. 4.

[3] On Origen's system, see further Hal Koch's excellent work, *Pronoia und Paideusis. Studien über Origenes und sein Verhältnis zum Platonismus*, 1932. One virtue of this work is that it seriously considers the question of the fundamental motif. This Koch finds in the *paideusis*-motif. The central idea in Origen's Christianity is that of the education and guidance of free, rational beings under Divine Providence. Origen has, Koch aptly says, transformed Christianity into pedagogical idealism. But the *paideusis*-motif derives from the Greek tradition. Eros and *paideusis* are, so to speak, interchangeable concepts. Koch deals with the problem of " Eros and Agape " too (pp. 33-35), and his conclusion is clear and unequivocal. Of Origen's attitude to the Christian idea of love he states: " Nowhere does it occur to him to make love, ἀγάπη, the basis of his idea of God. . . . And with this also corresponds his definition of the relation of man to God: here, *often in his terminology and always in reality, he*

7. GOD IS EROS—GOD IS AGAPE

Thus far, Origen's two main works, the "Contra Celsum" and the "De principiis," have furnished our material. The Homilies offer additional material, but not such as to alter our view of Origen's interpretation of Christianity.[1] Nevertheless, we must pay some attention to his *Commentary on the Song of Songs*. In it Origen gives those interpretations of the Song which gradually won for it a central place in the Christian doctrine of love. But what is more, in the prologue to his work he deals directly with the problem of "Eros and Agape."

In interpreting the Song of Songs, we must, according to Origen, bear in mind that it is intended exclusively for the "perfect," for Christian Gnostics, and can only be rightly understood by them. The words of Scripture generally, according to Origen's hermeneutic principles, have both a

---

has replaced the idea of Agape by that of Eros" (p. 33). "*The confusion of Eros and Agape is evident enough.* Without it Origen's conception of the destiny of the soul, which goes back to Plato's Phædrus, would be unthinkable " (p. 35 n.).

[1] W. Völker, it is true, insists, in his *Das Vollkommenheitsideal des Origenes*, 1931, that a too exclusive reliance on " Contra Celsum " and " De principiis " is the fundamental weakness of previous studies of Origen. He considers the Homilies to be sources of the highest value. For his own part, he makes special use of the 27th Homily on Numbers, about the Journeyings in the Wilderness, with Origen's allegory of the mystical ascent of the soul to God. On the basis of this usually ignored material, Völker tries to give a new picture of Origen. He is not the Hellenic philosopher, but the Christian mystic. The question, however, how far Origen was personally an intellectualist or a mystic falls quite outside our present enquiry. The evidence that can be used to show that he was a mystic shows, no less than the "intellectualistic " material, to what a large extent he was dependent on the Eros motif. Völker is open to the criticism that he is far too rash in concluding that " mysticism " means " Christianity." Against an older view, for which Origen was primarily the rational philosopher, he is undoubtedly right to lay more stress on the mystical element in Origen; yet it is difficult to see why, when considering the question of religious types, Völker regards " mysticism " and " ecstasy " as proof of a definitely Christian type. The mystical as well as the rational is contained in Hellenism. *Cf.* my article on *Den nyaste Origenesforskningen* in *Svensk Teologisk Kvartalskrift*, 1933, pp. 197-204.

literal meaning available to all, even to the uneducated, and a deeper, pneumatic meaning, reserved for Gnostics; but in the Song of Songs he finds clear proof that there are some portions of Scripture entirely lacking in literal meaning. Taken literally, the Song of Songs could only arouse vulgar Eros in the reader. Origen therefore expressly warns against putting this writing into the hands of simple Christians. For them it has no message at all. They, as the Apostle directs (Heb. v. 12 ff.), are to be fed with milk; the Song of Songs, on the other hand, offers that solid food which belongs to the perfect.[1]

Of what sort, then, is the love of which the Song of Songs speaks? For answer, Origen starts from what Plato and his followers say about the nature of love (Eros). It is the power that raises the soul from earth to the summit of heaven; the highest blessedness cannot be attained except by means of love's desire.[2] What the Platonists have written rightly and excellently, however, has been spoilt by fleshly men, who have understood what was said of the heavenly Eros as if it referred to vulgar Eros. But if such a thing could happen among the wise Greeks, then it is not surprising that the Song of Songs should suffer a similar fate among simple Christians.[3]

Origen is aware that Scripture avoids the word Eros.[4] It has good reasons for this. The implications of the word in common usage are such that the simple multitude would in-

---

[1] " In verbis enim Cantici Canticorum ille cibus est, de quo dicit Apostolus: ' perfectorum autem est solidus cibus.' " Comment. in Cant. Cantic., Prologus.

[2] "Apud Græcos quidem plurimi eruditorum virorum volentes investigare veritatis indaginem de amoris [=ἔρωτος] natura multa ac diversa etiam dialogorum stilo scripta protulerunt conantes ostendere non aliud esse amoris vim nisi quæ animam de terris ad fastigia cæli celsa perducat, nec ad summam posse beatudinem perveniri nisi amoris desiderio provocante." Ibid.

[3] Ibid.

[4] " Et in his ergo et in aliis pluribus locis invenies Scripturam divinam refugisse amoris [=ἔρωτος] vocabulum et caritatis [=ἀγάπης] dilectionisque posuisse." Ibid.

evitably misunderstand it as referring to "vulgar Eros." To guard against such misunderstanding, Scripture has chosen the unequivocal word "Agape."[1] All this, however, is important only in the case of simple Christians, of simpliciores or ἰδιῶται. The Song of Songs, on the other hand, is written for the perfect, for Gnostics; and now it is to be noted that while Scripture avoids the term, there is no intention of disapproving the fact of Eros, but merely of protecting it against the misunderstanding which is so easy. But for us Gnostics, Origen argues in effect, such precautionary measures are unnecessary. We may permit ourselves to call the thing by its right name and use the term Eros. *When the Gnostic finds the word Agape in Scripture, he should at once understand it as if Eros stood in its place, for that is the reality concealed under the protective disguise of Agape.*[2]

But, Origen continues, in some few passages, where misunderstanding is *a priori* excluded, Scripture itself can employ the term Eros and commend Eros love.[3] To this he gives the greatest weight, and his whole argument shows that it is vitally important for him to demonstrate the Christian legitimacy of the idea of Eros and the term Eros itself. With this in view, he searches through the Scriptures for passages containing the word Eros; but, as far as the New Testament is concerned, the result is entirely negative, the word does not occur. So Origen turns to the Septuagint; but even there his gain is small. He succeeds in detecting only two passages where there is at least a hint of Eros in

---

[1] " Videtur autem mihi quod divina scriptura volens cavere, ne lapsus aliquis legentibus sub amoris nomine nasceretur, pro infirmioribus quibusque eum, qui apud sapientes sæculi cupido seu amor [=ἔρως] dicitur, *honestiore vocabulo caritatem* [=ἀγάπην] *vel dilectionem nominasse.* . . ." *Ibid.*

[2] " Sic ergo quæcumque de *caritate* [=περὶ τῆς ἀγάπης] scripta sunt, quasi de *amore* [=περὶ τοῦ ἔρωτος] dicta suscipe nihil de nominibus curans; eadem namque in utroque virtus ostenditur." *Ibid.*

[3] " Interdum tamen, licet raro, proprio vocabulo amorem [=ἔρωτα] nominat et invitat ad eum atque incitat. . . ." *Ibid.*

the Platonic sense, and, significantly enough, both these passages are in the Wisdom literature.[1]

But Origen has not finished; these researches are merely a means to an end. He intends a complete and absolute identification of Platonic Eros and Christian Agape. In the "pneumatic" interpretation of Scripture, it is in general justifiable, Origen maintains, to substitute Eros for Agape; but the question arises whether this principle requires no qualification. Are we, for instance, justified in applying it in such a case as the Johannine "God is Agape"? Origen thinks we are, and finds support in a saying of the martyr Ignatius. As A. von Harnack has shown in his interesting study, *Der 'Eros' in der alten christlichen Literatur*,[2] a complete misinterpretation of the saying is involved. Ignatius writes: "For in the midst of life I write to you desiring death. My Eros has been crucified, and there is in me no fire of love for material things."[3] What can Ignatius have meant by the peculiar statement, "My Eros has been crucified"? What does he mean by Eros? The context leaves no room for doubt: "vulgar Eros" is meant, the desire for material and sensible things. This, Ignatius explains, has been crucified and rooted out of him, so that he can no longer desire anything that belongs to this transient world. Origen has misunderstood this[4] as referring, instead, to Christ, the Crucified. But if St. Ignatius could call Christ his Eros, then no objection can be made to calling God Eros, too. Origen

---

[1] Prov. iv. 6 and Wisd. viii. 2. Both speak of Wisdom: "Love her (ἐράσθητι αὐτῆς) and she shall keep thee" (Prov.); "Her I loved (ἐφίλησα) and sought out from my youth and I sought to take her for my bride, and I became enamoured of her beauty (καὶ ἐραστὴς ἐγενόμην τοῦ κάλλους αὐτῆς)" (Wisd.).

[2] Sitzungsberichte der Preussischen Akademie der Wissenschaften, Jahrg. 1918, i., pp. 81-94.

[3] Ignatius, Ep. ad Rom. vii. 2: ζῶν γὰρ γράφω ὑμῖν, ἐρῶν τοῦ ἀποθανεῖν. ὁ ἐμὸς ἔρως ἐσταύρωται, καὶ οὐκ ἔστιν ἐν ἐμοὶ πῦρ φιλόϋλον.

[4] The context makes Origen's interpretation quite impossible. ἐρᾶν is not used in the bad sense in the immediately preceding phrase, and might suggest that ἔρως is not, either; but the immediately following phrase is decisive: καὶ οὐκ ἔστιν ἐν ἐμοὶ πῦρ φιλόϋλον. See Harnack, *op. cit.*, p. 84.

has reached his goal. If John says: "God is Agape," it can with equal right be said: "God is Eros." The meaning is in both cases the same.[1] The connection between Christianity and Hellenistic piety (or, alternatively, the Platonic-Neoplatonic outlook)[2] is found. These two are, in Origen's view, one. But the character of the synthesis is determined by the Hellenistic element: Agape is interpreted on the lines of Eros.

Thus, in Origen, for the first time in the history of the Christian idea of love, we find *a real synthesis between the Christian and the Hellenistic views of love.* No later attempt at such a synthesis has gone beyond Origen in principle. Not even Augustine's *caritas*-synthesis does so. Almost all the ideas fundamental to it are to be found in Origen—at least in embryo. Like Augustine, Origen starts with the view that love is an elemental force found in all men.[3] The only question is, where it seeks satisfaction for its desire, in the spiritual or the material world. If in the former, love appears as "amor spiritus," if in the latter, it is "amor carnis"—exactly the same distinction as Augustine makes between "caritas" and "cupiditas."[4] Nor does Augustine

---

[1] "Non ergo interest, utrum amari dicatur Deus aut diligi, nec puto quod culpari possit, si quis Deum, sicut Johannes 'caritatem' [=ἀγάπην], ita ipse amorem [=ἔρωτα] nominet. Denique memini aliquem sanctorum dixisse, Ignatium nomine, *de Christo :* ' *meus autem amor crucifixus est* ' nec reprehendi eum pro hoc dignum iudico." Comment. in Cant. Cantic., Prolog.

Origen's mistake has borne interesting fruit through the centuries, not only in theological works—as, *e.g.,* Pseudo-Dionysius; *cf.* infra, p. 590—but in hymns and devotional literature influenced by mysticism. *Cf. e.g.* the hymn "Der am Kreuz ist meine Liebe, meine Lieb ist Jesus Christ " (1668), or " My Lord, my Love was crucified " (John Mason, 1645-94). And Johann Arndt says that Ignatius " always " called Jesus his love (*Vier Bücher vom wahren Christenthum,* 2 Buch, cap. xxvii.).

[2] We may recall that Origen's contemporary Plotinus (Enn. vi., 8, 15) directly asserts: " God is Eros "; *cf .supra,* pp. 197 ff.

[3] " Sed et hoc scire oportet quod impossibile est, ut non semper humana natura aliquid amet." Comment. in Cant. Cantic., Prolog.

[4] *Ibid. Cf.* in Cant. Cantic., Homilia i. 2: " Et quomodo est quidam carnalis cibus et alius spiritalis et alia carnis potio, alia spiritus, sic est quidam amor carnis a Satana veniens, alius amor spiritus a Deo exordium habens, et nemo

lack points of contact with Origen in his distinction between "uti" and "frui," and so on.

Still, it was not Origen's, but Augustine's synthesis which stamped its impress on the later history of the Christian idea of love. Even if Origen's doctrine of love could have been incorporated without difficulty into the churchly tradition, yet at other points, already established within the Church, his thought included far too much that was heretical for it to be able to gain acceptance and become the dominant Christian view. It needed a man as deeply rooted as Augustine in what was specifically Christian to assist that synthesis to victory.

---

potest duobus amoribus possideri. Si carnis amator es, amorem spiritus non capis." In Cant. Cantic., Hom. ii. 1: " Unus de animæ motibus amor est, quo bene utimur ad amandum, si sapientiam amemus et veritatem; quando vero amor noster in peiora corruerit, amamus carnem et sanguinem. Tu igitur, ' ut spiritalis,' audi spiritaliter amatoria verba cantari et disce motum animæ tuæ et naturalis amoris incendium ad meliora transferre secundum illud: ' ama illam, et servabit te, circumda illam, et exaltabit te.' " Note how Origen here again falls back on Prov. iv. 6.

VII

THE AGAPE TYPE IN IRENÆUS

1. IRENÆUS AND THE THREE FUNDAMENTAL DOGMAS OF THE EARLY CHURCH

AMONG the great ante-Nicene theologians Irenæus stands nearest, not only in time, but also in spirit, to primitive Christianity. He is important less as a new and creative exponent of Christianity than as one who, more than any other, has preserved direct contact with the primitive Christian Faith.[1] If Tertullian can be said to represent the Nomos type, and Clement and Origen the Eros type, Irenæus is, as truly, representative of the Agape type.

Irenæus is chief of the anti-Gnostic Fathers, and the polemic stamps his whole work. His life's work is essentially a defence of the primitive Christian Faith against heretical views. In this, his path is already prescribed by the preceding development. The idea of Agape, as might be expected in view of his relation to the older tradition, is found in him chiefly in connection with the three anti-Hellenistic dogmas of Creation, Incarnation, and the Resurrection of the flesh. He, like Tertullian, sets against the divisive and destructive doctrines of the heretics the firm and undivided tradition of the Church from the days of the apostles: " The preaching of the Church is true and stead-

---

[1] It is remarkable to what an extent Irenæus gathered up and united in himself what already existed, at least tentatively, in the earlier churchly theology. This has been particularly emphasised by F. Loofs in his *Theophilus von Antiochien Adversus Marcionem und die anderen theologischen Quellen bei Irenaeus*, 1930 (Texte und Untersuchungen zur Geschichte der altchristlichen Literatur xlvi. 2; 4 Reihe, Bd. 1). Of the literature on Irenæus may be mentioned—N. Bonwetsch: *Die Theologie des Irenäus*, 1925; W. Bousset: *Kyrios Christos*, 2 Aufl., 1921, pp. 333-362. E. Brunner: *Der Mittler*, 1927, pp. 219-233; and especially G. Aulén: *Den kristna försoningstanken*, 1930, pp. 38-69 (Eng. trans.: Christus Victor, S.P.C.K., 1931, pp. 32-51).

fast, in which one and the same way of salvation is shown throughout the whole world."[1] "As I have already observed, the church, having received this preaching and this faith, although scattered throughout the whole world, yet, as if occupying but one house, carefully preserves it. She also believes these points of doctrine just as if she had but one soul, and one and the same heart, and she proclaims them, and teaches them, and hands them down, with perfect harmony, as if she possessed only one mouth. For, although the languages of the world are dissimilar, yet the import of the tradition is one and the same. For the churches which have been planted in Germany do not believe or hand down anything different, nor do those in Spain, nor those in Gaul, nor those in the East, nor those in Egypt, nor those in Libya, nor those which have been established in the central regions of the world. But as the sun, that creature of God, is one and the same throughout the whole world, so also the preaching of the truth shineth everywhere, and enlightens all men that are willing to come to a knowledge of the truth. . . . For the faith being ever one and the same, neither does one who is able at great length to discourse regarding it, make any addition to it, nor does one who can say but little, diminish it."[2]

What, then, is the content of this unanimous faith and preaching? It is faith in God as Creator of heaven and earth, in the Incarnation, and in the Resurrection of the

---

[1] Contra hæreses, lib. V., cap. xx. 1: "Et ecclesiæ quidem prædicatio vera et firma, apud quam una et eadem salutis via in universo mundo ostenditur. . . . Ubique enim ecclesia prædicat veritatem."

[2] Contra hær., lib. I., cap. x. 2. From this it is seen that Vincent of Lerins' famous formula, " quod ubique, quod semper, quod ab omnibus creditum est," exists already in substance in Irenæus—cf. lib. IV., cap. xxxiii. 8: γνῶσις ἀληθὴς ἡ τῶν ἀποστόλων διδαχή, καὶ τὸ ἀρχαῖον τῆς ἐκκλησίας σύστημα κατὰ παντὸς τοῦ κόσμου, et character corporis Christi secundum successiones episcoporum, quibus illi eam, quæ in unoquoque loco est, ecclesiam tradiderunt." The great advantage of the Church, in Irenæus' view, is that (1) it has the *Scriptures* uncorrupted; (2) it has, above all, *love*—" et præcipuum dilectionis [=τῆς ἀγάπης] munus."

flesh, which, for Irenæus, virtually coincides with faith in the Father, the Son, and the Holy Ghost. " The Church, though dispersed throughout the whole world, even to the ends of the earth, has received from the apostles and their disciples this faith: She believes in one God, the Father Almighty, *Creator of heaven, and earth*, and the sea, and all things that are in them; and in one Christ Jesus, the Son of God, who *became incarnate for our salvation* (σαρκωθέντα : incarnatum pro nostra salute); and in the Holy Spirit, who proclaimed through the prophets the dispensations of God, and the advents, and the birth from a virgin, and the passion, and the resurrection from the dead, and the ascension into heaven in the flesh (τὴν ἔνσαρκον ἀνάληψιν) of the beloved Christ Jesus, our Lord, and His future manifestation from heaven in the glory of the Father to ' recapitulate ' all things (ἀνακεφαλαιώσασθαι τὰ πάντα) and *to raise up anew all flesh* (πᾶσαν σάρκα).[1]

Irenæus' criticism of the Gnostics and above all of Marcion, on the basis of these three fundamental dogmas, might seem superficially very much the same as Tertullian's. Yet its content is quite different, for its motivation is different. *Tertullian attacks Marcion essentially from the point of view of the Nomos motif, Irenæus from that of the Agape motif.*[2] Irenæus' use of the three dogmas shows that he knows how to give clear expression, at every point, to the idea of Agape.

1. The first, fundamental error of both Gnosticism and Marcion, Irenæus finds in their denial that God is creator of heaven and earth, in the distinction they make between the Creator and the Highest God, between the Demiurge, who produced this world, and the Father of Jesus Christ,

---

[1] Contra hær., lib. I., cap. x. 1. *Cf.* also lib. V., cap. xx. 1. It is very illuminating to compare Irenæus and Origen on this point. Both maintain the " Rule of faith," but Origen uses it simply in order to pass from it to the points not yet fixed by it, whereas for Irenæus the " Rule of faith " is centre and substance of his Christian thinking as a whole.

[2] Even where Irenæus is nearest to Tertullian, this distinction is still clear. *Cf. e.g.* Contra hær., lib. III., cap. xxv.; lib. IV., cap. xxviii.

who saves us from it.[1]   Behind this dualism lies a double
error: (1) the creation is separated from God, and (2) it is
connected with evil.   Irenæus rejects both parts.   He allows
no direct connection between sin and material existence; we
may neither suppose, with the Gnostics, that matter is in
some way the source of evil, nor conversely, with Origen,
that sin is the reason for the creation of the material world.
The ground of creation is in God Himself: it is His goodness and love.[2]   There can be no greater error, then, than to
make a sharp distinction between Creation and Redemption,
as if God had less to do with the former than the latter.
One and the same Divine love-will takes expression in both.
By the same Word by which He created the world, God has
also saved the world.[3]

When Irenæus makes God's love the ground of creation,
that is evidence of the extent to which the Agape motif
moulds his Christian thought.   The idea that existence ultimately has its ground in Divine love, can, it is true, be
found in piety that is influenced by Hellenism—we have
seen it in Gnosticism.[4]   But love, in that case, is always more
or less equated with desire; it is, so to speak, the Primal
desire, which creates the object of its longing.   With such a
view, however, Irenæus has nothing in common.   He is well
aware that the love which is the ground of creation is not
love that desires, but love that gives.   God has not created
man in order to satisfy His own needs, but to have someone
on whom to lavish His beneficence.[5]   Irenæus' idea of
Creation is thoroughly *theocentric*.   All things are of God.

---

[1] Contra hær., lib. I., cap. xxvii. 2.   *Cf.* lib. II., cap. i.

[2] Contra hær., lib. V., cap. xvii. 1: ἔστι δὲ οὗτος ὁ δημιουργός, ὁ κατὰ μὲν
τὴν ἀγάπην πατήρ. . . .

[3] Contra hær., lib. III., cap. xi. 1: " . . . per Verbum, per quod Deus
perfecit conditionem, in hoc et salutem his qui in conditione sunt, præstitit
hominibus."

[4] On love as the principle of Creation in Gnosticism, see *supra*, p. 306.

[5] Contra hær., lib. IV., cap. xiv. 1: " Igitur initio non quasi indigens Deus
hominis plasmavit Adam, sed *ut haberet in quem collocaret sua beneficia*."

God is love; therefore He has created all things, therefore He cares for all things. He has need of no one, but man has need of fellowship with Him,[1] and in His goodness and mercy He has also willed to take man into fellowship with Himself. As it was of unmotivated goodness God created man in the beginning, so the history of His dealings with the human race ever since witnesses to the same unmotivated goodness.[2] It is not we who have chosen Him, but He has chosen us, for our salvation; everything in God's relation to us bears witness to this.

As Irenæus allows no distinction between God the Creator and God the Redeemer, so he allows none between the God of the Old and of the New Covenant, the God of the Law and of the Gospel. These are not, as Marcion thought, two separate Gods, but one and the same. Irenæus is, of course, fully conscious that there is a fundamental difference between fellowship with God in the form it took before and after the coming of Christ, and he insists most strongly that everything has become new because the Word has become flesh. But that is not to say that we now have a new God. Christ has taught us to worship God in a new way, but not to worship a new God.[3]

Now here, if anywhere, Irenæus and Tertullian might seem to be at one, as both attack Marcion's dualism between the God of the Law and of the Gospel. Yet it must be said that Irenæus' criticism strikes far deeper than Tertullian's. For it starts not from the Nomos motif, but from the

---

[1] *Ibid.*: "In quantum enim Deus nullius indigens, in tantum homo indiget Dei communione." Cap. xiv. 2: "Ipse quidem nullius indigens; his vero qui indigent eius, suam præbens communionem."

[2] "Sic et Deus ab initio hominem quidem plasmavit propter suam munificentiam; patriarchas vero elegit propter illorum salutem." *Ibid.* In cap. xiv. 1 he also quotes John xv. 16.

[3] "Omnia enim nova aderant, verbo nove disponente carnalem adventum, uti eum hominem qui extra Deum abierat, adscriberet Deo; *propter quod et nove Deum colere docebantur; sed non alium Deum.*" Contra hær., lib. III., cap. x. 2. *Cf.* with this, Epist. ad Diognetum 3.

Agape motif. Tertullian, with his nomistic interpretation of Christianity, lacks understanding of just what is most Christian in Marcion; he is offended not merely by the Hellenistic, but equally by the Christian elements in Marcion's thought in so far as these are anti-nomistic. His attack on Marcion is thus to a large extent an attack on the Agape motif itself. Irenæus, on the other hand, meets Marcion on his own ground. He understands the idea of Agape no less well than Marcion: and in addition, he is considerably freer than Marcion from Hellenistic piety. So, starting from the Agape motif itself, he can show where Marcion's interpretation of Christianity falls short, and refute it from within. Marcion separates Law and Gospel so as to find room for love; Irenæus retorts that it is precisely *love* which binds them together. In both the Old and the New Covenant the Commandment of Love is the chief commandment. Jesus Himself brought no other and greater commandment, but simply renewed this one, when He bade His disciples love God with all their heart and others as themselves. Here, Irenæus holds, is the refutation of Marcion's talk about the "Stranger God." If Christ had come down from another Father, He would never have taken over the first and greatest commandment of the Law, but would have endeavoured by all means to give a still greater commandment from the perfect Father, and not make use of that given by the God of the Law.[1]

But does even this criticism really touch the deepest intention of Marcion? Granted that Irenæus starts from love, it is primarily regarded from the point of view of *commandment*; whereas, for Marcion, everything hangs in the last resort upon the paradox of God's love shown to us in Christ.

---

[1] Contra hær., lib. IV., cap. xii. 2. *Cf.* also cap. xii. 3: " In lege igitur et in evangelio quum sit primum et maximum præceptum, diligere Dominum Deum ex toto corde; dehinc simile illi, diligere proximum sicut seipsum: *unus et idem ostenditur legis et evangelii conditor.* Consummatæ enim vitæ præcepta in utroque Testamento quum sint eadem, eundem ostenderunt Deum."

Does not Irenæus criticise, after all, from a nomistic stand-point, so that he fails to touch Marcion? Irenæus has a reply to this. He shows that Marcion, although he wanted to affirm the Christian Agape motif, had not really understood it, but had weakened it. In severing the connection between this world and the Highest God and making Him the abso-lute " Stranger," Marcion's intention was to exalt God and make Him greater. But the effect was the opposite: Mar-cion has " shamelessly degraded " and lessened God.[1] He has not understood the depth of the Divine love, which has compassion not only upon the pitiable, but even upon those who by their own transgression had become enemies of God.[2] This is the deepest reason for Irenæus' insistence on the unity of the God who created us and the God who in Christ redeemed us. Otherwise the greatness of God's love is not perceived. It may be a great thing to show love to those who are complete " strangers," whom we have no obligation whatever to love. But God's love is still greater. He loves those who, as His creatures, had an absolute obliga-tion towards Him, yet rebelliously turned away from Him and spurned His will. " He, the same against whom we had sinned in the beginning, grants forgiveness of sins in the end."[3] This is the triumph of the Divine love.

2. Irenæus' second main objection to Marcion and Gnos-ticism is that they have no place for the Incarnation and the Cross. " According to the opinion of no one of the heretics was the Word of God made flesh. For if anyone carefully

---

[1] Contra hær., lib. I., cap. xxvii. 4: " . . . impudorate super omnes obtrectare Deum."

[2] " Est autem hic Demiurgus, qui secundum dilectionem quidem, Pater est; . . . cuius et præceptum transgredientes, inimici facti sumus eius." Contra hær., lib. V., cap. xvii. 1. Cf. supra, p. 396, n. 2.

[3] Ibid. " Utique quoniam hic est Pater noster, cuius eramus debitores, transgressi eius præceptum. Quis autem est hic? Utrumne incognitus aliquis, et nulli nunquam præceptum dans Pater? An vero qui a Scripturis prædicatur Deus, cui et debitores eramus, transgressi eius præceptum? . . . Idem ille, in quem peccaveramus in initio, remissionen peccatorum in fine donans."

examines the systems of them all, he will find that the Word
of God is brought in by all of them as not having become
incarnate (sine carne) and impassible."[1]   Against this
Irenæus, with remarkable penetration, sets his Incarnation
theology. How central this is for him, his continual return
to it shows.

It is easy to see why Irenæus just at this point is so bitterly
opposed to the Gnostics. He and they have two diametrically opposed conceptions, *two different Ways of salvation.*
Gnosticism teaches the *ascent of the soul* to the Deity,
Irenæus the *descent of God* to lost humanity; Gnosticism
teaches in the last resort *self-salvation,* Irenæus that salvation
in its entirety is a *work of God*; the Way of salvation in
Gnosticism is the Way of *Eros,* in Irenæus it is the Way of
Agape.

Irenæus' interest in affirming the idea of Incarnation is
strongly theocentric. What he means to say, first and last,
is that salvation is not our work, but God's. Away, then,
with every thought of self-salvation! "Not from us, but
from God is our salvation."[2]   There is no possibility for us
to work our way up to fellowship with God, but in the Incarnation of the Logos the foundation has miraculously been
laid for a new fellowship between God and the fallen human
race. From above the Divine salvation comes down to us.
Christ has come and in Himself recapitulated the whole
human race.[3]   The disobedience of the first Adam at the
tree in Paradise, Christ, as the second Adam, has remedied
through His obedience on the tree of the Cross.[4]   He has

---

[1] Contra hær., lib. III., cap. xi. 3.

[2] " Quoniam ipse Dominus erat qui salvabat eos, quia per semetipsos non
habebant salvari. . . . Non a nobis, sed a Deo est bonum salutis nostræ."
Contra hær., lib. III., cap. xx. 3.

[3] " Quoniam ipse est, qui omnes gentes exinde ab Adam dispersas et universas
linguas et generationem hominum cum ipso Adam in semetipso recapitulatus
est."   Contra hær., lib. III., cap. xxii. 3.

[4] " Dissolvens enim eam, quæ ab initio in ligno facta fuerat, hominis inobedientiam, obediens factus est usque ad mortem, mortem autem crucis; eam quæ

thus reconciled the human race with God, for what is true
of Christ is true also of the whole of the race whose head He
has become by the Incarnation.[1] What impelled Him to
enter into our lot, to take upon Himself our poverty and
make us sharers in His riches, was nothing other than His
love. "God's Logos, our Lord Jesus Christ, did, through
His transcendent love, become what we are, that He might
bring us to be even what He is Himself."[2] Thus to ascribe
salvation wholly to Christ means, according to Irenæus,
ascribing it wholly to God. Christ's work is, for Him, God's
own work. When Christ effects His recapitulation, it is
God Himself who in Himself recapitulates the old human
race.[3] Christ belongs entirely to the Divine sphere. "He
is Himself, in His own right, beyond all men who ever
lived, God, and Lord, and King Eternal, and Only-begotten,
and the Incarnate Logos."[4] He is God revealed for us,
descended to us, He is "God with us."[5] In His greatness
and wonderful glory God is inaccessible to us men; but in
His love He has revealed Himself to us and Himself come

---

in ligno facta fuerat inobedientiam, per eam quæ in ligno fuerat obedientiam
sanans." Contra hær., lib. V., cap. xvi. 3. ἐν μὲν γὰρ τῷ πρώτῳ Ἀδὰμ
προσεκόψαμεν, μὴ ποιήσαντες αὐτοῦ τὴν ἐντολήν· ἐν δὲ τῷ δευτέρῳ Ἀδὰμ
ἀποκατηλλάγημεν, ὑπήκοοι μέχρι θανάτου γενόμενοι. Ibid., cf. Epideixis 34.

[1] "Quando incarnatus est, et homo factus, longam hominum expositionem in
seipso recapitulavit, in compendio nobis salutem præstans." Contra hær.,
lib. III., cap. xviii. 1. "Et propter hoc . . . caro factum est, et pependit
super lignum, uti universa in semetipsum recapituletur." Lib. V., cap.
xviii. 3.

[2] "Propter immensam suam dilectionem [ἀγάπην] factus est quod sumus nos,
uti nos perficeret esse quod est ipse." Contra hær., lib. V., Præfatio.

[3] "Deus hominis antiquam plasmationem in se recapitulans, ut occideret
quidem peccatum, evacuaret autem mortem et vivificaret hominem." Contra
hær., lib. III., cap. xviii. 7.

[4] "Quoniam autem ipse proprie præter omnes, qui fuerent tunc homines,
Deus et Dominus et Rex æternus et Unigenitus et Verbum incarnatum prædicatur et a prophetis omnibus et apostolis et ab ipso Spiritu, adest videre
omnibus qui vel modicum de veritate attigerint." Contra hær., lib. III.,
cap. xix. 2.

[5] " . . . et hunc partum Deum esse nobiscum, et descendere in ea quæ sunt
deorsum terræ." Cap. xix. 3.—"Agnitio enim Patris, Filius." Lib. IV.,
cap. vi. 7.

down to us.[1]   This distinction between God in His sublimity and in His love is particularly characteristic of Irenæus. Every attempt from our side to approach God in His sublimity and heavenly majesty is doomed to fail. " Man cannot see God by his own powers ";[2] " God cannot be known without God."[3]   But now no one need be " without God."   We cannot ascend to Him in His sublimity, but He in His love has descended to us. What was impossible for men, God Himself has made possible by the miracle of the Incarnation. The advent of the Logos in the flesh is God's great work of love. In the Incarnation God's Agape manifests itself. So fellowship between God and men has been established; in the Incarnate Word we can now behold God. God Himself holds converse with us here upon earth.[4]

---

[1] " Igitur *secundum magnitudinem* non est cognoscere Deum: impossibile est enim mensurari Patrem; *secundum autem dilectionem eius* [κατὰ τὴν αὐτοῦ ἀγάπην] (hæc est enim, quæ nos per Verbum eius perducit ad Deum) obedientes ei semper discimus, quoniam est tantus Deus." Contra hær., lib. IV., cap. xx. 1. Irenæus returns again and again to this thought: " Unus igitur Deus, qui Verbo et sapientia fecit et aptavit omnia; hic est autem Demiurgus, qui et mundum hunc attribuit humano generi, qui *secundum magnitudinem* quidem ignotus est omnibus his, qui ab eo facti sunt: (nemo enim investigavit altitudinem eius, nec veterum, qui quieverunt, nec eorum qui nunc sunt) *secundum autem dilectionem* cognoscitur semper per eum, per quem constituit omnia. Est autem hic Verbum eius, Dominus noster Iesus Christus, qui novissimis temporibus homo in hominibus factus est, ut finem coniungeret principio, id est hominem Deo." Cap. xx. 4.   " Sed *secundum magnitudinem* quidem eius et mirabilem gloriam nemo videbit Deum, et vivet; incapabilis enim Pater; *secundum autem dilectionem* et humanitatem, et quod omnia possit, etiam hoc concedit iis qui se diligunt, id est videre Deum, quod et prophetabant prophetæ. Quoniam quæ impossibilia apud homines, possibilia apud Deum." Cap. xx. 5.

[2] "*Homo etenim a se non videt Deum.* Ille autem volens videtur hominibus, quibus vult et quando vult et quemadmodum vult. Potens est enim in omnibus Deus." *Ibid.*

[3] Contra hær., lib. IV., cap. vi. 4: ἄνευ θεοῦ μὴ γινώσκεσθαι τὸν θεόν. *Cf.* cap. xxxiii. 4: πῶς ἄνθρωπος χωρήσει εἰς θεόν, εἰ μὴ ὁ θεὸς ἐχωρήθη εἰς ἄνθρωπον;

[4] " Et huius Verbum naturaliter quidem invisibilem, palpabilem et visibilem in hominibus factum, et usque ad mortem descendisse, mortem autem crucis." Contra hær., lib. IV., cap. xxiv. 2.   ". . . prædicaverunt eius secundum carnem adventum, per quem commixtio et communio Dei et hominis secundum placitum Patris facta est, ab initio prænuntiante Verbo Dei, quoniam videbitur Deus ab hominibus et *conversabitur cum eis super terram.* . . ." Cap. xx. 4.

For Irenæus everything hangs upon *the reality of our fellowship with God* in Christ. But that means two things. First, it must be God Himself who comes to meet us in Christ and His work. "God cannot be known without God." If Christ were not one with God, then His advent into the world would not mean the coming of God to us. In spite of the Incarnation we should then have no real fellowship with God. Secondly, Christ's advent into the world must be indisputable reality. Irenæus has these two conditions in mind when he speaks of Christ as at once both God and man, and asserts that only so could He " unite man to God."[1] Now the second condition is as important as the first, and Irenæus most vigorously assails the docetic Christology of the heretics. If Christ only became flesh in appearance, then our salvation also would be merely apparent. And had His Passion been merely apparent and not real suffering, then He would have deceived us.[2] Here, too, Irenæus argues from the idea of love. What kind of love would it be that shrank from suffering? God's Logos has given us the commandment: "Love your enemies, and pray for them that hate you." It is easy enough to give such a commandment, if one knows oneself exempted from all suffering. But that was not the case with Christ; He Himself first fulfilled that commandment, when He suffered on the Cross and prayed for His persecutors. If we compare the Christ proclaimed by the Gospel, who really suffers on the Cross and prays for His tormentors, with the Christ of the Gnostics, " who flew away, and sustained neither injury nor insult," there can be no doubt as to which of them showed the greatest love.[3]

---

[1] Contra hær., lib. III., cap. xviii. 7: ἥνωσεν οὖν, καθὼς προέφαμεν, τὸν ἄνθρωπον τῷ θεῷ. εἰ γὰρ μὴ ἄνθρωπος ἐνίκησε τὸν ἀντίπαλον τοῦ ἀνθρώπου, οὐκ ἂν δικαίως ἐνικήθη ὁ ἐχθρός. πάλιν τε, εἰ μὴ ὁ θεὸς ἐδωρήσατο τὴν σωτηρίαν, οὐκ ἂν βεβαίως ἔσχομεν αὐτήν. Contra hær., lib. IV., cap. vi. 7: " . . . ab omnibus accipiens testimonium, quoniam *vere homo* et quoniam *vere Deus*." *Cf.* Epideixis 36 f.

[2] Contra hær., lib. III., cap. xviii. 6.

[3] Contra hær., lib. III., cap. xviii. 5.

3. Irenæus' third main objection to the heretics concerns the " Resurrection of the flesh." Again the same theocentric interest prevails, the same interest in Agape which, as we have seen, dominated his conception of the Creation, the Incarnation or the Cross. The heretics, following Hellenistic tradition, spoke of the "Immortality of the soul " as something inseparable from its " nature " or essence; but to Irenæus this is vain conceit, ingratitude to God and rejection of Him—" as if we had life from ourselves."[1]   God has a special purpose in first giving our life over to death and then again raising us to life.   " But learning by experience that we possess eternal duration from the excelling power of this Being, not from our own nature, we may neither undervalue that glory which surrounds God as He is, nor be ignorant of our own nature, but that we may know what God can effect, and what benefits man receives. . . ."[2]

With regard to the Resurrection, Irenæus follows the line of the Apologists, and his arguments are substantially the same; based on the *will and power of God*. His argument with the heretics reveals most instructively the incompatibility of Christian *belief in Resurrection* and Hellenistic *belief in Immortality*, and also the different fundamental religious motifs underlying them.   The heretics believe in the " Immortality of the soul,"[3] but reject any idea of the " Resurrection of the flesh."   Irenæus does the opposite; he asserts the " Resurrection of the flesh," but rejects—though not without certain touches of Hellenism—the idea of the " Natural immortality of the soul."   To the heretics two things were clear: (1) it was self-evident that man, as far as

---

[1] Contra hær., lib. V., cap. ii. 3: ἵνα μὴ ὡς ἐξ ἡμῶν αὐτῶν ἔχοντες τὴν ζωήν, φυσηθῶμεν καὶ ἀπαρθῶμέν ποτε κατὰ τοῦ θεοῦ, ἀχάριστον ἔννοιαν ἀναλαβόντες.

[2] *Ibid.*

[3] It should be observed that, while we use the accepted term "immortality of the soul " here, the Gnostics generally thought of the immortality of the Divine " pneuma."   *Cf.* Contra hær., lib. V., cap. xix. 2.

the higher, pneumatic part of him was concerned, could not perish; the life of immortality, eternal life, belonged to the human spirit simply because of its pneumatic, divine nature; (2) the idea of the " Resurrection of the flesh " was a pure absurdity : just as the nature of spirit is such that it cannot perish, so the nature of the material and sensible is such that it must inevitably disintegrate and disappear. Irenæus rejects both ideas, the former chiefly on the ground of God's will, the latter on the ground also of His power. Only God has life in and of Himself. So it can never be self-evident that life and immortality belong to man or to any part of him. All talk of man's " Natural immortality " means that man in his pride seeks to make himself like God.[1] Against this, Irenæus affirms that our life, present and future alike, is absolutely dependent on the will of God.[2] Our whole being therefore, spirit, soul, and body, possesses life because and for so long as *God wills* that we shall live; and when He sometime recalls us to life in the Resurrection, even then we shall live only because it is His will, and not by reason of any given necessity of our nature.[3] And his opponents' description of the " Resurrection of the flesh " as an absurdity, Irenæus finds to be simply a new attack on God's divinity—that is, on His Divine power. No doubt this seems an impossibility to men; but for God nothing is impossible. They reject the " Resurrection of the flesh " because they pay attention only to the weakness of

---

[1] " . . . inani supercilio iactaretur, quasi naturaliter similis esset Deo." Contra hær., lib. III., cap. xx. 1.

[2] " Ita ut sic initio fierent, et postea, ut sint, eis donat." Contra hær., lib. II., cap. xxxiv. 2.

[3] " Vivunt enim in quantum ea Deus vult vivere." Contra hær., lib. V., cap. iv. 2. " Sic et *de animabus et de spiritibus* et omnino de omnibus his, quæ facta sunt, cogitans quis, minime peccabit: quando omnia, quæ facta sunt, initium quidem facturæ suæ habeant, *perseverant autem quoadusque ea Deus et esse et perseverare voluerit.*" Contra hær., lib. II., cap. xxxiv. 3. " Deo itaque vitam et perpetuam perseverantiam donante, capit et animas primum non exsistentes dehinc perseverare, quum eas Deus et esse et subsistere voluerit." Cap. xxxiv. 4.

the flesh but not to *the power of God*, which awakens it from the dead.[1]

The above makes it plain that Irenæus, both in refuting the "Natural immortality of the soul" and in defending the "Resurrection of the flesh," has one and the same motive, his theocentric interest. For resurrection and eternal life he looks unwaveringly to God. In ourselves there is nothing that guarantees eternal life; we obtain it solely on the ground of God's will and as His gift. If Irenæus is here successor to the Apologists, the theocentric tendency is reinforced by his strong appreciation of Agape. It is just in the interests of the idea of Agape that he combats the idea of "Natural immortality." For if man imagines he possesses in himself what is in reality a gift of God to him, then "the love which God has towards man becomes obscured."[2] Neither Divine love nor Divine power is needed to give eternal life to one who already possesses it in virtue of his nature.

In face of this fundamentally clear and simple thought, it is astonishing to find Irenæus himself talking sometimes quite unconcernedly of the "Natural immortality" of the spirit or soul. He is surely inconsistent here. He sees in principle the danger of the Hellenistic theory and opposes it, but cannot in practice get rid of its influence. For Irenæus, the human being is a unity of spirit, soul, and body, and a real and complete man exists only in the union of these three[3]—he takes a similar "*totus-homo*" view to that of

---

[1] "Refutant igitur potentiam Dei et non. contemplantur quod est verbum, qui infirmitatem intuentur carnis, virtutem autem eiüs qui suscitat eam a mortuis, non contemplantur." Contra hær., lib. V., cap. iii. 2.   οὔτε οὖν φύσις τινὸς τῶν γεγονότων, οὔτε μὴν ἀσθένεια σαρκὸς ὑπερισχύει τῆς βουλῆς τοῦ θεοῦ. Contra hær., lib. V., cap. v. 2.

[2] "Ingratum enim magis eum hoc ei, qui eum fecerat, perficiens et dilectionem, quam habebat Deus in hominem [τὴν ἀγάπην, ἣν εἶχεν ὁ θεὸς εἰς ἄνθρωπον], obfuscabat, et excæcabat sensum suum ad non sentiendum, quod sit de Deo dignum, comparans et æqualem se iudicans Deo." Contra hær., lib. III., cap. xx. 1.

[3] "Anima autem et Spiritus pars hominis esse possunt, homo autem nequa-

Tertullian. Nevertheless, he regards it as fairly self-evident that spirit and soul cannot perish, and that only the body can be touched by the dissolution of death.[1]

It would take too long to detail the lines of thought in Irenæus, often somewhat diffuse, arising from this inconsistency.[2] But it is interesting to note that this very inconsistency makes him cling the more jealously to the " Resurrection of the flesh." For the more he favours the idea that spirit and soul are by nature such as to persist even after bodily death, the less support he has in this for his ultimate, theocentric intention. Only the " Resurrection of the flesh " remains as the manifestation of Divine power and love; and so the tendency, already detected in tne Apologists, when speaking of resurrection, to lay chief stress on the " Resurrection of the flesh," receives a further impetus. But in Irenæus it has a deeper religious motive. It is for him the ultimate *point d'appui* for the theocentric idea of Agape. For even if spirit and soul might be supposed to persist by reason of their natural qualities, its obviously transient nature excludes any such idea in the case of the body. When mortal and corruptible flesh becomes, in the Resurrection, immortal and incorruptible, obviously this transformation is not due to its own nature, but to the operation of the Lord, who

---

quam." Contra hær., lib. V., cap. vi. 1. " Neque enim plasmatio carnis ipsa secundum se homo perfectus est; sed corpus hominis, et pars hominis. Neque enim et anima ipsa secundum se homo; sed anima hominis et pars hominis. Neque Spiritus homo: Spiritus enim, et non homo vocatur. Commixtio autem et unitio horum omnium, perfectum hominem efficit." *Ibid.*

[1] " *Hæc* [*caro*] *enim est quæ moritur et solvitur ; sed non anima neque Spiritus.* . . . Superest igitur ut circa carnem mors ostendatur. . . . Hæc igitur mortalis." Contra hær., lib. V., cap. vii. 1.

[2] Attention has in some measure been drawn to this; *cf. e.g.* W. Bousset: *Kyrios Christos*, 2 Aufl., 1921, p. 359; and H. Koch: *Zur Lehre vom Urstand und von der Erlösung bei Irenäus.* Theologische Studien und Kritiken, Jahrg. 96-97, 1925, pp. 204 ff. But a thorough examination of the problem of " Resurrection and Immortality " in Irenæus is still needed. Especially valuable would be an examination of the " Image of God " in man (εἰκών and ὁμοίωσις) according to Irenæus.

can give the mortal immortality and the corruptible incorruptibility.[1] If man's body represents the very essence of mortality, it in particular is the object of the deed of Divine might, the Resurrection.[2] Here God's might can really triumph, here His strength is made perfect in human weakness. But if " the flesh " receives incorruptible life as a gift of God, and if, further, man is a whole and complete man only in and through the union of spirit, soul, and body, then what is said of " the flesh " applies to the whole man: not of himself, but by the Grace of God, man attains eternal life.[3] The basis of this whole argument is ultimately the belief in the " Resurrection of the flesh."

The whole content of Christianity is focussed in the " Resurrection of the flesh." Here all God's work reaches its completion. Both Creation and Redemption point to it as their goal: Creation, for God is to raise up on the Last Day the same flesh which He created in the beginning;[4] Redemption (the Incarnation), " for if the flesh were not in a position to be saved, the Word of God would in no wise have become flesh."[5]

---

[1] μετασχηματισμὸς δὲ αὐτῆς, ὅτι θνητὴ καὶ φθαρτὴ οὖσα, ἀθάνατος καὶ ἄφθαρτος γίνεται, οὐκ ἐξ ἰδίας ὑποστάσεως, ἀλλὰ κατὰ τὴν τοῦ κυρίου ἐνέργειαν, τὸ δύνασθαι αὐτὸν τῷ θνητῷ τὴν ἀθανασίαν, καὶ τῷ φθαρτῷ περιποιήσασθαι τὴν ἀφθαρσίαν. Contra hær., lib. V. cap. xiii. 3. " Quoniam autem corpora nostra, non ex sua substantia sed ex Dei virtute suscitantur. . . ." Cap. vi. 2.

[2] φανερώτατα περὶ τῆς σαρκὸς ταῦτα λέγων· οὔτε γὰρ ἡ ψυχὴ θνητόν, οὔτε τὸ πνεῦμα. Cap. xiii. 3.

[3] " Non enim ex nobis, neque ex nostra natura vita est, sed secundum gratiam Dei datur." Contra hær., lib. II., cap. xxxiv. 3.

[4] " Quoniam autem is qui ab initio condidit hominem, post resolutionem eius in terram promisit ei secundum generationem, Esaias quidem sic ait. . . ." Contra hær., lib. V., cap. xv. 1.

[5] " Si enim non haberet caro salvari, nequaquam Verbum Dei caro factum esset." Contra hær., lib. V., cap. xiv. 1.

2. THE LIMITATION OF THE IDEA OF AGAPE
IN IRENÆUS

Nowhere in the Early Church is the idea of Agape found in so pure a form as in Irenæus. His whole theology is saturated with the Agape motif: it is of love that God has created the world and designed men for fellowship with Himself, of love God's Logos has become flesh in order to "recapitulate" in Himself the fallen human race and reconcile it to God, of love God will at last in the Resurrection give eternal and incorruptible life to those created by Him and redeemed by Him. Even compared with Marcion's view, Irenæus' idea of love suggests a stronger appreciation of Agape. If Marcion is more uncompromising in working out what he conceives to be Christian love, Irenæus decidedly represents the purer type of Agape.[1]

Even his view of Agape, however, is not entirely untouched by alien motifs. We have already seen in him the influence of the Hellenistic conception of the "Natural immortality of the soul." But that is not all; the Eros motif affects the very centre of his thought, and has even put its seal upon

---

[1] G. Aulén (*Den kristna försoningstanken*, 1930, pp. 67 f.) aptly describes Irenæus' main position: "First, it should be emphasised that the work of Reconciliation is conceived entirely as a Divine work. The work of fighting and conquering the hostile powers is the work of the Incarnate Logos; but just as such it is a Divine work—not merely in the sense that God has taken the initiative, that the basis of it is Divine love and mercy, but in the sense that the active power in the deed itself is no other than God's ' Agape,' the Divine love itself. Decisive for his argument is this ' line from above downwards ': the Divine power ' descends,' enters into the world of sin and death, and there carries out the work whereby God reconciles the world to Himself. At the same time, this is the heart of Irenæus' Christology, which is inseparably bound up with his ' Soteriology.' It is particularly to be stressed that there is no question of any qualification or merits on man's part whatever, not even in the sense that Christ as man performs anything in the name of humanity. There is no other motive for what happens, no other power at work in what happens, than the Divine love alone." W. Schmidt takes a similar view in his *Die Kirche bei Irenäus*, 1934, p. 167, n. 1: "We find that he stands in principle on the line of Agape. His thought is completely theocentric."

the goal Irenæus sets for God's educative guidance of humanity, which in plain dependence on Hellenistic piety he describes as ἀφθαρσία and "deification." This idea is not, however, competitor to his theology of Incarnation, but directly connected with it. The Incarnation is the revelation of God's Agape, but its purpose is, in the last resort, the "deification" of man. To the question, plainly inspired by the idea of Agape: "ad quid enim descendebat?"[1] —Why did the Saviour descend to this world?—Irenæus gives several different answers, some dictated rather by the Agape motif, others by the Eros motif. The content of the latter may be conventionally formulated thus: *God became man in order that man might become God.*[2]

There is an illuminating exposition of this idea in the *Contra hæreses*, Book IV., Chapter XXXVIII. Could not God, Irenæus asks, have created man perfect from the beginning, as He is Himself? He answers: God could of course have given man such perfection, but as a creature he could not have received it. "For as it certainly is in the power of a mother to give strong food to her infant, but she does not do so, as the child is not yet able to receive more substantial nourishment; so also it was possible for God Himself to have made man perfect from the first, but man could not receive this perfection, being as yet an infant."[3] In His wisdom God has had regard to this. We are so eager to anticipate events; we will not "await the time of increase,"[4] we want to be as God from the start. But that is not God's way; He works with a distant aim. Step by step He leads us on to deification. In Creation He has bestowed on us our exist-

---

[1] "Ut quid [ἵνα τί, ad quid] enim descendebat?" Contra hær., lib. II., cap. xiv. 7.

[2] Contra hær., lib. IV., cap. xxxiii. 4: ἢ πῶς ἄνθρωπος χωρήσει εἰς θεόν, εἰ μὴ ὁ θεὸς ἐχωρήθη εἰς ἄνθρωπον. On this Bousset, *op. cit.*, p. 336, n. 4, remarks: "For χωρεῖν *cf.* Poimandres 32: εἰς ζωὴν καὶ φῶς χωρῶ (so speaks the initiate who experiences deification)."

[3] Contra hær., lib. IV., cap. xxxviii. 1.

[4] Cap. xxxviii. 4.

ence, as imperfect men no doubt, yet men who by means of the free will granted by God can progress towards higher goals. In the Incarnation God takes the next step, when He comes to us with the "perfect bread," the "bread of immortality,"[1] but comes in such a way as our human weakness can bear. Only after being trained by receiving Him are we ready to be raised to the Divine plane. Deification is ours only as a result of long development and education. It is an unreasonable and ungrateful demand, that we should from the beginning have been made gods. We may not leap over any of the stages God has appointed for us on our way to deification. First, nature must come into being, then the mortal be vanquished and swallowed up in immortality: that is the Divine ordinance.[2] "*Primo quidem homines, tunc demum Dii*"—"*First men, then gods.*"[3]

Why did Christ descend to us? In order that we might ascend to God. Christ's descent is the means of our ascent. Incarnation is the means of our deification. So he who despises the Incarnation deprives man of the ascent to God, deprives him of the condition for his deification.[4] This interconnection of the descent of the Logos and the ascent of man is vital for Irenæus. Testimony to its importance is the fact that it is the keynote of his great work *Contra hæreses.* In conclusion he writes: "For there is the one Son, who accomplished His Father's will; and one human race also in which

---

[1] Cap. xxxviii. 1.

[2] "Oportuerat autem primo naturam apparere, post deinde vinci et absorbi mortale ab immortalitate et corruptibile ab incorruptibilitate, et fieri hominem secundum imaginem et similitudinem Dei, agnitione accepta boni et mali." Cap. xxxviii. 4.

[3] *Ibid.*

[4] In this connection Irenæus uses the typical expression of Hellenistic Mystery-piety for man's ascent to God or deification: ἡ εἰς θεὸν ἄνοδος. *Cf.* lib. III., cap. xix. 1: ταῦτα λέγει πρὸς τοὺς μὴ δεξαμένους τὴν δωρεὰν τῆς υἱοθεσίας, ἀλλ' ἀτιμάζοντας τὴν σάρκωσιν τῆς καθαρᾶς γεννήσεως τοῦ λόγου τοῦ θεοῦ, καὶ ἀποστεροῦντας τὸν ἄνθρωπον τῆς εἰς θεὸν ἀνόδου, καὶ ἀχαριστοῦντας τῷ ὑπὲρ αὐτῶν σαρκωθέντι λόγῳ τοῦ θεοῦ. εἰς τοῦτο γὰρ ὁ λόγος ἄνθρωπος, ἵνα ὁ ἄνθρωπος τὸν λόγον χωρήσας, καὶ τὴν υἱοθεσίαν λαβών, υἱὸς γένηται θεοῦ.

the mysteries of God are wrought, ' which the angels desire to look into,' and they are not able to search out the wisdom of God, by means of which His handiwork, confirmed and incorporated with His Son, is brought to perfection; so that His offspring, the *Only-begotten Logos, descends to the creature* . . . and is contained by it; and, on the other hand, the *creature contains the Logos*, and *ascendᶜ to Him*, passing beyond the angels, and is made after the image and likeness of God."[1]

Thus strands from the Eros and the Agape motifs are woven together. The human is raised up to the Divine—Irenæus shares this idea with Hellenistic piety generally. The raising is not man's, but from first to last God's work—so the Agape motif proves, after all, determinative of his thought. Fellowship with God rests wholly on the miracle of the Incarnation, on the fact that in His love God has come down to us in Christ—here all is consistently conceived according to the scheme of Agape. And yet this fellowship is regarded as a fellowship on God's own level, on the level of holiness and perfection—this is Irenæus' tribute to the Hellenistic Eros motif.

[1] Contra hær., lib. V., cap. xxxvi. 3.

VIII

THE COMPROMISE

1. The Result of the Contests of the Second Phase

In the first contests, against Gnosticism and Marcion, the theology of the Apostolic Fathers and the Apologists had taken the lead. The result, in terms of· motif, was that not only the Eros, but also the Agape motif was seriously compromised. The Christian idea of love found no expression unmodified by nomism.

If now we try to estimate the result of the contests of the second phase, we may say at once that the situation is significantly changed, and that rather in favour of the Agape motif. It is now the Nomos and Eros motifs that are compromised: Nomos, due to Tertullian, whose schismatic relation to the Church was closely connected with nomism; Eros, due to Origen, whose many heretical opinions were influenced by Eros. In the next period, the outlook of the Church bears chiefly the impress of Irenæus, who represents in essentials, as we have seen, the Agape type. The Nomos type had its heyday in the first period of the post-apostolic age; in the second period the Agape type comes more into the foreground. But the Eros type is not forgotten. The theologians of the fourth century—we shall consider the three outstanding names, Methodius of Olympus (d. 311), Athanasius (at the Council of Nicæa 325, d. 373) and Gregory of Nyssa (d. after 394)—do not produce a simple development of Irenæus' position. Their theology is rather a compromise between Irenæus and Origen, between Agape and Eros, in which the influence of the latter becomes greater with the passage of time.

413

The existence of this *compromise* is testified by the fact that in all these theologians either different works or different arguments in the same work reveal now the Eros, now the Agape motif. There has been no real decision between them; neither has one superseded the other nor has a form compounded of both been created. Their relation to each other is fairly superficial, and they appear by turns without obviously cancelling each other out. Life is lived as a matter of course in both worlds alike. The resultant tension is unnoticed, inasmuch as the different principles are applied to different problems. In matters of long-standing dispute with Gnosticism there is a clear consciousness of opposition to Eros piety; here the Christian tradition dating from the Apologists is a mighty bulwark against alien influences. At points where no such tradition existed, however, the Eros motif is unhesitatingly adopted from contemporary thought. Consequently, it is not a real synthesis, but a compromise that is reached.

2. METHODIUS OF OLYMPUS

A singularly illuminating example of this double-sidedness is Methodius. Here we can actually delimit the occurrences of the different motifs. In his dogmatic work *De resurrectione* the Agape motif, in his ethical ascetic treatise *Symposium* the Eros motif is primary.

On Creation, Incarnation and the Resurrection of the flesh, Methodius follows the path marked out by the Apologists and Irenæus. Like the latter, he insists on the unity of Creation and Redemption. On this basis he vehemently attacks Origen's doctrine of " eternal Creation," his view of the sensible world as a penal and educative institution set up by God because of sin for the fallen spirits, his doctrine of *apokatastasis*, and so forth. He is altogether opposed to the spiritualising tendency of Origen and his disciples. Since sin has no closer relation to the body than to the soul, there is no occasion to contemn things bodily. They are the good creation of God, intended by Him for perfection no less than the spiritual side of our being. The Resurrection of the flesh holds, therefore, a central place in Methodius' theology. In all this the strong influence of the Agape tradition is discernible. Methodius' campaign against Origen is, so to speak, simply a new chapter in the war on the Eros motif which the Apologists and Irenæus had earlier to wage against Gnosticism.[1]

The *Symposium* presents an entirely different picture. In it the Hellenistic Eros motif has very nearly sole control.[2] If Methodius intended to produce a " Christian " counterpart of Plato's *Symposium* and to supersede Plato's idea of Eros by the ideal of " Virginity," which Methodius regards as the specifically Christian virtue, even so there is little to distinguish his view from ordinary Eros theory. Virginity simply assumes the functions of Eros. What Plato says of the " heavenly Eros " Methodius takes over and applies to Virginity.

Virginity, says Methodius, is something exceedingly great

---

[1] As Methodius has nothing essentially new to add in this matter, detailed evidence is unnecessary. For a thorough treatment of this side of his thought, see F. Boström: *Studier till den grekiska teologins frälsningslära*, 1932. *Cf.* also N. Bonwetsch: *Die Theologie des Methodius*, 1903.

[2] The title itself betrays the dependence on Plato, and this dependence is a matter not merely of form, but of content and foundation motif. As in Plato's *Symposium* each participant was to hold a discourse in praise of Eros, so in Methodius' *Symposium* each of the ten virgins partaking of a simple meal has to hold a discourse in praise of Virginity. Platonic influence is strongest in the 8th Discourse (Thekla). Virginity is here described as the god-like, or even the " divine " life (παρθενία is derived from παρ-θεία, Symp. viii. 1: παρθεία γὰρ ἡ παρθενία κατὰ μίαν ὑπαλλαγὴν καλεῖται στοιχείου). Virginity is the wings on which the soul rises to heaven, its goal is the contemplation of the Divine beauty, and so on. Now possibly Methodius cannot be held responsible for the contents of every discourse, any more than everything in Plato's *Symposium* can be said to reflect Plato's own view. But he clearly approves what is said in the 8th Discourse, since Arete at the end awards Thekla " the largest and thickest chaplet " as victor in the contest (Symp. xi.).

and wonderful,[1] the very greatest gift which man can offer to God.[2]   It is the straight and most direct way to heaven,[3] it leads upwards and bestows immortality.[4] The best evidence that the worth of virgin beauty[5] is superior to all else is its ability to win Christ's love.[6] The virgin soul alone has a right to the honour of the name "Bride of Christ,"[7] and Christ is not ashamed to confess His love for the beauty of her prime.[8] Her soul's glance draws Christ's Eros to herself, so that His heart takes wings and He is inflamed with desire towards the shining glory of her inner man.[9]

All of which shows clearly how in Methodius Virginity is most intimately connected with the idea of Eros.   It is nothing else but the Eros Way of salvation and the Eros ethic which he presents.   Through Virginity earthly love is done away.   Love that was previously directed downwards finds a higher object and a higher aim; it is sublimated and directed upwards towards the heavenly world.   Underlying this whole conception is the Platonic, Hellenistic doctrine of the Two Worlds; and the Platonic distinction between

---

[1] Symposium i. 1: μεγάλη τίς ἐστιν ὑπερφυῶς καὶ θαυμαστὴ καὶ ἔνδοξος ἡ παρθενία.

[2] Symp. v. 1: τὸ γὰρ μέγιστον καὶ ἐπιφανέστατον ἀνάθημα καὶ δῶρον, οὗ μηδὲν ἀντάξιον ἄλλο προσενέγκασθαι πάρεστιν ἀνθρώποις θεῷ, τὸν ἆθλον τῆς παρθενίας εἶναι πέπεισμαι διαρκῶς.

[3] Symp. v. 6: αὕτη γὰρ ὀρθὴ πρὸς οὐρανὸν καὶ σύντομος ὁδοιπορία. Cf. vi. 2.

[4] Symp. v. 5: . . . ἀναγωγὸν εἶναι τὴν παρθένον.—οὐ γὰρ μικρὸν εἰς ῥᾳστώνην ἀφθαρσίας ἁγνεία, ἀνωφερῆ τὴν σάρκα πρὸς ὕψος αἴρουσα. Symp. viii. 4.

[5] Cf. the mode of address frequently employed in the Symposium: ὦ καλλιπάρθενοι.

[6] Symp. vii. 1: ἐρᾷ γὰρ ὁ λόγος οὐδενὸς τῶν σαρκός, ὅτι μὴ πέφυκεν ἀποδέχεσθαί τι τῶν φθειρομένων, οἷον χεῖρας ἢ πρόσωπον ἢ πόδας, ἀλλ' εἰς αὐτὸ τὸ ἄϋλον καὶ πνευματικὸν βλέπων εὐφραίνεται κάλλος.

[7] Symp. vi. 5: νυμφεύομαι τῷ λόγῳ καὶ τὸν ἀΐδιον τῆς ἀφθαρσίας προῖκα λαμβάνω στέφανον.

[8] Symp. vii. 1: ὅθεν δὴ καὶ ἐρᾶσθαι τοῦ κάλλους τῆς ἀκμῆς αὐτῆς ὁμολογεῖν οὐκ ἐπαισχύνεται. Christ is therefore also called "the Lover of beauty," ὁ ἐραστὴς τῆς ὥρας. Ibid.

[9] Symp. vii. 2: ὦ αὕτη, τῷ ἐπεράστῳ σου βλέμματι τῆς συνέσεως ἀνεπτέρωσας ἡμῶν τὴν καρδίαν εἰς πόθον.— . . . οἱονεὶ τὸ τοῦ ἔσωθεν ἀνθρώπου τῆς καταστολῆς αἴγλην ἀποστίλβοντος ὠρέχθαι σημαίνων. Ibid.

"heavenly Eros" and "vulgar Eros" reappears. Indeed, Methodius says explicitly that the aim of Virginity is to attain to the "heavenly Eros."[1] If love is otherwise dragged down to earth, owing to the weight of human nature, and adheres to its object, Virginity gives it wings, so that it can mount up to the heavenly regions, "to a pure atmosphere, and to the life which is akin to that of angels. Whence also they, first of all, after their call and departure hence, who have rightly and faithfully contended as virgins for Christ, bear away the prize of victory, being crowned by Him with the flowers of immortality."[2]

There is a deep cleavage between the Agape view of the *De resurrectione* and the Eros view of the *Symposium*. To explain the co-existence of such diverse trends, the two writings have sometimes been assigned to different stages in Methodius' development: the *Symposium* to his youth, when he was still under the influence of Plato and Origen; the *De resurrectione* to a later period when, emancipated from this influence, he had become a determined opponent of Origen and protagonist of the anti-Hellenistic churchly tradition. This may possibly be correct, but it is quite unnecessary as an explanation of the double-sidedness we are speaking of. It is enough to observe that two quite distinct spheres are involved. The *De resurrectione* deals with a question about which the Church already had a firm tradition. Thanks to this, in the matter of Creation, Incarnation and Resurrection the Eros motif has always had difficulty in gaining ground. It was recognised as the enemy, and the weapons to be used were known. The *Symposium*, on the other hand, deals, at least apparently, with an entirely different question—namely, the ethical conduct of the

---

[1] Symp. vi. 2: αἰνίσσεται γὰρ διὰ τούτων τὰς ἐπὶ πέρατα παρθενίας ἐπισπερχομένας ἐλθεῖν καὶ πάντα εἰς τὸ συμπληρωθῆναι τὸν ἔρωτα τοῦτον κοσμίως δρώσας. Otherwise, "Eros" in Methodius usually means "vulgar Eros"; cf. Symp. v. 5; viii. 2; x. 1; xi.

[2] Symp. viii. 2.

Christian, especially the ideal of Virginity. On this point, no firm tradition existed, and there is more uncertainty of judgment. Elements of Eros theory could easily steal in and be taken for the Christian view. Methodius is therefore the starting-point not only of a series of Christian authors who sought to imitate Plato's *Symposium*, but also and especially of the strong tradition of Christian " Bride-mysticism."[1]

If the co-existence of the Eros and the Agape motifs in Methodius was possible because they were applied to different sets of ideas, what was the mutual relationship of these sets of ideas? Methodius adopts the usual method of bridging the gulf between these motifs: Agape becomes the means, Eros the end; and in this case the Incarnation is the means, the virgin life the end. The Logos, he says, left His heavenly Father and descended to us in order, through the " trance "[2] of the Incarnation and Passion, to bring us to the stage of Virginity. There God's education of the human race achieves its end and the saving work of Christ its fulfilment. " For truly by a great stretch of power the plant of Virginity was sent down to men from heaven."[3] But this did not happen from the very beginning. First, God commanded the human race to multiply and fill the earth. That done, God began to consider how the human race " might now proceed from one point to another, and advance nearer to heaven, until, having attained to the very greatest and most exalted lesson of Virginity, they should reach to perfection."[4] It was to bring humanity to this perfection that Christ came. In both His teaching and life He has set before us the ideal of Virginity,

---

[1] Here, of course, he could refer to statements of Origen—*e.g.*, in Comment. in Cant. Cantic. and De oratione xvii. 2.

[2] Symp. iii. 8: . . . μετὰ τὴν ἔκστασιν τοῦ Χριστοῦ, ὅ δή ἐστι μετὰ τὴν ἐνανθρώπησιν καὶ τὸ πάθος.

[3] Symp. i. 2.

[4] *Ibid.* Methodius conceives this educative process in six stages: (1) marriage of brothers and sisters (from Creation to Abraham), (2) polygamy (from Abraham to the prophets), (3) monogamy, (4) prohibition of marital unfaithfulness, (5) demand for moderation even within marriage, (6) absolute virginity (through Christ).

and so can rightly be called ἀρχιπάρθενος.[1] Even when, in accord with the tradition of the Church, he speaks of the work of Christ as a victory over the devil,[2] the line of thought just indicated is for Methodius still the main thing. All the devil's efforts are directed to dragging us downward;[3] Christ, on the other hand, shows us the way upwards.[4] Before Christ came all men were captives and thralls of the devil, but since Christ has come and shown us the ascetic life and its all-surpassing glory, the kingdom of the devil is fallen, his grim tyranny is overthrown.[5] The devil has now no power to prevent the ascent of the re-born to God.[6] So the saving work of Christ and the ideal of Virginity fashioned by the Eros motif are combined. The two are, in fact, one. Salvation means the imitation in our own life of that virgin purity which Christ once manifested in His life. The Incarnation of Christ has no real meaning for us until He is born anew in each one of us.[7]

[1] Symp. i. 5: ἀρχιπάρθενος . . . γέγονεν ὁ λόγος ἐνανθρωπήσας τῆς ἐκκλησίας. In Symp. i. 4, Methodius asks: Why did no one of the many patriarchs and prophets and righteous men who taught and did many noble things, either praise or choose the state of virginity? He answers: Because it was reserved for the Lord alone to be the first to teach this doctrine; for it was fitting that He who is arch-priest, arch-prophet and arch-angel should also be ἀρχιπάρθενος.

[2] Symp. viii. 7: διὰ τοῦτο ἐγεννήθη καὶ κατῆλθεν αὐτὸς ἀπὸ τῶν θρόνων τοῦ πατρός, ἵνα τὸν δράκοντα χειρώσηται μείνας προστρέχοντα τῇ σαρκί.

[3] Symp. viii. 10: . . . ἵνα μὴ ἀπατηθῇ πρὸς τοῦ δράκοντος βρίθοντος κάτω.

[4] ἄνω πρὸς ὕψος. Ibid.

[5] Symp. x. 1: ἀφ' οὗ γὰρ ὁ Χριστὸς ἐδίδασκεν αὐτὴν ἀσκεῖν ἡμᾶς καὶ ἐμήνυσεν ἡμῖν τὸ ἀνυπέρβλητον κάλλος αὐτῆς, ἡ βασιλεία τοῦ πονηροῦ καθῃρέθη, πρότερον ἀεὶ πάντας αἰχμαλωτίζοντος καὶ δουλουμένου . . . ἀφ' οὗ δὲ Χριστὸς ἐνηνθρώπησε καὶ παρθενίᾳ τὴν σάρκα κοσμήσας ὥπλισεν, ὁ ὠμοτύραννος ἄρχων τῆς ἀκρασίας ᾑρέθη καὶ εἰρήνη καὶ πίστις κρατεῖ.

[6] Symp. viii. 10: ἀλλ' ἀστοχεῖ καὶ σφάλλεται τῆς ἄγρας, ἄνω πρὸς ὕψος ἁρπαζομένων τῶν ἀναγεννωμένων " πρὸς τὸν θρόνον τοῦ θεοῦ " · ὃ δή ἐστιν, ἄνω περὶ τὴν θείαν ἕδραν καὶ τὴν ἀσκανδάλιστον ὑπόβασιν τῆς ἀληθείας αἴρεται τὸ φρόνημα τῶν ἀνακαινισθέντων, τὰ ἐκεῖ βλέπειν καὶ τὰ ἐκεῖ φαντάζεσθαι παιδαγωγούμενον, ἵνα μὴ ἀπατηθῇ πρὸς τοῦ δράκοντος βρίθοντος κάτω· οὐ γὰρ αὐτῷ θέμις τοὺς ἄνω νεύοντας καὶ τοὺς ἄνω βλέποντας ἀφανίσαι. Notice the multiplicity of ways of expressing ascent: ἄνω πρὸς ὕψος—ἄνω περὶ τὴν θείαν ἕδραν—αἴρεται—τὰ ἐκεῖ—ἄνω νεύοντας—ἄνω βλέποντας.

[7] Symp. viii. 8: ἐπειδὴ τοὺς χαρακτῆρας καὶ τὴν ἐκτύπωσιν καὶ τὴν ἀρρενωπίαν εἰλικρινῶς τοῦ Χριστοῦ προσλαμβάνουσιν οἱ φωτιζόμενοι, τῆς

Although at first sight Methodius seemed to be guided in certain questions by the Agape motif, in others by the Eros motif, our enquiry has shown that in both cases the question is one and the same; it has merely been put under different headings. The three fundamental dogmas of Creation, Incarnation and the Resurrection of the flesh imply a definite view of the content of salvation: they are expressions of the Agape Way of salvation. But the ideal of Virginity, too, includes a definite view of the content of salvation: it is an expression of the Eros Way of salvation. When he puts these two together, it is ultimately one and the same thing, salvation, Methodius is concerned with in both cases; only, in the one case the tradition of the Early Church led him to give it a more Christian stamp, whereas in the *Symposium*, under Hellenistic influence, salvation is conceived in terms of " heavenly Eros." He was clearly never aware of any tension between the two views.

That being so, it is not surprising that, even when he uses the word Agape, Methodius often puts an interpretation on it whose proper context is that of Eros. Agape is desire directed upwards, the desire for incorruptibility and immortality. Since by itself it is altogether too weak, God has sent Virginity as its ally, to urge it on and support it.[1] " Flying on the heavenward wings of Virginity "[2] the soul can now mount up to God and " enter in exulting into the

---

καθ' ὁμοίωσιν μορφῆς ἐν αὐτοῖς ἐκτυπουμένης τοῦ λόγου καὶ ἐν αὐτοῖς γεννωμένης κατὰ τὴν ἀκριβῆ γνῶσιν καὶ πίστιν, ὥστε ἐν ἑκάστῳ γεννᾶσθαι τὸν Χριστὸν νοητῶς. " For to teach the Incarnation of the Son of God by the Holy Virgin, without confessing that He also comes into the Church as into His flesh, is not perfect. For each one of us must confess not only His Advent into that holy flesh which was born of the pure Virgin, but also *a like Advent into the spirit of each one of us.*" De sanguisuga viii. 2 f. On this point, too, Methodius is a pioneer of mysticism.

[1] Symp. iv. 4: χρησιμωτάτην γὰρ καὶ ἐπίκουρον εἰς ἀφθαρσίας κτῆσιν τὴν παρθενίαν ὁ θεὸς ἐδωρήσατο, σύμμαχον ἀποστείλας τοῖς ὀριγνωμένοις καὶ ποθοῦσι, καθὼς ὁ ψαλμῳδὸς ὑφηγεῖται, τὴν Σιών, ὃ δή ἐστι τὴν ἔκλαμπρον ἀγάπην.

[2] Symp. viii. 12: πτερουμένη τοῖς οὐρανοπόροις τῆς παρθενίας πτεροῖς.

bride-chamber."[1]   And there it beholds a wonderful beauty that cannot be described.   Up there is "Agape itself" along with the rest of the Ideas, there the tree of Agape grows beside that of Sophrosyne.[2]

3. Athanasius

It has rightly been said of Athanasius that his history coincides with that of the fourth century.[3] And, indeed, we find in him the same double-sidedness found in Methodius and characteristic of the fourth century in general. Athanasius won fame and importance far beyond the fourth century by his stand against Arianism: in this he is decidedly on the side of Agape. But apart from this he has also been extraordinarily important as a pioneer of the ascetic life and monasticism, in which he is no less decidedly on the side of Eros.

It is during the Arian controversy that the Agape motif becomes increasingly clear in Athanasius.[4] He is an excellent illustration of the value of controversy for insight into the essential nature of Christianity. The theology of Athanasius, however, and the course of the Arian controversy are both well known, and we may confine ourselves here to a general indication of the motif-content of the Nicene theology, of which Athanasius was the chief representative.

The Christological controversies of the Early Church have

[1] *Ibid.*

[2] Symp. viii. 3: εἶναι γὰρ αὐτὴν δικαιοσύνην καὶ αὐτὴν σωφροσύνην, *ἀγάπην αὐτὴν ἐκεῖ.*—εἶναι γὰρ δένδρον τι σωφροσύνης αὐτῆς, εἶναι ἀγάπης. *Ibid.* Thus Agape is fitted into the ordo-salutis-scheme of Eros, now as a stage of the ascent, now as its goal. " For having put off darkness and sanctified (illumined ?) in soul, we advance stage by stage, from . . . unbelief to searching the Scriptures . . . from thence *into the inextinguishable fire of love,* whence kindled we proceed to the desire for what is better, till we come to the summit —that is, to the sanctification of the Holy Ghost." De Lepra xiii. 4.

[3] A. Harnack: *Lehrbuch der Dogmengeschichte,* Bd. II., 4 Aufl., 1909, p. 21.

[4] It is significant that it was only when the controversy had been going on for some time that Athanasius came to lay great stress on the crucial word of Nicene theology, ὁμοούσιος.

often been regarded as quarrels about irrelevant metaphysical formulations meaningless for the real religious life. Nothing could be further from the truth. Indeed, very definite religious values were at stake. It was a contest between the Hellenistic and the Christian spirit, between a Hellenistic and a Christian conception of the meaning of fellowship with God. The Christological dogma of the Early Church is not a doctrinal construction of free speculation, but is the result which issued from this contest. Once this is realised, the old dogmatic formulæ gain vastly in interest. In the stiff, fossilised formulations can be traced the strife of mighty spirits and the pulse of the religious life itself.

The main purpose of early Christology was to assert the reality of fellowship with God through Agape, against prevalent Hellenistic ideas. In Christ God Himself has opened this fellowship to us: that is the theme of the old Incarnation-theology. But when Hellenistic ideas step in, they threaten in two different ways to make our fellowship with God illusory: first, if it was not God Himself, but a being of a lower order who came to us in Christ; secondly, if Christ was not a real man, but came in appearance only to us in our world. First, to regard Christ as a lower, created being comes very naturally to a mind cast in Hellenistic mould. God was the one enthroned in distant transcendence, and a series of intermediate beings came between Him and the world. What more natural than to interpret the Christian belief that God has come to us in Christ as if Christ were just such an intermediate being? This was what Arianism held. But, secondly, the docetic view of the Incarnation was also natural to the Hellenistic mind. If we are to say that Christ became man—and even Hellenism sometimes thinks of a saviour coming with a message from the higher world— it is all-important that the Divine saviour himself is completely untainted and unfettered by the lower, material world, from which he is to set free the souls of men.

Sharply opposed to such Hellenised views of Incarnation, the Early Church seeks to give unqualified affirmation to the Johannine idea, of the Word who was God and who became flesh. In Christ God Himself meets us, but He meets us in a real human life. Redemption means, not that God in Christ gives us instructions and an example of how to free ourselves from the conditions of our temporal life and raise ourselves up to fellowship with Him, but that God in His love has condescended to us, entered into our temporal conditions, and instituted fellowship with us. If Christ's earthly life was but apparently an ordinary human life, then the love He manifested in His life and death would be but an apparent love. We can only speak seriously of God's love to us in Christ if Christ is " of one substance with the Father " (ὁμοούσιος τῷ πατρί), for only then have we any right to see in Christ's love God's own love. But be He never so much " of one substance with the Father," who is love, there would still be no real love and fellowship if it was merely in appearance that He submitted to the conditions of human life and took upon Himself our burdens. Such is the religious content of the Nicene theology as affirmed by Athanasius and finally expressed in the formula of Chalcedon (A.D. 451) which says of Christ that He is " of one essence with the Father as regards His Godhead, and at the same time of one essence with us as regards His manhood."

Athanasius displays the same exultant spirit that is distinctive of Greek Christianity to this very day, the spirit of Easter.[1] The Divine life itself has come down to us in Christ. In His death and resurrection He has brought to nought the power of death, set free us who were thralls of sin and death, and brought life and immortality to light. It

---

[1] *Cf.* N. v. Arseniew, *Ostkirche und Mystik*, 1925, p. 1: " The *joy of the Resurrection*—that is the basal note which sounds through the entire *Weltanschauung* of the Eastern Church." " This song of victory, this jubilant, all-transfiguring *Easter joy* . . . this is the innermost soul of the Church of the East." *Ibid.*, p. 31.

is God Himself who in Christ accomplishes the saving work. This is the very foundation of Athanasius' theology. In opposition to Arian theory it gives remarkably clear expression to the Agape Way of salvation.

A very different impression is gained if we disregard Athanasius' polemical position and consider only his positive view of Christianity, as it appears in his early works, *Oratio contra Gentes* and *Oratio de incarnatione verbi*, or in the *Vita S. Antonii* which gives a good idea of his ascetic ideal. His dependence on Hellenistic thought is at once evident. Nor is this surprising, for Athanasius, after all, lived and worked in Alexandria, and it would have been astonishing had he been less influenced by the great Alexandrian tradition.

In the light of this, Athanasius grounds fellowship with God in man's original likeness to God—on the old Hellenistic and mystical principle that "like attracts like," a principle also found, he believes, in the biblical story of Creation, where man is created in the image of God (Gen. i. 26). This original endowment made it possible for man, through the co-operation of God's grace and his own powers, proudly to hold converse with God and lead a life truly blessed and immortal. "For having nothing to hinder his knowledge of the Deity (*i.e.*, Vision of God), he ever beholds, by his purity, the Image of the Father, the Divine Logos, after whose image he himself is made."[1] By the power of reason he could rise above the sense-world and all corporeal ideas, and enter into direct relations with the Divine things and τὰ νοητά in heaven. Man can, however, attain to God by

---

[1] Oratio contra gentes ii.; Migne, PG, vol. xxv., p. 5 D: ἵνα . . . ἔχων τὴν τοῦ δεδωκότος χάριν, ἔχων καὶ τὴν ἰδίαν ἐκ τοῦ πατρικοῦ λόγου δύναμιν, ἀγάλληται καὶ συνομιλῇ τῷ θείῳ, ζῶν τὸν ἀπήμονα καὶ μακάριον ὄντως τὸν ἀθάνατον βίον. οὐδὲν γὰρ ἔχων ἐμπόδιον εἰς τὴν περὶ τοῦ θείου γνῶσιν, θεωρεῖ μὲν ἀεὶ διὰ τῆς αὐτοῦ καθαρότητος τὴν τοῦ πατρὸς εἰκόνα, τὸν θεὸν λόγον, οὗ καὶ κατ' εἰκόνα γέγονεν.

this path only if his spirit has no concern with things corporeal, is untouched by that desire which is evoked from without, by the sense-world, but communes wholly and solely with itself on high.[1] " Then, transcending the things of sense and all things human, it is raised up on high; and seeing the Logos, it sees in Him also the Father of the Logos, taking pleasure in contemplating Him, and ever renewed in its desire towards Him."[2] For in its purity the soul " is in a position to see God in itself as in a mirror."[3]

No further analysis is needed. The motif which finds expression here is unmistakable, for Eros is in evidence at every point. But, the question arises, how does this relate to Athanasius' strong interest in the Incarnation, mentioned above?

What has been said of the unmediated vision of God refers to man in his original state, as he was created by God. Had this state continued, man would have been able of himself to know God and find his own way to fellowship with Him. This was possible, however, only if he neglected things of sense and concentrated on his own pure spirituality and God alone. Instead, men used the freedom of choice God had given[4] so as to turn away from God. They " began to seek

---

[1] Oratio contra gentes ii.; Migne, PG, vol. xxv., p. 8 A: . . . ὑπεράνω μὲν τῶν αἰσθητῶν καὶ πάσης σωματικῆς φαντασίας γινόμενος, πρὸς δὲ τὰ ἐν οὐρανοῖς θεῖα καὶ νοητὰ τῇ δυνάμει τοῦ νοῦ συναπτόμενος. ὅτε γὰρ οὐ συνομιλεῖ τοῖς σώμασιν ὁ νοῦς ὁ τῶν ἀνθρώπων, οὐδέ τι τῆς ἐκ τούτων ἐπιθυμίας μεμιγμένον ἔξωθεν ἔχει, ἀλλ᾽ ὅλος ἐστὶν ἄνω ἑαυτῷ συνὼν ὡς γέγονεν ἐξ ἀρχῆς.

[2] Ibid.: τότε δή, τὰ αἰσθητὰ καὶ πάντα τὰ ἀνθρώπινα διαβάς, ἄνω μετάρσιος γίνεται, καὶ τὸν λόγον ἰδών, ὁρᾷ ἐν αὐτῷ καὶ τὸν τοῦ λόγου πατέρα, ἡδόμενος ἐπὶ τῇ τούτου θεωρίᾳ, καὶ ἀνακαινούμενος ἐπὶ τῷ πρὸς τοῦτον πόθῳ.

[3] Ibid., p. 8 B: ἱκανὴ δὲ ἡ τῆς ψυχῆς καθαρότης ἐστὶ τὸν θεὸν δι᾽ ἑαυτῆς κατοπτρίζεσθαι. This is Athanasius' interpretation of the Beatitude: " Blessed are the pure in heart, for they shall see God " (Matt. v. 8).

[4] From the beginning there is a duality in man's nature: (1) he is created *out of nothing*, and (2) he is created *in the image of God*. ὁ μὲν γὰρ θεὸς οὐ μόνον ἐξ οὐκ ὄντων ἡμᾶς πεποίηκεν, ἀλλὰ καὶ τὸ κατὰ θεὸν ζῆν ἡμῖν ἐχαρίσατο τῇ τοῦ λόγου χάριτι. Or. de inc. verb. v., p. 104 C. Correspondingly, he has two possibilities: (1) as created *out of nothing* (that which is not) he is actually by

things nearer to themselves. But nearer to themselves were the body and its senses."[1] Their connection with God, the true Being, having been thus severed, they fell victims to death and corruption. What was God to do now? Was He to let men, in spite of their transgression, remain immortal? Then God would be a liar, since He had threatened them with death if they transgressed His commandment. Or was He to let men fall victims to death? Then God's plans would be thwarted and His work brought to nought. Why, then, did He create them at first? If they were to return to the "nothing" out of which He had created them, it would have become Him better never to have made them at all.[2] There is only one way out of this dilemma: the Incarnation. By it God's honour and veracity were upheld, for the Incarnate Logos took death upon Himself so that the consequence of sin was death, just as God had said. By it, also, God's work was saved from destruction, for the Incarnate Logos restored the corruptible to incorruption. Man had fallen back, through his transgression, into the original "nothing" given by nature, and had lost the likeness to God given by God's grace, and only the same Logos of God who created him of nothing in the beginning, could restore him from the "nothing" caused by sin.[3] The image of God by itself would have sufficed to give men knowledge of God,[4] if only

---

nature mortal; (2) as created *in the image of God* (*i.e.*, in the likeness of that which is) he could have become immortal. ἔστι μὲν γὰρ κατὰ φύσιν ἄνθρωπος θνητὸς, ἅτε δὴ ἐξ οὐκ ὄντων γεγονώς. διὰ δὲ τὴν πρὸς τὸν ὄντα ὁμοιότητα, ἣν εἰ ἐφύλαττε διὰ τῆς πρὸς αὐτὸν κατανοήσεως, ἤμβλυνεν ἂν τὴν κατὰ φύσιν φθοράν, καὶ ἔμεινεν ἄφθαρτος. . . . Or. de inc. verb. iv., p. 104 C. The decision as to which of these possibilities shall become actuality, God has placed in man's own hands. He has given him freedom and the right of self-determination, has made him αὐτεξούσιος (Or. contra gentes iv., p. 9 C). He has given him power to choose in either direction (*cf.* Or. de inc. verb. iii., p. 101 B: . . . τὴν ἀνθρώπων εἰς ἀμφότερα νεύειν δυναμένην προαίρεσιν).

[1] Or. contra gentes iii., p. 8 C.   [2] Or. de inc. verb. vi., p. 105 D f.
[3] Or. de inc. verb. vii., p. 108 D, and xiii, p. 120 B.
[4] Or. de inc. verb. xii., p. 116 D: αὐτάρκης μὲν γὰρ ἦν ἡ κατ᾽ εἰκόνα χάρις γνωρίζειν τὸν θεὸν λόγον, καὶ δι᾽ αὐτοῦ τὸν πατέρα.

they had been able to direct their gaze upwards; but they had lost this capacity, and held their gaze downward to the sense-world instead.[1] Not even in seeking God could they alter their direction, but they sought Him down below, among the created things. What else could the Logos do, then, when He would help them, but come as an ordinary man, assume a body like theirs, derived from below?[2] Like a good teacher, He takes account of their real position and stoops to their low level. "For seeing that men, having rejected the contemplation of God, and with their eyes downward, as though sunk in the deep, were seeking about for God in nature and in the world of sense, feigning gods for themselves of mortal men and demons, the Saviour, the Logos of God, in His love for humanity takes to Himself a body and as man walks among men; He takes to Himself also all the senses of men, to the end that they who think that God is corporeal may, from what the Lord effects by His body perceive the truth, and through Him learn to know the Father."[3]

So the Incarnation introduces Agape into the context of Eros. Athanasius' thought runs therefore in principle as follows: since man could no longer raise himself to the heavenly Eros, which in itself would be the right Way of salvation, the normal Way to fellowship with God, God must come down to him in Agape, must in Christ hold converse with him as a man among men. The idea of Agape and the Incarnation thus holds a secondary place; yet in this place it is taken quite seriously. Athanasius stresses again and again that Christ really descended to our level, submitted to our corruptibility, suffered our death,[4] and that He

---

[1] Or. de inc. verb. xiv., p. 121 B: οὐκέτι μὲν ἄνω, κάτω δὲ τοὺς ὀφθαλμοὺς ἐσχήκασιν.

[2] Ibid. ὡς ἄνθρωπος ἐπιδημεῖ, λαμβάνων ἑαυτῷ σῶμα ὅμοιον ἐκείνοις, καὶ ἐκ τῶν κάτω.

[3] Or. de inc. verb. xv., p. 121 C.

[4] εἰς τὴν ἡμετέραν χώραν. Or. de inc. verb. viii., p. 109 A. ἀλλὰ παραγί-

did all this by reason of His love.[1] Still, in the last resort Christ descends to our human level in order to enable us to ascend to the Divine level. The descent of Agape is the means, the ascent of Eros the end. Just as for Irenæus God's Agape reveals itself in the Incarnation, but does so, in Hellenistic fashion, with a view to the " deification " of man,[2] so for Athanasius, who allows Eros a much more dominant rôle, this last is even more true. If God's Logos has descended to us, it is in order that we might ascend to God. " He became man that we might become divine."[3]

νεται συγκαταβαίνων τῇ εἰς ἡμᾶς αὐτοῦ φιλανθρωπίᾳ. *Ibid.* καὶ τῇ φθορᾷ ἡμῶν συγκαταβάς. *Ibid.*, p. 109 B. καὶ τοῦτο φιλανθρώπως ποιῶν, ἵνα, ὡς μὲν πάντων ἀποθανόντων ἐν αὐτῷ, λυθῇ ὁ κατὰ τῆς φθορᾶς τῶν ἀνθρώπων νόμος. . . . *Ibid.*, p. 109 C.

[1] As Origen, so Athanasius in speaking of the love of God and Christ prefers to use the term φιλανθρωπία, often in connection with ἀγαθότης. Or. de inc. verb. i., p. 97 C, and xii., p. 117 B.

[2] Cf. supra, p. 410.

[3] . . . ἵνα ἡμεῖς θεοποιηθῶμεν. Or. de inc. verb. liv., p. 192 B. Cf. Or. contra arianos ii. 70; PG vol. xxvi., p. 296; iii. 33, p. 393 A. ὡς γὰρ ὁ κύριος, ἐνδυσάμενος τὸ σῶμα, γέγονεν ἄνθρωπος, οὕτως ἡμεῖς οἱ ἄνθρωποι παρὰ τοῦ λόγου τεθεοποιήμεθα (Migne, after other MSS, τε θεοποιούμεθα). iii. 34, p. 397 B. Θεοὶ διὰ τὸν ἐν ἡμῖν λόγον. iii. 25, p. 376 C. It is true he speaks of man's θεοποίησις with a certain reserve. Christ is called the Son of God and God φύσει καὶ ἀληθείᾳ, we are so called only κατὰ χάριν. iii. 19, p. 361 C f. He objects to the Arians that their position logically leads to the claim: " We shall ascend to heaven and be like the Most High." When he finds this will to ascend in the heretics, he is well aware of its diabolical presumption and folly; but when he tries to explain where the error lies, he reduces it to this, that the Arians claim to possess by nature what is only given by grace. τὰ γὰρ κατὰ χάριν διδόμενα τοῖς ἀνθρώποις, ταῦτα θέλουσιν ἴσα τῆς τοῦ διδόντος εἶναι θεότητος. *Ibid.*, iii. 17; p. 360 A. Ascent and deification remain man's goal. Athanasius thinks he adequately safeguards the distinction between divine and human by emphasising that God possesses His θεότης in and of Himself, whereas man obtains his θεότης by grace.

With regard to the deification of man, also, the Eastern Church has faithfully preserved the Athanasian type. *Cf. e.g.* Stefan Zankow, *Das orthodoxe Christentum des Ostens*, 1928, p. 44 f.: " Orthodox Christianity stresses both the Incarnation of God and the *deification* of man by means of that Incarnation. The most intimate and the everlasting union of God and man for our salvation in the Divine-human Person of Jesus Christ is the historical foundation of the new reality of Redemption, of the deification of humanity and the transfiguration of the world. This basic idea runs like a vital nerve through the whole realm of the faith and life of the Orthodox Church."

In addition, Athanasius is the great advocate of Virginity[1] and monachist piety—a fact particularly revealing for the structure of his thought. As the author of the *Vita S. Antonii*, Athanasius has helped perhaps more than any other to mould the ascetic ideal of Christianity. It is significant that it was the story of the hermit Antony which was the occasion of Augustine's conversion. One day, Augustine relates, he was visited by a fellow countryman, an African, one Ponticianus, who held a high office at the Imperial court. Ponticianus told him how two friends of his at the court had been won for the ascetic ideal through reading the *Vita Antonii* and had been enabled to renounce the world in order to devote themselves wholly to the service of God as hermits.[2] This story made an extraordinary impression on Augustine. He retired within himself and thought with shame: " The unlearned start up and ' take heaven by force,' and we, with our learning, and without heart, lo, where we wallow in flesh and blood !" And so there follows the great revolution in his life—as in the case of countless others under the direct influence of the *Vita Antonii*.[3]

---

[1] Athanasius finds one of the best proofs of the divinity of Christ in the fact that He has succeeded as no other in winning humanity to the virtue of Virginity. *Cf.* Or. de inc. verb. li., p. 185 D f.

[2] Augustini Confessiones, lib. VIII., cap. vi. 15.

The very words used to describe the new attitude of the two men reveal the Eros tendency: " Et ambo iam tui *ædificabant turrem* sumptu idoneo relinquendi omnia sua et sequendi te " (*Ibid.*). The comparison of the hermit's life with the building of a tower is probably not due solely to Luke xiv. 28 (" Quis enim ex vobis volens turrim ædificare, non prius sedens computat sumptus ? . . ."). Other associations may well have played their part. The simile of building a tower is apt when Christianity is interpreted on the lines of Eros. The Stylite ascends his tower or pillar in order to get as near heaven as possible. *Cf.* K. Holl, *Gesammelte Aufsätze zur Kirchengeschichte*, Bd. II., 1928, p. 396: " The monkish striving to come near to God is given a naïve, outward interpretation when the Stylite climbs on to a pillar in order to lessen the distance between himself and heaven."

[3] " Ita rodebar intus et confundebar pudore horribili uehementer, cum Ponticianus talia loqueretur. Terminato autem sermone et causa, qua uenerat, abiit ille, *et ego ad me.*" *Ibid.*, cap. vii. 18. " Hortulus quidam erat hospitii nostri. . . . Illuc me abstulerat tumultus pectoris, ubi nemo impediret ardentem litem, quam mecum aggressus eram, donec exiret qua tu sciebas, ego autem non." *Ibid.*, cap. viii. 19.

4. Gregory of Nyssa

Gregory of Nyssa, finally, is of particular interest. He, too, has the usual double-sidedness, though with far greater emphasis on the Eros motif. It was due to him and the other two "Cappadocians"—Basil the Great and Gregory of Nazianzus—that the Nicene theology finally won through, and to that extent the Agape motif finds a place, at times a really large place, in his thought. And yet he "hellenises" unblushingly, so that his outlook is in many ways reminiscent of Origen and Neoplatonism.

For the part played by *the Agape motif* in Gregory of Nyssa we must go to his *Great Catechism*, which mainly treats of the Incarnation. Here the idea of Agape finds a clear and forceful expression rarely equalled in the Early Church. Gregory has an unusually keen eye for the paradox in the idea of Incarnation and Divine descent. "Why, then, did the Deity descend to such humiliation? Our faith is staggered to think that God, that incomprehensible, inconceivable, and ineffable reality, transcending all glory of greatness, wraps Himself up in the base covering of humanity."[1] Gregory finds the answer in *the Divine love*. "If, then, love (ἡ φιλανθρωπία) be a special characteristic of the Divine nature, here is the reason for which you are in search, here is the cause of the presence of God among men."[2] Although Gregory, following Origenist tradition, uses the word φιλανθρωπία instead of Agape, it is plainly the Agape motif he has in view. But he goes still further. It might be thought that God's descent to the level of man was incompatible with Divine omnipotence, or that this latter was *concealed* in Christ's Incarnation and Passion; but Gregory asserts to the contrary that the Divine power is

---

[1] Oratio catechetica magna, cap. xiv.; Migne, PG, vol. xlv., p. 45 D.
[2] *Ibid.*, cap. xv., p. 48 A.

never more palpable and compelling than in this very descent.[1] That great and sublime things are done by the power of God is not a matter for wonder; that is of the nature and essence of Divinity. But the descent to lowliness reveals "a superabundance of power," for it shows that not even the nature of the Divine itself can set a limit to its power. For as "it is the peculiar property of fire to tend upwards (ἡ ἐπὶ τὸ ἄνω φορά), no one deems it wonderful in the case of flame to see that natural operation. But should the flame be seen to stream downwards, like heavy bodies, such a fact would be regarded as a miracle, namely how fire still remains fire, and yet by this change of direction in its motion (ἐν τῷ τρόπῳ τῆς κινήσεως) passes out of its nature by being borne downward. In like manner, it is not the vastness of the heavens, and the bright shining of its constellations, and the order of the universe, and the unbroken administration over all existence that so manifestly displays the transcendent power of the Deity, as this condescension to the weakness of our nature."[2] The simile of the flame is the more interesting as Gregory uses it quite differently in other contexts. Elsewhere, flame whose nature is to strive upwards serves as a symbol of the Eros tendency in man.[3] Here, however, in portrayal of the wonderful descent of Divine love, he takes the simile of the flame which contrary to its nature sinks down, and so by contrast gives extraordinary vividness to the meaning of Agape.

It is nevertheless not the Agape but *the Eros motif* that really characterises Gregory's thought. Here we meet the attitude of pure mysticism, with its whole apparatus of concepts that were traditional ever since Philo and Plotinus. There is the ecstatic Vision of God and the "bright dark-

---

[1] *Ibid.*, cap. xxiv., p. 64 B: πρῶτον μὲν οὖν τὸ τὴν παντοδύναμον φύσιν πρὸς τὸ ταπεινὸν τῆς ἀνθρωπότητος καταβῆναι ἰσχύσαι, πλείονα τὴν ἀπόδειξιν τῆς δυνάμεως ἔχει, ἢ τὰ μεγάλα τε καὶ ὑπερφυῆ τῶν θαυμάτων.

[2] *Ibid.*, p. 64 C f.

[3] *Cf. infra*, p. 445 f.

ness,"[1] and we hear of a " seeing by not seeing,"[2] a " knowing by not knowing," of a " sober intoxication,"[3] and so on. Gregory's great and ever-recurrent theme is *fellowship with God according to the scheme of ascent.*

Even the choice of subjects for his writings bears unequivocal witness to this tendency.

In the *Mystica interpretatio vitæ Moysis* (De vita Moysis) he depicts the mystical ascent of the soul to God on the basis of the narrative of Moses' life and especially of his ascent to God on Mount Sinai.[4] The fact that no irrational animal was allowed to approach the mountain is given the deeper meaning that in contemplating things spiritual it is necessary to rise above the knowledge given through the senses.[5] He who will ascend to behold the heavenly things must purify himself from every sensible and irrational emotion before he dares the ascent of the holy mountain. " For theology is in truth a steep mountain and difficult of access, so that the great multitude can scarcely reach the foot of the mountain; but if anyone is a Moses, he can ascend the mountain."[6] With Moses he can enter into the " bright darkness " where God Himself dwells. Fellowship with God begins, it is true, by being a light for man by contrast with the darkness of the sense-world; but everything ends at the last in the Divine darkness. Only when we have left behind not merely all that belongs to the senses but reason

---

[1] ὁ λαμπρὸς γνόφος. De vita Moysis; PG, vol. xliv., p. 377 A. ὁ θεῖος γνόφος. In Cant. Cantic., Homilia xi.; PG, vol. xliv., p. 1000 D.

[2] De vita Moysis, p. 377 A: ἐν τούτῳ γὰρ ἀληθής ἐστιν εἴδησις τοῦ ζητουμένου, τὸ (?) ἐν τούτῳ τὸ ἰδεῖν, ἐν τῷ μὴ ἰδεῖν.

[3] ἡ θεία τε καὶ νηφάλιος μέθη, δι' ἧς ἐξίσταται αὐτὸς ἑαυτοῦ. In Cant. Cantic., Hom. x., p. 992 A. ἡ ἀγαθή τε καὶ νηφάλιος μέθη. Ibid., Hom. v., p. 873 B. Cf. H. Lewy: *Sobria ebrietas. Untersuchungen zur Geschichte der antiken Mystik*, 1929.

[4] De vita Moysis, p. 372 D f.: . . . κατὰ τὴν τῆς ἱστορίας τάξιν τῇ ἀναγωγικῇ προσαρμόσαι τὸ νόημα.

[5] Ibid., p. 373 C.

[6] Ibid., p. 373 D f. Ibid., p. 376 A: ὄρος γάρ ἐστιν ἄναντες ὡς ἀληθῶς καὶ δυσπρόσιτον ἡ θεολογία, ἧς μόλις ὁ πολὺς λεὼς τὴν ὑπώρειαν φθάνει (εἰ δέ τις Μωϋσῆς εἴη, γένοιτο ἂν καὶ ἐπὶ τῆς ἀνόδου).

itself as well, and are lost in the invisible and inconceivable —only then do we behold God.[1]

To the same theme Gregory returns in his work *On the Beatitudes*.[2] Since Jesus spoke these words on a mountain Gregory will interpret each Beatitude as a stage in the spiritual mountain ascent,[3] or as a step upwards to the Vision of God and union with God. So his second discourse begins: "Those who wish to ascend a stair raise themselves, when they have mounted the first step, from that to the next above; the second step leads them again to the third, this to the next, this in turn to the next. And in this way he who ascends finally arrives, by always raising himself from the step on which he is to the next one, at the top step. Why do I begin with this introduction? It seems to me that the Beatitudes are arranged as the rungs of a ladder, and that this makes the successive ascent easy of contemplation."[4]

Gregory's work on the Song of Songs[5] is particularly interesting in this connection. It, too, is constructed wholly according to the scheme of ascent.[6] The Song of Songs, Gregory thinks, is the best guide to philosophy and the knowledge of God.[7] It is the breviary of Bride-mysticism, it contains, so to speak, the "philosophy of Bride-mysticism."[8]

[1] *Ibid.*, p. 376 D f.

[2] De beatitudinibus; PG, vol. xliv., p. 1193 ff.

[3] De beatitud., Oratio i., p. 1196 A: ἐπειδὴ οὖν ἀναβαίνει εἰς τὸ ὄρος ὁ κύριος . . . οὐκοῦν δράμωμεν καὶ ἡμεῖς πρὸς τὴν ἄνοδον.

[4] De beatitud., Or. ii., p. 1208 C f.

[5] In Cant. Cantic.; PG, vol. xliv., pp. 755-1120.

[6] This work swarms with expressions for the soul's ascent to God, of which the most frequent and characteristic may be mentioned. Often two or more are used together. For ἀναγωγή see Hom. v., p. 864 C; for ἀνάβασις, iv., p. 852 C; xv., p. 1109 D; v., p. 876 C; ix., p. 968 A; iv., p. 852 B; ix., p. 969 A; ix., p. 968 C; for ἄνω, ἄνειμι, ἄνοδος, ix., p. 968 C; iv., p. 852 D; xv., p. 1109 D; xii., p. 1029 C; v., p. 877 A; ix., p. 968 B; xi., p. 997 B; viii., p. 941 C; for ὕψος, ὑψόω, ὑψηλός, see further v., p. 864 A; ix., p. 968 C; ix., p. 968 B; vi., p. 889 C.

[7] In Cant. Cantic., Hom. ii., p. 788 C: πάλιν πρόκειται ἡμῖν τὸ ᾆσμα τῶν ᾀσμάτων, εἰς πᾶσαν θεογνωσίας καὶ φιλοσοφίας ὑφήγησιν.

[8] ἡ δὲ κατὰ ἀναγωγὴν θεωρία. Hom. v., p. 864 C. φαμὲν τοίνυν δόγμα τι τῶν ἀστειοτέρων τὴν ἐν τοῖς ῥητοῖς τούτοις φιλοσοφίαν διὰ τῶν ἐπαίνων τῆς νύμφης ἡμῖν παρατίθεσθαι. Hom. xv., p. 1109 A.

Here Gregory follows in the steps of Origen and Methodius. Like Origen, he uses the terms Eros and Agape interchangeably " without troubling about words," since they are simply different names for one and the same reality.[1] Describing how the soul is seized with love for God and Christ, he employs the old Eros metaphor and says it is wounded with " Love's arrow "; and it is significant that he speaks now of " Eros' arrow,"[2] now of " Agape's arrow."[3] Christ is " Agape's Archer "[4] who adroitly aims at the soul and does not miss his mark;[5] but He is also one who pierces the soul with " Eros' arrow."[6]

It seems, then, that Gregory uses the words Eros and Agape without distinction;[7] but did he never reflect on the relation between them? First, we must note that in the above quotations where the idea of Agape is clearly implied he uses the term φιλανθρωπία instead of Agape.[8] In the work on the Song of Songs the position is peculiar. Actually he is governed almost throughout by the Eros motif. As the word Agape, however, is used by his text, it seemed that he should use it too, yet he felt it was vague and indefinite. But

---

[1] Cf. supra, p. 389, n. 2.

[2] τὸ βέλος τοῦ ἔρωτος. Hom. xiii., p. 1048 C.

[3] τὸ βέλος τῆς ἀγάπης. Hom. v., p. 860 A. There is also found " Agape's sweet arrow," τὸ γλυκὺ τῆς ἀγάπης βέλος. Hom. iv., p. 852 B.

[4] ὁ τῆς ἀγάπης τοξότης. Hom. xiii., p. 1044 B.

[5] Hom. iv., p. 852 A: ἐπαινεῖ τὸν τοξότην τῆς εὐστοχίας, ὡς καλῶς ἐπ' αὐτὴν τὸ βέλος εὐθύναντα.

[6] Hom. xiii., p. 1048 C. By changing the picture Gregory makes man represent the arrow, which Christ, " Agape's Archer," puts to the bowstring and shoots at the mark on high.

[7] As further evidence we have: σώζεται δέ πως ἐν τοῖς λεγομένοις, ὡς ἐν γαμικῇ θυμηδίᾳ, ἡ ἀγαπητικὴ φιλοφροσύνη, δι' ἀμοιβῆς παρ' ἀμφοτέρων ἀλλήλοις τὴν ἐρωτικὴν ἀντιχαριζομένων διάθεσιν. Hom. ix., p. 956 A. φόβῳ καὶ οὐκ ἀγάπῃ . . . φόβῳ δουλικῷ, καὶ οὐχὶ ἔρωτι νυμφικῷ. Hom. xv., p. 1116 B. ἀγάπησον ὅσον δύνασαι ἐξ ὅλης καρδίας τε καὶ δυνάμεως, ἐπιθύμησον ὅσον χωρεῖς. προστίθημι δὲ θαρρῶν τοῖς ῥήμασι τούτοις καὶ τὸ ἐράσθητι. Hom. i., p. 772 A.

[8] The same is true in cases where Gregory touches on the idea of Agape or the descent of Divine love in his exposition of the Song of Songs. Here, too, he uses as a rule φιλανθρωπία. Cf. e.g. Hom. x., p. 988 A: ἡ δὲ κατάβασις τὸ τῆς φιλανθρωπίας ἔργον διασημαίνει.

Eros he found as a technical term in the Hellenistic tradition which in all essentials he was following. Hence he readily adopts the term Eros when speaking of love in a pregnant sense. And in one place he defines the relation between Eros and Agape thus: *a heightened and intensified Agape is called Eros.*[1] But just as Origen is somewhat hesitant about putting Eros on equal terms with Agape, and feels obliged to defend his action,[2] so Gregory is similarly hesitant. As he goes on it becomes clear that he was at least to some extent conscious that his statement was peculiar, and needed explanation. No one, says Gregory, as he seeks to forestall a very probable objection, need be ashamed of being wounded by this arrow of Eros, for it is not anything that has to do with bodily and material existence. That wound is rather one to be proud of, since the heart is thereby inflamed with love for things immaterial.[3] Gregory seeks thus to strengthen his case for letting Eros stand in the place of, or even higher than Agape, by pointing out that not the vulgar Eros but the heavenly Eros is meant.

It would be easy from Gregory's writings to multiply proof that his thought is dominated by the upward tendency.[4] The question which concerns us here, however, is simply how Gregory supposes fellowship with God to be brought about.

Like Athanasius, but to a far higher degree, Gregory founds man's fellowship with God upon his original likeness to God and kinship of nature with Him. He assumes the

---

[1] *ἐπιτεταμένη γὰρ ἀγάπη ἔρως λέγεται.* Hom. xiii., p. 1048 C.

[2] *Cf. supra,* p. 391, n. 1, especially " nec puto quod culpari possit. . . ."

[3] In Cant. Cantic., Hom. xiii., p. 1048 C f.

[4] We may recall that in his " In psalmorum inscriptiones " Gregory says that the five books of the Psalter represent five stages on the way up to the Divine life. For an impression of this " Philosophy of the Psalter " (ἡ κατὰ τὴν ψαλμ-ῳδίαν φιλοσοφία) see the beginning of chap. viii., PG, vol. xliv., p. 465 C f. Here Gregory has reached the fifth stage of the ascent; we are taken to the " highest peak," the " topmost step of contemplation," and we hear of wings stretched out for flight, of the " eagle-nature " which fastens the eye of the soul upon the brilliance of the light and mounts aloft.

axiom that " like attracts like," and recalls the Platonic and
Neoplatonic idea of the " eye like to the sun in nature."[1]
Just as the bodily eye can see and take in light from without
only because it itself contains a beam of light, so too man,
if he is to be able to know God, must possess in his nature
something akin (συγγενής) to God.[2] Therefore God, as
Scripture testifies, has created man in His own image so that
" by means of the like it sees the like."[3] What then must
man do in order to get into touch with God? Gregory
advises: " If thou wilt know God, know first thyself!"
Enter within thyself and consider thine own nature; there
thou hast a picture of God's nature.[4] " Know thyself " thus
means: " Know the nobility of thy nature and thine inner
worth, know the divinity that dwelleth in thee."[5] To do
this is not easy, however, for man's nature is difficult to
penetrate and interpret.[6] It is, so to say, a mixture of two
worlds, of the immaterial, immortal soul, and of the material
body, composed of the four elements.[7] Consequently, man
is dragged downwards by his bodily nature; he finds it easy
to see external things, but himself as he really is he cannot
comprehend. And yet to know oneself is the indispensable
condition for knowing God. He who will " philosophise
about God," says Gregory, must start not from external
things, but from within himself.[8]

Nevertheless, Gregory insists that man's likeness to God
must not be understood as if the soul were identical with

---

[1] Cf. supra, p. 194.

[2] De infantibus qui præmature abripiuntur; Migne, PG, vol. xlvi., p. 173 D.

[3] Ibid., p. 176 A: ὡς ἂν, οἶμαι, τῷ ὁμοίῳ βλέπειν τὸ ὅμοιον.

[4] Quid sit, Ad imaginem Dei; PG, vol. xliv., p. 1332 A: εἰ βούλει γνῶναι θεὸν, προλαβὼν γνῶθι σεαυτόν· ἐκ τῆς σαυτοῦ συνθέσεως, ἐκ τῆς σαυτοῦ κατασκευῆς, ἐκ τῶν ἐντὸς σεαυτοῦ. εἴσιθι ὑποδὺς ἐν σαυτῷ.

[5] κατάμαθε σεαυτοῦ τὸ τίμιον. In verba, Faciamus hominem ad imaginem et similitudinem nostram, Oratio i.; PG, vol. xliv., p. 260 B.

[6] Quid sit, Ad imag. Dei, p. 1328 A.

[7] Ibid., p. 1328 B: . . . ὥσπερ τινὰ μικτὸν κόσμον συγγενῆ τῶν δύο κόσμων.

[8] εἰ φιλοσοφεῖν περὶ τοῦ κατ' εἰκόνα καὶ ὁμοίωσιν θεοῦ βούλει, οὕτω φιλοσόφησον, οὐκ ἐκ τῶν ἐκτὸς, ἀλλ' ἐκ τῶν ἐντός σου. . . . Ibid., p. 1340 B.

God.[1] He will not be responsible for such a blasphemy.[2] There is an absolute distinction between the Divine and the human, and it must be upheld: God is the archetype, man merely the copy.[3] So when man contemplates God in the depths of his own being, it is but the reflection of God that he sees, just as we can see the whole orb of the sun in a mirror and get a correct picture of it, though on a small scale.[4] But between ourselves and God there is also this fundamental difference, that as created beings we must direct our desire to the Beautiful and seek to acquire it, whereas God is exalted above all desire. He does not need to seek anything outside Himself since He already possesses all things in Himself. In true Platonic spirit Gregory writes: "Since our nature is indigent of Beauty, it always reaches out after what it lacks. And this longing is the desire that lies in our constitution."[5] God, on the other hand, is the fulness of all Good and is the Beautiful in itself. "Therefore He looks only at Himself; and He wishes only for what He has, and has already all that He wishes and longs for nothing that is outside Himself."[6]

This natural *desire* in man, aroused by the sense of his own deficiency and reaching out towards the Beautiful, is plainly the same reality which Plato calls *Eros*; Gregory, however, calls it alternately ἐπιθυμία and ἀγάπη. Thus *Agape* means for him *fundamentally love in the sense of desire*;[7] constitutive of it is its connection with the Beautiful and its ceaseless effort to win this for itself.[8]

---

[1] De anima et resurrectione; PG, vol. xlvi., p. 28 A: οὐ γὰρ δὴ ταὐτόν ἐστι τῷ θεῷ ἡ ψυχή.

[2] *Ibid.*, p. 41 B: μὴ ταὐτὸν εἴπῃς . . . ἀσεβὴς γὰρ καὶ οὗτος ὁ λόγος.

[3] *Ibid.*, p. 44 A: ἐπειδὴ καὶ νοητῆς οὐσίας ἐστὶν εἰκών, μὴ μέντοι τὴν αὐτὴν τῷ ἀρχετύπῳ τὴν εἰκόνα λέγειν.

[4] *Ibid.*, p. 41 C.   [5] *Ibid.*, p. 92 C.   [6] *Ibid.*, p. 93 A.

[7] He expressly defines it: τοῦτο γάρ ἐστιν ἡ ἀγάπη, ἡ πρὸς τὸ καταθύμιον ἐνδιάθετος σχέσις. *Ibid.*, p. 93 C. On the connection between ἐπιθυμία and ἀγάπη cf. also Quid sit, Ad imag. Dei, etc.; PG, vol. xliv., p. 1336 B: . . . διὰ μὲν τοῦ ἐπιθυμητικοῦ πρὸς τὴν τοῦ θεοῦ ἀγάπην συνάπτηται.

[8] . . . τῆς ἀγαπητικῆς διαθέσεως, φυσικῶς τῷ καλῷ προσφυομένης. De

Agape is the yearning in every man for what can make his life richer and happier. But it can seek its good in two different directions; it can "by reason of a false judgment concerning the good, be balked of it, or by reason of a right judgment, find it."[1] The former happens when the search is directed downwards towards the sense-world, the latter when it is directed upwards towards God. The danger of life in the world is that men are tempted to pursue the shadows of the sense-world. In order to avoid this the virgin life is recommended.[2] It is not, however, intended that desire should be abolished outright. For desire is an integral part of man's nature, indeed it actually belongs to the image of God in man.[3] Even if the Agape-desire happens for the moment to be misdirected downwards towards things sensible and irrational,[4] that is no reason for wishing to tear it up by the roots; to do so would be to "pull up the wheat with the tares" (Matt. xiii. 29). "Therefore the wise husbandman leaves this growth that has been introduced amongst his seed to remain there, so as to secure our not being altogether stripped of better hopes by desire having been rooted out along with that good-for-nothing growth. If our nature suffered such a mutilation, what will there be to lift us up to grasp the heavenly delights? If Agape is taken from us, how shall we be united to God?"[5]

---

anima et resurrect.; PG, vol. xlvi., p. 93 C. The peculiar phrase ἡ ἀγαπητικὴ διάθεσις is thus synonymous with ἡ ἐρωτικὴ διάθεσις. For ἀγαπητική= ἐρωτική cf. supra, p. 434, n. 7.

[1] De anima et resurrectione, p. 92 C.

[2] De virginitate; PG, vol. xlvi., pp. 317 f.

[3] καὶ τοῦ μὲν δημιουργικοῦ τοῦ θεοῦ τὸ κατ' εἰκόνα ἐστὶ τὸ τῆς ψυχῆς ἐπιθυμητικόν· ἡ γὰρ ἐπιθυμία εἰς πρᾶξιν ἄγει. Quid sit, Ad imag. Dei, etc.; PG, vol. xliv., p. 1336 C.

[4] De anima et resurrect.; PG, vol. xlvi., p. 65 A: ἥ τε τῆς ἀγάπης δύναμις τῶν νοητῶν ἀπέστη, περὶ τὴν τῶν αἰσθητῶν ἀπόλαυσιν πέρα τοῦ μέτρου ὁλομανήσασα.

[5] Ibid.: ἡ τῆς ἀγάπης ἀφαιρεθείσης, τίνι τρόπῳ πρὸς τὸ θεῖον συναφθη-σόμεθα;

Desire is not to be rooted out, but *purified* and directed to the right objects—that is, to that which is in itself Beautiful, or God. Desire (Agape), by its very nature, turns in its intention towards the Beautiful, and likewise the Beautiful by its very nature arouses desire and draws it to itself.[1] These two, desire and the Beautiful, are meant for one another and must find one another. Their union can be hindered only if the sense-world comes between and draws desire to itself. But if desire has been purified from all taint of sense, there is no longer anything to distract it, no obstacle to its union with God. "If then," writes Gregory, "the soul is purified of all evil, it will be entirely in the sphere of the Beautiful. The Deity is in very substance beautiful; *and with the Deity the soul will therefore enter into communion in virtue of its purity.*"[2]

Our question is now answered as to how Gregory of Nyssa believes fellowship with God to be brought about. At every point the answer indicates the Eros Way of salvation. Fellowship with God is fellowship on God's own level, the level of holiness.[3] It is a fellowship to which man gains access "in virtue of his purity" and because he is by nature

---

[1] *Ibid.*, p. 89 B: τὸ γὰρ καλὸν ἑλκτικόν πως κατὰ τὴν ἑαυτοῦ φύσιν πάντος τοῦ πρὸς ἐκεῖνο βλέποντος.

[2] *Ibid.*

[3] How literally Gregory means this, the following shows. "By this prayer (the fifth clause of the Lord's Prayer) the Word of God prescribes what sort of man he must be who is to draw near to God: he hardly seems any longer to be within the bounds of human nature, but makes himself like God by his virtue (οὐκέτι σχεδὸν ἐν ἀνθρωπίνης φύσεως ὅροις δεικνύμενον, ἀλλ' αὐτῷ τῷ θεῷ διὰ τῆς ἀρετῆς ὁμοιούμενον). . . . If anyone, therefore, imitates the special characteristics of the Divine nature, he himself becomes in a sense God, a copy of whom he hereby clearly shows himself to be. Now what does the Word teach us? That we first through our works gain confidence to pray for forgiveness for the sins we have committed." De oratione Dominica, Or. v.; PG, vol. xliv., p. 1177 A f. To be able to enter into fellowship with God, we must first have made ourselves akin to Him by our virtue: χρὴ τῷ κατ' ἀρετὴν βίῳ τὸν θεὸν οἰκειώσασθαι. *Ibid.*, Or. ii., p. 1144 B. First we must purify our lives from sin; when that is done we may dare to pray to God and call Him our Father: οὐκοῦν ἐπικίνδυνον πρὶν καθαρθῆναι τῷ βίῳ τῆς προσευχῆς ταύτης κατατολμῆσαι, καὶ πατέρα ἑαυτοῦ τὸν θεὸν ὀνομάσαι. *Ibid.*

akin to God.[1] Our enquiry has confirmed what we said above, that Agape in Gregory is but another name for what is otherwise called Eros. Gregory's treatment of the words "God is love" points to the same conclusion. Since Agape is desire, and since no desire can exist in the self-sufficient, all-possessing Deity,[2] then it ought really to be impossible to speak of Agape in God. Plotinus once had a similar difficulty with the idea of Eros: Eros is desire, and as such ought to have no place at all in the Divine life. Yet Plotinus says "God is Eros." God is Eros to Himself; He loves Himself and enjoys His own beauty and perfection.[3] In Gregory we find the same argument almost word for word. "God is Agape"; that is, God is Agape to Himself; He enjoys the beauty and perfection which He finds in Himself: "For the life of the Supreme Being is Agape, seeing that the Beautiful is necessarily loved by those who know it; but the Deity knows Himself, and this knowledge becomes love."[4] So the Divine life revolves ceaselessly within itself, knowing itself and loving itself. In this sense we may say that God is Agape: ἀεὶ ἡ θεία ζωὴ δι᾽ ἀγάπης ἐνεργηθήσεται.[5]

5. Eros Symbols in Gregory of Nyssa

In controversy it is extremely valuable for a religious motif to have at its disposal easily understandable and suggestive pictures and symbols. The importance of symbols as means of campaign and conquest cannot be overrated. Theoretical discussions and doctrines are more difficult to grasp, and

---

[1] " Since every nature attracts what is akin to it, and humanity is akin to God and bears God's image in itself, so the soul is of necessity attracted to the kindred (συγγενής) Deity." De anima et resurrectione, p. 97 B.

[2] Ibid., p. 96 A: . . . ἐπιθυμίας ἐν ἐκείνῳ μὴ οὔσης διὰ τὸ μηδέ τινος τῶν ἀγαθῶν ἔνδειαν ἐν αὐτῷ εἶναι.

[3] Cf. supra, pp. 197 ff.

[4] ἡ δὲ γνῶσις ἀγάπη γίνεται. De anima et resurrectione, p. 96 C.

[5] Ibid.

even when understood they often leave the personal life untouched, whereas an appropriate symbol can immediately grip and convince without any proof. It is easily grasped and remembered, and even if its exact meaning is not fully comprehended, it still has remarkable power to fire the imagination and engage the will. Perhaps much of the reason for the success of the Eros motif is to be found in its easily accessible and well-developed symbolism.

We have seen how the strength of the Eros motif increases through the compromise theology of the fourth century, until it becomes, if not the only, at least the decisive factor in Gregory of Nyssa. He loves to talk in pictures and parables and is a master of symbols. By way of illustration we may recall how he depicts the paradox of the descent of Divine love under the figure of the flame which, contrary to its nature, sinks downwards. This figure was used in the service of the Agape motif; but the great majority of his pictures and symbols are intended to give expression to the Eros motif. In conclusion, therefore, it will not be out of place to gather together some of the most common and important Eros symbols.

1. *The Heavenly Ladder.* The idea of a ladder by which the human soul can climb to the higher world was prevalent in the mystery religions, and Plato's *Symposium* made the heavenly ladder part of the indispensable stock-in-trade of Eros metaphysics and Eros piety. We find it in Aristotle and Neoplatonism, in Gnosticism and Origen, and it underlies the general world-view, modelled on the " Alexandrian world-scheme," of late antiquity and the Middle Ages. It was only natural that Gregory of Nyssa should make abundant use of this symbol. He likes to picture the Christian life as a ladder on which the human soul, by its own power or with Divine aid, has to raise itself " methodically " step by step up to God. So the Bride in the Song of Songs

is led up on high by the Logos on the ladder of Virtue.[1]
This is primarily the ladder of Merit, but the same symbol
is also used for the ladder of Contemplation. We have seen
that Gregory regards the Beatitudes as a ladder set up for us
by Christ, upon which our meditation can ascend to the
Divine majesty. He finds a type of this " ladder of the
Beatitudes "[2] in Jacob's ladder. " It was the virtuous life
which was shown to the Patriarch under the figure of a
ladder, in order that he himself might learn and also impart
to his descendants, that one can ascend to God only if one
always looks upwards and has a ceaseless desire for the
things above, so that one is not satisfied with what has
already been attained, but counts it as loss if one cannot
reach that which is higher. Here the sublimity of the Beatitudes ranged one above another makes it possible for us to
draw near to God Himself, the truly Blessed, who is enthroned above all blessednesses. Just as we draw near to the
wise through wisdom, and the pure through purity, so we
approach the Blessed by the way of the Beatitudes. For
blessedness is in truth that which is distinctive of God,
wherefore also Jacob saw God enthroned upon a ladder. To
participate in the Beatitudes is nothing other than to participate in the Deity, to whom the Lord leads us up by means
of what has been said."[3] Gregory's whole theology is,

[1] ὁρῶμεν τοίνυν ὥσπερ ἐν βαθμῶν ἀναβάσει χειραγωγουμένην διὰ τῶν
τῆς ἀρετῆς ἀνόδων ἐπὶ τὰ ὕψη παρὰ τοῦ λόγου τὴν νύμφην. In Cant. Cantic.,
Hom. v.; PG, vol. xliv., p. 876 B. On the heavenly ladder and ladder symbolism
see supra, pp. 174, 185, 188 f., 221, 230.
[2] ὁ πρὸς τὰ ὑψηλότερα τῆς τῶν μακαρισμῶν κλίμακος χειραγωγῶν
ἡμᾶς λόγος. De beatitudinibus, Or. iv.; PG, vol. xliv., p. 1232 D.
[3] De beatitudinibus, Or. v.; PG, vol. xliv., p. 1248 D. This passage is
interesting not simply for the κλῖμαξ-symbol, but in several other respects too:
(1) By an abundant variety of expressions for ascent—πρὸς τὰ ὑψηλότερα—
ἀνιόντας—ἐπαίρουσα—πρὸς τὸν θεὸν ὑψωθῆναι—πρὸς τὰ ἄνω βλέποντα—
τὴν τῶν ὑψηλῶν ἐπιθυμίαν—τοῦ ὑπερκειμένου—ὕψος τῶν ἐπ' ἀλλήλων
μακαρισμῶν—πάσης ἐπεστηριγμένῳ μακαριότητος—ἀγάγει—it splendidly
illustrates the tendency on which Gregory's whole interpretation of Christianity is
based. (2) It combines the idea of " the heavenly ladder of Merit (Virtue)" with
that of " the heavenly ladder of Contemplation." (3) It shows as clearly as can be

strictly speaking, nothing but an attempt to answer the question which he has himself formulated thus: Where is this Jacob's ladder to be found? Where is the fiery chariot that can take us, as once the prophet Elijah, up to heaven?[1]

2. *The Wings of the Soul.* A graphic and inevitable illustration of the Eros Way of salvation is that of the wings which lift up the soul to participation in the Divine life. Its use was the more obvious since Eros theory had always stood in close connection with the astral religion of antiquity. Before beginning its heavenly journey the soul must be purified from all taint of things corporeal, whose weight would otherwise drag it down and bind it to the material world. But further, it must be furnished with wings to bear it aloft, through the ocean of air, through the planet spheres, up to the heaven of the fixed stars and to the abode of the Deity, high above all change and movement. This Eros symbol, too, had been developed by Plato, in the famous myth of the *Phædrus.* Gregory cannot accept Plato's view in its entirety, and rejects particularly the idea of the transmigration of souls, yet he readily uses the symbol of the wings of the soul. An interesting example is found in his exposition of the opening words of the Lord's Prayer. Referring to Ps. lv. 6, but utterly misrepresenting its sense, he cries: " Who will give me these wings so that I can in the spirit mount aloft to a height answering to these words? So that I leave the whole earth beneath me, cross the whole intervening ocean of air, reach the beauty of the ether and ascend to the stars and behold their wonderful order! So that I do not stop even here, but pass beyond these also and come outside all those things that are subject to motion and change, and finally come to that absolutely immutable nature, that power

---

that Gregory's theology is (to use Luther's phrase) a " theologia gloriæ ": God's wisdom is grasped by our wisdom, His purity by our purity; we learn to know God's nature in that by the heavenly ladder we " climb up to God's majesty."

[1] *Ibid.*, Or. vi., p. 1272 D.

exalted above all motion, which guides and sustains all that has existence, all that depends upon the ineffable will of the Divine wisdom!"[1]

Now Gregory perceived that these lofty notions and the assertion that it is possible to behold God in His majesty, apparently conflict with both Old Testament and Christian tradition. Through Moses God says: "No man can see me and live" (Ex. xxxiii. 20), and with this "the great John" and "the sublime Paul" also agree (Jn. i. 18; 1 Tim. vi. 16).[2] Gregory attempts to resolve the contradiction which he has rightly observed between his own Hellenistic ideas and the biblical view on this point, by arguing as follows. Christ, after all, has said: "Blessed are the pure in heart, for they shall see God." But what use would that be to us, if we lacked the elementary qualifications for such a Vision of God? "Does the Lord really enjoin upon us something that is beyond our nature, and does He exceed with His splendid commandment the measure of human strength? No, that is by no means the case. He does not command those to fly, to whom He has not given wings in Creation."[3] Surely John, Paul and Moses were pure in heart? Then we must assume, despite their declarations to the contrary, that they also beheld God.

3. *The Ascent of the Mountain.* Besides the two old Eros symbols of the heavenly ladder and the wings of the soul, Gregory has a number of new ones. Of these his most characteristic is the symbol of the mountain ascent, which we have already seen him use to represent the Christian life. It was from a *mountain* Jesus spoke the Beatitudes, thereby

---

[1] De oratione Dominica, Or. ii.; PG, vol. xliv., p. 1140 B f. *Cf.* De beatitudinibus, Or. ii., p. 1209 A: ἀλλ' εἰ πτερωθείημέν πως τῷ λόγῳ, καὶ ὑπὲρ τὰ νῶτα τῆς οὐρανίας ἀψίδος σταίημεν—the usual Eros idea of mounting on the wings of the soul *beyond* the vault of heaven. *Cf.* also De virginitate, cap. xi.; PG, vol. xlvi., p. 365 C.

[2] De beatitudinibus, Or. vi., p. 1264 C.

[3] *Ibid.*, p. 1265 D: οὔτε γὰρ πτηνοὺς γενέσθαι κελεύει, οἷς τὸ πτερὸν οὐκ ἐνέφυσεν.

showing that they are to be understood as different stages in our spiritual mountain ascent, as steps in our ascent to God: God bade Moses ascend the *mountain* to Himself, so giving us a type of the spiritual ascent, which begins with purification at the foot of the mountain and ends in the Divine " bright darkness " at the top; and so on.

4. *The Arrow*. When the Bride in the Song of Songs says: " I am sick of love " (cap. ii. 5), this can only mean that she had been wounded by Christ with " Love's arrow," Gregory thinks. Therefore the words which follow—" His left hand is under my head, and his right hand doth embrace me " (ver. 6)—must also refer to the " Archer," Christ, and show how He sets about bending the bow and shooting the arrow. But this changes the picture. At first it was the Bride who was wounded by the arrow; now the Bride herself, that is, the soul purified and seized with heavenly love, is the arrow. " Therefore she says: ' His left hand is under my head,' whereby the arrow is directed to the mark. But ' his right hand doth embrace me,' and draws me to Him, and makes me light for the ascent."[1] Gregory thinks this gives him the true meaning of " the philosophy of the divine ascent " as it is found in the Song of Songs.[2] The human soul is the arrow which is set upon the bowstring by Christ and shot towards the heavenly mark; but the force which carries it aloft is love's (Agape's = the heavenly Eros') longing.

5. *The Flame*. We have seen the metaphor of the flame used as a symbol of the Agape motif—the flame which contrary to its nature burns downwards. But that is an exception. As a rule the flame is a symbol of the Eros motif. One example must suffice: Gregory's explanation of " Blessed are the meek." He starts from the view that two opposite tendencies strive for the mastery in man, the

[1] In Cant. Cantic., Hom. iv.; PG, vol. xliv., p. 852 D.
[2] . . . ὡς ἂν, οἶμαι, κατὰ ταὐτὸν ἐν τοῖς διπλοῖς αἰνίγμασι τὰ περὶ τῆς θείας ἀναβάσεως ὁ λόγος φιλοσοφήσειεν. *Ibid.*, p. 852 C.

downward and the upward tendencies, the attraction to evil and the attraction to good. The first is best illustrated by a *heavy body*: it does not move at all in an upward direction, but downwards it moves all the more as its own weight hastens its fall. The second is best illustrated by a *flame*: in accord with its nature it strives upward, but displays no movement at all in a downward direction. The same applies to virtue: it strives to mount ever higher and higher. Since, however, the evil, downward tendency preponderates in us, the immobility of meekness is already a proof that the good tendency is on the way to victory. "Blessed are the meek," therefore, because meekness (which Gregory virtually identifies with apathy), in that it refuses to be dragged down by the passions, is proof of upward movement.[1]

6. *The Chain of Love.* According to Gregory, as we have seen, desire is not simply a force that drags man downwards; it also plays a certain part in his ascent to God. Without desire, Gregory holds, there would be nothing " which could lift us up to union with the heavenly." Therefore he does not intend that desire should be rooted out of us. It only needs to be purified and directed upwards. In one passage he illustrates this function of desire in the ascent, by the simile of a " chain, which draws us up from earth towards God."[2] If we add that desire, ἐπιθυμία, in Gregory's view is synonymous with ἀγάπη, we are thus given the idea of " the chain of love." This simile is introduced rather by the way, and cannot be quoted as specially characteristic of Gregory; but it is interesting to find a symbol which is later of some importance in Proclus and Dionysius the Areopagite and further on in the Middle Ages, already present in Gregory of Nyssa.

---

[1] De beatitudinibus, Or. ii., p. 1213 C: τὸ γὰρ ἡσύχιον ἐν τούτοις τῆς πρὸς τὰ ἄνω κινήσεως μαρτυρία γίνεται.

[2] . . . ὅτι δι' ἐπιθυμίαν πρὸς τὸν θεὸν ἀγαγόμεθα, οἷόν τινα σειρὰν κάτωθεν πρὸς αὐτὸν ἀνελκόμενοι. De anima et resurrectione; PG, vol. xlvi., p. 89 A.

II

THE COMPLETION OF THE SYNTHESIS

CHAPTER TWO

THE CARITAS-SYNTHESIS

I

AUGUSTINE'S POSITION IN THE HISTORY OF RELIGION

1. The Christian Idea of Love in a New Phase

THE development of the Christian idea of love in the first four centuries might well seem to have exhausted its possibilities. At the outset, an absolutely new fundamental motif of religion and ethics, the Agape motif, stands in sharp contrast to the contemporary fundamental motifs of Judaism and Hellenism, Nomos and Eros. But inevitably these three are soon brought into contact. A person of Jewish antecedents views the Christian idea of Agape in a different light from one who comes to it with Hellenistic prepossessions. Hence there arise different types of the Christian idea of love, moulded in some cases more by the Nomos motif, in others by the Eros motif, while yet others more faithfully preserve the primitive Christian Agape motif. These types rival one another with varying measures of success and defeat, though none finally supersedes the rest. The result is a compromise containing clear reminiscences of the Agape motif, though this is so far modified as to be scarcely any longer an independent motif. The idea of Agape seems to have lost its original force and to be destined to disappear.

The continued history of the Christian idea of love, however, shows that this is far from the case. Just when its resources seem exhausted, it begins a new and vigorous development to which all that has gone before is but the prelude. The renewal comes through Augustine, for whom several circumstances combine to make him see Christian love with new eyes. He perceives that love is the very heart of Christianity, and there is scarcely a word of the New Testament that he does not use repeatedly in expounding Christian love. Beyond question, here is one of the most important turning points in the whole history of the Christian idea of love, and perhaps the most radical of all, in view of its results.

Augustine's originality can usually be questioned, but his doctrine of love is a really *new contribution*. He has a unique capacity for assimilating the most varied sorts of material, and even though he is not a merely passive borrower, such a receptive and eclectic attitude cannot but limit his originality to a large degree. Nor is this receptivity absent in his view of love; almost all the materials for it, and frequently the plans for its construction also, are drawn from earlier sources. Yet here more than elsewhere he has succeeded in leaving his personal impress on the borrowed material. The plan of the whole is so solid and coherent that his original and creative work cannot be denied. After Augustine the Christian idea of love is no longer the same as before.

Further, Augustine's view of love has exercised by far the greatest influence in the whole history of the Christian idea of love. It even puts the New Testament view of love in the shade. New Testament texts continue to form the basis of discussion, but they are *interpreted* in accordance with Augustine. Ever since his time the meaning of Christian love has generally been expressed in the categories he created, and even the emotional quality which it bears is largely due to him. Not even the Reformation succeeded in making any serious alteration. In Evangelical Christendom to the present day, Augustine's view has done far more than Luther's to determine what is meant by Christian love.

This universal influence has been possible because of Augustine's peculiar position in the history of religion. He lives on the frontier of two separate religious worlds, those of Hellenistic Eros and primitive Christian Agape, and his significance lies chiefly in the fact that *these worlds really meet in his person and form a spiritual unity*. Naturally, Augustine does not stand alone as regards this synthesis; some of the foremost men of the Early Church were occupied with the very same problem. But none succeeded like Augustine. Generally speaking, the two fundamental motifs made no real inner contact in the other attempts at synthesis, or else when these attempts were in a measure successful, they failed for other reasons to determine future development—Origen is a case in point. The streams of Eros and Agape meet in Augustine; yet he does not receive passively what they bring to him. He lives actively in both worlds with his whole soul, so that the two motifs are brought into a mutual relationship which is far from superficial. The conflict between them is really settled, but not in such a way that either motif finally defeats and expels the other. If the Agape motif gains ground as Augustine develops, the Eros motif is not correspondingly thrust aside. On the contrary, *both* assert their influence throughout his development, and both together mould his definitive view. In the nature of the case, therefore, this view contains not only strong tensions, but real inner contradictions.

In Augustine *a new view of love emerges*. The meeting of the Eros and Agape motifs produces a characteristic third which is neither Eros nor Agape, but *Caritas*. Both Eros and Agape have contributed substantially to it, but it is itself new and unique. It is neither the primitive Christian love-motif expressed in terms of a Hellenistic flavour, nor is it the common Eros theory barely concealed under phraseology from the Christian tradition. Caritas is, if we may say so, both and neither of these. It is neither Eros nor Agape, but the *synthesis* of them; and it is a genuine synthesis, because while it contains elements of both motifs, it is not merely the sum of these, but forms a new, independent unity. Now it may be questioned whether a single view really can be constructed out of such different materials, whether such disparate motifs can be harmonised; in other words, whether one single concept can comprise all that Augustine means when he speaks of Caritas. That, however, is a separate question, and it must not obscure the fact that for Augustine himself they did become a unity. How this was possible is ultimately less a logical than a psychological problem.

2. Love as the Centre of Augustine's Interpretation of Christianity

Augustine tried to subsume Christianity as a whole under the aspect of love. Christianity is for him purely and simply the religion of love. The New Testament, of course, clearly puts love in the centre; it continually emphasises fellowship with God as a fellowship founded upon God's spontaneous and unmotivated love, and it centres the ethical demand on a love to God and neighbour which corresponds to this fellowship with God. But without a doubt, it is primarily due to Augustine that both Catholic and Evangelical Christianity take it as axiomatic that Christianity is a religion of love—of love in the sense of Caritas. For Augustine's conception has become normative of what this "religion of love" is understood to mean, which is not so much that Christianity is Agape-religion as that it is Caritas-religion.

For Augustine the whole of Christianity turns upon this one thing, *Caritas*. What then is Caritas? A detailed analysis will be made later; here we may take a preliminary and general survey. On which of the different forms of love—God's love, love to God, or love to neighbour—is Augustine's Caritas-view based? It is beyond question that when Augustine speaks of Caritas, he always thinks primarily of *love to God*. It is vital to keep this in mind if we are to avoid being misled by the rich variety of his view of love. Augustine has also much to say of *God's* love and grace; but it is not for him, as for Paul, the foundation on which all Christian love rests. Indeed, God's love itself has as its aim love to God; God reveals His love to us ultimately in order that we may learn rightly to love Him : it was to teach us to love God that Christ came into the world.[1] The emphasis falls decidedly on love to God, as is even more clearly shown by the relation between love to God and love to neighbour. When he speaks of love to God, Augustine often adds, in accordance with Christian tradition, the commandment of love to neighbour; but this has no independent place and meaning for him. It is really included already in the commandment of love to God, and this determines its limits. Augustine regards love to neighbour as fully legitimate only in so far as it can be referred ultimately, not to the neighbour, but to God Himself. When he resumes the subject of love to God, we notice at once that he has come to what is really central for him. Here he is really at home, and into his words he pours the whole passion of his soul. In the words of the Psalm : "Mihi adhærere Deo bonum est," he finds the adequate expression of his relation to God; in the abandon of the heart's undivided love he will cleave to God as his highest and only good.[2]

---

[1] " Quae autem major causa est adventus Domini, nisi ut ostenderet Deus dilectionem suam in nobis, commendans eam vehementer ?"   De catechizandis rudibus, lib. I, cap. iv. 7. . . . " Si ergo maxime propterea Christus advenit, ut cognosceret homo quantum eum diligat Deus; et ideo cognosçeret, ut in ejus dilectionem a quo prior dilectus est, inardesceret." Cap. iv. 8; Migne, 40, pp. 314 f.

Augustine's works are cited from " Corpus scriptorum ecclesiasticorum latinorum " (=CSEL) in so far as they are available in that edition; otherwise from Migne, PL, vols. 32-46.

[2] Epist. CLV, iii. 12.—Confessiones, lib. VII, cap. xi. 17.

Caritas, love to God, however, is not merely the religious, but also the ethical centre of Christianity. Caritas is the root of all real good, just as its opposite, fleshly desire, is the root of all evil.[1] Augustine has thus found a coherent view of the Christian ethical life, which delivers him from the atomism of legalistic ethics. Love to God is the central virtue, of which the old cardinal virtues are simply particular instances.[2] Only one thing is really enjoined upon the Christian—namely, love.[3] Where love is, no other precepts are requisite. So he can say: "Love, and do what thou wilt."[4] On the Commandment of Love hang not only the law and the prophets, but the entire Holy Scriptures.[5] In this respect there is, he holds, complete harmony between the Old and New Testaments, inasmuch as both culminate in love to God. The difference is simply this: in the Old Testament God *requires* love, in the New He *gives* what He requires.[6] Even so, the emphasis is not on the giving, but on the fulfilment of the Commandment which it makes possible. Law and grace point each to the other, yet with the fulfilment of the law as the ultimate aim.[7] The replacement of the Old Covenant by the New does not mean a radical change in the character of fellowship with God. Man's love to God is still the main thing, only the intervention of grace has improved its position. The Command-

---

[1] "Quomodo enim radix omnium malorum cupiditas, sic radix omnium bonorum caritas est." Enarratio in Psalmum XC., i. 8; PL 37, p. 1154. *Cf.* De gratia Christi et de peccato originali, I., xviii. 19; and xx. 21. In epist. Ioannis, tract. vii. 8. Contra Fortunatum, 21. De agone christiano, cap. i.

[2] De moribus ecclesiæ catholicæ, lib. I., cap. xxv. 46; PL 32, p. 1330 f. Epist. CLV., iv. 13, 16.

[3] "Non autem præcipit Scriptura nisi caritatem." De doct. christ., lib. III., cap. x. 15; PL 34, p. 71.

[4] "Dilige, et quod vis fac." In epist. Ioannis, tract. vii. 8; PL 35, p. 2033.

[5] De catechiz. rud., lib. I., cap. iv. 8; PL 40, p. 315.

[6] "Per fidem confugiat ad misericordiam dei, ut det quod iubet"; De spiritu et littera, cap. xxix. 51. *Cf.* the whole argument of this work of Augustine; especially cap. xvii.-xxx.

[7] "Lex ergo data est, ut gratia quæreretur, gratia data est, ut lex inpleretur." *Op cit.*, cap. xix. 34; *cf.* De gratia Christi et de pecc. orig., lib. I., cap. ix. 10.

ment of Love is no longer written on tables of stone, but
has been transferred to man's heart. Augustine delights to
quote Rom. v. 5: "The love of God hath been shed abroad
in our hearts through the Holy Ghost which was given unto
us."[1] When God through the Holy Spirit sheds love abroad
in our hearts, He gives what He commands: "Da quod
iubes, et iube quod vis."[2]

Love is Augustine's criterion for all things Christian. This
is perhaps most evident when he uses the idea of love to
refute his opponents. For instance, in asserting the Divine
authority of the Old Testament against Manichæan denials,
he finds it sufficient proof to point out that the Commandment of love to God and neighbour is found in the Old
Testament.[3] His strongest argument against the schismatic
Donatists is that by cutting themselves off from the Catholic
Church they abandon love. He who is an enemy of unity
has no part in the Divine love, nor has he the Holy Spirit.[4]
How central love is for Augustine, and how he makes it his

[1] De spiritu et litt., cap. xvii. 29.   There is hardly any text which Augustine
quotes oftener than Rom. v. 5, especially in the above connexion.   Free will
and the precepts of the law must be supplemented by the shedding abroad of
love in the heart through the Holy Spirit, if the soul is to be fired with the right
love to God as its " highest and immutable Good " (summum atque immutabile
bonum); cf. op. cit., cap. iii. 5.

[2] Conf., lib. X., cap. xxix. 40.

[3] De moribus eccl. cath., lib. I., cap. xxviii. 56 f.; PL 32, p. 1334.

[4] " Ecclesia catholica sola corpus est Christi, cuius ille caput est saluator
corporis sui.   Extra hoc corpus neminem uiuificat spiritus sanctus, quia, sicut
ipse dicit apostolus, caritas dei diffusa est in cordibus nostris per spiritum sanctum,
qui datus est nobis.   Non est autem particeps diuinæ caritatis, qui hostis est
unitatis.   Non habent itaque spiritum sanctum, qui sunt extra ecclesiam ";
Epist. CLXXXV., xi. 50.   " Quis autem uere dicit se habere Christi caritatem,
quando eius non amplectitur unitatem ?"   Epist. LXI. 2. " Caritas enim
christiana nisi in unitate ecclesiæ non potest custodiri."   Contra litteras Petiliani,
lib. II., cap. lxxvii. 172.   " Caritas ista non tenetur, nisi in unitate ecclesiæ.
Non illam habent divisores. . . .   Cupiditas enim cupit dividere, sicut caritas
colligere."   Sermo CCLXV., cap. ix. 11.   To the question of the Donatists:
" What have we less than you ?" Augustine answers: " Hoc solum minus habetis,
quod minus habet qui caritatem non habet."   De baptismo, lib. I., cap. xiv. 22;
cf. ibid., cap. vii. 9 to x. 14.   Cf. Contra Cresconium, lib. II., cap. xii. 15 to
xvi. 20; and also In ev. Joannis, tract. vii. 3.

standard of judgment, is further demonstrated by his exegetical canon, *that everything in Scripture must be interpreted in accordance with love*.[1] He himself gives this principle the very widest application and does not shrink from even the most forced interpretations. The whole content of Scripture is Caritas; interpreting it in this light, we cannot possibly go wrong. Even if we should happen to read a meaning other than the author's into a particular text, we need not fear that we shall miss the main mark. We should be like a man who strays from the road, yet goes across the fields to the same point to which the road leads.[2]

[1] De catechiz. rud., cap. xxvi. 50; PL 40, p. 345.

[2] " Sed quisquis in Scripturis aliud sentit quam ille qui scripsit, illis non mentientibus fallitur: sed tamen, ut dicere coeperam, si ea sententia fallitur, qua ædificet caritatem, quæ finis præcepti est, ita fallitur, ac si quisquam errore deserens viam, eo tamen per agrum pergat, quo etiam via illa perducit." De doct. christ., lib. I., cap. xxxvi. 41; PL 34, p. 34. *Cf.* the same idea in Conf., lib. XII., cap. xviii. 27 and cap. xxx. 41 f.

The following examples will give an idea of what happens to Augustine's exegesis when he applies his rule that everything in Scripture must be interpreted in accordance with love. In John iv. 40 Jesus is said to have stayed *two days* with the Samaritans after His conversation with the woman at the well: this, according to Augustine, means " mystically " that Jesus gave them the *two Commandments of Love*: " quo numero dierum mystice commendatus est duorum numero præceptorum, in quibus duobus præceptis tota lex pendet et prophetæ." In ev. Jn., tract. xvi. 3; *cf.* tract. xv. 33; and tract. xvii. 6. The number two is taken in general as referring to the Commandment of Love. It is of a deep mystical significance that the widow cast just *two* mites into the treasury (Luke xxi. 2) or that the Good Samaritan gave *two* pence to the host (Luke x. 35). Christ gave His disciples the Holy Spirit after the Resurrection, when He breathed on them and said: " Receive ye the Holy Ghost " (John xx. 22). On the day of Pentecost the Spirit was given a second time. Why was the Holy Spirit given *twice*? To teach us the two Commandments of Love. " Una caritas, et duo præcepta: unus Spiritus, et duo data." Sermo CCLXV., cap. vii.-viii.

The man Jesus cured at Bethesda had been sick for thirty-eight years. Why just so long? Answer: the number forty signifies the perfect life; Moses, Elijah, Christ—all fasted forty days. Moses represents the Law, Elijah the Prophets, Christ the Gospel. In Law, Prophets, and Gospel alike, then, the number forty means fasting, abstinence from sin, and a perfect life. But in what does the perfect life consist? The Apostle answers: " Love is the fulfilling of the Law " (Rom. xiii. 10). " If, then, the number forty means the fulfilment of the Law, and if the Law is only fulfilled in the twofold Commandment of Love, why dost thou wonder that he was sick, who was short of forty by two?" And when Jesus had healed the man, He gave him two commands: (1) " Take

Love is the one infallible sign of real Christianity. Augustine has a predilection for the Pauline formula, " Faith, hope, love,"[1] to describe the content of Christianity, but love alone is the really decisive factor. Both faith and hope can be present without our relation to God being right. " The Devil believes, but he does not love." On the other hand: " Where love is, what can be wanting? Where it is not, what can possibly be profitable?"[2] " When it is asked whether a man is good, one does not ask what he believes or hopes, but what he loves."[3]

The meeting of the Eros and the Agape motifs in Augustine's doctrine of Caritas is thus not merely one point among others; it concerns the very heart of his conception of Christianity. We shall therefore examine the parts played by the

---

up thy bed !" and (2) " Walk !"; that is, He taught him love to neighbour and love to God. Why in this order ? In the Law, love to God is the first and great Commandment. In the *fulfilling* of the Law, the order is reversed. We begin with love to the neighbour whom we see; thereby we merit to see God; by love to our neighbour we purify our eye for seeing God. " Take up thy bed !" thus means " Love thy neighbour." But why is the neighbour likened to a bed ? Because when the man lies ill, the bed carries him, but when he gets well, he carries the bed. The Apostle says : " Bear ye one another's burdens, and so fulfil the law of Christ " (Gal. vi. 2). " When thou wast sick, thy neighbour had to bear thee; thou hast become well, bear then thy neighbour ! . . . So ' take up thy bed.' But when thou hast taken it up, do not remain here, but ' walk.' By loving thy neighbour and ˌ aring for him, thou dost perform thy going. Whither goest thou, if not to the Lord God, to Him whom we ought to love with all our heart and all our soul and all our mind ? For we have not yet come to God, but we have our neighbour with us. Bear him, then, with whom thou goest, that thou mayest come to Him with whom thou desirest to abide. So ' take up thy bed and walk.' " In ev. Jn., tract. xvii. 4-9. " Portamus proximum, et ambulamus, ad Deum." Tract. xvii. 11; PL 35, p. 1533. *Cf.* tract. xli. 13; PL 35, p. 1700.

Arbitrary exegesis and number-symbolism are in no way surprising. We are accustomed to similar and worse things, particularly in Gnostic literature; but we find them also in the literature of the Early Church. The interesting thing is to see how this arbitrary exegesis in Augustine is used to make everything point to Caritas.

[1] *Cf.* especially the " Enchiridion ad Laurentium sive de fide, spe et caritate," which is intended to give an elementary exposition of the Christian faith and life under these three main headings.

[2] In ev. Jn., tract. lxxxiii. 3; PL 35, p. 1846.

[3] Enchiridion, cap. cxvii. 31; PL 40, p. 286.

two motifs, and see how he managed to make at least an apparent unity of them in his Caritas doctrine.

3. NEOPLATONISM AND CHRISTIANITY IN AUGUSTINE

The question of the influence of the Eros and the Agape motifs on Augustine's life and religious outlook seems to be very closely connected with the much-disputed question of the influence of Neoplatonism and Christianity on his inner development. He took over the Eros idea substantially from Neoplatonism, and what he possesses of the idea of Agape he has obviously got from the New Testament, especially from the Pauline writings.

Now it is true that on his way to Christianity Augustine passed through a variety of schools, each of which left its mark on him. If here we single out Neoplatonism, we do so because his own relation to Neoplatonism is quite different from his relation to the rest. Neoplatonism is a school he does not leave; even as a Christian he never breaks with it. All his life he remains a Neoplatonic Christian, or, if you will, a Christian Platonist. He has no need to set Christianity and Neoplatonism in opposition; he thinks he can find a remarkably large measure of agreement between them. He is convinced that if Plato and his disciples could live their lives over again in his time they would accept Christianity; *the change of but a few words and phrases* would bring their views into entire harmony with it.[1] How easily he makes the transition is illustrated by his treatment of the Christian belief in resurrection in relation to the Platonic doctrine of immortality. In the early centuries the Church had been acutely conscious that Platonism and Christianity could not be reconciled on this point. Augus-

---

[1] " Itaque si hanc vitam illi viri nobiscum rursum agere potuissent, viderent profecto cuius auctoritate facilius consuleretur hominibus, *et paucis mutatis verbis atque sententiis christiani fierent*, sicut plerique recentiorum nostrorumque temporum Platonici fecerunt." De vera religione, cap. iv. 7; PL 34, p. 126.

tine too is conscious of the difference, but it is not irreconcilable; it is not the clash of two totally different fundamental motifs, and he can pass from one to the other with
relative ease. It would require no more than an agreement
between the Platonic philosophers on certain points where
they differed among themselves, to bring their conception
very nearly into line with the Christian belief in resurrection.[1]

These are but a few examples of how Augustine mixes
Christianity and Neoplatonism, and we shall see many more.
But the question now arises concerning the importance of
the fact that he thus came to Christianity as a Neoplatonist,
especially as regards his conception of what Christian love
means. First, we may notice the risk, and it is no slight
risk, which the Neoplatonic contribution involves. In
Augustine there is a blending of motifs on a large scale.
He has done more than any other, by combining things
Neoplatonic and Christian, to import the Eros motif into
Christianity and to procure ecclesiastical sanction for it. It
was not without reason that Karl Holl described Augustine
as "one of the corrupters of Christian morality."[2] If
Augustine's view is judged by the primitive Christian idea
of Agape, only one verdict is possible: the Christian idea of
love has suffered seriously through being combined with the
Neoplatonic Eros motif.

But to do Augustine justice, there is more to be said. His
view of love must be compared with that of his immediate
predecessors, and then the situation is at once altered. We
discover how much Augustine has done to deepen the
Christian idea of love, and we find that Neoplatonism has
played a positive part towards this. It has in fact helped

---

[1] " Singula quædam dixerunt Plato adque Porphyrius, quæ si infer se com-
municare potuissent, facti essent fortasse Christiani." De ciuitate dei, lib.
XXII., cap. xxvii.

[2] K. Holl: *Gesammelte Aufsätze zur Kirchengeschichte*, Band I. *Luther*, 1921,
p. 139.

Augustine to see more deeply into the essential nature of
the Christian love-motif; and it has done this, oddly enough,
not in virtue of other elements which it contains, but precisely in its capacity as Eros theory. Indeed, we might say
that, *for Augustine, Neoplatonic Eros has become the means
of discovering Christian Agape.* The increased depth in
Augustine's doctrine of love is very marked by comparison
with the often quite trivial expositions of the Commandment of Love found in the Apologists and Tertullian. The
impulse towards this deepening came, without doubt, from
the New Testament, but not from it alone. What Augustine
found in the New Testament would never have been enough
by itself to give love the place it holds for him. It was only
because he came to Christianity by way of Neoplatonism
that he became aware of the centrality of love in Christianity.
He was not ignorant of Christianity before he met Neoplatonism, but there is nothing to suggest that Christian love
made any deep impression on him at that time. It is Neoplatonism that makes the difference. In it he meets a view
dominated throughout by the thought of love (Eros), and
he is gripped by it in a way that is decisive for his whole
life. When afterwards he comes in this frame of mind to
Christianity, it is as if scales fall from his eyes. Christianity
too, he finds, puts love in the centre—another sort of love,
but that does not trouble him yet. Augustine approaches
Christianity with the Eros theory as a divining-rod, and by
its aid he detects in Christianity a source where it will repay
him to bore.

The significance of Neoplatonism for Augustine's interpretation of Christianity is thus twofold. Due to it, at
least in part, is his possession of considerably deeper insight
than his predecessors had into the Christian love-motif; at
the same time, it forms a barrier beyond which his understanding of that motif cannot pass. Augustine's view of
love is an illuminating example both of the liberating and

stimulating effect which a new spiritual situation can have, in so far as it produces awareness of something new; and also of the restricting and retarding effect which it can have, in so far as the limitations imposed by the situation itself cannot be overcome. Neoplatonism is Augustine's situation. It opens to him a new horizon, enables him to look with new eyes upon the Christian love-motif. At the same time it limits his horizon, so that he is unable to discover the real depth of that motif and to see how it completely abolishes the Neoplatonic Eros motif.

The problem of "Neoplatonism and Christianity" has often been discussed in recent years with reference to the part played by these two elements in Augustine's "conversion." The *Confessions* have long been regarded as an authentic account of his religious development. Confidence in them, however, has been seriously shaken of late by the observation that Augustine's writings from the time immediately following his "conversion" give a picture of his spiritual condition very different from, or even contradictory to, that in the *Confessions*. Since the *Confessions* were written quite a long time after the development they describe, and are, moreover, a retrospective interpretation of that development, prior importance must naturally be ascribed to the earlier works. What this means for our view of Augustine's inner development is still strongly disputed. Some have held that Augustine's "conversion" is a conversion rather to Neoplatonism than to Christianity; others hold that Augustine is perfectly right when, as a mature Christian, he looks back to his "conversion" as the point at which he came through to Christianity, and that the earlier works do not contradict him on this point.

It would take too long to go into this question here,[1] and

---

[1] On this question see J. Nörregaard: *Augustins Bekehrung*, 1923, and K. Holl: *Augustins innere Entwicklung* (*Gesammelte Aufsätze zur Kirchengeschichte*, III, 1928, pp. 54-116).

it is not necessary for our present purpose. We are, it is true, concerned with the meeting of Christianity and Neo-platonism in Augustine's most characteristic doctrine, his conception of love; for his attempt to fuse Eros and Agape into one is at the same time an attempt to unite Christianity and Neoplatonism. Yet we can ignore the historical problem of his development, since we are not interested in distinguishing between one stage at which Augustine must be called a Neoplatonist, and another at which we find him a fully developed Christian. Neoplatonism never ceased to be an important factor in his spiritual life, even after he became a Christian. And this is as true of his general religious sentiment as of the theoretical statement of his religious outlook. What interests us is the actual meeting of the two different religious motifs and their relation to one another in his " Christian " life and " Christian " outlook.

But this has an important bearing on the sources for our

Of the abundant literature on Augustine we may mention further:—H. Reuter: *Augustinische Studien*, 1887. A. Harnack: *Augustins Konfessionen* (Reden und Aufsätze I, 2 Aufl. 1906, pp. 49-79); *Die Höhepunkte in Augustins Konfessionen* (Aus der Friedens- und Kriegsarbeit, Reden und Aufsätze, Neue Folge III, 1916, pp. 67-99); *Reflexionen und Maximen*, 1922. W. Thimme: *Augustins geistige Entwickelung*, 1908. J. Mausbach: *Die Ethik des heiligen Augustinus*, 1909. H. Scholz: *Glaube und Unglaube in der Weltgeschichte*, 1911. E. Troeltsch: *Augustin, die christliche Antike und das Mittelalter*, 1915. J. Hessen: *Die unmittelbare Gotteserkenntnis nach dem heiligen Augustinus*, 1919; *Augustinus und seine Bedeutung für die Gegenwart*, 1924. G. Ljunggren: *Zur Geschichte der christlichen Heilsgewissheit*, 1920. J. Geyser: *Augustin und die phänomenologische Religionsphilosophie der Gegenwart*, 1923. R. Reitzenstein: *Augustinus als antiker und mittelalterlicher Mensch* (Vorträge der Bibliothek Warburg, 1922-23), 1924. E. Salin: *Civitas Dei*, 1926. G. Aulén: *Den kristna gudsbilden*, 1927, pp. 98-126. Cuthbert Butler: *Western Mysticism*, 1927. M. Schmaus: *Die psychologische Trinitätslehre des hl. Augustinus* (Münsterische Beiträge zur Theologie, hrsg. von F. Diekamp und R. Stapper, H. 11), 1927. H. Arendt: *Der Liebesbegriff bei Augustin* (Philosophische Forschungen hrsg. von K. Jaspers, 9), 1929. M. Grabmann and J. Mausbach: *Aurelius Augustinus. Festschrift der Görres-Gesellschaft*, 1930. É. Gilson: *Introduction à l'étude de Saint Augustin*, 1931. W. Theiler: *Porphyrios und Augustin*, 1933. A. Dahl: *Odödlighetsproblemet hos Augustinus*, 1935. A. Petzäll: *Etikens sekularisering, dess betingelser inom kristen spekulation med särskild hänsyn till Augustinus*, 1935.

study. If we were describing the different stages in his development, the *Confessions* would have to be used with some caution as a historical source. As it is, the *Confessions* are for our purposes a source of the greatest value and trustworthiness. In them Augustine passes judgment on his development from the Christian standpoint he has reached, and so we may expect here his verdict on the problem of Eros and Agape. It is his judgment and the standards by which he judges that particularly claim our attention. As he is applying "Christian" standards, these standards will show best of all what Christianity means for him; and the *Confessions* have this further advantage, that they reveal the immediate significance of Eros and Agape for his religious life.

II

AUGUSTINE'S VITAL PROBLEM: THE SETTLEMENT OF THE ISSUE BETWEEN THE EROS AND THE AGAPE MOTIFS

1. The Eros Motif in Augustine's Religious Development

Love is unquestionably central in Augustinian Christianity; but it is not easy to say what kind of love it is, whether its features are mainly those of Eros or those of Agape. At first sight Eros seems to predominate, and this impression is confirmed by a glance at Augustine's development as described by himself in the *Confessions*.

Plato describes progress on the path of Eros as follows: "The right way of Eros, whether one goes alone or is led by another, is to begin with the beautiful things that are here and ascend ever upwards aiming at the beauty that is above, climbing, as it were, on a ladder from one beautiful body to two, and from two to all the others, and from beautiful bodies to beautiful actions and from beauty of actions to beautiful forms of knowledge, till at length from these one reaches that knowledge which is the knowledge of nothing other than Beauty itself."[1] This, in brief, is the Platonic Way of salvation; it is the *ordo salutis* of Eros doctrine.

Although Augustine means to take a Christian view of his development in the *Confessions*, he provides in fact a singularly clear example of what Plato calls "the right way of Eros." Augustine's earlier development is particularly dramatic; he passionately embraces a doctrine and as abruptly

---

[1] Symposium 211. *Cf. supra*, p. 174.

abandons it. Yet, running through these apparently aimless veerings from one point of view to another, there is a remarkably strong continuity. There is something permanent amid the change; something virtually unaltered accompanies him through all his different phases: it is the Eros point of view. It was not Neoplatonism that introduced him to it; he had it from the beginning, and it dominates him equally as a Manichæan, as a Neoplatonist and as a Christian. His spiritual life from first to last bears in a high degree the stamp of Eros.

Augustine dates the beginning of greater stability in his spiritual life from his acquaintance with Cicero's *Hortensius*. Through the study of this book he was gripped by the philosophic Eros, which in later retrospect he identifies with Christian love to God. " With an incredible fervour of heart," he writes, " I yearned for the immortal wisdom, and I began to arise in order to return to Thee. . . . How did I burn, O my God, how did I burn with desire to soar from earth to Thee, and I knew not what Thou wouldest do with me. For with Thee is wisdom. But love of wisdom is in Greek called philosophy, and with this that book inflamed me."[1] Afterwards he made Neoplatonic Eros, love for the Divine, so deeply and inwardly his own that it became, so to speak, the very core of his being.

That is how Augustine began, and so he continued. That crisis which is usually called his conversion produced no essential change. It falls entirely within the framework created by Eros piety, and Augustine himself describes it as the second act of what happened to him when he was gripped by the philosophic Eros. What he then wanted but could not achieve—namely, to contemn things earthly, to turn his longing wholly to the supersensible, and to rise on the wings of the soul to the sphere of the Divine—this

---

[1] Conf., lib. III., cap. iv. 7; *cf.* De beata vita, i. 4: " tanto amore philosophiæ succensus sum, ut statim ad eam me ferre meditarer."

became a reality at his conversion.[1] True to the Neoplatonic scheme of salvation as this change is, Neoplatonism had been unable to effect it; for although it adequately showed him what ought to be the object of his love, that object was too abstract and remote to hold him permanently. Neoplatonism had kindled in him love to God, but that love was rather a fleeting mood than a permanent disposition. Augustine himself describes it as follows : " I was amazed that I already loved Thee and not a phantasm instead of Thee. Yet I did not persist to enjoy my God, but now I was drawn to Thee by Thy beauty, now borne away from Thee by my own weight."[2] On the Eros ladder which Neoplatonism showed him, he could ascend from the beauty of the corporeal world, through the world of the soul and reason, to the eternal and immutable Being, and in a moment of trembling vision glimpse the Divine itself.[3] Augustine never doubts that Christian love to God is the same as Platonic Eros and that the Way of Eros leads ultimately to the same God as Christianity proclaims—only as yet he lacks staying

---

[1] " Quoniam multi mei anni mecum effluxerant—forte duodecim anni—ex quo ab undeuicensimo anno ætatis meæ lecto Ciceronis Hortensio excitatus eram studio sapientiæ et differebam contemta felicitate terrena ad eam inuestigandam uacare." . . . " Illa te adhuc premit umerisque liberioribus pinnas recipiunt, qui neque ita in quærendo adtriti sunt nec decennio et amplius ista meditati." Conf., lib. VIII., cap. vii. 17, 18. These considerations, together with the story of the Egyptian hermits, were the occasion of Augustine's conversion. Notice the metaphor of the " wings of the soul," reminiscent of Plato's *Phædrus*.

[2] Conf., lib. VII., cap. xvii. 23.

[3] The importance of the Eros motif as the starting-point of Augustine's doctrine of salvation appears most clearly in Conf., lib. VII., cap. xvii. First, he identifies Platonic Eros and Christian love to God. In what follows we find almost all the characteristic features of Eros doctrine: the beauty of temporal things (pulchritudo corporum terrestrium), the ascent from these step by step (gradatim a corporibus) to that which *is*, unchangeable (ad id, quod est; inconmutabilem), recollection (memoria tui; non mecum ferebam nisi amantem memoriam), the trembling contemplation of the beauty of the Divine (in ictu trepidantis aspectus), its fascinating power of attraction (rapiebar ad te decore tuo) and the downward gravitation of the body (diripiebar abs te pondere meo). As biblical support for the idea that it is the body that weighs down the soul and hinders its ascent to the Divine and its enjoyment of full fellowship with God, Augustine quotes here, as often elsewhere, Wisd. ix. 15.

power. " I lacked strength to hold my gaze fixed on Thee, and in my weakness was struck back and returned to my accustomed ways."[1] Then comes the *conversion*, and *its primary significance is that the inconstant Eros mood is elevated to a stable and permanent Eros disposition.*

What is true of the beginnings of Augustine's religious life and of the maturity it reaches in his " conversion " is equally true of the heights it attains later. There too the Eros motif is the main factor. We may recall the conversation Augustine had with his mother, a few days before her death, about the kingdom of heaven. The whole spiritual attitude it expresses has its prototype in the ascent to the Divine of the soul that is fired with Eros.[2] Step by step the way leads through the various spheres of the material world up to the human spirit; then beyond that, to a still higher sphere, to the great silence where there is unmediated apprehension of God Himself.[3] True, in certain respects this differs from the Neoplatonic tradition, and in particular the ecstatic absorption in God is lacking; yet it is impossible to doubt that the entire scheme of this ascent is determined by the Eros motif.

[1] Conf., lib. VII., cap. xvii. 23.
[2] Conf., lib. IX., cap. x. The same attitude of Eros is also found in Augustine's various expositions of the content of Christianity; *cf.*, *e.g.*, De doctrina christiana, De vera religione, De moribus ecclesiæ catholicæ, De libero arbitrio, De beata vita. We have already met similar ideas, as, *e.g.*, in Gregory of Nyssa; *cf.* *supra*, pp. 443 f.
[3] " Perambulauimus gradatim cuncta corporalia et ipsum cælum, unde sol et luna et stellæ lucent super terram. Et adhuc ascendebamus interius cogitando et loquendo et mirando opera tua et uenimus in mentes nostras et transcendimus eas." Conf., lib. IX., cap. x. 24. That this attitude of Eros reflects Augustine's real view is very evident from the detailed answer he gives in Conf., lib. X., cap. vi.-xxviii. to his repeated question: " Quid amo, cum deum amo ?" Here he describes the way to God almost exclusively in terms derived from the realm of the Eros motif.

2. THE AGAPE MOTIF AS A BASIC FACTOR IN AUGUSTINE'S OUTLOOK

It would however be quite unjust to Augustine to conclude from the above that he is exclusively a representative of Eros piety for whom the Agape motif plays but little part. He has a multitude of ideas and opinions which are undoubtedly to be traced back to the Agape motif. He, more than any of the Fathers of the Early Church, has given a central place to Christian love in the sense of Agape.

His doctrine of *Grace* and *Predestination*, above all, shows this to be so. He speaks much of Divine grace as "præveniens" and "gratis data";[1] and what is that but a proclamation of God's Agape? The Augustinian doctrine of Predestination also, from one point of view, is the most emphatic confession of the unmotivated and spontaneous nature of Divine love. Augustine has taken seriously the idea: "You have not chosen me, but I have chosen you." In spontaneous love God has chosen us before we turned in faith and love to Him. "This," says Augustine, "is that ineffable grace. For what were we, when we had not yet chosen Christ and, consequently, did not love Him? . . . What else but unrighteous and lost?"[2] Paul's word: "God commendeth his own love toward us, in that, while we were yet sinners, Christ died for us" (Rom. v. 8), has by no means escaped Augustine. For him, too, God's love is paradoxical and "incomprehensibilis."[3]

When Augustine speaks of God's love, he appears at times to break away from the Eros-scheme. According to Eros

---

[1] "Misericordia ejus prævenit nos." In ev. Jn., tract. lxxxvi. 2; *cf.* tract. lxxxii. 1; De patientia, cap. xxi. 18; Sermo CLXXVI., cap. v. 5. Further evidence is unnecessary; Augustine's writings abound in such statements.

[2] In ev. Jn., tract. lxxxvi. 2. *Cf.* also the passage from the "De patientia" mentioned in the previous footnote.

[3] In ev. Jn., tract. cx. 6.

theory it is, strictly speaking, impossible to talk of God's love at all, for Eros-love always presupposes imperfection, a need as yet unfulfilled. It looks, indeed, like a conscious attack on Eros theory when Augustine, in order to show the precise nature of Divine love, distinguishes between two sorts of love, a love that is due to the dryness of need and longing (indigentiæ siccitate) and a love that springs out of the fulness of goodness and benevolence (beneficentiæ ubertate), or, otherwise expressed, *amor ex miseria* and *amor ex misericordia.*[1] What is the difference between these two, if not that between Eros and Agape? Augustine seems to be well aware that God's love to us must be distinguished from Eros-love. *God's love is a love of mercy and of the fulness of goodwill.* Eros-love ascends and seeks the satisfaction of its needs; Agape-love descends in order to help and to give. Just because of its unmotivated and spontaneous character—or, in Augustine's own words, because God loves " ultro "—God's love has so much more power to kindle the response of love in man. Man can make no claim to God's love. If it is given to him, that rests upon a Divine miracle. God, the highest Judge, condescends to sinful man.[2] This line of thought is rather isolated in Augustine, but it is remarkable that it occurs at all in so definite a form. In view of such statements, especially if we also recall the central importance of the idea of Grace and Predestination, we can no longer doubt that Agape is a basic factor in the religious life and thought of Augustine.

A further proof, and one of the strongest, of Augustine's interest in Agape is his energetic affirmation of *the idea of*

[1] " Ibi enim gratior amor est, ubi non æstuat indigentiæ siccitate, sed ubertate beneficentiæ profluit. Ille namque amor ex miseria est, iste ex misericordia." De catechiz. rud., cap. iv. 7.

[2] " Jam vero si etiam se amari posse a superiore desperabat inferior, ineffabiliter commovebitur in amorem, si ultro ille fuerit dignatus ostendere quantum diligat eum, qui nequaquam sibi tantum bonum promittere auderet. Quid autem superius Deo judicante, et quid desperatius homine peccante ?" *Ibid.*

Incarnation. In all ages, this idea has always been a safe-guard of the Agape motif. By the Incarnation of the Son, God Himself has come down to us in the world of trans-ience and sin. This formed the permanent centre of Augustine's Christian thought. The prominence of the idea of Incarnation in the writings immediately following his " conversion " is striking—the more so since these writings are otherwise so definitely Neoplatonic in character, and there is scarcely any idea for which Neoplatonism has less room than that of Incarnation.[1] If Augustine's conversion meant, as we saw above, the full emergence of the idea of Eros, we can now state that it also meant, in a measure, the emergence of the idea of Agape. That love which descends in order to help and to give, which is spontaneous and un-motivated, was not alien to Augustine. Yet he never knew Agape in its Christian fulness.

We now come to the great and fatal contradiction in Augustine's view of love. He wanted to maintain both Eros and Agape at once. He was unaware that they are diametric-ally opposed to each other and that the relation between them must be an Either—Or; instead, he tried to make it a Both—And. But this was not done without tension and conflict.

3. The Settlement of the Issue between Eros and Agape

In the seventh book of the *Confessions* we can read be-tween the lines how Augustine settled the issue between Eros and Agape. He describes here what he found and did not find in Neoplatonism. He found God and the eternal world, and was fired with Eros for the Divine. But he is himself too weak, and God is too remote for him to attain. "When I first knew Thee, Thou didst draw me up to

[1] *E.g.*, Contra Academicos, lib. III., cap. xix. 42; De ordine, lib. I., cap. x. 29, and lib. II., cap. v. 16.

Thee . . . but my weak sight was beaten back when Thou didst powerfully shed Thy rays upon me, and I trembled with love and awe and found myself to be far off from Thee."[1] *Neoplatonism had been able to show him the object for his love and longing, but not the way to gain it.* Between God and man is a gulf which man cannot bridge. In Eros man is bound to God but cannot reach Him. The wings of yearning are not strong enough to bear him up to the Eternal. Augustine has no doubt that Eros is the way to God, but he has begun to doubt whether we, as we actually are, can gain access to Him by that way. If we are to find God, He must Himself come to meet us—but of that Neoplatonism knew nothing. Of God and His nature, of man's Eros for Him, indeed, of the Word of God which in the beginning was with God—of all these he could read in the writings of the Neoplatonists.[2] "But that the Word became flesh, and dwelt among us, I read not there," says Augustine.[3] These writings might tell him that the Son was in the form of God, but that He emptied Himself and took the form of a servant, that He humbled Himself and became obedient unto death, that God spared not His own Son but delivered Him up for us all—"those books do not contain."[4] *In Neoplatonism he finds human Eros which tries to take heaven by storm, but he misses God's Agape which descends, and without which Eros cannot attain to God.*

The strange thing is that Augustine never sees that Christian Agape is the direct opposite of Neoplatonic Eros,

---

[1] Conf., lib. VII., cap. x. 16: "O æterna ueritas et uera caritas et cara æternitas! Tu es deus meus, tibi suspiro die ac nocte. Et cum te primum cognoui, tu assumsisti me, ut uiderem esse, quod uiderem, et nondum me esse, qui uiderem. Et reuerberasti infirmitatem aspectus mei radians in me uehementer, et contremui amore et horrore: et inueni longe me esse a te." This recalls the famous semi-physiological description in Plato's "Phædrus" (251) of the condition of one who is gripped by Eros. The atmosphere of both is the same; here, as there, we find the "radiance" of Beauty, the "trembling" of love, the mingled love and awe, the pining that gives the lover no rest day or night.

[2] Conf., lib. VII., cap. ix. 13.   [3] *Ibid.*, cap. ix. 14.   [4] *Ibid.*

and these two motifs agree no better than fire and water. He seeks a compromise which will do justice to both. Even when he has become aware of God's Agape, he still lives with his whole soul in the realm of Eros. Agape is simply added as a new element to what he already possessed, and the validity of the latter is never questioned; Agape is fitted into the framework of Eros. Agape is a necessary corrective, without which Eros cannot reach its goal.

What, then, is the fault in Eros, which must be corrected? It is, in a word, the *superbia* that is always bound up with Eros. The soul's ascent to the higher world easily produces a feeling of self-sufficiency and pride—as Augustine knew by experience. Neoplatonism had taught him to know God and had kindled his love to God, but it had also called forth his pride.[1] When the soul in the rapture of Eros leaves the earthly and transient far below and ascends ever higher, it is seized with a "*Hochgefühl*" which is nearly akin to superbia. It begins to feel it has already attained, becomes self-sufficient and forgets the distance between itself and the Divine. But such dreams are a cause of its never reaching the goal.

In the light of Christianity, Augustine finds Neoplatonic Eros subject to a peculiar contradiction: *Eros is man's longing to get beyond all that is transient and even beyond himself, up to the Divine; but the ascent provokes superbia and self-sufficiency, with the result that man remains after all within himself and never reaches the Divine.*[2] Looking back on what Neoplatonism had taught him, Augustine will not deny that it showed him the right goal, but he asks: "Where was that love which builds on the foundation of humility, which is Christ Jesus? Or when should these

---

[1] Conf., lib: VII., cap. xx. 26.

[2] "Viderunt quo veniendum esset: sed ingrati ei qui illis præstitit quod viderunt, sibi voluerunt tribuere quod viderunt; et facti superbi amiserunt quod videbant." In ev. Jn., tract. ii. 4.

books teach me it?"[1] When he came from this to the Holy
Scriptures (or, as he puts it, "When I had been tamed by
Thy books"), he found that there is a fundamental opposition between the Neoplatonic and the Christian spirit: on
the one side there is *superbia*, on the other *humilitas*.

The only real cure for this superbia which prevents Eros
reaching its goal is God's Agape, His love in sending His
Son, who humbled Himself even to the death of the Cross.
In this context, Augustine can perceive the "unmotivated"
character, the paradox of God's love. It was not strictly fitting that He who was God should take the form of a servant
and suffer death upon the Cross; the Incarnation is a condescension on God's part which is incomprehensible to us.
Yet it was necessary, "that there might be a way for man to
man's God through the God-man."[2] Nothing less than
God's Agape could break man's superbia. Augustine's keen
interest in the Incarnation is connected with the fact that it
is for him an evidence of God's Agape, but he is interested
in Agape chiefly as *exemplum humilitatis*. Nothing can
reveal and overcome man's superbia like God's humilitas,
nothing shows how far man had strayed from God so much
as the fact that he could only be restored through an incarnate God.[3] "To cure man's superbia God's Son descended and became humble. Why art thou proud, O man?
God has for thy sake become humble. Thou wouldst per-

[1] Conf., lib. VII., cap. xx. 26. In "the love which builds on the foundation
of humility" (ædificans caritas) there is a reminiscence of Paul's words in 1 Cor.
viii. 1: "Gnosis puffeth up, but Agape edifieth" (caritas ædificat). *Cf.* on
this *supra*, p. 134. Augustine's thought here can be expressed thus : Eros, taken
by itself, puffeth up ; only in conjunction with Agape does it become a love that
edifieth.

[2] De ciuitate dei, lib. XI., cap. ii.

[3] " . . . ut humana superbia per humilitatem Dei argueretur ac sanaretur,
et demonstraretur homini quam longe a Deo recesserat, cum per incarnatum
Deum revocaretur, et exemplum obedientiæ per hominem Deum contumaci
homini præberetur." Enchiridion, cap. cviii. "Credimus pro nobis Deum
hominem factum, ad humilitatis exemplum, et ad demonstrandam erga nos
dilectionem Dei." De trinitate, lib. VIII., cap. v. 7.

chance be ashamed to imitate a humble man; imitate at least the humble God."[1]   God's Agape, or as Augustine prefers to say, God's humilitas, is the antidote to man's superbia.[2]

According to Augustine, the relation between Agape and Eros is therefore as follows. Eros, left to itself, can see God and feel itself drawn to Him.   But it sees God only at a remote distance; between Him and the soul lies an immense ocean, and when the soul imagines it has reached Him it has simply entered, in self-sufficiency and pride, into the harbour of itself.   But for pride, Eros would be able to bring the soul to God.   Here Agape must come to its assistance: God's humilitas must vanquish man's superbia.   For even if all other ties that bind the soul to things earthly and transient are broken, its ascent will not succeed so long as it is infected with superbia.   By superbia the soul is chained to itself and cannot ascend to what is above itself.   *It is the task of Agape to sever this last link of the soul with things finite.*   When a man has been freed from himself under the influence of God's humilitas, then the ascent succeeds. There is no longer anything to drag the soul down.   The humility of Christ, the Cross of Christ, bears it over the ocean to its fatherland.

To sum up, we may quote Augustine's own words from

---

[1] " Ut ergo causa omnium morborum curaretur, id est superbia, descendit et humilis factus est Filius Dei.   Quid superbis, homo?   Deus propter te humilis factus est.   Puderet te fortasse imitari humilem hominem, saltem imitare humilem Deum."   In ev. Jn., tract. xxv. 16.   " Vitiorum namque omnium humanorum causa *superbia* est.   Ad hanc convincendam atque auferendam talis medicina cœlitus venit: ad elatum hominem per superbiam, *Deus humilis descendit* per misericordiam."   De peccatorum meritis et remissione, lib. II., cap. xvii. 27. " Magna est enim miseria, *superbus homo*; sed major est misericordia, *humilis Deus.*"   De catechiz. rud., cap. v. 9.

[2] " Itaque filius dei hominem adsumpsit et in illo humana perpessus est. Hæc medicina hominum tanta est, quanta non potest cogitari.   Nam quæ superbia sanari potest, si humilitate filii dei non sanatur?"   De agone christiano, xi. 12.   " Hoc enim nobis prodest credere, et firmum atque inconcussum corde retinere, *humilitatem* qua natus est Deus ex femina et a mortalibus per tantas contumelias perductus ad mortem, *summum esse medicamentum quo superbiæ nostræ sanaretur tumor.*"   De'trinitate, lib. VIII., cap. v. 7.

his exposition of the first chapter of the Fourth Gospel: "These things, too [that all things were made by the Word], are found in the books of the philosophers: and that God has an only-begotten Son, through whom are all things. They could see that which is, but they saw it from afar: they would not hold the humilitas of Christ, in which ship they could have arrived safely at that which they were able to see from afar; and they despised the Cross of Christ. The sea has to be crossed, and dost thou despise the Wood? O, proud wisdom! thou laughest at the crucified Christ; it is He whom thou sawest from afar: ' In the beginning was the Word, and the Word was with God.' But why was He crucified? Because the Wood of His humiliation was necessary for thee. For thou wast puffed up with pride, and hadst been cast out far from that fatherland; and by the waves of this world the way has been cut off, and there is no means of crossing to the fatherland, unless thou be carried by the Wood. Ungrateful one! thou mockest Him who has come to thee that thou mayest return. He has become the way, and that through the sea. . . . Believe in the Crucified, and thou shalt be able to arrive thither. For thy sake He was crucified, to teach thee humilitas."[1]

[1] In ev. Jn., tract. ii. 4.

III

ANALYSIS OF THE IDEA OF CARITAS

1. Acquisitive Love as the Ground-form of Human Life

FROM the above it is plain that Augustine's view of love is based on the two old love-motifs of Eros and Agape. Both were living realities for him, and helped to mould his conception of love. Yet this conception is not merely a compromise between the two rival motifs; it is an essentially new view of love, the idea of Caritas. We must now see in greater detail what this means.

In Augustine the word "love," *caritas*, means something quite specific, but it is not easy to express in a simple formula what it means. "Caritas" includes *a whole complex of ideas*, and we must have these actually before us to see what Augustine means by it. Hence it is necessary, instead of giving a brief definition, to make a thorough analysis of the idea of Caritas in order to discover its constituent ideas.

Such an analysis must start from the idea which is fundamental for Augustine, that *all love is acquisitive love.*[1] To love means to direct one's longing and desire to an object by the possession of which one expects to be made happy.[2] The idea of love as desire and its connection with the search for happiness betray Augustine's original Eros-attitude and the eudæmonism of the philosophy of late antiquity. In Cicero's *Hortensius*, the book which first aroused in Augustine a living philosophical interest,[3] he had found the

[1] "Amor appetitus quidam est." De diversis quæstionibus XXCIII., qu. xxxv. 2.
[2] "Unde se fieri putat beatum, hoc amat." De disciplina christiana, cap. vi.
[3] De beata uita, cap. i. 4; Conf., lib. III., cap. iv. 7. *Cf. supra*, p. 465.

statement: "Certainly we all want to be happy." This statement played an important part in Cicero's argument as a fact which even the most hardened sceptic must admit; it was indisputable, and therefore a specially good starting-point for a philosophical discussion.[1] His own personal feeling that the satisfaction of the craving for happiness was the deepest problem of existence, predisposed Augustine to accept this ancient conception, and it remained amid all changes one of the corner-stones of his thought. When all things are shaken, *one* fact stands immovable—namely, that all men want to be happy. Now this fact might well seem far too unlike, or at least irrelevant to Christianity, to serve as its foundation. Nevertheless it is especially important for Augustine, as it satisfies his apologetic requirements for recommending Christianity to its adversaries. To them he can say: You want your own happiness, but it is not to be found where you seek it; only the happiness which Christianity gives fully answers your need; in aiming at your own happiness, you are unwittingly reaching out towards Christianity.

By connecting love so closely with the desire for happiness, Augustine finds it possible to regard *love as the most elementary of all manifestations of human life.* There is no one who does not seek his own happiness; and for Augustine this is synonymous with: "there is no one who does not love."[2] The variety of objects on which different men set their love may be infinite; one seeks his happiness in one thing, another in another, but all are alike in that they love, that they seek their own happiness. It is so obvious that the desire for happiness and blessedness is found in all men, that

---

[1] " Itane falsum erit, unde nec ipse (cum academicis omnia dubia sint) academicus ille Cicero dubitavit, qui cum vellet in Hortensio dialogo ab aliqua re certa, de qua nullus ambigeret, sumere suæ disputationis exordium, *Beati certe*, inquit, *omnes esse volumus?* Absit ut hoc falsum esse dicamus." De trinitate, lib. XIII., cap. iv. 7.

[2] " Nemo est qui non amet." Sermo XXXIV., cap. i. 2.

it needs no proof; it is an axiom upon which all are agreed.[1] The man of the world perversely loving transient things, and the Christian loving God and eternal life, are really both striving after the same advantage. They both seek a happy life, although they think they find it in such different things.

The most diverse things can be made objects of desire and love; but Augustine does not mean that the nature of the object plays no part in this connection, and that love selects its object with sovereign freedom. Love, according to him, is by no means free and sovereign over against its object. On the contrary, it is precisely the object that, by its nature, evokes love, inflames desire, awakens longing. Only that which is in some respect *good* or advantageous, only that which is a "bonum," can be loved. Why? Because only this can exercise upon the soul that power of attraction which is an essential element in all love. To love is to seek one's good in the beloved object. An object can only be loved if it can be conceived as including this good in itself. It is, however, not enough that it should simply be a "bonum" in general, but it must be, or be conceived as, a "bonum" *for me* who am the lover. Since love means that I seek the satisfaction of my own need, it follows that I can only love *my* "bonum." This is not contradicted,

---

[1] "Beate certe omnes vivere volumus; neque quisquam est in hominum genere, qui non huic sententiæ, antequam plene sit emissa, consentiat." De moribus eccl. cath., lib. I., cap. iii. 4. "Omnium certa sententia est, qui ratione quoquo modo uti possunt, beatos esse omnes homines uelle." De ciu. dei, lib. X., cap. i. "Nota est igitur omnibus, qui una uoce si interrogari possent, utrum beati esse uellent, sine ulla dubitatione uelle responderent." Conf., lib. X., cap. xx. 29. "Omnis autem homo, qualiscumque sit, beatus vult esse. Hoc nemo est qui non velit, atque ita velit, ut præ cæteris velit; imo quicumque vult cætera, propter hoc unum velit." Sermo CCCVI., cap. ii. 3. "Beatos esse se velle, omnium hominum est. . . . Beatos esse se velle, omnes in corde suo vident, tantaque est in hac re naturæ humanæ conspiratio, ut non fallatur homo qui hoc ex animo suo de animo conjicit alieno; denique omnes id velle nos novimus." De trinitate, lib. XIII., cap. xx. 25. "Et ego qui vobiscum loquor, vitam volo et dies bonos: quod quæritis vos, hoc quæro et ego." Sermo CVIII., cap. iv. 4. De doct. christiana, lib. I., cap. xxiii. 22.

according to Augustine, by the evident fact that men often love what is evil; for in that case, it is not really the evil that they love, but the benefits they think they can gain from it. Even in evil, man loves nothing other than his "bonum"; evil as such, in its capacity as "malum," can never be an object of love. It is not the evil in evil that man loves, but the good, which is never entirely absent even in evil.[1]

Desire, acquisitive love, is the ground-form of all human life whatsoever. Our whole life, Augustine believes, exhausts itself in a ceaseless pursuit of advantages. This is as true of the life of the righteous as of the sinner. When Augustine takes desire and the longing which is centred in the self and its interests, as the chief marks of all human life, even of the highest, he intends no disparagement of humanity; it is simply a way of saying that we, unlike God, have not life in ourselves and of ourselves, but from Him. *Desire is the mark of the creature;* it is grounded in God's own will and plan. God alone is the Immortal who has life in Himself; therefore He needs nothing that is outside Himself. God has His "bonum" in Himself, and that is why there cannot be found in Him any need or desire. He is the Absolute Being and likewise the Highest Good. Thus there cannot exist anything good which He does not already possess: this is God's self-sufficiency and autarky.[2]

It is quite different with created life, human life: this has not its "bonum" in itself; its existence depends entirely on something which is outside it. It *does not already possess* its "bonum," but must first *seek* it, and this it does through love—that is, through the desire that is set upon the acquisition of this good. So, far from being evil and reprehensible, desire—here we are only concerned with desire as such, apart from the object to which it is directed—is in the highest degree good and praiseworthy, inasmuch as it gives expres-

[1] Sermo XXI. 3.   [2] De vera religione, cap. xviii. f., 35 ff.

sion to man's actual position as a created being. If man ceased to desire, it would mean that he supposed he possessed his "bonum" in himself and no longer needed to seek it elsewhere; it would be the same as an attempt to arrogate to himself something of the Divine self-existence and self-sufficiency.

In the above line of thought, elements from antiquity and from Christianity are strangely interwoven. In ancient fashion, the Divine life is thought of as self-sufficient, reposing entirely in itself and enjoying its own perfection and blessedness; it is absolute rest, exalted above all change. With this is combined the Christian idea of Creation. God, who has His "bonum" in Himself, steps outside Himself in creative activity, brings forth life and fills that life with His good.

For Augustine, however, the distinction between the creature and the Creator coincides with the metaphysical distinction between *time and eternity*. It may seem odd that Augustine often indulges in all kinds of speculations about the nature of time, which appear irrelevant for religious purposes. The explanation is that he sees his speculation about time and eternity as one with the properly religious ideas which we dealt with above.

It is characteristic of human life that it is lived in time and therefore is subject to continual change and decay. We cannot deny all reality to life in time, but it is reality of a lower order. Time includes three moments: past, present and future. But we cannot say of all these moments that they possess reality or that they *are*. The future *is not yet*, and the past *is no more*. Only the present *is*. But not even this *is* in the deepest sense of the word, for in the next moment that which now is has ceased to be, has changed into something past, something which is no longer. The future is a ceaseless threat to the present; the future turns the present into the past and robs it of its reality. Only a present which cannot become a past, *is* in the deepest sense of the word. Such a present does not exist in time, but only in eternity. Eternity knows no past, present and future. In eternity there is only the eternal Now, the eternal present, which is not threatened by any future.[1]

All this sheds a new light on Augustine's conception of acquisitive love as the ground-form of human life in general. Man is confined within temporal existence, he has not his " bonum " in himself, but must seek it outside himself. By acquisitive love he seeks his " bonum "—that is, he reaches out from the present with its imperfection towards something future from which he expects satisfaction. Love is his longing set upon that which is not yet. Even should he attain the object of his desire so as to have it as a present possession, he does not really *possess* it, for he is in perpetual danger of losing it. The future casts its threatening shadow into the present and prevents man from enjoying what he has, for it is of the nature of time to deprive us of what we love.[2] Even if a man gained all he desired in this temporal life and were sure of not losing it during his lifetime, the stream of time bears him inexorably towards *death*, which means the great loss of all things. If he lacks his " bonum " in the present, he lives with his desire in the future; if he possesses what he thinks to be his " bonum " in the present, even then he lives in the future, fearing that it will rob him of what he now has. In neither case does he live in the present. Yet it is nothing but the present which his love and longing seek; this is clearly the case, if we put together three propositions which Augustine takes for granted: (1) love seeks its " bonum," but (2) this is the same as that which is, and (3) only the present *is*. Now the creature is such that the present and that which *is* slip out of his hands. Only God and the eternal *is*. The Creator's

---

[1] *Cf.* on this, Conf., lib. XI., cap. xiv. 17 ff.
[2] " Tempora surripiunt quod amamus." De vera rel., cap. xxxv. 65.

tense is present, the eternal Now; the creature's tense is preterite and future.[1] But this is merely another way of saying that God has His "bonum" in Himself, whereas man as a created being must seek his good outside himself. It is not given to him to live only by his own resources; like a parasitic growth, he must affix himself to something else. But the nature of this other thing to which he affixes himself is not a matter of indifference. It is all-important that the object upon which he sets his love and longing should really be a "bonum," and thus be able to give him the nourishment and satisfaction which he needs and seeks.

2. Caritas and Cupiditas

In our analysis of the idea of love in Augustine, we have so far dealt simply with what he thinks characteristic of, and common to, all love whatsoever. We may summarise the result thus: (1) All love is acquisitive love. (2) This acquisitive love is the most elementary and fundamental phenomenon in human life. God has created man such that he *must* desire, *must* love and long for something. Since God has reserved to Himself the privilege of "being sufficient for Himself" and has forbidden man to "be sufficient for himself," this is a plain indication to man that he should seek and desire his "good," his "sufficiency," in something which does not originally belong to him.

We must now go on to note that in itself this acquisitive love is neither good nor bad; to desire is simply human, an expression of the fact that man is a temporal being, belonging to the sphere of created things. The opposition between

---

[1] "In omni prorsus agitatione creaturæ duo tempora invenio, præteritum et futurum. Præsens quæro. . . . Præteritum et futurum invenio in omni motu rerum: in veritate quæ manet, præteritum et futurum non invenio, sed solum præsens, et hoc incorruptibiliter, quod in creatura non est. Discute rerum mutationes, invenies Fuit et Erit: cogita Deum, invenies Est, ubi Fuit et Erit esse non possit." In ev. Jn., tract. xxxviii. 10.

good and evil, between a *right* and a *wrong* love, first appears in connection with the question of the object of the love. That love is right which sets its desire on a *right object*—that is, on an object which really can satisfy man's needs; that love is wrong which is directed to a *wrong object*—that is, to an object which is unable, or only apparently able, to satisfy man.

Upon what *objects*, then, can love be set?

There are ultimately only two possibilities: " Omnis amor aut ascendit aut descendit."[1] Behind the manifold things on which love can be set, there is an inescapable Either—Or: love is directed either *upwards* towards God, the Creator, or *downwards* towards created things. This gives Augustine his fundamental contrast between Caritas and Cupiditas. *Caritas is love directed upwards, Cupiditas is love directed downwards. Caritas is love of God, Cupiditas love of the world. Caritas is love for the eternal, Cupiditas is love for the temporal.* The reason why love can take these contrary courses is that man is by nature both a spiritual and a fleshly being. He is the highest of the creatures, and so both possibilities are open to him; in Caritas he can raise himself up to his Creator, and in Cupiditas he can sink down into the lower creation. Man's spirit seeks to wing its way up to the eternal and find its happiness there, but his bodily and fleshly nature binds him by its weight to the earthly and temporal and prevents his flight.[2]

Man has to choose between Caritas and Cupiditas, between directing his love up to the eternal or down to the temporal. What makes this choice so serious is that we ourselves are

[1] Enarratio in psalmum cxxii. 1. " All love either ascends or descends."

[2] " Intellexit ubi esset, quia per fragilitatem carnis suæ ad illam beatitudinem volare non posset; circumspexit pondera sua; . . . *Spiritus sursum vocat, pondus carnis deorsum revocat. . . . Quomodo volabo?* quomodo perveniam?" Enarr. in Ps. lxxxiii. 9. Here, as often, Augustine quotes the passage from Wisd. ix. 15, influenced by Greek thought, about the body that weighs down the soul. *Cf. supra*, p 466, n. 3. Other instances of his use of this passage are De ciu. dei, lib. XIX., cap. xxvii.; In ev. Jn., tract. xxi. 1; and especially tract. xxiii. 5.

transformed into conformity with that which we love. Love binds us to the beloved object, which enters as our " bonum " into us and sets its stamp upon our self : we become like the object we love. By loving God, we become as gods; by loving the world, we ourselves become merely a bit of world, and so the Scripture rightly calls evil men quite simply " the world."[1] When man reaches up in Caritas towards the eternal, he himself becomes filled, so to speak, with eternity; if he sinks down in Cupiditas into the created things, he becomes filled with what is lower and more transient than himself.[2]

Caritas and Cupiditas, however, are not on an equal footing, and they have not each the same right to lay their claim upon man. Both by reason of man's true destiny and in the nature of the case itself, *Caritas is the only right love.*

First let us look at the question from the point of view of *man's destiny.*

Since God has put man in an intermediate position between two worlds and so given him the possibility of directing his love by his own choice either upwards towards heaven or downwards towards the world, it might seem as if the choice were a matter affecting only man himself. God has ordered it so that man is not " sufficient for himself," but must seek his " good " outside himself; He has also placed man where there is within his reach both a greater " good " which he can only attain by great effort, and a lesser " good " which he can have with little trouble. It appears to be his own affair whether he pretentiously chooses the greater good or more modestly contents himself with the smaller. That is not Augustine's opinion. The choice is, of course, free inasmuch as man has the possibility of choosing in both directions. But if he chooses to direct his love downwards, he has

---

[1] " Inde acceperunt nomen, ex eo quod amant. *Amando Deum, efficimur dii : ergo amando mundum, dicimur mundus.*" Sermo CXXI. 1. *Cf.* In ev. Jn., tract. ii. 11, and De doct. christiana, lib. I., cap. xii.

[2] In ev. Jn., tract. i. 4.

thereby fallen short of his God-given destiny. It was not without purpose that God gave him the highest place in creation. The very fact that He made man walk upright instead of bowed down like the irrational beasts, which have to seek their food on the earth, is a clear indication of what his destiny is. We must seek the nourishment of our soul and our " good " above. It is incongruous to have the face looking upwards and the heart downwards. The form given to man at creation exhorts him : Sursum cor !¹

By God's ordinance, the good which is to be the object of man's longing is *above* him.² So he must direct himself *upwards,* and in love (Eros) raise himself up to that good. But all too easily, earthly good can confuse his mind and drag his love *downwards* to itself. He becomes bowed down to earth, he becomes " *curvatus,*" as Augustine expresses it.³

Caritas, however, is the only right sort of love, not only

---

¹ " Belluas enim Deus prostratas in faciem fecit, pastum quærentes de terra : te in duos pedes erexit de terra. Tuam faciem sursum attendere voluit. *Non discordet cor tuum a facie tua. Non habeas faciem sursum, et cor deorsum.*" Sermo de disciplina christiana, cap. v. " Bonum est sursum habere cor." De ciu. dei, lib. XIV., cap. xiii.

² " Sicut enim non est a carne sed super carnem, quod carnem facit uiuere: sic non est ab homine, sed *super hominem, quod hominem facit beate uiuere.*" De ciu. dei, lib. XIX., cap. xxv.

³ " Et *quando se homo pronum facit ad terrenas concupiscentias, incurvatur quodammodo ; cum autem erigitur in superna, rectum fit cor ejus, ut bonus illi sit Deus.*" Enarr. in Ps. l. 15. " Noli relicto superiore bono, *curvare te ad inferius bonum.* Rectus esto, ut lauderis: quia laudabuntur omnes recti corde. Unde enim peccas, nisi quia inordinate tractas res quas in usum accepisti ? Esto bene utens rebus inferioribus, et eris recte fruens bono superiore." Sermo XXI. 3. " Quid est autem *curvari* ? Non se posse erigere. Talem invenit Dominus mulierem per decem et octo annos curvam: non se poterat erigere. Tales sunt qui in terra cor habent. At vero, quia invenit mulier illa Dominum, et sanavit eam, habeat sursum cor. In quantum tamen curvatur, adhuc gemit. Curvatur enim ille qui dicit: Corpus enim quod corrumpitur, aggravat animam, et deprimit terrena inhabitatio sensum multa cogitantem." Enarr. in Ps. xxxvii. 10. The words about the body weighing down the soul are quoted from Wisd. ix. 15—on this see *supra,* p. 466, n. 3, and p. 483, n. 2.
It is of interest to compare Augustine and Luther on this point. For Augustine, sin consists in the fact that man is bent down to earth (curvatus); and Luther, too, can say that sinful man is " curvatus." But this means for Luther something quite different; it means that man is egocentric, that his

because of this positive Divine ordinance, but because of *the nature of the case itself*. Desire is so constituted that it can only reach its goal in the form of Caritas. It is only in appearance that there are two ways of satisfying desire.

This is plain from the definition of desire as a necessary feature of created life. The Divine life is self-sufficient (sufficit sibi), it reposes in itself and has its "bonum" in itself. God's *possession* of everything that can possibly be called good makes it impossible for Him to need or desire anything. What the Divine life thus *possesses*, the creature must first *seek*; it does this by desire, the simple effort to possess oneself of one's "bonum." The difference between God and the creature is that that which exists in God as an immediate unity, has fallen apart in the creature and can only be restored to unity by a special act. The happy life, beata vita, is characterised by the fact that "need" and "bonum" coincide completely and form an indissoluble unity. This is so with God from the start; for man, as a created being, it is the goal that looms in the distance, to which he draws near by the act of desire (love). All our striving, all our desire, has really but one end: to destroy the dualism between "need" and "bonum." There is nothing of this dualism in God. He is absolute rest and absence of need. It is strictly not correct, according to Augustine, when Scripture says that God rested on the seventh day. God does not need to rest, He is Himself rest, *quies*.[1] For

---

will is determined always by his own interest and so is bent upon itself (" incurvatus in se "). In Augustine, the sinful soul is " *bent down* " *to earth*; in Luther, it is " *bent upon itself*." The difference is clearest of all if we notice how this situation is thought to be changed. For Augustine it happens when the soul directs its desire upwards towards God and the heavenly world. Luther has discovered that even the soul that is turned towards heaven can be bent upon itself—that is, if it is governed by desire and longing. " Even in heaven they only seek their own," he can therefore say. It is from this point of view that he criticises Catholic piety.

[1] *Cf*. De ciu. dei, lib. XI., cap. viii., and lib. XXII., cap. xxx. " Tu autem bonum nullo indigens bono semper quietus es, quoniam *tua quies tu ipse es*." Conf., lib. XIII., cap. xxxviii. 53.

us the situation is different. The unity that is the foundation of a happy life has been destroyed. We stand on the one side with our need, and on the other, separated from us and outside us, is our " bonum." It is the task of desire or love to bridge this gulf and place our " bonum " in our hands, so as to restore the original unity necessary for a happy life. When desire has performed its function of uniting " need " and " bonum," man has achieved absence of need and perfect rest. In this sense, *quies* is the key-word of Augustine's thought.[1] God is Himself " quies," eternal rest. " Quies " is also the ultimate aim of man in all his striving, no matter what object the individual may pursue.[2] So long as man has not attained this end, he wanders about restlessly pursuing his "bonum." It is against this background that we must understand Augustine's famous saying: "Thou hast made us for Thyself, and our heart is restless till it finds rest in Thee."[3]

When I love or desire a particular object, that does not mean that I desire it simply or unconditionally. I desire it only on the tacit supposition that it can serve as my " bonum," satisfy my need and let my restless seeking come to rest. Desire itself, so understood, contains in itself the standard by which we can distinguish between what is and

[1] Thus the idea of *quies* embraces Augustine's Confessions from the first chapter to the last; *cf.* in cap. i.: " inquietum est cor nostrum, donec requiescat in te," and in the last chapter: " tua quies tu ipse es."

[2] So certainly as every man seeks his own happiness and joy, he is striving ultimately to attain perfect rest. Even war exists to lead to peace. · *Cf.* De ciu. dei, lib. XIX., cap. xi.-xiii. " Sicut nemo est qui gaudere nolit, ita nemo est qui pacem habere nolit. Quando quidem et ipsi, qui bella uolunt, nihil aliud quam uincere uolunt; ad gloriosam ergo pacem bellando cupiunt peruenire." Cap. xii. Little as man can ever free himself from the elementary desire for happiness, just as little can he free himself from the will to *quies* (pax): the two are at bottom one, and possess something of the necessity of natural law. " . . . quodam modo naturæ suæ legibus." " Non amare tamen qualemcumque pacem nullo modo potest. Nullius quippe uitium ita contra naturam est, ut naturæ deleat etiam extrema uestigia." *Ibid.*

[3] " Fecisti nos ad te et inquietum est cor nostrum, donec requiescat in te." Conf., lib. I., cap. i. 1.

what is not worth loving. Anything whatever may become an object of desire; but not everything is of such a nature that we can *rest* in it and find complete satisfaction.

What must be the nature of the object that can give man rest and satisfaction? It must obviously be a "bonum," or else it would be impossible to love or desire the object. But this point is irrelevant to the present question, for simply to state that love can only be directed to a "bonum" does not explain the difference between Caritas and Cupiditas. Both alike seek their satisfaction in a "bonum." If Cupiditas, which loves created things, is a wrong sort of love, that is not because created things are evil. All that God has created is good. What is wrong with Cupiditas is not that it seeks its "good" in something evil, but that it seeks its "good" in a far too small and insignificant good, which is incapable of giving real and final satisfaction.

To explain why created things can never offer full satisfaction to man's thirst for rest and blessedness, Augustine refers to the old idea that God has created everything *out of nothing*. This idea he interprets in a peculiar way. God is the Absolute Being, which is identical with the Absolute Good. Between this Absolute Being and its diametrical opposite, "nothing," created things exist as a *Relative Being*. *As created by God*, they have Being and are Good; *as created out of nothing*, they can decline in Being and Goodness.[1] By turning away from God, the creature sinks ever

---

[1] "Hoc scio, naturam Dei numquam, nusquam, nulla ex parte posse deficere, et *ea posse deficere, quæ ex nihilo facta sunt.*" De ciu. dei, lib. XII., cap. viii.; *cf.* lib. XII., cap. i. "*Quare deficiunt?* Quia mutabilia sunt. Quare mutabilia sunt? Quia non summe sunt. Quare non summe sunt? Quia inferiora sunt eo a quo facta sunt. . . . Ipsum enim quantumcumque esse, bonum est; quia summum bonum est summe esse. Unde fecit? *Ex nihilo.*" De vera rel., cap. xviii. 35. "*Sed uitio deprauari nisi ex nihilo facta natura non posset. Ac per hoc ut natúra sit, ex eo habet quod a Deo facta est; ut autem ab eo quod est deficiat, ex hoc quod de nihilo facta est.*" De ciu. dei, lib. XIV., cap. xiii. "Unde colligit non ob aliud res deficere uel posse deficere, nisi quod ex nihilo factæ sunt. . . ." Epist. cxviii. 15.

deeper down towards the "nothing" out of which it was raised by creation. It is this sinking, this loss of Being and Goodness, that is for Augustine the meaning of *evil*.[1] Evil is nothing but "privatio boni."[2] If, then, evil means decrease of Good and Being, a creature's good ("bonum") consists in the increase of its Being. When a man sets his love and his desire on a certain object as his "bonum," this simply means that he is trying to possess himself of that object so as to supply the lack of Being which is inherent in his existence as a creature, and so to insure himself against the risk of annihilation which threatens everything that only possesses relative Being. Now what does it mean if man, to whom God has given the highest place in the created hierarchy of higher and lower Being—that is, the place nearest God and farthest from "nothing"—what does it mean if man does not seek his "bonum" in God by way of Caritas, but seeks it by way of Cupiditas in some temporal object? It means that he tries to supply his lack of reality by means of something which possesses still less reality than himself. That is the great and fatal contradiction in all Cupiditas-love: in its capacity as desire, it seeks ultimately to fill man with reality and deliver him from the threatening "nothing"; but it tries to accomplish this by binding him to things which more and more drag him down from

---

[1] Since God is Absolute Being and Absolute Good, and since "nothing" is the diametrical opposite of Being, one might expect "nothing" to be identical with evil. But that is not what Augustine means. His opposition to Manichæism led him to hold that evil must not be thought of as an independent substance. Evil, unlike Being and the Good, has not a *causa efficiens*, but only a *causa deficiens*. "Quæ tamen quanto magis sunt et bona faciunt, causas habent efficientes; in quantum autem deficiunt et ex hoc mala faciunt, causas habent deficientes." De ciu. dei, lib. XII., cap. viii. When Being ceases, evil also ceases. It can only exist so long as there is some Being which it can, so to speak, prey upon and reduce. "Ac per hoc nullum est quod dicitur malum, si nullum sit bonum. Sed bonum omni malo carens, integrum bonum est; cui verum inest malum, vitiatum vel·vitiosum bonum est: *nec malum unquam potest esse ullum, ubi bonum est nullum.*" Enchiridion, cap. xiii.

[2] "Quid est autem aliud quod malum dicitur, nisi *privatio boni*?" Enchirid., cap. xi.

his higher estate towards "nothing."[1]   Cupiditas is *false* love not merely because it is *wrong*—that is, forbidden by God—but also because it is *senseless*.   When I love or desire something, that means I want to win something which I do not already possess.   But when man cleaves to the world in Cupiditas, he wins nothing he does not already possess.   He may gain certain outward objects which were not previously in his possession; but in the last resort he desires these not in themselves, but as a means to his rest and happiness, since he expects from them an increase of his own Being and a guarantee against the risk of annihilation.   But how can they offer him any such thing?   The world belongs, like himself, to the sphere of the created and transient; its Being is mixed with nothingness to an even higher degree than his own.   How could it increase his Being?   In virtue of the rule that a man becomes like the object he loves, the man who devotes himself in Cupiditas to the world, himself becomes "world," loses the higher Being and higher Goodness which he had as the highest of the creatures, and sinks ever deeper down towards "nothing."   But that was certainly not what the man really desired.

It is clear that not any and every "bonum" can satisfy man's need.   As created by God, temporal things are good, but when He created them He never intended them to be objects of man's love and desire in which man should seek his "sufficiency."[2]   It is most perverse if, in order to satisfy its need, the soul has recourse to what is less and emptier than itself; for if this is not in itself evil, it has at any rate no *quies* to give.   We now come back to the question with

---

[1] " Vita, quæ fructu corporis delectata negligit Deum, *inclinatur ad nihilum*." De vera rel., cap. xi. 22.   " Tanto utique deterior, quanto ab eo, quod summe est, ad id quod minus est, uergit, ut etiam ipsa minus sit; quanto autem minus est, tanto utique fit *propinquior nihilo*."   Contra Secundinum 15.   Augustine emphasises this point most particularly in his attack on Manichæism.

[2] " Omnis creatura Dei bona est, et illic peccatum non est, nisi quia male uteris."   Sermo XXI. 3.

which we started: What must be the nature of the object that can give man perfect rest and satisfaction? It is by now obvious what Augustine's answer must be. It can be summarised in the following two points:

1. Real rest and satisfaction can only be found in *the highest good*; man cannot be content with anything less. If by pursuing some lower good he is prevented from seeking the highest good, then that lower good is no longer a good for him; it hinders him from attaining that which could satisfy him to a still higher degree. So long as anything higher and better is conceivable, it is this that must be sought. Man can only find rest at the final goal, but only that which is the highest good, "summum bonum," can be the final goal.[1]

2. Real rest and satisfaction can only be found in that which is also *the immutable, inalienable good*. Actually, this is already included in the idea of a highest good, but Augustine often affirms it independently. If I had reached the highest good, but there were still a risk of losing it, that would be the end of rest: I should live in continual fear. Real "quies" can only exist along with the secure consciousness that the good I possess is an eternal and inalienable good, a "bonum incommutabile." Happiness without perman nce cannot be my "bonum" any more than a permanent life without happiness.[2] Only in these two elements together do I possess the "bonum" which really can satisfy me.

[1] " Bonorum summa, Deus nobis est. Deus est nobis summum bonum. Neque infra remanendum nobis est, neque ultra quærendum." De moribus eccl. cath., lib. I., cap. viii. 13.

[2] " Non ergo magnum est diu vivere, aut semper vivere: sed magnum est beate vivere." Sermo CXXVII., cap. i. 2. " Nullo modo igitur esse poterit vita veraciter beata, nisi fuerit sempiterna." De trinitate, lib. XIII., cap. viii. 11. " Sine immortalitate non potest esse [beatitudo]." *Ibid.*, cap. vii. 10. " Cum ergo beati esse omnes homines velint, si vere volunt, profecto et esse immortales volunt: aliter enim beati esse non possent. Denique et de immortalitate interrogati, sicut et de beatitudine, omnes eam se velle respondent." *Ibid.*, cap. viii. 11. *Cf. supra*, p. 478, n. 1.

When this two-fold standard, deduced directly from the nature of desire, is applied to the objects that offer themselves for desire, it at once appears that created things do not stand the test. In the whole of creation there is nothing that can reasonably be called the highest good, nor is there anything permanently and inalienably good. God, on the other hand, fulfils both requirements: (1) *He is the highest good*, inclusive of all good—that is, all that can possibly be sought and desired. God is not a particular good, but is the actual Goodness in all that is good[1]; He is reality, and as such, "ipsa veritas," "ipsa bonitas" and "ipsa pulchritudo"; (2) *He is the eternal and immutable*; one who has found Him and has Him as his highest good, need never fear to lose it. In a word, *God is at once "summum et incommutabile bonum,"* the highest and immutable (inalienable) good.[2]

Augustine found among created things no "bonum" sufficiently high, and at the same time sufficiently sure and reliable, to be made with any confidence his "bonum"; but before God and His perfection and eternity he must exclaim: "What can be not only *better*, but also *more sure* than this 'bonum'?"[3] Here man has what can wholly

---

[1] "Quid autem eligamus, quod præcipue diligamus, nisi quo nihil melius inuenimus? Hoc Deus est, cui si aliquid diligendo uel præponimus uel æquamus, nos ipsos diligere nescimus. Tanto enim nobis melius est, quanto magis in illum imus, quo nihil melius est." Epist., CLV., iv. 13. "Bonum hoc et bonum illud: *tolle hoc et illud, et vide ipsum bonum,* si potes; ita Deum videbis, non alio bono bonum, sed *bonum omnis boni.* . . . Sic amandus est Deus, non hoc et illud bonum, sed ipsum bonum." De trinitate, lib. VIII., cap. iii. 4. "Te invoco, Deus veritas, in quo et a quo et per quem vera sunt, quæ vera sunt omnia. . . . Deus beatitudo, in quo et a quo et per quem beata sunt, quæ beata sunt omnia. Deus bonum et pulchrum, in quo et a quo et per quem bona et pulchra sunt, quæ bona et pulchra sunt omnia." Soliloquia, lib. I., cap. i. 3.

[2] De doct. christiana, lib. I., cap. xxxiii. 37. "Nullo modo dubitamus, si quis beatus esse statuit, id eum sibi conparare debere, quod semper manet nec ulla sæuiente fortuna eripi potest. . . . Deus, inquam, uobis æternus esse semper manens uidetur? . . . Deum igitur, inquam, qui habet, beatus est." De beata vita, ii. 11. *Cf.* De diversis quæstionibus octoginta tribus, qu. xxxv.

[3] "Quid esse non solum melius, sed etiam certius hoc bono potest?" De moribus eccl. cath., lib. I., cap. xi. 18.

satisfy him. "Desire" has found its "bonum"; the dualism is overcome. This could not be said when it sought its satisfaction in temporal things. Desire means that man seeks to gain something which he does not previously possess. It loses its meaning when man sets his desire, his Cupiditas, upon temporal things; for even if he gains these, he really gains nothing beyond what he already has : he is himself a created and transient being, and from created and transient things he can only reap corruption. But just as desire in the form of Cupiditas unites us with transient things, so in the form of Caritas it unites us with God and the eternal world. *Only then has desire any real meaning,* for it brings man into relation with something which he does not possess in himself,[1] but needs to acquire : in himself he is a created and transient being, but by union with God he gains eternal life and eternal "quies," for which his soul hungers and thirsts : "inquietum est cor nostrum, donec requiescat in te" (*Conf.,* I. i. 1). Desire—the most fundamental and elementary phenomenon in human life—finds its meaning only when it is directed to God; in other words, *God is the only right and natural correlate to man's desire.* The whole stream of love must therefore flow to Him and not even the smallest tricklet must run away elsewhere; as the highest good, God cannot suffer anything to be loved beside Himself.[2] It is also unnecessary to desire anything apart from Him, since all that is worth loving and desiring is found in fullest measure in Him.[3] As He is sufficient for Himself, so He is also sufficient for us : "Ipse *sufficit* tibi; præter illum nihil sufficit tibi."[4]

[1] De trinitate, lib. VIII., cap. iii. 4. *Cf.* De vera rel., cap. x. 19: "Æterno enim Creatori adhærentes, et nos æternitate afficiamur necesse est."

[2] "Quidquid aliud diligendum venerit in animum, illuc rapiatur, quo totus dilectionis impetus currit . . . [dilectio] Dei quæ *nullum a se rivulum duci extra patitur,* cujus derivatione minuatur." De doct. christiana, lib. I., cap. xxii. 21.

[3] De vera rel., cap. xlviii. 93.

[4] Sermo CCCXXXIV. 3. *Cf.* Sermo XXIII., cap. x. Sermo CLXXVII. 9:

It has by now become clear that the difference between Caritas and Cupiditas is not one of *kind*, but of *object*. In kind, Caritas and Cupiditas, love of God and love of the world, correspond most closely.[1] Love is desire and longing whether it is directed to temporal things or to God and the eternal. For Augustine love is a longing indifferent in itself, whose quality is determined by the object to which it is directed. It can be the highest thing—if it is directed to the highest, to what is really worth loving and desiring, to God; but it can be the lowest—if it is directed to the lowest, to temporal, transient things. Love is the elementary motive power in all human action, good and bad alike. The main thing, therefore, is that man should see through the worthlessness of worldly things and the folly of desiring anything so transient, and in order to have his hunger really satisfied should turn his desire to that which eternally abides. The idea that love is an ethically indifferent force which becomes ethical or unethical according to the nature of the object it desires is at times given very vigorous expression by Augustine. He says, for instance: "What is it that effects even the evil in man, if not love? Show me a love that is idle and effects nothing. Vices, adulteries, crimes, murders, all kinds of excesses—is it not love which produces them? Purify therefore thy love: conduct the water which is flowing into the sewer, to the garden instead. Such a strong urge as it had to the world, let it have to the Creator of the world."[2] Caritas-love, which is the same as

---

"Ipse ergo sufficit, solus sufficit, de quo dictùm est, 'Ostende nobis Patrem, et sufficit nobis." Enarr. in Ps. cxxii. 12. In this connection Augustine loves to quote Philip's request to Jesus, Jn. xiv. 8: "Lord, shew us the Father and it sufficeth us." He takes this to mean that the Vision of God, "visio Dei," is the only thing that is sufficient for us, "quod sufficit nobis." *Cf. infra*, p. 509.

"Deus restat quem si sequimur, bene; si assequimur, non tantum bene, sed etiam beate vivimus." De moribus eccl. cath., cap. vi.

1 "His consideratis quid magnum uita æterna iubeat amatoribus suis, cum se iubet sic amari, quem ad modum hæc amatur a suis?" Epist. cxxvii. 4.

2 "Quid enim de quoquam homine etiam male operatur, nisi amor? Da mihi vacantem amorem et nihil operantem. Flagitia, adulteria, facinora,

the good will, is distinguished from Cupiditas-love, which is the root of all evil, not absolutely and qualitatively, but merely in virtue of its object. In both cases it is a question of acquisitive love. "Love, but see to it *what* you love. Love to God and love to neighbour is called Caritas; love of the world and love of temporal things is called Cupiditas."[1] We must be converted from false Cupiditas-love, but the conversion (conversio) consists simply in turning love's desire from a lower to a higher object, in conducting the water from the sewer to the garden (converte ad hortum!). The soul which vainly sought its desired happiness in the world must turn to God and seek in Him the satisfaction of its desire. Betrayed by the world in its quest for riches, honour and life, it turns its back upon this world and seeks satisfaction in another, where these advantages can be gained, but in a still higher form, and for perpetuity.[2] To sacrifice the temporal world for the eternal, therefore, can also be described by Augustine as an act of prudence.[3]

---

homicidia, luxurias omnes, nonne amor operatur? Purga ergo amorem tuum: aquam fluentem in cloacam, converte ad hortum: quales impetus habebat ad mundum, tales habeat ad artificem mundi." Enarr. in Ps. XXXI. ii. 5.

[1] "Amate, sed quid ametis videte. Amor Dei, amor proximi, caritas dicitur: amor mundi, amor hujus sæculi, cupiditas dicitur." *Ibid.*

[2] "Diuitiæ si diliguntur, ibi seruentur, ubi perire non possunt; honor si diligitur, illic habeatur, ubi nemo indignus honoratur; salus si diligitur, ibi adipiscenda desideretur, ubi adeptæ nihil timetur; uita si diligitur, ibi adquiratur, ubi nulla morte finitur." Epist. cxxvii. 5. It should be noted that these words occur in direct connection with the thought of the Commandment of Love and (Rom. v. 5) of the love shed abroad in our hearts through the Holy Spirit.

With reference to the idea of conversion, K. Holl remarks: " It was Augustine who established the word and idea of ' converti ' in the vocabulary of Western Christianity " (*Gesammelte Aufsätze zur Kirchengeschichte*, iii., p. 83). We may add that Augustine is the starting-point of the tradition according to which the meaning of conversion is the transference of *desire* to a new *object*. In this respect Augustine's own conversion is typical.

[3] " Prudenter intellegis, quod in hoc mundo et in hac uita nulla anima possit esse secura." Epist. cxxx. 1. " Dicatur hæc prudentia, quia prospectissime adhærebit bono, quod non amittatur." Epist. clv. 12. *Cf.* Expositio quarundam propositionum ex Epistola ad Romanos xlix.: " Definitio enim prudentiæ in appetendis bonis et vitandis malis explicari solet. . . . Eadem namque animæ natura et prudentiam carnis habet, cum inferiora sectatur; et prudentiam spiritus, cum superiora eligit."

In the light of the above, it is easy to understand the peculiar idea which is fairly often found in Augustine, that *even man's sins and iniquities are in the last resort expressions of his—admittedly misdirected—search for God*. What, asks Augustine, is sinful curiosity but desire for knowledge? But I can only acquire reliable knowledge by turning to the eternal. What is pride but desire for power? But real power is only won by seeking God's kingdom in Caritas. What does sensual desire long for but rest? But rest is found only where no need or corruption exists—that is, only in the eternal life.[1] The sinner's mistake is not that he pursues riches, honour, power, pleasure and other advantages for his own sake; for these are but different aspects of the "quies" and blessedness which he as a created being should and must desire : his mistake is that he seeks this where it is not to be found. The very insatiability of vice shows that man is meant for eternity; for it is this that prevents his ever being satisfied with anything temporal, and ceaselessly drives him on in his fruitless search for happiness. In a word, *what* the sinner seeks is *right*, but he seeks it *in the wrong place*. What the sinner seeks is right, for he, like all other men, seeks life and good days; he seeks blessedness, but blessedness is nothing other than God : thus in the midst of his sin he is really seeking God, though he himself is not conscious of it and does not seek Him in the right place.[2] Augustine says:

---

[1] " Quid est autem unde homo commemorari non possit ad virtutes capessendas, quando de *ipsis vitiis* potest ? Quid enim appetit curiositas nisi cognitionem, quæ certa esse non potest, nisi rerum æternarum et eodem modo se semper habentium ? Quid appetit superbia nisi potentiam, quæ refertur ad agendi facilitatem, quam non invenit anima perfecta nisi Deo subdita, et ad ejus regnum summa caritate conversa ? Quid appetit voluptas corporis nisi quietem, quæ non est nisi ubi nulla est indigentia et nulla corruptio ?" De vera rel., cap. lii. 101.

[2] " Ita fornicatur anima, cum auertitur abs te et quærit extra te ea quæ pura et liquida non inuenit, nisi cum redit ad te. Peruerse te imitantur omnes, qui longe se a te faciunt et extollunt se aduersum te. Sed etiam sic te imitando indicant creatorem te esse omnis naturæ et ideo non esse, quo a te omni modo recedatur." Conf., lib. II., cap. vi. 14. *Cf.* the complete argument in Conf.,

"When I seek Thee, my God, I seek the blessed life "[1]; but he could equally well say: When I seek the blessed life, I seek Thee, my God. Augustine had no difficulty with this identification of the quest for happiness with the quest for God. From his fundamental axiom that all men without exception seek their own happiness[2] he unhesitatingly drew the conclusion, not only that all men love, but also that *all without exception love God*, whether they know it or not.[3] The sinner does not know it, and so he roams about in the temporal sphere; nevertheless it is really God whom he seeks even there, for he seeks his happiness, and happiness is God. Even Cupiditas, even the love which turns away from God, is in the ultimate analysis love to God, although man is unaware of that fact.

In such circumstances, it is not surprising that the distinction between Caritas and Cupiditas, which at first seemed so sharp and clear, becomes in the end very vague. In the course of our exposition, we have had to add one qualification after another which has made the contrast less sharp. The substance of the matter may be summarised in the following four points:

---

lib. II., cap. vi. 13-14. "Non est requies, ubi quæritis eam. *Quærite quod quæritis, sed ibi non est, ubi quæritis.* Beatam uitam quæritis in regione mortis: non est illic. Quomodo enim beata uita, ubi nec uita?" Conf., lib. IV., cap. xii. 18. "Quod quæritis, et ego quæro; sed non ibi quæritis ubi possimus invenire. Ergo audite me, ubi possimus invenire: vóbis non tollo, *locum vobis ostendo*: imo sequamur omnes eum qui novit ubi sit quod quærimus. Sic et nunc, quia desideratis vitam et dies bonos, non possumus vobis dicere: Nolite desiderare vitam et dies bonos; sed illud dicimus: Nolite hic quærere in hoc sæculo vitam et dies bonos, ubi boni esse non possunt. . . . Desiderium ergo vestrum, quo vultis vitam et dies bonos, non solum non reprimo, sed etiam vehementius accendo. *Prorsus quærite vitam, quærite dies bonos : sed ubi possunt inveniri, ibi quærantur.*" Sermo CVIII., cap. v. 5. *Cf.* De trinitate, lib. XI. v; and Sermo CLVIII. 9: "Quid hic quærebas? Divitias? Avare, quid enim tibi sufficit, si Deus ipse non sufficit? Sed quid amabas? Gloriam, honores? Deus tibi erit gloria."

[1] Conf., lib. X., cap. xx. 29.

[2] On this, *cf. supra*, pp. 477 f.

[3] "*Deus quem amat omne quod potest amare, sive sciens, sive nesciens.*" Soliloquia, lib. I., cap. i. 2.

1. At first sight, Caritas and Cupiditas seem to represent a sharp dualism of upward-directed and downward-directed love, love of God and love of the world, love for the eternal and love for the temporal.

2. The distinction is softened, however, when we notice that Caritas and Cupiditas stand on the same ground: the *nature* of the love is the same, though the object in either case is different. The nature of the love is in both cases the same, because Caritas as well as Cupiditas is acquisitive love; both alike seek only their own "bonum." But the object of the love is different, for Caritas, unlike Cupiditas, does not seek its "bonum" in the temporal, but in the eternal.

3. Even with regard to the *object*, the contrast is somewhat weakened by the emphasis on the common nature of all love, as being the quest for happiness and desire for "quies." If we look beyond the immediate, concrete object of love to the intention of all love to reach a final "quies," then all love seems to be set upon a common object. In this sense, all love is ultimately love to God, and the difference between various sorts of love is reduced to a matter of where and how and with what success this common object is sought. Caritas seeks God and finds Him because it seeks in the right place; Cupiditas seeks Him (for even it seeks its "quies"), but does not find Him, because it seeks Him in the wrong place and cleaves to His creatures instead of to Himself.

4. In formal confirmation of this modification of the contrast between Caritas and Cupiditas, we may add a fourth point. The contrast between Caritas and Cupiditas is almost of the nature of a formula in Augustine; yet since they really represent one and the same kind of love which is simply set on different objects, this fact has coloured even his mode of expression. Convinced as he is that Cupiditas is the very root of all evil,[1] that does not prevent him from speaking of a

---

[1] "Quomodo enim radix omnium malorum cupiditas, sic radix omnium bonorum caritas est." Enarr. in Ps. xc. 1, 8.

good Cupiditas—that is, a Cupiditas directed to right objects, to eternal things.[1]   And in the " De doctrina christiana " he makes the peculiar statement that *not even Caritas, although it is the fulfilment of the Law, can possibly be a right love if it is not directed to the right objects.*[2]   No doubt this should be regarded rather as an inexact use of terms—by Caritas Augustine means a love directed to God and the eternal, which cannot turn to false objects without ceasing to be Caritas; and by Cupiditas he means a love directed to temporal things, which cannot turn to the right objects without ceasing to be Cupiditas.   But what clearer proof could there be that Caritas and Cupiditas are distinguished not in kind, but by their objects, than this talk of a right Cupiditas and a wrong Caritas?

Before leaving a question so important for Augustine as that of Caritas and Cupiditas, we must briefly consider the relation of his idea of Caritas to the Eros motif or, alternatively, the Agape motif.   Even if Augustine's distinction between Caritas and Cupiditas does not entirely lack points of contact with New Testament Christianity,[3] there cannot be the slightest doubt that his doctrine of love, so far at least as our analysis has yet dealt with it, rests substantially on the foundation of Eros and has very little in common with Agape-love.   The fact that he thinks of all love as fundamentally acquisitive love speaks plainly enough.[4]   Behind

[1] " *Cupiditas rerum æternarum* et felicitatis æternæ." Sermo XXXII., cap. xxii.

[2] " *Nec ipsa, quæ præcepti finis et plenitudo legis est caritas, ullo modo recta esse potest, si ea quæ diliguntur, non vera, sed falsa sunt.*" De doct. christiana, lib. IV., cap. xxviii. 61.   *Cf.* also the idea of " *carnalis caritas,*" which appears—though in a slightly different sense—in Sermo IV., cap. iii. 3.

[3] *Cf.* especially 1 Jn. ii. 15, which contrasts love for God and love of the world. On this, see Part I., pp. 115 f.   In the De vera religione, cap. iii. 4, Augustine himself collects a series of New Testament texts which he thinks are in direct line with Platonism and therefore support his interpretation of Christianity. The passages he quotes are: John i. 1-3; Matt. vi. 19-21; Gal. vi. 8; Luke xiv. 11 ; Matt. v. 39 and v. 44; Luke xvii. 21; 2 Cor. iv. 18; 1 John ii. 15-16.

[4] *Cf. supra*, pp. 175 ff.

Caritas we detect the "heavenly Eros" of Platonism, behind Cupiditas "vulgar Eros."[1]   The contrast between the two forms of love is very much the same in Augustine as in Neoplatonic Eros doctrine : it is the contrast between love directed upwards and love directed downwards, between love for the eternal and love for the temporal.

Into this scheme, built as it is on Eros theory, the Christian Commandment of Love is now introduced.   To do this is not difficult so far as love to God is concerned, since Augustine is convinced that the ascending love which Neoplatonism had taught him is essentially the same as the love required in the Commandment : " Thou shalt love the Lord thy God with all thy heart."   Such an identification, however, can obviously be made only at the expense of the Christian idea of love ; for if Christian love is thought of as a form of " acquisitive love " and interpreted to mean that we seek our own " bonum " in God, then the theocentric character of the Christian Commandment of Love is undoubtedly lost.   Even though God is described as the *highest* good, this does not alter the fact that He is degraded to the level of a means for the satisfaction of human desire.   " Love to God," as interpreted by Augustine, loses a good deal of its original Christian meaning.   Even so, it must not be overlooked that the relation to God culminating in Caritas is far more Christian than we should judge simply from Augustine's theoretical treatment of the idea of God, which often contains little more than ordinary Hellenistic ideas of God as True Being and Highest Good.—With the Commandment of love to neighbour Augustine has more difficulty.   Caritas is essentially desire directed to God ; and if that is what love to God means, it is not easy to rank love to neighbour with it.   Yet Augustine does so ; he says, for instance : " Love to God and love to neighbour are called Caritas."[2]   But when he does so, love to neighbour seems like an alien intrusion, present only because

---

[1] *Cf. supra*, pp. 50 ff.   [2] Enarr. in Ps. XXXI. ii. 5.

Christian tradition requires it. There is at all events nothing in the primary definition of the idea of Caritas to make the introduction of love to neighbour necessary.

Augustine's doctrine of Caritas is undeniably one of the most interesting and important junctures in the whole history of ideas. In it antiquity and Christianity are remarkably interwoven. Antiquity taught Augustine to ask the eudæ-monistic question, with its ideal of freedom from all need and its demand for an absolutely undisturbed *quies*; and it could be shown point by point how his thought rests almost throughout on the foundations of antiquity. *In the history of ideas, Augustine's Caritas-theory must be regarded as a continuation of the endless discussions of ancient philosophy about what is the " highest good."* To this question different philosophical schools had given different answers: the highest good is the momentary pleasure of the senses; or it is a spiritualised enjoyment of life; or it is the independence of the self, its exaltation above the vicissitudes of fortune; and so forth. The demands had become more and more exacting with regard to what might be accounted the highest good. Why is it impossible at a more advanced stage to recognise pleasure as the highest good? Because pleasure is far too fleeting and easily turns into its opposite. The highest good must be something enduring, something really dependable. This entire discussion lies behind Augustine's conception.[1] He puts the question in the customary way: What is the highest good? Where can I find my real " bonum "? But

---

[1] In Sermo CLVI., cap. vii., Augustine gives an interesting definition of the difference between ancient philosophy and Christianity. Common to all is the question: what is the good for man ? The Epicureans, according to Augustine, find this good " in voluptate corporis," the Stoics " in virtute sua "; in Christianity, on the other hand, " fruitio Dei " is the highest good. " Dicebat Epicureus: Mihi frui carne, bonum est. Dicebat Stoicus: Mihi frui mea mente, bonum est. Dicebat Apostolus: Mihi autem adhærere Deo, bonum est." The difference between Epicureanism, Stoicism and Christianity is, for Augustine, the same as the difference between " secundum carnem vivere," " secundum animam vivere " and " secundum Deum vivere."

to this old question he has found a new answer, as follows:
"Mihi adhærere Deo bonum est." *God*, and He alone, is
the highest good. "He is the source of our happiness, He is
the end of all desire"[1]; in union with Him I find all that I
need. Against all views which seek the highest good in
this-worldly advantages, Augustine sets his *transcendent
eudæmonism*.

Augustine obviously got his *question* from ancient
philosophy. But where did he obtain his *answer*? Was it
from Christianity? That at any rate was his own view of his
relation to ancient philosophy and to Christianity. The
philosophers have disputed what the highest good is;
Christianity comes with the right answer. God is the highest
good; and therefore Christianity commands that we shall
love and desire Him alone.[2] But if we accept Augustine's
own estimate and take it that antiquity and Christianity are
related in him as question to answer, we should recognise
that he over-simplifies the matter in two ways. First,
Augustine's new answer is not so very new; there are parallels
to it here and there in the thought of late antiquity—especially
in Neoplatonism. Secondly, it means a radical transformation of the Christian idea of God, if that idea is used as the
answer to the cudæmonistically conceived quest for the
"highest good."

As regards the *question*, Augustine's Caritas doctrine is
primarily a link in the ancient discussion about man's highest
good; as regards the *answer*, *it forms just as decided a link in
the history of Christian ideas, especially in the history of the
Christian idea of love*. In the doctrine of Caritas the Christian
idea of love enters upon a new phase, since the Christian

---

[1] "Ipse enim fons nostræ beatitudinis, ipse omnis adpetitionis est finis . . . ad
eum dilectione tendimus, ut perueniendo quiescamus, ideo beati, quia illo fine
perfecti." De ciu. dei, lib. X., cap. iii.

[2] "*Bonum enim nostrum, de cuius fine inter philosophos magna contentio est,
nullum est aliud quam illi cohærere. . . . Hoc bonum diligere in toto corde, in
tota anima et in tota uirtute præcipimur.*" De ciu. dei, lib. X., cap. iii.

commandment of love to God—naturally cast in quite a new mould—is made the answer to man's inevitable desire. Man seeks by nature nothing but his happiness. He asks: Where shall I find my "bonum," where shall I find my "highest good"? The Christian Commandment of Love, according to Augustine, implies no condemnation of this egocentric and eudæmonistic question. It says rather: "Love (*i.e.*, desire), but see to it what you love; thou shalt love the Lord thy God with all thy heart," for He alone is that "bonum" which can really satisfy your desire.

Augustine has tried to bring about a fusion of very heterogeneous elements in his doctrine of Caritas, a fusion of ancient eudæmonism with Christian love, of the desire of Eros with the devotion of Agape. The meaning of this synthesis is, in brief: *the Christian Commandment of Love gives the final answer to the question of ancient philosophy about the "highest good."* In this union the Christian idea of love is the losing partner, and that is simply because ancient thought is allowed to put the question.

3. FRUI AND UTI

According to Augustine, there is only one object that man has any real right to love—namely, God. The right form of love, Caritas, is in essence love of God. It is man's duty to love God "with all his heart and all his soul and all his mind." But when all his capacities and powers are thus claimed for love to God, there is nothing left in him which is, so to speak, free to love anything else. The love of God excludes all other love, it "suffers not a tricklet to be drawn off from itself, by the diversion of which its own volume would be diminished."[1]

The question arises, however, whether it is really true that love for the creature necessarily conflicts with love for the

---

[1] De doct. christiana, lib. I., cap. xxii. 21.

Creator. If those things which surround us in the world were in themselves evil, then naturally all love of them would be bad. But according to Augustine this is not so: as created by God the world is good, even if its goodness is admittedly only relative. Does not love for the Creator itself, then, require that I should also love His work? Can we not conceive of such a love for the creature as would simply be an expression of our love for God, and which, so far from diverting from Him anything of the stream of love, would actually, though by a detour, conduct it in its completeness to Him?

Augustine has faced this question and tried to answer it by distinguishing two sorts of love: *Frui* and *Uti*, a love which "enjoys" and a love which "uses" its object. To *enjoy* (frui) is to love something *for its own sake* (diligere propter se), to *use* (uti) is to love something *for the sake of something else* (diligere propter aliud).[1] The relation between Frui and Uti is therefore that between end and means. When I "enjoy" an object, I make it the absolute end of my striving, I seek nothing else beyond it; when I "use" an object, though I love and value it, I do so not for its own sake, but because in the last resort I love something else, and regard the object I am using as a means to attain the enjoyment of this.[2]

Augustine illustrates the difference between Frui and Uti as follows. If we are in foreign parts, but can only feel happy in our own country, we have to *use* a carriage or ship to get there; but it is our own country that is to be *enjoyed*. Yet it may happen, he continues, that the journey itself so appeals

---

[1] " Frui enim est amore alicui rei inhærere propter seipsam. Uti autem, quod in usum venerit ad id quod amas obtinendum referre, si tamen amandum est." De doct. christiana, lib. I., cap. iv. 4. " Si enim propter se [diligimus], fruimur eo, si propter aliud, utimur eo." *Ibid.*, cap. xxii. 20.

[2] " Summum id dicitur, quo cuncta referuntur; eo enim fruendo quisque beatus est, propter quod cetera uult habere, cum illud iam non propter aliud, sed propter se ipsum diligatur." Epist. CXVIII. iii. 13.

to us that we forget our fatherland; then the journey has ceased to be an object for use and has become one for enjoyment, it has changed from a means into an end; instead of being valued for the sake of something else, it is now valued for its own sake. This is the situation of us men in our temporal life: we live in an alien land and are " absent from the Lord " (2 Cor. v. 6). The world is given to us to be used as a means and vehicle for our return to God. So we must really use it only as such a means, and not, seduced by its false attractions (perversa suavitate), begin to devote ourselves to it and enjoy it as if it were already our " bonum " and our fatherland.[1] If it is merely used, the world can help us on the way of Caritas to God; but if it is enjoyed, it becomes a hindrance and drives us on the way of Cupiditas away from God.

We must now ask how the distinction between Frui and Uti is related to that between Caritas and Cupiditas, which is so fundamental to Augustine's thought. It is evident that the two pairs of ideas are not directly synonymous: Caritas and Cupiditas are distinguished as right and wrong love; Frui and Uti have nothing immediately to do with this distinction. There is a right enjoyment, but also a wrong one, just as there is both a right and a wrong use. What decides, then, between right and wrong in this case? Augustine finds the answer in the definition of " enjoyment " and " use." Enjoyment is an absolute love, use a relative one. Now since everything should be loved according to the value it possesses, it obviously follows that the absolute should be loved absolutely, the relative relatively. The purpose of our love to God must therefore be enjoyment of God, " fruitio Dei "; to wish to use God would plainly be wrong, for it would mean loving the Absolute with a merely relative love. But it would be an equal error to wish to enjoy the world: that would mean loving the relative with an absolute love;

[1] De doct. christiana, lib. I., cap. iv. 4.

the only right thing to do with the world is to " use " it.[1]
Since the two pairs of ideas, Caritas—Cupiditas and Frui—
Uti, overlap one another, there are four possible relations of
love open to a man.   There is a *right enjoyment*—that is,
enjoyment of God—and a *wrong enjoyment*—that is, enjoyment of the world; there is a *right use*—that is, use of the
world—and a *wrong use*—that is, use of God.   The wrong
sort of love arises because a man turns to enjoyment and use
objects not meant for those purposes: he enjoys what by
nature ought to be used, and uses what ought to be enjoyed.
Both Caritas and Cupiditas are thus a combination of enjoyment and use, but in directly opposite directions.   *Caritas
enjoys God and uses the world, Cupiditas enjoys the world
and uses God.*   Augustine himself thus formulates the right
and the wrong relation to God and to the world: " Good
men use the world in order to enjoy God, whereas bad men
want to use God in order to enjoy the world."[2]

So long as only the contrast between Caritas and Cupiditas
is considered in Augustine's doctrine of love, it might seem
to include no more than a simple Either—Or, either God or
the world.   But when to this fundamental contrast the new
pair of opposites, Frui—Uti, is added, the Either—Or becomes a richly varied system of objects of love.   All created
things, from that which is nearest God to that which is
nearest " nothing," have been endowed by God with a
higher or lower degree of being and so with a higher or

---

[1] " Omnis itaque humana perversio est, quod etiam vitium vocatur, fruendis
uti velle, atque utendis frui.   Et rursus omnis ordinatio, quæ virtus etiam
nominatur, fruendis frui, et utendis uti."   De div. quæst. octoginta tribus,
qu. xxx.

[2] " Boni ad hoc utuntur mundo, ut fruantur Deo; mali autem contra, ut
fruantur mundo, uti uolunt Deo."   De ciu. dei, lib. XV., cap. vii.   " Ea re
frui dicimur, quæ nos non ad aliud referenda per se ipsa delectat; uti uero ea
re, quam propter aliud quærimus (unde temporalibus magis utendum est, quam
fruendum, ut frui mereamur æternis; non sicut peruersi, qui frui uolunt nummo,
uti autem Deo; quoniam non nummum propter Deum inpendunt, sed Deum
propter nummum colunt)."   'De ciu. dei, lib. XI., cap. xxv.

lower degree of goodness. To this "*order of natures*" love
has to adapt itself. Augustine has found a new test for distinguishing right love from wrong. Right love carefully
observes the "order of natures" established by God at
Creation, and so loves every object strictly in accordance
with the value it possesses; wrong love pays no respect to the
natural order of values. Thus the difference between Caritas
and Cupiditas receives further definition: Caritas is an
"*ordered love*" (dilectio ordinata), Cupiditas is an "*unordered love*" (dilectio inordinata). Caritas retains, of
course, its fundamental character of love to God, but the
description of it as "ordered love" makes it more specific
and guards it against misunderstanding. For Caritas also
can love created things, but not with such a love as is
properly given to God alone; it "uses" the world, and loves
it only as a means for ascending to God. Even when Caritas
loves created things, God is its ultimate aim. Of him who
has such an "ordered love," Augustine says: "He neither
loves what he ought not to love, nor fails to love what he
ought to love, nor loves that more which ought to be loved
less, nor loves that equally which ought to be loved either
less or more, nor loves that less or more which ought to be
loved equally."[1] Caritas therefore, as "ordered love," first
carefully *assesses the worth* of the various objects, and then
gives to each object just as much love as this worth evokes.[2]

What has been said of Caritas as "ordered love," finds—
mutatis mutandis—an exact parallel in Cupiditas as "unordered love." Cupiditas, too, retains its fundamental char-

---

[1] De doct. christiana, lib. I., cap. xxvii. 28. " Sicut enim bona sunt omnia,
quæ creauit Deus, ab ipsa rationali creatura usque ad infimum corpus, ita bene
in his agit anima rationalis, *si ordinem seruet* et distinguendo, eligendo, pendendo
subdat minora maioribus, corporalia spiritalibus, inferiora superioribus, tem-
poralia sempiternis. . . . Cum enim sint omnes substantiæ naturaliter bonæ,
ordo in eis laudatus honoratur, peruersitas culpata damnatur." Epist. CXL.,
ii. 4. " Hæc est perfecta justitia, qua potius potiora, et minus minora diligimus."
De vera rel., cap. xlviii. 93.

[2] De doct. christiana, lib. I., cap. xxvii. 28. One who has an " ordered love "
is described as " rerum integer æstimator."

acter; it is love of the world. But in the last resort, the
error of Cupiditas is not that it loves things in the world;
these may be loved, so long as the love given to them corresponds to their degree of goodness. The error of Cupiditas
is that it loves with an "unordered love"; it does not
enquire into the natural order, but loves these low things
with such a love as should be reserved for God.[1]

The distinction between love as Frui and love as Uti thus
serves a double purpose. *On the one hand*, it insists that all
love must have its ultimate goal in God. Whatever is a
"bonum" may be loved, but only that may be enjoyed in
which eternal blessedness is to be found—that is, only God
Himself, only the Holy Trinity.[2] The idea of "fruitio Dei"
is an expression of the strongly theocentric tendency which
marks Augustine's thought. It has the important task of
preventing God from being made into a means to some
other end. God must be loved for His own sake, as an end
in Himself and a terminus beyond which we do not seek to
pass, but in which our desire comes to rest; for eternal
blessedness is nothing else but "fruitio Dei" and "visio
Dei." This is the only thing in existence which can be loved
absolutely *freely*—that is, without seeking to gain something
else by it.[3] That is what Augustine means by his repeated

---

[1] " Deficitur enim non ad mala, sed male, id est non ad malas naturas, sed ideo
male, quia *contra ordinem naturarum* ab eo quod summe est ad id quod minus
est." De ciu. dei, lib. XII., cap. viii. " Cum enim bona sit, et bene amari
potest et male: *bene scilicet ordine custodito, male ordine perturbato.*" Op. cit.,
lib. XV., cap. xxii. " Quapropter, etiam in ista corporis voluptate invenimus
unde commoneamur eam contemnere; non quia malum est natura corporis,
sed quia in extremi boni dilectione turpiter volutatur, cui primis inhærere fruique
concessum est." De vera rel., cap. xlv. 83. " Unde enim peccas, nisi quia
inordinate tractas res quas in usum accepisti ? *Esto bene utens rebus inferioribus,
et eris recte fruens bono superiore.*" Sermo XXI. 3.

[2] " Eadem quippe Trinitate fruendum est, ut beate vivamus." De trinitate,
lib. VIII., cap. v. 8. " Res igitur quibus fruendum est, Pater et Filius et Spiritus
sanctus, eademque Trinitas, una quædam summa res." De doct. christiana,
lib. I., cap. v. 5. " In his igitur omnibus rebus illæ tantum sunt quibus fruendum
est, quas æternas atque incommutabiles commemoravimus." *Ibid.*, cap. xxii. 20.

[3] " Ista visio non vitæ hujus est, sed futuræ; non temporalis, sed æterna. . . .
Ad istum fructum contemplationis cuncta officia referuntur actionis. Solus

exhortation to love God "gratis." It does not mean that love to God is to be an unselfish love in the sense that it has ceased to be acquisitive love; any such love is, for Augustine, quite simply non-existent. To love God "gratis" means that we are not to seek Him as a means for gaining other advantages; indeed, He comprises in Himself all advantages, and so is the one in whom we can find our sufficiency.[1] To say that God is to be loved "gratis" is only another way of saying that God may not be "used."

The distinction between Frui-love and Uti-love makes it possible, *on the other hand*, to avoid excluding the creation from the sphere of right love. So long as we think only of an absolute love, there is no room for any but direct love of God. The idea of "Uti" has thus the important task of making love relative so that it can be directed to the creature as well, without sin. So Augustine finds room for a love for temporal things, which need not compete with love for God but can be taken into its service. As for the time being we have to live our life here in the world, it is good to be able to find in it not merely an alien land, but also a lodging where we can rest for a while.[2] But it is, we note, only for a while, and only in order to gain strength for a continued pilgrimage. Real rest, the final *quies*, is found only in God. When we take a rest in the world, we must above all remember the exhortation: "Use the world; let not the world hold thee captive."[3] By "rest" in this connection, we can mean no more than when we say our foot "rests" on the ground when walking; it rests only to be raised again the next moment and take us further on our way. Even the

---

est enim liber; quia propter se appetitur, et non refertur ad aliud. . . . Ibi ergo finis qui sufficit nobis. Æternus igitur erit: neque enim nobis sufficit finis, nisi cujus nullus est finis." In ev. Jn., tract. ci. 5.

[1] "Hoc est Deum *gratis amare*, de Deo Deum sperare, de Deo properare impleri, de ipso satiari. Ipse enim sufficit tibi; præter illum nihil sufficit tibi." Sermo CCCXXXIV. 3.

[2] In ev. Jn., tract. xl. 10.   [3] *Ibid.*

Christian at such times of rest may find some pleasure in earthly things; yet these are never his native land, but merely an incidental recreation and a lodging for the traveller.[1] We can devote a certain relative love to things in the world; yet this is none the less evidence of the weakness of our love of God, and has its dangers. The recreation of the moment can all too easily become a serious distraction, so that we lose sight of our final goal. The ideal would be to have no need to devote any time or thought to temporal things. If we really loved God as we ought, we should not love anything *at all* in the world[2]—that is Augustine's final word on this question.

The purpose of the distinction between the ideas of "Frui" and "Uti" was to make love of the world relative, partly by depriving it of its absolute character, partly by relating it to love of God as means to end. The result, however, was that not only love of the world but all love whatsoever—including Frui-love—was made relative. Augustine defines "Frui" thus: "*amore* alicui rei inhærere propter se ipsam." Love, amor, is here plainly a means to an end. Apply it to love to God, and we see at once how this becomes relative. The idea of "Frui" was intended to guarantee the absolute meaning of love to God, but in fact it makes its relativity all the clearer. In Caritas, God is loved for His own sake, as the highest good, the object which gives final blessedness. But the blessedness does not consist in *loving*—that is, desiring and longing for the

---

1 " Sic est autem requies voluntatis quem dicimus finem, si adhuc refertur ad aliud, quemadmodum possumus dicere *requiem pedis* esse in ambulando, cum ponitur unde alius (altius ?) innitatur quo passibus pergitur. Si autem aliquid ita placet, ut in eo *cum aliqua delectatione voluntas acquiescat*; nondum est tamen illud quo tenditur, sed et hoc refertur ad aliud, ut deputetur non tanquam patria civis; sed *tanquam refectio, vel etiam mansio viatoris*." De trinitate, lib. XI., vi. 10.

2 " Non amat multum nummum, qui amat Deum. Et ego palpavi infirmitatem, non ausus sum dicere, Non amat nummum; sed, non multum amat nummum : quasi amandus sit nummus, sed non multum. *O si Deum digne amemus, nummos omnino non amabimus !*" In ev. Jn., tract. xl. 10.

highest good—but in *possessing* it.[1] Blessedness does not consist in Caritas directed to God, but in that "*fruitio Dei*" to which Caritas is to bring us. But that means that Caritas is made relative and ranked as a means—inevitably, since all love, as Augustine thinks, is desire. We possess blessedness "non amando, sed fruendo," says Augustine.[2]

It looks as though Caritas ought to have only interim significance, so long as we are in the world, far from our desired goal, separated from our "bonum." In the eternal life, where faith is exchanged for contemplation and enjoyment of God, visio et fruitio Dei, there would scarcely be any room for love. Having already obtained our "bonum," and obtained it for ever, we could hardly reach out in love for anything more. We have reached our goal; eternal rest (quies) is here; and the very meaning of this quies is that desire is for ever quenched: man no longer needs to seek his "bonum," but possesses it. Perfect fruitio Dei means in principle the cessation of love. Alongside this idea, however, there is often found in Augustine quite the opposite idea, that love is to increase when we at length see God face to face.[3] Only then shall we really know what we possess in God as our summum bonum; and the more we *know* Him, the more we are bound to *love* Him.[4]

---

[1] "Nemo tamen beatus est, qui eo quod amat non fruitur." De ciu. dei, lib. VIII., cap. viii. "Secutio ·igitur Dei, beatitatis appetitus est: consecutio autem, ipsa beatitas. At eum sequimur diligendo, consequimur vero. . . ." De mor. eccl. cath., lib. I., cap. xi. 18.

[2] De ciu. dei, lib. VIII., cap. viii. ("Not by loving, but by enjoying").

[3] "Plus ergo amabimus cum viderimus, si potuerimus amare et antequam videremus." Sermo XXI. 1. "Si amamus credendo et non videndo, quomodo amabimus videndo et tenendo?" Sermo CLVIII. 9. "Amor ergo quietus in vultu Dei, quem modo desideramus, cui suspiramus, cum ad eum venerimus, quomodo nos accendet? In quem nondum visum sic suspiramus, cum ad eum venerimus, quomodo illuminabit? . . . Non autem desines amare, quia talis est quem vides, qui nullo te offendat fastidio: et satiat te, et non te satiat. Mirum est quod dico." Enarr. in Ps. lxxxv. 24. *Cf.* Retractationes, lib. I., cap. vi. 5 (vii. 4): ". . . nisi forte putatur caritatem dei non futuram esse maiorem, quando uidebimus facie ad faciem."

[4] For the relation between "knowing" and "loving" *cf.*, *e.g.*, De trinitate,

Not even the ideas of "Uti" and "Frui" were able to deliver Augustine from the prevalent Hellenistic Eros theory. When he says we are to use the world in order to attain the enjoyment of God, he has the same idea as Plato had in urging us not to be captivated by the beautiful things in this world, but to use them as a ladder on which to ascend to the higher world.

4. THE ASCENT TO GOD

Love has a function in the world of the spirit analogous to that of the law of gravitation in the material world. By the "order of natures" everything has its given place in the universe. Man has been appointed by God to the highest place in creation; and this is a token that he should direct his desire upwards. As the material body is dragged downwards by its weight, so the soul is enabled by Caritas to ascend to God.[1] Here upon earth man may well think Caritas a weight: the law is usually considered heavy and difficult, and that affects Caritas which is the fulfilment of the law. But if from one point of view it is man who bears Caritas as a burden, from another it is Caritas that bears him. On "the wings of Caritas" he is lifted up to heaven.[2] To take another of Augustine's similes: "Just as olive oil

---

lib. X., cap. i. f.   ". . . quanto notiores tanto utique cariores." Epist. xcii. 1. "Porro si quanto maior notitia tanto erit maior dilectio." De spiritu et lit., cap. lxiv. "Proinde hoc primum præceptum iustitiæ, quo iubemur diligere deum ex toto corde et ex tota anima et ex tota mente, cui est de proximo diligendo alterum consequens, in illa uita inplebimus, cum uidebimus facie ad faciem." *Ibid.*

[1] " Si essemus lapides aut fluctus aut uentus aut flamma uel quid huius modi, sine ullo quidem sensu adque uita, non tamen nobis deesset quasi quidam nostrorum locorum adque ordinis adpetitus. *Nam uelut amores corporum momenta sunt ponderum, siue deorsum grauitate siue sursum leuitate nitantur. Ita enim corpus pondere, sicut animus amore fertur, quocumque fertur.*" De ciu. dei, lib. XI., cap. xxviii.

[2] "Habent enim et aves pennarum suarum sarcinas. Et quid dicimus? Portant illas, et portantur. Portant illas in terra, portantur ab illis in cœlo. . . . Porta ergo pennas pacis, *alas accipe caritatis.* Hæc est sarcina, sic implebitur lex Christi." Sermo CLXIV., cap. v.

cannot be kept down by any liquid, but bursts through all and leaps up and floats on top, so Caritas cannot be kept down, but must of necessity mount upwards."[1] This upward tendency dominates the whole of Augustine's interpretation of Christianity. It is human aspiration at its best that we see in Caritas, the form both natural to it and well-pleasing to God. The whole life of a Christian is a never-ceasing ascent with the vision and enjoyment of God as its ultimate goal.

When Augustine speaks of ascent, his problem is in general how man is to raise himself from the sense-world to the pure spirituality of God. And we can distinguish in Augustine a *three-fold mode of ascent*: by the ladder of Virtue, of Speculation and of Mysticism.

1. It may seem peculiar that Augustine, who lays such stress on grace, can speak as easily as he does about human merit (meritum) and can actually describe the way to fellowship with God as an ascent by the *ladder of Virtue*.[2] In ex-

---

[1] " Sic et caritas non potest premi in ima; necesse est ut ad superna emineat." In ev. Jn., tract. vi. 20.   It is in accordance with this that Augustine interprets 1 Cor. xii. 31, which he cites in the following form: " adhuc supereminentiorem viam vobis demonstro."

[2] In the De doctrina christiana, lib. II., cap. vii., Augustine speaks of the seven stages or steps of virtue: timor dei, pietas, scientia, fortitudo, consilium misericordiæ, purgatio cordis, sapientia.   Their meaning is, briefly, this.   The ascent begins with the fear of death and judgment, for " the fear of the Lord is the beginning of wisdom "; this teaches us to crucify our flesh with its superbia. At the next step we learn to hold fast to Scripture and submit to it, even if we do not yet fully understand it.   At the third step we reach real insight into the meaning of Scripture and see that everything in it points to love (*cf. supra*, pp. 238 ff.)—that is, love for God with all one's heart and love for one's neighbour and for oneself as included in love for God.   At the fourth step man receives strength to turn his back on the transient, and set his love wholly upon the eternal things (" et inde se avertens convertit ad dilectionem æternorum, incommutabilem scilicet unitatem eamdemque Trinitatem ").   This was primarily a matter of love to God, but at the fifth step we see its meaning as regards love to neighbour; here man learns to practise love and mercy towards his neighbour, till his love finally culminates in love to enemies.   Thus prepared, man can mount to the sixth step.   Here he has virtually reached fellowship with God, for since he has purified his heart he is able to behold God as much as He can be beheld in this life.   There remains but one step to the final consummation, which consists

planation of this, it has often been pointed out that the idea of merit had dominated Western Christianity ever since Tertullian, and that even Augustine could not wholly resist the force of this tradition, much as it conflicted with his basic doctrine of grace. But true as this may be, it is inadequate to explain the place given to the idea of merit in Augustine. It is in any case a doubtful procedure thus to select certain elements as basic doctrine and others as alien additions. The idea of merit and the idea of virtue as a way to God are no alien additions to Augustine's thought, but belong organically to it. It is only when we see these apparently conflicting elements in the unity they actually have in Augustine that we get a faithful picture of his thought. It may be easy enough for us to find two trains of thought, one of grace and the other of merit and virtue; but for Augustine himself there was no tension between them. There could not be, for he held that "when God crowns our merits, it is nothing other than His own gifts that He crowns."[1] What binds grace and merit together is Caritas. Caritas is on the one hand that gift which man receives by grace, on the other hand it is "the fulfilling of the law" and so the sum of all virtues. The ascent by the ladder of Merit or Virtue is therefore nothing but the ascent of Caritas itself.[2]

---

in the enjoyment of the eternal wisdom itself ("Talis filius ascendit ad sapientiam, quæ ultima et septima est, qua pacatus tranquillusque perfruitur ").

[1] Epist. CXCIV., cap. v. 19. "Et ipsa tua merita illius dona sunt." Enarr. in Ps. cxliv. 11. "Quia et ea quæ dicuntur merita nostra, dona sunt ejus." De trinitate, lib. XIII., cap. x. 14. "Dei dona sunt merita tua." De gestis Pelagii, 35. "Quod ergo præmium immortalitatis postea tribuit, dona sua coronat, non merita tua. . . . Coronat autem in nobis Deus dona misericordiæ suæ." In ev. Jn., tract. iii. 10. Cf. Conf., lib. IX., cap. xiii. 34.

[2] "Et exaltatus est super plenitudinem scientiæ, ut nemo ad eum perveniret, nisi per caritatem: plenitudo enim legis caritas. . . . Volavit super pennas ventorum. Illa autem celeritas, qua se incomprehensibilem esse monstravit, super virtutes animarum est, quibus se velut pennis a terrenis timoribus in auras libertatis attollunt." Enarr. in Ps. xvii. 11. In Ps. xviii., to which Augustine here refers, the Lord is said to descend. Augustine changes this, partly by the aid of his Latin text, to an ascent: God has ascended so high above all things so

2. Another means of ascent is the *ladder of Speculation*. Since by reason of sin we could not see the eternal nor draw near to God in our own strength, He has come in His mercy to our aid: He has made us a ladder of created things by which we can mount up to Him.[1] On the basis of Rom. i. 20, Augustine has worked out a complete *theologia naturalis*. God has arranged the universe as a great " order of natures."[2] By its aid we can, in admiration for the Creator's might, traverse His works from the lowest to the highest and so finally reach the Creator Himself, to whom all these things point us. With one voice they cry to us: " We are not thy God; *seek above us*."[3] If according to Plato it is the beauty of things that arouses Eros in man and drives him to reach out longingly towards that which is in itself Beautiful, so in Augustine, too, it is the beauty of created things that leads our gaze up to their Creator and kindles our Caritas to Him. The man who lives in the spirit is at an intermediate stage: if he turns his attention downwards, he finds the corporeal world; if he turns it upwards, he finds God.[4] So the important thing is that our spirit should look in the right direction—upwards. God is not a corporeal being. If we would find Him, we must not seek Him here below, but

---

that man shall be able to approach Him only by the ascent of Caritas or, which is the same thing, by the ascent of virtue. " Per caritatem, hoc est, per virtutem." Enarr. in Ps. cxxi. 12.

[1] Enarr. in Ps. cxliv. 8. " Transcenderat omnia cacumina terrarum, transcenderat omnes campos æris, transcenderat omnes altitudines siderum, transcenderat omnes choros et legiones angelorum. Nisi enim transcenderet ista omnia quæ creata sunt, non perveniret ad eum per quem facta sunt omnia." In ev. Jn., tract. i. 5.

[2] " Et gradibus quibusdam ordinavit creaturam, a terra usque ad cœlum." Enarr. in Ps. cxliv. 13.

[3] " Non sumus deus tuus; quære super nos." Conf., lib. X., cap. vi. 9. " Neque in his omnibus, quæ percurro consulens te, inuenio tutum locum animæ meæ nisi in te." Ibid., cap. xxxx. 65.

[4] " Tu si in animo es, in medio es: si infra attendis, corpus est: si supra attendis, Deus est." In ev. Jn., tract. xx. 11. " . . . atque esse quamdam medietatem inter Deum et corpus, animam." Ibid., tract. xxiii. 6.

ascend in meditation above everything that belongs to the corporeal world. But our ascent is not finished even when we have transcended the corporeal sphere and reached the world of the spirit. God is a spirit, but not a mutable spirit like us. If we would come to Him, therefore, we must ascend above all that belongs to the world of mutable spirit as well.[1] The chief stages on the speculative Way to God are thus briefly given: "Transcend the body and taste the spirit; transcend the spirit and taste God."[2]

3. Nearly akin to the speculative ascent is the ascent by the *ladder of Mysticism*. It is hardly possible to draw any sharp distinction between them, for in Augustine the mystical ascent is largely on the same lines as the speculative. Yet the picture would be incomplete without mentioning the mystical ascent. First, we may recall Augustine's conversation with his mother at Ostia, which substantially follows the anagogical scheme of mysticism.[3] The idea constantly recurring in Augustine, that man must seek God within himself,[4] points in the same direction. Here he enters on the path characteristic of mysticism in all ages, the introspective Way to God. " Higher up " and " further in "

---

[1] " Non est Deus corpus, non terra, non cœlum, non luna, non sol, non stellæ, non corporalia ista. Si enim non cœlestia, quanto minus terrena ? Tolle omne corpus. Adhuc audi aliud: non est Deus mutabilis spiritus. Nam fateor, et fatendum est, quia evangelium loquitur, Deus spiritus est. Sed transi omnem mutabilem spiritum." In ev. Jn., tract. xxiii. 9.

[2] " Transcende et corpus, et sape animum: transcende et animum, et sape Deum." In ev. Jn., tract. xx. 11. " Attolle te a corpore, transi etiam te." *Ibid.*

[3] Conf., lib. IX., cap. x. 23-25. *Cf. supra,* p. 467.

[4] " Agnosce in te aliquid, quod volo dicere, intus, intus in te; . . . descende in te, adi secretarium tuum, mentem tuam, et ibi vide quod volo dicere, si potueris. Si enim tu ipse a te longe es, Deo propinquare unde potes ?" In ev. Jn., tract. xxiii. 10. " Non enim valde longe pergo in exempla, quando de mente tua volo aliquam similitudinem dare ad Deum tuum; quia utique non in corpore, sed in ipsa mente factus est homo ad imaginem Dei. In similitudine sua Deum quæramus, in imagine sua Creatorem agnoscamus. Ibi intus, si potuerimus, inveniamus hoc quod dicimus." *Ibid.* " Et ecce intus eras et ego foris et ibi te quærebam et in ista formosa, quæ fecisti, deformis inruebam. Mecum eras, et tecum non eram." Conf., lib. X., cap. xxvii. 38.

become interchangeable terms for him.[1] At the beginning of the road that leads to fellowship with God, stands the exhortation γνῶθι σεαυτόν. By entering into himself and examining his own nature, Augustine thinks he can pierce the mystery of the Holy Trinity.[2] To know oneself is to know God, to abide in oneself is to abide in God. When man departs from God, he can no longer abide in himself; he begins to set his love upon what is outside himself and sinks deeper and deeper into transient things.[3] Conversion begins when he enters into himself again, for he can only abide in himself if at the same time he returns to God.[4] To return to oneself is to return to God, and to return to God is in the deepest sense to return to oneself.

The above might easily give the impression that Augustine's Way of salvation was in the main the same as the Platonic and Hellenistic Way. But that is by no means the case. Even if the general structure is the same, the Hellenistic theory of salvation is left behind at decisive points. Both starting-point and goal have acquired a quite different meaning.

The starting-point of the Hellenistic theory of salvation is the belief in the divine origin and nature of the human spirit. To this Augustine is most strongly opposed; man is not a disguised divinity. He is most concerned to keep the distinction clear between God as Creator and man as His creature. God remains God and man man. Augustine is always con-

---

[1] " Tu autem eras interior intimo meo et superior summo meo." Conf., lib. III., cap. vi. 11.

[2] Cf. De trinitate, lib. X.

[3] " Incipit enim deserto Deo amare se, et ad ea diligenda quæ sunt extra se, pellitur a se. . . . Jam vides quia foris es. Amare te cœpisti: sta in te, si potes. Quid is foras? . . . Cœpisti diligere quod est extra te, perdidisti te. Cum ergo pergit amor hominis etiam a se ipso ad ea quæ foris sunt, incipit cum vanis evanescere, et vires suas quodam modo prodigus erogare. Exinanitur, effunditur, inops redditur." Sermo XCVI., cap. ii. 2.

[4] " Ecce unde ceciderat a se, ceciderat a patre suo: ceciderat a se, ad ea quæ foris sunt exiit a se. Redit ad se et pergit ad patrem, ubi tutissime servet se." Ibid.

scious of the distance between them. He expressly rejects—
despite its attraction for a Hellenistic mind—the interpretation of the Old Testament Creation-story which makes it
mean that God breathed into man a part of His own Spirit.
The spirit of life which God breathed into man was not
God's own Spirit, but a created spirit.[1]

As the starting-point is different, so is the goal. Since
Augustine recognises no original identity between the Spirit
of God and the spirit of man, the goal cannot be for him
their mystical absorption in one another. Even if the mystical
ascent, mentioned above, includes a tendency to the ecstatic,[2]
there is no question of the complete absorption of the soul
in God. The distinction between God and man is never
abolished; even at the highest point of spiritual life the distance is preserved. The goal of the Christian life is the indwelling of the Triune God in us, but " the Trinity is in us
as God in His temple, but we are in Him as the creature in
its Creator."[3]

5. Caritas and Gratia. Our Ascent and God's Descent

In Caritas man was to ascend to his Creator in order to
possess in Him his " summum et incommutabile bonum."

[1] " . . . non ait Græcus πνεῦμα, quod solet dici Spiritus sanctus, sed πνοήν,
quod nomen in creatura quam in Creatore frequentius legitur." De ciu. dei,
lib. XIII., cap. xxiv. " Sicut autem nos possumus non de nostra natura, qua
homines sumus, sed de isto ære circumfuso, quem spirando ac respirando ducimus
ac reddimus, flatum facere cum sufflamus: ita omnipotens Deus *non de sua
natura* neque subiacienti creatura, sed etiam de nihilo potuit facere flatum, quem
corpori hominis inserendo inspirasse uel insufflasse cōnuenientissime dictus est,
incorporeus incorporeum, sed inmutabilis mutabilem, quia non creatus creatum."
Ibid.

[2] " . . . attingimus eam modice toto ictu cordis." Conf., lib. IX., cap. x. 24
" . . . extendimus nos et rapida cogitatione attingimus æternam sapientiam
super omnia manentem." *Ibid.*, cap. x. 25. *Cf.* also *supra*, p. 466, n. 3.

[3] " Ac per hoc et cum in nobis sunt Pater et Filius, vel etiam Spiritus sanctus,
non debemus eòs putare naturæ unius esse nobiscum. Sic itaque sunt in nobis,
vel nos in illis, ut illi unum sint in natura sua, nos unum in nostra. Sunt quippe
ipsi in nobis, tanquam Deus in templo suo: sumus autem nos in illis, tanquam
creatura in Creatore suo." In ev. Jn., tract. cx. 1.

But the greater the distance between the Creator and man, His creature, the more difficult is the ascent of Caritas. Has man any power to raise himself to God, or is he doomed as a created being to set his love on the created things around him? In the struggle between Caritas and Cupiditas, is not the latter bound to prevail? Can man really achieve such a Caritas as the Commandment of Love requires?

Augustine had occasion to think out this problem, partly in relation to the Pauline theology of grace, but more especially in connection with his campaign against Pelagianism. In the latter he found a moralistic view of Christianity which in the matter of fellowship with God put all the emphasis on the human side. Pelagius does not deny the importance and necessity of Divine grace, but "grace" is reduced to little more than the following three points: (1) At creation God gave man free will, in virtue of which he can always choose the good. (2) Further, He has graciously made man's choice easier by showing him, in His law and above all in the example of Christ, the good which he has to realise. (3) When man has nevertheless chosen evil, God's grace is shown in that He forgives the sin, thus making it possible for man's free will to begin afresh without being burdened by the past.[1]

Augustine attacks this Pelagian conception of grace most vigorously. A "grace" which includes only the three elements mentioned—freedom of the will, the law and the forgiveness of sins—is of no service to us. What use is formal

---

[1] Pelagius especially objects to any idea of original sin. This is connected with his insistence on the freedom of the human will, which may be said to be the basic idea of his outlook. Unlike Augustine, he regards the life of the will not as a connected whole, but rather in an atomistic fashion. He is less concerned with the total attitude of the will than with the single, isolated act of will. Sin is therefore regarded not as perverseness of will, but merely as individual sinful action, and it is overcome by man's deciding for the good in virtue of that freedom of choice which is every moment at his disposal. This decision is equally thought of as an individual act.

freedom of the will with its abstract possibility of decision in different directions, when we are surrounded in real life by the sense-world with all its allurements, which drag our desire downwards and inexorably fetter us to transient things without any external compulsion, but by means of the pleasure they arouse?   Again, what use is it that we learn in the law and through the example of Christ how our desire ought to be directed upwards to the heavenly things, when these in their remote transcendence leave us cold and unmoved?   And what use is it, finally, that God in His grace and mercy forgives us the sins we have hitherto committed, if for our future activity we have only the resources of free will, which are inadequate to free our desire from lower things and direct it to the heavenly?   If grace is to have any real value for us, it must be a *power* intervening in our actual life, really effective here and now.   Augustine does not admit that Pelagius' " deistic " idea of grace is real grace.   It merely means that God has so ordered it from the beginning that we can fend for ourselves.   Augustine sets an effective grace in place of this—grace as the personal intervention of God Himself in our life.   It is not that he rejects free will and the law—for him, too, these are necessary, since without free will it would be impossible to speak of a good or evil life at all, and without the law we should not know how we ought to live[1]—but what he wants to emphasise is that these are *not enough*.   And he reserves the word " gratia " for the Divine intervention which is necessary over and above these.[2]

How is it, then, that the law and free will together are

---

[1] " Quod cum ostendero, profecto manifestius apparebit bene uiuere donum esse diuinum non tantum quia homini deus dedit liberum arbitrium, sine quo nec male nec bene uiuitur, nec tantum quia præceptum dedit, quo doceat quemadmodum sit uiuendum. . . ."   De spiritu et lit., cap. v. 7.

[2] " Neque scientia divinæ legis, neque natura, neque sola remissio peccatorum est illa gratia, quæ per Jesum Christum Dominum nostrum datur, sed ipsa facit ut lex impleatur, ut natura liberetur, ne peccatum dominetur."   De gratia et lib. arb., cap. xiv. 27.

unable to lead man to the good? This is the answer: The law cannot be fulfilled by·fear, but only by love.[1] Even if man outwardly does the good, but does it from fear of punishment and not from love of God, then he does it with a servile mind and not with a free and unconstrained heart, and it is no better than if he did not do it. "For that fruit is not good which does not come from the root of Caritas."[2] *What is necessary is that the will should really be won for the supernatural good.* This can never be brought about by any legal command, but only by a new desire driving out the old, by Caritas overcoming Cupiditas. The sweetness of pleasure must be vanquished by something yet sweeter.[3] So all turns finally on the question how we are to gain possession of this Caritas, which is the "fulfilling of the law" and the root from which all good grows. Pelagius affirms that man can produce Caritas in himself; Augustine denies it. "He who asserts that we can possess God's Caritas without God's aid, what else does he assert than that we can possess God without God?"[4] If man had originally been a divine being,[5] we could have spoken of a natural upward attraction dwelling in him even as he is now; but Augustine rejects this Hellenistic idea and holds that man is a created being who as such belongs to the rest of creation. Further, through

---

[1] "Venerat autem tempus ut impleretur lex per dilectionem; quia a Judæis non poterat impleri per timorem." In ev. Jn., tract. vii. 10. Of the Old Testament Augustine says, *ibid.*, tract. iii. 14: "Non erat ista [gratia] in Veteri Testamento, quia Lex minabatur, non opitulabatur; jubebat, non sanabat." The law commands: Love not the world, and so on. But that which man, bound by the law, would not bear, Christ, though not bound by the law, has taken upon Himself for our sake. "Hæc est gratia, et magna gratia."

[2] "Quod mandatum si fit timore pœnæ, non amore iustitiæ, seruiliter fit, non liberaliter et ideo nec fit. Non enim fructus est bonus, qui de caritatis radice non surgit." De spiritu et lit., cap. xiv. 26.

[3] Conf., lib. IX., cap. i.

[4] De patientia, cap. xviii. 15. "Unde est in hominibus caritas Dei et proximi, nisi ex ipso Deo? Nam si non ex Deo sed ex hominibus, vicerunt Pelagiani: si autem ex Deo, vicimus Pelagianos." De gratia et lib. arb., cap. xviii. 37.

[5] We may recall that such a view was held by Pelagius' disciple, Cælestius: "Si anima non potest esse sine peccato, ergo et deus subiacet peccato, cuius pars, hoc est anima, peccato obnoxia est." De gestis Pelagii, cap. xviii. 42.

the Fall man has cut himself adrift from God and sunk down into transient things; and so he naturally seeks his "bonum" in the temporal things about him. In the abstract, it is true, his intermediate position between the higher and lower worlds gives him the possibility of choice in both directions; but in his present situation only one of these possibilities can in fact be realised. Ever since the Fall there has dwelt in his nature a downward attraction, and he cannot direct his longing to the eternal. He does not possess any Caritas in himself, and if he is to gain it, it must be given to him by a special Divine act of grace, it must be infused into his heart from without.

This idea of the infusion of grace and love (infusio caritatis) has often been taken to prove that Augustine's conception of grace was magical and naturalistic. Thus Harnack says: "The love of God is infused into the soul in portions."[1] The root error of Augustine's doctrine of grace is supposed to lie in its "objective character" (ihres *dinglichen* Charakters)[2]; indeed, he is accused of believing that "love can be poured in like a medicine."[3] Similarly, W. Herrmann finds the weakness of Augustine's idea of grace in the fact that he failed to make it psychologically intelligible how man is converted by the grace of God which meets us in the historical Christ, and was content to think of grace as a mysterious power.[4] But here the need for caution is in-

---

[1] A. Harnack: *Lehrbuch der Dogmengeschichte*, Bd. III., 4 Aufl., 1910, p. 84: "Die Liebe Gottes wird in Stücken der Seele eingeflösst."

[2] *Op. cit.*, p. 84: "Just because he laid so great a stress on Grace through Christ (gratia per Christum), while conceiving it to consist of portions or instalments of Grace, he was the means of establishing, along with the perception of its importance as beginning, middle and end, the delusion that Grace had an objective character (der Irrwahn ihres *dinglichen* Charakters)."

[3] *Op. cit.*, p. 88.

[4] W. Herrmann: *Ethik*, 5 Aufl., 1921, p. 96: "Augustine leaves us in the dark as to how the decisive turning is effected in the human consciousness. . . . Even so, Augustine does not describe how a new fire is kindled in the heart of the individual when he comes to know Christ and experiences His power. The idea that there is a general power of Grace and that this is connected with

dicated by the very fact that Augustine's idea of the "in-fusion" of Caritas is directly connected with Paul's saying in Rom. v. 5 that "the love of God hath been shed abroad in our hearts through the Holy Ghost which was given unto us." Nothing was further from Augustine's intention than a magical or naturalistic idea of grace. If we are to apply the alternative "magical and naturalistic" or "personal and psychological," then it is the latter that describes Augustine's view. Caritas is infused into our hearts, not in a manner that is unconnected with our relation to God, but by the fact that the Holy Spirit is given to us. It is not true to say that in his doctrine of grace Augustine has missed the "psycho-logical" point of view. On the contrary, it was just this that attracted his special attention, and he was at great pains to make clear that process of conversion by which man is led from Cupiditas to Caritas. This is most evident from the way in which he managed to introduce Divine grace into the scheme of the psychology of desire.

How, then, did Augustine suppose this infusion of love to take place? The situation from which he started was briefly as follows. As a creature, man must seek his "bonum" outside himself, either in the higher or the lower world. The higher world can offer an eternal and infinite bonum; the bonum of the lower world, however, lies within easiest reach. Since man is as he is, the competition between the two can only be unequal. The lower world rushes in and captivates man by the pleasure it arouses in him, and by comparison the heavenly good seems so remote and unreal that it can take no firm hold on man's soul. By His law, it is true, God has bound man to the supernatural good and bidden him set his longing upon it in Caritas; but this is merely an external bond, not to be compared with that

everything that derives from Christ, ·was sufficient for him and for many Christians after him. They thus represented to themselves as a mysterious power that personal life which really helped them."

inward bond of desire by which the things of the world hold man captive to themselves. The reason why the eternal cannot seriously compete with the temporal is that man is outside its magnetic field, so to speak. Temporal things lie so near to him that they ceaselessly draw and allure him. The poet is right that " Everyone is drawn by his own pleasure "; for when pleasure with its inner enticement is present, all goes smoothly and almost automatically.[1] If the eternal is to gain such power over man, then it must come *near* him, so near that its power of attraction becomes greater and more irresistible than that which proceeds from temporal things. It is just this that has happened in the *Incarnation*. It has bridged the gulf that separated man from his Creator. God, our eternal bonum, is now no longer far from us; in Christ He has come to us in the midst of our temporal world, and come so near to us that every temporal bonum must pale beside this bonum. This revelation of God in Christ is the power that attracts us.[2] " Thou showest a green twig to a sheep and thou drawest it. Nuts are shown to a boy and he is drawn."[3] That is an illustration of God's dealings with us men. When He wishes to draw us to Himself, He uses Christ as the means, and so we can rightly speak of " the Father's drawing." He Himself is remote from us in His heavenly majesty, but in Christ He has come quite near to us, and thanks to Him and His Incarnation our heavenly bonum is no longer at an unattainable distance, but is as near to us as temporal things.[4]

This totally alters man's position as regards the choice

---

[1] In ev. Jn., tract. xxvi. 4.

[2] " Ista revelatio, ipsa est attractio." *Ibid.*, tract. xxvi. 5.

[3] " Ramum viridem ostendis ovi, et trahis illam. Nuces puero demonstrantur, et trahitur: et quo currit trahitur, amando trahitur, sine læsione corporis trahitur, cordis vinculo trahitur." *Ibid.*

[4] " Cum ergo longe a nobis esset immortalis et justus, tanquam a mortalibus et peccatoribus, descendit ad nos, ut fieret nobis proximus ille longinquus." Sermo CLXXI., cap. iii. 3., " Venit Christus mutare amorem, et de terreno facere vitæ cœlestis amatorem." Sermo CCCXLIV. 1.

between the lower and the higher world. Previously, free will had only the abstract possibility of choice and was bound in fact to choose the lower world because of its greater power of attraction; but now through " the Father's drawing," the higher world also becomes a reality to be reckoned with. Through the Incarnation of Christ we are drawn into the magnetic field of the eternal world and may taste something of the sweetness of the heavenly life. " There is a certain pleasure of the heart (voluptas cordis), to which that heavenly bread is sweet."[1] Previously, our supernatural bonum was found only in the form of an obligatory law and for that very reason could not seriously engage us; now it is an active force which irresistibly draws our innermost being. " If those things exercise attraction which among earthly delights (inter delicias et voluptates terrenas) are revealed to their lovers," Augustine says, " then does not Christ, revealed by the Father, draw? What does the soul more strongly desire than truth? For what should it have a greedy appetite, why wish the palate within to be healthy for judging what is true, if not in order to eat and drink wisdom, righteousness, truth, eternity?"[2] When God gives Himself to us in Christ, He gives us at once the object we are to love and the Caritas with which to love it.[3] The object we are to love is Himself, but Caritas also is Himself, who by the Holy Spirit takes up His abode in our hearts.[4] Even the fact that we love God is itself entirely a gift of God.[5]

---

[1] In ev. Jn., tract. xxvi. 4.

[2] *Ibid.*, tract. xxvi. 5. " An vero habent corporis sensus voluptates suas, et animus deseritur a voluptatibus suis ?" *Ibid.*, tract. xxvi. 4.

[3] " Dedit se ipsum quem dileximus: dedit unde diligeremus. Quid enim dedit, unde diligeremus, apertius audite per apostolum Paulum: Caritas, inquit, Dei diffusa est in cordibus nostris. Unde ? num forte a nobis ? Non. Ergo unde ? Per Spiritum sanctum qui datus est nobis." Sermo XXXIV., cap. i. 2.

[4] " Quia Spiritus sanctus Deus est, amemus Deum de Deo." *Ibid.*, cap. ii. 3.

[5] " Prorsus donum Dei est diligere Deum. . . . Diffundit enim caritatem in cordibus nostris amborum Spiritus, per quem Spiritum et Patrem amamus

What, then, is the place and significance of grace in Augustine's thought? Two points will supply the answer.

1. From one point of view, grace (gratia) is the key-word of Augustine's interpretation of Christianity. Everything in our life depends ultimately on God's grace. This is as true of the natural as of the Christian life. We have nothing of ourselves, all of God. "Before thou wast man, thou wast dust; before thou wast dust, thou wast nothing."[1] And before God took us for His children, we were sinners and children of wrath. By God's grace we have been brought into existence, by God's grace we have been justified.[2] It is called grace because it is given for nothing, with no preceding merit on our side.[3] Augustine may say that by faith and good works we are to merit eternal life as a reward, but he means in no way to detract from Divine grace. Even faith is a gift of God's grace, and if by it we "merit" eternal life, that simply means that we receive "grace for grace." The good works we do are not really our own but God's, which He works in us by His grace.[5] Both our faith and our works rest wholly upon grace, which is the ground of their possibility. Augustine never tires of saying in different ways that God's grace *precedes* (prævenit) all our works. Above all, the Incarnation is the great evidence of God's

---

et Filium, et quem Spiritum cum Patre amamus et Filio. Amorem itaque nostrum pium quo colimus Deum, fecit Deus." In ev. Jn., tract. cii. 5.

[1] Enarr. in Ps. cxliv. 10.

[2] "Attendamus ergo gratiam Dei, non solum qua fecit nos, verum etiam qua refecit. Cui ergo debemus quia sumus, illi debemus quia et justificati sumus." *Ibid.*

[3] "Ubi audis, *gratia*, Gratis intellige. Si ergo gratis, nihil tu attulisti, nihil meruisti." *Ibid.*

[4] "Cum promerueris Deum vivendo ex fide, accipies præmium immortalitatem, et vitam æternam. Et illa gratia est. Nam pro quo merito accipis vitam æternam? Pro gratia. Si enim fides gratia est, et vita æterna quasi merces est fidei . . .; sed quia ipsa fides gratia est, et vita æterna gratia est pro gratia." In ev. Jn., tract. iii. 9.

[5] "Quid ergo? nos bene non operamur? Imo operamur. Sed quomodo? Ipso in nobis operante; quia per fidem locum damus in corde nostro ei qui in nobis et per nos bona operatur." Enarr. in Ps. cxliv. 10.

grace and love.[1]   "If God did not love sinners, He would not have come down from heaven to earth."[2]   No rational ground for this grace of God can be found.   Grace is a positive expression of God's will; we cannot give it a motive by referring it to anything else.   When we have said it is grace, we have said all there is to be said about it.[3]

It is at this point that Augustine is furthest from the Hellenistic theory which served as a starting-point for his doctrine of Caritas.   It looks as if he had in fact abandoned the Eros scheme and come to think wholly in terms of the Agape motif.   The proclamation of God's gratia, as we have it in Augustine, would seem to be the most unreserved proclamation of God's spontaneous and "unmotivated" love.   But it is not so; there is another side to his conception of grace, which will considerably modify the impression we have so far gained.

2. If God had not condescended to us in His *gratia*, we could never have ascended to Him in *Caritas*.   This is what makes grace so extraordinarily important in Augustine, but also limits it.   Without grace there is no access to God. Without grace, Caritas has no air beneath its wings for its flight to God.   Grace "prevents" our every deed—but as the means precedes the end.   *The end is and remains the ascent of Caritas to God.*   This brings us back to Eros.   All that was said above about Augustine's Way of salvation according to the scheme of ascent still holds good.   Grace has simply been introduced as the indispensable means of this ascent.   What the law and free will combined could not do, since our pleasure is bound up with earthly things, is done

---

[1] "Per ineffabilem gratiam Verbum caro factum est."   In ev. Jn., tract. lxxxii. 4.

[2] *Ibid.*, tract. xlix. 5.

[3] "Nam quæ major gratia Dei nobis potuit illucescere, quam ut habens unigenitum Filium, faceret eum hominis filium, atque ita vicissim hominis filium, faceret Dei Filium?   Quære meritum, quære causam, quære justitiam; et vide utrum invenias nisi gratiam."   Sermo CLXXXV., cap. iii. 3.

by God's grace coming to meet man with the eternal and supernatural bonum and awakening in him a longing for heaven. Grace does not annul the law, but gives what the law requires. Unlike the law, it does not merely enjoin the good; it awakens delight in the good.[1] Grace does not destroy free will, but simply gives it a new object and so a new direction and aim.[2] "Gratia Dei ex nolente volentem facit."[3] What was burdensome and difficult so long as it was expressed as law, now becomes easy and pleasant to us, since Caritas has come to dwell in our hearts by grace. What will a man not endure and suffer for love, if only he attains what he loves? Think how the lover of money or honour will forsake everything else to obtain what he loves. He does not even regard this as a sacrifice. And just so, the Caritas that is infused by grace brings it about that the ascent to God is not felt to be hard and troublesome, in spite of the effort it costs.[4]

Even if, in speaking of grace and the Incarnation, Augustine most emphatically asserts the Divine descent, this does not mean any real break with the Eros idea, as we have shown. He still conceives fellowship with God funda-

---

1 " Non obligatio, sed delectatio." In ev. Jn., tract. xxvi. 4. " Nos autem dicimus humanam uoluntatem sic diuinitus adiuuari ad faciendam iustitiam, ut præter quod creatus est homo cum libero arbitrio præterque doctrinam qua ei præcipitur quemadmodum uiuere debeat accipiat spiritum sanctum, *quo fiat in animo eius delectatio dilectioque summi illius atque incommutabilis boni, quod deus est.*" De spiritu et lit., cap. iii. 5. " Per fidem confugiat ad misericordiam dei, ut det quod iubet atque inspirata gratiæ suauitate per spiritum sanctum faciat plus delectare quod præcipit quam delectat quod inpedit." *Ibid.*, cap. xxix. 51.

2 " Liberum ergo arbitrium euacuamus per gratiam? Absit, sed magis liberum arbitrium statuimus. . . . Ac per hoc, sicut lex non euacuatur, sed statuitur per fidem, quia fides inpetrat gratiam, qua lex inpleatur, ita liberum arbitrium non euacuatur per gratiam, sed statuitur, quia gratia sanat uoluntatem, qua iustitia libere diligatur." *Ibid.*, cap. xxx. 52.

3 " The Grace of God makes a willing man out of an unwilling one." Opus imperfectum contra Julianum, lib. III., cap. cxxii.

4 Sermo XCVI., cap. i. 1: " Non est durum nec grave quod ille imperat, qui adjuvat ut fiat quod imperat. . . . Quidquid enim durum est in præceptis, ut sit lene, caritas facit."

mentally in accord with the scheme of ascent. Grace and
the Incarnation are simply the necessary means for it. *The
descent of Christ has as its aim our ascent:* God became
man that we might become gods.[1] How little the idea of
grace counteracts the Eros tendency is perhaps best shown
by the fact that Augustine—quite logically, since grace is
the same as *infusio caritatis*—can describe grace itself as
the ladder on which we may mount to the Divine life and
make our way to the heavenly fatherland.[2] There is thus
no real change in his attitude : *our* love to God is still
decisive for fellowship with God; only we cannot have this
love without the help of *God's* love, and so this too has its
appointed place in his thought.[3] The descent of God in
Christ to lost humanity is of the utmost importance; and
yet it has *no intrinsic value* for Augustine. In other words,
*Augustine is not really interested in the causal, but only in
the teleological, motivation of the Incarnation.* Causal consideration of the Incarnation stops at the miracle of the
Divine love itself; the main point in the Incarnation is that
God, the Holy One, condescends in mercy to the sinner
and wills to have fellowship with him. The teleological
consideration also maintains, it is true, that the Incarnation
is the revelation of Divine love, but the main point is that
this has happened in order that we may be enabled to
ascend to Him. In the former case the centre of gravity is
God and His love which descends and gives itself; in the

1 " Ut enim non sis homo, ad hoc vocatus es ab illo qui propter te factus est
homo. . . . Deus enim deum te vult facere: non natura, sicut est ille quem
genuit; sed dono suo et adoptione." Sermo CLXVI., cap. iv. 4. " Homo
propter nos factus, qui nos homines fecit; et assumens hominem Deus, ut homines
faceret deos." Sermo CCCXLIV., 1.

2 " Facit [gratia Dei] illi gradus quibus ascendat. . . . Ergo ascensus in
corde tuo sint dispositi a Deo per gratiam ipsius. Amando ascende: inde
cantatur Canticum graduum." Enarr. in Ps. lxxxiii. 10. Epist. CIV., iii. 11.

3 " Ut diligeremus, dilecti sumus." Sermo CLXXIV., cap. iv. 4. " Quæ
merita bona tunc habere poteramus, quando deum non diligebamus ? Ut
enim acciperemus dilectionem, qua diligeremus, dilecti sumus, cum eam nondum
haberemus." De gratia Christi, xxvi. 27.

latter, it is man and his acquisition of the means he requires for his spiritual self-assertion and his ascent.

Thanks to his anti-moralism and his eudæmonism, a theocentric and an egocentric tendency are peculiarly interwoven in Augustine's doctrine of grace. In his anti-moralism he is decidedly theocentric. We have nothing of ourselves, all of God's grace. Caritas, which is the fulfilling of the law and the root of all good, is not part of our natural endowment, nor can we in any way acquire it. It must be given to us from outside by God as an unmerited grace; it must be infused into our hearts by the Holy Spirit. In all this, our gaze is turned unwaveringly towards God. But now the idea of Caritas is set in a eudæmonistic scheme, in terms of the psychology of desire, which is just as decidedly egocentric. When Caritas has been infused into a man's heart, he still continues to seek the satisfaction of his desire, though he seeks it no longer in the things of sense, but in a supernatural bonum. Here our gaze is turned unwaveringly upon our own self and what can satisfy its needs.

Augustine's constant objection against the Neoplatonists is that they did not know the Incarnation and had no place for grace. He plainly wants to find room for the Christian Agape motif. Yet he does not take this opportunity of completely dismissing the Neoplatonic doctrine of salvation. Even as a Christian he retains the Way of salvation of Eros. He builds it into his Caritas doctrine and fills it out with his doctrine of grace. Caritas, which as upward-directed love bears the essential stamp of " heavenly Eros," is the only right way to God. But so long as Caritas is merely commanded by the law, it is unproductive and an impassable way for us. Something more is needed, a dynamic moment, which overcomes sloth and our natural resistance to the ascent. This occurs when God in His grace infuses Caritas into the heart. Gratia is the motor which alone can set our heavenly Eros in motion, the *power* which makes the ascent successful.

These ideas made Augustine the founder of the Catholic doctrine of grace. His combination of Gratia and Caritas, God's descent and our ascent, created the *synthesis* between the primitive Christian and the Hellenistic idea of salvation, between the Ways of salvation of Agape and of Eros, which became predominant in the Mediæval Church. In many points the Catholic Church has rejected Augustine's ideas about grace,[1] but in its basic idea of grace as " infused love " which makes our ascent to God possible, it has faithfully continued the course Augustine began.[2]

In Caritas, both tendencies—upwards and downwards—are united. The *foundation* of the life of Caritas is Divine grace; but this is the same as Incarnation, descent, humilitas, and so the Christian life also is marked by humilitas. But the *goal* of the life of Caritas is to attain to God in His sublimity, to reach up with love's longing towards His per-

---

[1] *Cf.* J. Mausbach: *Die Ethik des heiligen Augustinus*, 2 Aufl., 1929, Bd. I., p. 43: " Yet not everything that the vigorous mind of Augustine discovered in dealing with dogma has been accepted by the Church as a permanent gain. The very title of ' doctor gratiæ ' bestowed on him is not to be understood as if his doctrine of Grace and Predestination had Catholic features in every detail. Augustine emphasises ' in many utterances the work of God's grace in man, the nothingness of human will and ability, and man's entanglement in sin, more sharply than is compatible with the maintenance of the moral self of human nature, with the result that both in his own time and even now, centuries later, the greatest misunderstandings and errors have arisen.' And this is not merely a question of the sharpening of language in controversial exposition, but partly of one-sidedness and crudity of thought."

[2] Instructive in this respect is K. Adam: *Das Wesen des Katholizismus*, 4 Aufl., 1927. In dealing with justifying Grace as " the infusion of love," he repeatedly states that this kindles a new Eros in man. " On the contrary, from the Catholic point of view, Grace is a vital force which awakens and summons the powers of man's soul, his understanding, his will, his feeling, and fires them with a *new Eros* " (p. 197). " It is a sort of overflow of the eternal, infinite love in me. That is the *new Eros*, the new strong and steadfast will, the new Divine fulness, holy love " (p. 198). " It is true that by certain subjective signs and by earnest self-examination he can ascertain with moral certainty whether he is at the moment impelled by the *new Eros*, and so whether he is a child of love, a child of God " (p. 200).

fection; therefore, there is also an upward tendency in the Christian life. To use a simile of Augustine's which admirably illustrates this duality: Caritas is like a tree, which stretches its roots deep down into the earth, but only in order to be able to stretch its top the higher towards heaven.[1] There is no one who does not wish to be exalted, says Augustine, but we too easily forget that the way to exaltation passes through humilitas.[2] It was to teach us this that Christ descended to us and humbled Himself. From Him we are to learn to descend in humilitas and so find the way that leads to exaltation.[3] "Descendite, ut ascendatis et ascendatis ad deum."[4]

Augustine thus teaches a *theologia humilitatis*, but merely as a means for rising to a *theologia gloriæ*. He is rightly called "doctor gratiæ," but his *theologia gratiæ* finds its significance in his *theologia caritatis*.

6. Amor Dei and Amor Sui

Caritas is in essence *love to God*. Yet according to Augustine, *all* love—even that which is directed to God—is acquisitive love and so, in a certain sense, *self-love*. What then is the relation between these two, love of God and love of self, amor Dei and amor sui?

This is one of the most complicated questions in Augus-

---

[1] "Arborem attendite: ima petit prius, ut sursum excrescat; figit radicem in humili, ut verticem tendat ad cœlum. Numquid nititur nisi ab humilitate? Tu autem sine caritate vis excelsa comprehendere; sine radice auras petis?" Sermo CXVII. 17.

[2] "Nam quis non velit ire ad exaltationem? Omnes delectat celsitudo: sed humilitas gradus est. . . . Dominus autem ostendit gradum." Sermo XCVI., cap. iii. 3.

[3] "Vis capere celsitudinem Dei? Cape prius humilitatem Dei. . . . Cape ergo humilitatem Christi, disce humilis esse. . . . Cum ceperis humilitatem ejus, surgis cum illo." Sermo CXVII. 17. For the ascent and descent see also Enarr. in Ps. cxix. 2.

[4] Conf., lib. IV., cap. xii. 19. "Descend that you may ascend and ascend to God."

tine. We can find at least apparent contradictions. It is not difficult to find statements which put the two kinds of love *in absolute opposition to one another*: amor Dei is the root and source of all good, amor sui the essence of sin and the root of all evil. On the other hand, the thought very frequently occurs, that *love to God and self-love harmonise in the best possible way*. Indeed, the connection between them is sometimes so intimate that it is tempting to speak of an identification of amor Dei and amor sui.

These contrary tendencies are especially important, because we can arrive at quite different ideas of Augustine's thought according as we take the one or the other to be ultimately decisive for him. If we take amor Dei and amor sui to be mutually exclusive, then Augustine's thought will appear strictly *theocentric*, whilst if we take them to be identical, his thought will just as certainly appear *egocentric*. Karl Holl has taken this latter view in his book *Augustins innere Entwicklung*, and has accordingly characterised Augustine's entire outlook as pure eudæmonism. Others have attempted to show that this is a one-sided and unjust judgment, and have naturally pointed to the theocentric element as decisive.

Before going on to examine this question, we may assert quite generally that these two lines of thought do exist in Augustine. Neither of them can be eliminated in the interests of simplicity and uniformity; nor is it enough simply to state that there is a contradiction in Augustine, and then to select one line as being characteristically Augustinian, while the other is an accidental deviation. We must first ask whether it is conceivable that Augustine so crudely contradicted himself. It is not difficult, of course, to show that contrary tendencies helped to mould his thought, for he lives in two separate worlds with heterogeneous motifs. But it is one thing to say this and quite another to credit him with such an obvious contradiction as to assert in one place what he denies in another, and to do this not simply in an isolated instance, but throughout the whole of his writings. Furthermore, the point in question is of the most vital importance for Augustine. Amor Dei is equivalent to Caritas. It cannot be a matter of indifference to him whether this is the opposite of self-love or an expression of self-love. If we think he so flagrantly contradicted himself in the matter which is of central importance to him, then it is the clearest proof that we have not rightly understood him. We cannot be content simply to state the contradiction and then invent a main line from which there are various deviations. We have only reached a real understanding when we see how the apparently contradictory statements are the consequences of Augustine's fundamental conception.

We come, first, to that line of thought according to which amor Dei and amor sui are *opposites*.

How seriously Augustine meant this contrast, we may judge from the fact that he constructed his great work *De Civitate Dei* on the basis of it. The dualism of the two realms, the kingdom of God and that of the world, " Civitas Dei " and " Civitas terrena," goes back to that of amor Dei and amor sui.[1] God alone *is* from eternity to eternity. By His creative act He produces a host of relatively independent beings, angels and men. His purpose in this is to set up a kingdom of God. That which distinguishes this kingdom and makes it the kingdom of God is the fact that in it God is " all in all." As He is the " omnium substantiarum

---

[1] " Fecerunt itaque ciuitates duas amores duo, terrenam scilicet amor sui usque ad contemtum Dei, cælestem uero amor Dei usque ad contemtum sui." De ciu. dei, lib. XIV., cap. xxviii.   " In hac [ciuitate Dei] autem nulla est hominis sapientia nisi pietas, qua recte colitur uerus Deus, id expectans præmium in societate sanctorum non solum hominum, uerum etiam angelorum, ut sit Deus omnia in omnibus." *Ibid.* " Profecto ista est magna differentia, qua ciuitas, unde loquimur, utraque discernitur, una scilicet societas piorum hominum, altera inpiorum, singula quæque cum angelis ad se pertinentibus, in quibus præcessit hac amor Dei, hac amor sui." De ciu. dei, lib. XIV., cap. xiii.

auctor et conditor,"[1] so the happiness of every creature depends solely on its unbroken connection with Him.[2] Severed from Him, it is subject to annihilation; it can have permanence only by constantly receiving reality and " bonum " from God. But there has already been a falling away in the world of angels. Instead of receiving all from God and humbly acknowledging their dependence on Him, certain angels turned away from God to themselves, as if they possessed their " bonum " in themselves.[3] This fall of the angels marks the beginning of the kingdom of the world, which is in conflict with the kingdom of God. Just as the principle of the Civitas Dei is amor Dei, love set upon and cleaving to God, so the Civitas terrena has its principle in amor sui—that is, the self-sufficiency of the creature whereby it puts itself in God's place as its own " bonum " and imagines it has " enough " in itself (sufficere sibi).

The Civitas Dei is intended, however, to embrace not only angels but also the human race. The kingdom of God exists, so to speak, at a higher heavenly and a lower earthly level. It is God's will that it should include the immortal angels and mortal men in a holy fellowship where all possess their " bonum commune " in God and live by His grace alone.[4] But through the Fall of the first men the kingdom of the world enters into the lower level as well. " Eritis sicut di "— " Ye shall be as gods "—such was the temptation that led to the Fall of the first men. This reveals the common essence

---

[1] De ciu. dei, lib. XII., cap. i. " Author and Creator of all essences."

[2] " Beatitudinis igitur illorum causa est adhærere Deo." *Ibid.*

[3] " Alii sua potestate potius delectati, uelut bonum suum sibi ipsi essent, a superiore communi omnium beatifico bono ad propria defluxerunt." *Ibid.* " Proinde causa beatitudinis angelorum bonorum ea uerissima reperitur, quod ei adhærent qui summe est. Cum uero causa miseriæ malorum angelorum quæritur, ea merito occurrit, quod ab illo, qui summe est, auersi ad se ipsos conuersi sunt, qui non summe sunt; et hoc uitium quid aliud quam superbia nuncupetur." *Ibid.*, lib. XII., cap. vi. *Cf.* De vera rel., cap. xiii. 26.

[4] De ciu. dei, lib. XII., cap. ix.

of all sin; for in whatever form sin may appear in a particular case, it always means the same thing: man turns away from God to himself, amor Dei gives place to amor sui. Man refuses to seek his "bonum" in God, and behaves as though he possessed it in himself. The purpose of man's existence is that God should be his "supreme and true principle"; sin is man's proud insistence on being his own "principle."[1] In this sense, Augustine can say that all sin has its root and origin in pride, superbia, by which man seeks to put himself in God's place.[2] Self-sufficiency, which in God is the expression of His divinity,[3] in man is sin. Real self-sufficiency, absence of need and autarky, is to be found only in God. It is idle fancy for man to think he himself possesses it,[4] but it is a fancy with serious consequences for the whole of his life, for it puts an end to his interest in God; he no longer sees that he must fly to God for his "bonum," but remains in himself. But in the nature of the case, he *cannot* in the long run remain in himself: he cannot be satisfied with his own emptiness.[5] So, having severed his connection with God, he is driven irresistibly towards the things he finds outside himself in the world. There is a strict logic in sin, and the man who has begun to fall is compelled to fall ever deeper. The Fall begins when man turns from God to amor sui. "*Prima hominis perditio fuit amor sui.*"[6] But then he cannot remain in himself, and the second 'stage of the Fall comes when he begins to seek his good in the world and so sinks ever deeper

[1] "Hinc enim et delectauit quod dictum est: Erîtis sicut di. Quod melius esse possent summo ueroque principio cohærendo per obœdientiam, non suum sibi existendo principium per superbiam." *Ibid.*, lib. XIV., cap. xiii.

[2] "Vitiorum omnium humanorum causa superbia est." De peccatorum merit. et remiss., lib. II., cap. xvii. 27. *Cf.* De trinitate, lib. XII., cap. ix. 14. De natura et gratia, cap. xxix. 33.

[3] *Cf. supra*, p. 479.

[4] "Quid est enim, dicentes se esse sapientes, nisi a se habere, sibi sufficere? Stulti facti sunt: merito stulti." Sermo CL., cap. viii. 9.

[5] "Inanescunt qui placent sibi de se." Conf., lib. X., cap. xxxix. 64.

[6] Sermo XCVI., cap. ii. 2.

down into transient things.[1] Amor sui is not merely one sin among others, but the sin of sins.[2] " Secundum se ipsum vivere " is characteristic of the kingdom of the world, "secundum Deum vivere " of the kingdom of God.[3] Augustine comes very near to destroying the Eros scheme here, for he also attacks the common idea of Eros theory that evil is to be traced to corporeality.[4] His use of the terms

[1] " Incipit enim deserto Deo amare se, et ad ea diligenda quæ sunt extra se, pellitur a se. . . . Jam vides quia foris es. Amare te cœpisti: sta in te, si potes. . . . Cœpisti diligere quod est extra te, perdidisti te. Cum ergo pergit amor hominis etiam a se ipso ad ea quæ foris sunt, incipit cum vanis evanescere." *Ibid.*

[2] This absolute opposition of *amor Dei* and *amor sui* and the description of amor sui as the root of all evil make it natural to ask what is the relation of this contrast to that between *Caritas* and *Cupiditas*; for Augustine says of Cupiditas, too, that it is the root of all evil, " radix omnium malorum " (*cf. supra*, p. 454, n. 1). As a matter of fact, it is the same contrast in both cases, only that here it is taken a step further back. The fundamental opposite of amor Dei (or Caritas) is amor sui. But since the man who has turned away from God cannot remain in himself, he is driven out from himself to the temporal things and is landed in Cupiditas. But the deepest root of all evil, its primal source, is and remains self-love. " Hæc omnia mala ab eo velut fonte manant, quod primum posuit, seipsos amantes." In ev. Jn., tract. cxxiii. 5.

[3] " Arbitror tamen satis nos iam fecisse magnis et difficillimis quæstionibus de initio uel mundi uel animæ uel ipsius generis humani, quod in duo genera distribuimus, unum eorum, qui *secundum hominem*, alterum eorum, qui *secundum Deum* uiuunt; quas etiam mystice appellamus *ciuitates duas*, hoc est duas societates hominum, quarum est una quæ prædestinata est in æternum regnare cum Deo, altera æternum supplicium subire cum diabolo." De ciu. dei, lib. XV., cap. i. " Homo ita factus est rectus, ut non secundum se ipsum, sed secundum eum, a quo factus est, uiueret, id est illius potius quam suam faceret uoluntatem." *Ibid.*, lib. XIV., cap. iv. *Cf.* this whole chapter, which is entitled " Quid sit secundum hominem, quid autem secundum Deum uiuere."

[4] It is not the corruptible flesh that has dragged the soul down into sin, but the sinful soul that has made the flesh corruptible. " Verum tamen qui omnia mala animæ ex corpore putant accidisse, in errore sunt. . . . Tamen aliter se habet fides nostra. Nam corruptio corporis, quæ adgrauat animam, non peccati primi est causa, sed pœna; nec caro corruptibilis animam peccatricem, sed anima peccatrix fecit esse corruptibilem carnem." De ciu. dei, lib. XIV., cap. iii. There are the rudiments here of a " totus-homo " view—in conscious opposition to Platonic theory and in spite of Wisd. ix. 15 which he quotes. We must not regard " the flesh " as the cause of sin, but must have regard to " uniuersa hominis natura " (*ibid.*). Salvation, too, concerns the whole man. *Cf.* Augustine's polemic against the Neoplatonist Porphyry, De ciu. dei, lib. X., cap. xxxii.: " Hæc uia *totum hominem* mundat et immortalitati mortalem ex omnibus quibus constat partibus præparat."

" secundum spiritum vivere" and "secundum carnem vivere" to describe the difference between the two kingdoms has ultimately nothing to do with the contrast which Eros theory makes between the spiritual-rational and the corporeal-sensible, although naturally we do at times catch a slight echo of this in Augustine. "Secundum carnem vivere" is the same as "secundum se ipsum vivere" and that is why it is sin.[1] Not corporeality, but egocentricity is the deepest root of sin.[2]

We have now seen one line of thought in Augustine, according to which amor Dei and amor sui are in sharp opposition; we must proceed to look at the other, according to which they *harmonise* in the best possible manner.

The idea is found in Augustine, not merely in isolated instances, but constantly recurring, that self-love and the love of God ought properly to coincide. It is one of his favourite ideas, and agrees excellently with his outlook as a whole. If we remember that for him all love is acquisitive love, and that God is "summum bonum," it is not surprising that even love to God should be a kind of amor sui, and that amor sui, rightly understood, can find full satisfaction only in that which is the "highest good"; so that, with a certain logic, amor sui leads on to amor Dei. Self-love, says Augustine, impels me in all my activities; it is only self-love which impels me to seek my bonum. But if I seek it in anything temporal, I am ultimately deceived. I wanted my own welfare, but got what was my misfortune: it was a false, an ill-

---

[1] " Non enim habendo carnem, quam non habet diabolus, sed uiuendo secundum se ipsum, hoc est secundum hominem, factus est homo similis diabolo: quia et ille secundum se ipsum uiuere uoluit, quando in ueritate non stetit." De ciu. dei, lib. XIV., cap. iii.

[2] It is sometimes said that sin according to Luther is (unbelief or) *egocentricity*, according to Augustine *superbia*. This is quite right, but it is misleading inasmuch as superbia *is* amor sui—that is, egocentricity. Man should have his centre, his bonum, in God; but in superbia his centre is in himself. On the other hand, it is plain that "egocentricity" has a quite different meaning in the two instances.

informed self-love that impelled me. *Right* self-love cannot seek its bonum in anything but God, and it is my own loss if I do not love Him.[1] By amor Dei or Caritas I serve my own best interests; for that love is set upon *God*, the " highest good," which I thus gain *for myself*. So if I do not love God, it only shows that I do not *rightly* love myself.[2] Amor Dei and amor sui are so much one thing that they grow and decline with one another. The more I love God, the more I love myself too.[3]

Self-love is not directly commanded by the Commandment of Love, which only speaks of love to God and neighbour. According to Augustine, this is not because self-love is contrary to God's will, but because a special commandment about it was unnecessary—for several reasons. First, it is our nature to love ourselves.[4] Secondly, the Commandment of Love in

---

[1] " Vis audire unde diligas te ? Ex hoc diligis te, quia Deum diligis ex toto te. Putas enim Deo proficere, quod diligis Deum ? et quia diligis Deum, Deo aliquid accedit ? et si tu non diligas, minus habebit ? Cum diligis, tu proficis: tu ibi eris, ubi non peris. Sed respondebis, et dices, Quando enim non dilexi me ? Prorsus non diligebas te, quando Deum non diligebas, qui fecit te. Sed cum odisses te, putabas quod amares te. Qui enim diligit iniquitatem, odit animam suam." Sermo XXXIV., cap. v. 8.

[2] " Si non diligit Deum, non diligit seipsum." In ev. Jn., tract. lxxxvii. 1. " Quid autem eligamus, quod præcipue diligamus, nisi quo nihil melius inuenimus ? Hoc Deus est, cui si aliquid diligendo uel præponimus uel æquamus, *nos ipsos diligere nescimus.* Tanto enim nobis melius est, quanto magis in illum imus, quo nihil melius est." Epist. CLV., iv. 13. ". . . si nosmet ipsos diligere illum diligendo iam nouimus." *Ibid.,* iv. 14. " Uidelicet ut intellegeretur nullam esse aliam dilectionem, qua quisque diligit se ipsum, nisi quod diligit deum. Qui enim aliter se diligit, potius se odisse dicendus est." *Ibid.,* iv. 15. " Nisi diligat deum, nemo diligit se ipsum." Epist. CLXXVII. 10. " Qui ergo se diligere novit, Deum diligit: qui vero non diligit Deum, etiam si se diligit, quod ei naturaliter inditum est, tamen non inconvenienter odisse se dicitur, cum id agit quod sibi adversatur, et se ipsum tanquam suus inimicus insequitur." De trinitate, lib. XIV., cap. xiv. 18. " Vero solus se novit diligere, qui Deum diligit." De mor. eccl. cath., lib. I., cap. xxvi. 48.

[3] " Nos autem ipsos tanto magis diligimus, quanto magis diligimus Deum." De trinitate, lib. VIII., cap. viii. 12.

[4] " Ut se quisque diligat, præcepto non opus est." De doct. christiana, lib. I., cap. xxxv. 39. " Ergo, quoniam præcepto non opus est ut se quisque et corpus suum diligat, id est, quoniam id quod sumus, et id quod infra nos est, ad nos tamen pertinet, inconcussa *naturæ lege diligimus,* quæ in bestias etiam

both its parts really does speak of self-love. I cannot love God without at the same time loving myself.[1] Therefore, when the Commandment of love to God was given, it was unnecessary to stress self-love by a special commandment.[2] The Commandment of love to neighbour speaks still more clearly of self-love; for it expressly says, " Thou shalt love thy neighbour *as thyself.*" How can a man possibly love his neighbour if he does not even love himself? Self-love is both the pre-condition and the measure of our love to our neighbour.[3]

But we can go still further and say that self-love is not merely included in love to God and to neighbour as an equivalent third; it is in the last resort the very foundation of all the rest. Man is so made that he cannot help loving himself.[4] But the important thing is that his self-love should be guided into the right path—that is, directed to God as his

---

promulgata est; restabat ut de illo quod supra nos est, et de illo quod juxta nos est, præcepta sumeremus." *Ibid.,* cap. xxvi. 27.

[1] Non enim fieri potest ut seipsum, qui Deum diligit, non diligat: imo vero solus se novit diligere, qui Deum diligit. Siquidem ille se satis diligit, qui sedulo agit, ut summo et vero perfruatur bono: quod si nihil est aliud quam Deus, sicut ea quæ dicta sunt docuerunt, quis cunctari potest, quin sese amet, qui amator est Dei." De mor. eccl. cath., lib. I., cap. xxvi. 48. " In eo quippe nosmet ipsos diligimus, si deum diligimus." Epist. CXXX. vii. 14.

[2] " Quia igitur nemo nisi deum diligendo diligit se ipsum, non opus erat, ut dato de dei dilectione præcepto etiam se ipsum homo diligere iuberetur, cum in eo diligat se ipsum, quod diligit deum." Epist. CLV. iv. 15. " Se autem spiritualiter diligit, qui ex toto, quod in eo vivit, Deum diligit." De vera rel., cap. xii. 24. " Quis autem diligit animam suam? Qui diligit Deum ex toto corde suo, et ex tota mente sua." Sermo XC. 6.

[3] " Cum dictum est, Diliges proximum tuum tanquam teipsum, simul et tui abs te dilectio non prætermissa est." De doct. christiana, lib. I., cap. xxvi. 27. " Iam uero quia duo præcipua præcepta, hoc est dilectionem Dei et dilectionem proximi, docet magister Deus, in quibus tria inuenit homo quæ diligat, *Deum, se ipsum et proximum,* adque ille in se diligendo non errat, qui Deum diligit: consequens est, ut etiam proximo ad diligendum Deum consulat, quem iubetur sicut se ipsum diligere." De ciu. dei, lib. XIX., cap. xiv. " Qui enim non diligit Deum, quomodo diligit proximum tanquam seipsum; quandoquidem non diligit et seipsum?" In ev. Jn., tract. lxxxiii. 3. " Prius vide, si jam nosti diligere te ipsum." Sermo CXXVIII., cap. iii. 5.

[4] " Sic itaque condita est mens humana, ut . . . nunquam se non diligat." De trinitate, lib. XIV., cap. xiv. 18.

bonum.[1] Augustine can actually say that the Commandment of love to God was given to teach us rightly to love ourselves.[2] He knows a motive for love to God, and this motive is egocentric. Amor Dei commends itself as the right sort of love, because only so can man successfully love himself. When he loves God, he does so ultimately in order to obtain satisfaction for the demands of self-love.[3] Self-love embraces human life from beginning to end. It drives man both on the road away from God and on the road back to Him. The Fall begins with amor sui. Since man loves himself more than anything else, he refuses even to be subordinate to God. But when he is adrift from God and tries to remain in himself, the same amor sui drives him out of himself; self-love teaches him the impossibility of being content with the fiction of his own resources. He must go out into the world to seek his bonum. And when the world betrays him, it is again self-love that impels him to return. As a prodigal son, he "returns to himself"—not, however, in order to remain in himself, but to go to his Father, where all that his amor sui desires is to be found in abundance and securely possessed.[4] The road that leads away from God is that of false self-love; the way to God is that of true self-love.

The importance of self-love in Augustine's thought is best seen from the way in which he uses it as the foundation for his doctrine of the Trinity.[5] "God is love." Man is made

---

1 " Jam enim se non diligit perverse, sed recte, cum Deum diligit." *Ibid.*

2 " Ut enim homo se diligere nosset, constitutus est ei finis, quo referret omnia quæ ageret, ut beatus esset; non enim qui se diligit aliud uult esse quam beatus. Hic autem finis est adhærere Deo." De ciu. dei, lib. X., cap. iii. " Diligite Dominum, et ibi discite diligere vos." Sermo XC. 6.

3 " Qui autem se propter habendum Deum diligunt, ipsi se diligunt: ergo *ut se diligant, Deum diligunt.*" In ev. Jn., tract. lxxxiii. 3.

4 " Reversus ad semetipsum, ut non remaneret in semetipso, quid dixit? Surgam, et ibo ad patrem meum. Ecce unde ceciderat a se, ceciderat a patre suo: ceciderat a se, ad ea quæ foris sunt exiit a se. *Redit ad se, et pergit ad patrem, ubi tutissime servet se.*" Sermo XCVI., cap. ii.

5 On Augustine's doctrine of the Trinity in general, see M. Schmaus: *Die psychologische Trinitätslehre des hl. Augustinus* (Münsterische Beiträge zur

in God's image; and if we would gain insight into the nature of the Divine life, it is necessary, according to Augustine, to find analogies from the life of the human soul, and especially from those human activities which bear the stamp of love. Three things can be distinguished in every act of love : (1) the lover, (2) the object loved, and (3) love itself, which is the bond of union between the lover and the beloved object.   In Augustine's own words : we must distinguish between *amans*, *quod amatur* and *amor*.[1]   These three, which in the concrete act of love are one, give a picture of the inner life of the Trinity.[2]   These general considerations, however, are not enough for Augustine; he wants to see the Trinitarian love mirrored in a special form of human love, and he selects human *self-love*.[3]   This is the more remarkable, as it is particularly difficult to reach a trinitarian view from this starting-point; for in self-love the subject and object, amans and quod amatur, are identical, and the three elements of love are reduced to two.[4]   That Augustine nevertheless insists on this starting-point shows more than anything else how fixed and central in his thought the idea of amor sui is.   As self-love is fundamental to all human life, so here it is assigned to the Divine life itself.   The inner life of the Trinity is moulded by that love with which God ceaselessly loves

---

Theologie hrsg. von F. Diekamp und R. Stapper, H. 11), 1927.   As the question of love is extraordinarily important for Augustine's idea of the Trinity, and as his thought on this point includes many problems as yet unsolved, a special study of " Love and the Trinity " in Augustine is much to be desired.

[1] " Amor autem alicujus amantis est, et amore aliquid amatur.   Ecce tria sunt; amans, et quod amatur, et amor.   Quid est ergo amor, nisi quædam vita duo aliqua copulans, vel copulare appetens, amantem scilicet, et quod amatur ?" De trinitate, lib. VIII., cap. x. 14.

[2] " Sed ubi ventum est ad caritatem, quæ in sancta Scriptura Deus dicta est, eluxit paululum Trinitas, id est, amans, et quod amatur, et amor."   *Ibid.*, lib. XV., cap. vi. 10.

[3] *Cf.* esp. De trinitate, lib. IX., cap. ii.

[4] " Quid, si non amem nisi me ipsum ? nonne duo erunt; quod amo, et amor ? Amans enim et quod amatur, hoc idem est, quando se ipse amat: sicut amare et amari, eodem modo idipsum est, cum se quisque amat.   Eadem quippe res bis dicitur, cum dicitur, Amat se, et amatur a se."   *Ibid.*

Himself—though naturally not with a love that desires and seeks its bonum in something else, but with a love that contemplates and enjoys its own perfection.[1]

Both the lines of thought we have described—(1) amor Dei and amor sui as absolute opposites, and (2) amor Dei and amor sui as ultimately identical—are equally essential to Augustine's outlook. He himself felt a certain tension between them, but was not led to abandon either. He cannot explain how they agree, yet he never doubts that they do. He maintains both and sees in their co-existence an inevitable paradox. "We must love, not ourselves, but Him"—of that he is certain. But if we obey this command, if we cease loving ourselves and set all our love upon God, Augustine is equally convinced that this is the best possible way of loving ourselves. "For in some *inexplicable* way, it is a fact that he who loves himself and not God, does not love himself; and whoever loves God and not himself, does love himself. For he who cannot live of himself, will certainly die if he loves himself. Consequently, he does not love himself who loves himself to his own loss of life. But when anyone loves Him by whom he lives, he loves the more by not loving himself, since he ceases to love himself in order to love Him by whom he lives."[2]

Yet this matter is not such a paradox nor so inexplicable as Augustine imagines and asserts. The whole difficulty arises because he uses the term "amor sui" in two different

---

[1] "Quid est autem amare se, nisi sibi præsto esse velle ad fruendum se." *Ibid.*

[2] In ev. Jn., tract. cxxiii. 5. *Cf.* the parallel argument in De ciu. dei, lib. XIV., cap. xiii.: "Bonum est enim sursum habere cor; non tamen ad se ipsum, quod est superbiæ, sed ad Dominum, quod est obœdientiæ, quæ nisi humilium non potest esse. Est igitur aliquid humilitatis *miro modo* quod sursum faciat cor, et est aliquid elationis quod deorsum faciat cor. Hoc quidem *quasi contrarium uidetur*, ut elatio sit deorsum et humilitas sursum. Sed pia humilitas facit subditum superiori; nihil est autem superius Deo; et ideo exaltat humilitas, quæ facit subditum Deo. Elatio autem, quæ in uitio est, eo ipso respuit subjectionem et cadit ab illo, quo non est quidquam superius, et ex hoc erit inferius. . . . Ipsum quippe extolli iam deici est."

senses, to indicate the *nature* and to indicate the *object* of the love.

As regards the *nature of love*, Augustine never doubts that all love is acquisitive love. The whole meaning and content of love is just this, that it seeks *its own bonum*. Paul says (1 Cor. xiii. 5): "Love seeketh not its own"; but such an idea is excluded for Augustine by his primary definition of love. For him, it is the mark of love to seek its own, "quærere quæ sua sunt."[1] In this widest sense, all love is "amor sui." And "amor sui," so conceived, need naturally not conflict with "amor Dei" as defined by Augustine; or rather, they *cannot* conflict, for the simple reason that they have no common denominator, and are not on the same level. "Amor sui" speaks of the nature, "amor Dei" of the object of love. "Amor sui" simply means that love desires its bonum, and so in the nature of the case it finds its fulfilment only when it seeks as its object that which is by nature the highest good, summum bonum. Thus self-love is predisposed from the start to resolve itself into love of God. Only that "amor sui" which is equally "amor Dei" is real and successful "amor sui."

It is very different when "amor sui" indicates the *object of love*. Then "amor sui" and "amor Dei" are on the same level and are absolutely opposed to each other. There are two rival objects of love. If we seek our bonum in the one, we cannot seek it in the other. If I set my love's longing upon God, I do not set it upon my own self: if I imagine I possess my bonum in my own self, I am prevented from seeking it in God.

The following diagram will make Augustine's meaning clear and show the difference between the two senses in which he uses "amor sui":

[1] Augustine interprets the Pauline "caritas non quærit quæ sua sunt" as follows: "non sua quærit *in hac vita*." Enarr. in Ps. cxxi. 12. By this qualification he makes even Paul agree that all love ultimately seeks its own.

The nature of love:	The object of love:
All love is *amor sui* 1 : it seeks *its own* bonum (= quærit quæ sua sunt)	(1) in God: amor Dei. (2) in itself: *amor sui* 2. (3) in the world: amor mundi (amor sæculi).

Of these, (1) *amor Dei* is the right kind of love; for it seeks its satisfaction in a *real bonum*, in the only thing that is without qualification worth seeking, in God. (2) *Amor sui* 2 is a false love; for it seeks its bonum in a *fiction*, it imagines it possesses its bonum in itself, is sufficient for itself (sufficere sibi), and so stops in its own emptiness. (3) *Amor mundi* (amor sæculi) is a false love, for it seeks its good in a *substitute*; it seeks its satisfaction in something which is indeed a bonum, but which by reason of its relativity can give no real satisfaction.

Rightly understood, there is no contradiction here in Augustine. All love is by nature acquisitive love and, in this general sense, " amor sui "; but this does not alter the fact that its object ought to be God, and that the right kind of love must consequently be described with reference to its object as " amor Dei." Yet although Caritas, the right kind of love, has as its object not itself but God, and so *from the point of view of its object*, is not " amor sui " but " amor Dei "; nevertheless, like all love, it seeks its own bonum, and so *with reference to its nature* it must be described as " amor sui." Combining these two points, we have the simple statement: in Caritas I seek *my own* bonum, but I seek it in *God*, and *not in myself*. This sentence expresses both the affinity and the difference between amor sui and amor Dei.[1]

[1] In Caritas I seek *my own* bonum (=amor sui 1), but I seek it in *God* (=amor Dei) and *not in myself* (=amor sui 2). If we apply the distinction between the two kinds of amor sui to the passage quoted above, which Augustine himself thought " inexplicabilis," it becomes transparently clear: " For in some inexplicable way it is a fact that he who loves himself (amor sui 2) and not God does not love himself (amor sui 1); and whoever loves God (amor Dei) and not himself (amor sui 2), does love himself (amor sui 1). For he who cannot live of

The above exposition makes it possible to answer the much-disputed question whether Augustine's thought is essentially theocentric or egocentric. The answer is two-fold : (1) from the point of view of the *object*, Augustine's view of love is markedly *theocentric*, in so far as no other object may compete with *God* for our love; (2) with regard to the *nature* of the love, his view is just as markedly *egocentric*, for even in God I seek *my own* bonum.

But did Augustine really mean this? So often he insists that our love to God is only right when we love Him " gratis," for His own sake alone and not in order to gain anything else. So often we find him saying that God is to be " all in all." Surely his thought is thoroughly theocentric here. Yet looked at more closely, that is not quite what these phrases imply. As regards " gratis amare " and " gratis diligere," we have already seen what they mean.[1] To say that God is to be loved " gratis " is simply another way of saying that He is not to be used, not to be sought as a means to some other end; He himself is our reward, our sufficiency, our " bonum."[2] Nothing in this goes beyond the distinction

---

himself, will certainly die if he loves himself (amor sui 2). Consequently, he does not love himself (amor sui 1) who loves himself (amor sui 2) to his own loss of life. But when anyone loves Him by whom he lives (amor Dei), he loves (amor sui 1) the more by not loving himself (amor sui 2), since he ceases to love himself (amor sui 2) in order to love Him by whom he lives (amor Dei)." When amor sui coincides with amor Dei, it is always a question of amor sui 1; when it is opposed to amor Dei, then it is a question of amor sui 2.

[1] *Cf. supra*, pp. 508 f.

[2] " Si amas, gratis ama: si vere amas, ipse sit mercedes quem amas." Sermo CLXV., cap. iv. 4. " Si gratiam ideo tibi dedit Deus, quia gratis dedit, gratis ama. Noli ad præmium diligere Deum; ipse sit præmium tuum." In ev. Jn., tract. iii. 21. " Quid est gratuitum ? Ipse propter se, non propter aliud. Si enim laudas Deum ut det tibi aliquid aliud, jam non gratis amas Deum." Enarr. in Ps. liii. 10. " . . . ut simul colatis et diligatis Deum gratis: quia totum præmium nostrum ipse erit, ut in illa vita bonitate ejus et pulchritudine perfruamur." De catechiz. rud., cap. xxvii. 55. " Primo amare Deum gratis; hæc est enim pietas: nec sibi extra illum ponere mercedem, quam exspectet ex illo. Illo enim melius est nihil. Et quid carum petit a Deo, cui Deus ipse vilis est ? . . . Gratis ergo amandus est Deus." Sermo XCI., cap. iii. 3. " Nullo modo merces quæreretur ab eo qui gratis amatur, nisi merces esset ipse

between Frui and Uti, but even Frui-love is acquisitive love and, as such, is egocentric. An analysis of the statement that God is to be "all in all," leads to the same conclusion. Augustine seeks to interpret it word for word. God is to be *all*: that means that God, as the summum bonum, includes in Himself not merely some, but all advantages, every thing that a man can possibly desire. So we must not seek our bonum partly in Him and partly in something else. God wills to be all.[1] But He wills to be all *in all*. God is *my* bonum, but what He is for me He ought to be for every man. As summum bonum He is also "bonum commune," the bonum that is enough for all. When God has become that, the end is attained. "Then there will not be anything lacking for desire, when God shall be all in all."[2] Thus these ideals also agree perfectly with Augustine's basic conception, which we outlined above.

We have seen above that " amor sui " bears two different senses :

amor sui 1 = to seek one's own bonum,
amor sui 2 = to seek one's own bonum in oneself.

---

qui amatur." Sermo CCCXL. 1. " Hoc est Deum gratis amare, de Deo Deum sperare, de Deo properare impleri, de ipso satiari. Ipse enim sufficit tibi; præter illum nihil sufficit tibi. Noverat hoc Philippus, quando dicebat: Domine, ostende nobis Patrem, et sufficit nobis." Sermo CCCXXXIV. 3. " Hoc est gratis amare, non quasi proposita acceptione mercedis; quia ipsa merces tua summa Deus ipse erit, quem gratis diligis: et sic amare debes, ut ipsum pro mercede desiderare non desinas, qui solus te satiet; sicut Philippus desiderabat, cum diceret, Ostende, etc." Enarr. in Ps. cxxxiv. 11. " Nolite aliquid a Deo quærere; nisi Deum. Gratis amate, se solum ab illo desiderate. Nolite timere inopiam: dat se ipsum nobis, et sufficit nobis. Philippum apostolum audite in Evangelio: Domine, ostende nobis Patrem, et sufficit nobis." Sermo CCCXXXI., cap. v. 4. *Cf. supra*, p. 493, n. 4.

[1] " Sic diligunt justi, hoc est gratis, ut alia præter illum non exspectent bona, quoniam ipse erit in omnibus omnia." In ev. Jn., tract. xci. 4.

[2] " . . . perducturus eos ad illum finem qui sufficiat eis, ubi satietur in bonis desiderium eorum. Tunc enim aliquid desiderio non deerit, quando omnia in omnibus Deus erit." In ev. Jn., tract. lxv. 1. " Quando ergo erit quod Apostolus dicit in fine, ut sit Deus omnia in omnibus. . . . Ipsum enim debes gratis amare, qui ipse te poterit pro rebus omnibus satiare." Sermo CCCXXXIV. 3.

In the former sense, all love is amor sui: to love is to seek one's own bonum. But this gives no indication whether it is a right or a wrong love; that is determined by the *object* upon which the love is set. That love is right whose object is God, and wrong, whose object is one's own self (or the world). But a further complication arises, since even within the sphere of the right kind of love we can speak, according to Augustine, of a threefold object of love, and one of these objects is precisely one's own self. Caritas, whose object and ultimate aim is in principle always God, can be concretely directed either to God, to oneself or to one's neighbour.[1] This gives us a new scheme:

The nature of the right love:	The object of the right love:
All *right* amor sui 1 is *amor Dei* (Caritas): this is love	(1) to God: amor Dei (in the narrow sense). (2) to one's own self: amor sui 3. (3) to one's neighbour: amor proximi.

Caritas is in all circumstances amor Dei, whether its direct object is God, so that it is amor Dei in the narrow sense, or its immediate object is one's own self or one's neighbour; and the reason for this is that Augustine is able to apply his scheme of Uti and Frui here: we love God for His own sake, ourselves and our neighbour for God's sake.[2] Plainly, this gives us a third sense for amor sui:[3]

amor sui 3 = to love oneself in God.

---

[1] In De ciu. dei, lib. XIV., cap. vii., Caritas is described as "amare Deum et . . . secundum Deum amare proximum, sicut etiam se ipsum."

[2] "Ex una igitur eademque caritate Deum proximumque diligimus: sed Deum propter Deum, nos autem et proximum propter Deum." De trinitate, lib. VIII., cap. viii. 12. "Deum igitur diligimus per se ipsum et nos ac proximos propter ipsum." Epist. CXXX., vii. 14. "Ipsum amemus propter ipsum, et nos in ipso, tamen propter ipsum." Sermo CCCXXXVI., cap. ii. 2. ". . . diligendum esse Deum propter Deum, et proximum propter Deum." De doct. christiana, lib. II., cap. vii. 10. "Ipso solo sic delectabimur, ut nihil aliud requiramus; quia et in uno ipso fruemur, et in nobis invicem ipso fruemur. . . . Quid aliud in nobis quam Deum debemus diligere." Sermo CCLV., cap. vii. 7.

[3] The difference between amor sui 1 and amor sui 3 is obvious. If the former

7. LOVE TO NEIGHBOUR. GOD'S LOVE

Besides love to God and self-love, we have just mentioned love to neighbour. This brings us to an important problem in Augustine's view of love. Where the Eros motif predominates, there is no difficulty in speaking of love in the two first-mentioned forms—of love to God: for Eros is the ascent of the soul to the eternal world; or of self-love: for Eros is acquisitive love. But the two remaining forms of love, love to neighbour and God's love, cause difficulties from this point of view.[1]

It is therefore very illuminating to see how Augustine deals with *love to neighbour*. He had no independent place for it in his outlook as a whole, which is strongly marked by the Eros motif; yet its importance both in the New Testament and Christian tradition made him unable to ignore it. He had therefore to find a place for it by referring it to something else. So he refers it partly to love for God and partly to self-love.

It is a basic idea of Augustine's that the commandments of love to God and to neighbour are not really two, but *one single* command. God is the only worthy object for our love. When God commands us to love our neighbour, we are not strictly to love our neighbour, who is not worthy of such love, but God in our neighbour. Love to neighbour is really just a special instance of love to God. Augustine says: " He who in a spiritual way loves his neighbour, what

---

is that comprehensive love which includes amor Dei as one of the possibilities it may realise, then amor sui 3 is in turn included as a special instance within amor Dei. But no less evident is the difference between amor sui 2 and amor sui 3. Both have reference to the object of love, but amor sui 2 denotes a wrong love that is in competition with amor Dei, whereas amor sui 3 denotes a right love that can be put under the head of amor Dei according to the scheme of Uti-Frui.

[1] *Cf. supra*, pp. 211 ff.

does he love in him but God?"[1] We are not to love our
neighbour as he now is, but as he will be when God is all in
all. We find the pattern for our love to our neighbour in
the way in which Christ loved us, and of this Augustine
says: "What was it but God that He loved in us?" As the
doctor does not strictly love the sick man in his present
miserable state, but loves health which he wants to restore
in him, so Christ does not strictly love us as we now are,
but loves us in consideration of the good and perfect beings
we may yet become through Him.[2] It is obvious that this is
something quite different from what the New Testament
means by love. Augustine has no room for a love to neighbour which is, in the strict sense of the word, unmotivated.
Even when he says that Christian love to neighbour is not
simply the naturally motivated love for a kinsman, friend or
benefactor,[3] but is love for the neighbour precisely as a man,[4]
he still does not mean an unmotivated love in the primitive
Christian sense. The love he means is not concerned with
the neighbour in his concrete situation, but with his
"nature" as created by God; and further, love finds a
motive even here in the thought of the potential worth in
the neighbour, which may in future become actual. The
Christian ought to love all men, since none can know what
a man may become tomorrow who today is evil.[5]

---

[1] In ev. Jn., tract. lxv. 2. Cf. De fide et operibus, cap. x. 16; cap. xiii. 20;
cap. xiv. 25.

[2] In ev. Jn., tract. lxv. 2.

[3] "Et dilectio ista temporalis est. . . . Magis enim est inhumanum, non
amare in homine quod homo est, sed amare quod filius est: hoc est enim non in
eo amare illud quod ad Deum pertinet, sed amare illud quod ad se pertinet."
De vera rel., cap. xlvi. 88.

[4] "Quapropter, cur iste non invictus sit hominem diligendo, cum in eo nihil
præter hominem diligat, id est creaturam Dei ad ejus imaginem factam, nec ei
possit deesse perfecta natura quam diligit, cum ipse perfectus est?" Ibid.,
cap. xlvii. 90.

[5] "Omnes ama; quoniam nescis quid cras futurus sit qui hodie malus est."
De catechiz. rud., cap. xxvii. 55. "Sapientem animam atque perfectam talem
diligat, qualem illam videt; stultam non talem, sed quia esse perfecta et sapiens
potest." De vera rel., cap. xlviii. 93.

The connection between love to neighbour and self-love
Augustine sees in the form of the commandment itself:
Thou shalt love thy neighbour *as thyself*. Self-love is the
pattern and measure of love to neighbour.[1] He who does
not love himself cannot love his neighbour either. As
" ordinata dilectio," the right kind of love begins with oneself,[2] though it does not stop there, but goes on to one's
neighbour.[3] It widens itself to embrace first our nearest
kin, then strangers, and finally enemies.[4] But even so, there
is no question of any unmotivated love.[5] Just as we saw
above that love to neighbour was a special instance of love
to God, so now we may describe it as a special instance of
self-love. Augustine has adopted the old idea that love to
neighbour and almsgiving have the effect of blotting out

---

[1] " Regulam diligendi oximum a semet ipso dilector accepit." De ciu.
dei, lib. I., cap. xx.

[2] " Qui enim vult ordinate dare eleemosynam, a se ipso debet incipere, et
eam sibi primum dare. . . . Quod judicium et caritatem Dei cum Pharisæi
præterirent . . . et ideo non dabant eleemosynas a se incipientes, secumque
prius misericordiam facientes. Propter quem dilectionis ordinem dictum est,
Diliges proximum tuum tanquam te ipsum." Enchiridion, cap. lxxvi. 20.
" Prius vide, si jam nosti diligere te ipsum; et committo tibi proximum, quem
diligas sicut te ipsum." Sermo CXXVIII., cap. iii. 5.

[3] " Sic te dilige, et diliges proximum tanquam te ipsum." De disciplina
christiana, cap. v. 5.

[4] " Propinquior est tibi frater quam nescio quis homo. . . . Extende
dilectionem in proximos, nec voces illam extensionem. Prope enim te diligis,
qui eos diligis qui tibi adhærent. Extende ad ignotos, qui tibi nihil mali fecerunt.
Transcende et ipsos; perveni, ut diligas inimicos." In ep. Jn. ad Parthos,
tract. viii. 4.

[5] The ultimate reason why there can be no unmotivated love in Augustine
is that he knows of no love that is not *acquisitive*. His sole alternative is Uti
and Frui. Only God may be " enjoyed." In comparison with God, therefore,
our neighbour, like all other created things, must be an object for " use." Comparing man with the rest of creation, however, we may again apply the distinction
between Uti and Frui, though in a relative sense only. The material creation
we must only " use," our neighbour and ourselves we may " enjoy," though
only in a relative way, only " in God." *Cf*. De trinitate, lib. IX., cap. viii. 13:
" Cum ergo aut par nobis, aut inferior creatura sit, inferiore utendum est ad
Deum; pari autem fruendum, sed in Deo. Sicut enim te ipso, non in te ipso
frui debes, sed in eo qui fecit te; sic etiam illo quem diligis tanquam te ipsum.
Et nobis ergo et fratribus in Domino fruamur."

sin.[1]   Love to enemies is especially meritorious.[2]   God has
commanded us to love our neighbour.   By fulfilling this
commandment, we are brought a step nearer God.[3]   Love
to neighbour is the ladder on which we can mount up to
God.[4]   Thus we " use " our neighbour " in order to enjoy
God."[5]

For its *content* also love to neighbour depends entirely on
self-love.   When he who understands what true self-love is,
receives God's command to love his neighbour as himself,
this can only mean that he is to try and help his neighbour
to love God.[6]   If right self-love means that I love God as my

---

[1] Enchiridion, cap. lxxii. 19: " Multa itaque genera sunt eleemosynarum, quæ
cum facimus, adjuvamur ut dimittantur nostra peccata."   On love to neighbour
and almsgiving as atonement for sin *cf. supra*, pp. 248 and 260 1.

[2] " Sed ea nihil est majus, qua ex corde dimittimus, quod in nos quisque
peccavit. . . .   Multo grandius et magnificentissimæ bonitatis est, ut tuum
quoque inimicum diligas."   Enchir., cap. lxxiii. 19.   For love to enemies, *cf.*
Sermo LVI., cap. x. f.

[3] " Diligendo proximum, et curam habendo de proximo tuo, iter agis.   Quo
iter agis, nisi ad Dominum Deum, ad eum quem diligere debemus ex toto corde,
ex tota anima, ex tota mente?   Ad Dominum enim nondum pervenimus, sed
proximum nobiscum habemus.   Porta ergo eum, cum quo ambulas; ut ad eum
pervenias, cum quo manere desideras."   In ev. Jn., tract. xvii. 9.

[4] " A dilectione autem proximi tanta quanta præcipitur, *certissimus gradus* fit
nobis, ut inhæreamus Deo."   De musica, lib. VI., cap. xiv. 46.   " . . . ut
nullus certior gradus ad amorem Dei fieri posse credatur, quam hominis erga hominem caritas."   De mor. eccl. cath., lib. I., cap. xxvi. 48.   " Ista sunt *quasi
cunabula caritatis Dei*, quibus diligimus proximum; ut quoniam dilectio proximi
malum non operatur, hic ad illud *ascendamus* quod dictum est, Scimus quoniam
diligentibus Deum omnia procedunt in bonum."   *Ibid.*, cap. xxvi. 50.   The
saying of Paul in Rom. viii. 28, that " all things work together for good to them
that love God," Augustine interprets to mean that everything—and here
primarily love to neighbour—serves as a means to the attainment of their
" bonum," the vision and enjoyment of God..   We may also recall the passage
quoted above (p. 295) from De doct. christiana, lib. II., cap. vii., where love to
one's neighbour and one's enemy is the fifth rung in the ladder of virtue and
a preparation for the Vision of God.

[5] " Nos vero invicem nostri miseremur, ut illo perfruamur."   De doct.
christiana, lib. I., cap. xxx. 33.

[6] " Iam igitur scienti diligere se ipsum, cum mandatur de proximo diligendo
sicut se ipsum, quid aliud mandatur, nisi ut ei, quantum potest, commendet
diligendum Deum?"   De ciu. dei, lib. X., cap. iii.   " In eo quippe nosmet
ipsos diligimus, si deum diligimus, et ex alio præcepto proximos nostros sicut
nosmet ipsos ita uere diligimus, si eos ad dei similem dilectionem, quantum in
nobis est, perducamus."   Epist. CXXX., vii. 14.

summum bonum, it follows that I must wish my neighbour also to obtain a share in that bonum.[1] "For you do not love him as yourself, unless you try to draw him to that bonum which you yourself are pursuing."[2] God is the source of our blessedness and the goal of all effort. Whoever has found his bonum in Him must for God's sake also wish others to come to this bonum,[3] that nothing of the stream of love may be wasted.[4] God is not only *my* bonum, but the *common* bonum of all creatures, not "bonum proprium," but "bonum commune."[5]

Love to neighbour thus occupies an insecure position in Augustine: in principle there is no place for it in his scheme of love, yet the influence of the New Testament compels him to include it. Something similar is true also with regard to *God's love*.

God is defined, in the manner of Eros theory, as the "summum bonum," the object to which all desire ought to be directed; and this fact naturally influences the conception of God's love. Augustine often quotes 1 Jn. iv. 16: "God is Caritas." But its meaning is not the same for him as for its author; it concerns *God's self-love*. "God is Caritas" means (1) that the Divine life—amans et quod amatur et

[1] "Quia . . . ille in se diligendo non errat, qui Deum diligit: consequens est, ut etiam proximo ad diligendum Deum consulat, quem iubetur sicut se ipsum diligere." De ciu. dei, lib. XIX., cap. xiv. "Ea autem est regula dilectionis, ut quæ sibi vult bona provenire, et illi velit." De vera rel., cap. xlvi., 87.

[2] "Te autem ipsum salubriter diligis, si plus quam te diligis Deum. Quod ergo agis tecum, id agendum cum proximo est; hoc est, ut ipse etiam perfecto amore diligat Deum. Non enim eum diligis tanquam teipsum, si non ad id bonum ad quod ipse tendis, adducere satagis. Illud est enim unum bonum, quod omnibus tecum tendentibus non fit angustum." De mor. eccl. cath., lib. I., cap. xxvi. 49.

[3] "Ipse enim fons nostræ beatitudinis, ipse omnis adpetitionis est finis. . . . Ad hoc bonum debemus et a quibus diligimur duci, et quos diligimuş ducere." De ciu. dei, lib. X., cap. iii.

[4] In De doct. christiana, lib. I., cap. xxix. 30, Augustine uses the simile of a man who values the art of a certain actor and so wishes everyone else to love this same actor, too.

[5] De lib. arb., lib. II., cap. xix. 52 f.

amor—centres upon itself in ceaseless self-love and in blessed enjoyment of its own perfection;[1] but it also means (2) that God is the object which gathers all Caritas, all heavenward love, to itself; in this there is something of the Aristotelian κινεῖ ὡς ἐρώμενον.

But this is only one side of the matter. On the other side, Augustine can speak of God's love in the strongest Agape-terms. Election, the Incarnation and the Cross contain for him a powerful proclamation of the Divine love. Augustine knows that God's love precedes all our love. This thought permeates his doctrine of Election. When we were sinners and displeasing to God, He loved us and thus made it possible for us to love Him and become well-pleasing to Him.[2] God's love is an incomprehensible miracle to us; it defies all explanation and motivation.[3] "For it was not from the time that we were reconciled to Him by the blood of His Son that He began to love us; He loved us before the foundation of the world."[4] In this connection Augustine quotes Paul's classical statement of Agape in Rom. v. 8, that Christ died for us "while we were yet sinners," and adds: "He therefore had love toward us even when we were practising enmity against Him and working iniquity. In a wonderful and divine manner, even when He hated us, He loved us."[5] And he finds the Incarnation and the Cross bearing the same testimony: "How hast thou loved us, good Father, who didst not spare Thine only Son, but delivered Him up for us sinners!"[6]

It is obvious that this last-mentioned idea of love cannot

---

[1] See what is said above (pp. 323 f.) about "amor sui" as the basis of Augustine's conception of the Trinity.

[2] "Displicentes amati sumus, ut esset in nobis unde placeremus." In ev. Jn., tract. cii. 5.

[3] "Quapropter incomprehensibilis est dilectio qua diligit Deus, neque mutabilis." In ev. Jn., tract. cx. 6.

[4] *Ibid.*

[5] *Ibid.*: "Proinde miro et divino modo et quando nos oderat, diligebat."

[6] Conf., lib. X., cap. xxxxiii. 69.

be contained within the scheme of love that Augustine took over from antiquity. His perplexity is significant when in the " De doctrina christiana " he is faced with the task of finding a place for God's love in his Uti-Frui scheme. He asks: " Does God love us in order to use us, or in order to enjoy us?"[1] The latter is out of the question, since God, who is the sum of all good and possesses all advantages, has no need of anything that belongs to us. Even the former has its difficulties. What sense could there be in saying that God's love to us means that He uses us, employs us as means? Nevertheless, Augustine feels compelled to decide that God " uses " us, for—he adds—" if He neither enjoys nor uses us, I am at a loss to discover in what way He can love us."[2] But the love both of enjoyment and of use is a " motivated " love. So it is not surprising that Augustine has difficulty in finding a place within this scheme for God's Agape, God's spontaneous, unmotivated love.

8. THE DOUBLE NATURE OF THE IDEA OF CARITAS. AMOR, DILECTIO AND CARITAS

There is a cleavage running right through Augustine's whole theory of love. Though he has contrived his synthesis so skilfully that it appears broadly as a unity, yet we have been able to show that there are different and conflicting tendencies at almost every point. He took over the scheme for his doctrine of love from ancient Eros theory, but primitive Christian Agape is also present in his thought as a constantly disturbing element which upsets the balance.

Amor sui is diametrically opposed to amor Dei and is the real root of sin: here there is the influence of the idea of Agape, at least to some degree. Yet amor sui, in a refined and sublimated form it is true, is accepted and preserved in

[1] De doct. christiana, lib. I., cap. xxxi. 34.
[2] " Si neque fruitur neque utitur, non invenio quemadmodum diligat." *Ibid.*

love to God itself, just as we find it in theories dominated by the idea of Eros.

Augustine is well aware that we have not chosen God, but that God chose us before we possessed any merit whatever to furnish a motive for His love: the idea of Agape taught him this, and he has given it most forceful expression in his doctrine of Election. Yet fellowship with God retains the character of a choice on man's part; God is measured by the standards of human desire, and since this shows Him to be the highest good (summum bonum), the sum of all that man can possibly desire, man decides to devote himself wholly to Him; thus by rational calculation and an act of preference, man chooses God: for that is what Eros demands.

Augustine can praise God's love for sinners, which descends to that which is lost. " If God had not loved sinners, He would not have descended from heaven to earth "[1]: this is the language of Agape. Yet God's love for sinners is not so unmotivated and inexplicable as it might appear. It is not strictly the sinner whom God loves, but the good that still survives in him and the perfection he may yet attain. God's love for the sinner is like the doctor's love for the sick: " What does he love in them but health, which he wishes to restore?"[2] When God loves us men, it is in the last resort nothing but Himself in us that He loves: Eros has compelled Augustine to provide this motive for God's unmotivated love.

The synthesis of the Eros and Agape motifs, which Origen had already produced but the Church would not then accept, is completed in Augustine's doctrine of Caritas in a form which the Church could accept without reservation. The parallel between Origen and Augustine, however, is not merely a matter of their fundamental attitude to the problem of " Christianity and Hellenism," but extends even to

<hr />

[1] In ev. Jn., tract. xlix. 5. [2] In ev. Jn., tract. lxv. 2.

terminology. In order to establish the Christian legitimacy of the term Eros, Origen tried to show that Eros and Agape were synonymous; Augustine is equally concerned to make " amor," the equivalent of Eros, a legitimate Christian term. To this end, he tries to prove that there is no difference between amor and Caritas.[1] No doubt, says Augustine, Scripture mostly uses the word " caritas " for love to God, but the term " amor " is also to be found.[2] The three terms, *amor, dilectio* and *caritas*, are used quite indifferently, without any of them representing exclusively a good or, alternatively, a bad love.[3] But the parallel with Origen goes even further. Origen found himself obliged to defend his identification of Eros with Agape against a widespread opinion that this meant a perversion of the Christian idea of love; Augustine finds himself in a similar situation. He says: " I thought I ought to mention this, since some are of the opinion that caritas or dilectio is one thing, amor another."[4] Origen had a double difficulty to overcome with regard to Eros: to the popular mind, it savoured of " vulgar Eros "; and because it was derived from Hellenistic philosophy there was also a certain tension between it and the Christian Agape. In Augustine, the position is somewhat simplified;

---

[1] The chief passage for this is in De ciu. dei, lib. XIV., cap. vii.

[2] " . . . quæ usitatius in scripturis sanctis *caritas* appellatur; sed *amor* quoque secundum easdem sacras litteras dicitur." *Ibid.* " Unde intellegimus, quod etiam cum dicebat Dominus: *Diligis me?* nihil aliud dicebat quam: *Amas me?* " *Ibid.*

[3] " Sed scripturas religionis nostræ, quarum auctoritatem ceteris omnibus litteris anteponimus, non aliud dicere amorem, aliud dilectionem uel caritatem, insinuandum fuit." *Ibid.* Augustine's chief concern is plainly to find room for " amor " as a description of love in the Christian sense. In his desire to get rid of the distinction between amor and dilectio, he tries also to show that dilectio (= ἀγάπη) can sometimes be used for a love that is objectionable from a Christian point of view. He therefore eagerly seizes upon 1 Jn. ii. 15, where love for the world and love for God are contrasted, the same word, dilectio, being used in both cases. On this he comments: "Ecce uno loco dilectio et in bono et in malo." *Ibid.* On 1 Jn. ii. 15, see *supra*, pp. 156 f.

[4] " Hoc propterea commemorandum putaui, quia nonnulli arbitrantur aliud esse dilectionem siue caritatem, aliud amorem. Dicunt enim dilectionem accipiendam esse in bono, amorem in malo." *Ibid.*

for whilst the first difficulty remains inasmuch as " amor " also tends to savour of " vulgar Eros," the second difficulty seems to have disappeared.   The " philosophers' " use of " amor " to denote their Hellenistic idea of love is so far from causing Augustine any difficulty, that he actually uses this as an argument for employing it to express Christian love. Since " amor " can mean not only " vulgar Eros " but also, thanks to the refinement of the " philosophers," " heavenly Eros," Augustine believes he finds the Christian idea of love in this " amor."[1]   Obviously, Augustine never considered whether Agape might not be something quite different even from " heavenly Eros " and from " amor in bonis rebus et erga ipsum Deum."[2]

[1] *Cf.* the similar reason for identifying Eros and Agape in Gregory of Nyssa, *supra*, p. 435

[2] " Uiderint philosophi utrum uel qua ratione ista discernant; *amorem tamen eos in bonis rebus et erga ipsum Deum magni pendere*, libri eorum satis loquuntur." De ciu. dei, lib. XIV., cap. vii.

AUGUSTINE, THE MIDDLE AGES AND
THE REFORMATION

AUGUSTINE's thought has suffered a peculiar fate. For his contemporaries and posterity he has been the great protector of the Church against heterodoxy. He made his name as the great teacher of the Church and won a central place in the subsequent development of doctrine, partly through his doctrine of Sin and Grace, developed in opposition to Pelagianism, and partly through his conception of community and Church, arising out of the Donatist controversy and expanded into a universal theory of history in his great work, *De civitate Dei*. But in both these respects his view did *not* subsequently prevail. Essential aspects of his theology of Grace and Predestination were directly rejected by Mediæval theology; and it is not his spirit that speaks in the world-empire of the Mediæval Church.

But, at another point that was really more central for him, his view has set its seal on the Catholic type of piety. That is, as regards the conception of Christian love. Here there was no controversy to sharpen his perception of what was specifically Christian. The materials for the construction of his theory came from different sources. He had found love in the form of Neoplatonic Eros—the soul's home-sickness for its heavenly origin, its bold flight up to the world that is beyond all transience, where all its yearning and desire reach full satisfaction, where its striving comes to rest for ever. He had also found love in the Christian Commandment of Love and in Christ's humilitas. In his view these two become one. It was the fact that Neoplatonism and Christianity appear to meet in the idea of love, which encouraged him to subsume the whole of Christianity under

the aspect of love. Here the Augustinian idea really did prevail in the Mediæval Church, and its idea of love comprised
the same elements in the same combination. Augustine's
attempt to unite Eros-love with an Agape-love presented
mainly in the form of humilitas, is found imbued with the
same spirit both in the ideals of Mediæval mysticism and in
the Scholastic doctrine of love.

Protestant historians of dogma have commonly held that
Paul, Augustine and Luther form an unbroken succession.
There is some support for this view. Paul was far more
important for Augustine than for anyone else in the Early
Church; and the men of the Reformation loved to appeal to
Augustine. Yet we have seen enough to know that such a
view is quite impossible. Augustine and Luther are *not*
principally on the same line. As against Luther, Augustine
is the man of *synthesis*, and it is in this that his strength lies.
In true Neoplatonic manner, he can portray the " ascent " of
the soul in the most glowing colours, and revel in the blessedness of the " Vision of God." On the other hand, like no
other since Paul, he can exalt and praise Divine grace, which
in absolute sovereignty, moved by its own love and mercy
alone, elects and saves those who in themselves are nothing
but vessels of wrath. *Augustine finds the synthesis of these
two in his doctrine of Caritas, and it is this very synthesis
which Luther smashes to pieces.*[1] When Luther ranges himself alongside Augustine, he does not do so without qualification. He says plainly what it is he values in him. In this

[1] A. Harnack's view of the relation between Augustine and the Reformation
is the direct opposite of this. For him, reformed Christianity represents synthesis
—the synthesis between the negative, world-denying spirit of Neoplatonism
and the " unclouded cheerfulness " of antiquity. " If it were possible to unite
in science and in the disposition, the piety, spirituality, and introspection of
Augustine, with the openness to the world, the restful and energetic activity,
and unclouded cheerfulness of antiquity, we should have reached the highest
level ! . . . Is it not in the same ideal that the meaning of evangelical and
reforming Christianity is contained, if it is really different from Catholicism ?"
H.D., vol. v., p. 110.

connection we may quote a characteristic utterance, preserved in Luther's *Table Talk*: "See then how great a
darkness is in the books of the Fathers about faith! . . .
Augustine writes nothing special about faith, except when
he disputes against the Pelagians. They woke Augustine up
and made him into a man."[1] This touches the crucial point.
Luther has an eye for the significance of controversy. It is
his opposition to Pelagianism that makes Augustine a pre-
cursor of the Reformation. But what he says positively in
his doctrine of Caritas only arouses Luther's hostility.

We do an injustice to Augustine's real view if, as has
often been done, we omit either of these two sides. We do
not make Augustine less great by recognising the duality of
his position and the difficulty of the task he set himself in
trying to unite things which by their nature cannot be united.
Indeed, it is only by recognising this that we realise the greatness of his work and the universality of his influence. At
the stage of development in which he stood, such a synthesis
was without doubt historically necessary; and he succeeded
so well that his synthesis held not only for himself, but for
his generation, and not only for his generation, but for a
millennium.

When the Roman Catholic Church claims Augustine as
its own, it is right inasmuch as he produced the synthesis
upon which Catholicism afterwards lived for centuries. Even
if the Eros motif prescribed the essential ground-plan of
Augustine's thought, yet he included so much of the Agape
motif in his idea of Caritas, that the question of the nature
and content of Christian love could not afterwards be left
alone. Augustine may thus be said to have been largely
responsible for the programme of the subsequent work of
Mediæval theology.

The Reformation can claim Augustine as its own with no
less right. For when, at the Reformation, the time came for

[1] Tischreden Nr. 3984; WA, Tischreden, Bd. 4, p. 56, 23.

the destruction of that synthesis which Catholicism in general
and Augustine in particular had contrived, the Reformation
could appeal to the same Augustine—that is, to those sides of
his thought which had not before prevailed. Evangelical
Christianity has every right to claim him as its own, because
when he wedded Platonism and Christianity in the manner
that his age required, he gave such a place to Divine grace
and love that he provided the explosive which the Reformation required, in order to shatter the Caritas-synthesis and
make room for the renewal of the Agape motif.

Yet in spite of all such considerations, it is not what unites,
but what divides them that ultimately decides the relation
between Augustine and Luther. What the former builds up,
the latter tears down, and erects on the vacant ground an
edifice of a totally different structure. In view of the central
importance of the idea of Caritas in Augustine, and since its
essential traits were faithfully preserved in the Mediæval
Church, the type of life it implies may be called Augustinian;
but Luther then is not so much the man in whom Augus-
tinianism finds its fulfilment, as the man who vanquishes it.

CHAPTER THREE

THE EROS MOTIF PASSES TO THE MIDDLE AGES

I

FROM PLOTINUS TO PROCLUS

1. THE MODIFICATION OF THE FUNDAMENTAL MOTIFS

THE Eros motif travelled by two main ways to the Middle Ages.

One route goes by way of Augustine. As we have seen, he produced a new view of love (Caritas) by fusing the primitive Christian Agape motif with the Neoplatonic and Hellenistic Eros motif. Mediæval theology now takes over the idea of Caritas, and so inherits something of the Eros motif slightly altered by passing through Augustine's hands.

Another route by which the Eros motif reached the Middle Ages, without such alteration, goes by way of *Pseudo-Dionysius*. If Augustine's Caritas is a new conception based on both Eros and Agape, we can hardly say there is anything but simple *confusion* in Dionysius: the Eros motif has inundated Christianity, and Christianity is literally absorbed in Neoplatonic Eros theory. This confusion was the end of a long development both in Christianity and in Hellenistic philosophy. It was possible only because both sides had approached one another and done their part to reduce the opposition between the two love-motifs.

To understand this process and how it came about, we must bear in mind that the relation between the Hellenistic and the Christian conception of salvation, between the Eros and Agape motifs, is originally one of *mutual hostility*.

From the point of view of a later time when the two motifs had already mingled, it is easy to think of Christianity and the idealist philosophy of late antiquity as spiritual movements so nearly akin that it should not be difficult for them to harmonise. But that does not represent the original situation. It is no accident that the first great literary antagonist, Celsus, happened to be a *Platonist*. Like Christianity, the more or less Platonising philosophy of late antiquity sought to answer the problem of salvation; but this common purpose only accentuated their sense that they were two rival views of salvation, and they looked upon one another from the beginning as adversaries. Later, when Neoplatonism comes on the scene, it engages in a contest with Christianity from the outset and tries to restore the old religion.[1] Christians were no less sensitive to the difference. We have repeatedly seen how carefully they guarded their belief in God as the Creator of heaven and earth, the idea of Incarnation, and the belief in the " Resurrection of the flesh "—all of them ideas which stand in sharpest contrast not only to Gnosticism, but equally to Platonism and all Eros theories whatsoever.

With time, however, the original sharpness of the contrast was lost, and Christianity and Neoplatonism began to converge. Historians of dogma have often pointed out how

[1] *Plotinus* himself felt the need of settling accounts with certain forms of Christianity, as the ninth book of the second Ennead shows; *cf.* also C. Schmidt: *Plotins Stellung zum Gnostizismus und kirchlichen Christentum*, 1901 (Texte und Untersuchungen zur Geschichte der altchristlichen Literatur, hrsg. von. O. v. Gebhardt und A. Harnack). Plotinus' disciple, *Porphyry*, attacks Christianity still more in his great polemic κατὰ χριστιανῶν. Only fragments of this work survive, scattered in the writings of the Fathers. Harnack has collected and published these in " Abhandlungen der Königlichen preussischen Akademie der Wissenschaften, Jahrg., 1916, Philos.-hist. Kl. " under the title: " *Porphyrios, ' Gegen die Christen,'* 15 *Bücher. Zeugnisse, Fragmente, Referate.*" Despite the fragmentary condition of Porphyry's extant works, it is not difficult to form an idea of the spirit which governs the criticism. Here, as in Celsus, its deepest objection concerns the descent and humility of Christ, the Incarnation and the Cross, and naturally also the Christian belief in Resurrection, especially the " resurrection of the flesh." *Cf.* fragg. nos. 65, 77, 84, 92, 94 (Harnack, *op. cit.*, pp. 86, 93, 96, 100, 101).

much Christianity took over from Neoplatonism. But that is only one side of the case. It is too easily forgotten that the relation was *reciprocal*, and that Neoplatonism was also influenced by Christianity. After a century or two, Neoplatonism is no longer the same as at its first appearance, and among the reasons for this is its co-existence with Christianity. The best example of the way in which these two forces live side by side and constantly make new contacts with one another is furnished by Origen. Himself a Christian, he becomes a pupil of Ammonius Saccas, the pioneer of Neoplatonism; and among his own pupils in the Christian Catechetical School in Alexandria he had some who held more or less Platonic views. It was probably the necessity of dealing with their problems that led Origen to a deeper study of Greek philosophy. And Origen is not an isolated case; he largely represents the general situation. Christians in no small numbers received instruction in the Neoplatonic philosophical schools, and Neoplatonists in the Christian schools.[1] Such personal connections are bound to reduce the differences somewhat. Christian theologians begin to " Hellenise "; Neoplatonic philosophers are infected with Christian thought.[2] How vague the distinction between

[1] In this process of fusion, it was Alexandria, the great centre of religious and philosophical syncretism, that took the lead. *Cf.* Überweg's *Grundriss der Geschichte der Philosophie*, Bd. I, 12 Aufl., 1926, hrsg. von K. Praechter, p. 635.

[2] What it is like when a Christian theologian " Hellenises " we know from Origen (*cf. supra*, pp. 369 f., 381-392) or from Gregory of Nyssa (*supra*, pp. 430, 432-446). In this connection we may recall Hypatia's disciple, Synesius of Cyrene, who on being elected bishop in 411, reserved to himself the right to hold a view at variance with the Christian tradition concerning the eternity of the soul and the world, and to give a spiritualising interpretation to the " Resurrection of the flesh." In the extant writings and hymns of Synesius, moreover, the Eros motif is absolutely dominant. For a concrete idea of how Christian thought invades Neoplatonic territory, it is enough to mention the Neoplatonist Hierocles, who in the fifth century pleads for the Christian idea of the creation of the world out of nothing by an act of the Divine will—an idea unheard of in Greek philosophy; *cf.* Überweg-Praechter, *op. cit.*, p. 641; and Zeller-Nestle: *Grundriss der Geschichte der Griechischen Philosophie*, 13 Aufl., 1928, p. 382.

Christianity and Neoplatonism became in time is also shown by the fact that it is hardly possible to tell whether the later Neoplatonists accepted Christianity or stood outside it.[1]

This process of fusion is the background and condition for Pseudo-Dionysius' view of love. He opens the door wide for Hellenistic Eros theory to enter into Christianity; but it is now no longer two intact motifs that meet: an Eros motif, modified and already affected by the Agape motif, joins hands with an idea of Agape that is itself disintegrating. Before dealing with this question, however, we must notice Proclus' view of love. In this we find the re-fashioned doctrine of Eros which Dionysius the Areopagite in the main adopts and transfers into Christian territory.

2. THE TRANSFORMATION OF THE DOCTRINE OF EROS IN PROCLUS

Plato and Plotinus are the great authorities whose thought Proclus simply wishes to reproduce and propagate. To give a complete exposition of Proclus' idea of love would simply mean a repetition of much that we have already said about the Eros motif in these two thinkers. We shall confine ourselves, therefore, to a comparison of Proclus with Plato and Plotinus, pointing out where he either develops or transforms the doctrine of Eros.[2]

---

[1] A comprehensive study of the important process of fusion between Christianity and Neoplatonism is still needed. For a general description of the period, *cf.* K. Praechter: *Richtungen und Schulen im Neuplatonismus*, 1910; W. Jaeger: *Nemesios von Emesa*, 1914; J. Geffcken: *Der Ausgang des griechisch-römischen Heidentums*, 1920.

[2] For an admirable characterisation of Proclus, see E. Zeller: *Die Philosophie der Griechen*, III. Teil, II. Abt., 3 Aufl., 1881, p. 784 ff.

With regard to Proclus' general philosophical position, see especially his " Elementatió theologica " (Στοιχείωσις Θεολογική), edited by E. R. Dodds: *Proclus, The Elements of Theology*, 1933. " In many ways a student of Neo-Platonism would be well advised to begin his reading with the brief but pregnant Στοιχείωσις Θεολογική " (A. E. Taylor: *Philosophical Studies*, 1934, p. 152).

1. *The transformation of the "Alexandrian world-scheme."* Compared with Plato's original idea of Eros, an important alteration takes place when Plotinus fits the doctrine of Eros into the "Alexandrian world-scheme." Plato is chiefly interested in the ascent of the soul to the higher world; but for Plotinus this is simply the second act of a cosmic process, of which the first act is the emanation of all things from the One. According to Plotinus and the "Alexandrian world-scheme," there are two movements in the cosmic process, and that in different directions: (1) "the downward way"—all that exists has emanated from the divine One—and (2) "the upward way"—all things stream back to their Divine source. Eros has a place only in the latter, the ascending movement, and the descent has an exclusively cosmological significance.

At this point Proclus goes a step further in the transformation of the doctrine of Eros. His thought, too, moves wholly within the "Alexandrian world-scheme"; but he is not content with the bare statement that the Many proceeds from and returns to the One: he wants to find a principle which will make this procession and return intelligible. Since the One brings forth the Many, Proclus thinks there is a causal relation between them: the One is the cause, the

---

Although this work of Proclus contains his doctrine of Eros from beginning to end, it is remarkable that the term itself nowhere seems to occur. Yet it is common in other writings of his. Of chief interest for our purposes is his *Commentary on the Alcibiades* (Procli in primum Platonis Alcibiadem commentarius; Procli Opera, ed. V. Cousin, tom. ii., 1820).

Of the literature on Proclus we may mention: H. Koch: *Pseudo-Dionysius Areopagita in seinen Beziehungen zum Neuplatonismus und Mysterienwesen* (Forschungen zur Christlichen Litteratur- und Dogmengeschichte, Bd. I., 2 und 3 Heft, 1900); H. F. Müller: *Dionysios, Proklos, Plotinos. Ein historischer Beitrag zur neuplatonischen Philosophie* (Beiträge zur Geschichte der Philosophie des Mittelalters, Bd. XX., Heft 3-4, 1918); A. E. Taylor: *The Philosophy of Proclus* (Philosophical Studies, 1934, pp. 151-191). For the direct influence of Proclus on the Middle Ages, cf. M. Grabmann: *Die Proklosübersetzungen des Wilhelm von Moerbeke und ihre Verwertung in der lateinischen Literatur des Mittelalters* (in M. Grabmann: Mittelalterliches Geistesleben. Abhandlungen zur Geschichte der Scholastik und Mystik, Bd. II., 1936, pp. 413-423).

Many emanating from it is the effect. Now as an effect, that which is produced is both to some extent identical with that which produces, and also distinct from it. It is identical in so far as it is what it is owing to its cause alone, in which it is thus completely contained. Yet it is distinct from its cause, something new and independent. In so far as that which is produced is identical with that which produces, it *remains* in the latter; in so far as it is distinct, it *proceeds* or departs out of this. But since that which is produced derives all its being from that which produces, then to the extent it has not remained in its cause, but has departed from it, it must have a tendency to *return* to its cause.[1] The *remaining, the procession and the return* (μονή, πρόοδος, ἐπιστροφή)—with this triadic scheme Proclus seeks to replace the "Alexandrian world-scheme" with its two parts. Actually, the difference is not so great; the basic theory is in both cases the same. Still, this transformation of the "Alexandrian world-scheme" is not unimportant; in this triadic form it had a great influence in certain directions on Mediæval theology, and this transformation corresponds closely with the changes in the idea of Eros effected by Proclus.

2. *The Eros that descends.* Although Proclus makes no claim to offer any new opinions of his own, but simply to interpret the thought of Pláto and Plotinus—his works are largely in the form of commentaries on Plato—yet with him the doctrine of Eros enters on a new phase.

In its original Platonic form, Eros is perfectly clear and simple: it is the love that directs its longing *upwards.* Eros is the desire of the lower for the higher, of the imperfect for perfection, of the mortal for immortality. Plato is quite

---

[1] πᾶν τὸ αἰτιατὸν καὶ μένει ἐν τῇ αὐτοῦ αἰτίᾳ καὶ πρόεισιν ἀπ' αὐτῆς καὶ ἐπιστρέφει πρὸς αὐτήν. Elementatio theologica, 35; ed. Dodds, pp. 38, 9. On the procession and the return, *ibid.*, 25-39, pp. 28-42. *Cf.* E. Zeller, *op. cit.*, pp. 787 ff.; Überweg-Praechter, *op. cit.*, pp. 629 ff.; W. Windelband: *Lehrbuch der Geschichte der Philosophie,* 9 and 10 Aufl., 1921, p. 211.

logical in refusing to speak of any Eros in the gods. Eros springs from the deficiencies of human life, which are to be removed in a higher form of existence; but just for that reason it is not applicable to the perfect, Divine life. Now we have observed in Plotinus[1] a certain modification of the idea of Eros, and that in two respects. He tells us not only how the lower yearns for the higher, but also how the higher " cares for the lower and adorns it "; further, he actually says that the Divine itself *is* Eros, not merely the object of Eros as it is in Plato. Yet there is here no real departure from the Platonic idea of Eros. The care of the higher for the lower is never related by Plotinus to the idea of Eros, and therefore could not influence it. As regards the statement " God is Eros," he makes this a matter of God's love for Himself; the Divine enjoys its own perfection, and such a form of self-love is obviously in the direct line of acquisitive love.

In Proclus the case is different. There is a plain departure from the old scale of values. The higher has begun to interest itself in the lower and to approach it with a view to helping and saving it. It is not easy to decide in detail what factors contributed to this result. Influences from both the ancient belief in Providence and the Christian Agape view have undoubtedly played a part. In any case, Proclus tells how the Divine comes down to and cares for human life, in a way that distinguishes him from earlier Neoplatonism and seems to approach Christian Agape tradition. There is, of course, nothing in his thought corresponding to the Christian idea of Incarnation—that has too many impossible associations for a Neoplatonist—but the fundamental spirit of Christianity has inevitably exercised a modifying influence on the ancient sense of values: it is no longer unworthy of the Deity to descend to the lower. This has its effect also on Proclus' doctrine of love. *Eros has changed its direc-*

[1] *Cf. supra*, pp. 194 ff.

tion. It is no longer merely an ascending love, but also and primarily a love that *descends*. Thus Proclus says something almost incredible in a Platonist: "*Eros descends from above, from the intelligible sphere down to the cosmic, and turns all things towards the Divine beauty.*"[1] The latter statement, that Eros turns all lower things towards that which is beautiful in itself, is an old and well-known Platonic view; but that Eros should stream down from above as a divine gift is an idea of which the original Eros theory was totally ignorant. But it is Proclus' basic assumption: "Whence should come love among men, if it were not first in the gods themselves? For everything good and saving that is found in souls has its determinate cause from the gods."[2]

It will easily be perceived how important this change of content in the idea of Eros is for its union with the idea of Agape. If Eros itself is a divine love which descends to bring salvation to man in his need, then there can hardly be an irreconcilable difference between the two views of love. The idea of Eros seems to have come so near that of Agape that they can be combined without difficulty.

3. *The Chain of Love.* In the fifth book of the third Ennead, Plotinus had given an allegorical interpretation of Plato's myth about the birth of Eros from Porus and Penia (Symposium 203). Here Plotinus says we must not speak merely of one Eros, but of many. There is one Eros that corresponds with the world-soul, but every individual soul also has its own special eros; and the relation of the individual eros to the all-embracing Eros is the same as that of the individual soul to the world-soul. Later Neoplatonists much admired this allegory, and there were a number of

---

[1] Procli in primum Platonis Alcibiadem commentarius, Procli Opera, ed. Cousin, tom. ii., 1820, pp. 141 f.: ἄνωθεν οὖν ὁ ἔρως ἀπὸ τῶν νοητῶν μέχρι τῶν ἐγκοσμίων φοιτᾷ, πάντα ἐπιστρέφων ἐπὶ τὸ θεῖον κάλλος.

[2] *Op. cit.*, p. 150.

attempts to imitate it. They play with this idea, and gradually the universe is filled with innumerable erotes. Proclus also stands in this tradition, but his demand for coherence and system will not let him be content with this multiplicity without unity; he seeks to bring order into this chaos of erotes, and the result is his theory of the Chain of Love. He thinks of the different sorts of erotes as bound together like links in a great *Eros-chain*, ἡ ἐρωτικὴ σειρά, which joins heaven and earth. The topmost link is fixed in the highest Divine order, and is thus connected with the highest spiritual beauty. The chain then passes down through the sphere of the lower gods, through the choirs of angels and hordes of demons, through the hosts of heroes, till it reaches ordinary human souls. Thus everything is in connection with the supernatural beauty and can receive something of its effluence. Eros streams down from above over all existence and allows it to participate in the higher life, towards which its desire is thereby turned.[1]

We have already seen in Gregory of Nyssa a hint of the Chain of Love.[2] But there is more than a hint in Proclus. The Chain stretching from heaven to earth is a figure he often uses.[3] It is of special interest because it so clearly reveals the new function of Eros as love that descends. The way between heaven and earth is now open in both directions. The Eros chain brings the divine forces of the higher world down to the lower,[4] and leads the Eros-longing of the lower world up to the divine world. It exists not merely so that the heavenly beauty can stream down to us, but also to furnish us with the means for our ascent.

4. *The ordo salutis of Proclus.* In the introduction to the

---

[1] *Op. cit.*, pp. 82-86. 　　　　　　　[2] *Cf. supra,* .p. 446.
[3] *Cf., e.g.*, Proclus in Parmenidem, ed. Cousin, tom. v., pp. 118, 155.
[4] *Cf.* Elementatio theologica, 140; p. 124, 1: πᾶσαι τῶν θεῶν αἱ δυνάμεις ἄνωθεν ἀρχόμεναι καὶ διὰ τῶν οἰκείων προϊοῦσαι μεσοτήτων μέχρι τῶν ἐσχάτων καθήκουσι καὶ τῶν περὶ γῆν τόπων. For this σειρά, *cf.* also Elementatio theol., 21, p. 24; and 129, p. 114.

commentary on the *Alcibiades*, Proclus states his conception of philosophy, and especially of Platonic philosophy. He says that its whole meaning is summed up in the inscription that stood over the door of the temple of Apollo at Delphi: γνῶθι σεαυτόν, "Know thyself." With self-knowledge, knowledge of God begins. To enter into oneself and know one's own nature is the beginning of the ascent to the Divine, ἡ ἐπὶ τὸ θεῖον ἀναγωγή.[1]

In what does Proclus suppose this ἀναγωγή, this ascent, to consist? The first step is for the soul to *purify itself* from the treacherous influence of things sensible; for the second, it must receive the *illumination* which streams to it from above, from the intelligible world. But there is yet a third step. Deep within itself the soul has something divine, which enables it ultimately to become *one* with the Divine itself. Proclus proceeds on the old principle that "only like attracts like." Through the noetic element in our nature we grasp the intelligible, through the divine in our nature we grasp God and become one with Him; we become ἔνθεοι and reach complete ἕνωσις with the One.[2] What Proclus here has to say about the three stages of the ascent, *purification, illumination and union*, κάθαρσις, ἔλλαμψις and ἕνωσις, is really nothing new. Elements of this view can be found as far back as Plato, and indeed as far back as the earliest Mysteries. Three main periods can be distinguished in the development which led to the doctrine of the mystical ascent and its stages as we have it in Proclus.

(1) The first period is that of the old *Mysteries*. Here we are entirely on religious ground. The first demand of the Mystery-religions was for purification: "Let him that is pure come hither." He who fulfils this first requirement participates next in the divine illumination; it is the task of the Mystery to mediate this, and it is often given sym-

---

[1] In primum Platonis Alcibiadem, ed. Cousin, tom. ii., p. 13.
[2] *Ibid.*, tom. iii., pp. 103 ff.

bolical expression by leading the initiate from a dark into a brightly lighted room. But illumination is not the final goal; this is only reached in the ecstatic union of the soul with the divinity itself. Thus in this earliest period we find in substance all the three stages of the soul's ascent.

(2) The second period begins when Plato transfers this idea into *philosophy*. For him the task of philosophy is primarily to achieve purification. If the soul is to behold anything of the higher world, it must keep itself as much as possible untainted by the corporeal-sensible, which only shows us shadow-images and no real being. That is the meaning of Plato's κάθαρσις. But illumination and union also find a place in him, though they tend to be confused. The real aim is to contemplate the Ideas, but at the highest stage Plato characteristically leaves dialectic with its discursive thought, and goes over to ecstatic experience; only in the "divine madness" does the soul become *one* with the Divine.

(3) In the third period the idea gradually returns to its religious origin. This is prepared for by Neoplatonism, which to a large extent bears the stamp of Mystery-piety. The task of philosophy becomes more and more the purification of the soul (Porphyry, Iamblicus). The place of Proclus in this evolution is particularly important. What Mystery-piety and philosophy had gradually worked out concerning the stages of the ascent is found in Proclus as a developed theory, ready to be taken over by *Christian mysticism*. As Plato had transferred this idea from Mystery-piety to philosophy, so Pseudo-Dionysius takes it over from Proclus and transplants it to Christian soil. Thus the Neoplatonist Proclus has gained an importance for Christian theology far surpassing that of most of the Fathers of the Church. His scheme of purification, illumination and union recurs throughout the centuries in Christian mysticism with its three ways: via purgativa, via illuminativa and via unitiva.

An unbroken line runs from the ancient Mysteries through Plato, Plotinus, Proclus, Pseudo-Dionysius and Mediæval mysticism down to our own time. It is strange how Catholic mysticism, in setting forth the Christian Way of salvation, even today has recourse to the venerable terms of ancient Mystery-piety and the anagogical scheme of salvation of the Neoplatonist Plotinus.[1]

5. *Eros, the power of cohesion in existence.* A survey of Proclus' Eros theory shows clearly that the idea of Eros has undergone a very radical transformation. What is most characteristic of Proclus' conception of love is briefly this: *Eros is the bond of union in existence.*[2] Eros is no longer simply the ascent of the individual soul, as in Plato, nor is it simply the upward tendency indwelling all existence, as in Aristotle, but it has a still more universal significance. Aristotle may be said to have transformed the Platonic idea of Eros into an all-embracing cosmic force; in a sense he already makes Eros into a bond of cohesion in existence, inasmuch as everything is set in motion towards the Divine by Eros, as by a spiritual force of gravitation. Yet even so, there is in this case—compared with Proclus' conception of Eros—only a more limited and one-sided movement. The fact that the universe, according to Aristotle, bears the stamp of Eros, only means that all lower things reach out after the higher and long to become like it. In Proclus, however, Eros is a *universal force of cohesion* in the most comprehensive sense of the term. Here the *whole* universe really does bear the stamp of Eros. It is not simply that the lower reaches up with the longing of Eros towards the higher, but

---

[1] *Cf., e.g.*, the book of devotion edited by H. S. Denifle, " *Das Geistliche Leben*," 6 Aufl., 1908, where the three main parts have the following titles: 1. The Way of Purification, 2. The Way of Illumination, 3. The Way of Union. In the preface this is said to be " appropriate even in the twentieth century."

[2] Eros as the cohesive element in the universe is described in many different terms. Here are a few from the commentary on the *Alcibiades*, tom. ii.: δεσμός (p. 117), σύνδεσμος (p. 173), συνδετικός (pp. 142, 189), συνάπτειν (p. 177), συναγωγός (p. 142), συνοχή (p. 190).

the higher also stoops down with the solicitude of Eros to the lower. Eros is a divine power of sympathy[1] which permeates reality in all its parts and unites them in all directions and at all levels: it binds together the higher with the lower, the lower with the higher, the equal with the equal. The gods have Eros for themselves and one another, the higher gods love the lower with the solicitude of Eros (προνοητικῶς), the lower gods love the higher with the longing of Eros (ἐπιστρεπτικῶς).[2] From the world of the gods Eros streams through the Chain of Love, down through all existence in all its stages, and "converts and brings together all things to the nature of the Beautiful"[3]; and through Eros all things return and ascend to their Divine origin. The whole cosmic process—remaining, procession and return—is thus under the dominion of Eros. Eros opens communications between the Divine and the mortal, not merely in one direction, as in Plato, from the lower to the higher, but in both directions: Eros is both the channel which conveys to us the Divine gifts, and the vehicle by which we can ascend to the higher world.[4] Eros is the bond "which unites all the gods with the spiritual Beauty, the demons with the gods and us with the demons and the gods."[5] There is nothing in the universe, whether higher or lower, that is not included in the movement of Eros, which is a movement towards everything else both in solicitude for it and in desire and longing for it. Thomas Aquinas took over essential parts of Proclus' thought which came to him through Pseudo-Dionysius, and he employs an expression which shows better than anything else what is meant here: love is a "virtus unitiva."

[1] In this connection we may recall the Stoic idea of a συμπάθεια or σύνδεσμος that holds together everything in the universe.

[2] *Op. cit.*, II., p. 153.

[3] ὁ δὲ [ἔρως] ἐπιστρέφων πάντα καὶ συνάγων εἰς τὴν τοῦ καλοῦ φύσιν. *Op. cit.*, II., p. 141.

[4] *Op. cit.*, II., pp. 189 ff.   [5] *Op. cit.*, II., p. 177.

II

DIONYSIUS THE AREOPAGITE

1. THE POSITION OF PSEUDO-DIONYSIUS IN THE HISTORY OF THE CHRISTIAN IDEA OF LOVE

ABOUT the year 500 we encounter a singular figure, the author of four books which were of the utmost importance for subsequent developments. These are, *On the Heavenly Hierarchy*, *On the Ecclesiastical Hierarchy*, *On the Divine Names*, and *On the Mystical Theology*.[1] He himself professes to be an immediate disciple of the Apostle Paul— namely, Dionysius the Areopagite, mentioned in Acts xvii. 34. In reality he lived about A.D. 500, and in all essentials is a disciple of Plotinus and Proclus. He adopted large portions of the latter's writings, often very nearly as they stood; the fundamental Neoplatonism is but scantily covered with an exceedingly thin Christian veneer. The unknown author's attempt to deceive Christendom as to his identity succeeded so completely, however, that the spurious works were universally regarded as genuine for a thousand years, and enjoyed almost canonical authority as being written by a disciple of Paul.[2]

[1] Besides these, there are ten letters by the same author. The works mentioned are referred to below as follows: CH, De cœlesti hierarchia; EH, De ecclesiastica hierarchia; DN, De divinis nominibus; MTh, De mystica theologia. The text used is Migne, PG, vol. iii.

[2] The time of their composition can be fixed with reasonable certainty as between 485 and 515. In 485 Proclus died; and it is his writings that Pseudo-Dionysius has largely plagiarised. The first known quotation from the Dionysian writings is in the monophysite Severus, who was Patriarch in Antioch from 512-518. When Severus' followers at Constantinople in 533 referred to the writings of Dionysius the Areopagite, the orthodox side asserted these to be spurious. But objections soon ceased, and by the end of the century belief in their genuineness was general. In particular, Maximus Confessor (d. 662) wrote a commentary on them and helped to establish their prestige. This remained undisputed

This was fraught with momentous consequences for the Christian idea of love. The ideas thus invested with apostolic authority were nothing but the common Hellenistic Eros theory. Now no one could help seeing that the Christianity of Dionysius was entirely different from that of Paul and of the New Testament in general; but this ceased to be disturbing when Dionysius' view was taken as being the deeper, " mystical " meaning of Christianity. The New Testament contained Christianity as proclaimed for simple people; Dionysius gave that secret " wisdom " which the Apostle spoke among the perfect (1 Cor. ii. 6). In his Caritas doctrine Augustine had effected a fusion of the Eros and Agape motifs; but in Pseudo-Dionysius the pure and unadulterated Eros motif assumes the position of the deepest spiritual meaning of Christianity.

2. The Fundamental Idea of Pseudo-Dionysius

The fundamental idea in Pseudo-Dionysius' thought is that adopted from Proclus, of a unitary force of Eros per-

---

until Laurentius Valla and Erasmus on stylistic grounds, and Luther on positive religious grounds, cast doubt upon their genuineness. Final proof of their spuriousness is given by two Roman Catholic scholars, H. Koch and J. Stiglmayr, who in the same year (1895) independently showed that an extensive section of the " De divinis nominibus," chapter 4, § 18-35, is a simple excerpt from a work of Proclus, extant in a Latin translation, the " De malorum subsistentia." Further researches have shown how largely Pseudo-Dionysius is dependent elsewhere, too, on Proclus. Of the literature may be mentioned: H. Koch: *Pseudo-Dionysius Areopagita in seinen Beziehungen zum Neuplatonismus und Mysterienwesen*, 1900 (Forschungen zur christlichen Litteratur- und Dogmengeschichte, hrsg. v. A. Erhard und J. P. Kirsch, Bd. I.); J. Stiglmayr: *Aszese und Mystik des sog. Dionysius Areopagita* (Scholastik, II. Jahrg., 1927, pp. 161-207); H. F. Müller: *Dionysios, Proklos, Plotinos. Ein historischer Beitrag zur neuplatonischen Philosophie*, 1918 (Beiträge zur Geschichte der Philosophie des Mittelalters, hrsg. v. C. Baeumker, Bd. XX.). In a couple of articles entitled " Der sog. Dionysius Areopagita und Severus von Antiochien " (Scholastik, III. Jahrg., 1928, pp. 1-27, 161-189), J. Stiglmayr argued that Pseudo-Dionysius is identical with Severus of Antioch. This thesis was strongly disputed by J. Lebon in the *Revue d'histoire ecclésiastique*, vol. xxvi., 1930, pp. 880-915; and Stiglmayr has tried to give it further support in Scholastik, VII. Jahrg., 1932, pp. 52-67.

meating the whole universe and holding all things together. Eros is not limited to a particular sphere, but is found at all levels, from the highest to the lowest. It is found in the Deity Himself, in the angels, in spiritual as well as in psychical beings; indeed, its operation extends right down to the physical world. But wherever found, its purport is the same: it is a "unifying and cohesive force."[1] It causes the solicitude of the higher for the lower, and the longing of the lower for the higher, and the mutual attraction of things on the same level, and it is the ground of the natural self-love of every being.[2]

Like Proclus, Dionysius says it is from the Deity Himself that Eros takes its rise. From above it streams down to the utmost limits of existence, and allows all creatures to participate in the mysterious powers of the Diety; but at the same time it turns the longing of all creatures up towards the Divine.[3]

High above the world in which we live, and high above all other existence, the divine One is enthroned in transcendent majesty, in absolute immobility and rest, always remaining in itself, inaccessible to all our conceptions. Of God there is really nothing that can be said; He is the Nameless.[4] All that is said of the Divine must therefore consist of negations, not as if the Divine itself were something negative, but because everything that is within our reach is negative; and this is true not merely of what falls within the sphere of

---

[1] τὸν ἔρωτα, εἴτε θεῖον, εἴτε ἀγγελικὸν, εἴτε νοερὸν, εἴτε ψυχικὸν, εἴτε φυσικὸν εἴποιμεν, ἑνωτικήν τινα καὶ συγκρατικὴν ἐννοήσωμεν δύναμιν. DN, cap. iv. § xv.

[2] Ibid. Cf. DN, cap. iv., § x.: καὶ τὰ ἥττω τῶν κρειττόνων ἐπιστρεπτικῶς ἐρῶσι, καὶ κοινωνικῶς τὰ ὁμόστοιχα τῶν ὁμοταγῶν, καὶ τὰ κρείττω τῶν ἡττόνων προνοητικῶς, καὶ αὐτὰ ἑαυτῶν ἕκαστα συνεκτικῶς. It is striking how he agrees with Proclus even in his choice of words; cf. supra, p. 570.

[3] μία τίς ἐστιν ἁπλῆ δύναμις ἡ αὐτοκινητικὴ πρὸς ἑνωτικην τινα κρᾶσιν ἐκ τἀγαθοῦ μέχρι τοῦ τῶν ὄντων ἐσχάτου, καὶ ἀπ' ἐκείνου πάλιν ἑξῆς διὰ πάντων εἰς τἀγαθόν. DN, cap. iv., § xvii.

[4] ἀνώνυμος. DN, cap. i., § vi. Cf. cap. i., § i.

our senses,[1] but also of our thoughts.[2]   By negating this when considering the Divinity, we approach its " *super*-substantial and *super*-divine and *super*-good " *being*.[3]   Just as it transcends all else, so it is beyond all affirmation and negation.[4] There is really only *one* thing Dionysius thinks he can state without qualification about the Deity : it is the *cause* (αἰτία) of all things, the source of everything beautiful and good, of everything, indeed, that exists.[5]   But this Divine causality includes both *causa efficiens* and *causa finalis* : God is at once the origin and ultimate goal of all things; from Him all things have streamed forth, and to Him all things stream back.[6]

When Dionysius calls God the *Good*, *Light*, the *Beautiful*, or *Eros*, he is really only saying the same thing in different ways.

To understand what Dionysius means by describing God as " the *Good*," we must first rid ourselves of all ethical associations.   God's " goodness " has nothing to do with His mercy and love in the Christian sense.   As is usual in metaphysical theories, for Dionysius " Being " and " Good " are identical.[7]   God's "goodness" means simply His "*causality*" —in the double sense named above : God is ἀρχή and πέρας (τέλος); He is the primal source and ultimate goal of all things.   God's goodness—that is, His fulness of reality—cannot remain simply within Himself; it overflows its banks, so to speak, and produces all other existence.   Just as it is not by any act of will, but simply by reason of existing, that the sun

---

[1] M Th, cap. iv.   [2] MTh, cap. v.

[3] MTh, cap. i., § 1.   In DN, cap. vii., § iii., Dionysius points to the order and arrangement of the universe as the way and the ladder by which we can ascend to knowledge of the Deity; but here, too, negation has the last word.

[4] οὐδέ ἐστιν αὐτῆς καθόλου θέσις, οὔτε ἀφαίρεσις . . . ἐπεὶ καὶ ὑπὲρ πᾶσαν θέσιν ἐστιν ἡ παντελὴς καὶ ἑνιαία τῶν πάντων αἰτία.   MTh, cap. v.

[5] ὡς αἰτίαν δὲ τῶν ὄντων, ἐπειδὴ πάντα πρὸς τὸ εἶναι παρήχθη διὰ τὴν αὐτῆς οὐσιοποιὸν ἀγαθότητα.   DN, cap. i., § iv.

[6] . . . ὡς αἰτίας, ὡς ἀρχῆς, ὡς πέρατος.   DN, cap. i., § vii.; *cf.* § v.

[7] DN, cap. v., § iv.

sends out its rays in all directions and illumines everything;
so the divine One also, solely by reason of its existence and
of the overflowing fulness of its being, must let its goodness
stream down and give rise to a world with different levels,[1]
whose reality and " goodness " diminish with their distance
from the primal Divine source of goodness.[2]   But if all that
exists has come into existence through the outflow of the
Good,[3] the Good is also the goal towards which all things
strive.   The desire of every creature is to be partaker in the
Good.[4]   All life and all existence wells up out of the fulness
of the Divine being; out of the undifferentiated One streams
an infinite multiplicity, but this is not dissipated; the Divine
" goodness " gathers all this multiplicity and leads it back to
its source.   The whole cosmic process moves in an eternal
cycle " for the sake of the good, from the good, in the good
and to the good."[5]   The cohesive force in it all is the Divine
" goodness," and therefore God may also be called the
" Prime gatherer of the dispersed."[6]

For the same reason, the Divine essence can also be called
" *Light* "; for light has the same two characteristics of outflow and return.   The source of light cannot conceal the
whole fulness of light within itself; by its very nature as
light, it must send out its rays in all directions.   But at the
same time these rays draw all eyes to themselves and lead
them back to the source of the light.   So it can be said of
light, too, that it brings together and unites and perfects.[7]

But the divine One is also called " the *Beautiful*."   This,

---

[1] DN, cap. iv., § 1.   [2] DN, cap. iv., § ii. f.

[3] DN, cap. iv., § iv.: καὶ τἀγαθόν ἐστιν, ἐξ οὗ τὰ πάντα ὑπέστη, καὶ ἔστιν,
ὡς ἐξ αἰτίας παντελοῦς παρηγμένα. . . .

[4] *Ibid.*

[5] ὥσπερ τις ἀΐδιος κύκλος, διὰ τἀγαθὸν, ἐκ τἀγαθοῦ, καὶ ἐν τἀγαθῷ,
καὶ εἰς τἀγαθόν.   DN, cap. iv., § xiv.

[6] ἀρχισυναγωγός ἐστι τῶν ἐσκεδασμένων.   DN, cap. iv., § iv.

[7] ἡ τοῦ νοητοῦ φωτὸς παρουσία συναγωγὸς καὶ ἑνωτικὴ τῶν φωτιζομένων
ἐστί, καὶ τελειωτική, καὶ ἔτι ἐπιστρεπτικὴ πρὸς τὸ ὄντως ὄν.   DN, cap. iv.,
§ vi.

however, adds nothing to what has already been said. For as " Being " and " Good " are identical, according to Dionysius, so also " the Good " and " the Beautiful " are identical.[1] So we are not surprised to have exactly the same thing repeated. The Beautiful is both the *causa efficiens* and the *causa finalis* of everything. By means of the Beautiful all things have come into existence;[2] but the Beautiful is also that which by its power of attraction sets all things in motion towards itself.[3] This is exactly the same idea as in the Aristotelian κινεῖ ὡς ἐρώμενον.[4]

All this goes to show that Dionysius is dominated by a single basic idea—namely, that all things have issued from God and return to Him. This idea asserts itself in every case, whether he speaks of the Deity as the One, Light, the Good or the Beautiful; but it only reaches its climax when he gives the divine One the name *Eros*.[5] This is the adequate term for the universal Divine power that holds the universe together.[6] Eros is the necessary correlate of " Being," " the Good " and " the Beautiful "; Eros is what gives the cosmic process its dynamic nature. If the divine Eros-forces were not diffused throughout the universe, it would be impossible to speak of " the Good " or " the Beautiful," since these are constituted essentially by the longing and desire they arouse— that is, by Eros.

---

[1] διὸ καὶ ταὐτόν ἐστι τἀγαθῷ τὸ καλόν. DN, cap. iv, § vii.

[2] καὶ ἀρχὴ πάντων τὸ καλόν, ὡς ποιητικὸν αἴτιον. *Ibid.*

[3] καὶ κινοῦν τὰ ὅλα, καὶ συνέχον τῷ τῆς οἰκείας καλλονῆς ἔρωτι. *Ibid.* "The Beautiful" gets its name (κάλλος), according to Dionysius, just because it calls (καλεῖν) everything to itself: καὶ ὡς πάντα πρὸς ἑαυτὸ καλοῦν (ὅθεν καὶ κάλλος λέγεται) καὶ ὡς ὅλα ἐν ὅλοις εἰς ταὐτὸ συνάγον. DN, cap. iv., § vii. When speaking earlier of "light" as a cohesive force, Dionysius tries to support his view with a similar etymological speculation. Thus the sun (ἥλιος) is said to have got its name because it "holds everything together (ἀολλής)" and brings together the dispersed": διὸ καὶ ἥλιος, ὅτι πάντα ἀολλῆ ποιεῖ, καὶ συνάγει τὰ διεσκεδασμένα. DN, cap. iv., § iv.

[4] *Cf. supra*, p. 184.

[5] This is dealt with exhaustively in DN, cap. iv., §§ vii.-xvii.

[6] καὶ ἔστι τοῦτο [ὄνομα] δυνάμεως ἑνοποιοῦ καὶ συνδετικῆς, καὶ διαφερόντως συγκρατικῆς ἐν τῷ καλῷ καὶ ἀγαθῷ. DN, cap. iv., § xii.

Wherever in the world we find any motion or striving, we can be sure that Eros is busy. The world is full of erotes, of individual Eros-forces. Here Dionysius is following Plotinus and Proclus, but, like the latter, he is particularly interested in the *unity* of this multiplicity. He tries to show that all the individual erotes derive from the one all-embracing Eros,[1] which is identical with the divine One, and that they are held together by this in an exactly determined relation to each other.[2] The origin and source of Eros is in the Divine being itself, which is perpetual causality. From it the divine Eros-forces are transmitted by the chain of causality or Eros down to the very lowest. Every creature has its determinate place as a link in this chain. Every such link is firmly enclosed within itself through self-love; but at the place it occupies in the chain it has a double task, to receive the divine Eros-forces from the next link above it and to transmit them to the next link below it. This is the meaning of Dionysius' monotonously reiterated principle that the higher cares for the lower, that the lower reaches in longing towards the higher, that things on the same level have fellowship with one another and that every creature is enclosed within itself in self-love.[3] Thus Eros is the principle of motion in the universe. It was Eros that prevented the divine One from remaining in itself and drove it to activity in accordance with its all-creative power, and it is Eros that drives everything which has proceeded from the divine One to turn back to the same.[4]

That is what Dionysius wants to express when he says that

---

[1] νῦν αὖθις ἀναλαβόντες ἅπαντας εἰς τὸν ἕνα καὶ συνεπτυγμένον ἔρωτα . . . . DN, cap. iv., § xvi.

[2] ἐπειδὴ τοὺς ἐκ τοῦ ἑνὸς πολλοὺς ἔρωτας διετάξαμεν, ἑξῆς εἰρηκότες. . . . *Ibid.*

[3] *Cf.* DN, cap. iv., § vii.; § x.; § xii.; § xiii.; § xv.

[4] αὐτὸς γὰρ ὁ ἀγαθοεργὸς τῶν ὄντων ἔρως, ἐν τἀγαθῷ καθ' ὑπερβολὴν προϋπάρχων, οὐκ εἴασεν αὐτὸν ἄγονον ἐν ἑαυτῷ μένειν, ἐκίνησε δὲ αὐτὸν εἰς τὸ πρακτικεύεσθαι κατὰ τὴν ἁπάντων γενητικὴν ὑπερβολήν. DN, cap. iv., § x.

Eros is *ecstatic*.[1] Eros does not permit the lover to remain in himself, but forces him out of himself to the beloved. In a certain respect Dionysius can find support for this in the old Eros tradition. That the soul seized with love for the Divine only attains final union with the Deity in an act of ecstasy, is old Platonic and Neoplatonic wisdom. But what is new in Dionysius—though Proclus had prepared the way for it—is that he even applies this idea to the Deity itself. God is Eros, and this means that He who is the cause of all things " through the beautiful and good Eros towards every-thing, by reason of the overflowing fulness of Eros-goodness, goes out of Himself owing to the care He has for all existence, and becomes, so to speak, bewitched by goodness, by ἀγάπησις and ἔρως."[2] Ecstatic love causes God to be drawn down to the lower world from the heavenly height where He is enthroned in absolute isolation from all else.[3] Now it looks as if certain reminiscences of the idea of Agape have influenced Dionysius—as they did Proclus before him—in his description of the Divine descent. But however that may be, it is plain that this love, even when it has thus changed its direction, still preserves the characteristics of Eros in its whole structure.

The fundamental thought of Pseudo-Dionysius' theory is thus briefly as follows. It is the idea of the Chain of Love that joins heaven and earth, that leads the divine Eros-forces down to the lower world, and that leads the whole desire of the lower world up towards the Divine again. Otherwise expressed, it is the idea of the μονή, πρόοδος and ἐπιστροφή of the divine One, the idea of the closed κύκλος in which the Divine life eternally revolves within itself without beginning and without end,[4] proceeding out of itself in perpetual

1 DN, cap. iv., § xiii.: ἔστι δὲ καὶ ἐκστατικὸς ὁ θεῖος ἔρως.
2 DN, cap. iv., § xiii.   3 *Ibid.*
4 ἐν ᾧ καὶ τὸ ἀτελεύτητον ἑαυτοῦ καὶ ἄναρχον ὁ θεῖος ἔρως ἐνδείκνυται διαφερόντως, ὥσπερ τις ἀΐδιος κύκλος. DN, cap. iv., § xiv.

"ecstasy," perpetually returning to itself, and at the same time perpetually remaining in itself.

3. THE HEAVENLY AND THE ECCLESIASTICAL HIERARCHY

It is the basic idea described above that is developed in detail in Pseudo-Dionysius' two works *On the Heavenly Hierarchy* and *On the Ecclesiastical Hierarchy*.

The *goal* of our life can be described briefly as *deification*, which means that we raise ourselves to the greatest possible likeness to God and to unity with Him.[1] A more apt description of Dionysius' conception of salvation than Plotinus' formula can scarcely be found : the Divine within us must be led up to the Divine in the All.[2] The only adequate name for the Deity is "the One," τὸ ἕν or ἕν θεῖον. But Dionysius can also speak of τὸ ἕν in man. It is the highest, divine part of his nature, the part by which he can comprehend and have fellowship with God, in accordance with the Hellenistic principle, approved also by Dionysius, that "like attracts like." Man's deification or ἕνωσις with God thus means that his ἕν becomes *one* with τὸ θεῖον ἕν. Fellowship with God[3] means for Dionysius a fellowship on God's own level, and presupposes the ascent of the soul through the three main stages : purification, illumination, and union.[4] To attain union with the One we must first *purify* ourselves from contact with all the multifarious divided life of sense. The scattered thoughts and desires must be collected. The soul must turn from outward things and retire into its own depths. If the divine One revolves within itself in an eternal cycle without beginning or end, then the soul should imitate this and turn inward to itself.

---

[1] ἡ δὲ θέωσίς ἐστιν ἡ πρὸς θεὸν ὡς ἐφικτὸν ἀφομοίωσίς τε καὶ ἕνωσις. EH, cap. i., §iii.

[2] *Cf. supra*, p. 194.

[3] ἡ κοινωνία πρὸς τὸ ἕν. EH, cap. ii., § v.

[4] CH, cap. iii., § iii.

" For the soul the cyclic movement means its entry into itself
from outward things and the gathering into unity of its
spiritual forces. As in a circle, this prevents it from going
astray and turns it away from the multiplicity of external
things and gathers it first of all within itself."[1] When the
soul is thus gathered in its inmost ground or, what is the
same thing, has mounted to its highest pinnacle,[2] where it
looks up, as from a watch-tower, towards the higher world,
then it is met by the Divine *illumination*. This leads on in
turn to *union*, which is attained in a state of ecstasy. This is
the stage of perfection : the soul has reached its goal, deification, θέωσις. Like " the divine Moses," it ascends to the
divine " bright darkness "[3] and beholds the Deity as He is;
but this beholding is a " seeing by not seeing," a " knowing
by not knowing."[4]

To make possible the attainment of this goal God has
founded the two hierarchies, the heavenly and the ecclesiastical.[5] Their task is to convey the divine gifts and forces
down through the universe, and to lead the lower beings up
to ἕνωσις and deification.[6]

---

[1] ψυχῆς δὲ κίνησίς ἐστι, κυκλικὴ μὲν ἡ εἰς ἑαυτὴν εἴσοδος ἀπὸ τῶν
ἔξω, καὶ τῶν νοερῶν αὐτῆς δυνάμεων ἡ ἑνοειδὴς συνέλιξις, ὥσπερ ἔν τινι
κύκλῳ τὸ ἀπλανὲς αὐτῇ δωρουμένη καὶ ἀπὸ τῶν πολλῶν τῶν ἔξωθεν αὐτὴν
ἐπιστρέφουσα καὶ συνάγουσα, πρῶτον εἰς ἑαυτήν, εἶτα ὡς ἑνοειδῆ γενομένην,
ἑνοῦσα ταῖς ἑνιαίως ἡνωμέναις δυνάμεσι, καὶ οὕτως ἐπὶ τὸ καλὸν καὶ
ἀγαθὸν χειραγωγοῦσα, τὸ ὑπὲρ πάντα τὰ ὄντα, καὶ ἓν καὶ ταὐτόν, καὶ
ἄναρχον καὶ ἀτελεύτητον. DN, cap. iv., § ix.

[2] This is the source of the ideas in Mediæval mysticism concerning the " ground
of the soul," the " scintilla animæ," " apex mentis," " vertex mentis," " in-
timus mentis sinus," " Fünklein," " Seelenburg," etc.

[3] ὁ θεῖος γνόφος, MTh, cap. i., § i.; ἡ τοῦ θείου σκότους ἀκτίς. *Ibid.*

[4] MTh, cap. ii. Dionysius shows himself here to be singularly akin to Gregory of
Nyssa; *cf. supra*, pp. 431 f.

[5] σκοπὸς οὖν ἱεραρχίας ἐστίν, ἡ πρὸς Θεόν, ὡς ἐφικτόν, ἀφομοίωσίς
τε καὶ ἕνωσις. CH, cap. iii., § ii. *Cf.* EH, cap. ii. 1.

[6] *On the Heavenly Hierarchy* begins characteristically by quoting Jas. i. 17,
which says that all good gifts come down from above, from the Father of lights.
Dionysius couples with this the idea, adopted from Proclus, of the πρόοδος and
ἐπιστροφή of the Divine. The radiance of divine light which reaches us by its
πρόοδος, fills us with its unifying force and so leads us back to the divine One.

The Heavenly Hierarchy has its archetype in the Divine being, and as God is triune, so the Heavenly Hierarchy, too, is arranged in three triads, 3×3 choirs of angels. The highest of these is in direct connection with the Deity.[1] In " divine and unwavering Eros " it reaches up towards the One and receives illumination direct from the primal source.[2] From this the divine forces are transmitted step by step down to the lower orders of angels; and it is a fixed principle that the lower order is led up to the Deity only through the mediation of the next higher.[3]

If the Heavenly Hierarchy is a copy of the Divine being with its πρόοδος and ἐπιστροφή, the *Ecclesiastical Hierarchy* is a copy of the Heavenly.[4] Here, too, the goal is the same—namely deification[5]—and the same fixed principle applies. Through the higher orders the Divine forces stream down to the lower, and when these have been made participant in the Good and Beautiful, according to their capacity, they are led through the mediation of the higher orders up to the Divine origin.[6]

Since the highest order in the Ecclesiastical Hierarchy is directly linked with the lowest in the Heavenly, the two Hierarchies together form a continuous chain which stretches from the highest heavenly to the lowest earthly things, as the diagram opposite shows.

The most interesting link in the chain is that which joins the two parts—that is, the Bishop or, as Dionysius prefers to say, the *hierarch*. The very name indicates the dominant

---

(ἐπιστρέφει πρὸς τὴν τοῦ συναγωγοῦ πατρὸς ἑνότητα, καὶ θεοποιὸν ἁπλότητα). CH, cap. i., § 1.

[1] CH, cap. vii., § iii.; *cf.* § iv.

[2] CH, cap. iv., § ii.: ὁ θεῖος καὶ ἀκλινὴς ἔρως.

[3] τὸ διὰ τῶν πρώτων τὰ δεύτερα πρὸς τὸ θεῖον ἀνάγεσθαι. CH, cap. iv., § iii. The task of the higher order is to be the mystagogue of the lower (. . . καὶ τῶν ἡττόνων εἶναι τοὺς θειοτέρους μύστας καὶ χειραγωγοὺς ἐπὶ τὴν θείαν προσαγωγὴν καὶ ἔλλαμψιν καὶ κοινωνίαν. *Ibid.*). EH, cap. v. 1, § iv.

[4] CH, cap. i., § iii. EH, cap. vi. 3, § v.

[5] EH, cap. i., § iv.   [6] EH, cap. i., § ii.

	The One		τὸ ἕν
The Heavenly Hierarchy	I.	Seraphim	σεραφίμ
		Cherubim	χερουβίμ
		Thrones	θρόνοι
	II.	Dominions	κυριότητες
		Powers	δυνάμεις
		Authorities	ἐξουσίαι
	III.	Principalities	ἀρχαί
		Archangels	ἀρχάγγελοι
		Angels	ἄγγελοι
The Ecclesiastical Hierarchy	I.	Bishop	ἱεράρχης
		Priest	ἱερεύς
		Deacon	λειτουργός
	II.	Monks	μοναχοί, θεραπευταί
		Baptised Christians	ἱερὸς λαός
		Catechumens	κατηχούμενοι

position he holds in the Ecclesiastical Hierarchy.[1]   In the hierarch the heavenly forces are concentrated; and in his overflowing "goodness" he permits these forces to flow, through his administration of the sacraments and his symbolic actions, to all who are set under him.[2] He is the "God-filled and divine man," possessor of the sacred Gnosis; it is through him that the different orders of the Ecclesiastical Hierarchy are purified and perfected.[3]   He holds the same position in the Ecclesiastical Hierarchy as God in the Heavenly.[4]   He is, so to speak, God on earth.   When the hierarch, "God-filled," leaves his place by the altar of God during the celebration of the Eucharist, and proceeds round

---

[1] ὡς ἱεραρχίας ἐπώνυμος.   EH, cap. i., § iii.

[2] αὕτη γὰρ ἡ καθολικὴ τῶν θείων εὐκοσμία καὶ τάξις, πρῶτον ἐν μετουσίᾳ γενέσθαι καὶ ἀποπληρώσει τὸν ἱερὸν καθηγεμόνα, τῶν δι' αὐτοῦ θεόθεν ἑτέροις δωρηθησομένων, οὕτω τε καὶ ἄλλοις μεταδοῦναι.   EH, cap. iii. 3, § xiv.

[3] οὕτως ἱεράρχην ὁ λέγων δηλοῖ τὸν ἔνθεόν τε καὶ θεῖον ἄνδρα, τὸν πάσης ἱερᾶς ἐπιστήμονα γνώσεως, ἐν ᾧ καὶ καθαρῶς ἡ κατ' αὐτὸν ἱεραρχία πᾶσα τελεῖται καὶ γινώσκεται.   EH, cap. i., § iii.; cf. EH, cap. v. 1, § v.

[4] CH, cap. xiii., § iv.   ὡς γὰρ ἅπασαν ἱεραρχίαν ὁρῶμεν εἰς τὸν Ἰησοῦν ἀποπεραιουμένην, οὕτως ἑκάστην εἰς τὸν οἰκεῖον ἔνθεον ἱεράρχην.   EH, cap. v. 1, § v.   What is said of God in 1 Tim. ii. 4 is applied to the hierarch in EH, cap. ii. 2, § i.

the temple, even to its remotest part, and thence returns to the altar, this is a symbol of God's own μονή, πρόοδος, and ἐπιστροφή.[1] But it is not only a symbol; for by this symbolical action he actually does the same thing as the divine One does in its procession and return. At the altar he becomes filled with the divine Eros-forces; these he carries out to the congregation (ἱερὸς λαός) and then, on his return to the altar, again enters into his ἕν and unites with τὸ θεῖον ἕν.[2]

By means of the two Hierarchies, the divine One has set up communications with us. In itself it always remains in its transcendence, but through the mediation of all the intervening " orders " the Divine forces are conveyed down to us, and our desire is led up to the Divine world. For the establishment of fellowship between us and the Divine, however, it is necessary for us to use the means thus provided, and to raise ourselves to the supernatural order. Fellowship with God does not occur on our level, but on the Divine level.[3] This is best shown by Dionysius' conception of prayer.[4] It might seem as if in prayer we drew God's blessing down to us. But that is not the case. God remains in His transcendence, and the effect of prayer is that we raise ourselves up to God and are united with Him. To make this clear, Dionysius employs the simile of a *brightly shining chain* that reaches down from heaven to us. If we were to climb up this, it might look as if we were drawing it down to us, but in reality we should be raising ourselves up to brighter realms.[5]

---

[1] EH, cap. iii. 3, § iii.

[2] *Ibid. Cf.* EH, cap. iv. 3, § iii.

[3] There is an occasional glimpse of the idea of Incarnation in Dionysius, as, *e.g.*, EH, cap. ii. 2, § i.; cap. iii. 3, § xiii. But even then it is still a question of θέωσις and fellowship with God on God's level.

[4] DN, cap. iii., § i.

[5] ὥσπερ εἰ πολυφώτου σειρᾶς ἐκ τῆς οὐρανίας ἀκρότητος ἠρτημένης, εἰς δεῦρο δὲ καθηκούσης, καὶ ἀεὶ αὐτῆς ἐπὶ τὸ πρόσω χερσὶν ἀμοιβαίαις δραττόμενοι, καθέλκειν μὲν αὐτὴν ἐδοκοῦμεν, τῷ ὄντι δὲ οὐ κατήγομεν ἐκείνην, ἄνω τε καὶ κάτω παροῦσαν, ἀλλ' αὐτοὶ ἡμεῖς ἀνηγόμεθα πρὸς τὰς ὑψηλοτέρας τῶν πολυφώτων ἀκτίνων μαρμαρυγάς. *Ibid.* For the " Chain of Love " in

4. Eros is "More Divine" than Agape

We have seen how Dionysius' thought is dominated by the Eros motif. When he finds the New Testament speaking of love, Agape, he can make no sense of it except by detecting Neoplatonic Eros behind it. Agape is for him simply a substitute for Eros in Proclus' sense of the word. Where love is concerned, Eros is the only reality he knows. He does speak of Agape, but this is entirely due to the fact that he found this word in the Christian tradition; and the way in which he speaks of it plainly proves that he found it a nuisance and would gladly have been rid of it.[1] But Dionysius is not merely uneasy in using the word Agape; he actively opposes its use. He does not interpret Agape as Eros simply in his thought, but he formally substitutes Eros for Agape. This attempt to oust Agape from the Christian vocabulary simply puts the seal on the fact that the spiritual reality signified by it is entirely foreign to Dionysius. He is clearly aware that he is taking a bold step, it is true.[2] He knows that in asserting Eros at the

---

Gregory of Nyssa, *cf. supra*, p. 446; and in Proclus, *supra*, pp. 570 f. Dionysius has another simile, too: if we are on board a ship and pull towards us a rope that is fastened to a rock, it is not the rock that is drawn to us, but we and the ship are drawn to the rock. *Cf.* also Clem. Alex., Strom. IV., cap. xxiii. 152, 2.

[1] In an essay on *Amour et extase d'après Denys l'Aréopagite* (in the *Revue d'Ascétique et de Mystique*, 6ᵉ Année, 1925, pp. 278 ff.) G. Horn has tried to explain what enabled Dionysius to replace the Christian word Agape by the term Eros. Horn suggests that the word Agape had grown weaker through use, and by the time of Dionysius had lost its force. To give expression to the full force of Divine love Dionysius therefore found it better to employ the word Eros. "Wishing to express the Divine love by a term in which all its force, all its life and all its emotion would be apparent, Dionysius would think he had found in ἔρως a more eloquent and arresting expression than ἀγάπη" (p. 279, n. 2). This ·explanation, however, seems both superfluous and misleading. For even if it is true that Agape had at this time largely lost its force, yet that was not the reason why Dionysius preferred to speak of Eros. Eros was the reality he knew, so he naturally preferred to speak of the thing by its right name. No other explanation is necessary.

[2] παρρησιάσεται δὲ καὶ τοῦτο εἰπεῖν ὁ ἀληθὴς λόγος, ὅτι καὶ αὐτὸς πάντων αἴτιος δι' ἀγαθότητος ὑπερβολὴν πάντων ἐρᾷ. DN, cap. iv., § x.

expense of Agape he seems to do violence to the Holy
Scriptures,[1] and that he can count on strong opposition from
many quarters in the Church.[2] Yet he urges his readers
not to be deterred by such difficulties from using the term
Eros.[3]

As we have already seen what positive interest Dionysius
had in replacing Agape by Eros, we may here restrict ourselves to the question of the support he could adduce against
his critics for demanding this substitution. Three arguments
in particular are prominent:

1. First, *Eros and Agape are synonymous*.[4] When the
critics refuse to replace Agape by Eros, Dionysius taunts
them with unreasonableness and stupidity in that they insist
on words and phrases, when the meaning is after all the
same[5]: as if it were impossible to express the same thing
with more than one word. Is it not permissible to describe
"the number four" as "twice two," or "the mother
country" as "the fatherland," and so on?[6] The identity of
Eros and Agape, however, is not simply Dionysius' own invention; he believes there is evidence for it even in the Holy
Scriptures themselves.[7] The passages he adduces are the
same as Origen used for a similar purpose.[8] In dependence
on Origen and with the same misinterpretation, Dionysius
also quotes the saying of Ignatius: "My Eros has been

---

[1] καὶ μή τις ἡμᾶς οἰέσθω παρὰ τὰ λόγια τὴν τοῦ ἔρωτος ἐπωνυμίαν
πρεσβεύειν.   DN, cap. iv., § xi.   πλὴν ἵνα μὴ ταῦτα εἰπεῖν δοκῶμεν, ὡς τὰ
θεῖα λόγια παρακινοῦντες. . . . *Ibid.*

[2] οἱ τὴν ἔρωτος ἐπωνυμίαν διαβάλλοντες. *Ibid.*

[3] ὥστε τοῦτο δὴ τὸ τοῦ ἔρωτος ὄνομα μὴ φοβηθῶμεν, μηδέ τις ἡμᾶς
θορυβείτω λόγος περὶ τούτου δεδιττόμενος.   DN, cap. iv., § xii.

[4] ταὐτὸ σημαίνοντες.   DN, cap. iv., § xi.

[5] ἔστι μὲν γὰρ ἄλογον, ὡς οἶμαι, καὶ σκαιὸν, τὸ μὴ τῇ δυνάμει τοῦ σκοποῦ
προσέχειν, ἀλλὰ ταῖς λέξεσι.   *Ibid.*

[6] ὥσπερ οὐκ ἐξὸν τὸν τέσσαρα ἀριθμὸν διὰ τοῦ δὶς δύο σημαίνειν . . . ἢ
τὴν μητρίδα διὰ τῆς πατρίδος.   *Ibid.*

[7] ἐμοὶ γὰρ δοκοῦσιν οἱ θεολόγοι κοινὸν μὲν ἡγεῖσθαι τὸ τῆς ἀγάπης
καὶ τὸ τοῦ ἔρωτος ὄνομα.   DN, cap. iv., § xii.

[8] Prov. iv. 6 and Wisd. Sol. viii. 2.   On these passages in Origen, *cf. supra*,
p. 390, n. 1.

crucified."[1] This identification of Eros and Agape makes it possible for Eros to replace Agape and oust it from its place; but it provides no positive reason why this must happen.

2. Here the second argument arises: *Eros is plainer and clearer than Agape.* In itself, neither word is superior to the other. All words and phrases belong to the lower, sensible sphere. When the soul has risen to the intelligible sphere,[2] and still more when it has reached union with the Divine,[3] it needs no words and sensible symbols. But so long as it is at the lower level and cannot dispense with the medium of words, clearer and plainer words[4] are naturally to be preferred to those that are less clear. Dionysius applies this principle to the two words Eros and Agape. No one rightly knows what Agape is: it is an empty sound,[5] a meaningless collection of letters; it is a sound produced by the lips and caught by the ears, but it cannot enter into the soul.[6] What Eros is, however, everyone knows. It presents a clear idea and sure guidance for the soul that wishes to raise itself up to God.[7]

3. But this pedagogical reason for preferring Eros to Agape was not in itself satisfactory for Dionysius; for from that point of view it could equally well be argued that Agape had the advantage, as Dionysius himself was fully aware.

---

[1] To preserve the fiction that he is Dionysius the disciple of Paul, he must naturally refrain from quoting Origen. Incautiously, however, he quotes " the divine Ignatius " (DN, cap. iv., § xii.), who also lived too late to be suitably quoted by Dionysius the disciple of Paul. It is astonishing that this fatal mistake did not betray the author for a thousand years.

[2] ἐπὶ τὰ νοητά. DN, cap. iv., § xi.

[3] . . . ὅταν ἡ ψυχὴ θεοειδὴς γινομένη, δι' ἑνώσεως ἀγνώστου ταῖς τοῦ ἀπροσίτου φωτὸς ἀκτῖσιν ἐπιβάλλῃ, ταῖς ἀνομμάτοις ἐπιβολαῖς. *Ibid.*

[4] οἱ σαφέστεροι λόγοι. *Ibid.*

[5] ἠχὴ ψιλή. *Ibid.*

[6] . . . καὶ λέξεσιν ἀγνώστοις, μὴ διαβαινούσαις εἰς τὸ τῆς ψυχῆς αὐτῶν νοερόν, ἀλλ' ἔξω περὶ τὰ χείλη καὶ τὰς ἀκοὰς αὐτῶν διαβομβουμέναις. *Ibid.*

[7] ὅταν δὴ ὁ νοῦς διὰ τῶν αἰσθητῶν ἀνακινεῖσθαι σπεύδῃ πρὸς θεωρητικὰς νοήσεις, τιμιώτεραι πάντως εἰσὶν αἱ ἐπιδηλότεραι τῶν αἰσθήσεων διαπορθ-μεύσεις, οἱ σαφέστεροι λόγοι. *Ibid.*

In his search for biblical support for the use of Eros, he could not help seeing that the Holy Scriptures are directly against him. They avoid the word Eros, and show a plain predilection for the word Agape, which Dionysius is attacking. He tries to explain this troublesome fact by reference to the pedagogical point of view. In principle, he holds, Scripture has no qualms about talking of Eros. The difficulty is that the idea of Eros is ambiguous: it can mean not only the heavenly, but also the vulgar Eros. For the simple multitude, who only know Eros in the latter sense, there is grave risk of completely misunderstanding any talk of Eros,[1] and Scripture has taken account of this. " On account of the stupid prejudice of such people " it avoids speaking of Eros in contexts where misunderstanding might arise, and employs instead the unambiguous word Agape.[2] Now it is interesting to notice that in this case Agape is the clear and unambiguous word, which from a pedagogical point of view is preferable to Eros. Quite evidently, when Dionysius wants Eros to displace Agape the pedagogical argument is not sufficient. He must assert the positive superiority of Eros as well. This he does in his third main argument: *Eros is more divine than Agape*.[3] As regards Divine things, Eros is the only adequate term, and since the sublime nature of these things makes misunderstanding impossible, the word Agape neither need nor ought to be used on this level. Since the name " Eros " is used of the Divine wisdom, we are delivered from the habit of thinking of Eros as something low, and are brought to a knowledge of " the true Eros," the heavenly Eros.[4] When, however, it is a question

---

[1] ἀχώρητον γάρ ἐστι τῷ πλήθει. τὸ ἑνιαῖον τοῦ θείου καὶ ἑνὸς ἔρωτος. DN, cap. iv., § xii.

[2] διὰ τὴν ἄτοπον τῶν τοιούτων ἀνδρῶν πρόληψιν. *Ibid.*

[3] καίτοι ἔδοξέ τισι τῶν καθ' ἡμᾶς ἱερολόγων καὶ θειότερον εἶναι τὸ τοῦ ἔρωτος ὄνομα τοῦ τῆς ἀγάπης. *Ibid.*

[4] διὸ καὶ ὡς δυσχερέστερον ὄνομα τοῖς πολλοῖς δοκοῦν, ἐπὶ τῆς θείας σοφίας τάττεται πρὸς ἀναγωγὴν αὐτῶν καὶ ἀνάστασιν εἰς τὴν τοῦ ὄντως

of the love that we as Christians owe to one another, then to prevent misunderstanding we may, on this lower, earthly level, use the more cautious and euphemistic term Agape.[1]

ἔρωτος γνῶσιν (so older editions, rightly; Migne has φρῶσιν misprint ?) καὶ ὥστε ἀπολυθῆναι τῆς ἐπ' αὐτῷ δυσχερείας. *Ibid.*

[1] *Ibid.*

III

FROM DIONYSIUS TO ERIGENA

1. THE LADDER OF PARADISE

FOR a thousand years after Dionysius the Areopagite, the ladder-symbolism characteristic of Eros piety sets its mark almost without question upon the general conception of Christian fellowship with God; but this was not due solely to the influence of Dionysius. Augustine, too, had represented the Christian life as an ascent to God by the ladder of Virtue, Speculation and Mysticism. But above all, the enormous influence of *monastic piety* in this respect cannot be ignored. The ascetic observances of the monk are regarded as a ladder set up from earth to heaven. In this connection it is interesting to recall the Monastic Rule of Benedict (*c.* 529). Here the story of Jacob's Ladder is applied to the central monastic virtue, humility. "If we wish to attain the pinnacle of the highest humility and quickly come to that heavenly exaltation to which the ascent is made by the humility of the present life, then we must by our upward-striving works erect that ladder which was revealed to Jacob in the dream."[1] The uprights of this heavenly ladder are our body and soul, and the rungs on which we mount are the stages of humility.[2] Benedict speaks of twelve such steps of humility. When the monk

---

1 " Unde, fratres, si summæ humilitatis volumus culmen adtingere et ad exaltationem illam cælestem, ad quam per præsentis vitæ humilitatem ascenditur, volumus velociter pervenire, *actibus nostris ascendentibus scala illa erigenda est, quæ* in somnio Iacob apparuit." S. Benedicti Regula Monasteriorum, cap. vii.; Florilegium Patristicum XVII. (ed. B. Linderbauer), 1928, p. 27, 11.

2 " *Scala vero ipsa erecta nostra est vita in sæculo,* quæ humiliato corde a Domino erigatur ad cælum; latera enim eius scalæ dicimus nostrum esse corpus et animam, in qua latera diversos gradus humilitatis vel disciplinæ evocatio divina ascendendos inseruit." *Ibid.*, p. 27, 17.

has traversed these, and thus travelled as far as humility can take him, he is ripe for the divine Caritas. He has attained the true love of God, in virtue of which it is then easy for him to fulfil God's will in all things.[1]

The outstanding document for the ascetical heavenly ladder of eremitic and monastic piety is the great work written by the monk of Mt. Sinai, Johannes Climacus, about the end of the sixth century—the κλῖμαξ τοῦ παραδείσου, *The Ladder of Paradise*.[2] Its particular interest for our purpose is the remarkable clarity with which it shows how the way to salvation and fellowship with God was conceived in these circles about the year 600. On the basis of the story of Jacob's Ladder (Gen. xxviii. 12), the soul's ascent to God is portrayed. The soul must continually die to the sense-world, and with great effort work its way up the thirty steps (" gradus ") that lead to God. At the first step the task of the monk is to free himself from his attachment to lower things; his heart must turn from this world and its empty joys. We are not, says John Climacus, called by God to a wedding-feast, but to grieve over ourselves.[3] " There is no rejoicing for the condemned in prison; nor is there for true monks any festival on earth."[4] Only mourning can really root out all love of the world from the heart and set man free from earthly things.[5] The " gift of tears " is therefore a glorious blessing. " Truly, he is free from the eternal perdition, who always thinks upon his death and upon his sins,

---

[1] " Ergo his omnibus humilitatis gradibus ascensis monachus mox ad caritatem Dei perveniet illam quæ perfecta foris mittit timorem, per quam universa quæ prius non sine formidinem observabat, absque ullo labore velut naturaliter ex consuetudine incipiet custodire." *Ibid.*, p. 31, 131.

[2] Joannis Climaci Scala paradisi, Migne, PG, vol. lxxxviii., pp. 632-1161.

[3] οὐκ ἔστιν ἡμῖν, ὦ οὗτοι, ἐνταῦθα ἡ τοῦ γάμου κλῆσις, οὐκ ἔστιν, οὔκουν· πάντως δὲ εἰς πένθος ἑαυτῶν ὁ καλέσας ἡμᾶς ἐνταῦθα ἐκάλεσε. Scala paradisi, Gradus VII.

[4] οὐκ ἔστι καταδίκοις ἐν φυλακῇ χαρμονή, καὶ οὐκ ἔστι μοναχοῖς ἀληθινοῖς ἐπὶ γῆς ἑορτή. *Ibid.*

[5] πένθος ἐστὶ κέντρον χρύσεον ψυχῆς πάσης προσηλώσεως καὶ σχέσεως γυμνωθέν. *Ibid.*

and who ceaselessly wets his cheeks with living tears."[1] Yet there are tears of different kinds, some produced by a deceitful and self-complacent mind, some flowing from pure love to God.[2] Only the latter enter into the question here. For John Climacus it is beyond all doubt that such tears, prompted by "all-holy Agape," are of great benefit to us.[3] The "baptism of tears" is more potent than ordinary Christian baptism; for if the latter purifies us from past sins, the former purifies us from all the sins we have committed since.[4]

To understand the ethical and religious ideal of John Climacus we must take note especially of the four top rungs of his heavenly ladder ("gradus" 27-30). The aim of the monk's efforts is to reach such a rest (ἡσυχία) and apathy as is a reflection of God's own rest. The average man does not attain so high; neither does the ordinary monk, but only he who lives his life in absolute isolation as a hermit, only the real "hesychast" (ἡσυχαστής). He and he alone perfectly represents the life of heaven by his manner of life. He is as an angel upon earth.[5] As the angels never cease to grow in Agape, so the hesychasts never tire of mounting continually higher on the Eros ladder, until they at last reach the level of the Seraphim and themselves become angels in the highest sense of the word.[6] The means to attain this is *prayer* ("gradus" 28), which is in essence the perfect ἕνωσις of man with God.[7] But it is faith that gives

---

[1] *Ibid.*

[2] κάθαρσις δὲ μᾶλλον καὶ ἀγάπης τῆς εἰς θεὸν προσκοπή. *Ibid.*

[3] ὅτι μὲν ἅπαντα τὰ κατὰ θεὸν ἡμῶν δάκρυα ὠφέλημα, ὁ ἀντιλέγων οὐδείς. *Ibid.*

[4] μείζων τοῦ βαπτίσματος μετὰ τὸ βάπτισμα τῶν δακρύων πηγὴ καθέστηκεν . . . τὰ δὲ [δάκρυα] τῆς παναγίας ἀγάπης, τὴν ἱκεσίαν προσδεχθεῖσαν ἡμῖν ἐμφανίζουσιν. *Ibid.*

[5] ἡσυχαστής ἐστι τύπος ἀγγέλου ἐπίγειος. Gradus XXVII.

[6] οὔποτε παύσονται τῇ ἀγάπῃ προκόπτοντες ἐκεῖνοι· οὐδὲ οὗτοι καθημέραν ἐκείνοις ἀμιλλώμενοι. οὐκ ἄγνωστος παρ' ἐκείνοις τῆς προκοπῆς ὁ πλοῦτος, οὐδὲ τούτοις τῆς ἀναβάσεως ὁ ἔρως. *Ibid.*

[7] προσευχή ἐστι κατὰ μὲν τὴν αὐτῆς ποιότητα συνουσία καὶ ἕνωσις ἀνθρώπου καὶ θεοῦ. Gradus XXVIII.

wings to prayer; without faith no one can fly up to heaven.[1]

At the 29th rung the hesychast may be said to have reached the stage of heavenly perfection.[2] He is free from all passions and possesses the divine *apathy*, which comprises in itself all virtues. Even if he still lives in the flesh, yet through apathy he has crossed the border into the other world and lives a heavenly life. He has God's essence dwelling in him,[3] for God is ἀπάθεια.[4] To possess this ἀπάθεια is to carry heaven in one's heart.[5] John Climacus can therefore—though he senses the boldness of the expression—speak of a " heaven on earth "[6] to which the hesychast has worked his way up.

There can be no doubt as to the motif under which this "Ladder of Paradise" must be placed. The gist of it all is the elevation of the human to the Divine; it is the usual Eros ladder of Hellenistic piety, the ladder of virtue and the mystical ascent. The goal reached by this ladder is the usual goal of Eros piety, ἡσυχία and ἀπάθεια, the soul's rest and exaltation above all passions. In apathy the hesychast has taken the " leap over the wall " and landed in the heavenly world, " in the bride-chamber of the royal palace."[7] He has arrived at the longed-for goal.

But there is still one stage left. Above the 29th rung with its apathy stands the 30th, where all centres round *Agape*.[8] One cannot help asking: what is the reason for the addition

---

[1] πίστις προσευχὴν ἐπτέρωσε· χωρὶς γὰρ ταύτης εἰς οὐρανὸν πετασθῆναι οὐ δύναται. *Ibid.*

[2] αὕτη οὖν ἡ τελεία τῶν τελείων ἀτέλεστος τελειότης. . . . Gradus XXIX.

[3] ὁ τοιαύτης καταστάσεως ἠξιωμένος, ἔτι ὢν ἐν σαρκί, αὐτὸν τὸν ἐνοικοῦντα. . . . *Ibid.*

[4] σχολάσατε καὶ γνῶτε, ὅτι ἐγώ εἰμι ὁ θεὸς καὶ ἡ ἀπάθεια. *Ibid.*

[5] οὐδὲν γὰρ ἕτερόν τι ἔγωγε ἀπάθειαν ὑπείληφα εἶναι ἀλλ᾽ ἢ ἐγκάρδιον νοὸς οὐρανόν. *Ibid.*

[6] . . . περὶ τοῦ ἐπιγείου οὐρανοῦ ἐκ θρασύτητος φιλοσοφεῖν ἀρχόμεθα. *Ibid.*

[7] δράμωμεν, ἀδελφοί, τῆς ἐν τῷ νυμφῶνι τοῦ παλατίου εἰσόδου τυχεῖν . . . ἐν τῷ θεῷ μου ὑπερβήσομαι τεῖχος. *Ibid.*

[8] Gradus XXX.

of this last step? The goal was already reached; the hesychast had come to the point on the heavenly ladder where he could make the transition to the heavenly existence. Why then this new stage? The answer is simple enough. At the top of Jacob's Ladder stands God Himself, of whom primitive Christian tradition says " God is Agape " (1 Jn. iv. 8, 16). If a man is to come to full fellowship and ἕνωσις with Him, he too must become Agape, and this happens at the topmost step. The hesychast is said to be an angel on earth, but " the status of angels is Agape."[1] The result of this is the peculiar idea that *at the top of the Eros ladder Agape is enthroned*. But naturally this is not primitive Christian Agape, as John Climacus' own definition of it shows. Agape is by nature " godlikeness," and its chief effect on the soul is to produce a certain " inebriation of the soul."[2] Now this already points in the direction of Eros, and shows that John Climacus does not know Agape in the primitive Christian sense, but has simply taken over the word from Christian tradition. And he himself is aware that the 30th Agape stage really adds nothing new to what is already given at the 29th. " Agape " and " apathy " are merely different names for the same thing.[3] When the hesychast has reached the stage of apathy he has really reached his destination. It should be added that even at the top step John Climacus uses the words Agape and Eros indifferently as if synonymous. But it is interesting that Agape is the chief name for the highest stage and the formal conclusion of the ladder. It is clear that Pseudo-Dionysius' efforts to extirpate the word " Agape " had entirely failed.

[1] ἀγάπη ἀγγέλων στάσις. *Ibid.*
[2] ἀγάπη κατὰ μὲν ποιότητα ὁμοίωσις Θεοῦ, καθ' ὅσον βροτοῖς ἐφικτόν. κατὰ δὲ ἐνέργειαν μέθη ψυχῆς. *Ibid.*
[3] ἀγάπη, καὶ ἀπάθεια, καὶ υἱοθεσία, τοῖς ὀνόμασι, καὶ μόνοις διακέκριται. ὡς φῶς, καὶ πῦρ, καὶ φλὸξ εἰς μίαν συντρέχουσιν ἐνέργειαν, οὕτω καὶ περὶ τούτων νόει. *Ibid.*

2. The Hierarchical-sacramental and the Practical-ascetical Heavenly Ladders

A comparison of Pseudo-Dionysius and John Climacus shows that although the idea of the ladder dominates both their views of Christianity, yet they stand on very different ground. In Pseudo-Dionysius the ascent is hierarchical-sacramental, in John Climacus and in monasticism generally it is practical-ascetical. The distinction is made very clear by the place assigned to monks and hermits in the two theories. Dionysius ranks them very low, next above the simple Christians but *below* the ecclesiastical office; here it is the bishop-hierarch who forms the link between heaven and earth, who brings the divine forces down to the lower world, and who in his own person raises this to heavenly perfection. In John Climacus, on the other hand, the hermit-hesychast occupies the highest place. He is an "angel on earth." Dionysius is chiefly interested in the objective hierarchical ladder which connects us with the higher world, and with the sacramental forces which make our ascent possible; John Climacus lays all stress on the moralistic-ascetic ascent.[1]

At first these two points of view exist side by side, sometimes with a certain tension,[2] but gradually they converge and coalesce. The one who did most to effect this was Maximus Confessor (d. 662), who was both a representative of monastic piety and a keen follower of Pseudo-Dionysius. As regards his relation to the latter, there are two things to note. First, it was largely on the authority of Maximus Confessor

[1] These two aspects might be described as a repetition, on Christian ground and in new circumstances, of the old difference between Plato's psychological-pedagogical idea of the ladder and the more cosmological idea of Aristotle and Neoplatonism : cf. on this, *supra*, pp. 174, 185, 196.

[2] Cf., e.g., Johannes Climacus: Scala paradisi, Gradus VII.: οὐχ ἁρμόζει πενθοῦσι θεολογία. διαλύειν γὰρ αὐτῶν τὸ πένθος πέφυκεν. ὁ μὲν γὰρ τῷ ἐπὶ θρόνου καθημένῳ διδασκαλικῷ ἔοικεν.

that the Dionysian writings came to be accepted in the Church.[1] They had at first been suspect in orthodox ecclesiastical quarters, and it was most important that a man like him, with an established reputation for orthodoxy, held them to be genuine and devoted himself to writing commentaries on them.   But, secondly, it is Maximus Confessor who furnishes the best proof that Dionysius had failed in his attempt to eradicate the word Agape from the Christian vocabulary.   No further evidence is needed than the title of one of Maximus' works: " Four Hundred Chapters about Agape " (κεφάλαια περὶ ἀγάπης).[2]

The above-mentioned double influence is also plain to see in Maximus' view of love.

From " the most holy and, in truth, divine interpreter Dionysius the Areopagite "[3] he has learnt that Eros and Agape are simply different names for one and the same reality and that the word Eros is " more divine " than Agape.[4]   Following him he asserts that it is as right to say that " God is Eros " as that " God is Agape,"[5] and he has no hesitation in calling God ἐπιθυμία.[6]   In general, he employs ἀγάπη, ἔρως, ἀπάθεια and ἐπιθυμία without distinction.[7]

---

[1] In the Prologus in opera Sancti Dionysii, Migne, PG, vol. iv., pp. 16 ff., Maximus answers objections to the genuineness of these works.   One of the most striking objections, as was mentioned above (p. 591, n. 1), is that he quotes Ignatius: " My Eros has been crucified."   But Maximus thinks he can explain even this satisfactorily; cf. Maximi in librum De divinis nominibus scholia, cap. iv., § xii.; PG, vol. iv., p. 264 C, D.

[2] Capita de caritate; PG, vol. xc.

[3] Mystagogia, introduction; PG, vol. xci.

[4] ὅτι ἡ ἀγάπη ἔρωτα δηλοῖ, καὶ ὅτι θειότερον ὄνομα τοῦ ἔρωτος.   Scholia in lib. De divinis nominibus, cap. iv., § xii.   ὅτι τὸ αὐτὸ δύναται ἀγάπη καὶ ἔρως.   Ibid.

[5] εἰ γὰρ ὁ ἔρως αὐτός ἐστιν ἡ ἀγάπη, ὡς προείρηται, γέγραπται δὲ, ὅτι θεὸς ἀγάπη ἐστί, δῆλον ὅτι πάντων ἐνοποιὸς ἔρως ἤτοι ἀγάπη ὁ θεός ἐστιν.   Ibid., cap. iv., § xv.

[6] ὁ θεὸς ἀγάπη ἐστί, καὶ ἐν τῷ ᾄσματι ὁμοίως ἀγάπη εἴρηται· καὶ πάλιν γλυκασμὸς καὶ ἐπιθυμία, ὅ ἐστιν ἔρως.   Ibid., cap. iv., § xiv.

[7] Capita de caritate, Centuria i. 2.   Cf. Centuria ii. 48.   Further, Eros and Agape are directly coupled: ὁ ἔρως τῆς ἀγάπης, Centuria i. 10.   ὁ ἀγαπητικὸς ἔρως, Schol. in lib. De div. nom., cap. iv., § xiv.

The influence of monastic piety is plain also in Maximus'
moralistic-ascetic interpretation of the idea of Agape, as
found in his brief but extraordinarily important work "Liber
asceticus."[1] Of particular interest for our purpose is the
way in which the *Incarnation* and *love* are here linked.
The starting-point is given by the question "Cur Deus
homo?"[2] Maximus answers this question by pointing to
love. The Incarnation is a means in the service of Agape.
But, be it observed, the love meant here is not the love God
shows to us, but the love He demands of us. The Incarnation is not primarily the manifestation of God's love, but
the necessary means for us to be able. to practise love as
the highest exercise of virtue. The stress falls entirely on
love regarded as *commandment.* To fulfil the double
Commandment of Love, it is necessary first to free oneself
from pleasure in earthly things and direct one's desire
towards the Divine;[3] furthermore, this lies within the bounds
of our possibilities. Secondly, a love to neighbour is required which extends even to enemies, to those who hate
and injure us. This is beyond the bounds of natural human
possibility. For even if man resolved to renounce everything in the world, it is still impossible for him to love his
adversaries unless he first understands "the Lord's intention."[4] Here the Incarnation comes to our aid. Christ, who·
by nature was God but by reason of His love became man,[5]
knew "the Lord's intention" and knew how the devil had
got men into his power by drawing them away from love
to God and neighbour. The purpose of Christ's Incarnation
was to deliver us from the power of the devil and to "lift

---

[1] Liber asceticus (λόγος ἀσκητικός); PG, vol. xc.
[2] τίς ὁ σκοπὸς ἦν τῆς τοῦ κυρίου ἐνανθρωπήσεως; Liber asceticus 1.
[3] *Ibid.*, 6.
[4] ἀδύνατόν τινα ἀγαπῆσαι τὸν θλίβοντα . . . ἐὰν μὴ τὸν σκοπὸν τοῦ
κυρίου ἐν ἀληθείᾳ γινώσκῃ. *Ibid.*, 9.
[5] Following the Origenist tradition (*cf. supra*, p. 158, n. 1, and p. 212, n. 1)
he uses not ἀγάπη but φιλανθρωπία of Christ's love. *Ibid.*, 10.

the ancient curse of Adam '"[1] by a complete performance of
love to God and neighbour. To make Christ fall, the devil
let loose all his temptations against Him. The first was in
the wilderness, where he tempted Him to prefer earthly
things before love to God.[2] Failing in this, he tried another
attack and tempted Christ to transgress the commandment
of love to neighbour. To this end he incited the Pharisees
and scribes against Him. But Christ, seeing through the
enemy's wiles and knowing what was at stake if He yielded,
would not be seduced into hatred of them. "What a wondrous war! Instead of hate He showed love, and through
goodness defeated the father of evil. Therefore He endured
so much evil at their hands, or rather, for their sake, and
fought as a man unto death for the Commandment of
Love."[3] But the same fight must be fought ever anew,
first by the apostles, now by us. The assaults of the demons
upon us always aim at making us in one way or another
break the Commandment of Love.[4] When we know this
and have realised what the struggle means, when through
Christ we have learned "the Lord's intention" and have
our pattern in Him, then we ought to exert our will to the
utmost to perform that complete love to God and neighbour
which makes us, too, beloved of God.[5] What was before
impossible for us, then becomes possible. So the Lord has
put our salvation into our own hands. Everything depends
on ourselves. "Our salvation rests now in our will."[6]

It could not have been said more clearly than in this last
sentence, that in spite of his talk of Agape, Maximus' whole
thought is shaped by the heavenly ladder of ascetical self-

---

[1] Ibid.

[2] . . . εἴ πως δυνηθῇ καὶ αὐτὸν ποιῆσαι τὴν τοῦ κόσμου προτιμῆσαι
ὕλην τῆς εἰς θεὸν ἀγάπης. Ibid.

[3] ὢ παραδόξου πολέμου ! Ibid., 12.

[4] ἐὰν οὖν καὶ σύ, ἀδελφέ, τοῦτον κρατήσῃς τὸν σκοπόν, δύνασαι καὶ σὺ
τοὺς μισοῦντας ἀγαπᾶν· εἰ δὲ μή γε, ἄλλως ἀμήχανον. Ibid., 15.

[5] Ibid., 15, 30, 42.

[6] ἐν τῷ θελήματι ἡμῶν ἐστι λοιπὸν ἡ σωτηρία ἡμῶν. Ibid., 42.

salvation. The reason why Christ became man is ultimately that we might become gods.[1] We are to ascend to the Divine apathy, which is unmoved by the world's seductions and is not disconcerted by the hostility of men, but preserves its composure and behaves alike towards all, both friends and enemies.[2] In spite of all external analogies, this view has nothing in common with the Christian Agape motif. Salvation does not here consist in God's merciful and forgiving love which condescends to us, but in the love and apathy practised by us, in virtue of which we ascend to God. Maximus Confessor expressly warns us against putting any trust in a supposed forgiveness of sins which is not grounded on the virtue of apathy. " May we not cherish such thoughts as minimise our sins and preach forgiveness for them. . . . The fruit of repentance is the apathy of the soul, and it is apathy that wipes out sin."[3]

3. The Cycle of Nature

For more than three hundred years the influence of Pseudo Dionysius was largely confined to the Greek world. From the beginning of the ninth century there was increased interest in the Dionysian writings, for which Maximus Confessor's commentaries were of some importance. For Western Christianity an extraordinarily important event was the gift of a copy of the Greek text of Dionysius' writings to Lewis the Pious by the Byzantine Emperor Michael II. in 827. A few years later the Latin translation of these opened the way for the victorious march of Pseudo-Dionysius through

---

[1] γενώμεθα θεοὶ δι' αὐτόν· διὰ γὰρ τοῦτο ἄνθρωπος γέγονε, φύσει ὢν θεὸς καὶ δεσπότης. *Ibid.*, 43.

[2] . . . πάντα ἄνθρωπον ἐξ ἴσου ἀγαπῆσαι. Capita de caritate, Cent. ii. 10. ὁ τέλειος ἐν ἀγάπῃ, καὶ εἰς ἄκρον ἀπαθείας ἐλθών, οὐκ ἐπίσταται διαφοράν . . . πάντας ἐξ ἴσου θεωρεῖ, καὶ πρὸς πάντας ἴσως διάκειται. *Ibid.*, Cent. ii. 30.

[3] ἀπάθεια δὲ ἐξάλειψις ἁμαρτίας. Liber asceticus, 44.

the West.[1] The one who did most to introduce Dionysius' opinions to the West, however, was Johannes Scotus Erigena. He made a new translation and commentary on Dionysius' writings, and in his own works, especially in the great *De divisione naturæ*,[2] put forward a view that is akin to Dionysius' thought.

Erigena begins this work by stating the famous principle that dominates the whole of it, the principle of the four forms of nature—(1) the nature that creates and is not created, (2) that which is created and creates, (3) that which is created and does not create, (4) that which does not create and is not created.[3] But this simply puts in a new guise the idea, familiar from Proclus and Dionysius, of the outflow of everything from God and its return to Him.[4] The first and last natures are nothing other than God Himself; as the source of all things He is the nature that creates and is not created, and as the goal of all things He is the nature that does not create and is not created. The other two natures are the universe that proceeds from Him and returns to Him. " Just as the whole river originally proceeds from the spring, and just as the water that rose up in the spring is always and without interruption poured out through its river-bed, how-

---

[1] An earlier and generally accepted view was that Johannes Scotus Erigena made the first translation into Latin towards 860. Rather more than ten years ago, however, G. Théry found a Latin translation which is a couple of decades older, made by the Abbot Hilduin of Saint-Denis. Later, the works of Dionysius were repeatedly translated into Latin during the Middle Ages. Specially important was Johannes Sarracenus' translàtion, since Albertus Magnus and Thomas Aquinas took its text as the basis for their commentaries on Dionysius. A survey of recent research in this field is found in M. Grabmann's *Die mittelalterlichen lateinischen Übersetzungen der Schriften des Pseudo-Dionysius Areopagita* (M. Grabmann: *Mittelalterliches Geistesleben*, Bd. I., 1926, pp. 449-468).

[2] Migne, PL, vol. 122. Of more recent literature on Erigena we may mention H. Dörries: *Zur Geschichte der Mystik. Erigena und der Neuplatonismus*, 1925. H. Bett: *Johannes Scotus Erigena*, 1925; P. Kletler: *Johannes Eriugena*, 1931.

[3] De divisione naturæ, lib. I. 1. *Cf.* lib. II. 1.

[4] " Quoniam vero ad eandem causam omnia, quæ ab ea procedunt, dum ad finem pervenient, reversura sunt, propterea finis omnium dicitur, et neque creare neque creari perhibetur." Lib. II. 2.

ever far it may extend, so also the divine goodness and the divine substance and life and wisdom and all that is in the source of all things, flows out first to the primal causes ('causæ primordiales') and bestows existence upon them; thereafter it streams through them in an ineffable manner down to their effects through the different stages of the universe, and it always flows through the higher to the lower, in order to turn back again finally to its source by a hidden way through the most secret pores of nature."[1]

In this cycle of nature, *man* occupies an important place. In a way that anticipates the Renascence conception, Erigena takes up the old idea of man as a microcosm. Man alone comprises in himself that which is found at all stages of existence. He possesses "intellectus" like angels, "ratio" like men, senses like animals, life like plants, and a material body like material things. Nothing in nature is alien to him. But his return to God, therefore, is equally the return of all things to the primal divine source.[2] Just as the entire sensible world has a tendency to return to its origin,[3] so in man, too, God has planted an ineradicable desire for blessedness, which drives man by a natural necessity to seek his highest good in his origin.[4] Erigena therefore says that every rational being, even in his perversity and sin, is really seeking God.[5] Even in

[1] Lib. III. 4.

[2] " Humana siquidem natura in universitate totius conditæ naturæ tota est, quoniam in ipsa omnis creatura constituta est, et in ipsa copulata est, et in ipsum reversura, et per ipsum salvanda. . . . Ibi intellectus, ibi ratio, ibi sensus, ibi seminalis vita, ibi corpus." Lib. IV. 5. " Ac per hoc non immerito dicitur homo creaturarum omnium officina, quoniam in ipso universalis creatura continetur. Intelligit quidem ut angelus, ratiocinatur ut homo, sentit ut animal irrationale, vivit ut germen, corpore animaque subsistit, nullius creaturæ expers. Extra hæc enim nullam creaturam invenis." Lib. III. 37.

[3] " Et non solum de partibus sensibilis mundi, verum etiam de ipso toto id ipsum intelligendum est. Finis enim ipsius principium suum est, quod appetit." Lib. V. 3.

[4] " Nihil aliud appetit, nisi summum bonum, a quo veluti principio incipit moveri, et ad quod veluti finem motum suum accelerat." Lib. V. 26.

[5] " Tota siquidem rationalis creatura, quæ propriæ in hominibus intelligitur subsistere, etiam in delictis suis perversisque anfractibus Deum suum, a quo est, et ad quem contemplandum condita est, semper quærit." *Ibid.*

fallen man the desire for blessedness survives, and this desire guides him aright—that is, to return to God.

Erigena develops his *doctrine of love* in connection with the question of God's immobility and immutability, and in very close dependence on Pseudo-Dionysius' view of love. As God is exalted above all motion and change, it is impossible, strictly speaking, to say that He either loves or is loved, since the former would imply activity on His part, the latter His subjection to external influence.[1] Nevertheless, according to Erigena, it is equally right to say that God both loves and is loved and that He actually is Himself *love* (Eros); but this means no more than that He is the *cause* of all love.[2] To say that "God is love," merely means that He is the principle of the "cycle of nature"; He is the nature from which all streams forth and to which all returns. But in God there can be no love in the sense of a movement of love. Himself unmoved, He sets all things in motion towards Himself solely by His beauty. Erigena illustrates this by two illuminating similes, of the magnet and of the light. Just as the magnet by its indwelling force attracts the piece of iron and sets it in motion towards itself without being itself in any way involved in the movement, and without being affected by the iron, so also the Deity as the cause of all things sets the whole universe in motion towards Himself; but what causes this motion in the universe is not a movement in God, but simply the magnetic attraction of the Divine beauty alone.[3] The same thing is illustrated by the

---

[1] "Vellem tamen apertius mihi suadeas, ut clare videam, dum audio Deum amare vel amari, nil aliud nisi ipsius naturam sine ullo motu amantis vel amati intelligam." Lib. I. 74. "Num ineptum incongruumque est, si quis putaverit, agere vel pati ipsi naturæ accidere, quæ in seipsa nullum motum ad agendum, nullum habile ad patiendum percipit ?" Lib. II. 28.

[2] "Merito ergo amor [ἔρως] Deus dicitur, quia omnis amoris causa est, et per omnia diffunditur, et in unum colligit omnia, et ad seipsum ineffabili regressu revolvitur, totiusque creaturæ amatorios motus in seipso terminat." *Ibid.*

[3] "Sicut ergo lapis ille, qui dicitur magnes, quamvis naturali sua virtute ferrum sibimet propinquans ad se attrahat, nullo modo tamen, ut hoc faciat,

simile of the light. This is itself immovable, yet it sets the eyes of all living creatures in motion and draws them to itself. Hence comes the illusion that the light itself is in motion, whereas all that really moves is the "rays of the eyes."[1] It is essentially the same idea as we find in the Aristotelian κινεῖ ὡς ἐρώμενον.

Love is the bond that holds together all things that exist,[2] and its inmost meaning is to draw all things back to God through the cycle of nature. The fundamental form of all love is the Divine *self-love*. Wherever we meet anything that can be called love, it is ultimately a question of that love with which God loves Himself.[3] Whether he who loves knows it or not, his love is but a moment in the all-embracing Divine self-love.[4] From this it is not difficult to see why Erigena had to assert that we both can and cannot say that God loves. *We can say it in the sense of Aristotelian and Neoplatonic Eros; we cannot say it in the sense of Christian Agape.* If only we may interpret love in accord with the idea of κινεῖ ὡς ἐρώμενον, there is no difficulty whatever; for then God's love, or the fact that He loves and is loved, merely means that He draws all love to Himself.[5] " He loves to be loved,"

---

se ipsum movet, aut a ferro aliquid patitur, quod ad se attrahit: ita rerum omnium causa omnia, quæ ex se sunt, ad seipsam reducit, sine ullo sui motu, sed sola suæ pulchritudinis virtute." Lib. I. 75. " Ipse enim solus vere amabilis est, quia solus summa ac vera bonitas et pulchritudo est." Lib. I. 74.

[1] Lib. I. 75.

[2] " Amor est connexio ac vinculum, quo omnium rerum universitas ineffabili amicitia insolubilique unitate copulatur. Potest et sic definiri: Amor est naturalis motus omnium rerum, quæ in motu sunt, finis quietaque statio, ultra quam nullus creaturæ progreditur motus." Lib. I. 74.

[3] " Et ad se omnia attrahit: moveri quoque dicitur, quoniam seipsam ad seipsam movet, ac per hoc seipsam movet, ac veluti a seipsa movetur. Deus itaque per seipsum amor est." Lib. I. 75.

[4] " Pati dicitur, quia vult ab omnibus amari, et seipsam amat in omnibus. Ipsa enim est substantialis et verus amor, et plusquam substantialis amor; et eum amant, quæcunque amant, sive sciant quia amant, sive nesciant." Lib. II. 28.

[5] " . . . quia eum omnia appetunt, ipsiusque pulchritudo omnia ad se attrahit." Lib. I. 74.

says Erigena.[1] And when we love God, it is not really we who love Him, but He who in and through us loves Himself.[2] The result is much the same as in Plotinus: God is Eros, but Eros to Himself.[3] In this sense Erigena has no hesitation in speaking of God's love. What he must avoid at all costs, however, is to permit God's love to mean a real love in the Christian sense, a descending and self-giving love. Such an idea is incompatible with Erigena's metaphysical system. For in this, self-love has the last word; it is anchored in the Holy Trinity itself. "If then the Holy Trinity loves itself in us and in itself, it is assuredly loved by itself in a glorious manner unknown to all created beings."[4] Thus the whole cosmic process becomes a link in that self-love in which the Divine being revolves within itself from eternity to eternity— an idea that Erigena took over from Pseudo-Dionysius. Erigena's importance for posterity, however, lay less in his own positive teaching than in the fact that his translations of Pseudo-Dionysius made the latter's works known to the Middle Ages.

[1] Lib. I. 75, with reference to a saying of Maximus Confessor. *Cf.* Lib. II. 28: ". . . quia vult ab omnibus amari, et seipsam amat in omnibus."

[2] "Non vos estis, qui amatis. . . . Ipse amat . . . seipsum in vobis." Lib. I. 76. "Amat igitur seipsum et amatur a seipso, in nobis et in seipso." Lib. I. 75.

[3] *Cf. supra*, pp. 197 ff.   [4] Lib. I. 76.

CHAPTER FOUR

THE MEDIÆVAL DOCTRINE OF LOVE

I

INTRODUCTORY

IT has long been customary to speak rather slightingly of the Middle Ages and their intellectual work; they have stood for barren scholasticism and dull theories that have nothing to do with vital spiritual life. This contempt seems partly due to the fact that in Evangelical quarters the Middle Ages have been measured by the Reformation instead of judged on their own ground. But probably a more cogent reason is the negative valuation of Mediæval scholasticism by the Renascence. This is the view that has largely prevailed and moulded general historical opinion about the Middle Ages. Intensive modern research, however, has led to quite a different estimate of the spiritual contribution of the Middle Ages.[1] Mediæval thinkers, in fact, did a great work and one of the utmost importance for the succeeding period. Not least, the Renascence itself, even if it will not acknowledge it, owes a very great debt of gratitude to the Middle Ages.

In stating the Mediæval doctrine of love, we encounter a difficulty at the outset, inasmuch as Mediæval Christianity as a whole is Caritas-religion and Caritas-ethics. Caritas is not simply one element in Christianity, according to Mediæval ideas, but the whole of it; in principle there is nothing that falls outside the sphere of Caritas. To give a faithful picture

---

[1] See especially *Beiträge zur Geschichte der Philosophie des Mittelalters. Texte und Untersuchungen.* In Verbindung mit G. von Hertling, F. Ehrle, M. Baumgartner und M. Grabmann hrsg. von Cl. Baeumker.

of the Mediæval doctrine of love, it would strictly be necessary to give an exhaustive account of mediæval religious and ethical thought—but this would take us beyond the range of our present study. We must confine ourselves to a very general outline of the Mediæval view of love; but the reason for this is not merely the necessity of limiting our material, and still less is it because the work of Mediæval theology in this sphere is too scanty to repay more detailed study. The decisive reason is that a more detailed account would tend to obscure the significant contribution of the Middle Ages to the history of the Christian idea of love. This contribution is quite apart from the divergences of opinion and keen rivalries that exist between the various Mediæval schools. These differences have been allowed to determine the historical picture of the Middle Ages far too much; for although they were vital enough to the rival parties, yet when seen in a larger perspective they are mere ripples on the surface, beneath which Mediæval spiritual life displays wide uniformity.

Accounts of the theology of the Middle Ages have often been given on the basis of such distinctions as these: Scholasticism and Mysticism, Platonism and Aristotelianism, Realism and Nominalism, Franciscan and Thomistic thought, and so on. But it is plain from what has been said, that these and similar traditional points of view must not dominate our study. As regards the idea that scholasticism and mysticism are contrary spiritual movements, this, like so many other wrong ideas about the Middle Ages, comes from the Renascence. The Renascence regarded scholasticism as its real enemy, in which it saw only an empty dogmatism out of touch with life, whilst it readily accepted mysticism as a free and direct expression of the religious life itself. This view is clearly untenable, however, since many of the foremost scholastics occupy a prominent place in mysticism, as names like Albertus Magnus, Thomas Aquinas and Bona-

ventura remind us.[1] And furthermore, it is exactly the same
fundamental motif that finds expression in both scholasticism
and mysticism. Something similar is also true of the contrast
between Platonism and Aristotelianism in Mediæval thought.
From the point of view of method the distinction may be
important, but if we turn our attention to the basic religious
and ethical motif, we find again that it is in both cases the
same. Of all the distinctions mentioned it can be said that
although they may give expression to a tension, perhaps even
an opposition, yet it is always an opposition on a common
basis, and the most important thing is not what divides but
what is held in common. It is this common ground—which
creates no stir in the Mediæval controversies since it is the
self-evident presupposition of all schools—that we must
attempt to discover and bring to the fore.

The Middle Ages are the age of tradition. Theological
interest is not so much concentrated on individual contributions, but everything is reduced to a great system in which
individual views form subordinate elements. This fact, too,
will influence our presentation. So far we have traced the
history of the Christian idea of love through the theories of
its chief representatives; but to apply this method to the
Middle Ages would only lead to endless repetition, and
would obscure the real contribution of Mediæval theology.
We shall deal, therefore, not with personal contributions, but
with the *problems* involved. The materials with which the
Middle Ages had to work were mainly given already in
tradition, especially in Augustine and Dionysius the Areopagite; but it is interesting to see how they deal with these
materials, how they detect the inherent difficulties and labour
to overcome them. At certain points the Middle Ages also

---

[1] M. Grabmann: *Die Geschichte der scholastischen Methode*, Bd. II., 1911,
pp. 94 f.: " The idea that scholasticism and mysticism denote opposites has
been exposed as a scientific myth by Denifle's epoch-making study of the
sources."

made a contribution of their own, almost entirely independent of earlier tradition, to the Christian doctrine of love.

Accordingly, we may focus our enquiry upon the following three main questions: (1) The general character of the Mediæval interpretation of Christianity, (2) the development of the Caritas doctrine, and (3) the original contribution of the Middle Ages to the doctrine of love.

II

THE MEDIÆVAL INTERPRETATION OF
CHRISTIANITY

1. Cosmology and the Upward Tendency

THE religious cosmology of the Middle Ages displays a
grand uniformity. It is dominated by a simple pictorial
scheme, the Alexandrian world-scheme, by the idea of the
ladder, and by the upward tendency. To what an extent
the Alexandrian world-scheme moulded the whole is
perhaps most clearly shown by the fact that it was this
scheme with its motion in two directions—the procession
of everything from God (πρόοδος) and its return to Him
(ἐπιστροφή)—which Thomas Aquinas followed in constructing his *Summa Theologiæ*. The Alexandrian world-scheme,
however, was determinative not only for scholasticism, but
at least equally for mysticism. Any of the great Mediæval
mystics would furnish proof of this, and here is one
example. When Henry Suso, in the last chapter of his
autobiography (*Seuses Leben*), wishes to give a brief summary of its contents and so of his mystical views in general,[1]
he centres it all upon the question of how the spirit streams
out from the Divine being and streams back again to it.
What is more, he appends a drawing to illustrate his argument, which is entirely dominated by the idea of the κύκλος
and the scheme of μονή, πρόοδος, ἐπιστροφή.

MEDIÆVAL CHRISTIANITY AS ILLUSTRATED BY HENRY SUSO.

Since this drawing illustrates remarkably well, not only the outlook of
Suso or Mediæval mysticism, but the whole conception of Christianity
characteristic of the Middle Ages, it is reproduced here. It is found

[1] The chapter in question (*Seuses Leben*, cap. liii.) bears the title " Diss
buches meinunge ein beschliessen mit kurzen einvaltigen worten." *Heinrich
Seuse, Deutsche Schriften*, hrsg. von K. Bihlmeyer, 1907, p. 190, 22.

facing p. 616. The following explanation will serve as a commentary on it.

The process begins in the top left-hand corner, where the " fathomless abyss " of the eternal Divine substance is shown as three concentric circles or "rings," with the explanatory comment: "*Diz ist der ewigen gotheit wisloses abgruende, daz weder anvang hat noch kein ende.*" Out of this proceed (top right-hand corner) the three Persons of the Godhead, the Holy Spirit coming between the Father and the Son as the bond of love that unites them—the Trinity of the Persons in essential Unity: "*Diz ist der personen driheit in wesenlicher einikeit, von dem cristanr gelob seit.*" Immediately beneath the Trinity is the figure of an angel, representing the first stage of the outflow of the Divine to the creature, the "outflow of angelic nature": "*Disú figur ist der ussfluzz engelschlicher natur.*" Beside the angel is a falling demon, to symbolise the Fall in the angelic world. The next stage of the Divine outflow is human nature, "fashioned after the Godhead": "*Diz ist menschlichú geschaffenheit gebildet nach der gotheit.*" Here, however, comes a parting of the ways. *Some* men turn their love to the world and its lusts, and this, the love of the world that ends in misery, is symbolised (bottom right-hand corner) by a dancing pair: "*Diz ist der welt minne, dú nimt mit jamer ein ende*"; and as a reminder of this, the Old Reaper (Death) is glimpsed in the background: "*Diz ist der tot.*" *Other* men, however, remembering the brevity and impermanence of life, turn to God, and by the way of purification, illumination and union reach perfection. This turning from the world to God is depicted (bottom centre) by a kneeling nun, who seeks God because this life is short: "*Minen ker vil ich zu got nemen, wan diz ist gar ein kurtzes leben.*" The pictures next on the left illustrate the way of the soul upwards. The great figure pierced by swords and arrows and surrounded by serpents and scorpions, who holds a crucifix in his right hand, shows how a man must die and be crucified with Christ: "*Ach lug, wie ich muz sterben und mit Cristus gecrutzget werden!*" Next, man is brought to "resignation," symbolised by a woman sitting collapsed in a chair with her eyes closed: "*Gelassenheit mich berovben vill, va min* [= *des Meinigen*] *ie waz ze vill.*" The figure above the crucifix represents contemplation: "*Die sinne sint mir entwúrcket, die hohen kreft sint úberwúrcket.*" But there still remains the highest stage, the mystical union of the soul with God. The uppermost figure shows how it begins as the human spirit raises itself with Divine aid and enters into the Son: "*Hie ist der geist in geswungen und wirt in der driheit der personen funden.*" But through its union with the Son it gains also unity with the Father by the mediation of the Holy Spirit, which is the bond of love. This union with the Triune God is depicted by the line which runs from the Son (left) via the Holy Spirit (centre) to the

Father (right). This is what Suso calls (*op. cit.*, p. 193, 11) "des Geistes Überfahrt, . . . denn er ist mit minnereicher Schauung in Gott vergangen" ("The passage of the spirit, . . . for it has passed away into God with loving contemplation"). At this point we find the following inscription: "*Ich bin in got vergangen, nieman kan mich hie erlangen*" ("I have passed into God; no one can reach me here"). Here all differentiation between one's own self and God disappears, just as between the Persons in the Deity. The spirit is absorbed into the eternal Divine substance; it has no longer any independence, but is simply the dwelling in which God resides, God's tabernacle. This is illustrated by the picture of a tabernacle, which at one point (*apex mentis*) touches the ring of the Divine substance; and here all things are forgotten, for it is fathomless and unbounded: "*In dem inschlag han ich aller ding vergessen, wan es ist grundlous unt ungemessen.*" (Suso's explanation of the picture is found in *op. cit.*, pp. 190 ff. For the interpretation of the inscriptions see K. Bihlmeyer's introduction, *op. cit.*, pp. 52* ff.)

This entire train of thought is based on the Alexandrian world-scheme in the form given to it by Proclus and Pseudo-Dionysius. It is an unusually clear example of a theory dominated by the idea of the μονή, πρόοδος and ἐπιστροφή of the Divine. The beginning and end coincide in the eternal Divine substance. "Daz begin und ende sind eins worden" (*op. cit.*, p. 193, 24). But between the beginning and the end is the procession of the spirit from, and its return to, God: "des geistes usgeflossenheit und wideringeflossenheit" (*op. cit.*, p. 190, 26).

Finally, an interesting detail. As the Deity itself is indicated in the picture by a large "ring," the highest divine element in created beings is indicated by a small "ring." "Dar umbe usser dem grossen ringe, der da betütet die ewigen gotheit, flússent us nah biltlicher glichnúst kleinú ringlú, dú och bezeichen mugen den hohen adel ire vernúnftikeit" (*op. cit.*, p. 192, 3). This "ring," which, on the figures in the picture, is drawn in the region of the heart, thus indicates the inmost being of man, the noble divine part of him, the "ground of the soul," the divine spark, God's own image in man, the "high nobility of his rationality," and so on. By means of this, man is connected with the Divine, and it is here that the inflow of the divine powers takes place. The falling demon has, however, lost his "ring," which means that there is no longer any divine part in him.

The religious temper of the Middle Ages can be summarily characterised by the phrase "the upward tendency." The view of the religious life as a ceaseless ascent, with fellowship with God on God's own level as its goal, does not, of course, make its first appearance in the Middle Ages. The Middle Ages are the age of tradition: behind them is the Platonic doctrine of the Two Worlds, and the idea that the soul is attracted up to the world of Ideas; there is the Aristotelian idea of the ladder, the conception of Eros as the spiritual force of gravity, and of the power of the Divine to draw all things to itself on the principle of κινεῖ ὡς ἐρώμενον; there are also the astral notions of antiquity, Neoplatonic ideas of spheres that revolve one above the other, Augustine's mysticism with his ideas about the stages of ascent, the hierarchies of Pseudo-Dionysius and John Climacus' Ladder of Paradise. And these are but a few of the streams that now unite to form a mighty river. The result is that passionate "sursum" which gives to the Mediæval conception of Christianity its characteristic content and colour.

This found its most moving and influential expression in Dante's *Divina Commedia*. The cosmology it presents is typically Mediæval, with its idea of the ladder and the upward tendency. The whole universe in its three main parts—heaven, earth (with purgatory) and hell—is constructed in a series of terraces. In Dante's company we traverse all these stages, from the lowest hell, where the Prince of the Abyss with his three jaws eternally rends to pieces the three arch-traitors Judas Iscariot, Brutus and Cassius,[1] up to the highest heaven, where the Triune God Himself is enthroned in light inaccessible to both sense and thought.[2] The journey through hell is undertaken mainly for the sake of information about that part of existence and is not a part of the Way of salvation; the Christian Way of salvation begins with purgatory and the ascent of the mount

[1] Divina Commedia, Inferno xxxiv. 55 ff., p. 413 f. Lines and pages are cited from the edition, with translation and notes, of A. J. Butler (Macmillan, 3 vols.: *The Purgatory*, 1880; *The Paradise*, 1891; *The Hell*, 1892).
[2] Paradiso xxxiii., pp. 420 ff.

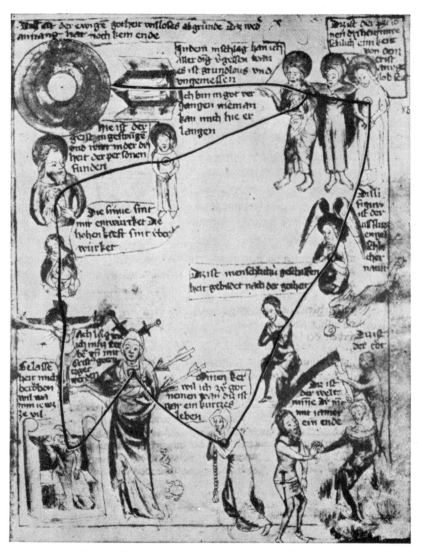

Suso : The procession and return of the Spirit.

(See pp. 613 ff.)

of purification. When, with great effort and by countless steps, the soul has mounted its seven terraces, and at each of them has been cleansed from one of the seven deadly sins,[1] it comes finally, at the top of the mountain, to the earthly paradise, from which the first men were driven out on account of their sin. But now, when the soul has passed through the purgatorial fire, sin is done away; the soul is pure and holy again[2] and ready for flight to the stars of heaven, ready to behold God in glory.[3]

What is it, then, that lifts and carries the soul in this ascent? Dante finds the explanation in the spiritual force of gravitation, the order that holds everything in the universe together, of which Proclus and Dionysius the Areopagite used to speak.[4] Everything in existence strives to return to its source. As fire by nature is drawn upwards, so the human soul is drawn to God.

> "And thither now, as to our seat
> Predestined, we are carried by the force
> Of that strong cord, that never looses dart
> But at fair aim and glad."[5]

By reason of its free will the soul, it is true, can be seduced by false pleasures and stray from the appointed path, directing its desire downwards, just as a flame can, contrary to its nature, be blown downwards accidentally by the wind. But that does not alter the fact that it is of the nature of the soul to ascend to God. It is as natural for the purified spirit to rise to the heavenly world as it is for a river to flow down from the mountain to the valley. If the soul freed from all alien impediments were to remain upon earth, it would be as strange as if fire were to rest on the ground.[6] Besides the

---

[1] Purgatorio ix. 112 ff., p. 108.

[2] Here he quotes Matt. v. 8: "Blessed are the pure in heart "; Purgatorio xxvii. 8, p. 335.

[3] Purgatorio xxxiii. 144 f., p. 421.

[4] On this and on what follows, *cf.* Paradiso i., pp. 10 ff.

[5] Paradiso i. 124 ff., p. 12. (Quoted above from Cary's translation.)

[6] Paradiso i. 136, p. 13.

influence of Proclus and Pseudo-Dionysius, we are reminded here of quite a number of ideas found in earlier tradition, such as Augustine's idea of the upward impulse of the soul fired by Caritas, or Gregory of Nyssa's idea of the ascending flame and the arrow of Eros or Agape which is fitted to the bow-string and shot towards its heavenly mark.

Arrived at the top of the mount of purification and the earthly paradise, however, Dante has covered only half his journey. He now continues his ascent, borne by the spiritual force of gravity, and makes a direct ascension into heaven. From sphere to sphere, from blessedness to blessedness he goes; and under the guidance of Beatrice he rises on the wings of the soul to the various planet spheres. In the highest of these, the heaven of Saturn, there meets his astonished gaze the shining golden Jacob's ladder, on which blessed spirits mount in the shape of a countless host of flames of light. This is the host of monks and hermits who in heavenly contemplation ascend to the throne of God.[1] He follows them[2] and comes through the heaven of the fixed stars and the crystal heaven to God's own heaven (Empyreum), where the Trinity itself is enthroned in an infinite sea of light, surrounded by the blessed. These, arranged in the form of a many-thousand-petalled rose, eternally contemplate and enjoy the Divine beauty.[3]

It is to be noticed that Dante's object was not to describe simply a subjective ecstatic experience of his own, but also to indicate what is the goal of human life in general. Our task is to turn our back on the lower existence and rise on the eagle wings of love to the heavenly world, in order

---

[1] Paradiso xxi. 28 ff., p. 276.   *Cf.* xxii. 68 ff., p. 290.

[2] Paradiso xxii. 100 f., p. 292.

[3] Dante's description of the ascent through the various heavenly spheres is linked closely with Pseudo-Dionysius and his nine angelic orders. *Cf.* Paradiso xxviii. 97-139, pp. 365 ff.; and ii. 112-123, pp. 24 f.   By adding to the seven planet spheres the heaven of the fixed stars and the crystal heaven (Primum mobile) he obtains nine heavenly spheres, each governed by its own order of angels, below the Divine heaven proper.

there to circle for ever about the Deity as the origin and ultimate goal of all things.

2. CHRISTIANITY AS CARITAS-RELIGION

The *Divina Commedia* is not only typically Mediæval in its "upward tendency," but it also represents with remarkable clarity the Mediæval conception of Christianity as *Caritas-religion*. Through the whole poem from beginning to end there runs like a golden thread the idea of God as love, "the eternal Love," "the first Love," the primal ground of Love.[1] It is *Divine love* which has created hell from all eternity,[2] which has made possible the progress and purification of souls in purgatory, which sets everything in the world in motion, and which is the goal of our desire and our enjoyment for ever in heaven. Love is the root of all virtues, and it is for lack of love we have to atone in purgatory.

But what kind of love is Dante talking about? Has it the essential traits of Eros or of Agape? The best answer is given by Dante himself, when interrogated (Paradiso xxvi.) by the apostle John as to the nature of love. It is as follows: It is of the nature of the good always to kindle love and to draw love to itself. The greater the "goodness" is, the greater the love that is awakened by it. Consequently God, who comprises in Himself all reality and all "goodness" so that every other good that exists is merely a reflection of His "goodness," must exercise a greater power of attraction than all else. In theory, human insight alone should bring us to love God, the highest and absolute Good, but in real life this love only comes into being by the help of Divine grace.

In this description of love the Augustinian Caritas-syn-

---

[1] Inferno iii. 6, p. 28; Paradiso xxxiii. 144, p. 430. *Cf.* Paradiso xxix. 18, p. 372; xxx. 52, p. 390; xxxii. 142, p. 419.

[2] Inferno iii. 6, p. 28.

thesis is easily recognised, though the Eros trait in it has been strengthened by the incorporation of the Aristotelian-Dionysian idea of love as the bond of union in the universe, and the idea of God as the ultimate principle of motion. Unquestionably, the most essential traits in this view of love are borrowed from the realm of the Eros motif; but there is also an important element of Agape present, inasmuch as love is regarded as a gift of Divine grace.[1]

After what has been said, it is hardly necessary to point out that when we call Dante's idea of love " Caritas," this Caritas is not to be identified—as has sometimes been done —with New Testament Agape. The problem involved in Mediæval Caritas theory is wholly obscured if the Caritas of Augustine and Dante is taken to be a simple interpretation of the New Testament idea of love, as H. Scholz assumes.[2] F. Heiler's judgment is sounder: " The Florentine poet, like Augustine and Aquinas, combines in his idea of God the Plotinian ἔρως with the primitive Christian ἀγάπη in a wonderful harmony, though the mystical element, it is true, predominates. In Dante, too, the apex of the theological pyramid is the sensitive and delicate mysticism of Plotinus."[3] This synthesis of Eros and Agape constitutes Dante's view of love, and that is why it can be quoted as

[1] Paradiso x. 83, p. 133. To ignore the Queen of Heaven and her grace in our attempt to ascend, says Dante, is like trying to fly without wings. Paradiso xxxiii. 13 ff., pp. 421 f.

[2] Scholz explains: " By love in the Christian sense we mean the love which we find in the Gospels. The love which *Paul* joined with faith and hope into a triple chord, in which love itself is the ground-tone. The love of which there are three classical interpreters: *Augustine, Dante, Pascal*. *Augustine's* Confessions, *Dante's* Divine Comedy, and *Pascal's* Fragments on the Nature of Christianity will, with the Gospels and *Paul*, provide the materials out of which we can construct the metaphysic of *Caritas*." H. Scholz: *Eros und Caritas*, 1929, p. 2. For the difference between the two problems " Eros and Agape " and "Eros and Caritas," see *supra*, pp. 55 f.

[3] F. Heiler: *Der Katholizismus*, 1923, p. 142. The Eros trait in Dante is still more strongly stressed by E. Wechssler: " What he here means is reproduced badly by *Liebe*, better by *Minne*, but best by *Eros*." *Vorträge der Bibliothek Warburg*, hrsg. von F. Saxl. *Vorträge*, 1921-1922, p. 90.

representative of the entire Mediæval doctrine of love. It is neither pure Agape nor pure Eros, but simply Caritas.

3. The Three Heavenly Ladders

To express its conception of what fellowship with God means and how it is attained, Mediæval theology has recourse to the ladder-symbolism that had become traditional since Augustine and Dionysius the Areopagite. For Mediæval thought it is self-evident that fellowship with God is a fellowship on God's level. If it is to be brought about, man must ascend above his present position, mount to the higher world, and in some way be conformed to that world; he must—to use the expressive word of Thomas Aquinas—become "deiformis." There are, in particular, three heavenly ladders for the soul's ascent known to the Middle Ages, and these are the same as we have already seen in Augustine.[1] We may call them: (1) The ladder of Merit; (2) the analogical ladder of Speculation; (3) the anagogical ladder of Mysticism.

1. *The Ladder of Merit—Merit and Grace.* Mediæval theology is a theology of merit. But this does not mean that it is not at the same time a theology of grace. On the contrary, it is characteristic of it that it regards as *one* these two things which, in the Evangelical view, are simply exclusive of one another.

The Way to God and eternal blessedness is that of human merit—on this, Mediæval piety and theology are entirely at one. "Man attains blessedness by a series of acts which are called merits," writes Thomas Aquinas.[2] But in saying this

---

[1] *Cf. supra,* pp. 513 ff.

[2] Summa Theologiæ, II. i., qu. v., art. vii.: "Homines autem consequuntur ipsam [beatitudinem] multis motibus operationum, qui merita dicuntur. Unde etiam, secundum Philosophum, beatitudo est præmium virtuosarum operationum." The argument is as follows: God does not need to acquire blessedness, for He possesses it in virtue of His nature; the angels acquire it by *one* meritorious

he does not intend to diminish the significance of Divine grace or to transfer the stress in the matter of salvation from God to man himself. On the contrary, he most emphatically rejects the idea that man might acquire blessedness in his own strength.[1] For Thomas, there is no contradiction between the idea of grace and the idea of merit, but each is a condition of the other. Merit is required of man, but he cannot achieve this merit unless Divine grace comes to his aid: *without grace no merit*—this is the general view of developed Mediæval theology, which in the main faithfully upheld the Augustinian principle: " when God crowns our merits, it is nothing but His own gifts that He crowns."[2] To speak of its strongly Pelagianising tendency, as Protestant historians of dogma have often done, hardly does justice to the Mediæval doctrine of grace. There is in the last resort far greater agreement between Mediæval theology and Augustine than is usually supposed. " Soli Deo gloria " and " sola gratia " are the hall-marks even of Mediæval theology. And, like Augustine, it can only speak of human merits because it sees in them effects proceeding from Divine grace, effects which cannot exist except on the basis of grace.

The basic idea in the varied and often very complicated Mediæval doctrine of grace is simple enough. All that God demands of a man can be summed up in a single command: that he shall love God with all his heart. Only action that springs from Caritas—that is, from a love entirely given to God—is well-pleasing to Him. But man, as he is by nature since the Fall, lacks this Caritas; his desire and longing are not directed to God and heavenly things, but to earthly things. When he acts on the basis of this natural disposition,

---

act, men by a number of such acts. Thomas's " Summa Theologiæ " and " Summa Contra Gentiles " are cited from the edition of Leo XIII.

[1] " Unde nec homo, nec aliqua creatura, potest consequi beatitudinem ultimam per sua naturalia." S. Th., II. i., qu. v., art. v., tom. vi., p. 51*b*. *Cf.* II. ii., qu. cxiv., art. ii., tom. vii., p. 346.

[2] *Cf. supra*, p. 514, n. 1.

therefore, nothing really worthy can result. If this is to happen, his inward man must be transformed. But such a transformation is outside the range of his own possibilities: he has no power to produce in himself this quality of love, this "habitus" of love. It can only be given to him as a gift by Divine grace. When God gives a man His Holy Spirit, the miracle happens, and God's own Caritas is shed abroad in his heart. At its deepest, grace means "the infusion of love," "infusio caritatis" or "infusio amoris." Through this act of Divine grace, man's whole existence is totally changed. "Love is the fulfilling of the law." When man has had love incorporated into his being, and Caritas has become the basic force in his life, then he is as God will have him to be. He is well-pleasing to God, and the foundation is laid for a life in accord with God's will. When he acts on the basis of this new disposition, this "habitus" of love, his works, too, become well-pleasing to God and come to be real merit ("meritum de condigno"). But it is to be noted that the works are meritorious solely because they flow from the Caritas-quality of the will, which is beyond human nature and only given by grace.[1]

Lack of space prevents us from going on to show how this fundamental thought finds different shades of expression in the different schools of Mediæval theology. What has been said, however, shows that the Mediæval doctrine of grace is simply a part of the Caritas theory taken over from Augustine, and a further development of certain tendencies in it. *The function of grace is to make possible man's ascent to God.* Without grace no merit—but when grace has been given and Caritas shed abroad in man's heart, he begins his

[1] "Quidquid est in merito, est a Deo." S. Th., I., qu. lxiii., art. v. ad 3, tom. v., p. 131. "Si autem loquamur de opere meritorio secundum quod procedit ex gratia Spiritus Sancti, sic est meritorium vitæ æternæ ex condigno. Sic enim valor meriti attenditur secundum virtutem Spiritus Sancti moventis nos in vitam æternam. . . . Attenditur etiam pretium operis secundum dignitatem gratiæ." S. Th., II. ii., qu. cxiv., art. iii., tom. vii., p. 347b.

ascent with new resources, and fellowship with God and eternal blessedness are his goal.

Two main objections have been levelled from the Protestant side against the Mediæval doctrine of grace: that it is impersonal and magical; and that it does not give grace the supreme place in the Christian life, but displaces it by other elements independent of grace. But neither of these objections touches the central point of the Mediæval conception of grace. The accusation of magic is levelled primarily at the idea of the *infusion* of grace. This idea is supposed to be the surest proof that grace is conceived impersonally and as a " thing," not personally and psychologically. But it is to be observed that the Middle Ages, like Augustine, took this idea directly from Rom. v. 5. And further, Mediæval theology took no small pains to show psychologically how the soul immersed in love of the world is seized by the aspiring Caritas-love, and how thus the psychological foundation is laid for a holy life. The alternative " magical or psychological " is altogether inapplicable to this subject. Grace in the Christian sense is nothing else but the Divine love itself; and we miss the point equally, whether we think of grace as an impersonal magical force, or as an effect in the soul, which is psychologically mediated and can be clearly understood. But no less misleading is the second objection, that grace is displaced by other and independent factors which are described as human merits. That is not what is meant by merit here. Merit is possible only on the basis of grace, and so there is no merit independent of grace. All is grace; even merit is in the last resort nothing else but grace.

The real and deep contrast between the Evangelical and the Mediæval conception of grace is as follows: the latter regards grace essentially as a means for man's ascent, whereas the former knows of no such ascent. The meaning of grace is plainly quite different according as fellowship with God is conceived in the Catholic manner as fellowship on God's level, or in the Evangelical manner as fellowship on our level. In the former case, grace is the Divine assistance man needs in order to be able to ascend to God; in the latter, it is the gracious condescension of God. In the former case, grace and fellowship with God are two different things: grace is the means, fellowship with God the end; in the latter case they coincide: grace is God's gracious will, in virtue of which He enters into fellowship with us sinners. In the former case, grace is a quality that is given to man; in the latter it is the good pleasure of God under which the man who is justified by God lives. In the former case, grace is the power which sets in motion man's upward-directed love, his Eros; in the latter case, it is the same as God's Agape.

Without grace, no merit—this is axiomatic for Mediæval theology. But what has just been said shows that this is only one side of the case. It is equally axiomatic that there is *no blessedness without merit.*[1] Grace makes it possible to win blessedness, but merit must win it. Grace is, so to speak, the starting-point for the ascent of merit. It is both the solid ground on which the ladder of merit can be raised, and the effective power that enables man to mount it step by step. Grace furnishes man with the requisite power, but that is not the end of the matter. Only the equipment for his ascent to God is given, and everything now depends on his making the ascent, too, a reality. By grace, Caritas is infused into man's heart, but this infusion is by no means an end in itself; it finds its end and its meaning only when man uses the possibility thus given for continually renewed acts of love towards God and the heavenly world. So, despite the fact that " grace " is the permanent foundation of all " merit," Mediæval piety largely assumes the character of

---

[1] " Homo ad beatitudinem pertingere non potest nisi per meritum."   S. Th., I., qu. lxii., art. iv., tom. v., p. 113*a*.

a climb up the ladder of Merit, with eternal blessedness as its goal.[1]

2. *The Analogical Ladder of Speculation.* Mediæval theology is in its whole structure speculative theology. This, too, is an expression of the upward tendency. By the ladder of religious speculation, theology has to ascend from the world of sense to God. The relation between God and the world is primarily conceived from the point of view of causality, starting from the general principle that there is always found in the effect something reminiscent of the cause.[2] Since God is "the first and universal Cause of all being," it is possible to detect in everything, in so far as it is a "being" at all, some likeness to Him.[3] It is the task of theology to search out these Divine "traces" in the universe and by their aid to rise to the contemplation of God Himself in His majesty. Naturally, we find no absolute likeness to the Divine within the created sphere. But everywhere in existence, from the highest to the lowest, there are *analogies* to the Divine life, clearer at higher, fainter at lower levels. By observing these analogies and working back from the effect to the first cause (via causalitatis), by negating the imperfect (via negationis) and positing the perfect (via eminentiæ) which the effect implies, we can arrive at a true, if never exhaustive and adequate, knowledge of God's nature.[4]

[1] "Si ergo volumus et nos cum eo ascendere, ascendendum nobis est in montes virtutum de vallibus vitiorum." Bernard of Clairvaux: Sermones de diversis, LXI. 1; Migne, PL, vol. clxxxiii.

[2] "Habent enim effectus suarum causarum suo modo similitudinem, cum agens agat sibi simile." Aquinas: Summa contra gentiles, lib. I., cap. viii., tom. xiii., p. 21a. "Cum enim omne agens agat sibi simile inquantum est agens, agit autem unumquodque secundum suam formam, necesse est quod in effectu sit similitudo formæ agentis." S. Th. I., qu. iv., art. iii., tom. iv., p. 54a.

[3] ". . . secundum aliqualem analogiam, sicut ipsum esse est commune omnibus. Et hoc modo illa quæ sunt a Deo, assimilantur ei inquantum sunt entia, ut primo et universali principio totius esse." *Ibid.*

[4] "Cognoscitur [Deus] a nobis ex creaturis, secundum habitudinem principii, et per modum excellentiæ et remotionis." S. Th., I., qu. xiii., art. i. The

The classical account of the speculative ascent is given in Bonaventura's *Itinerarium mentis in Deum*.[1] This work, despite its brevity, may be said to contain the sum total of his thought,[2] and from the religious point of view it is one of the profoundest things Mediæval theology produced. Such a work gives a far clearer and more direct impression of the spirit that governs the theology of the Middle Ages than the great Summæ and Sententiæ-commentaries. It is based entirely on the tradition from Augustine and Pseudo-Dionysius,[3] augmented in particular by the influence of Bernard of Clairvaux and Hugo of St. Victor. But under the living influence of the piety of St. Francis, which detected traces of God's power and love everywhere in the world, Bonaventura was able to fuse all this traditional material into an independent unity. He starts with St. Francis' vision of the six-winged Seraph in the likeness of the Crucified. In the light of his meditations on the soul's ascent to God,[4] he sees that

---

idea here indicated of an " analogia entis " is the key to the understanding of Thomas's doctrine of God in general. For the idea of " analogia entis " and its fundamental significance for Catholic thought, *cf*. E. Przywara: *Religionsphilosophie katholischer Theologie*, 1927, pp. 22 ff.

[1] Bonaventura's works are quoted from the Quaracchi edition.

[2] E. Gilson: *La philosophie de Saint Bonaventure*, 1924, p. 75: " The work which contains the sum of his most profound intuitions."

[3] From Augustine he took the basic idea itself, that of the speculative ascent. But he betrays also the influence of Pseudo-Dionysius at almost every point. Thus the " Itinerarium," like Dionysius' work " On the Heavenly Hierarchy " (*cf. supra*, p. 367, n. 6), begins by quoting Jas. i. 17 about " the Father of lights " from whom all "illuminationes " descend to us (Itin., Prologus 1, tom. v., p. 295*a*). The influence of Dionysius is also suggested—to give one more example—by the dominant position Bonaventura gives to the idea of the " hierarchisation " of the soul's capacities through the purification, illumination and perfecting (purgatio, illuminatio, perfectio) of the soul, and also by his modelling of the soul upon the nine angelic choirs; *cf*. Itin., cap. iv. 4-7. For the idea of " hierarchizatio," *cf*. In Hexaëmeron, collatio xx.-xxiii., tom. v., pp. 424-449, where this is the leading conception and where the dependence on Pseudo-Dionysius is equally complete. *Cf*. also E. Gilson, *op. cit*., pp. 431 ff.

[4] " . . . dum mente tractarem *aliquas mentales ascensiones in Deum*, inter alia occurrit illud miraculum, quod in prædicto loco [monte Alvernæ] contigit ipsi beato Francisco, *de visione scilicet Seraph alati ad instar Crucifixi*." Itin., Prologus 2, p. 295*b*.

the meaning of this vision can only be to give us instructions
about the way and the steps by which we have to mount to
God. The six wings of the Seraph signify the six steps which
the soul must traverse " in order to come to peace through
the ecstatic raptures of Christian wisdom."[1] That the Seraph
appeared in the likeness of the Crucified means that no one
can succeed in his ascent except through the Crucified.
" Christ is our ladder." We can come to God only through
the most burning love for the Crucified.[2] Here Bonaventura
points to St. Francis as the great example. In his case, love
for the Crucified had so wholly absorbed his spirit that it
even showed itself outwardly, for in the last years of his
life he bore on his own body the sacred wounds.[3]

To Bonaventura's contemplative mind, the whole universe
reveals itself as a huge ladder, given to us in order that we
may ascend to God by it;[4] and the aim of the work we are
discussing is to show how in all things, the lowest as well
as the highest, we can find something of God Himself. Now
there are three worlds, the sense-world " extra nos," the life
of our own soul " intra nos," and the eternal world " supra

---

[1] " Nam per senas alas illas recte intelligi possunt sex illuminationum suspen-
siones, quibus anima quasi quibusdam *gradibus vel itineribus* disponitur, ut
transeat ad pacem per ecstaticos excessus sapientiæ christianæ." Itin., Prolog. 3,
p. 295*b*. The words " gradibus vel itineribus " explain the purpose of the book
and its title. It is a guide-book for the soul on the road to God; it sets out to
describe the way and the steps, which begin here below among created things
and lead right up to God: " Effigies igitur sex alarum seraphicarum insinuat sex
illuminationes scalares, quæ a creaturis incipiunt et perducunt usque ad Deum."
Ibid. For Bonaventura, as for Augustine, " peace " (quies, pax) is the final
goal.
[2] " . . . ad Deum, ad quem nemo intrat recte nisi per Crucifixum." *Ibid.*
" . . . in Christo, *qui est scala nostra.*" Cap. i. 3, p. 297*a*. " Via autem non
est nisi per ardentissimum amorem Crucifixi." Prologus 3, p. 295*b*.
[3] *Ibid.*
[4] " In hac oratione orando illuminamur ad cognoscendum divinæ ascensionis
gradus. Cum enim secundum statum conditionis nostræ *ipsa rerum universitas
sit scala ad ascendendum in Deum.*" Cap. i. 2, p. 297*a*. " Et sic patet, quod
totus mundus est sicut unum speculum plenum luminibus præsentantibus
divinam sapientiam, et sicut carbo effundens lucem." In Hexaëmeron, Collatio
ii. 27; Bd. V., p. 340*b*.

nos."[1] Each of these shows us God, though in different ways and according to the degree of perfection of each. The irrational world shows us the *footprints* of God (vestigia) in the universe.[2] The size, number, beauty and order of things point to God as their author.[3] "He who is not enlightened by such a splendour of created things is blind." "Open therefore thine eyes, that in all created things thou mayest behold thy God."[4] But the manner in which we apprehend the sense-world also points us to God. Through the portals of the five senses, the entire world that surrounds us enters into us in perception and judgment.[5] Especially in judgment, which is subject to eternal rules, we can detect traces of God as the source of all truth and wisdom. Yet the sense-world and our conception of it can only provide analogies of a lower order. "By these first two steps we are led to behold God in His footprints, as it were in the manner of the two wings that are let down towards the feet."[6]

As yet, however, we are only in the forecourt. We enter the holy place when we enter into ourselves and contemplate our own spirit. Here God meets us in a higher way. We no longer see merely His footprints, but a more perfect analogy, for we are His image (imago Dei). Our natural endowments themselves contain an analogy to God's nature. God is love; but Divine love is for Bonaventura, as for Augustine and Pseudo-Dionysius, primarily the Divine self-love: it is the love within the Trinity, in virtue of which the Divine being—amans, quod amatur, amor—eternally circles about itself and is bent upon itself.[7] This has its analogy in

---

[1] Itin., cap. i. 2, p. 297a.

[2] This is treated in cap. i., which is entitled: "De gradibus ascensionis in Deum et de speculatione ipsius per vestigia eius in universo."

[3] Cap. i. 14, p. 299a.   [4] Cap. i. 15, p. 299b.

[5] Cap. ii. 3 ff., pp. 300a ff.

[6] Cap. ii. 11, p. 302b.

[7] *Cf. supra*, pp. 542 f., 582, 583 f., 607 f. Here we may recall Suso's characteristic phrase "widerboegung uf sin götlich wesen"; *Seuses Leben*, cap. li., p. 180, 20.

human self-love, and hence Bonaventura urges: "Go, then, into thyself and see how ardently thy spirit loves itself."[1] Here he finds a reflection of the most blessed Trinity.

Man, therefore, as he was created by God, possesses in the universe, and especially in his own spiritual endowments, the ladder by which he could ascend to the contemplation of God in His threefold form as Father, Word and Love.[2] But by Adam's Fall this natural ladder has been broken. Man's spirit is no longer an unspoiled copy of God; man's memoria, intellectus and desiderium are no longer turned inward towards himself, but outward towards the things of sense. To help us in this situation, the eternal Truth to which we could not rise has itself assumed human form in Christ. For us He has "become a ladder and restored the first ladder, which was broken in Adam."[3] We recover the possibility of ascent when the image of God in us is clothed with the three theological virtues, faith, hope and love. These bring order into the capacities of our soul; the soul is "hierarchised"— that is, it is purified, illuminated and perfected, and becomes a copy of the heavenly world with its nine angelic choirs. In this way, our own soul becomes like a ladder on which we can mount up to God.[4] "By these two intermediate steps [the 'image' given by nature and its renewal by grace] we enter into ourselves and behold God as in the mirror of the created images; and this is as it were in the manner of the two wings that are extended for flight."[5]

[1] ". . . ubi ad modum candelabri relucet lux veritatis in facie nostræ mentis, in qua scilicet resplendet imago beatissimæ Trinitatis. *Intra igitur ad te et vide, quoniam mens tua amat ferventissime semetipsam.*" Cap. iii. 1, p. 303*a*.

[2] "Dum igitur mens se ipsam considerat, per se tanquam per speculum consurgit ad speculandam Trinitatem beatam, Patris, Verbi et Amoris. . . ." Cap. iii. 5, p. 305*b*.

[3] "Non potuit anima nostra perfecte ab his sensibilibus relevari ad contuitum sui et æternæ Veritatis in se ipsa, nisi Veritas, assumta forma humana in Christo, fieret sibi scala reparans priorem scalam, quæ fracta fuerat in Adam." Cap. iv. 2, p. 306*a*.

[4] Cap. iv. 3 f., pp. 306*b* f.

[5] Cap. iv. 7, p. 307*b*.

But there still remain the two highest steps. God meets us not only in the universe and in our own spirit, but also in the world that is above us, the eternal world. And here He reveals Himself not merely in footprints or in images, but in the more adequate form of *light* (lumen).[1] When we entered into ourselves and beheld God in our own spirit, we passed from the forecourt into the holy place. Now we enter the holy of holies, where " the cherubim of glory stand above the ark of the Covenant overshadowing the mercy-seat."[2] According to Bonaventura, these two cherubim symbolise how God reveals Himself to us " as it were in the manner of the two uplifted wings ";[3] and this finds expression in the two chief names of God, " the Being " and " the Good."[4] The name " the Being " (" He who is ") reveals God's unity, whilst " the Good " asserts the triplicity of the Divine nature, inasmuch as this triplicity is a necessary condition for communication.

Thus, guided by lower and higher analogies we have come to the highest peaks of religious speculation. The mysteries of the Divine nature have been unveiled to enquiring contemplation. The six stages have been traversed and there seems to be nothing further to seek. The analogical ascent of speculation has attained its goal; and had Bonaventura's interest been exclusively speculative, he could have ended

[1] " *Extra* per vestigium, *intra* per imaginem et *supra* per lumen." Cap. v. 1., p. 308*a*.

[2] Cap. v. 1, p. 308. *Cf.* Heb. ix. 5.

[3] *Cf.* Exod. xxv. 19 f., and xxxvii. 7 ff.

[4] Of this Bonaventura says (cap. v. 2, p. 308*b*): " Damascenus follows Moses and says that God's first name is ' the Being ' (qui est). Dionysius follows Christ and says that God's first name is ' the Good ' (bonum)." The first passage referred to is Exod. iii. 14: " And God said unto Moses, I AM THAT I AM: and he said, Thus shalt thou say unto the children of Israel, I AM hath sent me unto you." The second passage is Luke xviii. 19: " None is good, save one, even God." From the account given above (p. 579 f.), we know in what sense Dionysius uses the name " the Good," and that it is not a Christian, but a Neoplatonic motif which it conceals. Here goodness is represented as communication, which means the overflow of the fulness of reality; it has nothing whatever to do with goodness in the Christian sense.

here. But he adds another chapter, for there is something beyond the six stages. This shows that the *Itinerarium* is really intended as a mystical writing—a fact of which there have been hints here and there already. Neither here nor elsewhere can a sharp distinction be drawn between the speculative and the mystical ascent.[1] As in Plato the final goal is not reached by discursive thought nor by dialectic, but only in a state of " divine madness,"[2] so Bonaventura holds that it is not speculative contemplation, but the mystical absorption in God, which brings us to our goal. Not by enquiring contemplation, but " per raptum " or " per excessum mysticum " we reach the peace (quies) that is the aim of our existence.[3] The six steps so far described are merely preparatory, like the six steps that lead up to Solomon's throne, or the first six days, in which the soul has to prepare itself to come finally to the Sabbath rest of the seventh day.[4] For this last ascent, Christ alone is " scala et vehiculum."[5]

That, according to Bonaventura, is the deeper religious significance of St. Francis' vision. "Like a second Jacob," Francis has been permitted to behold the heavenly ladder, and through him, by his example rather than his words, God now invites all really spiritually minded men to such an ascent and to the spirit's ecstasy.[6] After a couple of quotations from the " Mystical theology " of Pseudo-Dionysius, concerning the super-substantial and super-divine nature of the Trinity and the ascent into the Divine darkness, Bonaventura concludes his work with the following " exhortatio ": " Let us therefore die and enter into the darkness."[7] The goal is thus the usual goal of mysticism. Only,

---

[1] *Cf.*, *e.g.*, how these intermingle in Augustine, *supra*, p. 516.

[2] *Cf. supra*, p. 167.

[3] The title of cap. vii. is: " De excessu mentali et mystico, in quo requies datur intellectui, affectu totaliter in Deum per excessum transeunte."

[4] Cap. vii. 1, p. 312*a*.   [5] Cap. vii. 2, p. 312*b*.

[6] Cap. vii. 3, p. 312*b*.   [7] Cap. vii. 6, p. 313*b*.

Bonaventura has provided for it a speculative foundation constructed with unusual thoroughness.

3. *The Anagogical Ladder of Mysticism.* Vast as the available material is, we may here be quite brief. Mysticism is one of the best known and most discussed elements in Mediæval thought;[1] and, moreover, we have already in the preceding pages touched on a number of matters relating to it. One who knows Augustine and Pseudo-Dionysius knows in all essentials the general structure of the mysticism of the Middle Ages.

The ἀναγωγή of mysticism means an inner ascent. The mystic seeks the point within himself where he can make contact with God. This point, that which in the soul is akin to God,[2] is given many different names by the Mediæval mystics: "apex mentis," "vertex mentis," "scintilla animæ," "Fünklein," "Licht," "Hütte des Geistes," "Seelenburg," and so on.[3] This is the divine and uncreated element in the soul,[4] it is the peak of the soul to which man must climb if he is to come into contact with God, it is the Neoplatonic ἕν in man, which makes possible ἕνωσις with τὸ θεῖον ἕν.[5] But this height is not reached without

---

[1] For general purposes see J. Bernhart: *Die philosophische Mystik des Mittelalters*, 1922.

[2] For the idea of the soul's kinship with God, *cf. supra*, pp. 270, 281, 298, 323, 439 f.. For the idea of συγγενής and its connection with the idea of Eros, *cf.* p. 282 and p. 440, n. 1.

[3] A classical passage for this is in Meister Eckhart, hrsg. von F. Pfeiffer, 4. unveranderte Aufl., 1924, pp. 46 f. *Cf.* also F. Meerpohl: *Meister Eckharts Lehre vom Seelenfünklein*, 1926; O. Renz: *Die Synteresis nach dem hl. Thomas von Aquin*, 1911 (Beiträge zur Geschichte der Philosophie des Mittelalters, Bd. X.).

[4] According to the 27th·of the propositions condemned by the Bull of John XXII.; "In agro dominico," March 27th, 1329, Eckhart is stated to have taught: "Aliquid est in anima, quod est increatum et increabile"; Eckhart himself, however, denies that he had expressed such a view.

[5] "It is entirely one and simple, as God is one and simple." Eckhart, ed. Pfeiffer, p. 46, 12. "One and simple is this Citadel in every way." *Ibid.*, p. 46, 22. "See, in such measure as he is one and simple, so he comes into the one, which I here call a Citadel in the soul. . . . With that part the soul is like God, and otherwise not." *Ibid.*, p. 46, 40. *Cf.* J. Quint: *Die Überlieferung*

thorough preparation.[1] Here the old *ordo salutis* of mysticism, with its three stages of purification, illumination and
union, must be observed.[2] Mediæval mystics often complain

---

der deutschen Predigten Meister Eckeharts, textkritisch untersucht, 1932, pp. 125-
168, where the text of the sermon quoted here (No. VIII.) is examined.

Meister Eckhart is at present the most popular of the Mediæval mystics, and
it is tempting to devote more space to him as representative of the mysticism
of the Middle Ages. But for several reasons we shall not do so. (1) The condition
of the sources compels them to be used with the greatest caution and only after
thorough examination of every individual case. The text of Eckhart's German
works and sermons is dependent on notes taken by his audiences, and much
spurious matter has crept in. More recent research has shown that the text
edited by Pfeiffer is extremely unreliable. J. Quint, in the great work mentioned
above, has shown that no less than 2,000 emendations are necessary. H. Büttner
also leaves much to be desired, in the matter of reliability, in his *Meister
Eckeharts Schriften und Predigten, aus dem Mittelhochdeutschen übersetzt und
herausgegeben,* Bd. I.-II., 1903-1909. Further, Eckhart's Latin works give
a somewhat different picture of his thought from his German works. A
critical edition of his entire works is necessary before an account of his thought
can be given with any confidence. A critical edition of *Meister Eckeharts
sämtliche Schriften* is being issued by E. Seeberg, K. Christ, A. Spamer, J. Koch,
and J. Quint. And a French critical edition has been begun by G. Théry and
others. (2) Eckhart's influence in the Middle Ages was fairly limited; that of
Bernard of Clairvaux, Suso and Thomas à Kempis was far greater. *Cf.* H.
Boehmer: *Loyola und die deutsche Mystik,* 1921, pp. 7 ff. " It is not Plotinus
nor—what amounts to the same thing—Meister Eckehart, but Bernard, who is
the religious genius who has primarily determined the character of German
mysticism. Even in his own lifetime the influence of Eckehart was not so
extensive as that of the great Cistercian." *Ibid.,* p. 10. In view of this, it is
less suitable to cite him as representative. (3) A good deal of what has been
written in recent years about Eckhart (*e.g.,* A. Rosenberg's treatment of him in
the *Mythus des XX Jahrhunderts*) is so superficial and so much influenced by the
emotional thinking of " Aryan " romanticism, that for the avoidance of misunderstanding in giving an account of Eckhart's thought a thoroughgoing
purge would have to be undertaken; but for that this is not the place. Much
of what is now hailed as an expression of " the Nordic soul " (" die nordische
Seele ") and as a direct outflow of " elemental Germanic nature " (" urdeutsches
Wesen ") can be proved without difficulty to derive, often almost verbatim, from
the " tattered, servile, bastardised Augustine," from Rabbi Moses ben Maimon
and similar sources.

[1] " No one can be made perfect in a day." Theologia Germanica, cap. xiii.,
p. 45 (Eng. trans. by Susanna Winkworth; Macmillan, 1937).

[2] " Now be assured that no one can be enlightened unless he be first cleansed
or purified and stripped. So also, no one can be united with God unless he be
first enlightened. Thus there are three stages: first, the purification; secondly,
the enlightening; thirdly, the union." *Ibid.,* cap. xiv., pp. 46 f. This chapter
goes on to show how each of these three stages in turn includes three stages.

that men imagine themselves complete all too soon: "They desire to fly before they are fledged. They would fain mount up to heaven in one flight; albeit Christ did not so."[1]

Reference to Christ's Ascension as the pattern for the mystical ascent of the soul is not incidental; it is typical of Mediæval mysticism. It is perhaps clearest in Bernard of Clairvaux, who says, for instance: "When our Lord and Saviour Jesus Christ wished to teach us how we might ascend to heaven, He Himself did what He taught: He ascended to heaven. But as He could not ascend without first having descended, and as His simple divine nature, which can neither be lessened nor increased nor undergo any other change, did not permit Him either to descend or ascend, He took up into the unity of His person our nature— that is, human nature. In this He descended and ascended and showed us the way by which we, too, might ascend."[2] There is in us by nature an ineradicable desire to ascend and be exalted.[3] This desire is implanted in us by God Himself. Like Augustine,[4] Bernard sees in the upright form given to man at creation an evidence that he is meant by God to direct his desire upwards.[5] But in his attempt to raise himself up, the natural man takes the false path of pride and presumption, and so sinks ever deeper down. He can only be rescued when Christ shows him the right way. We are called to be followers of Christ. Even if during our earthly

---

1 *Ibid.*, cap. xiii., p. 45.

2 Bernard of Clairvaux; Sermones de diversis, LX. 1; PL, vol. clxxxiii.: "Dominus et Salvator noster Jesus Christus volens nos docere quomodo in cœlum ascenderemus, ipse fecit quod docuit, ascendit in cœlum . . . viamque nobis, qua et nos ascenderemus, ostenderet."

3 "Cupidi quidem sumus ascensionis: exaltationem concupiscimus omnes. Nobiles enim creaturæ sumus, et magni cujusdam animi." In ascensione Domini, Sermo IV., p. 310 C. "Omnes ascendere nitimur, omnes tendimus in sublime, sursum aspiramus omnes, omnes conamur in altum. . . ." Sermones de diversis, XXXIII. 1, p. 626 C.

4 *Cf. supra*, p. 485.

5 "Sunt autem qui alio modo sursum cor habeant, sicut fecit Deus hominem rectum." Serm. de div., XXXVI. 1, p. 637 D.

life this commonly and chiefly means that we are to follow Him in lowliness and humiliation, that is not all. Our "Imitatio Christi" is to include both humiliation and exaltation. We are to follow Christ in everything, not only when He descends in His incarnation, but also when at the Ascension He ascends into heaven.[1] To both Bernard applies the words in Lk. x. 37: "Go, and do thou likewise."[2] Incarnation and Ascension belong together as means and end. The Ascension alone gives the key to the mystery of the Incarnation. To the question, "Cur Deus homo?" (Why did Christ descend?), Bernard answers: by His descent (and subsequent ascent) Christ wished to teach us how we might ascend to heaven.[3] If we are urged to follow Him on the way of humility and humiliation, the purpose of this is that we might ascend like Him to the heavenly world. Even for Christ, humiliation was only a way and a means to ascend still higher. In His original heavenly exaltation He could not ascend higher, because of His divine nature; for there is nothing above God. But then He found by His descent a way in which He could still grow.[4] This must also be our way: through humiliation and humility to exaltation, "per humilitatem ad sublimitatem."[5] On these lines the

[1] "Quis docebit nos ascensum salubrem? Quis nisi de quo legimus, quoniam qui descendit, ipse est et qui ascendit? Ab ipso demonstranda nobis erat ascensionis via." Sermones de tempore, In ascensione Domini, Sermo IV. 6, p. 312 A. Cf. Serm. de div., XX., p. 592 ff.

[2] ". . . veniens incarnari, pati, mori, ne moreremur in æternum: propter quod Deus exaltavit illum, quia resurrexit, ascendit, sedet a dextris Dei. Vade, et tu fac similiter." In ascensione Domini, Sermo II. 6, p. 304 A.

[3] "Sic per incarnationis suæ mysterium descendit et ascendit Dominus, relinquens nobis exemplum, ut sequamur vestigia ejus." Serm. de div., LX. 2, p. 684 A. "Sic etiam oportebat Christum descendere, ut nos ascendere doceremur." In ascensione Domini, Sermo IV. 3, p. 310 C.

[4] "Christus enim cum per naturam divinitatis non haberet quo cresceret vel ascenderet, quia ultra Deum nihil est, per descensum quomodo cresceret invenit. . . . Neque enim ascendere potes, nisi descenderis." Ibid., Sermo II. 6, p. 304 A. "Quia non erat quo ascenderet, descendit Altissimus, et suo nobis descensu suavem ac salubrem dedicavit ascensum." Ibid., Sermo IV. 6, p. 312 A.

[5] ". . . ut per humilitatem ad sublimitatem ascendatis; quia hæc est via, et non est alia præter ipsam. Qui aliter, cadit potius quam ascendit; quia

Sermon on the Mount is also interpreted. The eight Beatitudes signify eight rungs of the mystical heavenly ladder, whose foot is here below while its top reaches up to heaven.[1] On this ladder we must ascend above ourselves and above everything in the world. Only then have we reached the goal of our "ascensio animæ" ("ascensiones in corde"),[2] when with the highest part of our spirit we reach the higher world and come to full and immediate union with God.[3] But this highest happiness is granted to man only in isolated and fleeting moments.[4]

---

sola est humilitas quæ exaltat, sola quæ ducit ad vitam." *Ibid.*, Sermo II. 6, p. 304 A.

[1] "Alterum proinde montem ascendas necesse est, in quo prædicantem audias, *scalam erigentem octo distinctam scalaribus, cujus summitas cœlos tangit.*" *Ibid.*, Sermo IV. 10, p. 314 C. The fact that there are eight rungs to the ladder here, whilst elsewhere a different number is given, is of minor importance; the essential thing for Bernard is that salvation is always conceived in the form of ascent. *Cf.* Serm. de div., LXI., p. 685 f.: "De quatuor montibus ascendendis"; CIII., p. 728 D.: "De quatuor gradibus, quibus electorum profectus distinguitur"; CXV., p. 741 A: "Unde et quatuor gradus ascensiones esse dicimus"; CXVIII., p. 742 C: "De septem ascensionis gradibus." Here also belongs Bernard's famous simile of the threefold kiss in Sermones in Cantica, III. 1; PL, vol. clxxxiii., p. 794. *Cf.* Serm. de div., LXXXVII. 1, p. 704 C.: "Tria sunt oscula: primum pedum, secundum manuum, tertium oris." *Cf.* also Bernard's work "De gradibus humilitatis," PL, vol. clxxxii. 941-958.

[2] Serm. de div., CXV., p. 740 D. In this connection we may recall the numerous mystical tractates which are found in the later Middle Ages under such titles as "De ascensionibus." *Cf.* also Richard of St. Victor: De gradibus caritatis, PL, vol. cxcvi., p. 1195 ff.; Wilhelm of St. Thierry: De natura et dignitate amoris; PL, vol. clxxxiv., p. 379 ff.

[3] "Nam ut in cœlum ascendas, prius necesse est levare te super te." In ascensione Domini, Sermo IV. 12, p. 315 C. "Sequere etiam ascendentem in crucem, exaltatum a terra, ut non solum super te, sed et super omnem quoque mundum *mentis fastigio* colloceris." *Ibid.*, Sermo IV. 13, p. 315 D. "Sic affici *deificari* est." De diligendo Deo, cap. x.; Selected Treaties of St. Bernard of Clairvaux, ed. Watkin W. Williams, 1926, p. 50.

[4] "Beatum dixerim et sanctum, cui tale aliquid in hac mortali uita raro interdum aut uel semel, et hoc ipsum raptim atque unius uix momenti spacio experiri donatum est. Te enim quodammodo perdere tanquam qui non sis, et omnino non sentire te ipsum et a temetipso exinaniri et pene adnullari, celestis est conuersationis, non humane affectionis." *Ibid.*, p. 48.

III

THE DEVELOPMENT OF THE CARITAS DOCTRINE

1. Augustine, the Middle Ages and Luther

THE Middle Ages have been quite naturally overshadowed in general estimation, at least for Protestants, by the two powerful religious personalities who immediately preceded and followed them. Augustine and Luther have been regarded as high points between which the intervening period was one of decline. Mediæval developments in the main have been interpreted as a progressive departure from Augustine until finally Luther, though with greater clarity than Augustine, brought out again the full significance of the deepest religious questions. But this view has been possible only because the different motifs on which Augustine's and Luther's thought is based have been ignored, while it has been taken for granted that in essentials there must be agreement between them. We have already had occasion to point out the error of this view in dealing with Augustine.[1] Augustine and Luther are fundamentally not on the same line. Augustine is the man of synthesis, Luther of reformation; and as for the Middle Ages, they mainly carry on the Augustinian synthesis, the Caritas-synthesis.[2]

A fatal objection to the traditional view emerged from K. Holl's studies of Augustine and Luther, which showed

---

[1] *Cf. supra*, p. 559 ff.

[2] Of the literature which deals directly with the Mediæval doctrine of love, the following may be noticed: P. Rousselot: *Pour l'histoire du problème de l'amour au moyen âge*, 1908; J. Klein: *Die Charitaslehre des Johannes Duns Skotus*, 1926; J. Kaup: *Die theologische Tugend der Liebe nach der Lehre des hl. Bonaventura*, 1927; R. Egenter: *Gottesfreundschaft. Die Lehre von der Gottesfreundschaft in der Scholastik und Mystik des 12. und 13. Jahrhunderts*, 1928.

that these two, despite all that may unite them, are widely separated at the very basis of their thought. Yet Holl never drew any conclusions from this with regard to his view of the Middle Ages. He still retains the old idea that the Middle Ages fall progressively below Augustine, though he modifies it to the extent of saying that it was Augustine who from the first gave the impulse to the decline. Holl starts from the New Testament commandment of love with all its absolute force. This had already been largely modified in Augustine owing to his eudæmonistic attitude. Neither love to God nor love to neighbour was affirmed with the rigour which Jesus gave them. Hence it arose that the demand for love was understood in a relative sense, and continued to be thus understood increasingly throughout the Middle Ages.[1]

There is, of course, something to be said for this view; and yet it does not give a satisfactory picture of the Mediæval contribution to the history of the Christian idea of love. It entirely leaves out of account the very problem which was central to the theological work of the Middle Ages, *the problem of unselfish love.* Here Holl pays the price for judging his subject by the standard of Kantian ethics. By this test, the limitation of the Middle Ages seems chiefly to be that they did not take the commandment of love seriously, whilst Luther's contribution consists essentially in the fact that he grasped its utterly radical nature. But in this way we are given a misleading idea of the relation of the Middle Ages to Augustine as well as to Luther. In the first place, we miss that element of Mediæval theology which goes beyond Augustine; and this applies particularly to the great problem just mentioned, the problem of unselfish love.

[1] K. Holl: *Augustins innere Entwicklung* (Gesammelte Aufsätze zur Kirchengeschichte III., 1928, pp. 54-116); *cf.* also *Gesammelte Aufsätze zur Kirchengeschichte* I., *Luther,* 2. und 3. Aufl., 1923,. pp. 161 f. The first edition of Holl's work on Luther (1921) does not contain this section on Augustine.

Secondly, Luther's thought is regarded too much from the point of view of *commandment*—that is, precisely from the theological point of view of the Middle Ages. For in taking the commandment of love seriously, Luther is still on the line of Mediæval theology. A view historically more correct is obtained, if we give to the problem of unselfish love the central place which it occupies in the Middle Ages themselves, and start with this problem in describing their doctrine of love. Then it becomes clear that Mediæval theology did indeed seek to take seriously the demand for love, for Caritas; and that just because of this it leads to the point where the Caritas-synthesis had to be destroyed by Luther. Mediæval theology felt the inner difficulties of the Caritas-synthesis it inherited, and it honestly tried to overcome them. As a matter of fact, it went as far with the problem as was possible from the starting-point Augustine had prescribed. It refined the doctrine of Caritas, but by doing so made its inner impossibility all the more patent. Thus in a certain way it played into the hands of the Reformation.

There is a great measure of continuity from Augustine to the Middle Ages, and also from the Middle Ages to Luther.[1] The Middle Ages tried most energetically to carry through the Augustinian synthesis, but they were at the same time anxious to give the specifically Christian idea of love as large a place as possible within it. If they failed, it was because of the inner impossibility of the synthesis. But by the very rigour of its demand for love, Mediæval theology made positive preparation without which the Reformation

[1] To how large an extent Mediæval theology lives on the Augustinian Caritas-synthesis can already be seen in Anselm of Canterbury and Petrus Lombardus. The latter's " Libri quatuor Sententiarum," in particular, carried the influence of Augustine into the most diverse schools of thought. As he deals with the doctrine of love in lib. iii., dist. xxvii.-xxxii., ed. Quaracchi, tom. ii, pp. 673-696, so the doctrine of love is found in corresponding sections of the many Mediæval commentaries on this work—a fact which much simplifies a survey of the Scholastic doctrine of love.

would have been impossible. The Middle Ages made the best that could be made of the idea of Caritas; they followed the path of Caritas as far as ever it led. But it was reserved for Luther to see that this path was impracticable, to abandon the idea of Caritas and to rediscover primitive Christian Agape as the only legitimate point of departure for the Christian doctrine of love.

2. THE PROBLEM OF UNSELFISH LOVE

The possibility of a pure and unselfish love of God became a burning question for Mediæval theology; and the reason was that it started like Augustine with the assumption that all love is acquisitive love and therefore, in the last resort, self-love. But if in every act of love man seeks his own bonum, how is it with Christian love, of which the Apostle says (1 Cor. xiii. 5) that it seeketh not its own? Especially in the case of love to God, the love must indeed be *pure* love for God and not simply self-love in disguise. For Augustine this problem had not arisen. He was convinced that love for God and true self-love must coincide: only by directing its desire to God as the summum bonum can self-love win true and enduring satisfaction. The fact that love to God thus receives an egocentric emphasis does not worry Augustine. He is satisfied so long as God is not " used " as a means to some other end, but is " enjoyed " as the final goal where we come to rest. This latter Augustine calls " loving God for His own sake," but he never considered the fact that the enjoyment itself is ultimately " for *our* own sake." Mediæval theology, however, did consider this fact. Whether and in what way self-love can co-exist with Caritas, was a serious problem for it.[1] In what follows

---

[1] " Utrum amor sui possit stare cum caritate." Alexander de Hales: Summa Theologica, Inqu. iii., tract. vi., qu. ii., cap. v., 714; ed. Quaracchi, iii., 1930, pp. 700 f.

we will take three examples of the way in which attempts were made to deal with this problem.

1. We turn first to Thomas Aquinas. He is the more interesting for our present question, as he keeps very close to Augustine and Dionysius the Areopagite.[1] He starts from the same point and goes a good deal of the way with Augustine. For Thomas, as for Augustine, all love is fundamentally acquisitive love;[2] love corresponds to the acquisitive will, and this latter to the natural quest for happiness. As surely as everyone loves himself and wants his own happiness, so surely must everyone be disposed, by nature and in accordance with reason, to love God above all things. Self-love properly understood must drive us to love God who, as the highest good, includes all that concerns our happiness.[3] The reason why we love God at all is that we need Him as our bonum;[4] indeed, Thomas does not hesitate to say : " Assuming what is impossible, that God were not man's bonum, then there would be no reason for man to love Him."[5] He agrees with Augustine, that whoever does not love God does not understand how rightly to love himself. When the sinner chooses and prefers earthly and transient good before God, who is the highest and permanent good, he does so because he is suffering from blindness to value. The difference

---

[1] A mere glance at Thomas's works shows how largely he depends on these two authorities. J. Durantel in his great study, *Saint Thomas et le Pseudo-Denis*, 1919, has shown in detail the relation of Thomas to Pseudo-Dionysius.

[2] " Amor est aliquid ad appetitum pertinens: cum utriusque obiectum sit bonum." S. Th., II. i., qu. xxvi., art. i., tom. vi., p. 188a.

[3] " Sic necesse est quod omnis homo beatitudinem velit. Ratio autem beatitudinis communis est ut sit bonum perfectum, sicut dictum est. Cum autem bonum sit obiectum voluntatis, perfectum bonum est alicuius, quod totaliter eius voluntati satisfacit. Unde appetere beatitudinem nihil aliud est quam appetere ut voluntas satietur. Quod quilibet vult." S. Th., II. i., qu. v., art. viii., tom. vi., p. 54a.

[4] " Non enim esset in natura alicuius quod amaret Deum, nisi ex eo quod unumquodque dependet a bono quod est Deus." S. Th., I., qu. lx., art. v. ad 2, tom. v., p. 104b.

[5] " Dato enim, per impossibile, quod Deus non esset hominis bonum, non esset ei ratio diligendi." S. Th., II. ii., qu. xxvi., art. xiii. ad 3, tom. viii., p. 223b.

between the good and the bad comes ultimately to this, that the good, guided by a right insight into their own nature and what is required for its happiness, rightly love themselves, whereas the bad are hindered by a false conception of their nature and cannot rightly love themselves nor consult their own highest interests. The good know that the chief part of their nature is reason (ratio), and that this finds full satisfaction and perfection only in the blessed contemplation of God (visio Dei). The bad, on the other hand, live in the error that the body and the senses are the chief part of their nature, and by this they evaluate things, by this the direction of their love is determined.[1] In this sense, sinners do not love themselves, for all that they do is to their own hurt; and yet love, which is the fundamental force in the universe, is not therefore eradicated from them. They continue to love themselves, only they do this in a perverted way.[2] To this self-love, which is never absent, Christianity can appeal; it reveals to man his true nature and goal, and thereby directs his love towards God and the eternal.

All the above is in closest agreement with Augustine. Like him, Thomas aims in his theological work at producing a unified view of Christianity subsumed under love. His basic idea can be summarised in two sentences: (1) everything in Christianity can be traced back to love, and (2) everything in love can be traced back to self-love. The idea that there is no other love than self-love is already included at the point where Thomas's doctrine of love begins, inasmuch as he

---

1 " Boni autem æstimant principale in seipsis rationalem naturam, sive interiorem hominem: unde secundum hoc æstimant se esse quod sunt. Mali autem æstimant principale in seipsis naturam sensitivam et corporalem, scilicet exteriorem hominem. Unde non recte cognoscentes seipsos, non vere diligunt seipsos, sed diligunt id quod seipsos esse reputant. Boni autem vere cognoscentes seipsos, vere seipsos diligunt." S. Th., II. ii., qu. xxv., art. vii., tom. viii., p. 203a. Cf. S. Th., II. i., qu. iii., art. viii., tom. vi., pp. 35 f.

2 " Naturalis amor, etsi non totaliter tollatur a malis, tamen in eis pervertitur." S. Th., II. ii., qu. xxv., art. vii. ad 2, tom. viii., p. 204a.

asserts that man can only love that which denotes a good for himself (" bonum suum ").

It did not escape Thomas, however, that his basic view of love accords badly with Christian love, which " seeketh not its own." He tries to overcome this difficulty in his usual way, by introducing a distinction which has since been of the very greatest importance for Catholic theology. Following the example of his teacher, Albertus Magnus, he introduces the Aristotelian doctrine of friendship into his doctrine of love.[1] He continues, it is true, to maintain that all love has its root in self-love; but he does not think it is therefore right to set down all love as selfish. We must distinguish between two kinds of love: *amor concupiscentiæ* and *amor amicitiæ*, acquisitive love and the love of friendship.[2] Caritas is a love of the latter sort. The Christian loves God, himself and his neighbour with the love of friendship or benevolence, " amor amicitiæ sive benevolentiæ." This lays the foundation for the doctrine, so important in the later Middle Ages, of " friendship with God."[3] Now it cannot be denied that the unity of Thomas's doctrine of love suffered from this addition.[4] As Thomas has answered affirmatively the question,

---

[1] Albertus Magnus writes: " Alii tamen aliter dicunt, distinguentes duplicem dilectionem, scilicet amicitiæ, et concupiscentiæ." The concern to put a limit to self-love by the use of the term " amor amicitiæ " appears already in Albertus. " Similiter non est bene dictum, quod aliquis se diligat dilectione amicitiæ: quia amicitia relatio est, quærens diversitatem in diligente et dilecto." Alberti Magni Opera omnia, ed. Borgnet, vol. xxviii., 1894, p. 537. It should be added that Augustine himself in one passage hints at the same idea: " Quidquid ad cibandum amamus, ad hoc amamus, ut illud consumatur, et nos reficiamur. Numquid sic amandi sunt homines, tanquam consumendi ? *Sed amicitia quædam benevolentiæ est.*" In epist. Jn. ad Parthos, tract. viii. 5; PL, 35, p. 2038.

[2] S. Th., II. i., qu. xxvi., art. iv., tom. vi., pp. 190 f.

[3] Cf. R. Egenter: *Gottesfreundschaft*, 1928.

[4] R. Egenter rightly comments (*op. cit.*, p. 19): " Difficulty arises from the fact that Thomas here, as also elsewhere, begins with the Aristotelian definition of love, which identifies it with benevolence. . . . This influence of Aristotle at a point where Thomas himself had reached clear distinctions, becomes subsequently most disagreeably noticeable, in so far as Thomas does not keep clearly distinct that which is supposed to denote the nature of love from that which

"Utrum amor sit in concupiscibili,"[1] and will not surrender his principle that all love is acquisitive love, it is undeniably strange that he can immediately afterwards give a new definition of love, based on Aristotle, as follows: "amare est velle alicui bonum."[2] What interests us here, however, is not this difficulty, but the fact that Thomas felt the tension between the Eros motif, on which his thought as a whole is based, and Christian Agape-love, and that he tried to find a solution with the help of the idea of "amor amicitiæ." It need hardly be said that this attempt was doomed to failure. Apart from the hopelessness of trying to express the meaning of Agape by the alien idea of "amicitia," it is obvious that this external corrective is unable to neutralise the egocentricity that is bound up with the very first premiss of the Thomistic doctrine of love. Further, when he adopts the idea of "friendship" from Aristotle, Thomas states with apparent satisfaction that Aristotle, too, derives friendship ultimately from self-love. For even if I love my friend for his own sake, I still only love what is for myself a "bonum."[3] In this way the unity of Thomas's doctrine of love is preserved. "Amor amicitiæ sive benevolentiæ" constitutes no threat to the doctrine that all love goes back ultimately to self-love and that man can only love that which is a "bonum" for himself. But at the same time, the place where Christian Agape-love, the love that seeketh not its own, was to find a refuge has disappeared.

2. The problem of unselfish love was attacked still more

---

indicates its consequences; and therefore the relations under discussion, which are in themselves very complicated, become still more obscure."

[1] S. Th., II. i., qu. xxvi., art. i., tom. vi., p. 188.

[2] *Ibid.*, art. iv., p. 190b. "To love is to wish somebody well."

[3] " Dictum est enim supra, quod unicuique est amabile, quod est ei bonum. Contra quod videtur esse, quod homo amat amicum illius gratia. Sed ipse [Aristoteles] respondet, quod illi, qui amant amicum, amant id, quod est bonum sibi ipsis. Nam quando ille, qui est bonus in se, est factus amicus alicui, fit etiam bonum amico suo. Et sic uterque, dum amat amicum, amat quod sibi bonum est." Eth. 8, 5.

vigorously by Bernard of Clairvaux in his *De diligendo Deo*.[1] This, too, begins with the usual Augustinian ideas. Love is the same as desire and longing (*appetitus*). It is of the nature of every rational being to strive restlessly after ever higher advantages.[2] Even if at first we set our desire upon the far too low and insignificant earthly things, yet the dynamic of desire itself, the fact that it is by nature unable to be content with anything lower, would in the end compel us to turn our desire to God as the "summum bonum" which includes in itself all the desired advantages, and in which alone desire can come to rest. When man has tried all temporal enjoyments and advantages and discovered their futility, there is nothing else for him to do but to take refuge in God.[3] But that is a long way round, and since life is short and our strength insufficient, we never arrive at the goal by it. If we insist on taking this way and refuse to turn to God before we have roamed through the sensible world, then Bernard recommends that we should at least shorten the way for ourselves by giving ourselves to these lower enjoyments only in imagination and thought, without demanding to experience them in reality.[1] Since self-love is thus the foundation-stone of human life, Bernard is confronted with the following problem: How can we get from self-love, which is man's natural condition, to a pure love for God? He answers this question—being a mystic, and accustomed to thinking in terms of ascent—by speaking of the *four stages or steps of love*.

Self-love is the beginning of all love whatsoever, and this is connected with the nature of man as a created being. Man ought, it is true, to set his love primarily upon his Creator, "but since human nature is frail and weak, man finds himself compelled by force of circumstances to serve himself first.

---

[1] Selected Treatises of St. Bernard of Clairvaux, De diligendo Deo, ed. Williams, 1926.

[2] De dilig. Deo, cap. vii., p. 34.　　　[3] *Ibid.*, p. 36.　　　[4] *Ibid.*, p. 37.

This is the carnal love by which *man loves himself for his own sake.*[1] This self-love is natural, but if it is allowed to proceed without restriction, it becomes a destructive force and threatens to get out of control. But its course is impeded by a commandment which says: Thou shalt love thy neighbour as thyself. " Thus the natural love becomes social when it is extended into what is common."[2] This is the first thing that happens to natural, carnal love: it is widened and begins to lose something of its exclusively egocentric character. But if love to neighbour is to be perfect, it must have its ground in God and in our love to Him. God awakens this in us by sending us sorrow and trials and then delivering us from them. So we discover our own helplessness and what we possess in God; and so it comes about that the carnally minded man, who loves no one but himself, begins to love God for the use he can make of Him. He is, indeed, still within the sphere of self-love, but, within this, love to God has also emerged as a possibility. Thus the first step (primus gradus amoris) is taken on the way from self-love to love for God. But when God continually renews His kindnesses toward us, our love towards Him, which was at first thoroughly egocentric, is deepened. Our heart is softened by His goodness, and we no longer love Him primarily for the benefits we obtain from Him, but for His own sake (secundus gradus amoris). And the more familiar we become with this intercourse with God, the more that deepened love prevails, till we finally attain a perfectly *pure* love to God and God is loved solely for His own sake (tertius gradus amoris). But there still remains the highest stage, in which the soul, as it were drunk with Divine love, entirely forgets itself and even loves itself only in God. This state belongs strictly to the heavenly existence alone, and

---

[1] " Et est amor carnalis, quo ante omnia homo diligit seipsum propter se ipsum." Cap. viii., p. 42.

[2] *Ibid.*, p. 43: " sic amor carnalis efficitur et socialis cum in commune protrahitur."

under earthly conditions it is attained only in rare and solitary moments (quartus gradus amoris).[1]

The way by which we have to ascend from natural self-love, through the four stages of love, to pure unselfish love for God can be set out thus:

Amor carnalis   : diligere se propter se.

Gradus amoris
- 1: diligere Deum propter se.
- 2: diligere Deum non propter se tantum, sed et propter Ipsum.
- 3: diligere pure Deum propter Ipsum.
- 4: diligere se propter Deum.

By constant sublimation and purification, self-love is thus transformed into its opposite, pure love for God. At the highest stage every hint of false self-love has disappeared. In so far as man can still be said to love himself, he does so only in God and for God's sake.

3. In giving an account of the problem of unselfish love, we must not forget the contribution *Mediæval mysticism* made towards combating the egocentric relation to God.[2] This finds chief expression in the demand for the *mortification of the self* (mortificatio). What above all keeps man far

---

1 "*Primus gradus amoris*: . . . Fit itaque hoc tali modo, ut homo animalis et carnalis, qui preter se neminem diligere nouerat, etiam deum uel propter se amare incipiat, quod in ipso nimirum (ut sepe expertus est) omnia possit que posse tamen prosit, et sine ipso possit nichil. *Secundus gradus amoris*: . . . At si frequens ingruerit tribulatio ob quam et frequens ad deum conuersio fiat et a deo eque frequens liberatio consequatur, nonne et si fuerit ferreum pectus uel cor lapideum totiens liberati, emolliri necesse est ad gratiam liberantis quatinus deum homo diligat non propter se tantum sed et propter se ipsum? *Tercius gradus amoris* : Ex occasione quippe frequentium necessitatum, crebris necesse est interpellationibus deum ab homine frequentari, frequentando gustari, gustando probari quam suauis est dominus. Ita fit ut ad diligendum pure deum plus iam ipsius alliciat gustata suauitas, quam urgeat nostra necessitas. . . . Iste est tercius amoris gradus, quo iam propter se ipsum deus diligitur. *Quartus gradus amoris*: Felix qui meruit ad quartum usque pertingere, quatinus nec se ipsum diligat homo nisi propter deum." De dilig. Deo, cap. viii.-x., pp. 41-47.

2 " But God rejoiceth more over one man who truly loveth, than over a thousand hirelings." Theologia Germanica, cap. xxxviii., p. 136.

from God is false self-love. Mysticism clings to this old idea, but at the same time applies it far more widely and rigorously. What is wrong with self-love is that man claims independence over against God.[1] So long as any of this self-will remains in him, he cannot attain perfect union with God. He must do violence to his nature,[2] empty himself of all that is his own, be stripped of all self-will. His life must take the form of "ein Entwerden."[3] His ego must be killed and annihilated;[4] only so can he pass into God and become *one* with Him.

In this conception elements from the spheres of the Eros and the Agape motifs are strangely interwoven. The thought of the love that seeketh not its own,[5] and the basic Christian idea of sin as in very essence selfishness[6]—these have clearly had an influence; and so we can speak of a certain Agape-

---

[1] "On this sin—namely, that man too inordinately loves himself—almost all depends, whatsoever is thoroughly to be overcome." Thomas à Kempis: De imitatione Christi, lib. III., cap. liii. 16, ed. P. E. Puyol, 1886. "What did the devil do else, or what was his going astray and his fall else, but that he claimed for himself to be also somewhat, and would have it that somewhat was his, and somewhat was due to him? This setting up of a claim and his I and Me and Mine, these were his going astray and his fall. And thus it is to this day. What else did Adam do but this same thing? It is said, it was because Adam ate the apple that he was lost, or fell. I say, it was because of his claiming something for his own, and because of his I, Mine, Me, and the like." Theol. Germanica, cap. ii. f., pp. 7 f. *Cf.* cap. xlix., pp. 191 f.

[2] De imitatione Christi, lib. III., cap. xlviii., 38, p. 289.

[3] *Seuses Leben*, kap. IL; ed. K. Bihlmeyer, p. 164, 11.—"My son, the more thou canst go out of thyself, so much the more wilt thou be able to enter into me." *Cf.* De imit. Chr., lib. III., cap. lvi., 1.

[4] "For in whatsoever creature this Perfect shall be known, therein creature-nature, qualities, the I, the Self and the like, must all be lost and done away." Theol. Germanica, cap. i., p. 5. "The annihilation of the spirit; its passing away into the simple Godhead." *Seuses Leben*, cap. xlviii., p. 162, 26 f.

[5] "And where a creature loveth other creatures for the sake of something that they have, or loveth God for the sake of something of her own, it is all false Love; and this Love belongeth properly to nature, for nature as nature can feel and know no other love than this; for if ye look narrowly into it, nature as nature loveth nothing beside herself." Theol. Germanica, cap. xlii., pp. 165 f. "Nature loves nature and means itself." *Seuses Leben*, cap. il., p. 165, 1.

[6] "Adam, the I, the Self, Self-will, Sin, or the Old Man, the turning aside or departing from God, do all mean one and the same thing." Theol. Germanica, cap. xxxvi., p. 130.

trait here. But it is also plain that the basic idea behind this conception, giving it coherence and meaning, is not the idea of Agape, but of Eros: it is the idea of God as the undifferentiated One, as essential Being and the Highest Good, from which all things flow forth and to which all things must return; it is the idea of God as the Unmoved, which sets all other things in motion;[1] the idea of the spirit which strives upwards, and the flesh that drags downwards.[2] This Neoplatonic background gives to the struggle against the selfish ego a content that is alien to Christianity: it attacks not only selfishness, but selfhood (" Ichheit," " Selbstheit "). The result is that in the midst of its struggle for unselfish love, mysticism proves to be the most refined form, the acme of egocentric piety.[3] It is the highest triumph of one's own will when the self sinks into the Deity, and when in the traditional manner of mysticism we can simply say: " God is I " or " I am God."

The Mediæval solution of the problem of Caritas thus consists in the sublimation of acquisitive love or self-love into pure love for God. The whole structure of the Mediæval view of love recalls a Gothic cathedral, where the massive stone rests firmly on the earth and yet everything seems to aspire upwards. The foundation of this view of love is something as earthly and human, far too human, as natural self-love. Yet this self-love contains a persistent tendency to ascend. Self-love drives man to seek satisfaction for his desire; but since this is by nature insatiable, it can never be content with a lower, temporal good. The man who properly understands himself is thus driven with an inner necessity by natural self-love to direct his desire upwards to the Divine. Self-love is the force that drives man upwards, and it reaches its culmination in love to God; this latter offers the highest

---

[1] Theol. Germanica, cap. i., pp. 2 ff.

[2] " Dum spiritus sursum, et caro quærit esse deorsum." De imitat. Chr., lib. III., cap. xlviii. 20, pp. 287 f.

[3] Cf. Anders Nygren: Urkristendom och reformation, 1932, pp. 108 f.

and most perfect satisfaction to the desire of self-love for the eternal. Now as we have seen, Mediæval theology was clearly aware of the difficulty of achieving a *pure* love for God, a love that seeketh not its own, on this basis. But this did not lead to any thorough revision of the Caritas-synthesis. Neither Thomas's " amor amicitiæ " nor Bernard's " quatuor gradus amoris " nor the " mortificatio " of mysticism were able to shake the traditional doctrine of love from its foundation of Eros. The solution was sought on the lines of sublimation: the initial egocentricity should be neutralised by a heightened demand for purity in one's love to God. The extreme consequences of this view are drawn by Occam and Biel. These reject imperfect penitence, the attritio that rests on fear and acquisitive love (amor concupiscentiæ), and they demand as the condition of forgiveness and fellowship with God perfect penitence, the contritio that is informed by Caritas (*i.e.*, based on amor amicitiæ);[1] and they further insist that man can " ex puris naturalibus " exercise such a pure love to God and love God more than himself. But with this they have brought the doctrine of Caritas to its most refined form as regards the question of unselfish love for God, and the point is reached where the tension between the motifs included in it becomes intolerable. Just by the attempt to find as much room as possible for Christian love, which seeketh not its own, they succeeded in producing a doctrine of love moralistic in the extreme and as remote as possible from the Agape-love of Christianity.

3. GOD IS AMOR SUI—GOD IS AMICITIA

It is the more remarkable that Mediæval theologians felt so clearly the tension in the Caritas-synthesis, since they gener-

---

1 On the problem of " attritio-contritio " cf. M. Premm: *Das tridentinische " diligere incipiunt,"* 1925; J. Périnelle: *L'attrition d'après le concile de Trente et d'après S. Thomas d'Aquin,* 1927; C. Feckes: *Die Rechtfertigungslehre des Gabriel Biel und ihre Stellung innerhalb der nominalistischen Schule,* 1925.

ally had no definite knowledge of the elements from which this synthesis was originally constructed. They lacked the linguistic advantage of the first centuries, when in places where Greek was spoken the words ἔρως and ἀγάπη themselves made confusion difficult. When there are two different words for love, it is less easy to forget that there are two different sorts of love. We can see this in Origen and Pseudo-Dionysius; for even if these two do all they can to identify Eros and Agape or to replace Agape by Eros, at least they need to *defend* this procedure.[1] The situation is quite different where Latin is spoken. It is true that ἔρως has its counterpart in " amor "; and in Augustine's assertion that amor, dilectio and caritas are synonymous, we still detect something of the old issue between ἔρως and ἀγάπη.[2] But not least through the influence of Augustine, the term " amor " received, so to say, ecclesiastical dignity. No apology is needed for using it of Divine things; it has no longer, as ἔρως has, an ambiguous sense to be explained and defended. In the Middle Ages, the connection between the two words was largely forgotten; Erigena is one of the few who realise that behind the ecclesiastically approved term " amor " the ἔρως of Plato and Neoplatonism is concealed.[3]

Interesting proof of the change that has taken place is found in Thomas's commentary on Pseudo-Dionysius' *De divinis nominibus*.[4] When Dionysius defends his use of the word ἔρως by reference to the two passages in the Septuagint, where, if not the word ἔρως itself, at least a kindred word occurs, Thomas cannot see what it is all about. It is a puzzle to him why anyone should need to defend such a correct and accepted theological term as " amor." He therefore

---

[1] *Cf. supra*, pp. 389 ff., 589 ff.   *Cf.* also pp. 435 f. on Gregory of Nyssa.
[2] *Supra*, p. 557 f.
[3] *Cf. supra*, pp. 606 ff.
[4] " In librum Beati Dionysii De divinis nominibus expositio "; cited here from Thomas ab Aquino: Opera, tom. x., Venetiis, 1593.

takes Dionysius to mean that the writers of Scripture have used the two words for love (amor and dilectio) quite generally and without distinction.[1] And as regards the two passages of Scripture, Thomas is clearly surprised that Dionysius should have picked on just these two.[2]

But although the old double formula " God is Eros " and " God is Agape " had lost its point in the Middle Ages, there is still something in a measure corresponding to it, inasmuch as Mediæval theology speaks of God's love both as self-love and as the love of friendship. As interpretations of the statement " God is love," both ideas are found in this theology: " God is amor sui " and " God is amicitia."

If the Mediæval doctrine of love seeks to overcome human self-love and reach an unselfish love for God, yet it has no hesitation in characterising *God's* love as self-love. We have already seen how it was to human self-love that Bonaventura turned for an analogy to God's love: " Go, then, into thyself and see how ardently thy spirit loves itself "—here, he thinks, we have a picture of the most blessed Trinity.[3] And the position is no different in Thomas Aquinas. He has learnt from Pseudo-Dionysius that God is primarily love to Himself.[4] This shows more plainly than anything else that the Eros motif and its corresponding scale of values is the ruling factor here. Augustine had already taught that love as " ordered love " must take account of the worth of its object; and that is the view of Mediæval theology, too: the greater the " bonum," the greater the love.[5] But it follows from this

---

1 " Et dicit, quod sibi videtur, quod conditores sacræ scripturæ *communiter* et indifferenter utuntur nomine dilectionis et amoris." Cap. iv., lectio ix., fol. 19 D.

2 After citing Dionysius' evidence for the word " eros," Thomas adds: " Et multa alia dicuntur ad laudem amoris in scripturis." *Ibid.*, fol. 19 C.

3 *Cf. supra*, p. 630, n. 1.

4 " Deus dicitur amor et amabilis, quia ipse amat motu suiipsius, et adducit se ad seipsum." In lib. B. Dionysii De div. nom. expositio, cap. iv., lectio ix. " Deus est suus amor." *Ibid.*

5 " Sic Deus diligit bonum, et majus bonum magis diligit, et maxime bonum maxime diligit." Albertus Magnus: Summa Theol., I., qu. lxiv., ad quæst.

that God as the " *summum* bonum " must love Himself most of all.

The part played by this idea in Mediæval theology is best seen in Richard of St. Victor, in his famous proof of the Trinity from the idea of love. The basis of the whole proof is the idea that love must not be " unordered." If God is love, the object of His love cannot be men; for to love with the highest love that which did not deserve such a love would be to exhibit an " unordered " love." But we may not postulate such a thing in God. " The Divine person could not have the highest love towards a person who was not worthy of the highest love."[1] So a second person was needed within the Deity, in order that there might be an object on which the Divine love could be set without limit. The unquestioned premiss of this argument is that God's love must not be an " unordered " love. It must not, as Agape does, leave the scale of values out of account, but like Eros it must be guided by the worth of the object. Richard of St. Victor has no room for the New Testament idea that the highest love is precisely that which loves those who are *not* worthy of it (Rom. v. 8). In other words, Richard will not allow God's love to be spontaneous and unmotivated, to be Agape. The result is that in the last resort it can only be conceived as Divine self-love, as God's " amor sui."

Yet even here there is a certain counterbalance to this in the idea of amicitia. For it is not only man who loves God with " amor amicitiæ "; the " friendship " is mutual, and

iii. ad 1; Opera omnia, ed. A. Borgnet, vol. xxxi., p. 658. " Pater Filium summe diligit. . . . In aliis autem tanta est dilectio, quantum est bonum quod diligitur in eis." *Ibid.*, ad quæst. iii. ad 4, p. 658.

[1] " Inordinata enim caritas esset. Est autem impossibile in illa summæ sapientiæ bonitate caritatem inordinatam esse. Persona igitur divina summam caritatem habere non potuit erga personam, quæ summa dilectione digna non fuit. . . . Certe solus Deus summe bonus est. Solus ergo Deus summe diligendus est. Summam ergo dilectionem divina persona exhibere non posset personæ quæ divinitate careret." De Trinitate, lib. III., cap. ii., PL, vol. cxcvi., pp. 916 f.

even God loves man with a love that bears the marks of
" amor amicitiæ."[1]   Indeed, we may go so far as to use the
idea of friendship to describe the nature of God.   In his
work, *De spirituali amicitia,* which is largely dependent on
Cicero's *De amicitia* and is intended as a Christian counterpart to it, the Cistercian Abbot Ælred of Rievaulx declares,
though with a certain hesitation, that " *God is amicitia.*"[2]
But friendship, therefore, is also the best heavenly ladder.[3]

4. Fides caritate formata—Fellowship with God on God's Level

It is most characteristic of Mediæval piety that it assumes
as a matter of course that fellowship with God is fellowship
on God's level.   Holy God and sinful man are incompatible.[4]
If they are to enter into relations with one another, man must
first be conformed to God.   By the ladder of merit, contemplation and mysticism he must ascend to the level of God's
holiness; he must become " deiformis " or " gottförmig," as
the technical term is in mysticism.   But the motive force in
this ascent is *Caritas.*[5]   " If he has not love, then he will not
become godlike or deified (vergottet)."[6]   A concise summary

[1] " Caritas . . . est quædam amicitia hominis ad Deum, per quam homo
Deum diligit et Deus hominem; et sic efficitur quædam associatio hominis ad
Deum."   Thomas Aquinas: Scriptum super Sententiis M. Petri Lombardi,
lib. III., dist. xxvii., qu. ii., art. i. 108, ed. M. F. Moos, 1933, p. 857.

[2] " O quid est hoc ? dicamne de amicitia quod amicus Jesu Joannes de caritate
commemorat: *Deus amicitia est ?*"   Beati Ælredi Abbatis De spirituali amicitia,
lib. I.; PL, vol. cxcv., p. 669 f.

[3] " . . . amicitia optimus ad perfectionem gradus existit."   *Ibid.,* lib. II.,
p. 672 A.   " Quomodo ad Dei dilectionem et cognitionem gradus quidam sit
amicitia, paucis adverte."   *Ibid.,* p. 672 B.

[4] " Nec in uno domicilio pariter morabuntur tanta munditia, et immunditia
tanta."   Bernard of Clairvaux: Sermones de tempore, In festo pentecostes,
Sermo III. 5, p. 332 B.

[5] " Caritas causa est et mater omnium virtutum."   Petrus Lombardus:
Libri IV. Sententiarum, lib. III., dist. xxiii.; cap. ix.; ed. Quaracchi, vol. ii.,
1916, p 661.

[6] Theol. Germanica, cap. xli., p. 159.   The title of this chapter is: " How
that he is to be called, and is truly, a Partaker of the Divine Nature (ein vergot-

of this conception is found in the extraordinarily apt and expressive formula " fides caritate formata." With respect to the justification of the sinner and his entry into fellowship with God, it is true that the Pauline language about " justification by faith " can be used. But it is never a question of faith pure and simple, but of faith in so far as it is perfected by love.[1] The decisive thing for man's justification is not faith, but love, Caritas. That is what is meant when, on the basis of the Aristotelian distinction between " form " and " matter," use is made of the formula " fides caritate formata," faith " formed " by Caritas. The form—in Aristotelian thought— is the thing of value which, by imprinting its stamp upon the matter, imparts value to this too. This idea is now applied to the relation between faith and love, fides and Caritas. Faith is the matter, and as such it is insubstantial and powerless. Love is the form, the formative principle, which by setting its stamp or " forma " upon faith, gives to faith, too, worth and real being.[2] So it is ultimately not by faith, but by love, that man is justified and comes into fellowship with God. And this, for fairly obvious reasons, was bound to be the result of the traditional view of Caritas. The whole requirement of the law is summed up in the commandment of love to God and love to neighbour. " Love is the fulfilling of the law." If this love is found in man, then all righteousness is thereby fulfilled. To the degree in which Caritas is found in his heart, man is no longer a sinner, but is

---

teter Mensch), who is illuminated with the Divine Light, and inflamed with Eternal Love, and how Light and Knowledge are nothing worth without Love."

[1] " Et ideo caritas dicitur forma fidei, inquantum per caritatem actus fidei perficitur et formatur." Thomas Aquinas: Summa Theol., II. ii., qu. iv., art. iii., tom. viii., p. 46b.

[2] " Fides sine caritate non potest elicere actum meritorium quem caritate veniente elicit. Ergo caritas dat fidei aliquam vim. . . . Sed fides fit decora, ut Deus eam acceptat, per caritatem. Ergo caritas format fidem." Thomas Aquinas: Scriptum super Sent. M. P. Lombardi, lib. III., dist. xxiii., qu. iii., art. 1, quæstiuncula i., p. 741. " Inquantum actus fidei est ex caritate, secundum hoc est Deo acceptus." Ibid., solutio i. ad 3, p. 744.

fundamentally holy, even if a good deal still remains to be done practically, by the sanctifying permeation of his whole life by Caritas. Thus according to the formula " fides caritate formata," God justifies man and takes him into fellowship with Himself on the ground of the Caritas which He finds in him. Therefore, even granted that God Himself has infused this Caritas into man's heart, the idea still remains intact, that God will have nothing to do with any but the holy and the righteous. *Thus " fides caritate formata " becomes the classical expression in Catholicism for fellowship with God on God's own level, on the basis of holiness.*[1] If God is to be able to have dealings with a sinful man, He must first, so to speak, *remake* him, so that he becomes something other than he was. The Way to fellowship with God, according to this view, proceeds through two stages: *first,* God must transform the sinner, and by the "infusion of love " (infusio caritatis) make him into a holy man; *then* He can receive this remodelled and now holy man into His fellowship. Even if Thomas Aquinas affirms that the four elements included in justification—(1) the infusion of Grace or Caritas, (2) the movement of the free will towards God, (3) the movement of the free will away from sin, (4) the forgiveness of sins[2]—occur simultaneously in time, and can only be distinguished in thought, yet it is his unshakable conviction that the infusion of Grace or Caritas as cause and condition of the other elements is, in point of fact, prior in relation to them.[3] These two things, the simultaneity of the elements and the priority of the infusion of grace, Thomas

---

[1] On this problem as a whole, see Anders Nygren: *Försoningen,* 1932, chap. vi., pp. 27-44.

[2] S. Th., II. i., qu. cxiii., art. vi., tom. vii., p. 336*a.*

[3] " Prædicta quatuor quæ requiruntur ad iustificationem impii *tempore quidem sunt simul,* quia iustificatio impii non est successiva, ut dictum est: sed ordine naturæ unum eorum est prius altero. Et *inter ea naturali ordine primum est gratiæ infusio*; secundum, motus liberi arbitrii in Deum; tertium est motus liberi arbitrii in peccatum; quartum vero est remissio culpæ." *Ibid.,* art. viii., p. 339*b.*

thinks he can reconcile as follows. Through the infusion of love, the soul receives a new form or quality. But in the same moment as this form is present, there immediately begins an activity in accordance with it. Just as fire, the very moment it is kindled, leaps upward, so it is with Caritas. When the flame of love is kindled in man's heart by the infusion of Caritas, it can do no other than mount on high. But the very moment it rises to God, it also breaks loose from sin. For the man thus created anew by Caritas, there occurs as the fourth element, forgiveness of sins and fellowship with God.[1] And with this, justification has attained its end; fellowship with God on the basis of holiness is realised.

---

[1] " In eodem instanti in quo forma acquiritur, incipit res operari secundum formam: sicut ignis statim cum est generatus, movetur sursum." *Ibid.*, art. vii. ad 4, p. 338*b*.

IV

NEW CONTRIBUTIONS TO THE DOCTRINE
OF LOVE

MEDIÆVAL theology made its most important contribution
to the Christian doctrine of love in developing the doctrine
of Caritas, especially in its work on the problem of unselfish
love. This is the starting-point not only for the theories of
the Roman Catholic Church, which were finally fixed at
Trent, but also for the "disinterested love" of Quietism;
and in some measure the work of the Middle Ages on the
doctrine of love may be said to have created the conditions
both for the renewal of the Eros motif in the Renascence and
for the renewal of the Agape motif in the Reformation.

But Mediæval theology also made more independent and
original contributions to the Christian doctrine of love. Two
things in particular are outstanding: *"minne"-piety* and
passion-mysticism. These introduce a change in the conception of love by no means insignificant, though this change
is in both cases rather a matter of emotional than of intellectual content.

1. MINNE-PIETY

Both Christian Agape and Greek Hellenistic Eros in their
original form represent a "heavenly love," though in very
different senses. Agape is heavenly love, Divine love, which
descends in mercy from heaven to us. But Eros, too, in its
original meaning has a right to the name of heavenly love.
For Plato is anxious to distinguish "the heavenly Eros" from
all downward-directed, sensual love whatsoever. Platonic
and Neoplatonic Eros is a love that is directed to heaven.
Even if it cannot quite deny all connection with sensual love,

yet it is so sublimated that the very nature of the love undergoes a radical transformation. The difference between the
vulgar and the heavenly Eros is not merely that the one is
turned to sensible, the other to super-sensible objects, but
when love thus changes its object it likewise changes its own
character. It sheds the traces of elementary sensual impulse;
it becomes spiritualised, and the whole of the lower sphere
of love is substantially eliminated. Sensual love has no place
in a discussion of love in the religious sense, whether in the
context of the Eros or of the Agape motif.[1] Caritas, which
is the synthesis of these two love-motifs, has also in the main
preserved the "heavenly" orientation. It is desire, which
as regards its object is directed upwards, and as regards its
nature is spiritualised.

Just at this point, however, a significant change occurs in
the Middle Ages, a change so radical as to cause a partial
alteration of the fundamental spirit. This was due to the
influence of the secular love-poetry which flourished at the
Mediæval courts under the name of Minne-poetry.[2] Originally, nothing but an earthly, sensual love is celebrated in
these love-poems, but in course of time it passes more and
more into a sublimated, spiritualised love—though always on

---

[1] Here we disregard the isolated instances in the history of the Christian idea of
love when vulgar Eros has intruded, as, e.g., in Gnosticism ; cf. supra, pp. 303-310.
[2] See especially E. Wechssler: Das Kulturproblem des Minnesangs, Bd. I.:
Minnesang und Christéntum, 1909. The origins of Minne-poetry are very
obscure. Different scholars have traced it to very different sources: to the
influence of ancient love-poetry (Ovid, Horace), to Arabic influence and so on.
Cf., apart from Wechssler, K. Vossler: Die göttliche Komödie. Entwicklungs-
geschichte und Erklärung, Bd. I., 1907; K. Vossler: Der Minnesang des Bernhard
von Ventadour (Sitzungsberichte der Königl. Bayrischen Akademie der Wissenschaften, 1918); K. Burdach: Über den Ursprung des mittelalterlichen Minnesangs, Liebesromans und Frauendienstes (Sitzungsberichte der Preussischen
Akademie der Wissenschaften zu Berlin, 1918; reprinted in K. Burdach: Vorspiel.
Gesammelte Schriften zur Geschichte des deutschen Geistes, Bd. I. 1: Mittelalter,
1925, pp. 253-333); S. Singer: Arabische und europäische Poesie im Mittelalter,
1918; H. Brinkmann: Geschichte der lateinischen Liebesdichtung im Mittelalter,
1925; H. Brinkmann: Entstehungsgeschichte des Minnesangs, 1926. A critical
review of the problem is given by E. Rooth: Den provensalska trubadurpoesiens
uppkomst. Gamla och nya teorier (Vetenskaps-Societetens i Lund årsbok, 1927).

the basis of sensual love—and into a romantic yearning and adoration, which sees its object as much as possible in the dim light of the ideal. At least in a substantial measure, this process of sublimation went on under the influence of the traditional doctrine of Caritas, of which certain characteristics have plainly been used as a pattern.[1] Just as *Caritas*, according to Augustine and Mediæval theology, is the most important of the three theological cardinal virtues, the central virtue from which all the other virtues spring[2]— "radix omnium bonorum caritas est"—so now *Minne-love* in its sublimated form fulfils the same function: "Minne is a treasury of all virtue" ("Minne ist aller Tugend ein Hort"). *Die hohe Frauenminne* passes into *Marienminne,* and this into *Christusminne* and *Gottesminne.*

Minne-poetry largely worked with ideas taken over from Christian theology; but it also, in its turn, reacted upon this theology. The blending of the sensible and super-sensible which is characteristic of Minne-poetry comes to set its impress, especially in certain circles among the mystics, upon the conception of Christian love, giving it a trait of sensuality which hitherto had been in the main alien to it. Ever since Augustine, Christianity had commonly been regarded as Caritas-religion; this now comes to mean that Christianity is *Minne-piety*. The Christian relation to God is now conceived in its entirety as Gottesminne, in the sense just explained. The soul which seeks fellowship with God, "die minnende Seele," can be portrayed as the beautiful queen for whom God and Christ have a yearning desire. Christ is the bridegroom of the soul, at which He shoots His arrows of love and so produces in it a pleasing smart. Christ

---

[1] *Cf.* E. Wechssler, *op. cit.*, p. 386: "We have seen how 'Minne,' the cardinal virtue of the Court, has approximated in many respects to *Caritas*, the cardinal virtue of the Church. The love of the Singer for the Lady, too, was a love that served and was ready for sacrifice: for this and other reasons an interaction was possible."

[2] *Cf. supra*, p. 454.

and the soul can be described as a pair of lovers, who enjoy each other's company with "lovely chatter, soft caress" (" holdes Plaudern, sanftes Streicheln "). Fellowship between God and the soul is often described by the figure used in the old mystery religions, the figure of a spiritual marriage (ἱερὸς γάμος).

From the above it is clear that this Minne-piety, which was cultivated with particular enthusiasm in the Mediæval nunneries, meant a reinforcement of the Eros motif, with a certain tendency towards vulgar Eros. The power which this strongly sensual and weakly sentimental idea exercised over Mediæval minds is perhaps best indicated by the fact that the chief document of this piety, Suso's *Büchlein der Ewigen Weisheit*,[1] was one of the most widely used books of devotion in the Middle Ages. It has been aptly said of Suso: " His spiritual love for God is clothed in forms which are thoroughly reminiscent of the secular love-lyric. He is at once both minnesinger and monk. Wackernagel rightly calls him a 'minnesinger in prose and in the spiritual realm.' "[2]

2. PASSION-MYSTICISM

But Minne-piety is not the only original contribution of Mediæval theology to the Christian doctrine of love. There is also Mediæval Passion-mysticism, which we find primarily in Bernard of Clairvaux, but also in Suso and Tauler, for

---

[1] Seuse: Deutsche Schriften, ed. Bihlmeyer, 1907, pp. 196-325.

[2] *Deutsche Mystiker*, Bd. I.: *Seuse*, hrsg. von W. Oehl, p. 20. *Cf.* Bihlmeyer's introduction to Suso's works, p. 75*: " *He heaps upon it* [the eternal Wisdom] *what only earthly love can devise in the way of eulogies*: it is his heart's desire, the empress of his heart, his joyous Easter day, the heart's summer delight, his beloved hour. He believes himself wedded to it as Francis of Assisi was to Poverty, and he pours out the jubilation of his heart over this grace in words full of impetuous enthusiasm. He devotes to it, especially in the days of his ' blooming youth,' when his countenance was still fresh and blooming, a service full of moving tenderness such as was wholly in accord with his poetical, romantic temperament and his knightly, aristocratic training. And in this he felt himself inexpressibly blissful !"

example, and to some extent in Thomas à Kempis and the *Theologia Germanica*. Here, too, we may speak—perhaps even more than in the case of Minne-piety—of an original contribution affecting the fundamental spirit of piety. Here, as never before, the Passion of Christ is made central to the interpretation of Christianity. Men immerse themselves in every detail of the Passion and in the depth of Divine love revealed there. The whole of the Christian life becomes essentially "meditatio vitæ Christi," in which the emphasis is laid on the suffering and death, with a view to an "imitatio Christi" which shall transform the whole of life. From Christ's lowliness and humiliation we are to learn humilitas, and from His love that Caritas which is the condition of the vision and enjoyment of God which is the final goal of the Christian life. The question therefore arises : what did this concentration on the Passion of Christ mean for the conception of Christian love?

In the suffering and death of Christ Christianity has from the beginning seen the greatest work of God's love; at the Cross of Christ the Divine love is manifested in all the depth of its paradox as the Agape of the Cross (Rom. v. 8). Now when Mediæval Passion-mysticism so emphatically places the Cross of Christ again at the centre of Christianity, it would be easy to assume without further question that this means a victory for the Agape motif. Just as Minne-piety means a reinforcement of the influence of Eros, Passion-mysticism would then mean a reinforcement of the influence of Agape in the Mediæval doctrine of love. And in a measure we may say this is so. Concentration on the Passion of Christ undoubtedly helped to deepen understanding of the self-sacrificial Divine love. But at the same time the effect of this was neutralised in various ways, so that the result from the point of view of Agape must be said to be rather small. *In the first place*, it must not be forgotten that Passion-mysticism is at the same time *Bride-mysticism*. Its chief biblical text is

the Song of Songs.[1]   This brings it into alarming proximity
with Minne-piety.   These two can no longer be regarded as
relatively independent phenomena.   The sensual, and still
more the sentimental, strain in Minne-piety encroaches upon
and inundates Passion-mysticism also, giving to its meditation
on and love for Christ features that are all too human.   Both
as regards love and the Passion of Christ, Passion-mysticism
is governed by a fundamental spirit far removed from that of
the New Testament which says: "Weep not for me, but
weep for yourselves, and for your children" (Lk. xxiii. 28).
This spirit of Mediæval Passion-mysticism has prevailed not
only in the Catholic, but very largely even in the Evangelical
Church, a fact to which many of our Passion hymns bear
ample testimony.   *Secondly,* the idea of *imitatio* itself raises
an obstacle to the full apprehension of the Agape motif.
Even in His death on the Cross, Christ is regarded by the
Mediæval mystics primarily as "exemplum."   "In the Cross
is salvation, in the Cross is life"—but, be it noted, only in
the Cross which *we*, as we follow Christ, bear.[2]

[1] Bernard of Clairvaux: Sermones in Cantica; Migne, PL, vol. clxxxiii.,
pp. 785 ff.; Hugo of St. Victor: Soliloquium de arrha animæ; PL, vol. clxxvi.,
pp. 951 ff.
[2] Thomas à Kempis: De imitatione Christi, lib. II., cap. xii., p. 131.

III

THE DESTRUCTION OF THE SYNTHESIS

CHAPTER FIVE

THE RENEWAL OF THE EROS MOTIF IN THE RENASCENCE

I

EROS RE-BORN

DURING the whole of the Middle Ages, Eros had been a living reality—but it was *imprisoned* in the Caritas-synthesis. As perhaps the most important element in this synthesis, Eros had largely moulded the interpretation of Christianity without anyone realising what a transformation of Christianity it effected. In default of direct contact with the Greek sources for the Agape or the Eros outlook, the modificatory influence which each of these two motifs exercised upon the other was generally unperceived. The example already quoted from Thomas Aquinas' commentary on Pseudo-Dionysius' *De divinis nominibus* is typical. On the basis of his text, Thomas quite innocently discusses the question how far we can use, in the same sense and with equal right, the two words " dilectio " and " amor " to describe God's nature; and he never suspects that behind the "dilectio" and "amor" of the translation are concealed the ἀγάπη and ἔρως of the original. So he comments on Dionysius' great effort to bring the two love-motifs to terms, without ever knowing what the difficulty is which his author seeks to overcome. He never saw that the problem is not only how far we can say with the New Testament: "God is Agape," but also how far we are justified in saying with Neoplatonism: " God is Eros," with all that that implies.

Towards the end of the Middle Ages, however, the situation is entirely altered. Owing to the stream of Greek refugees, who in the middle of the fifteenth century came to Italy when the Turks conquered Constantinople, the West came into direct contact with Greek culture and language. The result was a greatly increased study of the Classics, and not least of ancient philosophy. "Ad fontes," back to the sources, was the watchword of the new age. But with regard to what more particularly these sources were, an indication is given by the establishment at that time of the "*Platonic Academy in Florence*," under the patronage of the Medici. We must not, of course, exaggerate the dimensions of this "Academy." It cannot be compared with a university or a place of higher public education; it was not an academy for scientific enquiry, nor a centre for really thorough research. It was rather an attempt to imitate the ancient philosophical schools, which were half philosophical societies, half mystery-associations. Perhaps the most important part of the activity of the Academy—that at least which has left the most significant traces—was the social gathering, the *philosophical symposium*.[1] The life of this Platonic Academy was Marsilio Ficino (born 1433, just half a century before Luther). The subject of his writings[2] in itself shows plainly that it is the old *Eros tradition* he wishes to renew. His works are largely composed of translations and commentaries on Plato,

---

[1] *Cf.* Marsilio Ficino: In convivium Platonis, de amore, commentarius. This work begins as follows: " Plato, the father of philosophers, departed hence after fulfilling 81 years, on his birthday the 7th November, at the end of a meal. This banquet, which was dedicated to the memory of both his birth and his death, was celebrated annually by the ancient Platonists down to the time of Plotinus and Porphyry. But after Porphyry these solemn meals were discontinued for a period of 1,200 years, until finally the illustrious Lorenzo de' Medici in our time resolved to restore the Platonic banquet." This resurrected symposium was celebrated for the first time on the 7th November, 1474. On this occasion nine Platonists were invited, " that the number of the Muses might be complete."

[2] Ficino's works are cited from M. Ficini Opera, Parisiis, 1641, tom. i.-ii. For Ficino's thought in general see especially W. Dress: *Die Mystik des Marsilio Ficino*, 1929 (Arbeiten zur Kirchengeschichte, hrsg. von E. Hirsch und H. Lietzmann, 14). For Florentine Platonism and its influence on the thought of the following period, see J. Nordström: *Georg Stiernhielm, Filosofiska fragment*, I. Inledning, 1924, pp. xliv ff.

Plotinus, Proclus and Pseudo-Dionysius. Ficino's interest centres primarily on the succession which transmitted the Eros motif to the Middle Ages; and if hitherto the influence of Augustine had kept the idea of Eros imprisoned in the Caritas-synthesis, Ficino now wishes to set it free in its original purity.

This brings us to the important point where the Caritas-synthesis is threatened with destruction. The tension between the two motifs included in it has become so strong that the synthesis must disintegrate. The result of the disintegration may be expressed thus: *the Renascence takes up the Eros motif, the Reformation the Agape motif.* The most clear and interesting example of the concern of the Renascence for Eros is provided by Marsilio Ficino.

Ficino's admiration for Plato knows no bounds. In his first extant work he speaks of Plato as "the God of the philosophers,"[1] and the same view prevails throughout his work. All his energy is devoted to bring back the old Platonic spirit again, and he is firmly and fully convinced that it is to this the future belongs. The enthusiasm and assurance with which he preaches his new gospel appear perhaps most plainly in his letter to the like-minded Cardinal Bessarion. "Come, already come is that age, Bessarion, wherein the divine majesty of Plato may rejoice and we, all his followers, exceedingly congratulate ourselves."[2] But he looks at Plato with Neoplatonic eyes, and thinks that Neoplatonism is the logical development of what Plato had said less explicitly. Plato was, he says in the letter to Bessarion, the first to receive the precious gold from God. But, he continues, "when this gold was cast into the furnace, first of Plotinus, then of Porphyry and Iamblicus and finally of

---

[1] De Voluptate, Proœmium, tom. i., 1009a: "Plato, quem tanquam Philosophorum Deum sequimur atque veneramur."

[2] "Venerunt, iam venerunt sæcula illa, Bessarion, quibus et Platonis gaudeat et numen et nos omnis eius familia summopere gratularemur." Epist., lib. I. tom. i., 602b.

Proclus, then the dross disappeared in the fierce test of the fire, and the gold shone forth so much that it filled the whole world with wonderful radiance."[1]

In such circumstances it is not surprising that Platonic dualism and Neoplatonic mysticism occupy a large place in Ficino's thought. The soul is a stranger and sojourner here on earth, and man's misfortune is that this immortal divine soul is imprisoned in a mortal body.[2] Salvation consists in deliverance from the things of sense and the union of the soul with God. The soul attains its full redemption only in death. But even during this life we have to prepare ourselves for that. Here philosophy has its great task as a "meditatio mortis." And here, as so often in the realm of the Eros motif, philosophy and religion coincide.[3] Philosophy is a Way of salvation, the Way of Eros.[4] Through contempla-

[1] "Plato noster, venerande pater, cum in Phædro, ut te non latet, subtiliter et copiose de pulchritudine disputasset, pulchritudinem animi a Deo, quam sapientiam et aurum appellavit pretiosissimum, postulavit, aurum hoc Platoni a Deo tributum, Platonico in sinu utpote mundissimo fulgebat clarissime. . . Verum in Plotini primum, Porphyrii deinde, et Jamblici, ac denique Proculi, officinam aurum illud iniectum, exquisitissimo ignis examine excussis arenis enituit, usque adeo ut omnem orbem miro splendore repleverit." *Ibid.*, 602a.

[2] "Immortalis animus in corpore mortali semper est miser." Epist., lib. ii., tom. i., 661b.

[3] ". . . neque legitima Philosophia quicquam aliud quam vera religio, neque aliud legitima religio quam vera Philosophia." Epist., lib. I., tom. i., 651a.

[4] The influence of Eros in the Renascence is also shown by the keen interest taken in *astrology*. This has often been taken simply as an instance of the general "superstition" of the time, and thus one of the most important evidences we possess for Renascence religion has been obscured. In this learned superstition there is a scientific and a religious interest. It is the latter which is of importance here. Eros-piety and astral religiosity have in all ages gone hand in hand, whereas Agape rejects astral fatalism. It is no accident that the humanist Melanchthon attaches the greatest importance to astrological teachings, whilst Luther merely pours scorn on them: "Es ist ein dreck mit irer kunst." W. A. Tischreden, Nr. 5013, Bd. IV., p. 613, 6. It is the result of a fundamental difference in their religious attitude. *Cf.* A. Warburg: *Heidnisch-antike Weissagung in Wort und Bild zu Luthers Zeiten* (Sitzungsberichte der Heidelberger Akademie der Wissenschaften, Philos.-hist. Kl., Jahrg. 1920; reprinted in A. Warburg: *Gesammelte Schriften*, Bd. II., 1932, pp. 487-558). *Cf.* F. Boll und C. Bezold: *Sternglaube und Sterndeutung*, 4. Aufl., 1931, p. 117 f.; and W. Gundel: *Sternglaube, Sternreligion und Sternorakel*, 1933. "Christianity knows no gods and

tion, mysticism and ecstasy, we have daily to break the fetters that bind us to the sensible world.

But it would be quite wrong, as W. Dress in particular has shown, to assume from this that Ficino merely revives Neoplatonism.[1] It is true that Ficino himself liked to regard his work in this light, but there are elements in his thought which point in a very different direction, and closer investigation shows that it is these, and not the strictly Platonic and Neoplatonic elements, which are in the ascendancy. It is a question of the new emphasis which is laid on *man* in his temporal existence: empirical man is made, in a way such as never before, the centre of the universe. In a word, it is a question of the *human god*.

---

forces of destiny alongside or below the Highest; it refuses, as much as Science does, any investigation and calculation of God's will." Gundel, *op. cit.*, p. 158.

[1] W. Dress, *op. cit.*, pp. 76 ff.

II

THE HUMAN GOD

"Know thyself, O divine race in mortal dress." These
words, with which Ficino introduces his "letter to the
human race,"[1] give consummate expression to the key-note
of his thought. He bows in deepest reverence before himself
and the divine race to which he belongs.[2] It is the human
god whose worship he proclaims.

In itself, of course, Ficino's idea of man as a divine being
is nothing new. The devotees of Eros-piety have always
talked in such terms. From one point of view, the idea of
a divine part in man, the divine spark or whatever it may
be called, is the very foundation of Eros-theory, since according to this, salvation consists in the return of the divine part
in us to its origin in God. Yet this old idea takes on a new
shape and significance in Ficino. It takes a pronouncedly
anthropocentric form. Now it may be said that the idea of
Eros has been egocentric from the first; both in Plato and
Neoplatonism Eros is acquisitive love, and so is of an egocentric nature. But egocentric is not the same as anthropocentric. This is clear if we observe where the centre of
gravity lies in the different theories. In Plato and Neoplatonism it is placed in something objective, the Ideas or
the Divine world. Man may be fundamentally a divine
being, yet in his present situation he is a miserable prisoner.
The thought of what he lacks is predominant, and he does
not possess his high estate of himself, but it is derived solely
from the fact that he *participates in the higher world*. It is

[1] "Cognosce teipsum, divinum genus mortali veste indutum." Epist.
lib. I., tom. i., 642*a*.
[2] Ficino's letter to the human race bears the following characteristic title:
" Cognitio et *reverentia suiipsius* omnium optima." *Ibid.*

in this higher world that Platonic and Neoplatonic thought has its centre.

But now a complete change has taken place, from the objective to the subjective, from the transcendent to the immanent. Already in Erigena there are plainly the beginnings of this change,[1] and in the Renascence and Ficino it is an accomplished fact. The Renascence is characterised by an attitude clearly and consistently anthropocentric.

The chief document of this theory is Ficino's main philosophical work, *Theologia Platonica*, with the sub-title, *De immortalitate animorum*.[2] In the foreword to this work he announces that his main thesis is *the divine nature of the soul*.[3] In this he sees the fundamental dogma which Platonism and Christianity have in common.[4] As he goes on to expound this, he takes up the old idea of " the eye like to the sun in nature."[5] Just as the eye can only take in the light of the sun because it is itself of the same nature as the sun—" like attracts like "—so we can only have any idea of God because our nature includes a divine part. But

[1] *Cf. supra*, p. 605.

[2] M. Ficini Opera, tom. i., 74-414.

[3] Proœmium, p. 74a. " De divinitate animi " is also a theme which constantly recurs in Ficino's letters. *Cf.*, *e.g.*, Epist., lib. I. 601a and 642b; lib. II. 681b and 685; lib. VI. 789b; lib. VII. 891.

[4] In this connection Ficino quotes Augustine to the effect that the Platonists would only need to change a few words and phrases to bring their views into complete accord with Christianity; cf. *supra*, pp. 240 f. We may add that in setting forth the " Platonic theology," Ficino is not doing this in conscious opposition to Christianity. He is convinced that these two are in all essentials identical. Nor does his activity in the " Platonic Academy " indicate any conscious departure from Christianity. In the same year as the " Platonic Academy in Florence " was founded and Ficino finished his " Theologia Platonica " (1474), he took ecclesiastical office, after having been ordained priest the year before. Also, the common idea that Ficino's aim was to fuse together Platonic teaching and Christianity, or to prove agreement between them, must be said to be mistaken. This idea is based on the false notion that Platonism and Christianity appeared from the start as two independent phenomena to Ficino. But, in fact, their unity was already established.

[5] Theologia Platonica, Proœmium, 74a. *Cf.* lib. XIV., cap. viii. 310b. *Cf.* on this, J. Lindblom: *Det solliknande ögat.* (art. in Svensk teologisk kvartalskrift, 1927, pp. 230-247).

since the human soul never sees its own light so long as it is surrounded by the darkness of its bodily prison, and therefore often doubts its own divinity, there is nothing for us to do but to break our earthly fetters and "on Platonic wings, under the guidance of God, soar freely up to the spaces of ether, where we shall at once learn the sublimity of our nature."[1]

In what does this sublimity of our nature consist? It consists above all in the fact that man as a *microcosm* comprises in himself all the rest of the universe. This brings Ficino to the very heart of his thought, as even the tone of his speech shows. As by old habit, he can repeat the Platonic and Neoplatonic phrases, but so long as he does that, it all sounds rather traditional. It is quite different when he comes to his anthropocentric theme and the question of the world-embracing position of man. Then he speaks of what is his very own; then his tongue is loosed and oratory flows. He sings the praise of *Man*—but, be it noted, of empirical earthly man. For it is precisely as the earthly creature of sense which he is, that man is a microcosm. It is precisely in this capacity that he can be said to include all that there is in the macrocosm. Of the five stages which compose the universe, man occupies the middle one, and is thus *at the centre of the world*, so to speak. Below him are material things and "qualities," above him the angels and God. But he comprises all this in his own person; nothing in existence is alien to him. He rules the material things and "qualities," and unites himself with the angels and God.[2] Man is lord

---

[1] Theologia Platonica, lib. I., cap. i. 75.

[2] " Proinde, cum ascenderimus, hos quinque rerum omnium gradus, corporis videlicet, molem, qualitatem, animam, Angelum, Deum, invicem comparabimus. *Quoniam autem ipsum rationalis animæ genus inter gradus hujusmodi medium obtinens, vinculum naturæ totius apparet*, regit qualitates et corpora, Angelo se iungit et Deo, ostendemus id esse prorsus indissolubile, dum gradus naturæ connectit, præstantissimum, dum mundi machinæ præsidet, beatissimum, dum se divinis insinuat." *Ibid.*, 76a. *Cf.* lib. III., cap. ii. 116a, which has the following title: " Anima est *medius rerum gradus*, atque omnes gradus, tam

over the four elements: he treads the *earth*, ploughs the *water*, climbs up the highest tower into the *air* (not to mention the wings of Dædalus and Icarus), kindles *fire* and enjoys it on the hearth. But his capacity reaches still higher; with heavenly power he mounts up to heaven, and with more than heavenly mind he ascends above heaven.[1] Man is the God of the elements, the God of material things, the God of the earth; he is not merely God's representative on earth, but he is himself " *God upon earth*."[2] In thought he can penetrate the fabric of the universe and reconstruct God's whole creation and ordinances. It follows that his spirit is in essence almost identical with God's Spirit. Indeed, man could make the heavens, Ficino thinks, if only he had the necessary tools and had access to the heavenly material.[3] If one with all this before his eyes will not admit that the human soul is a *rival of God,* he is undoubtedly out of his mind, says Ficino.[4]

---

superiores quam inferiores connectit in unum, dum ipsa et ad superos ascendit, et descendit ad inferos." This idea is developed thus: " Si a Deo descenderis, tertio descensus gradu hanc reperis. Tertio quoque ascensus gradu, si supra corpus ascenderis, huiusmodi essentiam in natura summopere necessariam arbitramur." *Ibid.*

[1] " Terram calcat, sulcat aquam, altissimis turribus conscendit in ærem, ut pennas Dædali vel Icari prætermittam. Accendit ignem, et foco familiariter utitur et delectatur præcipue ipse solus. Merito cœlesti elemento solum cœleste animal delectatur. Cœlesti virtute ascendit cœlum, atque metitur. Supercœlesti mente transcendit cœlum." Theol. Platonica, lib. XIII., cap. iii. 289 f.

[2] " Deus est proculdubio animalium, qui utitur omnibus, imperat cunctis, instruit plurima. Deum quoque esse constitit elementorum, qui habitat colitque omnia. Deum denique omnium materiarum, qui tractat omnes, vertit et format. Qui tot tantisque in rebus corpori dominatur et immortalis Dei gerit vicem, est proculdubio immortalis." *Ibid.*, 290. " *Est utique Deus in terris.*" Lib. XVI., cap. vi. 369*a*. " Dei vicarii sumus in terra." Lib. XVI., cap. vii. 374*a*.

[3] " Cum igitur homo cœlorum ordinem unde moveantur, quo progrediantur, et quibus mensuris, quidve pariant, viderit, quis neget eum esse ingenio (ut ita loquar) pene eodem quo et author ille cœlorum ? ac posse quodammodo cœlos facere, si instrumenta nactus fuerit, materiamque cœlestem ?" Lib. XIII., cap. iii. 290*b*.

[4] " Quapropter dementem esse illum constat, qui negaverit animam quæ in artibus et gubernationibus est æmula Dei, esse divinam." *Ibid.*, 291*b*.

Since man is fundamentally a divine being, he cannot bear to see in God any perfection and power which he does not himself possess.[1] He is inflamed with desire to vie with God. Every attribute of God incites man to try to imitate Him. God is "primum ipsum verum et bonum," He is "auctor universorum," "super omnia," "in omnibus," "semper," and so on. But these are just what we strive to be.[2] Man is not satisfied, however, merely to be like God; he can in his "animi magnitudo" be content with nothing less than *becoming God* himself.[3] This attempt to raise himself to the Divine level is as natural to man as flight is to a bird.[4] And so we see, too, says Ficino, that man not only like all other things loves himself, but he also has a tendency to worship and adore himself as a god.[5] This tendency is so deeply rooted in human nature that it even asserts itself in the most insane men. It appears in the obstinate and stiff-necked way in which they stick to their own opinion, " as if it were a divine doctrine."[6] Ficino finds a further proof of man's divine nature and worth in the fact that those who have performed special service to the human race are

---

[1] So Nietzsche was not the first to think: " if there were gods, how could I endure not to be a god !" (*Thus Spake Zarathustra*, ii. 2). What is new in this idea is the hypothetical beginning, and the negative conclusion: " Thus there are no gods." It is not a far cry from Ficino to Nietzsche, who replaces God with the Superman, and to Feuerbach, who conceives God as the projection of man's wish-fantasy.

[2] Theol. Platonica, lib. XIV., cap. i. 299*a*.

[3] The whole of lib. XIV., 298-319, has as its theme: " *Quod anima nitatur Deus fieri.*" " In quo apparebit mira animi magnitudo, cui non satis fuerit æmulari Deum iis miris quos diximus modis, nisi etiam fiat Deus." Lib. XIV., cap. i. 298*b*.

[4] " Totus igitur animæ nostræ conatus est, ut Deus efficiatur. Conatus talis naturalis est hominibus non minus quam conatus avibus ad volandum." Lib. XIV., cap. i. 299*a*.

[5] *Cf.* lib. XIV., cap. viii. 310*a*, which discusses the subject: " *quod colimus nos ipsos ac Deum.*" " Primo, quod omnes non modo ut cætera faciunt cuncta, se diligunt et tuentur, verumetiam *colunt seipsos magnopere, et quasi quædam numina venerantur.*" *Ibid.*

[6] " Idem rursus, sed aliter agunt homines dementissimi, prout nimium placent ipsi sibi, pertinacissime in sua persistunt opinione, sententiam suam tanquam divinum decretum mordicus tenent." *Ibid.*, 310*b*.

glorified by all men as divine beings, and after death they are given divine adoration—of which we vainly seek any counterpart among the beasts.[1] For Ficino, this faith of man in his own divinity and man's worship of himself form the essential content of Christianity.[2]

[1] " Cuncti denique homines, excellentissimos animos, atque optime de humano genere meritos in hac vita, ut divinos honorant, solutos a corporibus adorant, ut deos quosdam Deo summo clarissimos, quos prisci Heroas nominaverunt. Tanta vero ad se et ad suos reverentia non apparet in bestiis, nedum vilioribus, sed neque etiam in maioribus. Atque hic primus est modus quo homines divinum imitantur cultum, videlicet quia seipsos ut deos colunt." *Ibid.*

[2] The view is sometimes put forward that Ficino's thought has a particularly Pauline tone. The reason for this very odd idea is probably that Ficino wrote a commentary on the Epistle to the Romans and that the formula " sola fide " occurs in it. But knowing Ficino's thought from the rest of his works, we should be inclined to doubt a priori the possibility of any Pauline influence. And the researches of W. Dress have fully justified this doubt. In his *op. cit.* he devotes an extensive section (pp. 151-216) to Ficino's commentary on Romans. Ficino himself, of course, was unaware of the gulf that separates his idea of religion from Christianity: he believes that with his Platonism he is simply laying a firmer foundation for the Christianity of the Church. But his commentary on Romans itself is extraordinarily clear evidence how little he really understood Paul. Ficino largely follows Aquinas's commentary on Romans. He has a certain advantage over Aquinas in his mastery of Greek, which enabled him to go back to the original text at certain points, and also in his finer psychological perception. And yet he obviously falls far behind Aquinas in comprehension of the theological problems of his text. He approaches the biblical texts with Platonic presuppositions and treats them as full of secret lore, like the formulas of the ancient mysteries. The way to the understanding of Scripture is described as a Neoplatonic-mystical ἀναγωγή with the mystagogue Paul as guide. As regards the formula " sola fide," Ficino is so far from taking it in a Pauline sense and approaching Luther, that he uses it to express a Neoplatonic idea of man's relation to God: " fide sola, ut Platonici probant, ad Deum accedimus. This must doubtless be translated: only by way of contemplation, through devotion of the soul, do we come to God. For fides represents the organ of our kinship with the prima intelligentia, which is also the primum agens." (*Op. cit.*, p. 200.) It should further be added that when Ficino speaks of " sola fides " he means nothing else but " fides caritate formata." Hence every hint of similarity between Ficino's thought and Luther's disappears. Dress sums up his conclusions on Ficino's commentary on Romans as follows: " What is revealed in his work gives us a shocking picture of the religious and theological helplessness and inadequacy of this first representative of the religious humanism of Italy when confronted with a testimony of primitive Christian piety " (*op. cit.*, p. 215). With this, the myth of Ficino's Paulinism can be removed from the order of the day. All that remains to Ficino is the anthropocentric, eudæmonistic conception of religion, which, in genuine Renascence spirit, puts man at the centre of the universe, and makes his own godlikeness and immortality the inmost heart of religion.

III

THE DIVINE SELF-LOVE

AFTER all that has been said above, it is hardly surprising that love in the Christian sense finds no place at all in Ficino's thought. The only love he knows is Eros-love, and that in its most elementary form of self-love. *All* love, whether God's love or man's love, is at bottom *self-love,* according to Ficino.

If God is called "love," it is not to say that He loves in the strict sense of the word, but only (1) that He is the *cause* of all love, and (2) that He *loves Himself.*[1] Here Ficino has adopted the Neoplatonic idea of love in the form given to it by Pseudo-Dionysius. God is Eros[2]—that is, Eros to Himself. As the highest good, He perpetually enjoys His own perfection.[3] And just as the Trinity centres upon itself

---

[1] " Præterea Deus appellatur amor [ἔρως], tum quoniam amorem in omnibus procreat, sicut a Peripateticis nominatur in sole calor, quoniam caloris est causa, tum etiam quia seipsum amat." In Dionysium Areopagitam De divinis nominibus, tom. ii. 49*a.*

[2] "Testantur hoc et Theologi veteres, qui amoris nomen [τὸ τοῦ ἔρωτος ὄνομα] Deo tribuerunt. Quod etiam posteriores Theologi summopere confirmarunt." In convivium Platonis, de amore, commentarius, Oratio I., cap. iv., tom. ii. 286*a.*

It is vastly interesting to compare Plato's text in the Symposium with Ficino's commentary on it. Ficino is not content merely to explain the meaning of Plato's words, but he brings in the whole of the tradition based on Plato, both from antiquity and Christianity. Consequently, he offers a splendid opportunity for a concrete study of all that in the course of time had attached itself to and nourished itself upon the Platonic doctrine of Eros, and also how this doctrine had been transformed and modified in the process. As our present study is primarily concerned with the Christian idea of love, our chief interest is naturally in the modification of Christian Agape by its confusion with Eros. But the matter could be viewed from the other side, to see how this confusion involved a modification of the original Platonic idea of Eros, an extraordinarily interesting question, but beyond the scope of this work.

[3] " Quapropter ipsum bonum in primis hoc habet, ut se velit summopere, sibique placeat, et tale sit omnino, quale vult ipsum." Theol. Platonica, lib. II., cap. xii., tom. i. 107*a.*

and is bent upon itself in eternal love—amans, amor, amatum[1]—so also that love which proceeds from God and permeates and holds together the whole universe in order finally to lead all things back to God, is simply an expression of His self-love.[2] And when God loves us men, it is because we are His work; in us also, God loves nothing but Himself.[3]

But as God is thus bent upon Himself in ceaseless love, so also is the human spirit, which imitates God in all things.[4] Here, too, self-love is the all-determining force. And not only is it so, but it ought to be so, according to Ficino.[5] Only on this basis can we speak of loving another person. For in the fellow-man whom we love, we recognise ourselves and love in him nothing other than ourselves.[6] Indeed, Ficino does not even shrink from reducing our love for God wholly to self-love. Love to God is the means, self-love the end—Ficino announces this unequivocally. Now there have, of course, been pointers in this direction in the earlier history of the idea of love. Augustine asserts that love for God and true self-love coincide. Yet there is a vast difference between the two ways of speaking about self-love. Augustine thinks of the self-love of the man who humbles himself before God, and finds in God his all and his "bonum,"

---

[1] "Est igitur penes Deum, amans, amor, amatum." In Dion. Areop. De div. nom., tom. ii. 49a. ". . . quo Deus se amando quasi circulo revolvitur in seipsum." *Ibid.* ". . . primus amor penes primum bonum ex ipso in ipsum circulariter se revolvens." *Ibid.*

[2] "Divina vero hæc species in omnibus amorem, hoc est sui desiderium procreavit. Quoniam si Deus ad se rapit mundum, mundusque rapitur: unus quidem continuus attractus est a Deo incipiens, transiens in mundum, in Deum denique desinens: qui quasi circulo quodam in idem unde manavit iterum remeat." In convivium, Oratio II., cap. ii., tom. ii. 287a.

[3] "Si Deus sibi ipse placet, si amat seipsum, profecto imagines suas et sua diligit opera. Diligit faber opera sua, quæ ex materia fecit externa. Amat multo magis filium genitor." Theol. Platonica, lib. II., cap. xiii., tom. i. 108b.

[4] "Mens reflectitur in seipsam." Theol. Platonica, lib. IX., cap. i. 198b. ". . . per se movetur, et in circulum." Lib. V., cap. i. 132.

[5] "Carissima enim sua cuique esse debent." Epist., lib. I. 654b.

[6] "Idcirco cum in amante se amatus agnoscat, amare illum compellitur." *Ibid.*, 655a.

saying: " Mihi adhærere Deo bonum est." But in the self-glorifying man of the Renascence, who believes he can " compete " with God and prefers to regard Him as a means at the disposal of the human god, we meet a self-love of a very different kind. Nowhere else has human self-love been preached in this sense and with such unprejudiced candour and naive self-conceit. Why do we love God? Ficino answers: "Ut nos ipsos præ cæteris amplectamur." All other things we are to love in God, but in God we love ultimately only ourselves.[1] It may seem strange that Ficino allows the chapter which, according to his own title, is to treat of *how we ought to love God*,[2] to conclude with a statement about *self-love*; and yet that is just as it should be, for self-love is in fact Ficino's last word.

[1] ". . . ut Deum primo in rebus coluisse videamur, quo res deinde in Deo colamus, resque in Deo ideo venerari, *ut nos ipsos præ cæteris amplectamur, et amando Deum nos ipsos videamur amavisse.*" In convivium, Oratio VI., cap. xxi., tom. ii. 315*a*.

[2] Oratio VI., cap. xxi. has as its title: " Quomodo Deus amandus," 315*a*.

CHAPTER SIX

THE RENEWAL OF THE AGAPE MOTIF
IN THE REFORMATION

I

LUTHER'S COPERNICAN REVOLUTION

1. THEOCENTRIC LOVE

THE deepest import of the great religious revolution that occurred in the Reformation, might be summed up briefly by saying that in this event theocentric religion asserted itself. In his campaign against Catholic Christianity,[1] Luther is governed by a completely uniform tendency. Whatever we take as our starting-point—his idea of justification, his conception of love or anything else—we are always led back to the same thing—namely, that *Luther insists, in opposition to all egocentric forms of religion, upon a purely theocentric relation to God*. In Catholic piety he finds a tendency which he cannot help regarding as a complete perversion of the inmost meaning of religion: the egocentric tendency. Here everything centres upon man himself, upon what he does and what happens to him. Salvation, God's own work, which He has reserved to Himself and accomplished through Christ, is transformed more or less into a work of man; righteousness is transformed from something God gives into something man achieves. At the same time, everything also centres upon man's own *interest*. Through the idea of merit, the good which he does is put into intentional connection with eternal blessedness, so that it comes to be regarded less as obedience to God, than from

---

[1] It will be evident in the following pages that the term " Catholic " is not used in the sense which it bears in the Creed.—*Translator's note.*

the point of view of the profit which it yields for man. Everything is measured by the standard of human desire and judged by the importance it has for man. This applies even to God Himself. When He is extolled as the highest good, summum bonum, that is simply a way of saying that, when measured by the standard of human desire, He proves to comprise all the desirable things that man can possibly wish. Luther's main objection to Catholic piety is always this, that it *puts man's own self in God's place*.[1] This tendency must first be rooted out if there is to be room for true fellowship with God, which has its centre in God Himself, God who gives everything and has a right to everything.

Luther feels himself to be the herald of theocentric religion in its campaign against all egocentricity whatsoever. With incomparable clarity he has expressed this opposition in the manifesto with which he introduces his lectures on Romans (1515-1516). Giving the "summarium huius epistole," he declares that there is something which is to be broken down and destroyed, and something contrary which is to be built up and planted. What is to be broken down and destroyed is everything " that is in us," all our righteousness and wisdom, absolutely everything in which we take a selfish delight. What is to be built up and planted is " everything that is outside us and in Christ." The righteousness by which God wills to save us, is not produced by us, but has come to us from elsewhere; it is not derived from our earth, but has come to us from heaven.[2]

[1] *Cf.* my *Urkristendom och reformation*, 1932, pp. 109-115 and 120-133.

[2] Römerbrief, ii., p. 3, 3 f.; 2, 4 ff.: " ' To pluck up, and to break down, and to destroy, and to overthrow,' namely, everything that is in us (*i.e.*, all that of ourselves and in ourselves pleases us), ' and to build and to plant,' namely, everything that is outside us and in Christ. . . . For God wills to save us not by domestic, but by extraneous righteousness and wisdom, not that which comes and springs from us, but that which comes from elsewhere into us, not that which originates in our earth, but that which comes down from heaven. Therefore it behoves us to be instructed in a righteousness altogether external and alien. Wherefore it is first necessary that our own and domestic righteousness should be rooted out."

It is fundamentally the same contrast which recurs as regards the idea of love. Luther has observed how the whole of the Catholic doctrine of love displays an *egocentric perversion*. Here, as so often elsewhere, moralism and eudæmonism have gone hand in hand to produce the same result. Moralism finds expression in the doctrine of love, chiefly by the fact that love is regarded essentially from the point of view of human achievement. However much Catholicism might speak of God's love, the centre of gravity in our relation to God was nevertheless placed primarily in the love we owe to God. "Die Liebe Gottes," the love of God, is less God's love to us than our love to God. Thus the moralistic attitude becomes at the same time egocentric. But eudæmonism also leads to the same egocentric result. In its Catholic presentation love never loses the marks of acquisitive love. It is therefore entirely logical that it should be traced back in the last resort to self-love.

This brings us to the point where Luther's significance in the history of the Christian idea of love becomes perfectly plain. *Against the egocentric attitude which had come to mark the Catholic conception of love, Luther sets a thoroughly theocentric idea of love.* When Luther wishes to say what love in the Christian sense is, he draws his picture not from our love, not from the realm of human love at all, but from God's love, especially as this has been revealed in Christ. But this love is not an acquisitive love, but a love that gives.

There is an inner connection and an exact correspondence between Luther's doctrine of justification and his view of love. *The very same thing which made him a reformer in the matter of justification, made him also the reformer of the Christian idea of love.* Just as justification is not a question of the "iustitia" in virtue of which God makes His demands upon us, but of the "iustitia" which He bestows, so Christian love is strictly not concerned with the love with which we love God, but essentially with the love with which

God Himself loves. Luther himself clearly saw this parallel between his view of justification and of love, as witness the often-quoted passage in the *Table Talk*, where he tells of his discovery of the true meaning of Rom. i. 17. In the less frequently quoted continuation of this passage, the parallel with reference to love is discussed.[1]

2. FELLOWSHIP WITH GOD ON OUR LEVEL

" Theocentric fellowship with God *versus* egocentric "— with this general formula we have given a preliminary state-ment of the meaning of the Reformation. To elucidate this a step further, we may add the following thesis: quite soon in the Early Church, and still more markedly in the Mediæval Church, fellowship with God was conceived as a fellowship on the level of God's holiness; but in Luther a Copernican revolution takes place, and fellowship with God now becomes a fellowship on our human level. In an acutely pointed paradox, Luther's conception might be ex-pressed by the formula, " *Fellowship with God on the basis of sin, not of holiness.*"

When God becomes for man a reality which he seriously

---

[1] Tischreden, Nr. 5518 (WA Tischreden, Bd. V, p. 210, 7 ff.): " I was long in error, and knew not how I was therein. I did know something, I dare say, and yet I knew nothing of what it was, till at last I came upon the place in Rom. i.: ' The righteous shall live by faith.' That helped me. Then I saw of what righteousness Paul speaks: there stood in the text ' righteousness '; then I put the abstract and concrete together and became sure of my case, learned to distinguish between the righteousness of the law and of the gospel. Before, I lacked nothing but that I made no distinction between law and gospel, held them to be all one, and used to say that Christ differed not from Moses save in time and perfection. But when I found the distinction, that the law was one thing, the gospel another, then I broke through. Then Doctor Pomeranus: I, too, began to change when I read concerning the love (charitate) of God, that its meaning was passive, namely, that with which we are loved by God. Before that, I always used to take love in the active sense. Doctor [Luther]: Aye, it is clear, charitate or dilectione ! I mean, that it is often understood of that with which God loves us. But in Hebrew the genitives of love (genitivi de charitate) are difficult. Then Pomeranus: But still, the rest of the passages afterwards explain those."

takes into account, so that he is disposed to come into a right relationship with Him, then it is quite natural for man to begin by asking how he can adjust his relation to God by his own conduct and efforts. In order to be able to meet God, the Holy One, man must seek in the highest possible degree to become holy himself. But in this very beginning, Luther sees the fundamental error of the religion of the natural man—namely, that he wishes to gain standing for himself before God. Whereas God wills to save us by a " righteousness from God " (Rom. x. 3), man seeks to " produce a righteousness of his own." The religion of the natural man consists in this, that he wishes to become good and holy, and by this means to enter into fellowship with God. But this is just the source of all his perverseness. It is a satanic temptation which, if we yield to it, leads us away from God and prevents us from receiving His love in Christ.[1] In us men there is an ineradicable will to order our relationship to God ourselves : " I would so like to be godly." But the error, the false relation to God, which it is the task of theology to overcome, lies already in this will.[2] For this intention, apparently so good and praiseworthy, has its deepest ground in man's unwillingness to live wholly upon God's " misericordia,"[3] in other words, upon God's Agape in Christ. In the will to purify oneself first, before one will take refuge in God, there lies a secret " præsumptio."[4] By so doing, man ascribes to himself the work which God has reserved to Himself, and which He carries out through

---

[1] " That is Satan, aided by our wisdom, nature, religion, which are born in us." WA 40, 2, p. 337, 6 f. *Cf.* p. 336, 11 f.

[2] " A most lively sighing goes on throughout the whole length of life, etc.: ' I would so like to be godly (fromm).' To conquer this natural disposition is the theological virtue." *Ibid.*, p. 339, 9 f.

[3] " Shall I not rather say ' Miserere mei '; for if I be godly, then I shall have no need of ' Miserere.' " *Ibid.*, p. 333, 3 f.

[4] " He walks in his presumption as a monk, and will first purify himself by his works." *Ibid.*, p. 333, 10 f. " It is an infernal thing not to be willing to run to God unless I feel myself pure from sins." *Ibid.*, p 333, 1 f,

Christ. For to give grace, forgiveness of sins, life and righteousness, together with deliverance from sin and death, is not the work of any creature, but belongs solely and alone to the Divine majesty.[1] When man nevertheless seeks to make it his own, this is an assault upon God's divinity. Luther cannot find words strong enough to warn us against this idea, apparently so godly but really so godless, of possessing our own holiness before God: " Thou holy Devil, thou wilt make me a saint."[2] God has revealed to us once for all the only right Way of salvation, when He sent His Son into the world and delivered Him up to death for sinners. We are following a false Way of salvation, when we seek to ascend up to God in heaven.[3] For in Christ He has descended to us. " For God's grace and His kingdom with all virtues must come to us, if we are to attain it; we can never come to Him; just as Christ from heaven came to us on earth, and not we from earth ascended to Him in heaven."[4] By this, God has plainly shown us that He will have nothing at all to do with holy men. A holy man is purely and simply a fiction, a make-believe human god.[5] When the devil tempts man to seek fellowship with God on the level of holiness, he should be repulsed with the words : " *Thou wilt make me holy; hast thou not heard tell that Christ was not given for holy men? . . . If I have no sin, then I need not Christ.*"[6] And so Luther can give his pastoral advice : " Beware of ever aspiring to such great purity that thou refusest to appear to thyself, nay to be, a sinner. For Christ dwells only in sinners. For *to this end He descended* from heaven,

---

[1] " Dare autem gratiam et remissionem peccatorum et vivificationem, iustificationem, liberationem a morte, peccatis non sunt opera creaturæ sed unius, solius maiestatis." WA 40, 1, p. 81, 4 ff.

[2] *Ibid.*, p. 88, 1.

[3] WA 40, 2, p. 329, 8 f.

[4] WA 2, p. 98, 25 ff.

[5] " God has nothing to do with holy men. A holy man is a fiction, like man-God, man-stone, -stock, -tree." WA 40, 2, p. 347, 9 f.

[6] WA 40, 1, p. 89, 1 ff.

where He dwelt in the righteous, *that He might even dwell in sinners.*"[1] It was not for imaginary, but for real sinners, that Christ died.[2]

Our fellowship with God, then, rests for us on the basis not of holiness but of sin;[3] and for God, upon His entirely unmotivated, groundless love, which justifies not the man who is already righteous and holy, but precisely the sinner.[4] There is no other justification than the justification of the sinner, no other fellowship with God than that on the basis of one's own sin and the groundless Divine love. In this sense, the justified Christian man is "simul iustus et peccator"[5]—in himself a sinner, but justified and taken into fellowship with God by the Divine love—that is, he is treated as only a man who is in himself righteous ought, in human judgment, to be treated. With this, Luther renews the primitive Christian Agape tradition, which at an early stage was interrupted in the Church, and restores Jesus' message of fellowship with God—"I have not come to call the righteous, but to call sinners" (Mk. ii. 17)—and Paul's gospel of the justification of the sinner.

Luther is fully aware of the revolutionary nature of this conception. He knows that by it he is pronouncing judg-

---

[1] "Cave, ne aliquando ad tantam puritatem aspires, ut *peccator* tibi videri nolis, immo esse. Christus enim non nisi in peccatoribus habitat. Ideo enim descendit de cœlo, ubi habitabat in justis, ut etiam habitaret in peccatoribus." *Dr. Martin Luthers Briefwechsel* (Enders), Bd. I., 1884, p. 29.

[2] "They are not feigned and counterfeit sins for which He died." WA 40, 1, p. 88, 2 f. "This is the most sweet mercy of God the Father, that He saves not counterfeit, but real sinners." WA 1, p. 370, 9 f.

[3] "But my Isaiah stands sure, the vanquisher of free will, and lays it down *that grace is given not to merits or the efforts of free will, but to sins and demerits.*" WA 18, p. 738, 25 f.

[4] "God wants nothing but sinners. If He is a justifier, then there must be righteousness (iusticia) with Him, that He may justify the ungodly." WA 40, 2, p. 327, 5 ff.

[5] "Thus a Christian man is both righteous and a sinner." WA 40, 1, p. 368, 26. "Thus a Christian man is both sinner and Saint." *Ibid.*, p. 368, 9. *Cf.* G. Ljunggren: *Synd och skuld i Luthers teologi*, 1928, cap. v.: Simul justus et peccator, p. 252 ff.; and R. Hermann: *Luthers These "Gerecht und Sünder zugleich,"* 1930.

ment not only on Catholic "work-righteousness," but on "all religions under heaven."[1]   Here there is no difference between Jews, Papists and Turks; in them all we find the same religious attitude, that false religion characteristic of reason (ratio), of which the basic idea is: " If I do this and that, God will be gracious to me."[2]   Ultimately, there are only two different religions, that which builds on faith in Christ, and that which builds on reason and one's own works.   These are absolutely opposed to one another: if we can deliver ourselves from sin and enter as holy men into fellowship with God, then Christ is superfluous.[3]   Christianity, therefore, is bound to regard this false religion as its real adversary.   Every attempt to make one's way to God by self-sanctification runs counter to the message of Christ's self-offering.   This latter falls like a thunderbolt and annihilates the righteousness which comes from the law.[4]   With this artillery—the message that Christ was given for our sins —we must demolish all the false, egocentric religions.[5]

---

[1] " Thus monasteries and *all religions under heaven* are condemned; all cults are condemned *inasmuch as they seek to furnish righteousness.*" WA 40, 1, p. 366, 3 f.

[2] " That is false religion which can be conceived by reason.   That is the religion of the Pope, Jews, Turks, like the Pharisee with his: " I give tithes," " I am not," etc.   He can go no higher.   There is no difference between the Jew, the Papist, the Turk.   Their rites indeed are diverse, but their heart and thoughts are the same: as the Carthusian thinks, so also does the Turk, namely, " If I do thus, God will be merciful to me."   The same passion is in the minds of all men.   There is no middle way between knowledge of Christ and human working.   After that, it does not matter whether a man is a Papist, Turk or Jew; one faith is the same as the other."   WA 40, 1, p. 603, 5 ff.

[3] '' If our sins can be taken away by our satisfactions and monasteries, what need was there for the Son of God to be delivered up for them ?"   WA 40, 1, p. 83, 12 f.

[4] " ' He hath given ' . . . ' Himself '; for what ?   For sins.   But [these words] are very thunderclaps from heaven against the righteousness of the law and of men."   *Ibid.*, p. 83, 4 ff.

[5] " With this artillery we must shoot down all cloisters and religions."   *Ibid.*, p. 83, 11 f.   The printed text of the same passage reads rather more fully: " With this sort of gunshot, engines of war and battering-rams, the Papacy must be destroyed and all religions, all cults, all works and merits of all nations must be overthrown."   *Ibid.*, p. 83, 27 ff.

To understand Luther at this point, we must observe that he does not unquestioningly regard everything that is religious as *eo ipso* valuable. The fact that a man turns away from the sensible and temporal life and devotes himself to the "spiritual," does not persuade Luther without more ado that he is on the way towards Christianity. For Luther, the distinction between "carnal" and "spiritual" has nothing to do with the traditional contrast of reason and sense,[1] of a higher and a lower part of man's nature. The natural man is "fleshly" in his whole being, in all that he does and is.[2] Not merely the sensible part of man, not merely that which is usually regarded as degrading and bad, but also the highest and best in him, and primarily this, is "flesh."[3] Even his righteousness, his religion and worship of God belongs to the realm of the "flesh."[4] So far from regarding these as a step away from sin, we must on the contrary regard them as "double sin."[5] For first and foremost, in spite of his imaginary righteousness, man is a transgressor of the law, if we

---

[1] It is to C. Stange's credit that he has given serious attention to the fundamental difference between Luther and Mediæval theology on this central question, and has also drawn out the consequences of this for Luther's thought in general. By a series of important studies, Stange thus anticipated K. Holl and provided an impulse for the Luther renascence in Germany. *Cf.* for our purposes, the following works of Stange in particular: *Die Heilsbedeutung des Gesetzes*, 1904; *Luthers älteste ethische Disputationen*, 1904; *Religion und Sittlichkeit bei den Reformatoren*, 1905; *Luther und das sittliche Ideal*, 1919; *Die Unsterblichkeit der Seele*, 1925. A substantial part of Stange's researches on Luther is now collected in his great work *Studien zur Theologie Luthers*, 1928.

[2] " . . . totum hominem esse carnem." WA 18, p. 742, 7. "All are flesh, for all savour of the flesh, that is, of what is their own, and are devoid of the glory of God and the spirit of God." *Ibid.*, p. 742, 19 f.

[3] "The principal part in man is flesh, or that which is most excellent in man is flesh." WA 18, p. 741, 23 f.

[4] "*Thus the highest righteousness, wisdom, will, understanding, is flesh.*" WA 40, 1, p. 244, 2 f. "And yet he says here that they, forsaking the Spirit, do now end in the *flesh, that is, the righteousness and wisdom of the flesh and of reason which seeks to be justified by the law—whatsoever is most excellent in man, apart from the Spirit, is called flesh, even religion itself.*" *Ibid.*, p. 347, 8 ff.

[5] "Therefore that righteousness is double unrighteousness, that wisdom double folly." WA 40, 1, p. 95, 4 ff.

consider the deepest meaning of the law; and secondly, he adds to this the sin of sins, by despising grace.[1] Nor does it improve matters that man imagines he is serving God by such righteousness. Indeed, it makes things still worse. Thus instead of the usual idea that because something is religious it is therefore valuable, Luther declares, with reference to fellowship with God on the level of holiness, that because something is religious it is therefore doubly sinful. To become " religiosus " in this sense is a horrible abomination.[2] It is to take the false Way of salvation, which simply leads man still further away from God and makes him still more unsusceptible to His grace. Before God we may not claim to be anything else but sinners.[3]

The deepest difference between Catholicism and Luther can be expressed by the following formulæ; in Catholicism: fellowship with God on God's own level, on the basis of holiness; in Luther: fellowship with God on our level, on the basis of sin. In Catholicism, it is a question of a fellowship with God motivated by some worth—produced, it is true, by the infusion of Caritas—to be found in man; in Luther, fellowship with God rests exclusively on God's unmotivated love, justification is the justification of the sinner, the Christian is " simul iustus et peccator." It is above all this last—Luther's assertion of the sinfulness remaining even in the justified man—which has caused offence in Catholic circles. " According to Luther, God accepts the sinner as

[1] " It is a most horrible sin to refuse to be justified by Christ. What is more grievous than to spurn the grace of God ? Or is it not enough to have spurned the law of God ? Have we not sinned enough in that we are transgressors of the law; are we to add *the sin of sins*, that we should spurn His grace as well?" WA 40, 1, p. 300, 7 ff.

[2] " Who can believe that it is so horrible a crime to become a monk ?" WA, 40, 1, p. 325, 1 f. The printed text of this passage reads: " But whoever would have believed or thought that it was so horrible and abominable a crime to become ' religiosus ' ?" *Ibid.*, p. 325, 16 f.

[3] " Flesh and all, we are to be called sinners." WA 40, 2, p. 340, 7. " Therefore we must always pray, for we are always sinners. . . . Over thy sin say thou a ' Miserere.' " *Ibid.*, p. 339, 8 ff.

righteous in such a way that the sinner remains a sinner "
(Denifle). This is in absolute conflict with Catholic Christianity, which, in accord with its upward tendency, seeks to
bring man into fellowship with God on the level of God's
holiness.

LUTHER'S VITAL PROBLEM: THE SETTLEMENT
OF THE ISSUE BETWEEN THE EROS AND
THE AGAPE MOTIFS

1. Synthesis and Reformation

In giving our account of Augustine's thought, we were able
to describe the settlement of the issue between the Eros and
the Agape motifs as the great problem of his life. The
primitive Christian and the Neoplatonic tradition equally
mould his interpretation of Christianity. The Ways of salvation of Eros and Agape meet in his person, and the result of
their meeting is his doctrine of Caritas. If we now use
exactly the same phrase—"the settlement of the issue between the Eros and the Agape motifs"—to describe Luther's
vital problem, this is to indicate that it is fundamentally the
same great problem with which Augustine has already
wrestled, which now enters a new phase and receives a new
answer in Luther. In Augustine, the issue between Eros and
Agape is decided in favour of synthesis; in Luther, in favour
of reformation. Augustine unites the two motifs in the
Caritas-synthesis; Luther shatters that synthesis.

It may perhaps seem strange to define Luther's vital problem as the settlement of the issue between Eros and Agape.
Luther himself did not use these terms, nor does he consciously seem to have considered the problem of love from
this point of view. Yet it is not difficult to see that this is
the problem with which Luther is in fact wrestling. Even
if he did not directly speak of Eros, he did, during an important period of his spiritual development, personally follow
the Eros Way of salvation in the form of Caritas. He tried

all three Mediæval heavenly ladders, and the whole tension between the Eros and Agape motifs was present for him in the idea of Caritas. The refinement of the idea of Caritas, which Mediæval theology produced, helped to open his eyes to the impracticability of this Way of salvation. He only reaches a solution of the difficulty, however, when he realises that the righteousness involved in man's justification is not a righteousness from us or in us, but "righteousness from God." This puts him on an entirely new Way of salvation, for "righteousness from God" is equivalent to God's Agape.

In what follows we shall merely indicate very briefly how this question is bound up with Luther's personal development, and illustrate by an example—that of the Sacrifice of the Mass and the Lord's Supper—its central significance for Luther's thought.[1]

2. THE STRUGGLES OF THE MONK AND CONTRITIO

That Luther's vital problem concerns the idea of Caritas and the tension this involves is very evident from the fact that Luther's decisive struggle in the monastery, which eventually led to a complete break with the Catholic Way

[1] Apart from C. Stange's works cited above, the following are particularly important for determining the general structure of Luther's thought: K. Holl: *Gesammelte Aufsätze zur Kirchengeschichte*, Bd. I.: *Luther*, 1921; E. Hirsch: *Luthers Gottesanschauung*, 1918; H. Boehmer: *Der junge Luther*, 1925; G. Aulén: *Den kristna gudsbilden*, 1927; G. Ljunggren: *Synd och skuld i Luthers teologi*, 1928; R. Bring: *Dualismen hos Luther*, 1929; W. von Loewenich: *Luthers Theologia crucis*, 1929; E. Vogelsang: *Die Anfänge von Luthers Christologie*, 1929; *Der angefochtene Christus bei Luther*, 1932; E. Seeberg: *Luthers Theologie*, i., 1929; P. Althaus: *Communio sanctorum*, 1929; R. Hermann: *Luthers These 'Gerecht und Sünder zugleich,'* 1930; P. Althaus: *Gottes Gottheit als Sinn der Rechtfertigungslehre Luthers* (Lutherjahrbuch, 1931); *Gottes Gottheit bei Luther* (Lutherjahrbuch, 1935).

Of the comprehensive literature on Luther, the following Swedish works may also be mentioned: E. Billing: *1517-1521*, 1917; A. Runestam: *Den kristliga friheten hos Luther och Melanchton*, 1917; Hj. Holmquist: *Luther, Loyola, Calvin*, 3rd edn., 1926; T. Bohlin: *Gudstro och Kristustro hos Luther*, 1927; S. von Engeström: *Luthers trosbegrepp*, 1933; H. Olsson: *Grundproblemet i Luthers socialetik*, i., 1934.

of salvation, was centred upon the question of Caritas and the possibility of a perfect penitence ("contritio") based upon it.

In trying to determine the cause and content of Luther's struggles as a monk, scholars have pursued very different courses and pointed to a series of different circumstances which may be thought to have played their part. As regards the main point, however, the sources leave us in no doubt at all as to what the deepest ground of this conflict was. It was the refinement of the Caritas doctrine by Mediæval theology,[1] which brought Luther to the point where this doctrine had to be broken down. He found this sublimated idea of Caritas in Occam and Biel, with their demand for a penitence and contrition based not merely on fear and acquisitive love, but on a pure and unselfish love of God. This demand becomes the more pointed when the authors mentioned affirm that man is able "ex puris naturalibus," by his natural powers alone, to love God above all things. It was this theory which Luther in the monastery tried to put into practice in his own life; it was not simply a theoretical problem for him, but a vital problem. It is in his attempt to achieve unselfish love for God and the "contritio" based on this, that the Caritas-synthesis breaks down for Luther. The more seriously he takes the commandment to love God with all his heart, and the more strict the demand that his love for God shall be pure and unselfish, the more impossible it becomes. It is not merely an external legalism of which Luther perceives the inner impossibility, but he has in view the highest and deepest of all commandments and the most inward of them, the Commandment of Love. In the meaning it acquires from the doctrine of Caritas, it becomes in its deepest and most spiritual form the heaviest possible burden,[2] capable more than anything

[1] *Cf. supra*, pp. 650 f.

[2] "But this understanding of the law spiritually is far more deadly, since it makes the law impossible to fulfil and thereby brings man to despair of his own strength and abases him, for no one is without anger, no one without lust: such

else of keeping man far from God. External commandments are easier to deal with, but the commandment which requires love with all the heart can only be a law which damns. In the monastery Luther learnt by personal experience that the Commandment of Love in its most intense and inward form is the most tyrannical law; indeed, it is a real devil for the troubled conscience.

Luther finds the solution of this vital problem only when he has learnt from Paul to make the right distinction between law and gospel, " discrimen inter legem et euangelium."[1] From the evidence of Scripture he realises that he, like the Church as a whole, has been following a false Way of salvation, the Way of Caritas. Our Caritas is not a way to God. Man is justified not by ascending to God in Caritas, but solely by receiving in faith God's love, which has descended to us in Christ. With this, the Caritas-synthesis has fallen to pieces, vanquished by God's Agape.

3. THE SACRIFICE OF THE MASS AND THE LORD'S SUPPER

It could be shown without difficulty how the Agape motif has set its seal on Luther's thought at every point. Here we shall confine ourselves to a single illustration of this fact, and refer to Luther's conception of the Lord's Supper.[2] In this, Luther has to fight a battle on two fronts, against the Catholic Church with its doctrine of transubstantiation and the sacrifice of the Mass, and against the spiritualising doctrine of the Lord's Supper taught by the " fanatical spirits "

---

are we from birth. But what will a man do, whither will he go, when oppressed by such an impossible law?" WA 1, p. 105, 14 ff.

[1] Cf. supra, p. 684, n. 1.

[2] On this subject cf. Y. Brilioth: Eucharistic Faith and Practice, Evangelical and Catholic, 1930, pp. 94 ff.; P. Althaus: Luthers Abendmahlslehre, Lutherjahrbuch, Jahrgang XI., 1929, p. 2 ff.; E. Sommerlath: Der Sinn des Abendmahls, 1930; G. Ljunggren: Luthers nattvardslära (Ordet och tron. Till E. Billing på hans sextioårsdag, 1931, p. 193 ff.).

(Schwärmer, fanatici spiritus). Luther's view has often been construed as an attempt to steer a middle course between these two extremes, the magical and the spiritualistic; against the former he denies any miraculous transformation, whilst he still insists, against the latter, upon the real presence of Christ in the Lord's Supper. Such an interpretation, however, in no way touches Luther's real meaning. He did not regard his view of the Lord's Supper as a via media, nor the two views which he attacked as two opposite extremes. Rather than opposites, they are simply different expressions of one and the same thing. Both are examples of the same false Way of salvation; in both cases the Lord's Supper, which is Christ's condescension to us, is transformed into an attempt on our part to mount up to God.

It is this perversion of the Lord's Supper which we find in the Catholic sacrifice of the Mass. In the Lord's Supper Christ has instituted His testament—that is, He wills to give us His gift there. This gift the Papists have turned into a sacrifice. But these two, sacrifice and testament, are mutually exclusive. We give the former, the latter we receive; the former comes from us to God, the latter from God to us.[1]

---

[1] ". . . that the Mass is not a sacrifice, but God's gift." WA 8, p. 515, 7. "If, however, thou discernest this sacrament, that it is a promise and not a sacrifice . . .," p. 518, 3. "From this observe now thyself the trickery of the priests, who of the testament have made a sacrifice. God imparts and gives to us, so they offer sacrifice: and that means nothing else but that they give God the lie or hold Him to be foolish in that He calls it a testament. For he who makes a sacrifice of it, cannot hold it to be a testament, because it is impossible that a sacrifice should be a testament; for we give the one but receive the other, the one comes from us to God, the other comes from God to us," p. 521, 26 ff. "Now I reckon, if we have rightly understood the foregoing things, how that the Mass is nothing other than a testament and sacrament in which God engages Himself to us and gives grace and mercy, then it will not do that we should make a good work or merit of it, for a testament is not a beneficium acceptum, but datum; it does not receive benefit from us, but brings benefit to us. Who has ever heard that he does a good work who receives a testament? He surely accepts a benefit for himself. Thus even in the Mass we give Christ nothing, but only take from Him." WA 6, p. 364, 16 ff. "So it cannot be that the Mass is a sacrifice, since we receive the one but give the other." WA 6, p. 523, 39 f. "There is now also a second scandal to be removed, which is much greater

In the Lord's Supper it is God who in Christ descends to us, in the sacrifice of the Mass we try to ascend to Him.[1] So the sacrifice of the Mass gives expression to the false Way of salvation, the Lord's Supper to the true Way. In the Lord's Supper there is given to us the forgiveness of sins; there we are met by God's self-giving love, God's Agape.

Now it is exactly the same objection which Luther has to bring against the spiritualising idea of the Lord's Supper taught by the " fanatical spirits." What is it that impels them to deny the real presence of Christ in the Lord's Supper? It is chiefly the idea that this would conflict with the glory of Christ. To uphold this glory, the significance of the Lord's Supper must be such that at its celebration we raise ourselves up in spirit to heaven, and there enter into fellowship with the glorified Christ. Luther puts into the mouth of his opponents these words: ": Seest thou not that heaven is high above, where Christ sits in His glory, and earth is far beneath, where His Supper is held? How can His body sit so high in glory, and at the same time be here below, letting itself be shamefully treated and handled with hands, mouth and belly as if it were a fried sausage? Would it be in keeping with the glorious majesty and the heavenly glory?"[2] But by such arguments the " fanatics " merely prove that they are on a false Way of salvation, that their theology is ultimately a " theology of glory " which seeks to mount up to God in His majesty. They are strangers to the deepest meaning of Christianity, which is revealed precisely in the Cross. If it offends us that Christ

---

and most specious, that is, that the Mass is everywhere believed to be a sacrifice which is offered to God," p. 523, 8 ff. " These two, therefore, must not be confused, the Mass and prayer, sacrament and work, testament and sacrifice, since the one comes from God to us through the ministration of the priest and demands faith, while the other proceeds from our faith to God through the priest and demands to be heard," p. 526, 13 ff.

[1] " Illud descendit, hoc ascendit," WA 6, p. 526, 16 f.

[2] WA 23, p. 115, 36 ff. " It would be a fine king of glory who let his body be thrown to and fro like this on the altar even by godless rascals." *Ibid.*, 155, 9 f.

comes down to us in the Lord's Supper and submits to shameful treatment by sinful men, then there is nothing in Christianity at which we might not take offence for similar reasons. Is the mystery of the Incarnation more acceptable to reason? How is it in keeping with the Divine majesty to suffer itself to be crucified and killed by sinful men?[1] But this is just God's greatest glory, that He for our sake has descended to the very depths, that He for our sake suffers and is shamefully handled both on the Cross and the altar.[2] God's glory consists in this, that He shows His love and beneficence toward us. Of this glory the "fanatics" have robbed God.[3] They deny Christ's love and grace and give Him instead the "glory" of sitting in a special place in heaven "like a bird in a cage."[4] For Luther, on the other hand, the Lord's Supper is the grandest epitome of the Gospel of the majesty of God's love.

*　　　*　　　*　　　*　　　*

The above indicates with what right, and in what sense, the settlement of the issue between the Eros and Agape motifs can be described as the vital problem of Luther's life. But this settlement involves two things. In the Caritas-synthesis he finds that union of the two motifs which it is his task to dissolve. But when this negative task is performed, he is confronted with the new task of putting in

---

[1] "How is it fitting that such majesty should suffer itself to be crucified by wicked rascals? O the God of flesh, O the God of blood, O the dead God, and so forth," p. 127, 13 ff.

[2] "The glory of our God, however, is this, that He for our sake lowers Himself to the deepest depths, into the flesh, into the bread, into our mouth, heart and bosom. And, moreover, for our sake He suffers Himself to be ingloriously treated both on the Cross and the altar," p. 157, 30 ff.

[3] "Now we poor fools hold that glory comes when someone manifests his virtue, goodness and beneficence to others. For to let oneself be honoured and served by others is a poor sort of glory and not a divine glory. So the fanatics might well be taken to school, to learn what glory means," p. 157, 2 ff.

[4] "First they deny and deprive Him of the love, grace and beneficence whereby He wills His body to be our food in the Supper bodily, and in exchange they grant Him to sit in a special place apart, like a bird in a cage," p. 159, 9 ff.

its place a doctrine of love which is wholly determined by the Agape motif which he has rediscovered. Here, the words quoted above from the introduction to Luther's lectures on Romans (1515-1516) are applicable: there is something to be broken down and destroyed, and something contrary to be built up and planted. Everything of our own is to be broken down and destroyed; and Luther sees this concentrated and intensified in the doctrine of Caritas, according to which man's love is the way to God. "Everything that is outside us and in Christ" is to be built up and planted; and Luther sees this concentrated in the love which comes to us in Christ and tries to find a way through us to our neighbour—that is, in Agape-love. We may therefore continue our study under the following two heads: (1) How the Caritas-synthesis is broken down; (2) how Agape-love is built up.

III

HOW THE CARITAS-SYNTHESIS IS BROKEN DOWN

1. The Campaign against the "Heavenly Ladders"

The Mediæval interpretation of Christianity is marked throughout by the *upward tendency*. This tendency asserts itself no less in the moralistic piety of popular Catholicism than in the rational theology of Scholasticism and the ecstatic religiosity of Mysticism. What puts these things, broadly speaking, on the same level in spite of all dissimilarities, is the upward tendency which they have in common. They all know a Way by which man can work his way up to God, whether it is the Way of merit known to practical piety, the ἀναγωγή of mysticism, or the Way of speculative thought according to the "analogy of being" (analogia entis). Man must mount up to God by means of one of the three heavenly ladders.

Against this upward tendency or ascent Luther makes his protest. He will have nothing to do with this "climbing up into the majesty of God." In place of this "theologia gloriæ" he demands a "theologia crucis."[1]

1. At the centre of Luther's struggle against the upward tendency stands his rejection of every idea of *merit*. When criticising the "good works" of Catholicism, he continually emphasises that it is not the works as such which are condemnable. They become condemnable owing to the *intention* which is connected with them. If the general Catholic view is that a good action is good and meritorious before God in the deepest sense, only when it is put into intentional connection with eternal blessedness, then it is pre-

---

[1] WA 1, p. 362. *Cf.* W. v. Loewenich: *Luthers Theologia crucis*, 1929.

cisely this intention, this motive, which according to Luther robs it of its value; indeed, it makes it condemnable.[1] One who does the good in order to win " merits " and promote his own blessedness is still not wholly devoted to the good itself. He uses it as a means for climbing up to the Divine majesty.[2] Only when this tendency is rooted out, and the good is done freely and straightforwardly " to the glory of God and the benefit of our neighbour," is it really good at all. Thus the idea of good works as a heavenly ladder is rejected. " In this sense we teach and praise our good works, not that we may ascend to heaven by them. For this must be the end for which they are to be done, not that they should serve us, so as to cancel sin and conquer death and attain heaven, but serve our neighbour, for his benefit and to supply his needs. The two are thus rightly divided, when we separate them as far and wide as heaven and earth are from one another; for God's works come down from above and give us nothing but heavenly and eternal blessings, but our works remain here below and furnish only what belongs to this earthly life and existence."[3] He who relies, in his relationship with God, on good works and merits, really makes himself God, " thrusts God from His throne and sets himself in His place," since

---

[1] WA 40, 1, p. 263, 10 ff.: " We ought to do this ! Good ! And then you will be saved ! No ! I grant that Christ is to be imitated, and the shedding of His blood; but by this I am not saved." WA 7, p. 33, 29 ff.: " From all this it is easy to understand how good works are to be rejected and not to be rejected, and how we are to understand all doctrines which teach good works. For when they contain the false appendage and perverse opinion that we are going to become godly and blessed through the works, then they are not good, but entirely damnable." WA 2, p. 491, 35 ff.: " Yet here it is to be noted that the Apostle does not condemn the works (of the law), as even Dr. Hieronymus teaches on this point, but trust in the works (of the law); that is, he does not deny the works, but he denies that anybody can be justified through them."

[2] WA 2, p. 493, 12 ff.: " For our righteousness looks forth from heaven and descends to us. But those ungodly men have presumed to ascend into heaven by their own righteousness and to bring from thence a truth which has originated among us from earth."

[3] WA 37, p. 662, 18 ff.

he ascribes to himself the work which appertains to God alone.[1] By giving us salvation in Christ, God has brought to nought all our attempts to ascend to heaven by our own works and merits. "For since Christ alone ascends into heaven, He who has also descended and who is in heaven, it is impossible that a Benedictine, an Augustinian, a Franciscan, a Dominican, a Carthusian, and such like should ascend to heaven."[2]

2. Luther is equally concerned to reject all attempts to ascend to God by the way of *reason and speculation*. He himself tried this way during his time in the monastery. One of the writings which he took as his guide at that time

---

[1] WA 40, 1, p. 363, 22: " They thrust God from His seat and put themselves n His place." *Cf.* p. 442, 22 ff.: " This divine virtue they have attributed to our works, saying: If you do this or that work, you will conquer sin, death and the wrath of God; and they have made us truly and naturally God. And by this fact the Papists have shown themselves under the name of Christ to be sevenfold greater idolaters than the heathen." P. 404, 29 ff.: " They deny faith and strive by their own works to make themselves blessed, that is, to justify themselves, deliver themselves from sin and death, conquer the devil and seize heaven by force. Which is simply to deny God and set themselves in God's place. For all these are works of the Divine majesty alone, not of any creature either angelic or human." P. 406, 17 ff.: " Wherefore, all hypocrites and idolaters essay to do those works which properly pertain to divinity and belong to Christ solely and alone. They do not indeed say with their mouth: I am God, I am Christ, yet in fact they arrogate to themselves the divinity and office of Christ. And so, in fact, they say: I am Christ, I am saviour, not only of myself, but also of others. And so the monks have taught and persuaded the whole world of this, that they can, by that hypocritical holiness of theirs, justify not only themselves, but also others to whom they communicate it." P. 405, 15 ff.: " Whosoever seeks righteousness by works apart from faith, denies God and makes himself God, for he thinks thus: If I do this work, I shall be righteous, I shall be victor over sin, death, the devil, the wrath of God and hell and shall attain eternal life. What, I ask, what else is this but to arrogate to oneself this work which belongs to God alone, and to declare oneself to be God? So it is easy for us to prophesy and most certainly to judge concerning all who are apart from faith, that they are not only idolaters, but idols which deny God and set themselves in the place of God." " But what else is this but to seize the name of Christ and attribute it to oneself and say ' I am Christ '? . . . And what can be more sacrilegious than this sacrilege? For he who says: ' I shall be saved through my works,' says nothing other than: ' I am Christ,' since the works of Christ alone save as many as ever are saved." WA 8, p. 619, 14 ff. *Cf. ibid.*, p. 599, 14 ff.

[2] WA 8, p. 618, 25 ff.

was Bonaventura's *Itinerarium mentis in Deum*[1]. From it he learned of the ascent by the analogical ladder of speculation. So when he later attacks so vigorously all ideas of such an ascent, he is speaking of things he knows from his own experience. It is not merely with reference to the unsearchable mystery of Divine predestination that he warns against "speculation on the Majesty."[2] Any attempt whatsoever "to climb into heaven by thinking" is doomed to failure.[3] There is no way by which man can reach God. The Way of speculation is as impassable as the Way of merit. If, even so, fellowship between God and man does exist, that is not because man has the power to mount up to God—though "ratio," reason, can never quite give up the idea that he has. It is rather because God condescends to man[4]—which to "ratio" is foolishness: "Oh, it is a ridiculous thing, that the One God, the high Majesty, should be a man."—it is because God through Christ makes for Himself a Way to man where there was no way. By means of

---

[1] *Cf. supra*, pp. 627 ff. WA, Tischreden I., Nr. 644, p. 302, 30 ff.: "The speculative science of the theologians is simply vain. I read Bonaventura on that subject, but he drove me nearly mad, because I wanted to experience the union of God with my soul (about which he talks nonsense) by the union of understanding and will. They are merely fanatical spirits." *Cf.* WA Tischreden I., Nr. 153, p. 72, 27 ff.

[2] WA 40, 1, p. 75, 9 f.: ". . . that we ought to abstain from speculation on the Majesty." P. 76, 9 ff.: "Thou oughtest not to ascend to God, but begin where He began, in the womb of His mother, ' made man and made,' and check thy affection for speculation. If thou wilt be safe and without danger of the devil and of thy conscience, know that there is no God at all besides this Man, and cleave to this humanity. That done, if thou hast embraced this Man and also cleaved to Him with thy whole heart, then in the matter of how we must act with God and towards God, abandon speculation on the Majesty. And in action against sin and death, abandon God, because He is intolerable here." *Cf.* WA 40, 2, p. 329, 8 ff.: ". . . who with their speculations ascend into heaven and speculate about God the Creator, etc. By that God be thou quite unmoved; he who will be saved, let him leave God in His majesty."

[3] WA 37, p. 38, 16 f. *Cf.*, p. 459, and p. 38, 35: ". . . to fly with their thoughts and flutter into the Divine being."

[4] WA 2 p. 98, 25 ff.: "For God's grace and His kingdom with all virtues must come to us, if we are to attain it; we can never come to Him; just as Christ from heaven came to us on earth, and not we from earth ascended to Him in heaven."

reason, ratio, man seeks in vain to ascend to God; in revelation, in the Word " which resounds down from above,"[1] in the Incarnation, God has descended to us. At the manger of Bethlehem reason receives its doom. Reason wants to " flutter up to heaven and seek God in His majesty "; " but here it comes down before my eyes. . . . Then indeed all reason must admit defeat and confess its blindness, in that it seeks to climb up to heaven and ventures to judge of Divine things, and yet cannot perceive what lies before its eyes."[2] God has willed to meet us only as " deus incarnatus et humanus deus."[3] And it is the Incarnation which is the very strongest evidence for the Evangelical Way of salvation. It is not we who are to raise ourselves up to God; He has come down to us in Christ. With this He has willed to put an end to the upward-striving tendency in us and terminate all our " attempts to fly "; He wills that in our search for God we should fasten our eyes upon this " deus incarnatus " in the fashion of His humiliation and His Cross.[4]

A concrete impression of the complete revolution which has taken place here is given by a comparison of Luther's exposition of John xiv. 8 ff. with Augustine's exposition of the same passage. Philip's words to Jesus, " Lord, show us the Father, and it sufficeth us," are used by Augustine as an example of the right way in which man ascends to God, to the vision and enjoyment of Him as the " summum

---

[1] WA 37, p. 39, 41; 40, 5 ff. [2] WA 37, p. 43, 6 ff.

[3] WA 40, 1, p. 78, 6.

[4] WA 1, p. 362, 15 ff. Sometimes, especially in studies of Luther which are under the influence of Ritschl, the fact that Luther points seekers after God to " the Man " Christ, has been taken to imply that Luther's interest was originally in the humanity of Jesus, and that for him, as for many representatives of a modern school of thought, this was the primary revelation of the Divine. But this is an interpretation of his words clean contrary to their obvious meaning. It never occurs to him to regard Christ merely as a man; He is " *deus* incarnatus," "humanus *deus*." Otherwise, to approach God through Christ would, in the last resort, be the same as to ascend from the human to the Divine, simply a new method of " climbing up to heaven "—the very thing, that is, which Luther refuses to allow.

bonum " which " sufficeth us."[1] For Luther, on the
contrary, these words of Philip are the typical example of
false theology, the " theologia gloriæ " with its mistaken
efforts to fly up to heaven to the Divine majesty; and he
sees in the answer of Christ a correction, which brings the
disciple back from these erroneous ways to the true theology,
the " theologia crucis."[2]

3. These objections of Luther's to the attempts to mount
up to God by the ladders of merit and of speculation are
also applicable, however, to the *mystical " ascent."* And
here, too, Luther reminds us that he can speak from his own
experience. He knows that it was Pseudo-Dionysius who
imported into Christianity these speculations about the unveiled Divine majesty. " This is their doctrine, given out as
the highest divine wisdom, into which I, too, was once in-
veigled, though not without great harm to myself. I exhort
you to detest as a veritable plague this Mystical Theology of
Dionysius and similar books."[3] And Luther's practical objection to Dionysius makes him clear-sighted, so that he can
expose him.[4] Whereas Dionysius had been venerated for a
thousand years as the Areopagite, the disciple of Paul,
Luther openly declares that Paul could not possibly have

[1] *Cf. supra*, p. 493, n. 4.
[2] " Then the apostle Philip (as somewhat more intelligent and keen than the
others) comes out with the great question, with which at all times the greatest
and wisest people have been very greatly concerned, studiously seeking and
enquiring what God is, and how we may know and attain to God. . . . Away
he goes with his own thoughts and flutters up into the clouds: ' Oh, if only we
might see Him as He sits up there among the angels !' " WA 45, p. 512, 6 ff.,
29 ff. " What hast thou to do with thine own thoughts and gaping up into
heaven? Hearest thou not what I say to thee? ' He that seeth me, seeth also
my Father ' . . . as Christ rebukes Philip: What sayest thou? ' Show us the
Father,' when thou seest and hearest me? Art thou not a great fool, that thou
thyself in the very devil's name wilt fathom how thou standest with God?"
Ibid., p. 518, 9 ff., 17 ff. *Cf.* also p. 515, 21 ff.
[3] WA 39, 1, p. 390.
[4] " But this same book of Dionysius is a new poem under a false title, as also
the book of Clement has a false title and was made by a rascally fellow long after
Clement." Art. Smalcaldici, ed. J. T. Müller: *Die symbolischen Bücher der
evangelisch-lutherischen Kirche*, 11. Aufl., 1912, p. 342.

had so uninspired a disciple. Dionysius, whoever he may have been, is more a disciple of Plato than of Christ, says Luther.[1] So it would be better not to have anything at all to do with his writings: "So little dost thou there learn of Christ, that on the contrary thou losest what thou perchance knowest of Him." And to this Luther adds: "I speak from my own experience."[2]

It is instructive to notice how Luther interprets such passages of Scripture as the Eros-piety of mysticism had otherwise taken for its own special use. Matt. v. 8: "Blessed are the pure in heart, for they shall see God," is an example. Long ago, Eros-piety had made this text its own. Here Scripture itself seems to point to the mystical contemplation of God (visio Dei) as the final goal of the Christian life. And does it not speak of a purification as the way to that goal— much as Plato speaks of the purification which is necessary in order to reach the vision of the self-subsistent Being and Beauty! But Luther will not be misled by this. He expounds this text not according to Eros, but according to Agape. He holds that there is no question of mystical purification here. "Thou mayest not climb up to heaven nor run into a cloister after it. . . . But that is a pure heart, which looks and thinks upon what God says." And equally little has the vision here spoken of anything to do with the mystical Vision of God. "That is far from what it means to see God, when thou comest toddling along with thy thoughts and climbest up to heaven. . . . To see His face, as the Scripture says, means rightly to perceive Him as a gracious,

---

1 "Plus platonisans quam Christianisans." WA 6, p. 562, 9 f. "Similarly, the Mystical Theology of Dionysius is pure fables and lies." Tischreden I., Nr. 153, p. 72, 33 f. "So the Mystical Theology of Dionysius is sheer nonsense. For just as Plato talks nonsense with his 'All things are Not-being and all things are Being,' and leaves it at that, so is this Mystical Theology with its 'Leave sense and understanding and ascend above Being and Not-being. In this darkness is there Being? God is all, etc.'" Tischreden I., Nr. 644, p. 302, 35 ff. Cf. Tischreden II., Nr. 2779aa and 2779bb, p. 654, 24 ff.
2 WA 6, p. 562, 11 f.: "Expertus loquor."

good (frommen) Father, to whom we may look for all good things. But this only comes through faith in Christ."[1]

Another passage which mysticism has delighted to use in proclaiming its gospel of Eros, is the story of the heavenly ladder which Jacob saw in his dream (Gen. xxviii.).[2] On the basis of this, love for God has again and again been spoken of as the ladder on which the soul has to mount up to God, and the stages through which it has to pass have been described. The " heavenly ladder " is, as we have seen above, the typical symbol of the mystical " ascent." Luther, too, has turned his attention to Jacob's ladder. But he has interpreted it in such a way that it no longer expresses the idea of Eros, but that of Agape. God has not willed us to raise a ladder in order to come up to Him; He Himself has prepared the ladder and come down to us. " Ipse descendit et paravit scalam." In Christ, God has come to meet us; Christ is the heavenly ladder and the " Way " furnished by God.[3]

---

[1] WA 32, pp. 325-328.

[2] " Oh, what error this text has caused, how many people it has deceived !" WA 14, p. 386, 18. Cf. also Luther's exposition of this passage, WA 9, pp. 407 ff.

[3] WA 16, p. 144, 2 ff.: " If He had willed to bring thee up to Himself by this way, He would have given thee a different Word. He Himself has descended and furnished a ladder; the Father suffered Him to be made a child and afterwards, as He grew into a man, He suffered Him to be crucified and to rise again. . . . Do thou let the Godhead be; thou hast enough to do with the humanity. If God sent Him down into the womb of the virgin, let be at that. His own words are: ' I am the way, the truth.' But they want to know whether they are predestinated. But He has not carried us into heaven. But first He descends and is made a babe, then is fastened to the Cross, etc. See what Philip said before the Supper, ' Show us the Father,' how he flew to and fro with his thoughts. Philip, here is the Father; if thou wilt seek elsewhere, thou wilt err. ' The Father is in me, and I . . . ,' which means, if thou wilt find the Father, it must be done through Me, otherwise it will not be done. He who wishes to seek by another way than My humanity, will err." Cf. the same passage in the printed text: " He will not have thee thus ascend, but He comes to thee and has made a ladder, a way and a bridge to thee. . . . He who is clever and wise, let him remain on this proffered path. He comes first to us and we do not first mount up to heaven to Him, but He sends the Son down into the flesh. . . . Wilt thou by another way climb up to heaven to God? He speaks: This way, brother, ' The Father is in me, and I in the Father '; keep thine eyes fixed on Me, through My humanity is the way to the Father." WA 16, p. 144, 16 ff.; 145, 15 ff., 25 ff.

Through Christ we have free access to God, and through Him the "ascent" which mysticism had vainly striven to achieve is accomplished.[1] But if Christ is *our way to God,* that is only because He is first and foremost *God's way to us.*

The distinction which Luther is making here, is no other than the distinction between Eros and Agape, between the Platonic, Hellenistic and the specifically Christian Way of salvation. Eros is man's way to God, Agape is God's way to man. Eros is egocentric, Agape theocentric fellowship with God. Luther himself was fully aware that his ultimate concerń was with these opposites. He knows that the Platonism which has invaded Christianity is the source of the rational "speculations on the Majesty"; it has transformed the Christian "theologia crucis" into a "theologia

---

[1] WA 40, 1, p. 79, 9 ff.: "We must ascend by Jacob's ladder, on which God leaneth, whose feet touch the earth hard by the head of Jacob. When thou wilt act and take thought concerning thy salvation, leave all thoughts of the law and traditions of philosophy, and fly to the manger and the bosom of His mother and behold Him sucking, growing up, dying." "Every ascent to the knowledge of God is perilous, except that which is made through the humility of Christ; for this is Jacob's ladder on which the ascent must be made. Nor is there any other way to the Father except through the Son." WA 4, p. 647, 19 ff. "Let us rather hear Paul, that we may learn Jesus Christ and Him crucified. For this is the way, the life and the truth; this is the ladder which leads to the Father." WA 6, p. 562, 12 ff. When Luther speaks of Christ as the ladder on which we come to God, he is far from suggesting the idea of fellowship with God on God's level. He simply never conceives of the Way to God as an ascent on our part. He merely adopts the language of his opponents about the "ladder" while denying its meaning by pointing us to Christ, very much as when he elsewhere attacks the "speculative theology" he can say that faith in Christ is "the true speculative theology." Tischreden I., Nr. 153, p. 72, 32 f. Naturally he does not mean that faith in Christ is modelled on the speculative theology, but that as the true "theology" it must drive out the false "speculative theology." So, too, here. God has descended to us in Christ, and has thereby broken down all our heavenly ladders. He alone is the Way and the "ladder." Römerbrief, ii., p. 132, 22 ff.: "'Being therefore justified by faith' and our sins being forgiven, 'we have access and peace,' but 'through Jesus Christ our Lord.' This also touches those who, in accord with the mystical theology, press into the interior darkness, leaving all thoughts of the Passion of Christ and desiring to hear and contemplate the uncreated Word before they have had the eyes of their heart justified and purified by the Word incarnate. For the Word incarnate is necessary first for purity of heart; and only when we have this are we transported through Him into the uncreated Word *per anagogen.*"

gloriæ," and theocentric Christianity into something ego-centric.[1] And Luther knows that it was Augustine above all, to whom he was otherwise so much indebted, who was primarily responsible for the prevalence of this outlook in Catholicism.[2]

2. THE CAMPAIGN AGAINST SELF-LOVE

Even the Mediæval idea of Caritas, as we saw above, contains in its way an attack on self-love. But the peculiar thing is that the self-love which is attacked is nevertheless retained as a basis for the doctrine of love as a whole. The over-selfish egoism of self-love is to be overcome by the sublimation of self-love into pure love for God. Luther's campaign against self-love is marked by a very different ruthlessness and intensity. Self-love is not to be ennobled and refined, but totally annihilated. The content of Luther's new view is best seen by contrast with Augustine's view, which was also the starting-point for the work of the Middle Ages.

Augustine stresses emphatically that self-love is the root of all evil especially in the *De civitate Dei*, when he traces the opposition between the kingdom of God and the kingdom of the world back to that between amor Dei and amor sui. But this refers, be it noted, only to the false, " un-

[1] WA 10, 1, 1, p. 202, 7 ff.: " All these are still human, *Platonic and philosophical ideas, which lead us out of Christ into ourselves*, whereas the Evangelist wishes to lead us out of ourselves into Christ. For he will not handle nor speak of the divine, almighty, eternal Word of God, except as in the flesh and blood that walked on the earth. He will not disperse us into the creatures which have been created by Him, that we should go after Him there and seek and speculate as the Platonists do, but he will gather us out of those same diffuse, wandering, volatile thoughts into Christ, as if he should say: Why dost thou run out and seek so far? See here, in Christ, the Man, is everything; He has made it all, in Him is life, He is the Word by whom all things were made; abide in Him, and thou wilt find it all."

[2] WA 10, 1, 1, p. 210, 14 ff.: " The Platonists first made Augustine of this opinion about this text, with their useless and nonsensical talk; though it appears so fine that they have been called the divine philosophers because of it. After that, Augustine has carried us all with him on this point."

ordered " (inordinata) self-love, which seeks its satisfaction in something other than God, in temporal and transient things. Besides this perverted self-love, Augustine speaks of a right self-love, which seeks its satisfaction in God Himself. This sort of self-love is so far from being opposed to love for God, that it is fundamentally equivalent to it. Thus for Augustine it is obviously not self-love as such, but only its wrong direction, which is sin and the root of sin, and he has to look for another criterion of sin. This other criterion he finds in the idea that evil is bound up with sensible and material things. As his nature is at once both spiritual and sensible, man is a citizen of two worlds. By God's appointment he has the highest good above him. He should, therefore, direct his thoughts and desires up towards the super-sensible, spiritual world. But now the sensible side of his being offers resistance, and seeks to drag him down and enchain him to temporal goods. Hence, when Augustine wishes to characterise the sinful man, he says that he is " curvatus." He is not, as he ought to be, erect and looking upwards, but crooked, bent down to the earth.

Despite all outward similarity between Augustine and Luther in these things, Luther's conception can be described as a direct antithesis to these ideas of Augustine. When Luther brands selfishness, self-love, as sin and as the essence of the sinfulness of sin, he means what he says without any qualification. He knows no justifiable self-love. In the commandment: " Thou shalt love thy neighbour as thyself," Augustine had actually held that a commandment of self-love was implied—even if it did not need to be expressly stated by a separate commandment, in view of man's natural inclination in that direction. Luther, on the contrary, asserts that the Commandment of Love involves the rejection and condemnation of all self-love whatsoever. It is of the greatest interest to notice how in his lectures on Romans Luther emancipates himself step by step from the Augustinian conception.

On the basis of Christ's words in John xii. 25, it is a fundamental principle for him that: " To love is the same as to hate oneself."[1] But against this there stands the universally accepted axiom that " ordered love begins with oneself," and there stands also the immense authority of Augustine. According to Luther, however, this is one of the ideas that have done most to lead us away from love.[2] Earlier in the lectures on Romans he has admitted that two interpretations of the commandment of love to neighbour are possible. It may be taken to mean that both things are commanded, to love one's neighbour and to love oneself. Or it can be understood so that only love to our neighbour is commanded, whilst the manner in which we love ourselves in obedience to our selfish nature is set forth as a pattern. To this Luther adds the comment that the latter interpretation pleases him better.[3] When he returns later to this question, he is more sure of the right interpretation of the Commandment. Now he ventures —though still with all " due respect for the Fathers "—to declare plainly that the interpretation which has prevailed ever since Augustine is false.[4] In commanding man to love his neighbour as himself, God has in no way commanded that man shall love himself. Self-love is, indeed, a vicious love (" vitiosus amor "), which must be destroyed. Never-

---

[1] Römerbrief, ii., p. 219, 8: " Est enim diligere se ipsum odisse."

[2] *Op. cit.*, p. 336, 5 ff.: " In the comment I have said that love (charitas) is amor not to oneself, but to one's neighbour. . . . Thus to please one's neighbour is not to please oneself. But this statement of Gregory and of ours seems to be contradicted by that famous distinction and order of loving. For, according to the blessed Augustine, even the Master teaches that ' first God is to be loved, then our soul, next our neighbour's soul, and lastly our body.' Thus, ordered love (charitas ordinata) begins with itself. The answer is, that just this is one of those things by which we have been carried away from love (charitate)."

[3] *Op. cit.*, p. 304, 1 ff.

[4] *Op. cit.*, p. 336, 22 ff.: " And so, saving the judgment of others and with due respect for the Fathers, in my opinion—I speak as a fool—that interpretation does not seem to be sound which is alleged concerning the precept of loving one's neighbour, whereby it is said that in the precept itself is the loving form with which one loves the neighbour, in that it says: ' as thyself.' Therefore they conclude: It is necessary that thou first love thyself and then, after the pattern of thy love for thyself, love also thy neighbour."

theless, it can serve as a pattern for the right kind of love to
our neighbour—just as rightly as Paul can use Adam as a
type of Christ. " Just as in Adam we are evil, so in Christ
we ought to be good."[1] This comparison does not alter the
fact that in one case it is a question of something evil, in the
other of something good. Similarly, here Jesus uses our
sinful self-love as an example of how we ought to love our
neighbour. " Thou shalt love thy neighbour as thyself. Not
as if thou oughtest to love thyself; for if that had been the
meaning, then it would have been commanded. But so far is
it from being commanded, that the commandment [of love to
one's neighbour] is, on the contrary, based on the prohibition
[of self-love]. So thou doest ill in loving thyself. From this
evil thou art delivered only when thou lovest thy neighbour
in like manner—that is, when thou ceasest to love thyself."[2]

---

[1] *Op. cit.*, p. 337, 8 ff.: " Therefore I believe that by this precept ' as thyself '
man is not bidden to love himself, but the vicious love is exposed wherewith
he loves himself in fact; that is to say, thou art wholly bent upon thyself and
turned to love of thyself (curvus es totus in te et versus in tui amorem), from
which thou shalt not be made straight, except thou entirely cease to love thyself
and, forgetful of thyself, love thy neighbour alone. For it is perversity that we
wish to be loved by all, and in all to seek our own (querere que nostra sunt);
but rectitude is as if thou shouldst do to all men that which thou perversely
wishest to be done to thyself, and shouldst do evil with as great zeal as thou hast
done good. By which, of course, it is not commanded to do evil, but [to show]
a similar zeal."

[2] *Op. cit.*, p. 337, 17 ff. *Cf.* WA 1, p. 654, 14 ff.: " And this the words of
Christ contain: He that loseth his life for My sake, shall find it. Accordingly,
when Christ says that we are to love our neighbour as we love ourselves, in my
judgment He is speaking of the perverse and crooked love (perverso et incurvo
amore) wherewith a man seeks nothing but his own (quæ sua sunt); which love
is not made straight unless it ceases to seek what is its own, and seeks what is
its neighbour's. This is the opinion of the blessed Paul, Phil. ii.: Not looking
each of you to his own things, but to the things of others. And 1 Cor. xiii.:
Charitas seeketh not its own. With these words he manifestly forbids self-love
(amorem sui). So the sense of the precept is seen to be, ' Thou shalt love thy
neighbour as thyself, that is, Thou lovest thyself alone and perversely, but if
thou wert to direct this kind of love to thy neighbour, then thou wouldst truly
love.' And this is plain from the fact that He does not command man to love
himself, which He would have done, of course, if self-love (amor sui) were good;
but He finds love of self (amorem sui) and transfers it to the neighbour, and so
sets it straight."

Luther has departed so far from the traditional idea, which discovers a *commandment* of self-love in the commandment of love to one's neighbour, that he finds this latter to contain a direct *prohibition* of every kind of self-love. Love to one's neighbour, he holds, has the task of completely dispossessing and annihilating self-love.

When stating what exactly man's corruption is, Luther uses Augustine's expression: man is crooked or "bent" (curvatus).[1] But this only makes Luther's divergence from Augustine the more plain. For it is immediately obvious that he uses this term in an entirely different sense from Augustine. When Augustine says man is "bent," "crooked," "curvus," "curvatus," he means that man is bent down to the earth, that he only knows and pursues the lower, temporal values. Luther, however, means that man has by nature a selfish disposition, that he does not deal straightforwardly, but in all his dealings is guided by consideration of their usefulness to himself. In other words, the will is not straight, but "crooked"; ultimately it turns back to itself.[2] Thus, when Augustine says man is "crooked," his idea is construed on the lines of Eros, and sin means being earthbound; when Luther uses the same expression, it is construed on the lines of Agape, for which sin primarily means selfish enslavement to oneself.

Luther's idea of sin is thus governed by his idea of love. "Love seeketh not its own." As the opposite of this, the essence of sin is that man does seek his own. Judged by this

---

[1] WA 18, p. 504, 10 f.: "A *crooked* spirit is the spirit of the flesh and of Adam, which in all things *is bent upon itself* and seeks its own; which is inborn in us." *Ibid.*, p. 491, 1: "The heart that is right towards God and *not bent upon itself* or anything other than God, is well grounded upon the eternal, and stands firm. . . . But the *crooked souls, bent upon themselves* with false opinion and deceptive good ideas, pride themselves upon themselves and not in God." WA 40, 2, p. 325, 7 f.: ". . . everything is *crooked* (incurvata); I seek in God and in all creatures what pleases myself."

[2] Luther's conception is characterised here by the following identifications: curvus=curvus in se=incurvatus in se (Römerbrief, ii., p. 184, 17 ff.)=versus in sui amorem ; *cf. supra*, p. 712, n. 1.

standard, the whole of natural human life proves to be under the dominion of sin, since it has universally the character of a quest for " its own," of " quærere quæ sua sunt."[1] From this point of view, sin is completely universal in extent. Sin has its seat not merely in man's sensible nature, but it embraces the *whole* man. And further, sin is not merely that which is commonly described as evil among men. Even the greatest and most praiseworthy deeds are sin, when judged by this standard; for they are done to man's own glory. Here the rule applies: the more generous—the more egocentric.[2]

But Luther goes yet a step further. Even *the very highest* which man can seek to attain—namely, fellowship with God itself—is polluted by the egocentricity which is inherent in everything human. It is this in particular which arouses Luther's hostility to Catholic piety, in which this egocentric fellowship with God has been, so to speak, reduced to a system. For when it seeks to build up love for God on the basis of self-love, what else is this but to " seek one's own

---

[1] WA 18, p. 742, 19 f.: " All are flesh, for all savour of the flesh, that is, of what is their own, and are devoid of the glory of God and the spirit of God."

[2] WA 18, p. 742, 36 ff.: " Moreover, it was at once apparent in the fashion of the work, that they did all these things for their own glory, so that they were not even ashamed to confess and glory that they were seeking their own glory. For with a consuming self-glory the Romans, on their own testimony, did whatever of good they did, and so also the Greeks, so also the Jews, so also every race of men. But though this may be honourable with men, with God nothing is more dishonourable; indeed, it is the most impious and highest sacrilege, because they did not act for the glory of God nor did they glorify Him as God, but with most impious robbery they robbed God of glory and attributed it to themselves, so that they were never more dishonourable and base than when they shone in their highest virtues. . . . Thou hast, therefore, that authoritative spirit, the principal part of man, striving after honourable things—that is, a thief of the Divine glory and a pretender to the Majesty—most of all when they are most honourable and most illustrious in their own highest virtues. Now deny that these are flesh and ruined by their impious mind !" *Cf.* also pp. 709 f., 731. *Cf.* E. Brunner: *Das Gebot und die Ordnungen*, 1932, p. 55: " It is because the bonum is ' good ' for *him*, man, that he wants it. And it is because he, man, realises *himself*, *his own* worth, his humanity, by doing his duty, that he does it. Everything turns for him upon the achievement of his own happiness and his own perfection; in short, upon himself."

even in God "?[1] Granted that man has freed himself from temporal desires and interests, *he is nevertheless still curvatus* —not, of course, in Augustine's sense, but in Luther's. Even in his relation to God, he is " bent upon himself."[2]

Now Luther was not blind to the fact that Catholicism could already claim to have seriously tried to overcome the selfish idea of love. He believes there is such an attempt in Augustine's distinction between " Frui " and " Uti," and another in the Scholastic doctrine of " amor amicitiæ."[3] But these are, to him, merely isolated efforts which cannot neutralise the fundamental perversion in the Catholic doctrine of love. The " School theologians " and Augustine have only seen it " from afar," and the foundation of their view of love, in spite of that, remains the same. Luther cannot be content to follow Scholasticism and Mediæval mysticism, and try to overcome selfishness by way of spiritualisation and sublimation. Eros retains its egocentric character, however it may be spiritualised and sublimated. It is not enough to give it God and the incorruptible things as objects of its love in place of corruptible, earthly things. For even so, it retains its selfish character and seeks its own, even in God. Luther has clearly seen that one does not arrive at Agape by refining and sublimating Eros. And what is it but an attempt to do this, when the Augustinian and Mediæval view of love seeks to build Christian love on the foundation of self-love? We must confront all such attempts with the question : " Do men gather grapes from thorns or figs from

[1] WA 18, p. 694, 16 f.

[2] Römerbrief, ii., p. 184, 17 ff.: " And this agrees with Scripture, which describes man as bent upon himself (incurvatum in se) in such a way that he turns to his own account (sibi inflectit) not only bodily, but even spiritual goods, and seeks himself in all things. And this crookedness (curvitas) is now natural, the natural vice and natural evil." *Cf.* Römerbrief, ii., p. 189, 21 ff.

[3] WA 46, p. 90, 3 ff.: " Of this our School theologians have also spoken, having seen something of the kind from afar, and they name two sorts of love, Amorem concupiscentiæ and amiciciæ, and St. Augustine names them Uti and Frui. Some, he says, love God from a good will; others, however, for the sake of their own ends."

thistles?" Can unselfish fruit be gathered from the tree of
selfishness? No, self-love, according to Luther, must be
plucked up by the roots, if the true Christian love, Agape, is
to find a place in us.

3. The Campaign against "Fides caritate formata"

The culmination of Luther's attack on the Caritas-synthesis is reached when he removes love outside the context
of justification entirely, and opposes the Catholic idea of
"fides caritate formata" with his assertion that justification
takes place "sola fide," by faith alone. If the Catholic view
is that man is justified by faith *and* love, with the stress on
the latter, then Luther replies that love must be completely
eliminated from this context. *In loco iustificationis* Caritas
is altogether out of place; there faith reigns alone—that is,
Christ alone. When Luther reads in Paul: "a man is
justified by faith, without the works of the law," he finds in
this not merely a rejection of all attempts to base fellowship
with God on external legalities. It is just as much a mistake to base it on a good disposition in man, whether this
is called love or anything else. If man is justified without
the works of the law, this applies not only to the outward
works of the law, but also and especially to love, which is
the fulfilling of the law.

Luther's attitude on this point has often been taken to
mean that in his concern to assert the importance of faith,
he came in some degree to set love aside. He holds that
the question of justification is at the very heart of Christianity; so if love has any central significance for him, we
might expect to find it just here. Yet, in fact, in this matter
of a man's justification, it proves to be Luther's whole concern completely to dismiss any thought of love. Consequently, it is easy to assume that Luther's relation to Augustine and the Middle Ages is such that he wished to replace

the "religion of love," which they proclaimed, by a "religion of faith." From the Catholic point of view, he has often been regarded as the destroyer of the Christian idea of love.[1] And even if Evangelicals have not been willing to subscribe to this judgment without more ado, yet Luther's treatment of love has been quite generally regarded as the weakest point in his thought, and his polemical position is held to have betrayed him into thrusting love too much into the background. Luther is supposed to have been so absorbed by his *religious* task that, to some extent, at least, he forgot the *ethical* side of Christianity. His indefatigable reiteration of the idea of "sola fide" is his religious strength, but this is said to be at the same time the source of his ethical weakness, in so far as it caused him to separate, more or less, not only the works of love, but love itself and the disposition of love from the basal relation to God. "Love has had to stand down in favour of faith"—such is a fairly universal view of this matter.

Now it must be said first of all, that the attempt to tone down Luther's conception by introducing the distinction between the works of love and love itself, as if only the former and not the latter ought to be excluded from the context of justification, means a complete abandonment of Luther's fundamental principles. Luther's objection to Caritas *in loco iustificationis* applies, as we said above, not only to external legalism, but equally to a quality or attitude of love presupposed in us. If Luther rejects all thought of basing man's fellowship with God on the good which man *does*, he is bound even more emphatically to reject the idea that man's fellowship with God is based on the good which man *is*. In this case Catholic criticism has seen more clearly when it says that Luther has logically no place for love, not only for the works of love, but for love itself, when estab-

---

[1] *Cf.*, *e.g.*, J. Mausbach: *Die katholische Moral und ihre Gegner*, 5. Aufl., 1921, pp. 154 f.

lishing fellowship with God in justification. If the Catholic
theory had been right in identifying the Caritas-synthesis
with Christian love, then it would be right to say that Luther
is the destroyer of Christian love; for there can be no doubt
that he is the destroyer of the Caritas-synthesis.

The fundamental error of both the above-mentioned views
is that they are guilty of a purely quantitative consideration
of the spiritual life. Faith and love are conceived as two
entities constant throughout the whole history of Christianity, and the distinction between different outlooks is
reduced to the question of how much importance is attached
to the one or the other of these sides of the Christian life.
Thus the question of Luther's significance for the Christian
idea of love is reduced to the essentially quantitative question of how large and how central a place in his thought he
gives to love. On one side it is held that Luther wishes to
be entirely rid of the idea of love in justification and the
establishment of man's fellowship with God; and the conclusion is immediately drawn that Luther's significance is
in the main destructive, since there is no place for the idea
of love in that which is for him the centre of the Christian
life. On the other side we find the firm conviction that the
idea of love has its settled place in the Christianity of the
Reformation, and all that is required is to show that it
actually is present even where it is not at once apparent.
This refers in particular to the fundamental relation to God,
and so it is necessary to try to introduce love here also—in
spite of " sola fides."

But to understand Luther's significance for the Christian
idea of love, we must first rid ourselves of the false assumption mentioned above. The idea of love is not a constant
phenomenon which we meet throughout the whole history
of Christianity; and the differences do not merely consist of
the different place and importance given to this idea.
Against the Scholastic doctrine of " fides caritate formata "

Luther insists on justification " sola fide ": but this contrast has not been in the least understood so long as it is taken as a matter of rivalry between faith and love, in which Luther takes the side of faith and Catholicism the side of love. So far from there being any rivalry between faith and love in Luther, it is truer to say that just because he took love out of the context of justification he consulted the interests of Christian *love* no less than of faith. As a matter of fact, " fides caritate formata " constitutes a threat not only to faith, but equally to the purity of Christian love. Luther has quite rightly seen that it is not Christian love, but a view of love contrary to it, which this formula expresses. The contrast between Luther and Catholicism, which at first appears to be the contrast between faith and love, is just as much a contrast between two fundamentally different conceptions of love. Only when this is observed can we reach a final answer to the question why Luther is so anxious to keep love at a distance where justification is concerned. At first sight it might seem to be a depreciation of love, as if only faith, but not love, were excellent enough to find a place in the fundamental relationship to God. But such an idea is a complete misunderstanding of Luther's meaning. It is certainly not because love is not high and divine enough, that Luther wishes to see it excluded from justification. If it only depended on its standing and excellence, Luther himself declares, he would be ready to set it alongside, nay, higher than, faith. Love is nothing other than God Himself, and therefore Luther can say of the man who abides in love, " that he and God become one cake (eine Kuche)."[1] Through faith we are children of God, but

[1] In WA 36, p. 423, 22 ff., Luther says of love, that it is " that one, eternal, unutterable good and supremest treasure which is God Himself. . . . Moreover, he that abides in love, abides in God and God in him, so that he and God become one cake." After this praise of the divine nature of love, he continues: " Now such words might well move not only the Papists, but also ourselves to say that faith alone does not justify, but also love. For he attributes so much to it, that he who abides in love abides in God and has God Himself; but he who

through love we are "gods," since to give in love is God's own nature.[1]

Thus it is absolutely impossible to say that Luther had any tendency to minimise and depreciate love. But why is he then so anxious to keep it apart from man's justification? Quite simply *because to do the contrary would mean a depreciation of love, a denial of Christian love.* To speak of love *in loco iustificationis* is to preach another and lower kind of love than the Christian. It is to deny and destroy Agape-love, and that in two ways. *First,* it is to deny love in the sense of God's "unmotivated," spontaneous love. For if love, as a quality to be found in man, has any place in the foundation of fellowship with God, if man is justified on the ground of Caritas discovered in him, then that is something which makes him worthy of fellowship with God, and this fellowship does not rest upon God's grace alone. To preach faith in Christ, on the other hand, is nothing else but to preach love—that is, God's love.[2] *Secondly,* to speak of love *in loco iustificationis* corrupts Christian love, looked at from the human point of view. It can no longer retain its purity, it becomes meritorious, a means governed by its end. Love *in loco iustificationis* cannot be anything but Eros, or man's way to God. Such a love is not "free."[3] Luther has discovered the Eros features

---

has God, has everything. But he has not here taken in hand to teach how we become righteous before God and come to grace or lay hold on the love wherewith He hath loved us through Christ—which cannot come to pass except through faith alone."

[1] Luther can declare the divine nature of love in the highest terms. It is " not of works nor human, yea not of angels nor heavenly, but God Himself." " God's children are we through faith, which makes us heirs of all divine blessings. But we are gods through love, which makes us beneficent to our neighbour, for Divine nature is nothing else but pure beneficence and, as St. Paul here says, kindness and love towards man, which showers its blessings lavishly upon all creatures daily, as we see." WA 10, 1, 1, p. 100, 17 ff.

[2] WA 10, 1, 1, p. 11, 18 ff.: The Gospel of Christ, " see, that is the great fire of God's love for us."

[3] In his work " Of the Freedom of a Christian Man " Luther summarises these two objections thus: " They are not free, and they insult the grace of God." WA 7, p. 33, 33 f.

of the Caritas-synthesis. He therefore has to destroy it to make room for Christian love. In justification we have to do with Christ alone. "Christ, however, is not my Caritas."[1] Christ is not my Eros, but God's Agape.

In breaking down the Catholic theory of "fides caritate formata" and ousting love from the place which Catholicism had been wont to give it in justification, Luther may be said to have been at the same time building up Agape-love. For in the process he was asserting both (1) God's Agape in its absolute sovereignty and groundlessness, and (2) Christian love in its purity, free from all egocentric calculations. But this already takes us into the next chapter and our last question.

[1] WA 40, 1, p. 240, 29 f. *Cf.* p. 240, 12 f. " I have not loved the Son of God and given myself for Him, as the sophists profess they love." WA 40, 1, p. 291, 15 f.

HOW AGAPE-LOVE IS BUILT UP

1. Amor Dei and Amor Hominis

It is beyond dispute that Luther regarded it as his main task to break down and destroy the classical Catholic idea of love, the Caritas-synthesis, which, by its connection with self-love and its upward tendency, proclaims its near kinship to the Eros motif. His criticism of the Catholic idea of love is radical and irrefutable. It has shown that the ambiguity which distinguishes the idea of Caritas is due to the fact that it is based upon two separate and mutually incompatible fundamental motifs. The two things which have been united for more than a millennium—the Eros and Agape motifs—the two things which together have formed the basis for the interpretation of Christian love, are now irrevocably divorced. It is made clear that the Caritas-doctrine has but little to do with specifically Christian love, and that its characteristics are substantially derived from the contrary fundamental motif.

Luther has succeeded in his work of destruction. The depth and finality of his criticism is due to the fact that it was not merely negative, but was undertaken from a positive point of view, for the purpose of asserting Agape in its specifically Christian meaning. But this brings us to the second question: Has Luther also succeeded in *building up* this other idea of love, or was the idea of Agape nothing more to him than a platform from which to criticise the idea of Caritas? Has he succeeded in giving a concrete portrayal of this love which is the opposite of egocentric Eros-love? Does there indeed exist any other love than that which builds on the foundation of self-love? Is it conceivable or possible in human life as human life is at present constituted?

If the last two questions are put to Luther, his immediate answer is essentially negative. The fact is that the resources of natural human life are exhausted in and with egocentric love. There is nothing in the life and activity of the natural man which does not bear the marks of " quærere quæ sua sunt," seeking its own. It is therefore wholly under the dominion of sin, and on that basis there is no possibility of manifesting love in the Christian sense of the word, a love that seeketh not its own, but loves God with all its heart and its neighbour as itself. In Catholicism this had been held possible, whether it was maintained with Thomas Aquinas that the assistance of Divine grace was necessary, or with Duns Scotus that man could attain to this love " ex puris naturalibus."[1] Luther takes particular exception to Duns Scotus' argument from self-love: since man by nature so exceedingly loves himself, who is a lower good, then he must be still more able by his natural powers to love above all things God, who is the highest good and as such worthy to be loved most of all. Luther at once sees the fallacy in this argument: it describes Christian love after the pattern of human, acquisitive love. It is a fundamental error to " arguere ab humanis ad divina " in this way, all the more so as the first premiss of the argument—man's self-love—is a devilish perversion.[2]

[1] Römerbrief, ii., p. 187, 21 ff. WA I, pp. 224, 34-225, 12.

[2] WA 40, 1, p. 459, 7 ff.: " If thou wilt compare the divine with the human, someone could say: These arguments are most weak—to argue from the human to the divine. Thus Scotus: a man can love God above all things; since he loves me, then he can love God more, for the greater the good, the more lovable it is. And he concludes that a man by his natural powers (ex naturalibus) can fulfil that law: ' Thou shalt love God with thy heart,' etc., because I am able to love a lesser good; as a peasant or a lansquenet will risk his neck for the sake of a florin, much more for God's sake." We can, of course, point to human situations as evidence of divine things—provided these human things are expressions of a divine " ordinatio." But that is not the case with self-love. " But as Scotus

But although, according to Luther, we may borrow no features from human love in order to portray Christian love, this in no sense means that Agape-love is a mere empty word. Love in the Christian sense is primarily God's own love, displayed in all His beneficent works, but chiefly through the giving of His Son. Here there is complete identity between God and love, love and God. " If anyone would paint and aptly portray God, then he must draw a picture of pure love, as if the Divine nature were nothing but a furnace and fire of such love, which fills heaven and earth. And again, if it were possible to paint and picture love, we should have to make such a picture as would be not of works nor human, yea not of angels nor heavenly, but God Himself."[1] " Then He pours out not sun and moon, nor heaven and earth, but His own heart and His dearest Son, and even suffers Him to shed His blood and die the most shameful of all deaths for us shameful, wicked, ungrateful people. How can we here say anything else but that God is nothing but an abyss of eternal love?"[2] From this Divine love Luther derives the features for his picture when he wishes to " paint " Christian love.

What, then, is the deepest difference between this Divine love and ordinary human love? With incomparable clarity Luther answers this question in the twenty-eighth thesis of the Heidelberg Disputation of 1518. It is true that he does not use the terms " Eros " and " Agape " to describe this contrast. Yet the passage may be said to contain one of the

argues: I love my lesser good—it is not an ordinance (ordinatio) of God, but a corruption (depravatio) of the devil," p. 461, 3 f.   Cf. WA 40, 1, p. 226, 8 ff.: " Thus Scotus argues: A covetous man can like money; if he can love the lesser good, then also the greater.   A man has by his natural powers (ex naturalibus viribus) the love for the creature—why not for the Creator?   This problem no Sophist has been able to resolve."   WA 1, p. 224, 28 f.: " The consequence is most absurd: erring man is able to love the creature, and therefore also God, above all things.   Contra Sco. Gab."

[1] WA 36, p. 424, 16 ff.

[2] Ibid., p. 426, 34 ff., according to the printed text; cf. Rörers Nachschrift, p. 426, 9 ff.

clearest delimitations of Eros and Agape, and the most apt description of the deepest characteristic of each. It runs: "*Amor Dei non invenit sed creat suum diligibile, Amor hominis fit a suo diligibili.*"[1] Human love is acquisitive love, and so is created by the desirable nature of its object. God's love is itself creative—*i.e.*, it makes something of that which is nothing. As regards human love, Luther knows that in his thesis he has said nothing but what is generally recognised and admitted by all, philosophers as well as theologians. As witness he invokes Aristotle—a typical representative of the Eros-tendency. Human love is distinguished by the fact that in all things it seeks its own and prefers to receive rather than to impart its good.[2] Divine love is the direct opposite of this. It seeks, above all, to impart from the fulness of its riches. Therefore it seeks out those who are sinners, evil, foolish and weak, and demonstrates its creative power in them by making them righteous, good, wise and strong. Just by seeking what is lost and in itself worthless, God's love demonstrates most plainly its spontaneous and creative nature. "For sinners are lovely because they are loved; they are not loved because they are lovely." Human love shuns sinners and seeks higher and more worthy objects for itself. But Christ says: "I came not to call the righteous, but sinners."[3]

---

[1] WA 1, p. 354, 35 f.

[2] WA 1, p. 365, 7 f.: "In omnibus querit quæ sua sunt et accipit potius bonum quam tribuit."

[3] Since "Disputatio Heidelbergæ habita" xxviii. is one of the main passages for Luther's doctrine of love, it is here quoted complete: "God's love (amor Dei) does not find, but creates, its lovable object; man's love (amor hominis) is caused by its lovable object. The second clause is evident and it is agreed by all philosophers and theologians that the object is the cause of the love. They assume with Aristotle that every power of the soul is passive and 'matter' (materiam) and that it acts by receiving—whereby he also testifies that his philosophy is contrary to theology, inasmuch as in all things it seeks its own (querit quæ sua sunt) and receives rather than confers good. The first clause is evident, since God's love (amor Dei) living in man loves sinners, the evil, the foolish, the weak, that it may make them righteous, good, wise and strong, and so it rather flows forth and confers good. For sinners are lovely because they

2. The Uniqueness of Christian Love

In answer to the question how far there exists any love other than egocentric, Luther can point first and foremost to this love of God and Christ for the lost. Here is a real love which does not seek its own, but gives and sacrifices. This is the criterion of Christian love. Until Luther's time, the features of Christian love had been drawn from human love, which was simply lifted up to a higher level, spiritualised and sublimated. Luther, however, has taken seriously the fact that Christian love is by nature wholly other than human love, and that its prototype is nothing else but God's Agape. Like this, it is spontaneous, unmotivated, groundless, creative. When this has been said, in principle everything has been said that there is to be said, according to Luther, about Christian love. Here we may set out a few of the most essential features of Christian love as Luther describes it. They are, as a matter of fact, simply an exposition of its spontaneous, creative nature.

1. Christian love is *spontaneous in contrast to all activity with a eudæmonistic motive.* Just as Christ has served us "freely and for nothing, and 'pleased not Himself' (ohne eigen Geniess)," so Christian love, too, is free from all selfish calculation or ulterior motive. It does the good, not in order to gain or increase its own blessedness, but "out of

---

are loved; they are not loved because they are lovely. So man's love (amor hominis) shuns sinners and evil men. But thus Christ: I came not to call the righteous, but sinners. And this is the love of the Cross (amor crucis) born of the Cross, which betakes itself not where it finds a good to enjoy, but where it may confer good upon the evil and the needy. For it is more blessed to give than to receive, says the Apostle. And so Ps. xli.: Blessed is he that considereth the poor and needy. Yet since the object of the understanding naturally cannot be that which is nothing—*i.e.*, the poor or needy—but that which *is*, the true, the good, therefore it judges according to appearance and accepts the person of men and judges according to the things which appear, etc." WA 1, p. 365, 1 ff.

free love and for nothing, to please God, not seeking nor regarding anything else, but that it thus pleases God."[1] But this makes it a free service to our neighbour as well. The fact that God's love for us is free and unmotivated carries with it the corollary that we love our neighbour also freely and without any selfish motivation.[2]

2. Christian love is also *spontaneous in contrast to all legalism*. The limitation of the law is just this, that it can never evoke a really free, willing and spontaneous action. The law meets us with its commands, as an imperative, and that is the very reason why it can never produce anything really good. It is in essence unproductive; indeed, it is at bottom self-contradictory. It requires free surrender to God's will; but just because it *demands*, it is an obstacle to this free, spontaneous surrender. The law has two motives at its disposal for compelling man to an outward fulfilment of the law: the fear of punishment and the desire for

---

[1] WA 7, p. 31, 6 ff. *Cf.* WA 6, p. 207, 26 ff.: " So a Christian man who lives in this confidence towards God knows all things, can do all things, dares all things that are to be done, and does it all joyously and freely, not in order to collect many good merits and works, but because it is his delight so to please God; and he serves God absolutely for nothing, content with this, that it pleases God."

[2] WA 7, p. 35, 25 ff.: " . . . and if he is now quite free [the Christian man will] willingly make himself into a servant again, to help his neighbour, to deal with and treat him as God through Christ has treated him himself; and all this for nothing, seeking nothing therein but the Divine pleasure, and thinking thus: Well now ! my God has given to me, unworthy and lost man, without any merit, absolutely for nothing and out of pure mercy, through and in Christ, the full riches of all godliness (Frömmigkeit) and blessedness, so that I henceforth need nothing more than to believe it is so. Well then, for such a Father, who has so prodigally lavished upon me His blessings, I will in return freely, joyously and for nothing do what is well-pleasing to Him, and also be a Christian towards my neighbour, as Christ has been to me; and I will do nothing except only what I see to be needful, useful and blessed for him, because I indeed through my faith have enough of everything in Christ.' See, thus there flows from faith love and delight in God, and from love a free, willing, joyous life to serve our neighbour for nothing. For just as our neighbour suffers want and is in need of our superabundance, so have we suffered want before God and been in need of His grace. Therefore, as God through Christ has helped us for nothing, so ought we through the body and its works to do nothing else but help our neighbour."

reward. But both of these rob the action of its spontaneous, unmotivated character, and prevent it from being a *real*— that is, a free and sincere—fulfilment of the inmost intention of the law.[1] Man can live for God in the deepest sense only when he is absolutely free from the rule of the law.[2] That which the law had to extort from him forcibly is then transformed into his free, spontaneous, willing action. The imperative of the law is exchanged for the indicative of the Gospel.[3] But this can only come about through faith in Christ or through the Holy Spirit—which means the same thing.[4] So long as man is under the law, the good has not

---

[1] WA 5, p. 33, 25 ff.: "This will, however, comes from faith in God through Jesus Christ. But the will that is constrained by fear of punishments is servile and violent, whilst that which is enticed by desire of rewards is mercenary and counterfeit. This will, however, is liberal, gratuitous and blithe; whence the people of Christ are called in Hebrew 'Nedaboth,' spontaneous, voluntary, liberal." *Cf.* WA 2, p. 489, 27 ff., WA 3, p. 17, 1 ff., and WA 7, p. 800, 25 ff.: "All together we are godly (fromm) unwillingly, or at all events with a false will, in that we are afraid of punishment and shame, or seek our own ends and pleasure therein. No one is godly purely for God's sake or solely because it is right and godly. Nature always will and must seek some reason why it should be godly; it cannot and may not be godly for godliness' sake, will not be satisfied with godliness as it should, but seeks to merit or escape something thereby. . . . For we ought not to be godly in order to merit or escape anything thereby; for such persons are all together mercenaries, servants and hirelings, and are not spontaneous children and heirs, godly for the sake of godliness itself alone—that is, for God's sake alone; for God is righteousness, truth, goodness, wisdom and godliness itself. And he who seeks nothing more than godliness, seeks and finds God Himself. He, however, who seeks reward and flees punishment, never finds Him, but makes reward his god. For that for which a man does anything, that is his god."

[2] WA 2, p. 499.

[3] WA 2, p. 492, 33 ff.: "Now we are not of the law, but the law is ours; and our works are not of the law, but of grace, from which freely and sweetly flow the things which the law previously extorted harshly and by force." WA 2, p. 596, 18 f.: "So the righteous is not obliged to live well, but he does live well, nor does he need the law to teach him to live well."

[4] WA 2, p. 587, 28 f.: "But this blithe disposition not the law, not nature, but faith in Christ Jesus effects." WA 7, p. 801, 21 ff.: "He who calls upon Christ in faith, has His name, and so the Spirit also assuredly comes to him. But when the Spirit comes, see, He makes a pure, free, blithe, joyous, lovely heart, which is godly (fromm) for absolutely nothing, seeks no reward, fears no punishment, but is godly only for the sake of godliness or righteousness itself, and does it all with joy." WA 10, 1, 2, p. 158, 25 ff.: "Now he who believes thereon receives

yet won complete power over him. The constraint he feels is evidence that he secretly entertains in his heart a contrary wish.[1] For spontaneity of action we can actually take the sinner as our example.[2] He has his delight in sin and performs it from inward inclination and gladly; he does not need to be attracted to it by promises of reward or threats of punishment. Similarly, man is completely won for the good only when he does the good spontaneously from inward inclination, and would do it even if it were not commanded in the law.[3]

3. The marks of Christian love described so far are largely negative. It is spontaneous—that is, it does not go back to either eudæmonistic or moralistic motives. But what is it, then, that sets it in motion? To this question Luther replies with his famous description of Christian love as " *quel-*

---

grace and the Holy Spirit, which makes the heart joyous and gay in God, and then he does the law voluntarily and for nothing, without fear of punishment and without seeking reward."

[1] Römerbrief, ii., p. 170, 33 ff.: " This the carnal man does not do, but he always dissents from the law and would rather (if it were possible) that there were no law. Thus he does not will good, but evil. And though he may work good (as I have said), yet he has no taste for it, since he works compelled by slavish fear, always having the contrary desire, if he might do it with impunity." WA 10, 1, 2, p. 156, 18 ff.: " If he rightly looked into his heart, he would find how he does all such things with distaste and constraint, because he is afraid of hell or seeks heaven—when he is not seeking something much less, such as honour, goods, health, and fearing shame or hurt or trouble. In brief, he would have to confess that he would rather live otherwise, did not the consequences of that life restrain him; for he would not do it purely for the sake of the law . . . he does not perceive the meaning of the law—namely, that it desires to be fulfilled with a joyous, free, blithe will."

[2] Römerbrief, ii., p. 172, 3 ff.: " But the flesh accomplishes this, since with delight and without repugnance and difficulty it works according to its lusts."

[3] WA 10, 1, 2, p. 156, 28 ff.: " Just as when thou askest an unchaste person why he does that work, he can give no other answer than: ' for the sake of the pleasure which he has in the work,' for he does it neither for the sake of reward nor of punishment, thinks not to gain anything by it, nor by it to escape any evil. Such delight the law wishes to find also in us, so that when thou askest a chaste person why he is chaste, he should say: ' not for the sake of heaven nor of hell, not for the sake of honour nor of shame, but for this cause alone, that I think it particularly excellent, and it pleases me heartily well, even were it not commanded.' "

lende Liebe," overflowing love. It has no need of anything at all to set it in motion from outside. It is not, like the world's love, a love aroused by the desirable qualities of its object. If it were, it would be merely a " geschöpfte oder geborgte Liebe," a derived or borrowed love. But as it is, it springs forth out of its own source, fellowship with God.[1]

4. But Luther immediately draws the implication from this, that this love is "*round and whole, the same* to one as to another" and without respect of persons.[2] It is, Luther holds, one of the most disastrous perversions love has suffered, when its value is judged by the value of its object. Christian love is the same whether it is directed to the godly or the ungodly, "just as the gold remains gold whether the good or the bad get it."[3] This trait, too, Luther has

---

[1] WA 36, p. 360, 8 ff.: " That is all a derived or borrowed love, that cleaves outwardly to the good which it sees in a person, and endures only so long as that same is there and can be enjoyed. This, however, must be an overflowing love (eine quellende Liebe), welling forth from within out of the heart like a fresh streamlet or brook which ever flows on and cannot be stopped or dried up or fail, which says: I love thee, not because thou art good (fromm) or bad, for I draw my love not from thy goodness (Frömmigkeit) as from an alien spring, but from mine own well-spring—namely, from the Word which is grafted into my heart."

[2] WA 10, 1, 2, p. 180, 3 ff.: " Against such unequal and piecemeal gentleness St. Paul speaks here, and desires that Christian gentleness be round and whole, the same to one as to another, be he friend or foe, forbearing everyone and forgiving everyone without any respect of person or of merit." *Cf.* WA 3, p. 77, 3 ff.: " But neither is this sufficient in God's sight, that a man should do good to the good and to his friends alone, but he must be roundly and universally the same to all, to good and bad, to friend and foe. For this is Christian godliness (pietas), to be equal to all, without discriminating according to the man and the favour of the flesh. Just as a fig-tree bears figs whether it stands among thorns or among roses, so the vine. For a good tree cannot produce bad fruit. But those who are friends to friends alone, are mixed. Concerning whom the Lord says: ' Do they collect figs of thistles?' So neither from fig-trees thorns. Since those are thorny to enemies, but agreeable to friends, therefore they are not whole and round and the same to all. Hence he adds: If I have requited them that recompense me evil. So the Lord teaches abundantly in Matt. v.: ' Be ye perfect,' that is, round and whole, like a circle. But those are like a semicircle or an arc, round to some and broken to others. And this the word ' Equity ' signifies. For without respect and distinction of persons he is the same to all who is equitable (equus)."

[3] WA 10, 1, 2, p. 180, 8 ff.: " For the silver did not turn to ashes when Judas the traitor got it. Thus all creatures and all that is of God is genuine and

derived from God's Agape. God does not allow His love to be determined or limited by man's worth or worthlessness. "For He maketh His sun to rise on the evil and the good, and sendeth rain on the just and the unjust " (Mt. v. 45). Thus the New Testament idea that the spontaneous, unmotivated, creative nature of Christian love is manifested supremely in love for enemies, has received new life in Luther.[1]

5. Having described Christian love as spontaneous, in the sense that it springs out of the right relation to God independently of what it may encounter from without, Luther seems to have gone as far as it is at all possible to go. Yet he still has something to add. For even behind love for sinners and love for enemies—that love which is apparently the least motivated of all—there *can* be a secret motive concealed, which robs the love of its spontaneity. For an example of this, we may turn to Augustine. When he speaks of God's love for the sinner, he is anxious to explain that it is not strictly love for the sinner himself, but for the good which, in spite of sin, still remains in him, and for the perfection which he can still attain. The idea that love has still something to hope for, something to gain, in the

---

remains the same for everyone. So also the forbearance attained in the Spirit remains forbearing, be it to friend or foe, to rich or poor. But the counterfeit nature behaves as if the gold should remain gold in the hand of St. Peter, but in Judas's hand become ashes. Thus rational and natural forbearance is forbearing towards rich and great, strangers and friends, and not towards all men. Therefore it is spurious, vain, false, hypocrisy, and pure fraudulence and an imposture in the sight of God."

[1] WA 36, p. 17 ff.: " Then it goes out lavishly and open to everyone who needs it, and meets both good and bad, friend and foe. Indeed, it is ready for enemies well-nigh most of all, as they have more need that I should help them out of their misery and sins, and especially in the highest good, that I should pray for them and do all that I can, that they also may become godly (fromm) and be redeemed from sin and the devil. See, that is a love welling out of the heart, not drawn into it, for he finds in that man nothing from which he might draw it; but because he is a Christian and grasps the Word which in himself is quite pure, the same makes his heart also so pure and full of honest love, that he lets his love flow out unimpeded towards everyone, be the person who or what he may."

sinner, thus supplies the final motive when all other motives
have disappeared. But Luther is anxious to eliminate even
this last motive. He allows himself no illusions suggesting
that love is always crowned with success in the end. But
is that to set a limit to Christian love? Is love to cease when
it realises that all its efforts in a particular instance are
doomed to failure? If so, then in the last resort it would
not be spontaneous and creative, but governed by consideration of the given circumstances. Against this Luther is
bound to protest. Christian love is by its very nature " *eine
verlorene Liebe*," a lost love. It is the direct opposite of
rational calculation. Even though again and again it finds
itself deceived, that is no reason why it should become hesitant and reserved. " For it is of the nature of love to suffer
betrayal."[1] Again it is the love of God and of Christ which
gives Luther the solution of the difficulty. For this love,
too, is in the highest degree a lost love, poured out upon
those who reward it with ingratitude. Only one of the ten
lepers returned to Christ and thanked Him for His beneficence; it was lost on all the rest.[2] Therefore the same is also
true of Christian love.[3] It is " a divine, free, unceasing, yea
indeed a lost love,"[4] which is prepared freely to find its

---

[1] WA 18, p. 652, 4 ff.: " Nor is there any danger if it be in error; for it is of
the nature of love to suffer betrayal, since it is exposed to all the uses and abuses
of all men, the general servant of good and bad, faithful and unfaithful, true and
false alike."

[2] WA 37, p. 148, 1 ff.: " So then you should say: I will suffer it and accept
the ingratitude. So Christ did, as thou seest here in the gospel; and so the Father
still does, for His sun shines on the good and the evil. But what if He should
say: I have let the sun shine so many years, and men do not recognise this
kindness; they are ungrateful; I will let it shine no longer and will let them die?"

[3] WA 37, p. 148, 7 ff.: " So must a Christian also do. . . . Say thou: I have
lost my kindness on that man; and here's another and I've done well to him, and
away he goes, too; then let the third come, and learn to say with Christ: ' Where
are the nine?' This is His reward: the tenth comes and acknowledges the
kindness and gives thanks. With this the Lord is content."

[4] WA 36, p. 435, 30 ff.: " It is not the way of Christians to go back and with-
draw the hand, but to go on and remain in love, that there may be a divine,
free, unceasing, yea, indeed, a lost love for people, and the kindness thus thrown
away. . . ."

kindness thrown away and lost, as also Christ has found.[1]
For how should Christian love fare better in this world than
the love of God and of Christ?[2]

3. THE CHRISTIAN AS THE CHANNEL OF GOD'S DOWN-POURING LOVE

The question we had to answer was how far Luther succeeded positively in building up the theocentric Agape-love.
The account given above seems to have shown that he did
succeed. He has been able to give an entirely concrete
picture of a love which is the direct opposite of the love that
"seeketh its own." And the features of this new kind of love
are derived from God's love. But there is still one question
unanswered—namely, whether this idea of Agape is merely
an ideal picture drawn from God's love, and having no
relation whatever to human life as it actually is. Is such a
love possible?

To this question, too, Luther's answer seems to be
primarily negative. He is perfectly aware that the love he
has described is no human love. "For such love is not a
natural art, nor grown in our garden."[3] Christian love is
not produced by us, but it has come to us from heaven.[4] The
subject of Christian love is not man, but God Himself, yet

---

[1] WA 36, p. 435, 13 f.

[2] WA 37, p. 148, 33 f.: " Christ Himself does not find people to be grateful
for so great a kindness; wouldst thou then have it better than He ?" *Cf.* WA 36,
p. 460, 6 ff.: " This must give us a joyous, laughing heart, so that we say: Why
should I have it better than my Lord? He gives the sun, kingdoms, peoples and
all things to all men, and what has He? That they curse Him, and crucify His
Son. That is a thanks written with black ink. Christ sweats a bloody sweat,
etc., and then is rewarded, alas, as He has not deserved; for they say that we are
saved by our works and not by Christ." P. 458, 18 ff.: " That, however, the
right love does not do; it allows nothing either good or bad, pleasant or painful,
to hinder it, but ever goes on with its love and does not see what the world does
nor what it deserves, but what God does and what He suffers for His love; and
it ever sings its little song: I have undertaken nothing for thy sake, but for the
praise of God and for thy best weal."

[3] WA 36, p. 436, 23 f. [4] *Cf. supra*, p. 682, n. 2.

in such a way that the Divine love employs man as its
instrument and organ. The Christian is set between God
and his neighbour. In faith he receives God's love, in love
he passes it on to his neighbour.[1] Christian love is, so to
speak, the extension of God's love. The Christian is not
an independent centre of power alongside of God. The love
which he can give is only that which he has received from
God. Christian love is through and through a Divine work.
Here Luther can speak in the loftiest and strongest terms. A
Christian is a " divine, heavenly man."[2] He who abides in
love is no longer "a mere man, but a god . . . for God
Himself is in him and does such things as no man nor
creature can do."[3] A Christian is called to be a Christ to
his neighbour.[4] Luther's saying that Christians are to be
" Gods and Saviours of the world " has, of course, nothing
to do with mystical " deification." It is his way of emphasising as strongly as possible the fact that the real subject of
Christian love is not man, but God Himself. This idea is

---

[1] This is, according to Luther, the entire content of Christianity: " These
two things, faith and love, or the receiving of kindness from God and the showing
of kindness to our neighbour." WA 10, 1, 1, p. 99, 20 ff. *Cf.* WA 45, p. 540,
7 ff.: " The first thing makes them to be reconciled with God and to have for
themselves all that they need. When they have this, then they, too, are to
become gods and saviours of the world through prayer, and so through the Spirit
of grace to become themselves children of God. Then as God's children they
must mediate between Him and their neighbour and serve and help others, that
they also may come to this."

[2] WA 36, p. 439, 35. *Cf.* p. 437, 30 ff.: " How could he now give greater
comfort or give love higher praise, than that it produces a divine man, who is
one cake with Him; a man who, when he loves his neighbour and forgives his
ingratitude and vexatious works if he spurns and plagues him for his kindness,
can glory that he has acted like a God. ' *Cf.* p. 437, 6 ff. (Rörer): " If thou so
livest, this is divine life—that is, God.Himself. How could he praise it more
highly? If he says: canst thou forgive thy neighbour his injury, knavery, etc.?
If thou canst remain kindly to him, thou hast acted like a God, who is in thee."

[3] WA 36, p. 438, 20 ff. *Cf.* p. 438, 4 (Rörer): " If thou canst keep thy heart
sweet, thou art a god, greater than all creatures."

[4] WA 7, 66, 34 ff.: " While we believe in Him, and are mutually and recipro-
cally each the other's Christ, doing to our neighbours just as Christ does to us."
Cf. p. 66, 3 f.: " And so I will give myself to be, as it were, a Christ to my
neighbour, just as Christ has shown Himself to me."

also clearly expressed in the simile which Luther loves to use in this connection.   In relation to God and his neighbour, the Christian can be likened to a tube, which by faith is open upwards, and by love downwards.   All that a Christian possesses he has received from God, from the Divine love; and all that he possesses he passes on in love to his neighbour. He has nothing of his own to give.   He is merely the tube, the channel, through which God's love flows.[1]   Here one cannot help thinking of Augustine's conception of love, and how utterly different it is from Luther's.   Augustine, too, can speak of the mediate position of man; but he means that man has the supersensible world above him and the sensible beneath.   Now love is, for him, in the category of desire, and therefore the love that is directed downwards is false and must be condemned; so he gives his exhortation : " Conduct the water which is flowing into the sewer, to the garden instead.   Such a strong urge as it had to the world, let it have to the Creator of the world."[2]   And this also sets its seal on Augustine's conception of love to one's neighbour.   Here, too, love must be directed upwards, so that it is not properly concerned with the neighbour himself, but really, in the last resort, with " God in the neighbour."   Luther, who has overcome the dualism of sensible and supersensible and has delivered Christian love from the category of desire, takes the directly opposite course.   He does not speak, like Augustine, of " using one's neighbour in order to enjoy God."   He does not speak of directing the stream upwards.   Indeed, Luther is not afraid to insist that *the stream of love must be directed downwards.*   For the love of which he speaks is not

----

[1] WA 10, 1, 1, p. 100, 9 ff.: " . . . faith and love, by which a man is placed between God and his neighbour as a medium which receives from above and gives out again below, and is like a vessel or tube through which the stream of divine blessings must flow without intermission to other people.   See, those are then truly godlike (gottformige, deiformis) men, who receive from God all that He has in Christ, and in turn show themselves also by their well-doing to be, as it were, the gods of their neighbours."   *Cf.* WA 45, p. 591, 29 ff.

[2] Augustine, Enarr. in Ps. xxxi. ii. 5 ; *cf. supra*, p. 494.

an acquisitive love, but Agape. All that can be called Agape
derives from God. From above His love comes down to us,
and it must pass on through us to our neighbour. " Amor
crucis ex cruce natus " does not seek its own; and it has also
left behind the idea of " fruitio." " It betakes itself "—says
Luther, with an obvious thrust at Augustine's fruitio-love—
" not where it finds a good to enjoy, but where it may confer
good upon the poor and needy."[1]

Even love to God takes this downward direction which is
characteristic of Agape-love. " To love God is to love one's
neighbour."[2] " It is there God is to be found and loved,
there He is to be served and ministered to, whoever wishes
to minister to Him and serve Him; so that the commandment of the love of God is brought down in its entirety into
the love of neighbour. Now a check is thereby put to the
flying spirits and the limit is set. . . . For this was the
reason why He put off the form of God and took on the
form of a servant, that He might draw down our love for
Him and fasten it on our neighbour."[3]

Only when we have understood that Christian love, according to Luther, is God's own love, can we understand the
deepest meaning of Luther's oft-repeated statement that a
man must be blessed in order to be able to perform the good.
This is commonly interpreted in an exclusively eudæmonistic
way: only when a man is blessed, only when, assured of
God's grace, he has his own concerns and interests guaranteed, is he rich and free enough to be able to devote his
activities to the service of his fellow-men in love. Now it is

[1] WA 1, p. 365, 13 ff. *Cf. supra*, p. 725, n. 3.
[2] " Amare Deum est amare proximum." WA, Tischreden, Nr. 5906, Bd. 5,
p. 397, 7.
[3] WA 17, 2, p. 99, 18 ff. In WA 10, 1, 2, p. 122, 19 ff. Luther reminds us
that such expressions as " to serve Christ and to serve God " signify primarily
a " service which proceeds from Christ, not to Christ, and which comes not
from us but to us," and he adds: " In rare cases, however, he thinks also of the
service which proceeds *above itself to God*, but by far the most commonly of that
which proceeds *beneath itself to men*."

true that "blessedness" delivers a man from egocentric action, though not, however, because all egocentric interests are thereby satisfied, but rather because they are overcome and destroyed. For Luther, however, blessedness means no less than fellowship with God. Therefore, only one who by faith lives in that blessed fellowship with God is open to receive the supplies from above, which he is then able to pass on in love.

From this point of view, the idea common ever since Ritschl's time, that Luther failed to provide a satisfactory motivation for love to neighbour,[1] appears in a peculiar light. It is true that we look in vain for a teleological motivation of love in Luther. But we are not justified in looking for such a thing in him at all. The whole construction of his ethics is not teleological, but causal.

Equally mistaken is the statement sometimes made, that love in Luther does not appear to be as divine as faith. For who has emphasised the divine nature of love like Luther, who says that it is " not of works nor human, not of angels nor heavenly, but God Himself "? It can be disputed whether the question as to which is more divine, faith or love, would have any meaning for Luther. But if the question is asked, then it cannot be rightly said that love falls short. By faith we are children of God, by love we are actually " gods."[2]

[1] A. Ritschl: *Die christliche Lehre von der Rechtfertigung und Versöhnung*, III. Bd., 4. Aufl., 1895, pp. 481 ff. (Eng. trans.: *Justification and Reconciliation*, 1900). W. Herrmann: *Der Verkehr des Christen mit Gott*, 7. Aufl., 1921, pp. 264 ff. (Eng. trans.: *Communion with God*, reprinted 1930). J. Gottschick: *Luthers Theologie*, 1914, pp. 57 ff.

[2] WA 10, I, 1, p. 100, 17 ff., quoted *supra*, p. 720, n. 1.

CONCLUSION

IF we ask what is the significance of Luther in the history of the Christian idea of love, it is quite misleading to answer that for him faith stands at the centre, whereas Catholic piety has its centre in love. From the purely formal point of view, it is true, support can be found for this idea in Luther's opposition of his formula " faith alone " to that of Catholicism, " faith formed by love." Yet such an interpretation causes that which is in fact most important to be obscured. It fails to recognise that in the last resort it is two different views of love which here confront one another. In attacking the Catholic doctrine of love, Luther has no thought of putting an end to love. What he seeks to destroy is that interpretation of Christian love which finds expression in the idea of Caritas, which fundamentally contains more Hellenistic Eros-love than primitive Christian Agape-love. Here, as elsewhere, Catholicism is a *complexio oppositorum*, a synthesis of opposed fundamental motifs. In Luther, on the other hand, a clear distinction is made. His view of love is throughout determined by the Christian Agape motif. We look in vain here for any single feature of Eros. And we try in vain to think of any possible expression of the idea of Agape, which Luther has not found and used.

From each of the two points of departure, a comprehensive and universal theory of love has been constructed.

On the one hand—in Catholicism—the idea of acquisitive love is the bond which ultimately holds the whole together. The fact that self-love is at the centre here is most clearly shown in that it is actually located in God, in the Holy Trinity. In self-sufficient blessedness and majesty God is enthroned above the world. God's love means, in the first place, that the Divine being revolves within itself in self-love, and secondly, that it draws the desire of all other beings towards itself. In virtue of natural self-love, everything strives upwards. The whole of existence, therefore, presents the spectacle of a ceaseless ascent, an incessant pursuit of that which is higher. Only in God can the desire of created beings for blessedness come to rest: "Inquietum est cor nostrum, donec requiescat in te."[1]

On the other hand—in Luther—it is the religion and ethos of Agape that we meet. God is Agape. That is why He has come to us in His Son. Only at the Cross do we find God, but there we really find Him. "Theologia crucis" is the only true theology. It is thus He has revealed His heart to us, and shown that He is "eitel Liebe," pure love, "ein Abgrund der Liebe," an abyss of love. And this Divine love has likewise set its seal upon everything in the world, which derives from a Divine dispensation. Everything in creation obeys the law of love. There is no tree that bears fruit for its own use; the sun does not shine for itself. It is only man and the devil who in everything seek their own.[2] So far from self-love being a natural ordinance of God in nature, it is a devilish perversion. That which in all things only seeks its own, is thereby closed against God. But when through faith man becomes open to God, the love from on high obtains a free course to and through him. He becomes a "tube," which by faith receives every-

---

[1] Augustine, Conf. lib. I., i. 1.

[2] WA 5, p. 38, 11 ff.: "And to give fruit indicates that this blessed man, in love (which we see to be commanded in every law of the Lord), serves not himself, but his neighbours. For no tree produces fruit for itself, but it gives its fruits to others; indeed, no creature lives for itself or serves itself, except man and the devil. The sun does not shine for itself, water does not flow for itself, etc. So every creature observes the law of love, and its whole being is in the law of the Lord; for even the members of the human body do not serve themselves; only the disposition of the mind is ungodly. For this not only gives its own to no one, serves no one, wishes no one well, but it seizes all of everything for itself, seeking in all things, even in God Himself, what is its own (quærens quæ sua sunt)."

thing from God's love and then allows the Divine love to
stream out over the world. God's love has made a new way
for itself down to lost humanity. Once for all, and in a
decisive manner, this has come to pass through Christ. He
came to us in the form of a servant and in humiliation, yet
His majesty has not thereby grown less. He has rather revealed it in still greater glory. His majesty is the sacrificial,
self-giving majesty of love.

INDICES

INDEX OF SCRIPTURE REFERENCES

INDEX OF GREEK WORDS

748

INDEX OF PROPER NAMES

[Principal references are given in *italics*]

750

INDEX OF SUBJECTS

[Principal references are given in *italics*]

P.170.